Also by Sally Bedell Smith

IN ALL HIS GLORY

REFLECTED GLORY

DIANA

GRACE AND POWER

For *Love*
of *Politics*

FOR LOVE OF POLITICS

The *Clintons*
in the *White House*

Sally Bedell Smith

First published in Great Britain
2008 by Aurum Press Ltd
7 Greenland Street, London NW1 0ND
www.aurumpress.co.uk

Published by arrangement with Random House,
an imprint of The Random House Publishing Group,
a division of Random House, Inc., New York.

A catalogue record for this book is available from the British Library.

ISBN 978 1 84513 337 5

10 9 8 7 6 5 4 3 2 1

2012 2011 2010 2009 2008

This book is printed on paper certified by the Forest Stewardship
Council as coming from a forest that is well managed according to
strict environmental, social and economic standards.

*Front-matter photographs: Paul J. Richards/AFP/Getty Images
(page a), Robert McNeely/William J. Clinton Presidential Library (pages b–c,
d–e), Ron Edmonds/AP Images (pages f–i)*

*Title-page photograph: Robert McNeely/William J. Clinton
Presidential Library*

Book design by Barbara M. Bachman

Printed by MPG Books, Bodmin, Cornwall

The truth is most politicians are not candid with people.

They try to act like they hate politics—and oh, this is a burden,

I just had to do it. When the truth is most of them love it and

wouldn't do anything else on a dime if they could avoid it.

—*Bill Clinton*

Introduction

———

ONE EVENING IN THE WINTER OF 1998, BILL AND HILLARY CLINTON invited a small group of friends to watch a movie in the theater at the White House. Since the beginning of the Clinton presidency, invitations to these evenings had become badges of status, and they promised an opportunity to spend informal time with the First Couple. Everyone gathered outside the luxurious screening room in the East Wing, grabbed some soda and popcorn, and then found places amid the rows of 51 beige upholstered seats.

Typically, the Clintons showed films that were about to open in theaters, making guests feel like insiders. But on this night, the film was a three-year-old comedy, *Something to Talk About*, starring Julia Roberts, Dennis Quaid, and Kyra Sedgwick.

The President and First Lady sat in two of the four large armchairs in the front row, and the guests settled themselves for a welcome respite from weeks of headlines about the President's involvement with Monica Lewinsky, a twenty-four-year-old White House intern. Five days after the story had broken on January 21, Bill Clinton had stood before television cameras, wagged his finger, and emphatically denied having had sexual relations with "that woman, Miss Lewinsky." The next day, Hillary had blamed the accusations on a "vast right-wing conspiracy" of enemies. Since then, both Clintons had resolutely gone about their business and maintained silence on the subject, even as lurid and specific details of the Lewinsky story emerged in the press. The movie screening came as the Clintons socially "resurfaced following the Monica revelation," recalled Mary Mel French, the Chief of Protocol, one of the guests that evening.

Something to Talk About began promisingly enough, with scenes of domestic bliss in a southern town, among them the bantering and early-morning rituals of Grace Bichon (Roberts), the manager of her family's prosperous horse farm; her husband, Eddie (Quaid), a real-estate developer; and their adorable preteen daughter, Caroline. But the plot took an ominous turn when Grace and Caroline drove through town and saw Eddie outside his office building, kissing a beautiful blonde and walking away with her, arm in arm. Observing her mother's fury, Caroline asked, "Is Daddy in trouble?" "Big trouble," said Grace.

"You marry a guy whose nickname in college was Hound Dog," said Grace's sister, Emma Rae (Sedgwick), "what did you think was going to happen?" In the inevitable confrontation the next day, Emma Rae kneed Eddie in the groin and called him a "lying sack of shit," while Grace told him, "You don't know how it feels to be made a big, fat fool of." Grace's revenge, from a recipe invented by her eccentric Aunt Rae, was a dinner of salmon with mint mustard sauce laced with emetics. "It's not lethal," explained Aunt Rae. "It will, however, make him sick as the dog that he is. . . . I call it homeopathic aversion therapy. . . . Sometimes a little near-death experience helps them put things in perspective." On cue, Eddie fell violently ill, retching and screaming in agony as Grace rushed him to the hospital.

Afterward, in the White House Family Theater, "Bill and Hillary were completely silent. We all wanted to slide under our chairs," recalled French, a friend of both Clintons from Arkansas who herself had been through a bruising divorce several years earlier. "Nobody said anything as we all got up to leave. I happened to be next to Hillary when we were walking out. She slipped her arm through mine and whispered to me, 'I'll tell you what. We should have that concoction. You should mix it up first and give me a portion.' We burst out laughing and couldn't stop."

HILLARY CLINTON'S ABILITY to laugh at such a moment of peril for her marriage—and her husband's presidency—not only signaled an awareness of her husband's philandering but showed that "she was trying to make the best of a lot of things," recalled French. "She knew my circumstances, and I knew some of hers."

That moment offered a revealing glimpse into a relationship that has fascinated and often mystified the American public. The intensity of the Clintons' ambitions and the complexities of their marriage and political partnership had a profound impact on his presidency. In many respects, Bill and Hillary strengthened each other as "force multipliers." Hillary's mother suggested that for them, one plus one equaled "a third kind of entity." Both had trained as lawyers and were equally versed in public policy. As President, Bill was the "principal," and Hillary's designated role as First Lady was to serve his interests. But they were equals in their personal relationship, and she had her own policy agenda, with sufficient resources and staff to pursue it. This created the impression, particularly in the first two years of the Clinton Administration, that the White House was the site of a copresidency, with overlapping agendas.

The Clintons' temperamental differences and the tensions in their marriage intruded on policy, politics, and personnel in their presidential years. The Monica Lewinsky episode was the most egregious instance, but disquieting undercurrents were evident from the beginning. "There is a saying, 'If Mama's not happy, nobody is happy,' " said one top administration official. "You could read her weather forecast on his face." Had the Clintons divorced, they would have been more fathomable. Instead, as Mary Mel French noted, "The Clintons are complicated because they stayed together."

Bill was forty-six years old when he entered the White House, and Hillary was forty-five. They declared themselves the Baby Boomer version of Franklin and Eleanor Roosevelt, but the way they operated was more akin to John F. Kennedy and his brother Bobby, who served as Attorney General and operated as a de facto Vice President while serving as the President's eyes and ears and closest advisor. "Eleanor Roosevelt was strong, but she did not try to beat men at their own game," observed former Kennedy aide and Roosevelt biographer Arthur M. Schlesinger. "Hillary does."

Bill and Hillary Clinton came to the presidency with a long history of consulting each other on virtually every consequential policy and political decision. This pattern continued in the White House years, especially in areas in which Hillary had a strong interest. Mickey Kantor, a longtime friend who served as U.S. Trade Representative and Commerce Secretary in the Clinton Administration as well as as an informal counselor when the Clintons were embattled by scandal, said, "Their lives had been so entwined, both personally and professionally, it has always been hard to distinguish who played what role. In the end, she had the first and last word when it was something important. . . . There was no issue I was around that she wasn't critical to."

Hillary considered Bill a "force of nature." Yet nearly everything about him was contradicted by something else. His wide-ranging intellect could be overridden by lapses in everyday common sense. He was by turns empathetic and self-absorbed, focused and undisciplined, cerebral and priapic, idealistic and cynical, honest and evasive, inspiring and mortifying. Above all, he was intuitive.

"He was capable of constant emotional scans of everyone in the room in real time while he was thinking," recalled one close Clinton associate. "He could recognize, quantify, and calibrate a response to the emotional state of the person with him." With his "Iron John misty look" and lip-biting contemplation, he resembled a "girly man. . . . Part of his personality is sissy and womanish," observed Gene Lyons, a sympathetic Arkansas journalist. Yet another side of him was classic alpha male, supremely self-confident and exuberant with political power. In the Oval Office, he could display toughness and a fearsome temper. Political consultant James Carville warned against being misled by Bill's "quarter inch of softness. . . . You'll break your finger if you mistake that for going all the way through."

The downside of Bill's magnetism was his compulsive need to seduce. For example, he made several lame plays for Laura Tyson, the fetching chairman of his Council of Economic Advisers. "Once we were talking about an article I had written," Tyson recalled, "and he said, 'You should come over and show me your article.' I thought, 'This is bizarre.' So I said, 'I'll just send it over.'" Another time at a White House dinner he commented on her alluring evening gown, saying, "You'd better not wear that to work," to which she replied, "Of course I'll never wear this to work." Said Tyson later, "It is pretty good protection if you don't let on any sign that this [a play] is happening. It will go away."

Bill also had a propensity to dissemble that earned him enemies across the political spectrum. But he yearned to please people and win their approval, and he had a gift for conciliating and placating. Even friends who shunned him after the Lewinsky revelations eventually relented. "For six months I didn't speak to him," said Tunkie Riley, the wife of the Secretary of Education. "Then he got me again. I forgave him."

The ability to win forgiveness, which seemed to perpetuate his reckless behavior, had its origins not only in Bill's charm but in his own forgiving nature. "He so much needed forgiveness from others that he made lots of down payments," said a longtime friend. "He knew the interest on these payments was going to come back to him."

WITH HER COOL MANNER and formidable will, Hillary had to work harder to win people over. Her extreme earnestness conjured up images in the press of a high school "hall monitor" and the "Salvation Army sister" in *Guys and Dolls*. Early in the 1992 campaign, *The New Yorker* ran a cartoon of a woman shopping for a new jacket and saying, "Nothing too Hillary." Many men were put off by her give-no-quarter nature. The pollster Frank Luntz once said, "She reminds most men of their first wife — or mother-in-law."

She was as unsentimental as Bill was mushy. She once wrote to a college friend, "Unthinking emotion is pitiful to me." When Jacqueline Kennedy Onassis sent a check to Bill's presidential campaign in 1992, he immediately said, "We can't cash this." Hillary's reply: "Make a copy, and then cash it." Said Ann McCoy, a friend from Arkansas, "You get a hug from Bill and a solution from Hillary."

Hillary's powers of concentration and rigorous self-discipline became legendary. "You can see her sometimes almost censoring the first, and second and third thing that comes into her head," said her longtime friend Diane Blair. James Carville marveled that unlike Bill, Hillary was "attuned to the glory of the unspoken thought." Even Hillary has acknowledged having an "obsessive personality." One close friend referred admiringly to her "tunnel vision" — the ability to focus on a problem, analyze it, and make a firm decision. Her husband noted in the second year of his presidency with a wave toward his large Oval Office desk, "I might as well try to lift that desk up and throw it through the window as to change her mind."

Nor did Hillary feel compelled to explain her certitude — or much else about her thoughts and emotions. "She could be moody, but she would never stop moving forward," said Ann Stock, who served as White House

Social Secretary. "Hillary has complex layers. What you see is not what you get." This confounding opacity alienated the press and fueled a perception that she was withholding information during numerous investigations. In fact, playing the role of "hidden hand" was one she enjoyed. "She was extremely Machiavellian, a master of doing things that could not be traced back to her," recalled one close colleague. "She would say, 'Do this, but don't leave any fingerprints.'" Hillary's mother once observed, "She just does everything she has to do to get along and get ahead."

WHEN BILL CLINTON MET Hillary Rodham in the spring of 1971, each of them was already conspicuously successful. A student leader at Georgetown, he had arrived at Yale Law School after two years in England on a Rhodes scholarship. Hillary had won the TV quiz show *College Bowl* several times, and had landed in *Life* magazine in 1969 after making headlines as the first student commencement speaker at Wellesley. She was among only twenty-seven women in a class of 235 at Yale Law.

Early in her second year, Robert Reich, a Dartmouth graduate she had known for several years through anti–Vietnam War activities, introduced her to Bill, his friend from Oxford. "It didn't take," Reich recalled. Months later, Hillary seized the initiative in the law-school library, a now-mythic encounter with a Spencer Tracy–Katharine Hepburn flavor. Noticing Bill across the lounge, she first braced him for "staring" at her and then introduced herself.

Her directness and her impulse to force issues were to typify their relationship. Bill was "impressed and stunned" by her boldness. Looking beyond her unruly brown hair, unadorned features, Coke-bottle glasses, and baggy clothes, he found her "sense of strength and self-possession" alluring. "With Hillary there was no arm's length," he later wrote. "She was in my face from the start, and before I knew it, in my heart." She offered the sort of intellectual sustenance and challenge Bill needed. He heatedly told his mother after she spoke disparagingly of Hillary's looks, "I have to have somebody I can *talk* to. Do you understand that?"

To Hillary, Bill was a "big gangly guy" with long curly hair and full beard. She was drawn by a "vitality that seemed to shoot out of his pores," and she thought he looked "very imposing . . . like a Viking" ("which is perfect," comedian Jay Leno quipped years later, "because she reminded him of Iceland"). More than anything, Hillary sensed that unlike other men, Bill Clinton "wasn't afraid of me."

In some ways, they were an unlikely couple: the earnest Methodist overachiever who freely acknowledged "I don't do spontaneity" and the instinctively affable and loquacious charmer who made everything look easy. "They are very different except in their values and interests," said one of their oldest friends. "There are countless couples where opposites attract, but that is not what I would say about them. They just have different styles and manifestly intelligent and deeply political natures."

With their compatible credentials and tightly aligned liberal views, they impressed their peers as a power couple even at Yale. Hillary recognized Bill's raw talent and his potential for greatness. In 1974, while serving on the staff of the House Judiciary Committee's inquiry into the possible impeachment of Richard Nixon, she told her colleague Bernard Nussbaum that Bill Clinton would be president someday. After Nussbaum scoffed at the idea, she fiercely told him, "Someday you'll eat your words." Hillary could have been a high-powered Manhattan or Washington lawyer, but she followed Bill to Arkansas, married him in 1975, and supported his political trajectory through five terms as governor. While pursuing a career as a partner in Little Rock's prestigious Rose law firm, she oversaw Bill's campaigns and advocated for his policies.

The flaw in the romantic picture was his womanizing. His tomcat tendencies emerged before their wedding and persisted over the years. "The rumors about him were so many and so pervasive," said Arkansas journalist Max Brantley. "There is a saying in Arkansas: 'You are on the second floor and you think you can stand in front of the window naked because no one can see you.' Bill Clinton thought he was invisible. He had willing partners who didn't say anything."

Bill's extramarital activities nearly ruptured his marriage twice in Arkansas. After he lost his first reelection for governor in 1980, he was "recklessly chasing women," recounted Hamilton Jordan, then a prominent Democratic party operative who had been Chief of Staff for President Jimmy Carter. In 1981, when their daughter, Chelsea, was one year old, a friend overheard Bill singing her a lullaby: "I want a div-or-or-or-orce. I want a div-or-or-or-orce." Later in the decade, according to Bill's former Chief of Staff Betsey Wright, there was a "serious threat" to the marriage, and the Clintons came close to separating. In 1989, he sought professional help for what friends called his "problem." "I thought he had conquered it," Hillary said a decade later. "I thought he understood it, but he didn't go deep enough or work hard enough."

Since Bill's early days as Governor of Arkansas, Hillary had been dogged by rumors that she was a lesbian—based mainly on her assertive manner, her lack of interest in her appearance during adolescence and early adulthood, her indifference to flirting with men, her husband's chronic infidelity, and her entourage of women staffers, who called themselves "Herc and the girls"—a play on her initials, HRC—during the 1992 campaign and who then worked in "Hillaryland" in the White House.

But there was no evidence of any involvement by her with another woman. Hillary simply came from a family where women stuck together, and "she was really into her women friends, into impressing them with her brains and feminism," said Martha Sherrill, who wrote a series of astute profiles of Hillary early in the Clinton Administration. "You got the sense that men were complicated for Hillary, but women were not." At the height of the Monica Lewinsky scandal, a friend of Secretary of State Madeleine Albright noted in a journal, "Madeleine connects with HRC. There is no discussion of topic A, only lots of girl talk, lots of kinship, along the lines of 'we both know what assholes men can be.' It was sort of like, 'You don't have to tell me. I know. I don't have to tell you. You know.' That sort of thing."

BILL CLINTON LEFT a respectable official legacy by helping to balance the federal budget, reform the welfare system, promote democracy after the end of the Cold War, and expand American trade with the rest of the world. The United States enjoyed peace and prosperity that began to unravel only in the administration's final year with the stirrings of a recession and a gathering threat of terrorism. Bill and Hillary's biggest problems were personal, as they fought off accusations of misdeeds not only during the Arkansas years but in the White House as well. To be sure, they had rabid enemies eager to find fault, but they created many of their own difficulties.

He was the first President to give his spouse the lead role in one of his most important policies and install her in a West Wing office. But her proposal for a national health-care program failed spectacularly and led to a Republican resurgence on Capitol Hill. Hillary was the only First Lady to testify before a federal grand jury and to be repeatedly deposed as part of ongoing criminal and civil investigations. She joined the ranks of "those shiny divas who need only one name—Cher and Madonna and Charo and Ann-Margret," in the words of *New York Times* columnist Maureen Dowd. Bill and Hillary were the only First Couple to be fingerprinted by the FBI and to have their private quarters searched as part of a federal probe. Most humiliating, he was the first President to have a description of his genitals appear in the press, along with sordid details of his sexual activities.

Bill Clinton came perilously close to losing his presidency in 1998 following the release of Independent Counsel Kenneth Starr's report on the President's misconduct with Monica Lewinsky. That September, a number of key senators discussed asking him to resign. Democratic senator Bob Kerrey of Nebraska even called him four days after the report's release to tell him he should "begin thinking about leaving the White House" and that he had three options: "to resign, to plea bargain, or to await impeachment." Kerrey told the President he would be "healthier and happier" if he stepped down. But Bill later said, it "never entered my mind" to resign. Kerrey, along with other pundits and politicians, underestimated Bill and Hillary Clinton's tenacity as political warriors.

IN THE YEARS SINCE Bill survived his impeachment trial, a curious amnesia seems to have set in about the Clintons' years in the White House. Bill used to complain to intimates that historical greatness would elude him because he was not given the chance to make great decisions. The tragic events of September 11, 2001, had the effect of confirming his prediction. The attack on the American homeland and the ensuing conflicts in Afghanistan and Iraq eclipsed the traumas of the Clinton years. They passed like the moon across the Clintons' sun, and the blazing headlines that had tarnished Bill and Hillary—about Gennifer Flowers and Whitewater and Travelgate and the health-care fiasco and Monica Lewinsky and impeachment—wound up flickering on the penumbra, appearing in retrospect to be the mere peccadilloes that Bill and Hillary always claimed they were.

It was as if history skipped a beat, hurtling from the end of the Cold War under President Reagan and the first President Bush to the onset of the War on Terror under the second President Bush. As the bloody fighting in Iraq dragged on with no end in sight, the Clinton years underwent a revision in the country's emotional imagination, shedding their tawdry aspects and becoming a halcyon interlude. After leaving the White House, Hillary became a serious-minded senator and wrote a bestselling memoir. Bill followed with a bestselling memoir of his own and took on the role of international celebrity, the Muhammad Ali of politics, leading good causes and dispensing advice to Democratic politicians and prominent world leaders.

But as Hillary weighed her presidential prospects, a kind of reckoning approached. The Clintons could continue to live in their never-never land of political respectability, personal wealth, and relative privacy, shouting advice from the first row of the theater, or they could once again answer ambition's call and seek a return to center stage by recapturing the White House. As the Clintons knew only too well, a bid for the presidency would dredge up the past in ways that promised to be painful and diminishing. The press would reexamine old scandals and yellowing depositions, and thousands of bloggers, unfettered by the conventions of traditional journalism, would let their imaginations wander into the Oval Office in the mid-1990s and then wonder online, in postings that would be linked hither and yon, what Bill really did with his cigar and Monica Lewinsky. The American people would have to ponder a most unpresidential question: Did they really want Bill Clinton running loose in the White House, doing heaven knows what and influencing his wife in ways that could only be imagined?

When Hillary embarked on her campaign for the presidency in 2007, she and Bill knew it would prompt a reconsideration of their marriage and political partnership. Contemporaneous chroniclers had taken stabs at explaining their contradictory and fraught relationship, but they did so on the fly, while the sensational headlines were still fresh. Even if Bill and Hillary end up switching roles, their collaborative habits remain deeply rooted, and their years together in the White House offer strong clues as to how they would conduct themselves if they returned to 1600 Pennsylvania Avenue, just as stage directions for a theatrical production provide the outlines for its revival.

Regardless of whether Hillary's bid falls short, the Democratic candidate for the presidency in 2008 will have to answer for the Clinton legacy because it is the last record of Democratic executive leadership. This is an opportune moment, then, to try to unravel the mysteries of the Clintons' marriage and to assess the extent to which the country was governed by a copresidency from 1993 to 2001, a historical excavation that has not been undertaken to date.

The Clintons have volunteered information about their relationship when forced by circumstances, but otherwise they have declined to supply many details. Only in rare unguarded moments have some insights slipped out. After Bill published his memoir in 2004, he came close to defining their marital dynamic in a discussion with public-radio interviewer Terry Gross about the marriage of Franklin and Eleanor Roosevelt, who worked in tandem in the White House but led separate private lives after she learned about his affair with Lucy Mercer Rutherfurd.

Musing about Roosevelt, Bill Clinton said, "It is fascinating . . . how he and his wife had a very complicated relationship. They loved each other very much. They had a bunch of kids, but they had big pockets of estrangement between them and pain, and they rendered enormous service to this country because they stuck with what they had in common." Years earlier, after Hillary told her friend Ann Henry that Eleanor Roosevelt was her role model, Henry replied, "That's right, but Eleanor never found her voice until after that marriage was over—until she didn't care about the marriage."

This is neither a day-by-day account of the Clinton years nor a deep examination of the administration's policies, although an essential part of the story is Bill and Hillary Clinton's vigorous engagement with the issues of the day. Rather, the following pages will explore how two intelligent, ambitious, and complex people confronted the challenges they faced in the White House, how they worked together and separately, and how the push and pull of their marriage affected the presidency.

Although the Clintons years ago backed away from their "two-for-the-price-of-one" rhetoric, it remains impossible to consider either of them in isolation. The dilemma extends even to what to call them. Unless a publication uses the "Mr." and "Mrs." style, journalists struggle with awkward constructions, alternately referring to him as "Clinton," her as "Clinton," him as "her husband," her as "his wife," him as "President," her as "First Lady," then "Senator." Hillary herself has tried to finesse the problem by

inviting familiarity and calling herself "HILLARY" in her campaign literature. For the purposes of clarity and ease of reading, this book will refer to
them as "Bill" and "Hillary."

The key to understanding them is in their shared love of politics—the
intellectual and emotional bedrock of their relationship. From 1974 on-
ward, they have been united in a common quest: to win—and keep winning—political office. He savors the sheer joy of the political game, the
energy he gets from the outstretched hands, the connections with people
of every sort, the validation of a triumphant campaign, the ability to affect
events, the applause and adoration that come with being a political star.
For Hillary, politics has long been more utilitarian: a means to gain power
and enact programs she believes would make a difference. For more than
three decades, politics has bound them together when other aspects of
their lives showed signs of crumbling.

Politics may seem an odd foundation for a marriage, but for the Clintons it has served as the defining factor not only of their careers but also of
their friendships, their dinner-table conversations, their intellectual interests, and, to outsiders at least, their emotional lives. While questions endure about whether the Clintons love each other in the way of most
happily married couples, there is no doubt about their shared commitment
to public affairs and the Democratic party—and, ultimately, to the pursuit
of political power.

For *Love*
of *Politics*

Chapter One

—

TIME: *"John Kennedy said that after he was elected, he began to think in terms of who it was he had to have in the room when he made the really big decisions. For him, that was Robert Kennedy. Who is it for you?"*
BILL CLINTON: *"Hillary."*

WITH THAT SIMPLE ONE-WORD REPLY IN DECEMBER 1992, BILL Clinton adumbrated the complications that would bedevil his presidency. It showed his intention to expand his election victory—which he won with a mere 43 percent of the vote—to encompass Hillary, as if she had been on the ticket, too. Bill was giving her primacy even above his Vice President, Al Gore, a formidable politician with far greater experience. The President-elect was feeling understandably buoyant, and at such moments he could be incautious, saying more than he intended to. He was *Time's* "Man of the Year," and he was stating what was obvious to him and to Hillary.

Bill and Hillary had been using the first-person plural since his initial run for governor in 1978, when Bill told *The New York Times,* "Our vote was a vindication of what my wife and I have done and what we hope to do for the state." They were such a "working unit" in Arkansas that they became known as "Billary"—a term of disparagement as well as admiration. The areas in which they deferred to each other, their private roles, their spheres of political expertise, the way they presented themselves to the public—all these were set during Bill's long years as governor. So, too, were the habits and rhythms of their marriage: her tolerance of his philandering, for example, and his delegation of responsibilities to her. As in any marriage, each partner had domains of primacy. These arrangements traveled with them during the long campaign of 1992 and into 1600 Pennsylvania Avenue.

Bill Clinton's run for the presidency was a triumph of political skill, luck, intelligence, deception, resilience, and sheer endurance. It was a flawed victory in some crucial respects. His behavior had created doubts about his character, and he antagonized many potential allies. National political reporters were dazzled by Bill and Hillary's talent but also disillusioned by their apparent disingenuousness and inability to be forthright about themselves and their plans for the presidency. The Clintons were deeply shaken by the scrutiny of the press, an experience that colored their view of Washington and those responsible for telling their story. Bill doubtless would have lost the election without Hillary's unyielding support when his character was under attack. Her rescue of his candidacy had enormous public consequences, as it made him beholden to her in ways that pervasively influenced his administration's policies.

When Bill began thinking about running in early 1991, George H. W. Bush's approval ratings were hovering around 70 percent in the aftermath of the successful Gulf War. But with his sensitive political antennae, Bill picked up softness in that support. It was a time of uncertainty, economic weakness, and anti-incumbent sentiment. Bill was also reaching a point of diminishing returns in Arkansas; John Brummett, a savvy Arkansas political columnist, said Bill had been bored with his job since 1987. When he was reelected in 1990, he had faced stronger opposition than before. "The voters were getting tired of him," said political analyst Michael Barone. "For the Clintons it was up or out."

Bill caught some lucky breaks when his strongest potential rivals among moderate Democrats—Tennessee senator Al Gore, New Jersey senator Bill Bradley, and Delaware senator Joseph Biden—decided not to run. The most formidable liberal opponent, New York governor Mario Cuomo, was the favored candidate, but Bill calculated that he could skillfully position himself for the 1996 campaign if Cuomo won the 1992 nomination and lost the general election. Bill got lucky again when Cuomo announced in December 1991 that he would not run, which left a small field of opponents Bill later described as "less than compelling."

He shrewdly styled himself as a "New Democrat" who could broaden his appeal to include independent voters and Republican moderates by shifting away from the Democratic liberal orthodoxy that had consistently lost elections. As chairman of the Washington-based Democratic Leadership Council since 1990, he advocated ideological flexibility and a smaller but more open government that would provide opportunity for those who assumed responsibility—welfare recipients who took vocational training and found work, for example. Bill was in a sense turning the New Deal legacy around. Franklin Roosevelt had sought to use government regulation to save capitalism from its worst excesses. Bill was advocating a plan to rescue progressive government by using market forces to encourage economic growth.

The whispers about his reputation for womanizing continued, however, and Bill needed Hillary's steadfast backing to fend off potential assaults. In July 1991, he told her that he had been called by Roger Porter, a Bush Administration official who had jokingly invited him to join the Republican party two years earlier. Bill recounted to his wife that Porter—a "mild-mannered policy wonk" who later taught at Harvard's Kennedy School of Government—had told him that the Bush White House feared a Clinton candidacy and warned the Arkansas governor to "cut the crap" because the Republicans would "do everything we can to destroy you personally." Hillary took this threat as the opening shot in a declaration of war and later told the tale to Bob Woodward of *The Washington Post* as evidence of a concerted effort by the right wing to bring them down. The story became such an article of faith to the couple that Bill repeated a more elaborate version in his own memoir thirteen years later.

But the conversation never happened, according to Porter, who consulted phone logs and his "meticulous diary" to back up his emphatic denial. "Bill Clinton started telling other people about this phone call," said Porter. "Human beings are interesting. When they tell something enough, they begin to believe it even though it is not true. It was the story about what was behind Hillary's belief in a vast right-wing conspiracy. A lot of Bill Clinton's life is moving people by telling stories that help them see things the way he wants them to. If truth is a casualty, it is for a good cause, in his view."

In his own vivid account, Bill insisted that after their conversation that summer, "I never heard from or saw Roger Porter again until he attended a reception for the White House Fellows when I was President." In fact, Bill phoned Porter several days after his victory in November 1992 "to talk process." According to *Time* magazine's Dan Goodgame, Bill "quizzed Porter on his 1980 book, *Presidential Decision Making*," which recommended setting up a group similar to the National Economic Council—one of the Clinton Administration's most noteworthy accomplishments. Robert Rubin, the designated head of that council, also received advice about White House operations from Porter—hardly the behavior of an antagonist out to destroy a Clinton presidency.

AS BILL CONTINUED to mull his candidacy, he sought out Henry Cisneros, the former Democratic mayor of San Antonio who several years earlier had disclosed an extramarital affair and later reconciled with his wife out of duty to his family. "You have handled it the right way," Bill told Cisneros. "You are now bulletproof. Nobody can come back at you." Recalled Cisneros, "He discussed it as a political problem: I offered a model for how to do it—versus the morality of the situation."

Late in the summer of 1991, Bill was playing hearts with a group of friends in Little Rock when one of them asked how he would deal with the rumors about his extramarital activities. "Hillary and I have talked about it, and we know how to handle it," Bill said. "Hillary is very strong. We know what to do." Early in September, Hillary told Frank Greer and Stan Greenberg, two of their top strategists, that the "pervasiveness" of the rumors posed a danger and that their approach would be "acknowledging that past without confessing to it." Bill and Hillary thought they defused the issue two weeks later by telling a group of Washington reporters, "Our relationship has not been perfect or free from difficulties, but we feel good about where we are. . . . We intend to be together 30 or 40 years from now." Shortly afterward, Bill officially entered the race.

In an effort to divert attention from personal matters, Clinton campaign aide George Stephanopoulos memorably said, "Specificity is a character issue this year." He meant that Bill should be judged on the particulars of his policies, but the description became ironic as Bill's penchant for hairsplitting and dissembling about his private life emerged as defining flaws. Once, during a debate with former Massachusetts senator Paul Tsongas, a rival moderate, Bill sputtered, "You're always perfect," to which Tsongas replied, "Not perfect. But I *am* honest."

TSONGAS'S RIPOSTE WAS one of the few times an opponent got the better of Bill, who was by widespread agreement the most gifted politician of his generation. He was a natural, with all the advantages of an extrovert born in a southern culture that emphasized human drama. Even in his youth, he ran for office so relentlessly that he earned the nickname "Billy Vote Clinton." He was a rare combination of powerful intellect and animal instinct, a man who loved policy and people in equal measure. He was an effortless optimist who "carried springtime in his breast pocket." He drew energy from his audiences "like a helium balloon," said his close friend Terry McAuliffe. "He grows with the crowd and loves it." He reveled in storytelling, much of it hyperbolic. His great political gift was an easy comfort with anyone, whether head of state or farmworker. His charm was undeniably egocentric: he wanted his performance to be appreciated and admired. "He is always evangelizing for the church of Bill," said Arkansas journalist Max Brantley.

When working a crowd, Bill would lean forward and move in close to individuals, a maneuver that could be disconcerting because he invaded the other person's space. The "full intensity Clinton," as Robert Reich called it, was above all physical. He usually began with a conventional handshake, extending his right hand, which had remarkably long, tapered fingers—more suited to a pianist or a surgeon, Hillary noted. Or he would confer a special status by using both hands in an antlike clasp. Whether in the company of a man or woman, Bill couldn't resist grabbing elbows or biceps—"basic, reflexive moves," observed political reporter Joe Klein, indicating "he is interested in you. He is honored to meet you."

When asked a question, he often responded with a question, which instantly flattered his interlocutor. He knew how to pause and let words sink in, and then took care with his answers, emphasizing points of agreement. He would convey his pleasure with an enormous nonstop smile and a disarming comment. Or he might create an opening by unexpectedly summoning a singular personal detail. The second time he saw Sandy Robert-son, the founder of the influential Robertson Stephens investment bank, Bill said, "How's your house with the clipper-ship timbers?" recalling that Robertson lived in the oldest house in San Francisco. The intimacy was a mirage, but as *Newsweek*'s Jonathan Alter pointed out, "He wasn't pretend-ing to enjoy superficial relations with people. This is what he liked. It is sin-cere phoniness. He gets energy from the rope line."

The pollster Stan Greenberg identified the "powerful impression that Clinton listens to people" as the "strongest element" of his character. Yet astute observers could see other forces at work. "When you are talking to him, you feel you are here, and he is operating on various other frequen-cies and tunes you in from time to time," said Anthony Williams, who was mayor of Washington, D.C., for the last two years of the Clinton presi-dency. While Bill was always eager to hear and synthesize information, he liked to talk more than to listen. "He has the narcissist's gift of making con-versation about him feel like conversation about you," wrote Benjamin Barber.

But the way he talked was an invaluable political tool that combined academic and emotional intelligence. He had an unusual capacity to speak about complicated issues such as globalization in lucid and simple language, with an informality that prevented him from seeming preachy or pedantic. Another essential talent was his ability to read an audience and convert their fears into optimism. "After he had framed his policy discus-sions, he could feel the vibe," said Eric Liu, who worked as a White House speechwriter in the first Clinton term and was Deputy Domestic Policy Advisor in the second. "He was so good at enabling people in the room to hear him without throwing out defenses and filtering out what he was say-ing. This is the essence of a great communicator. The shorthand for this was 'I feel your pain.' He tried to find out who you were in the audience and give you a sense that he was like you."

HILLARY UNDERSTOOD NOT ONLY that the political process replenished her husband but that the intensity of crowds was "overwhelming" to her. Her staff members knew that she could be depleted by campaigning and ad-justed her schedule accordingly. "She needed more rest and more time to get ready," said one of her husband's aides. Her political style diverged from Bill's in many ways. She could be highly effective, but she suffered by comparison to him.

Despite her combative personality, she was more naturally reserved in the arena, standing ramrod straight, with perfect posture. While he would lunge to meet people, she tended to wait for them to approach and greet them with a firm handshake. Her cooler persona discouraged the sort of tactile familiarity that he welcomed. Little had changed since the day in 1973 when Arkansas lawyer Webster Hubbell first saw Bill "holding court" in the middle of a group of strangers while Hillary perched nearby on a rock, studying. Two decades later, at the end of a Washington fund-raiser for the Democratic Leadership Council shortly after Bill was elected president, Hillary sat patiently backstage while her husband mingled with the crowd for more than an hour. "For Bill Clinton politics is the fun part," said Terry McAuliffe. "She loves the issues in an intellectual way. . . . If Hillary could be reading policy papers and debating with specialists, she would be happy."

Nor did she have what Max Brantley called "Bill's catholic tastes." She preferred to associate with those she found intellectually stimulating or who shared common ground. "She would devote her time to people who interested her and were useful," said Brantley. With her friends and staff, Hillary could be funny and casual, but with large groups she was likely to be stiff and formal. She worked hard at meeting and greeting, though she often appeared dutiful rather than joyful.

"I'm not a good actress. My feelings show on my face," Hillary once told an interviewer. But, in fact, she became the master of the "game face." Watching her walk into a Washington party looking decidedly gloomy early in the third year of the Clinton presidency, an observer could see her pause at the threshold, gather herself, and rig her smile before briskly entering a room full of people. Her brother Hugh Rodham spoke of "her business face" as an important "facet" of her personality. "She is the most controlled and disciplined person I ever met," said a major Democratic party fund-raiser. "She is always on, like an assembly line. Every interaction we have had has been identical. There has been no good or bad mood. She has been totally steady—no peaks, no valleys."

Since her high school days in Park Ridge, Illinois, she displayed uncanny poise at the podium, speaking in seamless and well-organized paragraphs without glancing at a text. Dorothy Rodham said she pushed her daughter to learn public speaking because of her own stage fright—so severe "I couldn't speak in front of eight people." Hillary had the flatlander's accent of her native Midwest, overlaid with southern inflections and dropped "g"s that belied her education at Wellesley and Yale. Yet for all her years in the South, she lacked her husband's passion and his ability to move audiences with his words. Her demeanor was businesslike, her cadences careful and slow. While Bill savored his ability to wing it, her appearances seemed scripted and well rehearsed. She also lapsed into the language of social science, what one observer called her "fugues into technocratic prose," which included sentences such as "the country was trending in the wrong direction on so many indicators."

When Bill Clinton addressed an audience, his gaze ranged everywhere, connecting with individuals as he assessed the mood. Hillary's eyes often sought the distance over the heads of her listeners. She seemed more focused on the perfection of her delivery, almost as if she were listening to herself. She gave the impression of talking "at" her audience, not with them.

Well into middle age, Bill could count on his boyish effervescence to captivate people. But Hillary had no such luxury. To be girlish would seem frivolous. Bill's weeping and other public displays of feelings were similarly out of bounds for her. "Men can show emotion more, but for women in politics it has a more pernicious effect," said Mickey Kantor. "Emotions are seen as weakness, a signal that a woman is not in control." That disadvantage meant she could not indulge in the kinds of behavior that humanized her husband. She had no choice but to appear publicly buttoned-up, which made her less likable.

SHORTLY BEFORE THE presidential primary season began, Bill Clinton "found himself handling poisonous snakes," wrote *Time*'s Lance Morrow. "Ugly stories have a slithering life of their own." The first such tale from Bill's past surfaced in November 1991 when a Little Rock friend named Connie Hamzy told *Penthouse* that Bill had propositioned her in a hotel lobby. When aides queried Bill, he acknowledged knowing her but denied any sexual involvement. Hillary's reaction was chillingly succinct: "We have to destroy her story." The campaign secured affidavits from three of

Bill's colleagues who backed him up, and Hamzy's allegations quickly died. Not long afterward, Bill mused aloud to *Time*'s Michael Kramer, "I wish I could find a way to get all these stories out early, so I don't have to deal with them after I'm nominated, when they can be so distracting."

Bill soon got more than he wished for when the supermarket tabloid *Star* triggered a sensation in January 1992 by recycling allegations from a lawsuit filed during his 1990 campaign for governor. The report named five women, including Gennifer Flowers, with whom he supposedly had affairs. Bill told his aides that all of the women had already filed affidavits denying the charges. But George Stephanopoulos detected that Bill's manner was "less breezy" than he had been about Hamzy, "more agitated and insistent." The Clintons vigorously denied all the allegations and sent Hillary out to reiterate that they had a strong marriage that shouldn't be subject to public scrutiny. Campaign officials were struck that after a day counteracting the charges, Bill and Hillary were "practically giddy." Bill explained to his strategists, "Hillary and I have talked through this whole thing exhaustively. I knew they would try to do this." But George Stephanopoulos was disquieted when he watched his boss slip away with longtime aide Bruce Lindsey to make a call from a pay telephone—to Flowers, the staff would later learn.

A week later, after the *Star* offered Flowers a "six figure amount," she provided further details for a new installment headlined "My 12-Year Affair with Bill Clinton." "I never felt he was struggling with his conscience about breaking his marriage vows," she said. "Bill treated our relationship as if he were bulletproof." When she had asked him about the other women listed in the lawsuit, he had insisted to her that he had "retired"— the exact language he used several years later when queried by attorney Bob Bennett about the persistence of rumors about his philandering.

To buttress her story, Flowers produced tape recordings she had made over a fourteen-month period of telephone conversations with Bill. When she worried that she would be asked about their relationship, he said, "If they ever hit you with it, just say no and go on. . . . If everybody is on record denying it . . . no problem. . . . They don't have pictures." The date of that conversation was September 23, 1991, just ten days before he announced his candidacy. Bill also urged her to sign an affidavit "explaining, you know, you were approached by a Republican" and asked to allege a sexual relationship. On October 17, he blamed "Republican harassment" for "trying to break you and me."

After the Flowers story was published, George Stephanopoulos watched as Bill read the account. "He would seize on incorrect details and even managed a laugh when he found specifics he could disprove," the aide recalled. "But it was a nervous laugh; he was agitated, unsettled." Hillary was campaigning elsewhere, so Bill called her from a telephone at a New Hampshire airport. After the conversation, Bill was "a different man. He was calmer and ready to fight. He had, it seemed, made things right with his wife." According to one news report at the time, "there was no scorn or sense of betrayal in her voice; she had long since accepted her husband's past and focused on winning a political future that would reward them both."

The Clinton campaign struck back at Flowers quickly, zeroing in on purported inaccuracies in her education and work history and shaming the mainstream press for pursuing "trashy supermarket" journalism. Bill's statement that "the story is untrue" turned out to be a denial only of her assertion that they had a twelve-year affair. As President, he ultimately admitted under oath that he had been involved sexually with Flowers—"a relationship . . . that I should not have had." In those early days, he conceded that he had returned phone calls from Flowers but only because she was "frightened" and he wanted to help her. Even the Clintons' most ardent advocate in the press, Sidney Blumenthal, wrote in *The New Republic* that Bill "clearly . . . knows her as more than a vague acquaintance." Stephanopoulos "assumed without asking that something had happened between them in the past."

Most of the press gave short shrift to the most damning evidence: the audiotapes. Campaign surrogates challenged their authenticity, claiming that they had been doctored, which gave reporters an opportunity to deny reality. Even so, Bill apologized to Mario Cuomo after the tapes revealed that he had told Flowers that the New York governor "acts like" a Mafioso. And the voice was unmistakably Bill's, along with his digressions into political analysis. ("I'm at a terrible disadvantage in name recognition still, but we're coming up and so we're moving pretty well.") The way Bill managed Flowers—suggesting cover stories and affidavits—anticipated the tactics he was to use with Monica Lewinsky. In a televised interview, Hillary told

ABC's Sam Donaldson that her husband's dealings with Flowers had an innocent explanation: "Anybody who knows my husband knows that he bends over backwards to help people who are in trouble and is always willing to listen to their problems." Hillary's words uncannily foreshadowed her insistence six years later to Sidney Blumenthal—by then a White House aide—that Bill had "ministered" to Lewinsky because she was a troubled young woman.

Faced with plummeting poll numbers in New Hampshire, the campaign arranged an interview with Bill and Hillary on a special edition of *60 Minutes* to be broadcast following the Super Bowl game between the Buffalo Bills and Washington Redskins, ensuring the largest possible audience. Their strategy was a classic "nondenial denial"—as Stephanopoulos explained it, "the ultimate inoculation." Bill would tacitly admit he had strayed in the marriage but would refuse to offer any details or discuss the Flowers allegations specifically. When *60 Minutes* correspondent Steve Kroft suggested that the Clinton marriage was hollow, Bill shot back, "This is not an arrangement or an understanding. This is a marriage." But it was Hillary's comments that saved her husband's candidacy. "You know, I'm not sitting here, some little woman standing by my man like Tammy Wynette," she said. "I'm sitting here because I love him. . . . And you know if that's not enough for people, then heck, don't vote for him." Ironically, Hillary *was* following the country singer's advice and standing emphatically by her man. As the Wynette song said, "He'll have good times/Doin' things that you don't understand./But if you love him, you'll forgive him,/even though he's hard to understand."

The image of the couple side by side, along with Hillary's words, made a convincing performance. The Clintons left the impression that their problems were in the past—and if Hillary was unconcerned, voters shouldn't be bothered either. Stephanopoulos now "had doubts about Clinton" because he had "seen his flaws up close." But he and other aides were willing to suspend disbelief for the sake of their larger cause. Reporters backed off because any sex story made them nervous. They chose to overlook that the scandal involved more than a consensual sexual relationship, because under pressure from Flowers, Bill had arranged a $17,520 job for her with the State of Arkansas. *Newsweek*'s Jonathan Alter ruefully admitted six years later, "Everyone knew . . . that he was dissembling about Gennifer Flowers. . . . But it barely mattered. He was turning out to be a big star."

A few days before the New Hampshire primary, Bill appeared in the town of Dover to implore voters, "If you'll give [the election] to me. . . . I'll never forget who gave me a second chance, and I'll be there for you 'til the last dog dies." As Max Brantley saw it, "He showed he was capable of running through the pain." Bill recovered enough to post a second-place finish, with 26 percent behind 35 percent for Paul Tsongas, practically a favorite son who had survived cancer and captured the public imagination by emphasizing the dangers of a burgeoning federal budget deficit. When the Clintons got the results, Bill initially wanted to call Tsongas to congratulate him. But Hillary's fierce instincts kicked in. "No," she said. "*We're* declaring victory." So Bill named himself "The Comeback Kid," and his striking confidence, along with his skill as a campaigner and the weakness of his opponents, propelled him to easy victories in the South and in border states.

THE PRESS WAS ALSO willing to retreat from the Flowers story because so many national political reporters liked Bill. They admired his commitment to a serious role for progressive government and his virtuoso knowledge of issues. He also flattered writers by soliciting their opinions. After reading Garry Wills's *Lincoln at Gettysburg: The Words That Remade America*, for example, he called the author for ideas on how he could rein in his expansive rhetoric and learn to speak more concisely.

But he needlessly antagonized the press in the following months by resorting to half-truths and semantic gymnastics when questioned about his past. Asked if he had smoked marijuana in his youth, he first replied that he had "never broken the drug laws in America," which he later rationalized as a "tacit but awkward admission that I had tried it in England." It wasn't until he faced the correct question that he owned up to smoking marijuana while at Oxford, but he added that he "didn't inhale"—a statement journalists found preposterous. Bill tried to make light of his evasions by appearing on Don Imus's radio show to say, "I like to play the saxophone because you don't inhale." But reporters were not amused and took him to task for being dishonest.

A far more serious affront was his lying to the press about his avoidance of military service during the height of the Vietnam War. When the issue first arose late in 1991, Bill told reporters that he didn't get drafted. "He gave the impression, 'Gee, what a coincidence, a fluke that I didn't get drafted. If I had I would have served,' " recalled James A. Barnes, political reporter for the respected Washington weekly *National Journal*. When his induction notice surfaced on April 5, 1992, the press corps wondered how Bill could have forgotten something so momentous—especially since he was renowned for having such a good memory that he could reel off the childhood phone number of a friend. Bill had not told his staff about the induction notice either. "I've had blind dates with women I've known more about than I know about Clinton," campaign strategist James Carville said.

It also emerged that Bill had gamed the system by signing up for a Reserve Officer Training Corps program at the University of Arkansas School of Law. While he was still at Oxford, a lottery to determine eligibility for the draft assigned his birth date a high number, putting him out of danger. Shortly afterward, he withdrew from the ROTC program and applied to Yale Law School. In a letter, a copy of which was released eight days before the New Hampshire primary by the colonel who had supervised the ROTC program, Bill described his decision in moral terms but admitted he wished to ensure his future "political viability." He also revealingly wrote, "I want to thank you, not just for saving me from the draft." Not only had Bill failed to serve in Vietnam, he had escaped in a slippery way.

"Some reporters were really angry and resented what Clinton had done," recalled Dee Dee Myers, his press secretary during the campaign. "To me it was the draft that shaped everything. Flowers you could argue, 'Does it really matter?' On one level yes, because we need a leader with integrity. But in our national life this sort of thing had happened before. The draft was different. The Baby Boomer reporters could say Gennifer Flowers didn't matter, but dissembling on the draft they couldn't forgive. It changed the way the press viewed him. They became more skeptical." Thomas Friedman of *The New York Times* expressed these misgivings best when he observed that Bill Clinton had the "masseur's touch with the English language," but "sometimes you want to check your wallet when he's done talking—just to make sure all your credit cards are still there." Christopher Hitchens, writing in the liberal *Nation* magazine, criticized

Bill's uses of "plausible deniability" when confronted with awkward questions. "Beware a wet-lipped man with a thin-lipped wife," he warned.

The resentment was mutual. Bill's treatment by the press in Arkansas had been fairly tame and, in John Brummett's view, "lax" in the "coverage of the underlying financial angle of politics." Unlike the Washington press corps, Arkansas reporters also lacked the "ability or willingness to keep a story alive after the first or second telling." There had been some persistent critics in Little Rock, but Hillary had been instrumental in muting one of the strongest, columnist John Robert Starr. "Hillary was assigned to neutralize Starr by schmoozing," said Gene Lyons. "She would call every day and chat, pat him on the head." This was not a task she particularly relished. As the presidential campaign was beginning, Lyons recalled hearing Hillary launch into a "very honest and bitter diatribe about her fear and loathing of the press."

Once Bill stepped onto the national stage, "the TV cameras caught everything he did, and also caught the inconsistencies," said Max Brantley. "That was a change for him." Both Clintons felt "seared" by the coverage during the primaries. "After the Flowers and draft scandals, the environment changed," said a correspondent for a news magazine. "He became cautious, bitter, and angry, and she did, too. This had not been far beneath the surface, but they dragged it up quickly, and they used these feelings to make things hard on themselves." When the correspondent asked Bill about the question of trust, the candidate wheeled on him: "How dare you question me?" he thundered. "Before this race no one questioned me. Now everyone questions me." Bill denounced the "appalling . . . arrogance and relative hypocrisy" in political press coverage, which he said had gone into "free fall."

Like her husband, Hillary took offense whenever anyone doubted her intentions or her word. Her bitterness boiled over only days after the 60 Minutes appearance when she appeared at a Democratic fund-raising event, where talk-show host Larry King leered, "It's 10 o'clock, Hillary. Do you know where Bill is?" Hillary replied that she had heard "so many rumors this week, I can't keep track of them. . . . You may have even started some of them."

To Newsweek's Eleanor Clift, Hillary seemed a "burned out . . . automaton," no longer full of "spunk and fire" as she had been when she and Bill had first hit the campaign trail. Hillary railed at *Newsweek* about the "reductionist" tendencies of the sound-bite culture and about the superficiality and cynicism of the press, which she believed wanted to "get" her husband. In particular, the Clintons felt they were being targeted by Howell Raines, who was then the Washington bureau chief of *The New York Times*, because he was "jealous" of the success of a fellow southerner.

Despite his mistrust of Washington reporters, even Bill had to concede the "surprisingly positive press coverage in the general election." His pollster Stan Greenberg had recommended that Bill recast himself as a "human being who struggled, pulled his weight, showed strength of character." Bill had a compelling story in his rise from a harsh childhood in honky-tonk Hot Springs, Arkansas, where "the ordinary confrontation and conflict of daily life was not contained. It was either repressed or it exploded." His philandering father had died three months before Bill's birth; his mother, Virginia, had married five times, worked as a nurse anesthetist, caroused at nightclubs, and played the horses most every day; his stepfather had been an abusive, alcoholic womanizer; and his younger brother, Roger, had suffered from drug addiction that led to imprisonment for dealing cocaine. Bill learned to parcel out bits and pieces of this dysfunctional upbringing once he realized that being a little confessional could engender sympathy and improve his image. Gene Lyons observed, "Bill is a talkative person who you think is telling you a lot but who is not telling you much."

ONE SIGNIFICANT OMISSION from the public story was the tale of Bill and Hillary's financial entanglements in "the interwoven power structure of business and politics" of Arkansas. It was a culture in which the moral architecture was weak, and in which everyone assumed that "fixing" was a requirement for getting things done. The Clintons' connections helped them enrich themselves in the go-go 1980s, a period they were to denounce as the "greed decade" created by the policies of Ronald Reagan. To augment her $110,000 Rose salary, Hillary earned $64,700 annually from various memberships on corporate boards, including those of two of the state's biggest employers, Wal-Mart and TCBY Enterprises, which also paid the Rose law firm some $750,000 in fees. The TCBY chairman explained Hillary's presence on his board as "making sure he was in good grace with the people in power."

In that atmosphere, Bill and Hillary developed a sense of entitlement, an expectation that others would take care of them. They became accustomed to borrowing from banks operated by political friends and accepting favors from individuals and corporations, such as the free use of private airplanes. Their behavior would have attracted close scrutiny on the national stage, but in Arkansas it was simply business as usual.

The Clintons had most conspicuously crossed the line in 1978, when they joined their friends James and Susan McDougal in buying 230 acres along the White River in the Ozarks for a land-development scheme that was to be known as Whitewater. "If Reaganomics works at all, Whitewater could become the western hemisphere's Mecca," Hillary wrote to James McDougal in 1981. The cost of the property was $202,611, and although they were equal partners the McDougals picked up almost all of the mortgage payments. It was easy to see why the McDougals saw this as money well spent. At the time, Bill was the Arkansas attorney general, and he undeniably had a political future.

Instead of severing relations with the McDougals after Bill was elected governor, the Clintons kept the partnership going. The Whitewater venture lost money, and the Clintons allowed the McDougals to cover three quarters of the losses, even though James McDougal operated on the edge of financial propriety and posed a risk to their good name. One of Hillary's more questionable moves, which appeared to be a clear conflict of interest, was to represent James McDougal's financially precarious savings-and-loan bank, Madison Guaranty, before a state commissioner who had been appointed by Bill. (The bank eventually cost taxpayers $73 million when it collapsed in 1989.) McDougal later claimed that he had put Hillary on a two-thousand-dollar-per-month retainer as a favor because Bill had told him they needed the money—an assertion that both Clintons denied. What's more, based on financial information they had received from James McDougal, the Clintons had filed tax returns that contained improper deductions.

These murky financial dealings surfaced briefly during the primaries in a March 8, 1992, article by *New York Times* reporter Jeff Gerth. It was a byzantine account that Hillary blunted with the help of New York lawyer Susan Thomases and Webster Hubbell, a partner at the Rose law firm. Although Thomases discovered that Hillary had "numerous" conferences with officials at Madison Guaranty, she managed to suppress that aspect of the story, in part by telling Gerth they had incomplete records and could not locate Hillary's billing files—a blatant lie, since both Hubbell and his Rose colleague Vincent Foster had reviewed and annotated the billing records.

When the Gerth story broke, some of Bill's aides urged him to hold a press conference. But Hillary was adamantly opposed, and her argument prevailed. Thomases was delighted that the story was "incomprehensible." The press found no further angles to pursue, and Whitewater quickly disappeared.

Two days after the *Times* report, Bill swept the Super Tuesday southern primaries, and a week later he won Illinois and Michigan. He had a bumpy ride in New York, primarily because of his deceptive answers to the marijuana questions and some vestigial interest in the state of the Clinton marriage. Bill recalled that when he appeared on Phil Donahue's talk show, the host drilled him for twenty minutes about marital infidelity. "I gave my standard answer," Bill wrote. "He kept on asking. I rebuffed him and the audience cheered. He kept right on." Bill won the New York primary with 41 percent of the vote, effectively wrapping up his nomination.

HILLARY HAD SEVERAL incarnations in the 1992 campaign. During the primaries, the Clinton team emphasized her role as coequal. "Buy one, get one free," said Bill, a phrase emblazoned on campaign buttons to appeal to women who "loved the modern-marriage pitch," said George Stephanopoulos. Hillary reinforced the message, telling voters, "People call us two-for-one." Out on the stump, Hillary spoke out on issues ranging from industrial policy to agricultural price supports. In strategy sessions, she operated on a par with Bill's advisors. She edited Bill's speeches and helped craft his language for the debates. She frequently deployed personnel to take care of various problems and tasks. When she was dissatisfied with the media plan for the New Hampshire primary, she ordered that it be redone. She moved quickly in what one of her aides called "an unemotional, highly rational, still human, but strategic way of dealing with problems.

She sort of had her own war room that went into action at various times when there was a crisis." Betsey Wright called Hillary a "process person" who operated as the "facilitator for making certain that the decisions [Bill] is leaning toward are ironclad, and by asking him the questions and walking him through scenarios, and playing devil's advocate, she keeps other people from imposing things on him. She has the trial lawyer's [ability] to punch a hole in an argument." Aides learned that Hillary was "the closer": no decision was final until she had signed off on it.

Bill called Hillary every night at around 10:00, and "they would talk about what happened that day, about political strategy," said a campaign aide. "She did not call him; he called her." When George Stephanopoulos first met the Clintons at the governor's mansion, he was struck by their informality together. Bill was padding around the bedroom in his briefs, while Hillary was offering cogent analyses of the primaries. Stephanopoulos imagined "the two of them propped up late at night, passing their reading back and forth, arguing, laughing, educating each other, sharing a passion for ideas." Susan Thomases believed that "it took the staff a long time to accept how close they are," but eventually, when Bill and Hillary were campaigning separately, the staff would arrange for them to rendezvous in Little Rock for twelve or twenty-four hours together. "They would have a complete resuscitation," said one high-ranking campaign aide.

As the extent of Hillary's role became known, former president Richard Nixon was moved to observe, "Hillary pounds the piano so hard that Bill can't be heard." Hillary was defiant at the time, saying she did not understand why Jimmy Carter's wife, Rosalynn, had been criticized for sitting in on cabinet meetings. "So what if she did?" asked Hillary. Bill disclosed that he expected Hillary to be a major force in his administration. "We will try to decide what it is she ought to do, and then discuss it with ourselves, and then tell the American people and give them time to get adjusted to it," he said.

Hillary's principal political role in the campaign was to be her husband's advocate. Her essential approach, said Betsey Wright, was that "no attack should be left unanswered." When he faced the accusations of dishonesty about women, smoking marijuana, and the draft, "she would be the first to react by saying not 'You're a bad boy,' but 'How do we dig out of it? What are the alternatives?' " recalled Mickey Kantor. "She was there every time fighting for how to make it better, deal with the situation. With Gennifer Flowers, who knows the full truth? But still, Hillary was his advocate. She had a client, and she was in love with her client. That was a formidable combination. She would take her emotional reaction and turn it into the energy to resolve the problem."

After the Flowers episode, Hillary worked with Susan Thomases and Betsey Wright to contain any more "bimbo eruptions," as Wright described them. As Hillary's proxy, Thomases consulted New York litigator Bernie Nussbaum about their "legal rights, liabilities, how to collect facts, hire investigators," Nussbaum recalled. "It was a sensitive subject." Subsequently, the campaign secretly paid one hundred thousand dollars to Jack Palladino, a San Francisco private detective, to dig up dirt on women in Wright's "doomsday book." Palladino would convince them to sign affidavits denying they had been sexually involved with Bill, out of fear that their private lives might be exposed. "[The Clintons] were saying, 'this is the only way to fight them,' " recalled Webster Hubbell, who did research into the women. "Anyone who criticized the Clintons we wanted to know what was in their background and what might be in their closet. Immediately it was, 'who did she sleep with and who were her boyfriends?' "

Hillary stumbled during the Illinois primary when she seemed to express contempt for homemakers after being confronted with charges that Bill had directed state business to Rose because she worked there. Standing in front of Chicago's Busy Bee restaurant, she heatedly said, "I suppose I could have stayed home, and baked cookies and had teas, but what I decided to do was fulfill my profession, which I entered before my husband was in public life." She immediately backtracked, but as with the Tammy Wynette comment it was a moment of authentic expression. "I don't know how you do it. I could never stay home with three kids all day," she once told Vince Foster's wife, Lisa.

In the spring of 1992, campaign pollsters discovered in their surveys that voters disliked Hillary's outspokenness, and many thought the Clintons were childless. In a somewhat imprudent memo, Greenberg described "the Hillary problem": "more than Nancy Reagan, she is seen as 'running the show.' " The campaign developed a "Manhattan Project" to present what Stephanopoulos called "homey details" about the Clintons.

Only weeks later, the Clintons were on the cover of *People* with their twelve-year-old daughter, Chelsea. Hillary declined to say much of significance about herself, however. "Bill and I were raised not to talk about what happened in your life," she explained. "That was bad form. It was unnecessary." They stopped the "buy-one-get-one-free" mantra, which Hillary later insisted actually meant nothing. She said she "thought it was funny. . . . People started introducing me that way and stuff. It was just viewed as a humorous twist."

Beginning in July, Hillary receded into the woodwork and insisted that her only role would be a "voice for children." She became "the good wife of a candidate," Mary Boyle, a county commissioner in Ohio, observed to Felicity Barringer of *The New York Times*. "Basically she had been tamed." The public saw the first manifestation of the "Hillary Nod," a reaction that kicked in whenever her husband was speaking. Her head would bob rhythmically, and her expression would show deep concern. "It's an absorption technique," said Betsey Wright, but its effect was an implicit command for others to agree along with Hillary.

She remained a crucial player behind the scenes. Although she didn't interview the candidates for Vice President, Bill consulted Hillary, who "was in every key meeting," said Mickey Kantor. "She had her say. She saw the power in choosing Al Gore." The selection of the Tennessee senator, another progressive southern politician, was designed to give Bill some gravitas and intensify the generational appeal of the Democratic ticket: two telegenic and smart Baby Boomers with a "sort of sibling synergy."

The son of a prominent liberal senator, Gore had been educated at Washington's elite St. Albans School and at Harvard, and he had been a journalist before turning to politics. Gore and his wife, Tipper, took several successful campaign bus trips with the Clintons, where they bonded to such an extent that Tipper called Hillary her "long-lost sister." "If there is a subject under the sun that we haven't discussed, I don't know what it might be," said Al.

Only in the last weeks of the campaign did Hillary return to her more customary assertive manner in public. Speaking to a crowd in Cincinnati shortly before Election Day, she used "we" so many times that a reporter joked about how much he enjoyed listening to "Mrs. Wilson," a reference to the wife of Woodrow Wilson, who took over in the last year of his presidency when he was incapacitated. *The New York Times* observed, "the real Hillary Clinton ... popped back up in an interview with Ted Koppel broadcast on Election Day," when Bill and Hillary "sat side by side in their airplane seats, and twice, as Koppel directed questions to Bill, Hillary answered for him. Her husband did not seem to mind, nor even particularly to notice."

WHEN BILL AND HILLARY learned they had won the presidency, their first reaction was to laugh. Hillary said a friend told them the victory was "like the dog that keeps chasing the car and all of a sudden catches it." The final tally gave Texas billionaire Ross Perot 19 percent—the highest number for an independent candidate since Theodore Roosevelt ran on the Bull Moose ticket in 1912. George H. W. Bush came in at 37.4 percent. Clinton's 43 percent was the smallest total for a winner in eight decades. In 1968, Richard Nixon had won by 43.4 percent to Hubert Humphrey's 42.7 percent, with 13.5 percent for George Wallace as a third-party candidate. Most political analysts believed that without Perot, Bush would have won reelection. "Bill Clinton and I were very fortunate to have a significant third-party candidate that drew virtually all of his votes from the Republican nominee," Al Gore said more than a decade later.

At the time, Bill claimed the Perot voters as his own, viewing his victory as a mandate of 62 percent for an ambitious package of programs to be enacted in his first one hundred days, FDR style. Viewed another way, almost six out of ten voters favored either Bush or Perot. The 43 percent for Clinton-Gore should have flashed a yellow rather than a green light—for incremental rather than sweeping changes. Another cautionary signal was Bill's lack of coattails. The Democrats lost nine seats in the House, while gaining one in the Senate. It should have been a time for bipartisan moderation, for including Republicans and independents in the cabinet and pursuing the New Democratic centrism of the campaign. But the Democrats had been out of the Oval Office for twelve long years, and they were in an expansive mood, eager to return to their liberal roots. Confident in their abilities, inexperienced in the ways of Washington, Bill and Hillary viewed the Democratic hold on both Capitol Hill and 1600 Pennsylvania Avenue as a source of great power, rather than as a fragile base to be tended carefully lest it break apart.

Chapter Two

—

IN THE SEVENTY-EIGHT-DAY INTERVAL BETWEEN HIS ELECTION AND HIS inauguration on January 20, 1993, virtually every decision Bill Clinton made had a direct impact on his first two years in office. He brought his work habits and patterns of behavior from Arkansas virtually intact, assuming they would naturally translate to the presidency. And he plunged ahead with plans for a big role for Hillary, even as more cautious hands urged restraint.

While he made some of his best decisions in assembling the team to manage the economy, he blundered in other crucial selections. He often worked at cross-purposes, making promises and then reversing them, sending mixed messages about his priorities. *U.S. News & World Report* noted that his style appeared to "oscillate between excruciatingly slow deliberations and spasms of frenzied activity." He launched a controversial initiative—lifting the ban on homosexuals serving in the military—seemingly by accident, and he allowed individuals and groups to jockey for power.

In the welter of conflicting pronouncements, he lost much of the momentum of his victory. His speechwriter Michael Waldman forlornly concluded, "Of the wasted prospects in the Clinton presidency, the transition was not only the first, but in some ways, the worst." Waldman cited "enormous wasted energy" on "task forces and clusters. . . . Nearly all of it was make-work."

The irony was that Bill was an avid student of history and had read at least ten presidential biographies for guidance on successful transitions. He cited Ronald Reagan's disciplined approach as his model, specifying that he would "follow Reagan's pattern in establishing a limited set of priorities." George Stephanopoulos said that, like Reagan, his boss didn't want to get "sidetracked by side issues." Indeed, the Reagan transition was a paragon of efficiency and planning that began seven months before Election Day, with nearly one thousand people working on it. By contrast, the Clinton transition sometimes seemed to have a staff of two—Bill and Hillary—and their failure to delegate slowed the appointment process to a crawl.

AFTER DISGUISING HILLARY'S advisory role during the general campaign, Bill took pleasure in displaying it publicly. When asked if Hillary would attend cabinet meetings, Bill said, "I hope so. . . . She knows more about a lot of this stuff than most of us do."

Hillary signaled her intention to have wide-ranging influence when she took the unprecedented step of sitting in on *Time's* "Man of the Year" interview, which was published in the last week of 1992. She offered her own extensive observations on "the right balance between moving forward and not getting caught up in politicizing everything you do," as well as "how you create a culture within the government . . . trying not only to build teams but to create a shared vision." She praised the virtues of managing "not in a hierarchical way, [but] in a team approach" that encouraged "cross fertilization of people's abilities."

When Bill described their shared decision making and how "we have always . . . given our opinions and helped each other to think through problems," Hillary instantly jumped in to contradict him. "That's not the way we do it, actually," she said. "In the process of talking about things, which we do all the time, we change each other's mind a lot," although she hastened to add that while they might disagree on the means to carry out a decision, "I can't think of anything where I was really upset about what he did. We think so much alike, and our values are so much alike."

The Clintons received no shortage of suggestions about what role Hillary should have in the White House. She was precluded from holding any official position in the cabinet or on the West Wing staff by an antinepotism statute passed by Congress in 1967, after Bobby Kennedy's tenure as Attorney General, which "prohibited a president's relative from serving in a post under his jurisdiction."

Veteran Washington journalist Sally Quinn, an accomplished hostess who had seen presidencies come and go, cautioned in *Newsweek* that Hillary "has always used 'we,' but 'we' is the kiss of death in Washington." Quinn observed that it is also regressive and sexist: "If she pursues the 'we' of governing, she is in danger of perpetuating the image of the intelligent wife living through her husband." Quinn admonished her not to attend her husband's meetings, "nor should she allow herself to become a scape-goat." The worst outcome, she said, would be the development of "two power centers . . . his and hers." She predicted that the "infighting, gossip and backbiting" would be "unmanageable . . . distracting and damaging to the President." Quinn's advice was prescient and sound, but the Clintons ignored all of it.

Hillary's old friend Donna Shalala urged her to have a full-time job outside the White House, perhaps as a law professor at Georgetown University. "In one of my early conversations with Hillary, I told her it was not to her advantage to run policy," Shalala recalled. "I thought she would get hurt. She said no, she was going to do a policy role, but she would be careful. She thought she was part of earning the presidency, and she wasn't about to not share the opportunity."

As Bill and Hillary sorted out what specifically she would do at 1600 Pennsylvania Avenue, she participated in the transition decision making, which was officially coordinated by Warren Christopher, a rather diffident but steely corporate lawyer from California who had served as Deputy Secretary of State for Jimmy Carter. Christopher "was so circumspect he didn't even feel his own pain," said one longtime aide. Most of the staff members were in offices in downtown Little Rock and Washington, but what Hillary called the "nerve center" was the brick, neo-Georgian Arkansas governor's mansion.

The President-elect met with advisors in his book-lined study or a low-ceilinged family room in the basement, while Hillary conferred with Susan Thomases and other friends and aides elsewhere in the mansion, often around the kitchen table, to discuss West Wing office assignments and sort through candidates for White House jobs. "Susan Thomases was running the White House piece of the transition," said Dee Dee Myers. "Hillary wanted control, and Susan could say no to people." Hillary frequently joined her husband and the other transition leaders, and at the end of the day, once the teams had disbanded, the Clintons usually found themselves "poring over policy papers and résumés together." She was "more influential than Christopher, though she didn't appear on any flow chart," observed Sidney Blumenthal, writing in *The New Yorker*.

Bill focused his attention for nearly two months on choosing his cabinet officers, their immediate subordinates, and even the aides below them. He later admitted, "I did micromanage. . . . I personally interviewed them all." Hillary quizzed many of the candidates and offered some of them guidance on how to deal with her husband. Robert Rubin of Goldman Sachs had been an advisor and fund-raiser during the campaign before Bill tapped him to head the new National Economic Council. Rubin was in the British Virgin Islands on vacation when he received a call from Hillary a few days before Christmas. She wanted to talk to him about the need for Bill to focus on economic issues. "My impression was she was very well organized, practical, and hardheaded," Rubin recalled. "I thought he would be the leader, and she would be the manager."

Like presidents before him, Bill selected a mixture of old friends— many of them Arkansans—campaign stalwarts, and new recruits. He tapped at least a dozen fellow Rhodes Scholars, including two of his closest friends, Robert Reich and Strobe Talbott, as Secretary of Labor and as Ambassador-at-Large overseeing policies toward the former Soviet Union. Bill wanted people he could trust, although as *Newsweek*'s Jonathan Alter later wrote, what he really needed was "something more: a human dam to hold back the tide of his past."

Hillary assigned herself the task of ensuring that Bill kept his pledge to appoint more women and minorities than any previous president, to make his Administration "look like America." She pressed him to fill half of the senior positions with women. And she specifically urged her husband to make history by appointing the first woman to one of the "big four" cabinet posts. With Texas senator Lloyd Bentsen slated for Treasury, Warren Christopher for State, and Congressman Les Aspin for Defense, the Attorney General was the only open position. "The Attorney General was a big deal for Hillary," said a top campaign and transition aide. "She was very focused on it. Yet nobody they proposed was their own person. They didn't have a ready woman."

Never before had an incoming First Lady put so many allies in key positions beyond her own staff: Her old friend Bernard Nussbaum headed the White House Counsel's office, assisted by Vincent Foster and another Rose partner, William Kennedy, and her high school friend Kevin O'Keefe; Webster Hubbell was Deputy Attorney General; Donna Shalala was Secretary of Health and Human Services; Wellesley friends Eleanor Acheson and Jan Piercy were at the Department of Justice and the World Bank. Al Gore, by comparison, placed only one colleague, Carol Browner, as head of the Environmental Protection Agency, and two of his choices for cabinet posts were rejected.

For the most part, Hillary kept a low profile during the interregnum, although she did make an appearance when Bill invited Democratic congressional leaders George Mitchell, Tom Foley, and Richard Gephardt to a meeting in Little Rock. "She stayed the whole time," her husband said proudly afterward. "She talked a lot. She knew more than we did about some things."

Bill's appointment of Donna Shalala—a veteran academic administrator with little experience in health care—indicated to experts in the field that he would "call the shots on health care reform from the White House." While the Clintons held their plans for Hillary's job close to the vest throughout the transition, by December the dimensions of her role were becoming apparent to a few insiders.

Health care was not a logical choice for Hillary—the way education or welfare policy would have been. She had served as chairman of the Children's Defense Fund, a national advocacy group, and in Arkansas had run a commission to improve the public school system, which had been ranked among the worst in the nation. Her track record on health policy was limited to having helped her husband put together a program expanding medical care into rural areas of Arkansas and serving on the board of the children's hospital in Little Rock. Her knowledge, she later admitted, was that of "a concerned citizen."

But Hillary wanted to lead national health-care reform. It would be the "signature initiative" of the first term, restructuring the entire health-

insurance system and extending coverage to the thirty-seven million uninsured. It would allow Hillary to control the fate of eight hundred billion
dollars in annual spending—one seventh of the economy. What's more,
Bill made the extravagant promise that he would introduce comprehensive
health-care legislation within the first hundred days of his presidency. The
Clintons were swinging for the fences, attempting to secure a place in the
history books with a sweeping policy that would rival anything Roosevelt
had done. Their stunning ambition was matched only by the naïveté and
impracticality of their expectations and strategies.

The first glimmer of their plans came in a meeting of the economic advisors with the President-elect in Little Rock in mid-December. After a discussion of health care's status within the budget proposals, the group
reached a tentative agreement. Hillary was not in the meeting, but Ira
Magaziner, a management consultant who had known the Clintons since
college days, sat quietly in a chair against the wall. As the discussion came
to a close, he began to speak.

"Ira was talking about his vision of health care," recalled Laura Tyson,
Chair of the Council of Economic Advisers. Magaziner's comments derailed the consensus on how to handle the issue and unnerved the economic team. On the plane back to Washington, "Bob Rubin was pretty
upset," said Tyson, who recalled that he had at least one glass of scotch to
calm down. "Only later did the participants in the meeting realize that Ira
was Hillary's proxy, and he had a mandate to present her position," said another top administration official. It was the first evidence of Hillary using
others to convey her wishes and leave no "fingerprints." Around that time,
Bill confided to Donna Shalala that he was "thinking of putting Hillary in
charge" of his health-policy proposals. "That's interesting," Shalala replied,
in a tone transmitting her disapproval.

Publicly, Bill remained noncommittal. In a preinaugural interview
with *The New York Times*, he said only that "I don't want her to have a job
outside the White House. I want her to help me." He announced that
Hillary would have a West Wing office but regretted that "they won't let us
knock down any walls, so we've got to figure out what to do." Bill also concealed the role of Ira Magaziner as Hillary's deputy on the health-care project, which Magaziner officially accepted on January 10. When the top
White House staff positions were finally announced four days later, Maga-

ziner was described as "senior adviser for policy development," focusing on worker training, education reform—and health care.

ONE OF BILL'S BIGGEST miscalculations—as he later freely admitted—was dawdling in picking his White House staff. He didn't give these appointments his full attention until after Christmas, when he completed his cabinet selections. By the turn of the year, only one hundred out of three thousand executive-branch jobs had been filled, which put the Clinton team about three months behind schedule. Neither Bill nor Hillary appreciated the importance of the White House staff. "They didn't realize how structured an administration eventually becomes and how much more they had to rely on staff to carry out orders than in the campaign or in Arkansas," said Bruce Reed, a domestic policy advisor in the West Wing. As Bill took his time, his aides began to resent the secrecy of the process in which Hillary was an equal partner, assisted by Susan Thomases. The Clintons applied what *Time* called a "strict quota policy," with Thomases "vetoing strong candidates." They chose almost exclusively from the campaign ranks and Little Rock buddies—unlike the Reagan transition, which had successfully integrated campaign loyalists with Washington veterans. There were so many thirtysomethings that they earned the nickname "The Brady Kids."

With the exception of foreign-policy experts, Bill and Hillary generally avoided appointees from the Carter years, for fear of being linked to an administration that was rejected after one term. "It was a decision of some consequence," said a top White House official. "It forced into the hinterland at the State Department and elsewhere a number of people who were extremely talented and experienced in the ways of Washington. Clinton was instead surrounded by younger staff with little experience." Bill didn't recognize the weaknesses of his team at the outset. When he unveiled the group just six days before the inauguration, one official grandly compared it to "the most important dinner party ever."

For his Chief of Staff, Bill picked Mack McLarty, a friend from Hope, Arkansas, where Bill had been born and spent his early years. An efficient, courteous business executive who had never before worked with Bill, McLarty was skilled at bringing an array of viewpoints to the table for consideration. This was crucial to Bill's determination to maintain his intensely personal operating style—dominating every sphere of government, wanting to know everything, making all decisions himself. But as presidential scholar Stephen Hess observed, Bill did not grasp that Washington "is not Little Rock writ large, that he is not in a three-ring circus but a thousand-ring circus, and he can't be ringmaster of each." Yet Bill had resolved to be just that, citing his reading of *Lincoln on Leadership* by Donald Phillips, which he called a "private Bible about how to govern." His lesson from it was that Lincoln "was always out and about picking up information. . . . You've got to go find the facts for yourself, and many of the good ones come from outside your inner circle. . . . A strict formal structure just won't cut it."

Bill set up a "spokes of the wheel" organization, with him at the hub and an array of senior staff reporting to him, as some other presidents, notably John F. Kennedy, had done. Hillary approved of this "nonhierarchical" management based on her experience as a Wal-Mart board member, and she had shared her enthusiasm there with her husband. "I was always fascinated by the way those executives would sit around and have their meetings and take some issue and just talk it through to death and get every angle of it," said Bill. Hamilton Jordan, who had been Jimmy Carter's Chief of Staff, was among the experienced hands who advised against this approach, arguing that "a loose White House structure . . . generates mixed signals, screw-ups, inconsistencies and infighting." But Jordan's plea to George Stephanopoulos got a cool rebuff.

Watching Bill's dithering over appointments and failure to meet self-proclaimed deadlines, the press concluded that his operation was disorganized and confused. His relations with reporters deteriorated as they challenged him for reneging on what Michael Kelly of *The New York Times* called "blue-sky no-pain promises." He had breezily pledged on national television the previous June that after winning the election he would spend "two hard months . . . to present a 100-day legislative plan to Congress" that would include "investing in jobs and education . . . and providing a basic package of health care to all Americans." His plan, he said, could be "ready on the desk of Congress the day after I'm inaugurated." It all sounded so effortless and attainable, until he began to grapple with the

demands of his transition. He started shifting his rhetoric to scale back expectations, particularly what he could accomplish in the first hundred
days.

One of his most contentious disagreements with the press was his
pledge early in the campaign to cut the taxes of the "forgotten" middle
class—those making less than eighty thousand dollars per year—by 10 percent. He continued to promote the idea even when he knew it was unworkable after hearing new deficit projections in August. As late as a week
before Election Day, he said he would "absolutely not" consider postpon-
ing the tax cut. But afterward, when reporters pressed him at a news conference, he unwisely flashed his anger, claiming that "the press thought
the most important issue in the race was the middle-class tax cut. I never
did meet any voter who thought that." Reporters rebuked him not only for
backtracking but for trying to rewrite his own words. Bill vented about his
coverage to aides, some of whom began calling NBC the "Nail Bill Clinton" network.

It was an NBC reporter, Andrea Mitchell, who caught him off guard a
week after the election when she queried him about a promise that he actually meant to keep. She asked him if he still intended to lift the forty-
eight-year-old ban on homosexuals in the armed services, and he replied,
"Yes, I want to." It was an assurance he had made repeatedly over the previous year to gay groups, which were among his strongest supporters. David
Mixner, one of his close advisors and a friend with whom he had protested
the Vietnam War, was an openly gay advocate for the change. But in making that apparently offhanded comment, Bill failed to anticipate resistance
from military leaders—led by General Colin Powell, Chairman of the
Joint Chiefs of Staff—who were concerned about the impact of openly ho-
mosexual servicemen and women on discipline and morale.

Although he was to back away from "immediate repeal," wrangling over
the policy consumed an inordinate amount of time during the transition
and the first months of the presidency, as Bill tried to placate his gay supporters and satisfy a military establishment already wary of him for avoiding the draft and saying he would cut the defense budget. "Like so much
else in those first few months, it just seemed to spin out of control," said
George Stephanopoulos. "Gays in the military" became a defining policy
that reinforced Bill's image as a conventional liberal after running as a

moderate. "No thinking person would have taken that on as his first issue," said one of Bill's major financial supporters. "He did it because he was not an organized person."

THE CLINTONS RATTLED along through the transition without fully understanding the perceptions they were creating They made two whirlwind trips to Washington, D.C., for meetings and events, working out of a suite at the Hay-Adams Hotel, overlooking the White House. When old friends came to call, Bill and Hillary greeted them casually, she in her bathrobe, he in his jogging clothes—a scene those closest to the Clintons were to see frequently in the White House Residence.

On the first thirty-six-hour foray, Bill and Hillary visited George and Barbara Bush for White House tours and briefings. Then Bill struck a disquieting note when he kept the entire U.S. Supreme Court waiting for an hour. On consecutive evenings, the Clintons attended dinner parties hosted by Democratic power brokers Pamela Harriman and Vernon Jordan. A few weeks later, they dined at the home of *Washington Post* board chairman Katharine Graham. These get-togethers were designed to introduce Bill and Hillary to the movers and shakers in the capital. It seemed like a good first step. *The Washington Post* noted that the President-elect wanted to "reassure the Establishment that he is not coming to make war on them"—a judgment that turned out to be premature.

On Thanksgiving weekend, the Clintons traveled to Summerland, California, for a short holiday at the eight-million-dollar, four-acre oceanfront estate rented by Harry Thomason and his wife, Linda Bloodworth-Thomason—Arkansas friends with whom the Clintons were "as interconnected as laces in a shoe." The Thomasons were producers of the hit CBS comedy *Designing Women*, as well as of *Hearts Afire* and *Evening Shade*. In the campaign, Harry had helped stage the debates and Bill's appearance at the convention, while Linda had produced a short documentary about the candidate called *The Man from Hope*, which had redefined him as a poor small-town boy who became a "noble public servant." The Clintons were so pleased with the Thomasons' work that they gave them responsibility for producing the four-day inaugural celebration.

Rather than a restful retreat, the California trip became another cavalcade of meetings and public appearances that included a session with

Ronald Reagan in his Los Angeles office, followed by a tour through a shopping mall in Glendale. Bill spent two happy hours wading through a crowd of thirty thousand, wearing a wireless microphone to broadcast his comments over a loudspeaker. He played beach volleyball, making himself conspicuous as "the one with the white legs," in the words of a female player, and he attended a black-tie birthday party for Harry Thomason in Pasadena at the Ritz-Carlton, where he capped the evening by ordering room-service pizza at 2:00 a.m.

Two weeks later, Bill presided over a two-day conference in Little Rock on the state of the economy. The guest list ballooned from one hundred to some 350 economists and business leaders, and the nineteen-hour gab-fest—ten hours the first day, nine the second—was broadcast live on C-SPAN. Bill was in his element, the consummate moderator and "tireless master of a thousand briefs," offering a primer on "mega-issues and meta-issues." "You watch Bill Clinton and you think he has a Teleprompter in his head and he's just reading from it," said his friend Vernon Jordan. Washington political commentator Elizabeth Drew was more skeptical, noting that Bill "seemed to have a compulsion" about "showing how much he knew." Hillary was a visible presence, but she made no comments and contented herself with scribbling notes.

None of the participants challenged the President-elect's viewpoint. "Like peacocks on audition, several speakers fluffed their intellectual plumage," wrote Thomas Friedman in The New York Times. It was unclear what sort of lessons television viewers learned, and it could be argued that planning and staging the event distracted Bill and his advisors from necessary decisions. Nevertheless, Bill wanted to "create a political mood," said Friedman. Since the election, economic indicators had shown signs of an accelerating recovery—a "supreme irony," wrote Newsweek's Robert Samuelson. "The 'weak' economy helped elect Bill Clinton, but in many ways George Bush is leaving a strong economy." While these improvements had taken shape early in the fall, the actual numbers—a 3.9 percent growth rate for the third quarter, rising consumer confidence, lower inflation, a drop in unemployment, higher productivity—weren't available until after Election Day. Bill Clinton "lucked out," said Samuelson.

Bill and his team were nevertheless intent on enacting a package of spending on government programs to stimulate the economy, and they didn't want to back off. In his public statements, Bill had been downplaying the good news, but he needed reinforcement from an expert at the conference. So his advisors secretly called John White, a Harvard professor who wrote a deficit-reduction plan that had been presented by Ross Perot. "I was told they needed someone to deliver the hard message," White recalled. "They dumped the data on me and provided me with the graphics." His message was to caution against getting "giddy about a possible recovery."

In part because Perot's emphasis on cutting the deficit had appealed to so many voters, the incoming administration was giving the issue more attention. Revised estimates now pegged federal deficits through 1996 at $290 billion per year—about $100 billion higher than anticipated. But Bill was still more interested in "investments" in roads, bridges, mass transit, education, and training than in cutting popular government programs. He proclaimed "absolute consensus" on the need for spending. It fell to political scientist Elaine Kamarck, one of the original theorists of the moderate Democratic Leadership Council, to emphasize the other side when she told the President he would have only six months to start reducing the long-term deficit. Bill greeted her blunt comments with silence and a trace of annoyance.

At the close of the conference on December 15, Bill had just ten days to meet his self-proclaimed deadline of appointing the entire cabinet by Christmas. His biggest challenge was finding a woman to nominate for Attorney General. His first choice, U.S. Appeals Court judge Patricia M. Wald, withdrew from consideration after what one transition official described as a "long flirtation" in which Wald went "back and forth." Women's groups pressured Bill to choose from their lists, prompting him to denounce them as "bean counters" trying to impose their will. He had no enthusiasm for any of their contenders and rejected the last one on December 23. The next day he submitted his own choice, forty-year-old Zoë Baird, the chief lawyer for Aetna. Baird had been under consideration for White House counsel, and she was a protégée of Warren Christopher. Bill had interviewed her only two days before he appointed her, but he said he found her to be "tough, tenacious and gifted." Hillary had liked her as well and supported the choice. In any event, Baird was "the last woman standing."

There was no doubt that Bill rushed the selection. The team responsible for vetting Baird told Bill that a Peruvian couple living illegally in the

United States worked as her nanny and chauffeur. She had sponsored the pair for citizenship but had not paid the workers' Social Security taxes until recently. Bill understood what Baird had done and "did not think it was a problem," Dee Dee Myers later explained. He was buttressed by the reassurances of Christopher, whose judgment he respected. The choice was "emblematic of our early troubles," concluded George Stephanopoulos. "By turning it into a quota, we put ourselves in a box . . . scrambling to find the best female Attorney General rather than the best Attorney General period."

With the cabinet in place, Bill and Hillary celebrated their last Christmas in Little Rock. Bill did his usual flurry of last-minute shopping—four hours in the local mall—and battled sniffles and hoarseness that he blamed on the holiday greenery. He constantly complained about allergies, but Hillary knew her man's foibles. "He gets these colds, and he calls them allergies," she told Robert Reich. "That gets him off the hook for being irresponsible." Bill's brother, Roger, showed up in a white sports car heaped with gifts, and the whole family gathered in the governor's mansion for a dinner of turkey, ham, sweet potatoes, Irish potatoes, green beans, broccoli, Jell-O salad, and two kinds of pie. Bill gave Hillary and Chelsea birthstone rings—an opal for his wife and an amethyst for his daughter—and Hillary gave him a set of Ping golf clubs in a white leather bag. Perhaps appropriately, given the tax increases he contemplated for the wealthy, they watched *Robin Hood* on TV.

Bernie Nussbaum got the summons to join the Clinton team at the end of the first week of January. When he arrived, Bill was on his way home from Austin, Texas, where he had been meeting with Mexican president Carlos Salinas de Gortari, so Hillary interviewed him first in the basement family room. His subsequent conversation with Bill ran about an hour and was "in retrospect poignant," recalled Nussbaum, who warned him of the perils of the Independent Counsel Law, enacted in 1978 after the Watergate scandals. The statute had expired in December 1992, but Congress was expected to revive it in the coming year.

The law was originally intended to create an autonomous prosecutor, appointed by federal judges to investigate misdeeds by high government officials. In practice, these prosecutors had a history of running open-ended investigations with unintended consequences. "I told him the last few presidents had gotten into serious political trouble because of certain legal difficulties, and that the job of White House Counsel was to make sure it didn't happen to him—to watch out, be aware, and make sure things didn't blow up," said Nussbaum. Bill acknowledged the issue but didn't show great concern.

After the interview had concluded, Hillary returned to the family room, prompting Bill to say to Nussbaum, "If you were my lawyer, who would you represent if there was a divorce?" "Which one of you has more money?" Nussbaum replied.

"They started laughing," he recalled. "They had a playful relationship. This was a joke you make in front of a wife you have affection for."

Neither Nussbaum nor his new boss fully appreciated the potential legal pitfalls they faced. But Vince Foster, who was to serve as Nussbaum's deputy, had some idea. Foster had known Bill since his early childhood in Hope, and he had been Hillary's closest colleague at Rose. Several weeks earlier, Foster had been working intensively with another Arkansas friend, corporate lawyer James Blair, to expunge Bill and Hillary's financial records of their misbegotten partnership with the McDougals. The Clintons decided to sell their stake to Jim McDougal for one thousand dollars, which would be reported on their financial-disclosure forms. McDougal was so broke that he didn't have the money, so Blair loaned it to him. It fell to Foster to figure out how to handle the transaction—and the dangling questions about the Clintons' losses on the venture—on their 1992 tax returns.

THE MANTRA FOR THE 1992 campaign had been "It's the economy, stupid," and Bill had appointed a highly capable team to manage economic policy: Lloyd Bentsen at Treasury had extensive experience from his years as chairman of the Senate Finance Committee; Robert Rubin, the chairman of the new National Economic Council, had run Wall Street's most prestigious investment bank; Leon Panetta, director of the Office of Management and Budget, was a longtime California congressman who as head of the House Budget Committee had been known as "Mr. No of Capitol Hill." Rounding out the team were two economists, Laura Tyson, a liberal whom Rubin admired for her "common sense on economic issues," and Alice Rivlin, Panetta's deputy, who was such an advocate of slashing the deficit that she had endorsed Perot's plan during the campaign.

Bill listened to the experts in the days before he moved to Washington. In the view of Robert Reich, "The new president was slightly intimidated by Bentsen and Panetta because they knew the Hill." Bill was similarly deferential toward Rubin's knowledge of the financial world. "Bill had great confidence about politics, ideas, and economics," said Reich. "He knew the arguments. But in the workings of Congress and the day-to-day mentality of Wall Street, he was less sure, which gave the deficit hawks power." At his first major budget discussion on January 7 in the governor's mansion, Bill finally acknowledged that deficit reduction was the "threshold issue." "I don't think it was thirty minutes before he looked up and said, 'I get it,' " recalled Rubin. "It was an essential decision to sacrifice programs in the campaign to be strong on the fiscal side." At that moment, the idea of a middle-class tax cut disappeared for good.

Bill's decision to abandon other promises was less admirable. To some extent, he simply underestimated the Democrats in Congress, who had become accustomed to the power and prerogatives of their majority status there yet had not worked with a president from their own party in a dozen years. In his meeting with Democratic congressional leaders twelve days after the election, Bill had unwisely yielded to their insistence that he drop his pledge to reform campaign-finance rules and lobbying practices. Bill was mindful that Jimmy Carter had harmed himself by failing to reach out to the barons of Capitol Hill, but by caving so quickly to their wishes he came across as weak. His reversal also angered Perot supporters, who wanted to reduce the influence of special interests in Washington.

It was only in retrospect that Bill was to acknowledge some of the failings of his transition, primarily his giving "almost no thought to how to keep the public's focus on my most important priorities." But he didn't come to grips with the ways in which he and Hillary set the tone for the Clinton presidency by keeping important parts of their agenda secret, by working through back channels, by purposely making her role ambiguous, and by inhibiting staff members who feared their pillow talk. "There was an air of distrust in the White House generally," said a prominent Clinton Administration official. "It was a world of shadows on the wall. This is very important to realize. You were always trying to read the shadows on the wall. Nothing was ever made clear."

Chapter Three

—

Leaving Arkansas was emotionally draining for Bill Clinton. He wept as he sang "The Battle Hymn of the Republic" at his last service at the Immanuel Baptist Church, and he slogged through the rain in a final round of golf. With an entourage of eighteen friends and staff members, he jogged around Little Rock, displaying his "particularly southern style . . . a slow and ambling trot," stopping at his old haunts, Community Baker and McDonald's, hugging everyone in sight. He freed Chelsea's pet frog in the Arkansas River, slapped yellow Post-it notes on his favorite histories and biographies, to be moved to the shelves of the Oval Office, and kept an appreciative crowd waiting for nearly an hour and a half for his arrival at a ceremony in his honor at the Little Rock statehouse.

At 5:15 a.m. on Saturday, January 16, the day he was due to leave town, Bill made a private farewell—the sort of risky encounter that was to imperil his presidency five years later. He was visited in the mansion's basement office by Marilyn Jo Jenkins, an energy-company executive with whom he had a close relationship. State troopers who worked for him later made sworn statements that he and Jenkins had been seeing each other since the late 1980s. Trooper Danny Ferguson testified that he had escorted Jenkins to see Bill four times in the days before the Clintons left Little Rock. Bill had also phoned her frequently in the preceding years. One call, at 1:23 a.m. from a hotel in Virginia, lasted ninety-four minutes. It was in fact Jenkins who had posed the "serious threat" to the Clinton marriage that Betsey Wright described.

Both Jenkins and Bill later denied they had a sexual relationship, and she explained that he had only been helping her through a "personal crisis." But he ultimately admitted that he had been to her apartment ten times, and his lawyer, Robert Bennett, noticed that he had a "forlorn and wistful" look when he talked about her. Bill also eventually acknowledged giving Jenkins gifts that Christmas and confirmed the predawn rendezvous at the governor's mansion.

After a delayed departure that evening, Bill and Hillary spent the night in Charlottesville, Virginia. The next morning, they toured Monticello, the home of the President with whom Bill felt special kinship and whose name he proudly carried. The two men had similarly prismatic characters, and Bill once observed that Thomas Jefferson "understood the kind of complexity that we're facing today. He had a fertile, complex mind and he understood how to reconcile the bedrock principles and apply them to the facts of the case at hand." When he felt "some sense of despair" during his presidency, Bill read from Jefferson's Notes on the State of Virginia and from Daniel Webster's eulogy to Jefferson and John Adams, who both died on July 4, 1826. One admonition by Jefferson particularly resonated: It was the "duty" of a President's advisors "carefully to veil from the public eye the weaknesses, and still more, the vices of our character."

On Sunday, January 17, Bill and Hillary joined Al and Tipper Gore on a bus with the license plate HOPE for the 120-mile journey to Washington, reenacting the trip that Jefferson had made in 1801. After conducting an interview with Bill and Hillary, NBC Nightly News anchor Tom Brokaw lingered while the two couples sat around a table in the kitchenette in the front of the bus. "It struck me like a college-dorm bull session rather than an incoming administration," Brokaw recalled. "Hillary was not leading, but she was like a junior partner. It was Gore to Bill Clinton, and Hillary was gracefully part of the conversation. My Blink moment was that they were not as well prepared as they thought." As the bus neared Washington, the First Couple retired to the rear of the bus and "canoodled." "They were affectionate," said Brokaw. "That really sticks in my mind."

These moments of physical contact—the two of them holding hands, or Bill curling his arm around Hillary's shoulders or leaning his face against her temple—were witnessed by colleagues and the press. The image was companionate rather than passionate, as Al and Tipper Gore seemed to be, and to some extent reflected Bill and Hillary's mastery of what White House Press Secretary Michael McCurry called "the science of how they interacted publicly"—the well-practiced whisper, the peck on the forehead even in periods of terrible tension. But at other times they made tender gestures without seeming to know they were being observed. "I *have* seen affection between them when it was not staged," said Bev Lindsey, the wife of Bill's longtime aide. On one campaign swing, their friend Linda Aaker watched as Hillary ate an apple, and Bill reached over to take a bite. "It was not grabbing but rather done in a sharing way," said Aaker. "It was more intimate than watching people kiss."

Bill and Hillary had an appealing and youthful appearance. Bill stood just over six foot two, and his thick thatch of well-coiffed salt-and-pepper hair made him appear even taller. He had long arms, big hands, broad shoulders, size-thirteen feet, and an oversized head. His face was fleshy and surprisingly pink, his eyebrows pale, and his features irregular, although taken together he was nearly handsome, and certainly striking. His nose was slightly bulbous, his keen blue eyes were engulfed by heavy lids and prominent bags, and he had an ample and jutting jaw. His mouth seemed disproportionately small and pouty in repose—"the sexiest mouth I had ever seen," said Gennifer Flowers. His grin was incandescent and boyish, and he would go slack-jawed at moments of wonderment. When something provoked him, his lips tightened, and his chin protruded even farther.

Tipping the scales at 226 pounds, he was well beyond his college weight of 195. When his girth increased on the campaign trail, Harry Thomason bought him boxy new suits. As an overweight child, Bill had been dressed by his mother in too flashy clothes—one Easter in a pale short-sleeved shirt, "white linen pants, pink-and-black Hush Puppies, and a matching pink suede belt"—and his sartorial choices hadn't improved much over the years. He thought nothing of wearing a lavender T-shirt emblazoned with Hope's famous watermelons. For his last "Turkey Trot" five-kilometer race before Thanksgiving in Little Rock, he arrived in silver tights, blue shorts, and a white sweatshirt with "42" on his chest.

Like her husband, Hillary had a large head; Bill once observed that it "seemed to be too big for her body." At five foot four, she didn't seem particularly petite, however. Her figure was matronly, her legs thick. Once she recognized the importance of her appearance for Bill's political career, she had remade herself in characteristically systematic fashion during the 1980s, first taming her wild and frizzy hair, then transforming it from brown to blond after reading in Margaret Thatcher's autobiography that women of a certain age should go lighter (although her eyebrows remained dark and thick). She took to wearing headbands because they covered her brown roots, but during the 1992 campaign her advisors decided that she looked severe, vaguely resembling a suburban Republican. They orchestrated a makeover led by Linda Bloodworth-Thomason, who brought in Hollywood hairstylist Cristophe Schatteman, a former hockey player from Belgium. Cristophe chopped off five inches and gave her a soft page-boy with wispy bangs. *Designing Women* consultant Cliff Chally helped to change Hillary's wardrobe from the bold checkered suits that had been alternating with straight skirts, baggy sweaters, and black tights. Chally dressed her in subtly tailored ensembles in muted colors, including proper St. John Knits. "We needed things toned down because she's somebody with strong features and a strong personality and ideas, so you don't want too much noise going on," said Strobe Talbott's wife, Brooke Shearer, one of her campaign aides.

Hillary nevertheless remained uncertain about how to look as she experimented with her wardrobe and tried a dizzying variety of hairstyles, including "her hair on top of her head in a mass of blond curls," as described by Sally Quinn, "very Krystle in *Dynasty*, very un-Hillary." Hillary wondered as well, querying her old friend Sara Ehrman, "What did you think of my hair last night, that getup?" When her friend said she liked it, Hillary replied, "I think I looked like a dork. I did. I looked dorky."

The most dramatic change in Hillary's appearance had come in her thirties when she switched from the exceptionally thick glasses she had worn since age nine to soft contact lenses, revealing wide blue eyes that her husband considered "beautiful." She had a pretty profile, featuring a straight nose and strong chin. Her face was round; she had a generous mouth with a slight overbite and prominent buccal pouches that created the impression of a faintly dimpled smile. After years as what Lois Romano of *The Washington Post* referred to as "an overweight, underdressed policy wonk who hadn't seen daylight for a while," Hillary was one of the lucky few whose looks improve with age.

THE CLINTON INAUGURAL committee described its four-day celebration as "a cross between a State Dinner at the White House and a Crittenden County 'coon supper.'" The total cost came to thirty million dollars, about 50 percent more than originally budgeted. Although the Washington Establishment was ready to embrace the Clintons, the First Couple remained wary, despite their brief overtures during the transition.

Shortly after the election, Sally Quinn had advised the Clintons, "You have to run against 'inside Washington' to get in and you have to become inside Washington to stay in." Writing in *The Washington Post*, she urged them to follow the advice of Jack Watson, Jimmy Carter's last Chief of Staff, and "accept Washington's hospitality." "Don't paint everybody with the same dark brush," Watson said. Quinn wrote, "People want to befriend the new president and his people. Don't be naive about their motives, take advantage of them." Quinn's husband, Ben Bradlee, the former editor of the *Post*, had his own succinct advice: "Don't lie. If you get in a corner, don't talk. But don't lie either."

As Linda Bloodworth-Thomason told *The New York Times*, Hillary was going to be "watching on both sides. . . . She knows that Washington is treacherous." On his second day in town, during a five-hundred-thousand-dollar "Faces of Hope" luncheon at the Folger Shakespeare Library for fifty-three ordinary people he had met during the campaign, Bill painted the nation's capital with the "dark brush" Watson had cautioned against: "I'll remember that this town, which gets so caught up in itself, and who's in and who's out, who's up and who's down, and the gossip that's in the paper every day about the manipulations of power, doesn't amount to one hill of beans unless we are spending all the money that you send us, to try to help deal with your problems in an honest and forthright way."

Bill and Hillary also approved an attack on the press by the Thomasons. It was a five-minute video shown at the inaugural gala that featured clips of such political commentators as David Broder and Fred Barnes dismissing Bill during the primary campaign as a "loser" and "dead meat." The background music was Frank Sinatra singing George Gershwin's "They All Laughed." ("They laughed at us and how./But ho, ho, ho! Who's got the last laugh now?") The Clintons thought the film was funny—and were un-concerned that it would anger the Washington press corps.

In choosing to antagonize the Establishment rather than welcome it, Bill and Hillary had proxies in the Thomasons, who would say things that the Clintons thought. "We're bunker people," Linda admitted. "The four of us are good in the foxhole together." After *The New Republic* criticized her convention film, *The Man from Hope*, Linda fought back on her sit-com *Hearts Afire*, having one of her characters call Washington a "chau-vinistic, mean-spirited, pompous-ass town" and dismiss its elite magazine editors as "11 little old baby Harvard boys" who are "irrelevant, arrogant, snide and cynical and negative and . . . they're short." Rather than discour-aging her, the Clintons took pleasure in her barbs.

When the Thomasons unveiled their inaugural plans, reporters criti-cized the week's festivities as an extended political commercial designed to keep the press at bay. *New York Times* reporter Frank Rich called it the "Wal-Mart inaugural week, a ludicrous public display . . . a coronation produced by a sitcom producer." With their opulent bashes, the Demo-crats looked just like Republicans. Even self-proclaimed populist James Carville joined the "let-'em-eat-cake brigade" by hosting two lavish parties. With echoes of 1960s radical chic, the Clinton inaugural became "Wood-stock in a limousine."

HILLARY FORBADE BILL'S mother, his brother, Roger, and her brothers, Hugh and Tony, from talking to reporters, but their antics nonetheless cre-ated unwelcome sideshows. On the strength of his connections, thirty-six-year-old Roger—described by *The New Yorker* as "musically challenged" —landed a two-hundred-thousand-dollar contract with Atlantic Records and a deal with the Greater Talent Network to give motivational speeches. "Without the fact of the shared last name, I don't know if the deal would exist," said Peter Guber, chairman of Sony Pictures.

Roger had been arrested twice for minor scuffles since his release from prison after serving a little more than a year for dealing drugs, and he had nearly been sent back when he began using cocaine again. He had knocked around, working at a horse farm, in a convenience store, and on road con-struction before the Thomasons gave him a job on the set of *Designing Women*, where they could keep an eye on him. Now he had arranged to make his national singing debut with En Vogue at the MTV Rock and Roll Inaugural Ball. Wearing a tuxedo instead of his usual gaudily patterned drawstring pants, Roger's nasal voice failed to impress the crowd.

Hillary's portly younger brothers, known variously among the Clinton staff as "The Boys," "Da Bears," and "The Brothers Karamazov," embarrassed their sister when the press discovered that they had solicited ten-thousand-dollar donations from corporations such as Ford and Mobil to underwrite parties in their honor. "The Rodham brothers were a nightmare," said Mary Mel French, cochair of the inaugural. "They made all sorts of demands, and Hillary never crossed them or confronted them or denied them anything, which was odd, since she confronted Bill."

Bill's sixty-nine-year-old mother cut an eccentric and showy figure as she swept through parties, which she attended with her fourth husband, Richard Kelley. Bill's stepfather Roger had died of cancer twenty-five years earlier, and Virginia had also lost a third husband, Jeff Dwire, a hairdresser who had served nine months in prison for stock fraud, to complications from diabetes. Even in the throng, she was hard to miss with her extravagant spray of white hair fanning from her forehead through her otherwise coal-black teased coif. She wore sunglasses and a white fur coat to one evening gathering and flirted with Harry Belafonte and Mickey Rooney at another. Sitting in a box at the Arkansas Ball, she ordered a Chivas Regal on the rocks. When the waiter said there was no hard liquor, she replied with an incredulous smile, "Let me get this straight. My son was inaugurated President of the United States, and I can't have a drink?" Aides quickly arranged for a bottle of Chivas to be purchased at a nearby liquor store. No one knew she had terminal cancer that had recurred in the middle of the campaign, after a mastectomy two years earlier. She told everyone—including her sons—that she was being treated for a herniated disk, but in fact her cancer had spread to her spine, skull, pelvis, and legs, and she was in considerable discomfort.

The one family member who got a pass from the press was Chelsea. The most pointed commentary came over Bill and Hillary's decision to enroll her at Sidwell Friends, an elite private school. In Little Rock, her public school had been 59 percent black and 41 percent white, and Sidwell had a significantly lower minority presence. President Jimmy Carter said he was "very disappointed" that Chelsea wouldn't attend the "very low income" public school in Washington where his daughter, Amy, had been educated with "the servants of foreign ambassadors." But the Clintons said their choice was based on Sidwell's academic excellence.

At age twelve, Chelsea had a plain face, braces on her teeth, and a tangled mass of long, wavy hair. But behind the gawky presence was a sensibility honed by a life in the spotlight. She was born into politics and had never known anything different. "They talk to Chels like she's an adult," said Ann McCoy. From the age of six, Chelsea had to develop finely tuned antennae when her parents began doing a dinnertime drill in which they took turns pretending to be one of Bill's political opponents, saying he had "done a terrible job. He doesn't care about anybody. He's a bad person."

When the Gennifer Flowers story broke, Hillary took Chelsea to the supermarket, pointed at the tabloids, and "told her that what we heard was going to be in one of them." Hillary explained that she and Bill wanted their daughter "to feel she's a part of this." Chelsea watched the 60 Minutes interview about Flowers with Bill and Hillary and afterward said, "I think I'm glad you're my parents."

Several nights later, once the Flowers tapes had been broadcast on television and radio, Hillary was scheduled to appear on ABC's Primetime Live with Sam Donaldson. Bill was back in the governor's mansion with Chelsea and Mickey Kantor. "Mom is going on TV, and I want you to watch it with me," Bill told his daughter. "Here is my side of the story." It was a discomfiting performance. After Donaldson played part of the tape in which Flowers said, "Good-bye, darling" and Bill replied, "Good-bye, baby," Hillary simply denied reality, saying, "Oh, that's not true. That's just not true."

"That didn't happen?" Donaldson asked.

"Of course not," Hillary replied, adding that Flowers had "pretended that her life was ruined because somebody had alleged that she had a relationship at some point with Bill." In Little Rock, Kantor observed that "Chelsea watched and understood. This was how two parents worked it out under public scrutiny."

"Chelsea is a lot like her mother," said seventy-three-year-old Dorothy Rodham after the election. "She just makes the best of everything." Hillary was proud that their dinner-table role-playing had helped Chelsea "gain mastery over her emotions." Chelsea used to tell her friends, "Emotions aren't rational." It was a sentiment she picked up from her parents—echoing Hillary's years-earlier pronouncement that "unthinking emotion is pitiful to me." In the view of one of her friends, Chelsea was "a combination of her parents. Her mom is all about strength. If people are against you, you are stronger. Her mother had a strong survivor mentality." At the same time, "her dad used people to a certain degree, and Chelsea did the same. People would give things to Chelsea, offer their help. She knew the motivation, but she always accepted, she took their gifts. It was an unspoken thing." She idolized her father and admired his ability to "talk for hours, and she wanted to be like that. She liked to hear herself talk, and she liked having an audience. . . . Everyone was impressed by how polite and nice she was. Chelsea was always 'on,' and didn't let herself slip into a rude persona. She was properly raised, but she wasn't witty or easy."

FROM THE MOMENT they arrived at the Lincoln Memorial on Sunday the seventeenth, the Clintons seemed to be everywhere at once. They filled Blair House, the official government guest quarters across from the White House, with staff, family, and friends including Jim and Diane Blair and Bruce and Bev Lindsey. Hillary's mother and father settled into the Foreign Minister Suite. At eighty-one, Hugh Rodham had suffered a series of small strokes and was in a wheelchair, but he was beaming with pride. Chelsea and a group of schoolmates occupied the top floor. Aides set up a TelePrompTer in the library for Bill to practice his inaugural address. "We ran a continuous buffet," said Benedicte Valentiner, Blair House administrator. "The Clintons hardly went to bed."

On their first full day, the Clintons attended a two-hour "Call for Reunion" concert at the Lincoln Memorial, where Bill gazed in open-mouthed wonder as a group of star saxophonists played "Heartbreak Hotel." Along with the Gore family, the Clintons were joined by eighteen thousand people in a procession across the Arlington Memorial Bridge, where they rang a replica of the Liberty Bell as part of a nationwide "Bells for Hope" celebration. They brought some forty friends back to Blair House, and at 2:00 a.m. a butler found Bill asleep in an armchair in the library with a draft of the inaugural address in his lap.

The next morning, Bill awoke early for a jog before a marathon of speeches and appearances around the city that included four $1,500-ticket fund-raisers in the evening, followed by an inaugural prayer meeting at the First Baptist Church that didn't end until 1:15 a.m. The day before the inaugural was no less hectic, with a visit to the Kennedy grave site in Arlington National Cemetery and a "Celebration for Children" at the Kennedy Center with Hillary, Mister Rogers, and Markie Post, one of the stars of the Thomasons' *Hearts Afire*. While Bill had lunch at the Library of Congress with Democratic and Republican governors, Hillary strolled along the Mall to survey the "America's Reunion" festival she had planned. That evening, the Clintons were nearly an hour late for the inaugural gala at the Capital Centre. The concert was "excessive beyond one's wildest dread," wrote Tom Shales of *The Washington Post*. Bill and Hillary held hands as Barbra Streisand serenaded them with "Evergreen," and Bill sang along with "Rock My Soul." When Bill took to the stage, sitting on a stool under a bright spotlight like a lounge singer, he said, "Thank you for sharing with me my last night as a private citizen." "This man must have one of the highest embarrassment thresholds in the civilized world," wrote Shales. Afterward, the diminutive sex therapist Dr. Ruth Westheimer observed with ditzy prescience that once Bill Clinton solved the country's problems, "the sex will be superb."

Behind the scenes, preparation of the inaugural address was chaotic—a condition that was to typify the writing of Bill's important speeches in the following years. He had begun working with his staff weeks before, around the dining room table in the governor's mansion. "His words flew quickly and his southern accent thickened," recalled speechwriter Michael Waldman. "At the same time he seemed disorganized, even then exhausted by the task he had set out for himself." Two nights before the inaugural, the speech remained a jumble, as Bill continued to take suggestions at Blair House from "whoever managed to wander in," recalled George Stephanopoulos. Bill summoned two friends who were professional writers, Taylor Branch and Tommy Caplan, and both men pitched in with phrases and themes. With all his additions and amendments, Bill managed to double the length of the speech, creating a "rambling effort" that in the view of Stephanopoulos would "send a signal of indiscipline and self indulgence." So on inaugural eve after the gala, Bill sat with his staff clustered around, rewriting, cutting, and practicing until 4:30 a.m., as his vice president dozed upright in a chair.

The high-spirited mood of the week was slightly dimmed by events in Iraq. Starting at the end of December, American jets had been skirmishing with Iraqi aircraft challenging the zones in the northern and southern parts of the country where they had been forbidden to fly since the end of the Gulf War in 1991. These clashes escalated on the Monday before the in-augural, when George Bush launched a cruise-missile attack on a Bagh-dad military complex after the Iraqi government blocked access to United Nations inspectors monitoring weapons of mass destruction. In an inter-view with *The New York Times* a week before his inaugural, Bill had spoken about Iraq's tyrannical leader Saddam Hussein with what *The New Repub-lic* called "alarming innocence." "I believe in deathbed conversions," said the President-elect. "If he wants a different relationship with the United States and with the United Nations, all he has to do is change his behav-ior." It was one of the instances when Bill said too much as he was feeling confident and relaxed. Recognizing his misstep, Bill compounded the problem by accusing the newspaper of misquoting him, only to retreat when the *Times* produced a transcript. Al Gore counteracted the percep-tion of his boss's weakness by appearing on *Meet the Press* to say that Sad-dam should be removed from power because of his brutality toward his own people. Saddam reacted by praising the President-elect for his "anti-war past."

Inauguration day dawned cold and clear under a flawless cerulean sky. Bill was up at 7:00 a.m. for a national-security briefing that brought news of a daylong cease-fire in Iraq. He and his family went to the Metropolitan African Methodist Episcopal Church for a rousing prayer service, the first time a President-elect had gone to a predominantly black church on the morning of his inauguration. Bill sang "Holy Ground" and "Precious Lord, Take My Hand," at one point pausing to wipe away a tear. Inevitably, the Clintons were running late, and both showed signs of crabbiness as they left Blair House for the White House. A U.S. Park Police officer later said that he had been shocked to hear the First Couple exchange profanities — something their aides in Arkansas had been accustomed to hearing. Bill and Hillary arrived twenty-seven minutes late for coffee with George and Barbara Bush before taking the motorcade to the Capitol. While the Clin-tons waited in a holding room, members of Congress heard further sharp exchanges.

But out on the West Front in the sunshine on January 20, 1993, looking across the crowds toward the Washington Monument, Bill delivered a
crisp and simple inaugural address that lasted only fourteen minutes—a
model of concision compared to his fifty-five-minute acceptance speech at
the convention. As the outgoing President appeared impassive, Bill decried the way the country had "drifted" over the previous decade. Drawing
from his campaign rhetoric, Bill spoke of renewing America through individual responsibility and national service. "There is nothing wrong with
America that cannot be cured by what is right with America," he said, in an
unmistakable homage to John F. Kennedy, whose hand he had shaken
during a visit to the White House nearly three decades earlier. After taking
the oath of office, the new President gave a round of hugs to everyone except Chief Justice William Rehnquist. Hillary wore a royal-blue coat with
a high collar and a matching broad-brimmed hat that Robert Reich
likened to a UFO hovering over her. Soprano Marilyn Horne sang, and
Maya Angelou, Bill's favorite bard, read an inaugural poem, "On the Pulse
of Morning."

Following a precedent established by Jimmy Carter, the Clintons left
their limousine several blocks from the White House to walk along the parade route. But unlike their predecessors, Bill and Hillary only occasionally held hands—and then for just a few paces. The image of them ten feet
apart, waving separately to the crowds, offered an inadvertent insight into
their relationship. Hillary was "walking at her own pace, several yards out
of the shadow of a husband who had to stretch to cling to her hand if there
was hand-holding to be done," noted *The New York Times.*

The first party at the White House that night was given by Chelsea for
her Arkansas contingent, along with Al and Tipper's daughter Sarah and a
group of Washington friends. They tore from the basement to the top floor
seeking clues ("find the secret staircase") for a scavenger hunt organized by
the Residence staff, and ate a buffet dinner of pizza, potato chips, fruit
salad, and cookies in the Family Dining Room on the ground floor.

The inaugural balls offered a new politically correct diversity, with the
first one for homosexuals, as well as an anti–animal oppression party,
where people dressed as artichokes and broccoli. In the "anything goes"
Baby Boomer spirit, some men wore turbans, and others wore sneakers
with their tuxedos. Bill and Hillary stayed as long as they could at each of

the thirteen balls they visited. Dressed in a purple lace evening gown glittering with beads and a rhinestone clasp at the waist, her hair upswept in a French twist, Hillary danced with her husband eleven times.

Bill picked up the saxophone to play five tunes, including "Night Train" and "Your Mama Don't Dance." At one point, he declared, "I feel like I been rode hard and put away wet." At the last stop, the still-exuberant new President said, "We got no sleep last night, and we're still standing. We're defying gravity as you watch."

In one of the few quiet moments of the evening, Bill and Hillary excused themselves from the MTV ball to meet with James Riady, deputy chairman of his family's Lippo Group, an Indonesia-based financial conglomerate with extensive business in the family's native China. The Clintons had been friendly with the Riadys since the mid-1980s, when Lippo began working with the powerful Stephens Investment Bank in Little Rock. During 1992, the Riadys had contributed more than five hundred thousand dollars to the Democrats, and in the coming years James Riady and his employee John Huang were to visit the White House numerous times. Later in 1993, Riady arranged the President's meeting with Indonesian president Suharto to discuss trade matters of interest to Lippo, though during the campaign Bill had condemned the authoritarian leader's human-rights abuses as "unconscionable." But it was the Chinese connection that was to create problems for the Clintons. A Chinese government company owned a stake in a Hong Kong bank controlled by Lippo—one of many deals that prompted questions about improper influence by the Chinese in the Clintons' fund-raising for the 1996 presidential campaign.

When Bill and Hillary were finally driven through the White House gates, it was 2:15 a.m. The Thomasons were in the Lincoln Bedroom, and Bill's mother and stepfather took the Queen's Bedroom, while the Blairs joined Roger Clinton, the Rodham brothers, and Chelsea's friends in the seven guest rooms on the third floor. Hillary later wrote that she and her husband had "crashed into bed" because they had been "too tired to explore these grand new surroundings." Bill had a different memory. He knew he had to get up early but recalled that he was "too excited to go right to bed." With his typically irrepressible curiosity, he couldn't resist temptation. "I wanted to look around," he said. And so he did, starting a nocturnal pattern that persisted to his last day in office.

Chapter Four

—

COMPARED TO PRESIDENTS REAGAN AND BUSH, WHO RAN THEIR STAFFS like CEOs overseeing senior managers, the Clintons were like a pair of dorm parents supervising a collection of precocious adolescents who referred to the White House and its grounds as "the campus." Hillary wielded the rule book, but Bill let the kids have fun after curfew. Women routinely wore slacks, and young men favored open-necked shirts. Some male staff members sported earrings, beards, or ponytails as well. With his mop of black hair and baby face, thirty-one-year-old White House Communications Director George Stephanopoulos was the avatar of informality, known for chewing bubble gum in interviews.

Pizza boxes and takeout containers littered offices and conference rooms, and the thrumming guitars of R.E.M. filled the once-hushed corridors of the Old Executive Office Building (OEOB), where most of the White House staff worked. The White House Mess, previously a white-tablecloth preserve for senior staff, resembled a student union as twenty-something aides lined up, cafeteria style, to dine on taco salad and Oreo yogurt.

Officially, Bill was "Mr. President," but staff members referred to him as "The Big Guy," "Boss," or "Chief," and Hillary's staff affectionately called her "The Big Girl" and later "Big Mama." But Secret Service agents no longer used Bill's code name "Elvis," as they had during the campaign. Now the First Couple were "Eagle" and "Evergreen"—alternatively "POTUS" and "FLOTUS"—and Chelsea was "Energy."

The freewheeling tone came straight from the top, starting with Bill's casual view of the Oval Office, which his staff called "The Oval." Bill turned over its décor to Kaki Hockersmith, a Little Rock interior designer and longtime friend. She hung bright gold curtains trimmed in blue, replaced the muted rug with one of bright blue adorned by the presidential seal in the center, and covered the sofas flanking the fireplace in what speechwriter Michael Waldman called "alarming yellow and maroon" stripes. The color scheme echoed that of Washington's football team, prompting one wag to refer to the office as "The Redskin Room." Hillary had a hand in the adjacent private study, where Bill kept his collection of vintage wooden golf clubs and stacks of presidential golf balls. She hung a black-and-white photograph of herself with Chelsea behind the desk and set up a CD player so he could listen to Kenny G and Barbra Streisand. During Bill's early months in office, Chelsea could be glimpsed doing her homework in that hideaway—the very spot where Bill was later to have assignations with Monica Lewinsky.

At first, Bill spent as much time as he could in the Oval Office, sitting behind John F. Kennedy's desk, which he had had retrieved from storage. He selected the artwork, including a portrait of George Washington and a 1917 Childe Hassam painting of flags, placed busts of Abraham Lincoln, Franklin D. Roosevelt, and Harry Truman on shelves and tables, and spread around so many tchotchkes (presidential medallions, campaign buttons, a chunk of rock from the moon) that *Newsweek* observed that "the highest office in the land looks a bit like a Presidential souvenir shop." He delighted in giving tours of the office, regaling visitors with its history.

Yet he seemed to have little reverence for the atmosphere and ethos of the place. Shortly after his inauguration, he invited Annie Leibovitz in for a photo shoot, and to the consternation of veteran West Wing employees she blasted Eric Clapton's *Unplugged* from her boom box. When Tom Brokaw arrived one spring morning for NBC's "Day in the Life of the President" feature, Bill joined him after jogging with two members of Congress. "He was standing there in his shorts, all sweaty with his white thighs," Brokaw recalled. "He was showing off the Oval Office to these congressmen. It was not quite right."

Bill seemed determined to pull down the wall of mythology around the president, to shorten the distance between himself and the people. "I'm not one for rules," his mother once declared, and the same could be said for Bill. He dismissed signs of deference and wouldn't permit his staff to rise when he entered a room. In answer to a question during an appearance on MTV, he famously admitted that he wore briefs, not boxers. He would think nothing of sampling food from someone else's plate, inquiring, "You don't want that, do you?" "He eats like a Tasmanian devil," said Hollywood producer Mort Engelberg. During his first trip on Air Force One, three weeks after he took office, Bill phoned his childhood friend David Leopoulos to exclaim, "I am right over Arkansas! There's a full kitchen here!"

Bill's let-it-all-hang-out personality and improvisational style were magnified in the Washington fishbowl. After his helter-skelter transition, he said, "I can't make every decision. I have to have real discipline. . . . Very few people are efficient past about twelve hours of work. . . . Every major error I made in my life I made when I was really tired. I am going to impose real discipline on myself and our team in terms of when I quit at night so I can see my daughter and get a good night's sleep."

But he changed none of his old habits, particularly his reliance on only four hours of sleep per night, which was based on a theory he had heard from Carroll Quigley, a professor at Georgetown, who claimed that great leaders needed less sleep than ordinary men and sustained themselves by napping during the day. "If he could get by without any sleep, he would do it," said Terry McAuliffe. "To him, sleep is a total waste of time, a missed opportunity." Bill viewed what he called his "sleep deprivation" as a way to impress others that he was working harder than they were. "It was his creative improvising time, when he was thinking about issues," said Press Secretary Mike McCurry. But in the view of another senior administration official, Bill's inability to sleep was also "related to his insatiable need and the constant scheming that goes along with it." With his penchant for secrets, he found solace in the time he had spent alone since childhood, "wondering and worrying," as he put it. "Often I slept less just to get the alone time," he said.

Fueled by adrenaline, nocturnal Bill seemed to possess an extra generator that kicked in around 10:00 p.m. Dressed in jeans, a casual shirt, and sneakers, he would settle into his upstairs office in the Treaty Room, which he transformed from a décor of celadon hues and English chintz in the Bush years to a masculine library with dark-red ersatz-leather wallpaper and floor-to-ceiling bookcases. He installed his collections of ceramic frogs and photographs, including portraits of Abraham Lincoln and Winston Churchill, and he worked behind a large desk from the presidency of Ulysses S. Grant.

The TV was often tuned to sports or cable news as Bill caught his second wind. Sometimes he would stay up all night reading. He typically had a half-dozen books going at any one time, "gulping down literary caviar and pretzels with the same enthusiasm," noted *The New York Times*. His taste ran from history and biography to Walter Mosley murder mysteries, from Gabriel García Márquez's *One Hundred Years of Solitude* to Marcus Aurelius's Stoical *Meditations*, which he said he read every few years. Since his Arkansas days, he lugged around an oversize saddle-leather briefcase to accommodate his portable library.

In most books he made extensive marginal notes (including his distinctive backward check marks) in his thick left-hand scrawl, which would require translation the next day by his assistant, Nancy Hernreich. His briefing primers ran more than one hundred pages, rather than the dozen that suited his predecessor; on Friday evenings, he liked to devour the Department of Agriculture's acreage-planted reports. He seldom engaged in sustained activity, preferring to read, then pick up the phone, then catch a few minutes on C-SPAN, before lifting the receiver again.

The Washington political culture quickly became accustomed to his habit of making postmidnight phone calls to gather intelligence, issue directives, and hash over decisions, often revisiting matters that his advisors believed had been decided. He phoned Terry McAuliffe "to find out what went on that day." Or he jolted one of his key officials out of a deep sleep to discuss policy questions. Mike McCurry, who had to wake up at 4:30 a.m. each day, finally asked his boss to stop calling several hours after McCurry's bedtime, when Bill was watching the replay of the daily White House press briefing on C-SPAN. "I cut off a valuable feedback mechanism because he would give me pointers," said McCurry. "He would say, 'This is what you should emphasize.' He would advise me what to do to reflect his voice and tempo. It was always interesting. Sometimes it was just curiosity, or he would say, 'I've been talking to [Democratic senator Tom] Daschle, and the press on the Hill is going to be writing this story.' " Occasionally, Bill's interlocutor would hear the faint slap of playing cards and know that Bill was enjoying a game of solitaire as he chatted. During one phone conversation with Christopher Dodd, the Democratic senator from Connecticut realized that Bill had fallen asleep. "That never happened to me," said McAuliffe. "Maybe my voice is too loud."

Most mornings, Bill's staff had no idea what time he had gone to bed. If he was feeling energetic, he would awaken at 7:30 for a jog—the only way, he said, he could "shake awake." (His initial efforts to run on Washington's streets prompted massive traffic tie-ups, as well as security concerns, so friends contributed thirty thousand dollars to build a quarter-mile running track inside the driveway on the South Lawn.) More often, his staff had to coax him to the office by 9:00 a.m., first with a wake-up call, then with a more insistent plea by phone from Nancy Hernreich, and finally with a personal visit to the Residence from one of his top aides, usually his Chief of Staff, with whom he had his first meeting of the day.

Despite Bill's large reserves of stamina, his nighttime ramblings caused problems. At times, his exhaustion would impair his ability to make considered decisions. "He can barely stay awake at today's meeting," Robert Reich noted in mid-February 1993. "His eyelids droop and his pupils move up under them, leaving nothing but a narrow sliver of white eyeball." Bill tried to compensate by following the Quigley rule and catching a midday snooze for as little as fifteen or twenty minutes. In a ten-minute limousine ride he would even take what one colleague called a "micronap." But he suffered from the cumulative effects, to the point that Lloyd Bentsen rebuked him: "I watch your eyes just fog over. You're tired. You think you can go without sleep. You can't." When Bill was obviously fatigued, his staff tried various tactics to get his attention. One aide would start to speak about an important matter, then fall silent, prompting Bill to look up and say, "What?" Mack McLarty would "figuratively shake him and say, 'Wake up!'" John Podesta, Chief of Staff in later years, would say, "Mr. President, this is really important."

Bill could also turn irritable when he was overtired, blowing up at staff members over small matters. His profanity-fortified rages—"cusswords for five minutes," said Abner Mikva, one in a series of White House counsels—were legendary inside the administration. Bill's angry side surfaced in occasional moments of pique before the cameras, most famously his finger-pointing, jaw-clenched denial of involvement with Monica Lewin-

sky. His "purple fits," as the staff called them, were invariably disproportionate to the triggering offense. His admirers likened his eruptions to a summer
storm that cleared as suddenly as it appeared. Afterward, he compensated by
"going out of his way to be nice"—his customary dance of seeking forgiveness. "He could get really ugly," said Mel French. "Then it would pass, and
ten minutes later he would be hugging me, but he never apologized."

Those who bore the brunt of these quicksilver shifts were nonplussed
that he acted as if nothing had happened. In Arkansas, he once gave a pair
of earplugs to Betsey Wright, who frequently screamed back at him, as did
Hillary. During the transition, he blistered Robert Reich, who coolly
replied, "If you ever talk to me again that way I'm leaving." Bill softened
and changed the subject, saying, "Did you ever think we would be here?"

But mostly his friends and advisors rationalized his behavior. One longtime associate explained that Bill "was sharing his emotions, inviting you
in, so you knew how he felt." Others emphasized that the outbursts were
"nonpersonal"—directed at situations gone awry or his political enemies or
frustrations over his press coverage—and necessary for him to clear the air
and function effectively. But he also blew up childishly if he simply did not
get his way—when an aide once neglected to bring him a piece of pie from
a farm he had visited, for example. George Stephanopoulos considered
Bill's tirades "my daily companion" and felt a duty "to absorb the anger"
and divert the boss. He cataloged a half-dozen varieties of Bill's tantrums
(morning roar, telephone nightcap, slow boil, the show "for the benefit of
someone else in the room," the last gasp, the silent scream). When reports
of Bill's temper eventually began to appear in the press, Newsweek observed that Stephanopoulos was "more like a battered wife than a key
strategic advisor to the President."

Some aides thought his eruptions were pathological. "The way Clinton
gets so angry in the moment means a lot is going on—a frustration," said
one top advisor. "He is not satisfied with himself, and he projects that onto
other people." Years later, Bill explained that he was able to live "parallel
lives," which he described as "an external life that takes its natural course
and an internal life where the secrets are hidden." He traced his identity as
a "secret keeper" to his troubled upbringing, when he hid the chaos of his
household behind a sunny persona. He had difficulty, he said, "letting anyone into the deepest recesses of my internal life. It was dark down there."

He admitted that over the years his own anger had grown "deeper and stronger" and that he was "determined not to lose control," because "doing so could unleash the deeper constant anger I kept locked away because I didn't know where it came from."

Unlike in his public persona, the private Bill expended little effort on charming those who served him. Robert Reich bluntly told him that he would not work for him in the White House because he was so tough on subordinates. "He struck me as more quiet and moody and pensive in private settings than he exhibited in public," said Eric Liu, one of his speechwriters. Most of those who knew Bill followed a similar trajectory: "You first meet him, it is awe," said Dee Dee Myers. "He is so smart, such a quick study, big ideas, big appetites, big charisma, the laser focus on you. Then there is profound disillusionment, but then you move onto a sort of plateau about him." Ultimately, his sheer brainpower and magnetism covered a multitude of sins.

His intelligence tended to be inductive, drawing from his wide-ranging knowledge. "Bill Clinton has a remarkable intellect of a kind," said Robert Rubin. "His retentiveness is close to photographic. He has an amazing ability to understand things quickly, to connect the dots, to see relationships." Bill could pull nuggets out of his reading and display them readily in conversation. Rubin recalled the time that he and Lawrence Summers, Deputy Secretary of the Treasury, were discussing a new book on economics that Summers had just read. At an Oval Office meeting, the book came up and Bill said he had recently read it as well. Afterward, Summers said to Rubin, "I am a professional economist, and I could not have summarized the essence of that book as well as he did." Yet Rubin added, "Larry and I weren't able to figure whether Clinton has immense intellectual rigor or not. He can say *x* and what the implications are. But I'm not sure he has the discipline to think things through so when he has finished he has a careful, rigorous progression of thought. He has a very good analytic mind, but I'm not sure it is a disciplined mind."

Just as his childhood friends had visited his house "to watch him think," his Washington colleagues marveled at what Webster Hubbell called his "astonishing" multitasking: his virtuoso displays of simultaneously watching television, reading, signing photographs, flipping through mail, playing cards, eating, doing a crossword puzzle, and talking about issues. Some felt insulted by these juggling acts, seeing them as evidence of his self-absorption, especially during meetings when advisors were making presentations. But he was usually paying attention. "He absolutely could dual process," said Rubin. Bill "would circle back and pick up where you were and keep you on your toes," said Eric Liu. "It was inefficient but not frustrating. He was such a machine, he could still do that and give you an answer. It felt meandering. You were floating for a bit until he landed on what you were interested in and talking about."

But Bill also tuned out in meetings and seemed oddly passive—for complicated reasons that could be divined only by those who knew him best. David Leopoulos recalled that when Bill was a teenager "we would be playing cards, and he would be just gone. I would say, 'Bill, what time is it?' and wouldn't get an answer. It was like he was in a trance. Sometimes it would last for minutes. I would go away and come back. I think it had to be related to his problems, maybe fear or frustration about what to do. I couldn't understand it, and I tried to relate it to his brilliance. Maybe he was thinking of more important things."

So, too, in the Oval Office, Bill would seem "not entirely there," said one top advisor who sensed that Bill had either grasped a point more quickly than everyone else or had already made up his mind. At other moments, Bill seemed to power down, like a computer going into sleep mode to conserve energy. Sometimes he simply didn't feel ready to respond to a criticism or viewpoint. "He would pull back and chew on his glasses," said Mack McLarty. "Rather than saying, 'I am not ready to respond,' he would be passive." Bill disliked making difficult choices. Instead, he preferred to split the difference and have it both ways—to be a New Democrat and an old-fashioned liberal, to do everything instead of just a few things. "He was always looking for a way of turning an either/or question into a both/and solution," said domestic policy advisor William Galston.

When Bill was "on," he captivated his staff. He sought viewpoints from everyone, the more diverse the better—like an "eager and bright graduate student," Laura Tyson recalled. "He was not only open to ideas, but to bringing them forth from people," said Rubin. Yet perhaps because of his strife-filled childhood, these discussions had definite parameters. "He wanted to hear views, but he didn't like to hear arguments," said National Security Advisor Anthony Lake. "He was a healer, a consensus builder."

Although he tried to avoid conflict, Bill also couldn't bear unanimity—the main reason he organized his office horizontally, with a dozen or so people reporting directly to him. "He didn't like a precooked answer," said James Steinberg, Deputy National Security Advisor. "If everyone was agreeing, he would say, 'What have I missed?' " recalled Rubin. Bill entertained contrary views because he was supremely confident in his ability to synthesize information. He asked so many questions and played devil's advocate so effectively that he managed, as Liu observed, "in an open way to keep his cards close to the chest." Even when he knew less than everyone else, he understood his power and believed himself to be the smartest person in the room.

The incessant talker in Bill could readily dominate gatherings—when he was in what Strobe Talbott called "transmit mode, conducting a kind of Socratic dialogue with himself." His staff called these streams of consciousness "High Jabberwocky," when Bill would eagerly display his intellectual virtuosity, capacious memory, and ornate hundred-word sentences with dizzying connected clauses. "When he was coming at you that way, you had no idea what he was saying. He was not making complete sense," said one senior advisor. Laura Tyson saw these soliloquies as a kind of "catharsis" that preceded "a reasonable meeting and discussion." Bill would then quiet down, turn analytical, and sift through probabilities.

His lack of restraint and inability to set priorities created a chaotic atmosphere. By blurring the lines of authority, Bill fostered competing factions with conflicting objectives—liberals fighting against moderates. He created a "shadow staff" by giving carte blanche to the liberal "Gang of Four" political consultants from the campaign—Paul Begala, Mandy Grunwald, James Carville, and Stan Greenberg—each of whom was paid approximately $200,000 to $300,000 per year by the Democratic National Committee for their services. These outsiders-without-portfolio were strong allies of Hillary. They shaped communications strategies and political decisions, and to an extraordinary degree they dictated policies based on polling results and focus groups. Friends such as Harry Thomason and Susan Thomases also roamed freely with special White House passes. Even at the senior levels within the administration, "it was never entirely clear what your role—or anybody else's—was," wrote Rubin. This was particularly true in Hillary's case.

Jealousy, backbiting, and self-serving leaking were inevitable in what Stephanopoulos described as a "dysfunctional" environment. "There were independent actors at multiple levels," said a senior advisor. "People you thought were in league together were not. This White House was very complex. What was real was never clear. Clinton was such a force of nature, if you were drawn in, he drove you a little crazy." Stephanopoulos became a master leaker, speaking on the phone to *Washington Post* reporter Ann Devroy as often as ten times per day. He had a reputation for reading his boss's moods and slickly spinning his message. But the Thomasons were among the Clinton friends who questioned Stephanopoulos's loyalty. Linda Bloodworth-Thomason called the diminutive aide "George Step-on-All-of-Us," which made the Clintons laugh.

The favored metaphor for meetings among Clinton White House insiders at the time was of small children in a soccer game scrambling to reach the ball. The "struggles about who would be in the room were frequent and sometimes ferocious," wrote Rubin. Scores of people would crowd into conference rooms, many with no reason to be present. Bill's lifelong inability to set boundaries threw policy making into turmoil. Meetings scheduled for ten minutes routinely stretched to two hours as Bill pursued his favorite digressions. One session on Bosnia lasted seven hours without coming to a resolution. Rather than following a crisp checklist, Bill delayed decisions as long as possible, seeking more facts in pursuit of the "silver bullet" that would yield an optimal outcome. Because he so frequently revisited matters that were supposedly settled, *Newsweek* said he was "like a gardener who uproots his plants to see how well they're growing." After the leisurely pace of business in Arkansas, "he didn't realize the cycle of decision making as President was more accelerated," said Mack McLarty. Bill still wanted to keep up with everything as he had in Little Rock, and while his advisors challenged his policy ideas, they were reluctant to push him to delegate or to make decisions faster. Once when National Security Advisor Anthony Lake stood up to try to end a marathon discussion, Bill simply ignored him, and no one else moved. After standing for a few minutes, Lake quietly sat down.

With a trail of broken promises and policy reversals stretching back to the Arkansas statehouse, Bill continued to confound both opponents and allies who confused his listening with agreement. "A signature of his political technique was to begin his reply to almost any proposition by saying 'I agree with that' even when he didn't," wrote Strobe Talbott. "This default to agreeableness . . . was also a means, both calculated and intuitive, of disarming those he was trying to persuade, of pretending to begin a conversation on common ground in order to get there before it was over." Perhaps because of the force of his personality, few were able to listen carefully enough to pick up the signals. Hillary, who knew her husband's moods and rhythms best, had little patience for those who didn't. "If you go in expecting that someone who is sympathetic with you agrees with you, then that is a very naïve position to take," she said. "When he says, 'I understand,' or 'That's terrible,' that is no commitment, but an expression of understanding."

The most visible consequence of Bill's ragged management style was what his Arkansas staff had ruefully named "Clinton Standard Time," which had far greater repercussions than it had in Little Rock. Every day, said one of his top advisors, was "a long road with quite a few detours." No one was immune from the effects of his constant tardiness—not even a group of elderly Holocaust survivors, who left a White House reception after waiting under a tent in a rainstorm for two and a half hours. "It wasn't malicious," insisted White House Social Secretary Ann Stock. "It was his insatiable curiosity. He couldn't resist talking to people."

Even heads of state were forced to cool their heels. When British prime minister John Major arrived for his first visit to the Clinton White House on February 24, Bill wasn't there to greet his motorcade. "We got him up to the Green Room, and the President arrived twenty minutes late," recalled Chris Emery, one of the White House ushers. "That was a sign of things. If the British press had gotten hold of it, it could have been an international incident." A month later, it was German president Helmut Kohl's turn to be kept waiting by the American President. Protocol aides observed with rising concern as Kohl, an imposing three-hundred-pounder with a garrulous but abrupt personality, watched the clock in the Roosevelt Room, his face getting "redder and redder."

As with so much of Bill's self-indulgent behavior—his vacillating, his disorganization, his temper tantrums—everyone tolerated and accommodated his tardiness, as they had in Arkansas. His staff became better at building elasticity into his schedule to allow for the inevitable delays. They learned to stay at their desks until signaled that the POTUS was heading toward a meeting room. But he would never shake his dilatory ways, and he continued to linger in the moment while others impatiently tapped their feet. "Hillary could not do anything because that's just the way he was," said Mary Mel French. "Even the foreign leaders tolerated it because they enjoyed his conversation and what he knew about their country and the subject at hand and what he brought to the table. At first it made them mad, but then we were okay. He always took so much time with them."

HILLARY IMPOSED SOME general rules for White House conduct that Bill thwarted when he could. He had been spotted during the campaign looking "serene, stealing time to smoke a cigar and read a book." But during the transition he insisted: "I never smoke those things. I'm allergic to them. Besides, that's a bad example." He was yielding to Hillary's disdain for his cigar habit, which led to the first ban on smoking in White House history. For the most part, Bill adhered to the prohibition, extracting his nicotine by chewing on unlit cigars for hours during meetings and on the golf course. At least once, though, he disobeyed Hillary's diktat. On the night that Air Force Captain Scott O'Grady was rescued after being shot down in Bosnia, Bill and Tony Lake defiantly lit up celebratory smokes at 2:00 a.m. on the Truman Balcony. Lake recalled they smoked "very quietly so we wouldn't wake up the First Lady." And they just as carefully extinguished all traces of their cigars before going inside the Residence.

Bill had difficulty with Hillary's dietary proscriptions too. She shied away from the "six major southern food groups"—sugar, salt, butter, eggs, cream, and bacon grease—and instructed the kitchen to serve more vegetables (especially broccoli, which Bill's predecessor loathed), "a lot of fiber and a lot of fruit." She eventually brought in Walter Scheib, a "nutritionally literate" chef who emphasized organic foods and low-fat menus. But on the road Bill rarely missed a chance to grab some barbecued ribs or a cheeseburger or slice of greasy deep-dish pizza, and he kept up his steady infusions of Diet Coke. Mindful of his stepfather's struggles, Bill drank little alcohol, though. For toasts at official dinners, he usually had water in his wineglass.

Hillary organized her own White House life in methodical contrast to her husband's. She had three bases of operation: her new space in the West

Wing, a suite of offices on the first floor of the nearby OEOB, and the Residence. She spent virtually no time in the East Wing, the traditional terrain of the First Lady, where the social and correspondence offices were located.

Her redoubt in the West Wing caused intense curiosity. "People were anxious about it," said one of Hillary's aides. "They didn't know what it meant." She occupied a small corner on the second floor, with one window overlooking a tile roof and the Residence beyond. Bill may have mused during the transition about knocking down walls to accommodate her, but she ended up "about as far as you can get from the Oval Office and still be in the same building," noted *Time*. The office was thoroughly businesslike, furnished with a red-and-blue-striped sofa, a wingback chair, a modest desk, and a table piled with papers. A poster-sized photograph of her husband hung on one wall, and she kept a framed image of her role model, Eleanor Roosevelt, on a credenza, along with awards and other photos. She also installed a small bust of Eleanor downstairs in the Roosevelt Room, which had previously enshrined only Theodore and Franklin Roosevelt.

In the Residence, Hillary had two offices. For personal business—paying bills, writing letters—she used a study next to the master bedroom that had once been Jacqueline Kennedy's elegant dressing room. Hillary also kept an office on the third floor, down the corridor from the exercise room.

Hillary's aides congregated in the OEOB, where the atmosphere had the distinct feel of a sorority. The First Lady had never supervised a staff before the campaign, when she bonded with the small group of women in "Hillaryland," which was both a state of mind and a geographical space. This cadre expanded so much in the White House—to roughly thirty people—that she had more senior officials than the Vice President. Only one man served on her staff, press aide Neel Lattimore. Hillary called her advisors "upbeat, optimistic, positive problem-solvers," and they were all fiercely loyal, tight-lipped, and so brimming with esprit de corps that they wore special "Hillaryland" lapel pins.

Hillary's top assistants—Maggie Williams, Evelyn Lieberman, and Melanne Verveer—were liberal stalwarts and close contemporaries who had worked for the Children's Defense Fund and People for the American Way. The rest of Hillary's aides were overwhelmingly young, and their starry-eyed devotion was almost cultlike—in contrast to the jockeying and self-promotion that marked Bill's staff. While Bill liked to be surrounded with a lot of people who spent time with him in small increments, Hillary spent longer stretches with her tightly knit group. "They were all on the same perch, and their worlds revolved around her," said one of Bill's advisors.

Her twentysomething aides, especially her personal assistant, Capricia Marshall, and her scheduler, Patti Solis, were "morale boosters, not intellectual but calming," said one of Hillary's friends. "Hillary really liked having those two girls around. They helped pick out clothes. She was open with them, and they tried to keep bad news away."

Since her high school days, Hillary had operated easily in groups of women, and unlike her husband she was conscientious about engendering loyalty in those who worked for her and were essential to her well-being. More than ever, she maintained her lifelong capacity to deflect prying questions about herself, in part by turning attention to the personal lives of her staff, querying them about boyfriends and children or commenting on new haircuts. Capricia Marshall recalled that when she had a baby, "Hillary was always sending me plates of broccoli because she thought I wasn't eating enough nutritious food while I was breastfeeding."

Although Hillary effectively masked her own feelings, she pulled her advisors close by encouraging them to laugh as well as to vent their frustrations along with her. As in Arkansas, everyone called her Hillary, and they all spoke with an edge of superiority about the "White Boys" on Bill's staff—a name coined by Susan Thomases, whose frequent visits to Hillaryland earned her such labels as "King Kong Kibitzer," "Blunt Instrument," and "Bulldozer without a Clutch." Hillary commanded respect from her subordinates because, as one White House aide put it, "She was going deep with you. She was studying and reading, too." Above all, she made them feel that they were on a mission with her.

While Bill's moods vacillated, and he constantly kept his staff off balance by blurring their roles, Hillary was more predictable, and every advisor knew precisely what her role was. "There were no fights over territory," said Ann Stock. Yet in the meeting room or on the phone, Hillary was as intimidating as ever. "When Hillary leans forward, puts her elbows on the table in front of her and hunches her shoulders ever so slightly, this is international sign language for 'Be quiet,' " said a White House insider. She called staff members after hours to make trifling requests, and, according to White House chronicler Bob Woodward, she "frequently reduced her personal traveling aide to tears" when the assistant failed to produce something that Hillary needed. She had a temper, but instead of "making nice" afterward as Bill did, Hillary withdrew in cool silence.

It was striking that no one from Arkansas served on her staff, although several took positions elsewhere in the administration. "One time Hillary said, 'Mel, your problem is you just aren't mean enough,' " recalled Mary Mel French. "I couldn't work for her and keep our friendship. She is too dogmatic. She gets so *into* it that she ends up being mean. That is why she has to have such a young staff. They take it, and they bow and scrape. With Hillary, it is not intentional. It's just that she is so intense. She is a really nice person if you don't push her too far."

In the course of a day, Hillary was invariably on the move, striding from one office to another, holding a yellow legal pad and sheaves of notes and documents. In the corridors of the West Wing, she didn't mind being seen without makeup in her thick no-line bifocals, her hair carelessly combed. Her aides were in charge of the "First Lady Box," an eighteen-inch-square container stamped "First Lady" that contained all her pertinent papers and that she took on trips.

Hillary functioned more efficiently than her husband. She made many of her own calls on her cell phone, and she dispatched thank-you notes promptly. With a bedtime of 10:00 or 10:30, she was usually up and ready by 7:30 a.m., her ablutions accompanied by National Public Radio "blaring away," according to Bill. She tried to join Chelsea for breakfast and made an effort to exercise, logging time on a treadmill (3.5 mph, 4.5° incline) in the third-floor exercise room. She gathered her senior staff and by 9:00 a.m. was embarked on a full schedule. She conducted her meetings in the conference room in the OEOB or in the second-floor family quarters, either around the sofa in front of the large lunette window of the West Sitting Hall, or in the nearby Private Dining Room, where she and her advisors would spread the table with papers and several plates of food for nibbling. She often exhorted her aides to join her in sprinkling hot sauce on whatever they were eating, claiming that salsa and Tabasco gave her a boost of energy. She was such a devotee that when on the road she always carried a bottle with her for a late afternoon pick-me-up.

Hillary had few idle moments. "[Bill] would call people to chat," said Ann Stock. "She didn't so much." Like her husband, she had a habit of opening mail while she talked to people. She customarily made calls from her treadmill, issuing directions into a speakerphone between breaths.

Her management style was self-consciously "female"—what Ann Lewis called "circle or matrix management. . . . You encourage people to sit around the table and contribute." Her subordinates were all true believers, so she seldom heard a dissenting view. They might advise her to "do something about those bags under your eyes," but they avoided crossing her about significant issues. "If she wanted your opinion, she would ask," said one of her friends. "You didn't volunteer your opinion. Hillary had good, bright, hardworking, and devoted staff, but they wouldn't have a view of their own. The problem was they were all afraid to say no to her."

"Hillary is direct and organized," said Mickey Kantor. "When she goes into a meeting, she knows what she wants. There are no frolics and detours, as he does. She is more focused and directed and sometimes even with blinders." While Bill decided by meandering, Hillary did so by arguing. "If you would say something to Hillary and she wouldn't agree, she would challenge you," said Robert Rubin. "If he didn't agree, he would let it go." Hillary's discipline and linear thinking had made her a better law student than her husband, and she applied the same lawyerly approach in the White House.

Both Clintons had always had an appetite for mastering information, Bill in a gestalt manner, and Hillary in a more detailed and deductive way—breaking down an issue, analyzing it, and developing a plan to deal with it. Unlike Bill, she was meticulous about how well something was "papered," or backed up. Once she had marshaled the arguments, she made decisions more quickly than Bill did. "She didn't look back," said Ann Stock. "There was no second-guessing." Nor was she as enamored by the sound of her own voice as he was—nor was she as glib. "She thought before she spoke, and her speaking style was very deliberate," said Robert Reich.

Hillary's intelligence was easier to comprehend than Bill's because her mind worked in a conventional, applied way, while his was more supple, creative, and circuitous. Her literary tastes ran from law journals to bestselling novels such as *The Chosen* and self-help books, including *Reviving*

Ophelia: Saving the Selves of Adolescent Girls, as well as *The Cloister Walk* and other spiritual guides.

In school, if Bill and Hillary were taking the same course, Hillary "would attend all the classes, read all the assignments, outline her notes, study hard for the exam," said their friend Ellen Brantley. "Bill would stop by some of the classes, read a couple of the assignments while also reading other related things, and then write an exam that brought in some ideas that had been introduced in class, some outside—linking them in a very original way. And they'd both get an A." Not surprisingly, Hillary often read books after Bill had finished them because he underlined the most intriguing passages that she might not otherwise single out.

HILLARY WAS PREOCCUPIED with politics and policy, and she had little interest in the traditional First Lady domain of flower arrangements, White House décor, and guest lists—at least until she saw that an artful seating arrangement could serve political ends. When Ann Stock was interviewed for the job of social secretary, Hillary included Susan Thomases in the session. As the two women questioned her closely for an hour and a half, Hillary emphasized that the social secretary might look like a "soft job," but she considered it "one of the most political jobs . . . like running a small advertising agency and taking the day's message and translating it into events for the President and First Lady."

Both Clintons wanted their official entertaining to contrast with what they regarded as "the Republican way," said Stock. They would wait for sixteen months before giving their first State Dinner. (During the same period three decades earlier, when Democrats set the social tempo, Jack and Jackie Kennedy had a half dozen such events.) Instead, the Clintons preferred "working lunches," at which Bill could have policy discussions. Once they made a commitment to State Dinners, both Clintons took keen interests in the seating plans, which they would each rearrange three or four times until they were both satisfied. Hillary consulted frequently with Ann Jordan, the well-connected wife of Vernon Jordan, about all aspects of entertaining—music, table settings, and especially invitation lists. "Ann was very helpful with getting the right guests and having them sit in the right place," said Ann McCoy, who served as Deputy Social Secretary. "She came to the White House all the time." When Capricia Marshall eventually took over as Social Secretary in 1998 at age thirty-two, Ann Jordan "was like a fairy godmother," said one of Hillary's friends. "Ann helped her with everything." By then, Hillary was more involved as well, trying out sample menus and passing judgment on designs for tablecloths and centerpieces.

When it came to interior design, Hillary never had much of an eye. Her successor at the Arkansas governor's mansion, Betty Tucker, had wasted little time repainting the rooms from Hillary's color scheme, which Tucker said "needed to be quieter." Hillary brought her bold preferences to the White House Residence, where she gave Kaki Hockersmith latitude to spend more than three hundred thousand dollars to redecorate the Treaty Room and the Lincoln Sitting Room, along with other areas in the private quarters. The Lincoln Sitting Room, restored in tasseled and swagged Victorian style, was roundly mocked: "so ablaze in color, texture and pattern," wrote Maureen Dowd of *The New York Times*, "that even Belle Watling might feel at home."

Their private rooms featured quilts and rocking chairs, with accents from Arkansas including Hillary's embroidered "RAISE AND SPEND" throw pillow. The Clintons added bookshelves wherever they could to accommodate their collection of some five thousand volumes. The night tables flanking their queen-sized bed had phones with separate lines and were piled high with magazines, galleys, position papers, and books flagged with multicolored Post-it notes. The high-ceilinged room between the master bedroom and formal Yellow Oval Room became the Clinton "Family Room." What had once been used by FDR and JFK as a bedroom was now furnished with a television, card table, sofa, and armchair.

To replicate the atmosphere of the governor's mansion, Hillary had the butler's pantry on the second floor transformed into an eat-in kitchen with a wooden table and white wicker chairs. The refrigerator was stocked almost entirely with drinks—mostly diet ginger ale and Diet Coke, and the kitchen wasn't set up for food preparation. "The cooking gene in my family leapt from my mother to my daughter," she once said. "It hardly left a trace." Her best culinary efforts were chopping vegetables for salad, scrambling eggs, or making basic applesauce.

As they had in Little Rock, the Clintons relied on a professional chef for their everyday dining. They had an aversion to taking their meals in the formal second-floor Private Dining Room, so they usually ate breakfast and dinner in the kitchen with Chelsea. They had their food served plated, rather than by waiters from a salver, as the Reagans and Bushes had done.

Their favorite gathering place was the third-floor Solarium, which Chelsea's black-and-white cat, Socks, also made his new home. Kaki Hockersmith decorated it as a casual all-purpose room — what one friend called a "kids' hideout." It wasn't very big, but it had an expansive feel, with large windows facing south toward the Washington Monument, and gave way to a terrace where Hillary planted tomatoes and peppers in pots. Hockersmith arranged two sofas covered in a bold floral print, occasional chairs, and coffee tables, as well as an octagonal glass dining table with chairs on rollers. The emphasis was comfort rather than style: a big-screen television with surround sound and tables scattered with playing cards, Boggle and Scrabble games, bowls of popcorn and pretzels, and nesting dolls of the Clinton, Reagan, and Bush families. The room became the venue for numerous political and policy meetings with the Clintons' advisors, and whenever guests were in residence — which was more often than not — Bill and Hillary joined them for meals at the Solarium table.

EVEN IN THEIR SOCIAL LIVES, the Clintons "didn't waste a second," said Ann Stock. In the early months at the White House they ventured out to restaurants, such as Red Sage and the Bombay Club, and to the homes of friends, sometimes on the spur of the moment. Bill popped in to see Strobe Talbott and his wife, Brooke Shearer, after a speech at the nearby Shoreham Hotel, eager to "kick back from work." The President ate lamb chops and ice cream and played jazz tunes on a saxophone belonging to the Talbotts' teenage son Adrian, reveling in the spontaneity.

On another evening, Bill and Hillary joined a small group of African-American friends, most of them working for the new administration, for a home-cooked dinner hosted by Lani Guinier, a law professor they had known since Yale. "We knew that Bill Clinton was probably the very first President of the United States to have enough black friends to hold a party, not just convene a photo opportunity," Guinier recalled. The First Couple received gag gifts (a witch's hat, a fake hand), mugged for snapshots, and sang "America the Beautiful." It was an evening of bonhomie as Bill sprawled in a chair, convulsed with "big, body laughs," while Hillary, her hair pulled back with a headband, was at first "more demure" but eventually unwound and confided that she had been unsettled to have seen sharpshooters on the White House roof. Guinier sensed that Hillary "felt captured, maybe even imprisoned" in her new home.

Such get-togethers quickly became a rarity because of security concerns, and most of the Clintons' private entertaining revolved around small dinners, late-night games of hearts, and movie nights in the White House Family Theater, with films supplied by the Motion Picture Association of America, often accompanied by directors and actors such as Steven Spielberg and Tom Hanks. As the resident cineaste, Bill selected most of the movies; he had seen his favorite film, *High Noon,* nineteen times even before he arrived in the White House.

Bill particularly thrilled to the presence of Hollywood celebrities. When Barbra Streisand came for the night, she made calls from Bill's private study next to the Oval Office. He arranged briefings on the environment for Billy Crystal and Christopher Reeve and gave entertainers tours of the White House and Air Force One. *Time* noted after Bill had been in office several months, "The overnight guest list for the Lincoln Bedroom sometimes reads like the register at the Hotel Bel-Air."

On Friday afternoons, Bill alerted the social office to call twenty couples or so for light supper and a movie, and few declined. "The people around them were loyal to him, working for them, and also supporters," said Laura Tyson. "The gatherings were informal. It was fun. It was personal in a way. But you were part of their team, their entourage."

Topping the guest list were Arkansas transplants such as Webster Hubbell, Ann McCoy, Vince Foster, Marsha Scott, Mack McLarty, and Bruce Lindsey. They formed a tight group, deeply wary of the capital culture. At one Washington dinner party in February, *Time* reporter Margaret Carlson asked Vince Foster's wife, Lisa, if Hillary was "as scary as she seems." Lisa, looking at Carlson as well as several other journalists nearby, replied, "Not as scary as y'all."

Also included in the Clinton private parties were overnight guests such as the Thomasons and members of the Clinton and Rodham families. Hillary gave her brothers free rein in the White House, which Ann McCoy admitted "probably drove people crazy." "Hughie would show up in the worst outfits," said one of Hillary's longtime friends. "He weighs three hundred pounds, and he would be wearing shorts with golf balls on them and a T-shirt. He would sit in the Solarium, and Hillary wouldn't bat an eyelash. People would come all dressed up for dinner, and Hughie would waddle up in his shorts and fall asleep. She didn't apologize for him, and she didn't tell him to spruce up. I admire her for that."

During their social evenings, Bill and Hillary would circulate separately, and Bill took up a predictable pattern described by one frequent guest: "We were with a group of people, and Bill came up and started talking about NCAA basketball. It had nothing to do with what anyone was talking about. We all stood there and listened, hanging on his every word, and it was almost unendurably boring. But he was President, which was our whole reason for being there." Bill then walked to another group and unspooled the same monologue. "He wouldn't wait and engage in a conversation that was ongoing," said the guest. "He would just start talking."

One unusual quasi-social occasion occurred on March 8, 1993, when Bill invited Richard Nixon to the Residence to discuss Russia. Hillary and Chelsea were seated on the floor in the West Sitting Hall, sorting through cassettes of Academy Award–nominated films brought to them by their friend Kathie Berlin, an executive with MGM. It was the first time Nixon had been to the White House since he had been forced to resign nineteen years earlier by the impeachment inquiry in which Hillary had been a minor player. In his typically forgiving fashion, Bill figured that Nixon "had lived what I thought was a fundamentally constructive life.... I thought that he had paid quite a high price for what he did, and I just thought it would be a good thing for the country to invite him back." While Nixon's other successors had sought the former president's advice "on the QT," Bill "invited him in a public way, alerted the press and a White House photographer," recalled Nixon aide Monica Crowley.

Nixon expressed his gratitude for the invitation, complimented Hillary on her attempt to reform health care, and bantered with Chelsea about Sidwell Friends, which both of his daughters had attended. "I used to be a referee for field hockey," he said. "If you need somebody I hope you'll call me." Hillary was predictably "very impressed by his discipline in the way he had prepared just to say hello to us." Bill found it interesting that Nixon said "he identified with me because he thought the press had been too hard on me in '92 and that I had refused to die, and he liked that. He said a lot of life was just hanging on."

BILL'S OLD FRIEND David Leopoulos believed that "the job of the presidency" was "all Bill and Hillary talked about. Chelsea brought them both down to reality." But Chelsea engaged in shoptalk as well and often took part in Bill and Hillary's spirited exchanges about the issues of the day. In many ways, their family unit grew tighter in Washington, where their work and living spaces commingled. Although both Bill and Hillary chafed at the restrictions of the White House, Hillary also believed that "living above the store" ensured that Bill wouldn't stray. One of her friends told *Time* that Bill "was under a kind of White House arrest."

Chelsea could still say of her father, as she had in Little Rock, "He gives speeches, drinks coffee and talks on the telephone." But he made a point each night of going upstairs to the Residence for dinner at 7:30 or 8:00 before resuming work later in the evening. Hillary was usually home at 6:00 when Chelsea returned from the ballet class she took every day after school.

The décor of Chelsea's suite of rooms facing Pennsylvania Avenue—a bedroom with twin beds and a sitting room—was mature and understated: solid fabric with floral trimming, printed wallpaper from Scalamandré, and photos of ballet dancers. Capricia Marshall was responsible for organizing Chelsea's life from a cubbyhole office next to her bedroom. "She had sort of like the cool big-sister role," said one of Chelsea's friends. "She was young and hip and could talk to Chelsea about things her mom didn't want to talk to her about."

Once, when the nurse at Sidwell Friends needed to get permission to dispense an aspirin, Chelsea said, "Call my dad. My mom's too busy." The nurse did in fact reach the President easily, and he was only too eager to remain on the phone for a chat. But it wouldn't be fair to conclude that Hillary was any less involved in Chelsea's life than Bill. Hillary wrote that she was an "authoritative" rather than authoritarian parent, and their friend Diane Blair said mother and daughter had a "close, low-key relationship." Bill was naturally the more permissive parent, indulging Chelsea's night-owl habits. "Bill would go on and on about Chelsea," said their longtime friend Priscilla Eakeley. "He loved to talk about her. She could do no wrong."

Bill and Hillary were conscientious about participating in events at Sidwell Friends, and Hillary also joined in school skits and attended parties given by parents of Chelsea's friends. If anything, they were overly involved in Chelsea's homework—especially Bill, who once told a morning meeting, "I was up late working on the Mesopotamians." He didn't hesitate to tap the resources at hand—arguably the best in the country—to assist with Chelsea's assignments. When he asked Laura Tyson for help on some algebra problems, she referred him to economic-team members Paul Stiglitz and Alan Blinder. For an immigration project, George Stephanopoulos had to find some border guards to give Chelsea information. One of Bill's advisors recalled visiting the Residence and seeing a paper Chelsea had done on Shakespeare. "Bill and Hillary had redlined it and had written comments," said the aide.

The White House was hospitable to Chelsea's friends from Little Rock and Washington who came for sleepovers and movie nights. They congregated in the Solarium and worked out in the exercise room. When they used the Family Theater, they had to sweep up the popcorn afterward.

Hillary took a particular interest in the girls. "She was always evaluating and taking stock while talking to you," said one friend. "But I felt she was conversational. If I said something, she would respond." Bill, on the other hand, preferred to perform. "Her dad didn't ask questions," said the friend. "He was happy to tell stories and let you know what he knew." Once when a group encountered him on his way to a meeting, he stopped for fifteen minutes to regale them about his days as a student at Georgetown, when he had only twenty dollars a week to spend on food. As the girls listened wide-eyed, he told them he allocated a dollar a day during the week so he could have fifteen dollars on the weekends for dates. His dollar covered breakfast of two doughnuts and soda, a fruit-filled pie and soda for lunch, and a thirty-five-cent, three-inch-thick tuna sandwich and soda for dinner.

Both Clintons were adamant about shielding Chelsea from public scrutiny for as long as possible. They imposed a blackout on press interviews, and they even excluded her from the first White House Christmas-card photo, which was of Bill and Hillary in the State Dining Room. To some extent, this was a natural impulse to preserve her privacy. But despite their efforts to train their daughter to understand the dark motives of the Clintons' enemies, Hillary in particular felt considerable anxiety about the cumulative impact on Chelsea of "the inevitable fallout of her father's public career." The Clintons would struggle with these consequences through the entire presidency, and it was fated that Chelsea would suffer some damage.

Chapter Five

—

THE FIRST SIX MONTHS OF THE CLINTON ADMINISTRATION BEGAN WITH a heightened sense of hope, which was emphasized by the insistent incantation of Bill's birthplace, then drifted into disarray, and ended eerily with tragedy. It was, Hillary later said, a "brutal" time, when she often functioned on "automatic pilot." What should have been a honeymoon for the Clintons had its happy moments, primarily in the company of old friends, and important policy successes that were to reap later benefits. Bill had plans for the economy and for foreign policy that flowed from his appreciation of national and global trends, but much of his early time in office was characterized by embarrassing setbacks and controversies. By taking an activist, big-government approach, Bill and Hillary defined the Clinton presidency as traditionally liberal rather than New Democrat, and they were accused of overreaching their electoral victory.

It was Bill Clinton unbound, trying to solve too many problems with costly government programs, translating his 43 percent of the vote into what *Time* called an "imperial mandate to rearrange the planets." Rather than reining him in, Hillary abetted Bill's grandiose plans. At a Camp David retreat ten days after the inaugural, Hillary argued strongly for pursuing all of their policy objectives rather than scaling back, as some more experienced advisors counseled. "Why are we here if we don't go for it?" she asked. Her public pronouncements revealed "the steady but light wind of social consciousness, mostly blowing from the left," wrote Martha Sherrill in *The Washington Post*.

Clinton loyalists referred to this period as a time of "joyful chaos." "In the early days we had no idea what we were doing," admitted White House domestic-policy expert Bruce Reed. "It was mostly chaotic and frustrating. The President had an endless to-do list. Everyone had to work twice as hard to figure out how to get anything done."

ON JANUARY 21, 1993, Bill's first full day in office, Bill and Hillary had planned an ambitious round of receptions, starting with a public open house that began at 9:00 a.m. Two thousand people had been chosen from a postcard lottery to meet the Clintons and Gores and then tour the public rooms in the White House Residence, sipping hot chocolate and listening to a military band. But more than one thousand extra guests without tickets were admitted, and the Clintons gave up after shaking some 1,800 hands in three hours. "We just screwed all these people," Hillary whispered to her husband—a comment heard on network television. Wearing a wireless microphone, Bill went out to the South Lawn to soothe the dissatisfied lottery winners by speaking to them as a group. Once that crowd cleared out, one thousand Arkansans came through for three hours in the afternoon for a similar reception in the State Dining Room, where Bill and Hillary continued to greet well-wishers. At 5:30, five hundred members of the Democratic National Committee arrived for an hourlong open house in the East Room, followed by 250 friends and staff for a buffet dinner in the State Dining Room.

In between all the meeting and greeting, Bill had a country to run. The military had sent fighter planes to bomb Iraqi antiaircraft sites, and he faced a pressing political problem at home with a controversy over Zoë Baird, his nominee for Attorney General. To address the Baird situation, he called an unusual midday meeting in the Oval Office, attended by Hillary and Tipper as well as by his top advisors. A week earlier, *The New York Times* had disclosed Baird's employment of illegal immigrants and her delay in paying their taxes. Baird had initially bristled that she had merely committed a "technical violation" of the law, and Bill had stood by her. But her first round of confirmation hearings on the day before the inauguration had gone poorly, and angry constituents began complaining to senators. In the middle of lunch in the Capitol following Bill's swearing-in, Senate Judiciary Chairman Joseph Biden whispered to him, "I don't want to rain on your parade, but . . . within the next 24 hours I'll be calling to tell you you'll have to go to the wall personally to save this woman, or you're going to have to pull her down."

As they convened in the Oval Office, the Clintons were "frazzled" from the exertions of their nonstop receptions. Bill sat at his desk, while Hillary, wearing a pale-blue suit, stood nearby with a "hard look on her face," recalled George Stephanopoulos. When Bernie Nussbaum suggested that Bill fight for Baird, Hillary broke in to say, "No, he can't do that."

Nussbaum shot back, "When you abandon people, you send the message you can be rolled."

But the opponents had the upper hand. Baird was actually an unpopular choice among Democratic liberals, who objected to her support for tort reform and efforts to weaken the federal whistle-blower law—positions that differed from Bill and Hillary's views. "Baird had no constituency to rise up and support her," said a White House official who worked on the nomination.

The new President vacillated throughout the day, as Baird continued her testimony and tried to save her nomination. He aggravated the situation by letting Stephanopoulos tell the press that Bill's understanding of Baird's situation had been "murky," which reversed earlier statements that it was "fully disclosed." Finally, after midnight, Bill returned to the Oval Office, this time in sweatpants, to issue a statement accepting Baird's withdrawal and conceding that his review of her candidacy had been rushed.

IN THE FOLLOWING WEEKS, Bill stumbled once more before successfully nominating an Attorney General. Under pressure from Hillary to keep his commitment to appoint a woman, he first selected Kimba Wood, a federal judge in New York City. Wood's path to office seemed assured, since she had already been investigated by the FBI and confirmed by the Senate for her judgeship. Both Bill and Hillary interviewed Wood and were impressed by her qualifications and ability. Hillary's interview with Wood was more than twice as long as Bill's.

After Wood's name leaked on Thursday, February 4, Bill learned that she too had employed an illegal immigrant. The crucial difference from Baird's situation was that Wood had hired her nanny before the passage of the 1986 Immigration Reform and Control Act made such employment illegal, and the nanny became a legal resident under the amnesty provisions of the law. Wood had also paid all the required taxes on time. When Bill had earlier asked if she had a "Zoë Baird problem," Wood had accurately replied that she did not.

But Wood had run into what *The New Republic* called "the latest prejudice dredged up by talk show democracy." With Hillary's encouragement, Bill began furiously backpedaling from Wood's candidacy. "They didn't think the public would understand the distinction between Zoë and Kimba," said Dee Dee Myers. "There was blood in the water already with the Zoë thing. Here was another woman with a weird name and a nanny problem. The administration was already labeled incompetent. The feeling was to cut our losses and move on, leave it behind." Wood moved even faster, announcing twenty-four hours later her withdrawal from consideration. Her preemptive statement angered Bill, because it overshadowed the first unalloyed good news of his fledgling administration, his signing that day of the Family and Medical Leave Act.

Over dinner in the Residence the following Saturday evening, Bill, Hillary, and White House aides pored over lists of names, even resorting to the *Congressional Directory*, in pursuit of qualified women. The next night, at a meeting in the Oval Office after a birthday party for the actress Mary Steenburgen—an old friend from Arkansas—Bill suggested the state attorney for Dade County, Florida, fifty-four-year-old Janet Reno. She had been recommended by Hillary's brother Hugh, who had worked as a public defender in a special court for drug offenders that she had established.

The six-foot-two prosecutor nicknamed "Bigfoot" had grown up on the edge of the Everglades, where she cut down trees with a chainsaw to unwind, and owned thirty-five peacocks named Horace. Steely but shy, Reno was known for her independence and integrity, although her experience was limited to criminal law. She earned "mixed" reviews in her handling of race riots in Miami, and she had only squeaked by in elections against weak opponents.

Nevertheless, four days later Bill nominated her, and she was sworn in on March 12, not to leave office until her boss's departure in 2001. She would have a remote relationship with Bill, who came to regard her as "politically tone-deaf" and to resent her willingness to appoint special prosecutors to investigate him and his wife, as well as five members of his cabinet.

"Janet was a different kettle of fish," said Donna Shalala. "He didn't know her and didn't try." Bill suffered the consequences of making a politically motivated appointment to fulfill a promise he had made to his powerful wife. "I don't think Clinton believed he had a choice," said Dee Dee Myers. "He had painted himself into a corner, and he had to appoint a woman." Even Janet Reno eventually conceded, "Gender is the reason I'm here."

DURING THE CAMPAIGN, liberal standard-bearer George McGovern, on whose 1972 presidential bid both Clintons had worked, assured ideological soul mates that Bill's campaign was, in the words of Joe Klein, "a Trojan horse, a way to sneak 1960s liberalism past the American public." Once Bill took office, his behavior seemed to fulfill the prediction, as he marginalized some of his prominent allies from the Democratic Leadership Council and surrounded himself with liberal-minded advisors. According to Newsweek, his governing strategy was to solidify his Democratic base first, then tack right as he approached reelection.

Bill put down his most conspicuous markers of liberalism in the first ten days on the job. Two days after his inauguration, he signed four proabortion executive orders—a maneuver orchestrated by Hillary to coincide with the twentieth anniversary of Roe v. Wade, which Bill lauded for overturning laws against abortion. And after two months of bad publicity about his controversial plan to permit homosexuals to serve freely in the armed services, he accepted what he called an "honorable compromise." He would delay for six months an executive order banning discrimination against homosexuals while the military developed rules for implementing it. Instead of an outright ban, the military would not ask recruits about their sexual orientation, and homosexuals in the military could serve only if they kept their sexual preferences secret. "Don't ask, don't tell" was a classic Clinton finesse: gay soldiers would be fit to serve if they engaged in tacit deception. Neither the military nor the gay community was pleased with the outcome. Announcing his retreat on January 29, Bill "looked pale and uncertain" and "conveyed no sense of command."

Five days earlier, he had been considerably more cheerful as he unveiled an initiative that promised to vastly expand the federal government's role in health care—his most consequential shift to the left. He eventually proposed an administrative and regulatory apparatus that would create 105 new government entities and expand forty-seven others. His appointment of Hillary as head of the Health Care Task Force, which was charged with developing a plan to restructure the health-insurance system, took nearly all his top officials by surprise, including Al Gore. Bill was investing Gore with considerable responsibility, but his failure to confide in his vice president was a telling sign of the real pecking order.

It was just as Bill had said the previous March: He and Hillary had decided on her role and announced it once they took office, giving the American people "time to get adjusted to it." The task force consisted of six cabinet secretaries plus a group of senior White House officials, all of whom reported to Hillary, elevating her to an unparalleled policy-making position for a First Lady. "It was a clear indication we were betting the farm on health care," said Bruce Reed. "That raised the stakes in all sorts of ways."

Hillary told the task-force members that she and Bill had succeeded with education reform in Arkansas by targeting the education establishment as "the enemy." She intended to do the same with the health-care establishment, establishing a "war room" and making speeches accusing drug manufacturers, health-insurance companies, and doctors of "unconscionable profiteering" in their prices and fees. "The use of a 'war room' for health care was unprecedented," said Pamela Bailey, the president of the Healthcare Leadership Council. "It was symbolic of the way this was approached. It had never been done before, nor would it be again."

The task force was supposed to draw on the wisdom and experience of more than five hundred administration officials, congressional aides, and outside experts overseen by Ira Magaziner. But the basic "managed competition" blueprint for the plan was determined by Bill, Hillary, and Magaziner even before the inauguration. It would be a hybrid structure that used private insurance but with significant government involvement. Employers would be required to provide health insurance to their workers and subsidize the cost; employers and individuals would band together in large regional alliances and contribute to a fund to buy health insurance from partnerships of doctors, hospitals, and insurance companies; the unemployed and the poor would be covered by government subsidy; and federal regulatory boards would control costs and ensure standards of benefits.

The task force was designed by the Clintons "as a way to buy time and work out the details" of a comprehensive bill by May 1, 1993, while Bill and Hillary sold it to Congress and the public.

Hillary's task force gave the appearance of "big tent" inclusiveness. "I had about eighteen meetings with Ira Magaziner, and I had about two meetings with her," recalled Michael Bromberg, a veteran lobbyist for private hospitals. "They took copious notes, they listened almost to the point of absurdity, but every time I walked away it was, 'Gee, they took a lot of notes and they listened, but I don't think it's going to make any difference.' I mean, they were on a path, where they knew best, and they weren't going to change."

From the start, important groups such as the American Medical Association, along with some of the nation's leading health-care economists, were not consulted. "A lot of people didn't have a fair chance to speak in the process," said Robert Rubin. As a result, Hillary "galvanized every single sector of health care against her and aligned herself with a narrow slice of the left," said Pamela Bailey. "She worked with people she was comfortable with and shared her beliefs. She never reached beyond her comfort zone."

When confronted with dissenting views, Hillary responded with unbending certitude. Dr. Paul Ellwood, one of the architects of managed competition, met with Hillary to discuss his misgivings about price controls. "He said to her that many of the changes that she was hoping for are already happening," recalled his friend Senator Daniel Patrick Moynihan. "She said, 'No they are not.' He said that costs are already going down. She said, 'No they are not.' " Ellwood remarked sardonically to Moynihan that "he had studied the subject all his life, she had studied the subject three weeks and already knows more than he."

The flaws in the Clintons' top-down proposal began with its premise: that a vast, interlocking network of health-care services could be replaced, virtually overnight, with an all-encompassing scheme imposed by Washington. "We have many health-care systems in this country—different regions, different needs and approaches—not one health-care system," said political analyst Michael Barone. Social Security and Medicare were created to fill a void, but the Clinton plan envisioned dismantling something that worked for most Americans. Ira Magaziner anticipated some of the problems in a memo on January 26, predicting that critics would say price controls could hinder the quality of care, consumers would be limited in their choice of doctors and services, and those already covered by health-care plans would face reduced benefits at higher cost to accommodate subsidized care for the uninsured. Even in its early stages, the plan confounded not only Donna Shalala but Robert Reich, who noted his bafflement in his journal after one confusing briefing in April, adding, "not a good omen."

The President and First Lady said that their plan could be financed by controlling costs and cutting out waste, but few economists believed relying on efficiencies would work. When some members of the transition team suggested that universal coverage would swell the deficit and require from thirty to ninety billion dollars in new revenues each year, Bill asked them to revise their calculations. Since Bill was going to be raising tax rates overall, he knew he couldn't impose still more taxes to pay for health-care reform.

Yet the Clintons pressed ahead, following what Donna Shalala called a "crazy process" that took Magaziner twenty-two pages to spell out, including the prediction that Bill would need to make 1,100 decisions. Magaziner and Hillary divided the task-force consultants into thirty-four groups that passed through a half-dozen reviews called "tollgates." As many as one hundred people typically attended these sessions, one of which ran eighteen hours straight. Hillary insisted that as many women and minorities as possible participate in these "working groups." The consultants operated in their own hermetic world in the OEOB, apart from the White House staff, "dozens of propeller heads arguing out wonky details that didn't matter," said Bruce Reed.

Magaziner, a tall, somewhat spectral figure with an aloof and humorless demeanor, had a history of impractical ideas and a mind that "skitters like an ice cube on a hot stove," wrote Adam Zagorin in *Time*. "He assumed you were a fool if you asked a question," said Shalala. "Bill and Hillary were fascinated by him. They thought he was a genius."

Not only did the Clintons sanction Magaziner's convoluted organization, they insisted that the identities of its participants be kept secret, which angered the press, Democratic leaders in Congress, and the health-care industry. The Clintons also pursued a self-defeating political strategy. At an early White House meeting, Pat Moynihan, the chairman of the Senate Finance Committee, advised them to develop broad bipartisan support for such ambitious legislation with far-reaching effects. But on the advice of Senate Majority Leader George Mitchell, they decided on a "Democrats only" approach, relying on their party's comfortable majorities in the House and Senate. For a brief period, the Clintons sought to fold their health-care legislation into the overall budget bill, but Democrat Robert Byrd, the Senate's stickler on rules, vetoed the idea as unworkable.

Another strategic mistake was declining to fix the broken welfare system before tackling health care, which Moynihan and many other experienced hands, such as Mickey Kantor, advocated. Bill's campaign pledge to "end welfare as we know it" had bipartisan appeal. Welfare reform had been one of Bill's signature issues in Arkansas. He had collaborated with other governors to design programs to train welfare mothers and to provide incentives for business to hire them. He knew what worked and what did not, and the idea of instilling personal responsibility in welfare recipients was a linchpin of his New Democrat identity. He had a natural base of support among moderate Democrats as well as Republicans who had been pushing welfare reform for years. It was an attainable victory that would have solidified Bill's position as a centrist reformer and provided a building block for health care. But "the ongoing game plan," as described by one senior official, was that "Hillary would do health care for the first two years and then for the second two years she would do welfare."

Bill and Hillary made a crucial error by alienating Moynihan, one of the most knowledgeable legislators in Washington. He had irked them during the transition by decrying "the clatter of campaign promises being tossed out the window." From the election through the inauguration, neither of the Clintons nor any of their top aides had called to consult him. The outspoken senator was annoyed, telling *Time*'s Michael Kramer that his domain covered "everything the President cares most about— economic recovery, trade issues, health care, welfare, Social Security." "Big deal," a "top administration official" told Kramer, adding, "he's not one of us. . . . He's cantankerous but he couldn't obstruct us even if he wanted to. The gridlock is broken. It's all Democratic now. We'll roll right over him if we have to."

The article appeared on Monday, January 25, prompting a flurry of

West Wing activity. White House aide Rahm Emanuel (who was later elected to Congress from Illinois) called the senator's office to apologize, saying that if the anonymous culprit were discovered, "that person would be fired." When the President phoned later that day, he told Moynihan that he was "horrified" and "livid" and that "if they catch the bastard, he will be fired. . . . We know it was someone who didn't know us—some smart-ass."

Moynihan "would remember this slight and exact his revenge many times over the next few years," noted George Stephanopoulos. With that one anonymous quote, "it seemed as if our administration were revealing its self-satisfied self-destructive subconscious." Three and a half years later over dinner with Moynihan, Kramer disclosed the source of the inflammatory remark, telling the senator, "The 'big deal' quote was from Rahm Emanuel"—the man who vowed to fire the culprit—and "confirmed by Stephanopoulos."

THE PRESIDENT SPENT much of his time presiding over marathon budget meetings before settling on a proposal to cut the deficit by five hundred billion dollars over four years and to raise the top income-tax rate from 31 to 36 percent. Rather than applying it to those making $200,000 per year, as he had pledged during the campaign, this tax would edge closer to the middle class, hitting couples who made $140,000 in taxable income and individuals making more than $115,000 annually. He included a tax on energy consumption based on British thermal units (BTUs) that would hit the middle class but was also intended to promote conservation. And he removed the cap of $135,000 on wages subject to the Medicare payroll tax of 1.45 percent.

Bill's pollsters had concluded that voters never expected him to enact his promised tax cut for the middle class, so he felt comfortable once his abandonment of that pledge became known. But a USA Today–CNN poll at the end of January 1993 showed that two thirds of those surveyed expressed major concern about the loss of a middle-class tax cut. Republicans exploited this sentiment effectively, knowing that voters had a long memory for reversals that hit them squarely in the pocketbook.

Yielding to both Perot's influence and to the urgings of his economic advisors and Alan Greenspan, the chairman of the Federal Reserve Board,

Bill angered liberals by committing himself to deficit reduction. He accepted the theory that by slashing the deficit, he would convince Wall Street that he was intent on controlling inflation. In an atmosphere of higher confidence, bond traders would lower long-term interest rates, promoting demand for credit that could help expand the economy.

Bill griped in meetings about catering to "a bunch of fucking bond traders" and becoming an "Eisenhower Republican." But in other respects his proposals hewed to progressive principles. He targeted the military and the intelligence services for most of the cuts that would halve the deficit. The remainder would come from the tax hikes, which would also pay for new programs, including a $27 billion expansion of the Earned Income Tax Credit to help the poor and an additional $13 billion for Head Start.

Bill launched his economic plan with speeches scheduled two days apart in mid-February. Hillary's role in the two talks displayed her copresidential power more vividly than ever. Bill's initial ten-minute message, delivered from his desk in the Oval Office, reflected the "tax the rich" themes favored by his political consultants and his wife. He also took another swipe at the capital Establishment, declaring Washington to be "a place where common sense isn't too common." The next day, February 16, the stock market plummeted eighty-three points, its largest drop in fifteen months. Mack McLarty immediately urged Bill to modulate his rhetoric for the second address, to a joint session of Congress, on Wednesday evening, the seventeenth. Bob Rubin, meanwhile, picked up negative reaction from New York business leaders, and in a Wednesday-morning phone call told Bill he had to eliminate the populism.

By then, Rubin had established a special place for himself in the empyrean of advisors. With a fortune of well over one hundred million dollars, he lived in a suite at the elegant Jefferson Hotel, flew by private jet, never wore a watch, and kept his distance from White House social life, content to have what he called a "working relationship" with the President. The White House staff called Rubin "The Court of Appeals" for his outsize influence over economic policy that was belied by his slightly diffident manner. Bill considered him "understated and intense at the same time." "Clinton was more disciplined with Rubin than with the others," said journalist Jacob Weisberg, who collaborated with Rubin on a memoir.

Hillary considered Rubin "wonderful," at least in part because he had taken the time to give her private tutorials on the importance of the bond market. "I really paid attention to what he'd say," she recalled. "I don't know that I ever accepted it, but I certainly appreciated it."

Bill suggested to Rubin that he ask Hillary to make the necessary changes in the speech. Rubin went to her office three doors down the hall in the West Wing to tell her that the proposed remarks were not "sensible" and would undermine confidence. "Show me what you mean," Hillary replied. Rubin took her through the draft line by line, pointing out the problems. Ever the pragmatist, she grasped the importance of Rubin's view, so she took him with her to the Roosevelt Room, where Paul Begala was supervising the latest version. "All right, Paul, these are the changes," she announced and began dictating new sentences as she struck out phrases that suggested punishing the wealthy. "Hillary had a certain authority," Rubin recalled.

When Bill briefed television-network anchormen over lunch in the second-floor dining room of the Residence, "he seemed very engaged," recalled Tom Brokaw of NBC, "but it was more than a little improvisational. He liked being the center of attention, and he ate everything but the draperies."

Throughout the day, Bill edited the address, and an aide heard him singing to himself as he left the White House. He continued to consult with Hillary about language in the limousine as they drove along Pennsylvania Avenue. After the speech, Bill invited "the kids" to the Solarium, where he and Hillary greeted them with high fives and fed them carrot cake and cherry pie. After midnight as his advisors were leaving, Hillary surprisingly agreed to stay up with Bill and watch a rerun of his speech on C-SPAN.

The President's de facto State of the Union message was a success, but the sequence of events over those days revealed the difficulties caused by his tendency to hold contradictory ideas in his head at the same time. He created an unsettling impression by simultaneously advocating cutting and spending and by touting a smaller and more efficient government even as he promoted a dramatic and costly new health-care entitlement. He added to the confusion by pushing for his $16 billion "stimulus package"—pared back from an original $30 billion—at a time when many economists believed that a growing economy didn't need such a boost. Robert Reich, James Carville, and Paul Begala encouraged him to persist, as did Hillary, who liked the idea of "immediate results."

Despite the Democrats' dominance of Capitol Hill, Bill's economic package was a hard sell. Polls taken in the spring of 1993 indicated that voters preferred lower taxes and fewer services to higher taxes and more ambitious federal programs. The Republicans were united in their opposition to his tax increases, and conservative Democrats wanted more spending cuts. Both factions sent a harsh message when Senate Democrats couldn't muster enough votes to break a filibuster by Republicans against the stimulus package that they denounced as unnecessary spending dressed up as "investment." On April 21, Bill pulled the package, a major political setback. "The president had asked for something, and Congress, controlled by his own party, had refused his request," wrote Robert Rubin. Bill's approval rating began to plummet, hitting bottom by late May at 36 percent in a *Time* poll, the lowest rating for a postwar president at that point in his term. *Time* marked the moment with a cover story headlined "The Incredible Shrinking President."

BILL AND HILLARY'S JOINT decision making at the beginning of his presidency was as overt as it would ever be in the White House. "He would say, 'Hillary thinks this. What do you think?' " said Bernie Nussbaum, who worked closely with both of them. "They really were a partnership. She was the absolutely necessary person he had to have to bounce things up against, and he was that for her. I sensed a tremendous need for each other. They didn't have to see each other, but they would talk continually every day." In deference to her continuing role as Bill's "closer," staff members called Hillary "The Supreme Court." "We would always say, 'Has the Supreme Court been consulted?' " recalled Dee Dee Myers. Whenever Bill said, "let me think about it," aides knew he intended to call Hillary.

Nussbaum's successor as White House counsel, Abner Mikva, believed that Bill needed Hillary more than she needed him. "He depended on her completely," said Mikva. Besides frequently reaching to hold her hand, he could act "like a baby" around her, calling her "Hirree." "During the day I can see him anytime I want to," Hillary boasted to *Time*. One senior official who watched Bill and Hillary closely over the years concluded that Hillary provided "considerable intellectual energy as a constant engine for creativity and politics alongside his own. He routinely rejected a lot of what she offered up—gently and deftly as always—but she supplied raw material for his constant, never-at-rest needs, generating adulation and policy ideas for him, putting forward this, that, or the other."

Yet Hillary's routine participation in West Wing meetings upset the equilibrium of official White House life. She "had a real chilling effect," said one longtime aide, when she turned aggressive and assertive around Bill. Bernie Nussbaum observed that Bill "would try to avoid fighting with her if he could, deflecting her if he could. It was not easy. She would say, 'Do this or that.' He would then be more careful." When Bill went into what one advisor called his "rope-a-dope," his staff learned to recognize that, behind the scenes, Hillary opposed what others were advocating.

Senior advisors tried to chart how Hillary's anger affected her husband in a variety of ways. Ann Stock observed that "if they were furious with each other they got standoffish." Often, Bill would arrive at the Oval Office feeling buoyant, "almost whistling as he whipped through papers," recalled David Gergen, an advisor in the first year. The phone would ring, and Hillary would be on the line. "His mood would darken," wrote Gergen, "his attention wander, and hot words would spew out. Had we seen the outrageous things his enemies were saying about him now? . . . Why was his staff screwing him again? *What*, I would wonder, had she said to him now?"

Even more disconcerting were Bill's evening phone calls—what George Stephanopoulos called the "nightcap"—when Bill would chew out an advisor with Hillary nearby. "It was completely at odds with the emotional tenor of the relationship that person had with Bill," said one top official. "It was vicious. Then the tone would change completely and he would say, 'Why don't you come over and watch football?' The staff person wondered what happened, which was that she had been standing there and had been haranguing Bill. When she walked out of the room, everything changed."

In meetings, her dissatisfaction could curdle the atmosphere when she directed her ire at his subordinates. "It was her way of saying, 'You are incompetent, look at how your staff treats you,' " said White House advisor

Robert Boorstin. "Rather than insult him directly, she used the staff. . . . People were scared of her because they knew she could chop off their testicles if she so chose. You did not cross Hillary."

With a dozen or so of her husband's advisors gathered around, Hillary would typically let loose a tirade. David Gergen described the phenomenon: "She would launch a deadly missile straight at [Bill's] heart and just before it hit, the missile would explode, the shrapnel hitting the staff." Her wording had a common theme: that the President's men "were wimps," said one senior official. "It was clearly, 'You don't have balls, no guts. You don't fight back.' The language was so striking. It seemed that every criticism was dual purpose and could apply to him, but she at the last minute didn't apply it to him." Bill would react by flushing crimson and lashing out at his staff. "She knew how to press his buttons," said the senior official. "It was a conscious pattern. Her anger gave him permission to express his anger." At such moments, Bill would lose his intuitive ability to read the emotions of others in the room. "His emotions were under assault, and he couldn't divert energy to how others were feeling," said one of his advisors.

Bill's staff in Arkansas had been inured to Bill and Hillary's fierce arguing, but their Washington advisors found it "demoralizing," said Gergen, which "deepened the divisions between the Bill and Hillary camps," making their subordinates walk on eggshells. When the Clintons "got into a row . . . the rest of us sat in embarrassed silence." The most unnerving aspect of the Clintons' altercations was their use of profanity, especially "fuck" and "shit," particularly in Hillary's case because of her slightly pious air. "She can swear like a trooper," said one of her friends, who attributed her habit to "being raised in the Sixties." Still, when a White House aide forgot a podium for a Rose Garden event on CBS This Morning in May 1993, everyone was taken aback when Hillary yelled at Bill, "What the fuck goes on here! . . . What is your staff doing?"

Hillary's anger was bound up in the intricacies of her marital bargain, which engendered rivalry and resentment along with mutual dependence. Gergen believed the First Couple operated like a seesaw: When either of them went down, the other went up and dominated the situation. Another senior official discerned an "unspoken, not fully conscious or recognized, pattern of behavior. The loss of gratification or dignity or fulfillment of one aspect of their relationship—marital fidelity—made him give her gratification, dignity, and fulfillment in another aspect of their relationship." This "unarticulated trade-off" depended on Hillary's "desire for recognition in the world of intellect, policy making and leadership." She was willing to accept stature in that realm of her life "without necessarily accepting that it was at the expense of the intimacy and exclusivity of his emotional relationship with her." This formulation "explains both the pattern and continuing high level of anger on her part—her resentment and seething beneath the surface."

Given the fraught climate, no one was particularly surprised in February when a report surfaced in the *Chicago Tribune* that during a heated dispute between Bill and Hillary, a lamp had been smashed in the Residence. The anecdote came from the Secret Service, whose agents were posted within earshot of the family's living quarters on the second floor. The story rapidly molted into a claim that Hillary had actually "thrown a lamp" at her husband—an assertion she publicly denied and later joked about, saying she had a "pretty good arm" and would not have missed if she had thrown an object at anyone.

But she never directly addressed the particulars of the "smashed" lamp in the original account, and her private reaction at the time showed a frantic concern over a security breach and deep misgivings about the loyalty of the permanent Residence staff. "Hillary said, 'We have a lot of enemies and we have to fight back,'" Bernie Nussbaum recalled. "She became more hardened. We found we couldn't trust a lot of people like the Secret Service and the staff, leaking rumors about Hillary-and-Bill fights. Whether it was true or not, people were leaking."

Even before the lamp story, Harry Thomason, who had been staying in the Residence since the inauguration while he worked out of an office in the East Wing, had urged Hillary to replace the Secret Service agents. The White House chief of security told Hillary she was "overreacting," and Vince Foster concurred, so no reassignments took place. Now at Hillary's request, the agents switched their posts from the second floor to outside the elevators downstairs on the ground floor, and a new detail was installed.

AL GORE WAS AFFECTED most by Bill's reliance on his wife. It was a given in the White House, as Mack McLarty said, that everyone would "just have to get used to" the fact that Hillary along with Bill and Gore had to "sign off on big decisions." But having what Bruce Reed called "three forces to be reckoned with" added yet another layer of perplexity and rivalry to the West Wing, where advisors and cabinet officers knew they could lobby either the First Lady or the Vice President to reverse decisions by the President. David Gergen called the "three-headed system" a "rolling disaster."

During the transition, the conventional wisdom about the relationship between the President and Vice President shifted from adoring descriptions of generational bonding to the prevailing media view that Gore's influence would "inevitably diminish" now that his "Dudley Do-Right" image was no longer necessary to take the curse off "Slick Willie." An account in *The New York Times Magazine* shortly before the inauguration set out the new interpretation, noting that "Al Gore hasn't yet realized there is going to be a co-presidency but he's not going to be part of the co," and that, according to Susan Thomases, Gore "would have to adjust to a smaller role." The article came out of the blue, and the Gore camp detected the veiled handiwork of Hillary in its slant. It was an open secret that some of Hillary's advisors, Thomases in particular, nurtured dreams that Hillary, not Gore, would follow Bill in the presidency. "There are a great many people talking very seriously about her succeeding him," Betsey Wright admitted during Bill's first year in office. "Friends, Democrats, people out across the country think it is a very viable plan of action."

"Of course there were tensions," said one of the Clintons' longtime friends, who recalled private meetings in which Hillary encouraged her husband to discount Gore's advice by saying, "Bill, you are President. This is your administration." The threesome "at times had the feeling of a brother and sister trying to win the affection not of the father but of another, more powerful older brother," said this friend. Hillary had an obvious advantage over Gore because she and Bill had been on the same wavelength for so long that they communicated almost by telepathy. But Gore operated under the assumption that Bill took Hillary's advice only when she claimed an issue as her own, and only when Bill would suffer emotional consequences if he ignored her.

The Clintons resented the Gores because they were products of Washington, its prestigious private schools, and its social network, placing them on the A-list for elite Georgetown gatherings, including the annual New Year's Eve party hosted by Ben Bradlee and Sally Quinn. A friend of the

Clintons noted in a journal that Hillary once said with some bitterness, "Gore gets credit because he's a Washington insider and can play the game. Gore is not 'from some place called Arkansas.' "

While Hillary held unique sway with Bill, he nevertheless had a close and effective professional relationship with his Vice President. "Gore had more of an ability to influence the President than was acknowledged," said a Clinton advisor. Before taking office, the two men signed a written agreement setting out Gore's responsibilities for the environment, foreign affairs, national security, science, and communications policies, as well as a general advisory role.

Bill also committed to a private lunch with his Vice President every Thursday. Gore was particularly insistent on the lunches, held in the small dining room off the Oval Office, where he would arrive each week with a stack of material to cover. The lunches were forums for professional "wonk talk" as well as personal discussions that were almost therapeutic for Bill. The regularity of the lunches enabled Gore to stay close to Bill and maintain his effectiveness. Gore knew "if the relationship was not nurtured, it would become vulnerable," said one top White House official.

"They managed quite well," said Laura Tyson. "They took seriously dividing up the issues between them, so each could explain to the other and give advice to the other. On most issues they were in the same place, and ironically Al Gore was more of a fiscal conservative than Bill Clinton." James Steinberg, Deputy National Security Advisor, observed that "both loved detail and were hyperknowledgeable. . . . They both were the smartest kid in the class, but you didn't feel a huge sense of competition."

Unlike Hillary, who went on the attack in meetings, Gore avoided public disagreement with Bill. "The Vice President rarely spoke first and did not assert himself aggressively," said domestic-policy advisor William Galston. "When he offered advice, Bill listened very attentively, because it was usually good advice. Clinton was impressed by Gore's clarity and orderliness, the way his mind worked, that he had thought through exactly what he wanted to say and how to say it. Al said no less, no more, and shut up." Housing and Urban Development Secretary Henry Cisneros observed that Bill appreciated Gore's "analytical framework that is all-Harvard in its idiom, and the way he would bring out an elegant answer." Gore increased his effectiveness through his deference, his loyalty, and his determination to help the President make the best decisions. "Gore in small settings was a first-class questioner," said Health and Human Services Secretary Donna Shalala. "He would bring out the issues, and they would work to build consensus between them."

Bill's panoramic but haphazard intelligence often benefited from Gore's more rigorous and linear thinking. In some respects, Gore's cast of mind was similar to Hillary's in his quest for synthesis, his empirical thought processes, and his effectiveness in meetings, prompting one staff member to liken him to a "piece of artillery." Gore was known to take a pair of scissors and cut a memo to shreds, whittling it down to the most essential fragments that he arranged on his desk before emerging with a basic theory. "You just pray nobody sneezes," said EPA Administrator Carol Browner. But Gore and Hillary had dissimilar personalities. Most obviously, Gore had an ironic sensibility and appreciation for the absurd that both Bill and Hillary lacked. Asked how his routine had changed when he was forced to use crutches after injuring his Achilles tendon, he deadpanned, "It takes me twice as long to walk Socks."

Bill and Tipper, who shared the same birthday, were more outgoing than Al and Hillary. As a foursome, they got together for bowling and movies at the White House, dinners and concerts, and nights at Camp David. Tipper quietly went out of her way to help Hillary with suggestions about doctors, dentists, and other domestic matters. She introduced her to her friend Dana Buchman, a designer from Memphis, and immediately stopped wearing Buchman's clothes because Hillary wanted those styles to be "her look." When Hillary was upset over press coverage, Tipper would invite her to lunch at the vice-presidential mansion to commiserate. Tipper had a master's degree in psychology, and she frequently appeared at Hillary's side to discuss mental-health issues. Her presence, *The Washington Post* noted, "reinforces Hillary as a caring person."

Yet Hillary always had an undercurrent of competition with Al Gore that burst into the open from time to time. One day, when Gore and his team presented their plans for improving government efficiency, Bill asked so many questions that the meeting ran a half hour too long. As a result, Bill was late for a session in the Residence with Hillary and her health-care advisors. Feeling snubbed, Hillary lectured her husband on the importance of health care. Bill "retreated a bit," recalled a participant. "It took five minutes to get through that situation. . . . She was not pleased."

WORKING TOGETHER AND on parallel tracks, Bill and Hillary pursued their expansive agendas at full throttle. Bill crisscrossed the country to gather public support for his economic program, while Hillary lobbied for the health-care plan, buttonholing nineteen Senators and thirty-one Congressmen (all of whom received thank-you notes and signed photos afterward), making speeches, and soliciting medical horror stories from ordinary citizens in nine states. She nodded and listened attentively as she took extensive notes that she stuffed into a black shoulder bag. Besides her frequent consultations with her husband, she talked with Ira Magaziner three times per day. The Clintons both employed the "town meeting" format in an effort to circumvent reporters, whom they kept at arm's length.

Neither of the Clintons could shake their deep-seated dislike for the national press, even when the coverage was positive. At the outset, journalists generally wrote approvingly of Clinton policies, as well as of Bill and Hillary's public performances. Hillary initially benefited from glowing coverage, particularly in magazines such as *Good Housekeeping*, *Vogue*, *Parade*, *Family Circle*, and *People*, where cover articles portrayed her as a superwoman who successfully juggled the roles of wife, mother, and First Lady. *Time* called her an "icon of American womanhood."

But Hillary had needlessly antagonized White House reporters as early as inauguration day by ordering the door locked between the briefing room and the offices of the Press Secretary, which for the first time forced reporters to make appointments just to shoot the breeze with the communications staff. Hillary and Susan Thomases had originally attempted to move reporters into new quarters in the OEOB; shutting the door was Hillary's backup plan. Her intention, she said, was to permit her husband to be "free to walk around without reporters looking over [his] shoulder." Weeks later, she irritated a *New York Times* correspondent by insisting her interview be confined to questions about traditional First Lady duties. Veteran White House correspondent Helen Thomas declared that Hillary had "the biggest chip on her shoulder" and was "aloof."

The Washington press corps was not so much antagonistic as it was instinctively oppositional. Reporters directed their criticism at Bill and Hillary's private behavior or ways in which the First Couple had failed to live up to expectations. After several months, the press tired of Hillary's "power-walking down the corridors of the Capitol." *The Washington Post* noted she was "a hard pol to warm up to," speaking only in "bromides and political platitudes." Mickey Kaus, writing in *The New Republic*, warned of "creeping Rodhamism" and decried Bill's nepotism in giving his wife such control over his domestic policy.

Bill tended to vent about the media in private, reserving his public barbs for the ritualized humor that presidents employ in their speeches each spring at dinners organized by journalistic organizations. He liked to use jokes as "a stick that you beat other people up with," recalled Mark Katz, one of his humor writers. At his first White House Correspondents Association dinner, Bill spent much of the time sarcastically settling scores with his press adversaries, while the audience reacted with "swallowed nervous laughter."

Hillary was typically more direct. To an audience in Lincoln, Nebraska, that spring, she denounced the "unfair, unjust, inaccurate reporting that goes on from coast to coast." She reminded herself that Eleanor Roosevelt, too, had been excoriated for meddling in her husband's business. But in contrast to Hillary, Eleanor had refrained from whining about her treatment in the media. Eleanor had never taken a seat at the table the way Hillary did or enjoyed Hillary's freedom to weigh in on anything she wanted or received credit for her ideas as Hillary did from Bill. Still, Hillary liked to take her cues from the former First Lady. At a speech in Manhattan raising funds for an Eleanor Roosevelt statue in late February, Hillary was "unsmiling" and "joyless" as she took issue with her detractors. She referred to "all the conversations I've had in my head with Mrs. Roosevelt" in which she had asked, "How did you put up with this?" and "How did you go on day to day with all the attacks and criticisms that would be hurled your way?"

HILLARY'S LIFE TURNED upside down on March 19 when her father, Hugh Rodham, suffered a massive stroke. She began a bedside vigil in Arkansas, joined by her mother, her brothers, Chelsea, and the Thomasons, with visits from Bill on the weekends. The health-care task force proceeded under the direction of Ira Magaziner, who stayed in close phone contact with her. After sixteen days in Little Rock, Hillary and her family decided to take no further extraordinary measures to keep her father alive. She returned to Washington on Sunday, April 4, and was airborne two days later to Austin, Texas, for a long-scheduled appearance.

As Hillary contemplated her father's imminent death, she sketched out an uncharacteristically impassioned speech, which she delivered for a half hour without notes. She spoke of a "sleeping sickness of the soul" in America that required a new political discourse based on greater spirituality and kindness. The line was lifted from Albert Schweitzer, and her description of a "crisis of meaning" was the exact language Al Gore had used in an interview with *Time* the previous October, when he expressed his dismay that "many people feel that their lives no longer have a sense of purpose."

The following day, Hillary was in the West Wing with Bill for a meeting with economic, health care, and political advisors, many of whom were arguing for delaying the health-care plan, emphasizing that it was more important to get the job done right than to get it done quickly. She was preternaturally composed as she pressed to keep her program a top priority, while conceding that the deadline for completing the plan would have to slip slightly.

Later that night, Hugh Rodham died—five days after his eighty-second birthday—and the next weekend, the Clintons went back to Little Rock for the funeral and then to Pennsylvania for the burial service. Hillary kept her emotions in check, although Webb Hubbell sensed her exhaustion when "suddenly she leaned her head over gently" and rested it on the shoulder of Vince Foster.

When Hillary was growing up, her father had been impossible to please, a tightwad and a draconian disciplinarian. If Hillary forgot to replace the cap on a tube of toothpaste, Hugh Rodham threw the cap out the window, "even in the snow," and forced her to find it. Hillary later chose not to see such behavior as abusive but rather as her father's way of teaching the importance of avoiding waste. Hillary "took his harshness as a challenge," said one of her old friends. He was also a doctrinaire Republican, whose political coloration Hillary had adopted in her youth. Dorothy—who counted herself a "closet Democrat"—noted that her daughter "was active in Goldwater's and Rockefeller's campaigns, but it was pro forma."

She said she didn't think Hillary "was ever really conservative except in a fiscal sense."

After Easter Sunday at Camp David with her family, Hillary jumped back into a full schedule. In a congressional briefing on Wednesday, April 14, she was as pugnacious as ever, announcing, "I don't care how they do things here. If they can't take the truth, at least they're going to get it from me."

THE OPPORTUNITY TO comfort Hillary had given a boost to Vince Foster, who was having difficulty adjusting to the realignment of his relationship with her. In Little Rock, they had been coequals as litigators—and by Hillary's description "best friends." He reminded her of Gregory Peck playing Atticus Finch in *To Kill a Mockingbird*—reserved, upright, and utterly dependable. "People gravitated to him because he was also a world-class listener," recalled Webster Hubbell. "Women were drawn to Vince not just because he was smart and handsome, but because he seemed to keep secrets."

There were rumors that Hillary and Foster had been romantically involved, a subject Foster had brought up when he first met Bernie Nussbaum. Foster said there was no truth to it, and Nussbaum found him "totally persuasive." Asked later about her husband's fidelity, Lisa Foster said, "I just don't think somebody is a loving husband and treats me the way he would treat me if he's having an affair. . . . I don't think Hillary would do it. . . . The type of friendship she and Vince had was not a romantic one. . . . I think in a lot of ways he felt sort of protective of her. . . . I just think that they were close friends." Not surprisingly, Hillary had long relied on Foster as a confidant, telling him before the inauguration that she wanted to direct health-care reform and that she was going to "take command" and be "involved in this presidency"—a conversation he recorded in a journal. Foster, in turn, "idolized" Hillary and discussed his own private matters with her.

But now Hillary was his boss, and she had to deal with urgent matters such as fending off legal challenges to the secrecy she had imposed on her health-care task force. To further complicate matters, Foster was acting as personal attorney for both Bill and Hillary, a questionable activity for an employee of the executive branch. The pressures of these two roles were weighing on Foster, who was unsettled by Hillary's uncompromising demands, especially after the leak about the smashed lamp, when she braced him for being "too naïve" and "too nice" and for failing to act more forcefully when she first asked him to change Secret Service personnel.

Foster felt responsible for the lamp story and from that moment began calling Hillary "the client." In the view of Webster Hubbell, who by then was working as Deputy Attorney General, Hillary "became a very demanding client indeed." In March, Foster told Hubbell that Hillary had "snapped at him about the Health Care Task Force" after a lawsuit was filed against the group, ordering him, "Fix it, Vince!" The rebuke had "hurt him deeply," Hubbell later wrote. Foster also fretted about possible controversy over "excessive costs" in Hillary's redecoration of the Residence with Kaki Hockersmith.

The Clintons' Arkansas past awakened other concerns. Foster was still trying to straighten out the tax implications of their Whitewater investment; his files contained some hundred pages on the matter. He worried mostly that if they claimed a capital gain of one thousand dollars on their 1992 tax return for the year-end sale to McDougal, they might prompt an IRS audit because they had actually lost money on the nearly defunct property. Specifically—as they had stated since the Whitewater story had broken in March 1992—they had claimed losses of some sixty-nine thousand dollars. But in April 1993, their accountant could verify only $5,878 in losses; the Clintons made no effort to revise their past tax returns. Foster decided to simply show an erroneous thousand-dollar gain on the 1992 tax return. On one of seven pages of handwritten notes on Bill and Hillary's taxes, he wrote that Whitewater was "a can of worms you shouldn't open."

What's more, officials at the Resolution Trust Corporation (RTC), the federal agency responsible for cleaning up the finances of savings-and-loan banks that had collapsed in the 1980s, had been accumulating evidence for months against James McDougal and Madison Guaranty. By the spring, the agency was pressing the Justice Department to investigate Madison's failure, including the possibility that funds from the bank had been illegally diverted to Bill Clinton's gubernatorial campaign in the mid-eighties and that Bill and Hillary had intervened with state regulators to help McDougal keep the bank solvent. Bernie Nussbaum later said that Whitewater and Madison Guaranty weren't "on the radar screen" for him in the spring and summer of 1993. But back in Little Rock, Foster had worked on Madison business before Hillary, and during the 1992 campaign he and Hubbell had reviewed and annotated Hillary's billing records to determine the extent of her legal work for the bank.

There were also signs of trouble involving Hubbell, who had stolen nearly five hundred thousand dollars from his partners and clients at the Rose law firm in the late 1980s to pay off debts from a profligate lifestyle. While Hubbell had managed to conceal his embezzlement and sail through his confirmation for the Justice Department job, his former colleagues had turned up evidence of irregularities in his expenses—which two Rose partners mentioned to Foster in April. "Vince had secrets he was carrying, and they were weighing on him," said one of Foster's White House associates. "I know he knew about Webb Hubbell's problems. He told me that at the old law firm there were issues he had to focus on back there. I am pretty sure Vince knew all the details. There were conversations going on with the law firm, and Vince was shouldering that."

But it was an ill-considered personnel decision prompted in part by pressure from Hillary that "drove Vince batty," said Bernie Nussbaum. The chain of events began in February when Harry Thomason told the Clintons they should make changes in the travel office that served the White House press corps. Investigations by Thomason and others in the following months persuaded Hillary that the travel-office personnel were guilty of "financial mismanagement and waste" and should be replaced.

In a meeting with Foster on May 13, Hillary asked him if he was "on top of" the travel-office situation. He assured her that his colleague William Kennedy, a former Rose partner, was working on it. Foster noted afterward that Hillary's mood was "general impatience . . . general frustration." White House aide David Watkins recalled that Hillary said, "We need to have our people in there." Shortly afterward, Watkins wrote in a memorandum that after the blowup over the Secret Service earlier in the year, he believed "failure to take immediate action" on the travel office would not be "tolerated" by Hillary. "There would be hell to pay," he wrote, if they defied her wishes. "Hillary was precise and direct," said a White House aide. "Things were not moving fast enough. She didn't have a dog in the hunt, but she wanted to get it over with."

On May 19, Mack McLarty gave the order to fire the office's seven em-

Hillary consulting with Bill during an economic conference in Little Rock six weeks after his election as President in November 1992. *"She thought she was part of earning the presidency, and she wasn't about to not share the opportunity."*

Bill, Hillary, and Chelsea Clinton in Little Rock, Arkansas, on October 3, 1991, for Bill's announcement of his presidential candidacy.

"From the age of six, Chelsea had to develop finely tuned antennae."

Gennifer Flowers discussing Bill Clinton at a news conference in New York City on January 27, 1992. *"Bill treated our relationship as if he were bulletproof."*

Bill watches as Hillary talks to reporters on February 16, 1992, in New Hampshire. *"Aides learned that Hillary was 'the closer': no decision was final until she had signed off on it."*

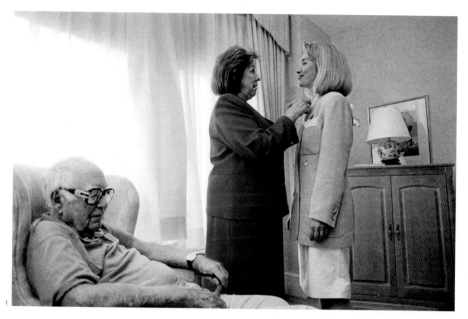

Dorothy and Hugh Rodham with their daughter, Hillary, in a Manhattan hotel in July 1992 during the Democratic National Convention. *"Hillary simply came from a family where women stuck together."*

Bill and Hillary with Al and Tipper Gore on a campaign bus tour, October 26, 1992. *"[Hillary] had her say. She saw the power in choosing Al Gore."*

Bill and Hillary celebrating in Little Rock on election night 1992.

"Like the dog that keeps chasing the car and all of a sudden catches it."

Bill meeting with his economic advisors on January 1, 1993.

"He was capable of constant emotional scans of everyone in the room in real time while he was thinking."

The Clintons with their
friends Harry and Linda
Thomason at a party in
Pasadena, California,
November 28, 1992.

*"We're bunker people.
The four of us are good in
the foxhole together."*

Bill and Hillary on
Fifteenth Street in
Washington, D.C., dur-
ing the inaugural parade
on January 20, 1993.

*"Hillary was 'walking
at her own pace, several
yards out of the shadow of
a husband who had to
stretch to cling to her hand
if there was hand-holding
to be done.'"*

Bill hugs his mother, Virginia Kelley, during the Arkansas inaugural ball as his stepfather, Richard Kelley, looks on.

"Let me get this straight. My son was inaugurated President of the United States, and I can't have a drink?"

Bill announces his appointment of Hillary as head of his Health Care Task Force on January 25, 1993, with management consultant Ira Magaziner (left of Hillary) as her deputy.

"We will try to decide what it is she ought to do, and then discuss it with ourselves, and then tell the American people and give them time to get adjusted to it."

11

The President and Vice President at their weekly lunch, February 1, 1993.

"When people ask me what it's like being number two at the White House, I tell them, 'She seems to enjoy it.'"

12

Bill with senior advisor George Stephanopoulos (right) during speech preparations on February 15, 1993.

"Linda Bloodworth-Thomason called the diminutive aide 'George Step-on-All-of-Us,' which made the Clintons laugh."

Bill confers with Robert Rubin, director of the National Economic Council and later Secretary of the Treasury.

"The White House staff called Rubin 'The Court of Appeals' for his outsize influence over economic policy."

Bill, Hillary, and Chelsea in the second-floor kitchen of the White House Residence.

"'The job of the presidency' was 'all Bill and Hillary talked about. Chelsea brought them both down to reality.'"

16

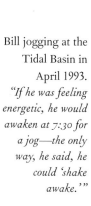

Bill jogging at the Tidal Basin in April 1993.

"If he was feeling energetic, he would awaken at 7:30 for a jog—the only way, he said, he could 'shake awake.'"

17

Hillary and Deputy White House Counsel Vincent Foster (second from left) talk to Bill and family friend Jim Blair (far right) in Little Rock on April 8, 1993, before the funeral of Hillary's father.

"Vince had secrets he was carrying, and they were weighing on him."

Bill at the G-7 summit at Akasaka Palace in Japan on July 8, 1993.

"He sounded positively Japanese when he declared, 'In hard times we shouldn't react like porcupines. We should open up like sunflowers.'"

Bill sailing on the yacht *Relemar* with Jacqueline Kennedy Onassis and Ted Kennedy in Martha's Vineyard, August 24, 1993.

"The well-heeled summer folk on the Massachusetts island embraced the Clintons with an unabashed enthusiasm denied them by the capital panjandrums."

Labor Secretary Robert Reich (far right) gestures to Treasury Secretary Lloyd Bentsen (left of Reich) as they inspect a replica of the White House made with LEGO toys during a South Lawn event to promote the North American Free Trade Agreement, October 20, 1993. *"Secretary Reich could almost live there!"*

Bill and Hillary celebrate with the Health Care Task Force on September 22, 1993, after the President's speech to Congress outlining their plan.

"She worked with people she was comfortable with and shared her beliefs. She never reached beyond her comfort zone."

Bill talking on the telephone in the Center Hall of the White House Residence on November 17, 1993. *"He has the narcissist's gift of making conversation about him feel like conversation about you."*

Paula Jones, a twenty-seven-year-old former Arkansas government employee, accuses Bill of sexual harassment during a news conference on February 11, 1994.

"Stephanopoulos was angry when he realized Bill had misled his advisors by saying he didn't recall meeting Jones and had never been alone with her."

In a series of makeovers, Hillary experiments with a persona to match her unparalleled copresident role.

"We sense that we aren't seeing the 'real' Hillary, and this makes us very nervous."

24

Mrs. Clinton's Hairstyles

JAN. 93

MARCH 93

MAY 93

JUNE 93

SEPT. 93

FEB. 94

APRIL 94

APRIL 94

NOV. 94

NOV. 94

25

26

Hillary and her "Hillaryland" staff in the dining room on the second floor of the White House Residence. *"She was really into her women friends, into impressing them with her brains and feminism. You got the sense that men were complicated for Hillary, but women were not."*

Monica Lewinsky, a twenty-two-year-old White House intern, greets Bill at his surprise forty-ninth birthday party on the South Lawn, August 10, 1995.
"His arm 'casually but unnecessarily' brushed against her chest."

27

The Clintons on a
seventeen-day summer
vacation in Jackson
Hole, Wyoming,
August 1995.

*"They picked
Wyoming because 'swing
voters liked outdoorsy
vacations,' although
Jackson Hole was hardly
a plebeian getaway."*

28

Hillary speaking at the
United Nations Fourth
World Conference on
Women in Beijing,
September 5, 1995.

*"The people there were
stunned. There was no
caution in that speech."*

29

Bill and Monica Lewinsky shortly after their second sexual encounter in his private office on November 17, 1995. *"It was the blow job that changed history. . . . There is no doubt that if Bill Clinton had kept his zipper up north instead of down south, Al Gore would have been elected President."*

The President and Vice President shake hands with Senator Bob Dole (left) and Representative Newt Gingrich (right) in the Oval Office during federal budget negotiations, December 19, 1995. *"Everyone said it was a win for Bill Clinton. But in fact Gingrich won the governing, and Clinton won the TV show with the shutdown."*

Hillary arrives at the U.S. District Court in Washington, D.C., on January 26, 1996, to testify before a federal grand jury.

"She displayed the toughness that Bill said was 'one of the reasons I loved her.'"

Bill playing golf with Hillary's brothers, Tony (left) and Hugh Rodham, in Coral Gables, Florida, April 29, 1996.

"The Rodham brothers . . . made all sorts of demands, and Hillary never crossed them or confronted them or denied them anything, which was odd, since she confronted Bill."

Bill with Laura Tyson, chairman of the President's Council of Economic Advisors and director of the National Economic Council during the first term of his presidency.

"You're the kind of girl back when I was in college I would have tried to get drunk."

ployees. The decision caused an uproar in the press over an absence of due process and allegations of cronyism when it emerged that a distant cousin of Bill would be put in charge and that Harry Thomason had been promoting a friend to get some of the White House air-charter business. William Kennedy aggravated the situation by inappropriately asking the FBI to help with the investigation, "direct contact," Hillary later conceded, that was a "serious breach of Washington protocol." The Thomasons did their friends in the White House no favors by appearing on ABC's *Good Morning America* to say that they made so much money—"a six-figure salary weekly"—that they hardly needed a piece of the White House air-travel business, which Linda called "sort of the equivalent of taking over a lemonade stand."

In the end, none of the charges against the employees stood up, and their precipitous and amateurish dismissals became a damaging test of Hillary's honesty under oath before federal investigators. She later said that others had misconstrued an "offhand comment," and she meant only to suggest that they "look into" questions about mismanagement. She insisted that she did not know the "origin of the decision" to remove the employees, that she had "no role in the decision," and that she "did not direct that any action be taken." But her recollection was at odds with a report issued in October 2000 after a lengthy investigation by the office of the Independent Counsel, which concluded that her statements had been "factually false" and that there was "overwhelming evidence that she in fact did have a role in the decision to fire the employees."

THE TRAVEL-OFFICE PROBLEMS came to a head in a month when the Clintons faced a cascade of troubles. The day before the firings, Bill was caught by White House reporters holding up traffic at Los Angeles International Airport for forty-five minutes while he got a two-hundred-dollar haircut on Air Force One from the Thomasons' Hollywood stylist, Cristophe Schatteman. The Clintons initially denied they had paid such an extravagant sum. Then Hillary claimed that Cristophe was on a "personal services contract," which was untrue. "When I asked how much that cost, Hillary said it was none of their [reporters'] business," said Dee Dee Myers. "The Clintons made it that much more difficult for themselves by making up the story about the personal-services contract." In fact, Bill, who had been accustomed to accepting favors in Arkansas, had received the haircut gratis, and the media caught him out, making much of his Hollywood pretensions. "The underlying truth," concluded George Stephanopoulos, was that Bill "had been self indulgent and insensitive to the image of having a Hollywood hairstylist cut his hair on a busy airport runway."

In the following weeks, Bill came under fire yet again for dumping a prominent nominee, this time his old friend Lani Guinier, with whom he had joyfully celebrated his first week in office. He had proposed her for Associate Attorney General for Civil Rights, but it turned out that her academic writing included a controversial interpretation of the Voting Rights Act that, in its advocacy of minority rights, seemed to undercut the democratic principle of one man–one vote. Bill waffled when asked how much of her work he had read. He had actually read more of it than he was willing to admit.

Fearful that he would be tagged for supporting an ultraliberal, Bill pressured her to withdraw her nomination; in this he had Hillary's full support. As he had with previous troubled nominees, Bernie Nussbaum pleaded with Bill "not to cut her loose." When Bill did, Guinier was furious, and she and the Clintons stopped speaking. In a book about the experience, she recounted being brushed off by Hillary in the West Wing just as her nomination was starting to collapse. "Hey Kiddo!" Hillary said, adding that she was thirty minutes late for lunch. *Newsweek* observed at the time that Guinier's "messy departure" illustrated Bill's "lack of constancy on almost every issue."

The President suffered an embarrassing rebuff in his efforts to quell sectarian unrest in the formerly socialist Yugoslavian federation, where Serbian troops had been slaughtering Muslims trying to establish their own independent country in Bosnia. Taking the advice of Al Gore and National Security Advisor Tony Lake, Bill agreed to a proposal to bomb Serbian military positions while helping the Muslims acquire weapons to defend themselves—the fulfillment of a pledge he had made during the 1992 campaign. But instead of pushing European leaders to sign on, he directed Secretary of State Warren Christopher merely to consult with them. When they balked at the plan, Bill quickly retreated, creating a "perception of drift." The key factor in Bill's policy reversal was Hillary, who was said to have "deep misgivings," and viewed the situation as "a Vietnam that would compromise health-care reform." The United States took no further action in Bosnia, and the "ethnic cleansing" by the Serbs was to continue for two more years, resulting in the deaths of more than 250,000 people.

At the end of May, *The New York Times Magazine* published a startling cover article in which Hillary elaborated on the speech she had given the previous month in Austin. Headlined "Saint Hillary," it was written by Michael Kelly, a perceptive and hard-hitting reporter who had been covering the Clintons for many months. Hillary and her aides had meticulously cooperated with Kelly in order to show how her spiritual journey had been influenced by the writings of liberal theologians and the guidance of ministers she admired. She talked about "the use of power to achieve social good," the existence of "evil people in the world," and the need to "have standards in our social community lives" that are based on the Ten Commandments and the Golden Rule.

The cover photograph starkly depicted her in a white voile suit and a pearl choker against a white background, her smile uncertain. At first, according to *Time*, "her staff loved the picture." But they soon resented its subtext of nunlike sexlessness. Hillary was upset that Kelly mocked her for preaching a "slightly incoherent . . . politics of meaning" and setting herself up as an arbiter of virtue in America in the "gauzy and gushy wrappings of new age jargon." She later shot back that the "elite media" didn't "know what to do with spirituality," which they denigrated because they were "scared of it." "I feel sorry for people like that," she said.

TO IMPOSE SOME ORDER and discipline in West Wing operations, create an image of centrism, and mollify a restive and resentful press, Bill brought veteran Republican strategist David Gergen into his inner circle on May 29. In separate interviews, both Bill and Hillary assured Gergen that they intended to pursue moderate policies and were eager to reach out to the political Establishment they had so willfully disregarded. At Gergen's urging, during June the Clintons hosted a series of twice-weekly dinners in the Residence for members of the national press and other influential Washingtonians. The President and First Lady tried their best to be gracious, offering cocktails on the Truman Balcony, first-run films such as *Sleepless in Seattle,* and the opportunity to mingle with such high-culture celebrities as Isaac Stern, Kathleen Battle, and Jessye Norman. For each evening, they invited forty people to dine on beef Wellington or "pan-seared lamb cushions," mesclun salad, and fresh apricot sorbet, and to be serenaded by the Army Strings.

Press reviews of the "charm offensive" were mixed. "This isn't dinner, it's damage control," observed *The Washington Post*. A few weeks later, Sally Quinn wrote that "many . . . who went to the White House with a hostile attitude came away starry-eyed. It is easy to spot the new friendliness in newspaper and magazine columns." But Quinn also quoted one reporter who admitted feeling "cheap and used." In the end, the Clintons abandoned the effort after the glow faded. "The chemistry didn't happen naturally," said one of Bill's senior advisors. "The press corps was not ready to put down its cudgels, and Bill Clinton was not ready to make peace."

Bill's blue mood lifted when he heard the tragicomic saga of a Virginian named John Wayne Bobbitt. After a domestic dispute on the night of June 23, Bobbitt's enraged wife, Lorena, chopped off his penis with a kitchen knife while he was sleeping, then threw it out of her car as she sped away from home. Police eventually found the severed organ by the side of the road, and doctors reattached it.

When the tale made headlines the next day, Bill regaled an Oval Office meeting with every detail, told with dramatic flourishes. "She suddenly looked down," the President said, "and she suddenly noticed it was still in her hand, and she was so startled, she just tossed it out the winder!"

"Did they get her for littering, Mr. President?" asked Eric Tarloff, the husband of Laura Tyson. Bill rattled on for a couple of sentences, stopped his monologue briefly, laughed, and said, "Litterin'. That's funny." Winding up the story, he said, "The doctors who reattached it say it may be okay, they aren't sure. But they said that if it turns black in the next two days, then it's hopeless."

"Mr. President," cracked Vernon Jordan, "that's just rank prejudice."

In the following days, Bill asked for regular bulletins on Bobbitt's postoperative progress, which he received with much merriment from Al Gore before morning meetings in the Oval Office.

ON SUNDAY, JULY 4, Bill and Hillary left for Tokyo to attend the G-7 summit, the sixteenth annual gathering of heads of state from the major industrial powers. That year, largely at Bill's insistence, Russian president Boris

Yeltsin was to be included in the discussions, although Russia was not an official member of the group. While the majority of Bill's attention had been on domestic matters, he had spent months nurturing a global initiative that included $28.4 billion from the G-7 nations for Russia and its former satellites, which had been struggling to form stable democracies since the breakup of the Soviet Union in 1991. In April, he had met with Yeltsin in Vancouver and promised an ambitious $1.6 billion aid package for Russia.

Bill regarded the chance to promote economic stability and democratic reforms in Russia as "the biggest foreign policy issue we'll have in this administration." He also knew he needed Yeltsin's cooperation to dispose of nuclear warheads located in Ukraine, a former Soviet territory. After initial wariness, the two leaders had bonded, calling each other "Beeeell" and "Boris."

Yeltsin had a serious drinking problem, and Bill's experience as the stepson of an alcoholic gave him an advantage in dealing with the Russian leader. Bill also appreciated his counterpart's combination of crudity and subtle intelligence, of sloppy emotion and cold calculation. "I suspected that there was more to his affinity with Yeltsin than being approximately the same height and shape and shoe size, or being the leaders of two countries that could blow up the world, or being fellow politicians who had to contend with obstreperous legislatures and hostile media," wrote Strobe Talbott. "The key as I saw it might be that Yeltsin combined prodigious determination and fortitude with grotesque indiscipline and a kind of genius for self-abasement. He was both a very big man and a very bad boy, a natural leader and an incurable screw-up. All this Clinton recognized, found easy to forgive and wanted others to join him in forgiving."

A week before leaving for Asia, Bill ordered the launching of twenty-three Tomahawk cruise missiles against the Iraqi intelligence-service headquarters in Baghdad. The air strikes were the President's response to "compelling evidence" uncovered by the CIA of an Iraqi plot to assassinate former president George Bush during a visit to Kuwait three months earlier. Bill made his decision in secrecy, excluding members of Congress and notifying world leaders only after the order had been given to strike. Jordan's King Hussein, on his first official visit to Washington, learned about the attack on CNN, which put him in a "very awkward position," wrote his wife, Queen Noor. While the low-level conflict with Iraq had proved an annoying distraction during the inaugural festivities, this time it gave Bill a chance to show he could be a muscular leader, not the man who had talked airily of placating Saddam Hussein and hoping for his redemption. White House officials were gratified when Bill's approval ratings rose into the mid-forties the next week.

Bill followed that success with a starring role at the G-7 meeting, where he dazzled world leaders with his energetic advocacy of foreign aid and expanded world trade. He made personal overtures to each leader and sounded positively Japanese when he declared, "In hard times we shouldn't react like porcupines. We should open up like sunflowers." But Bill didn't take over every discussion, as might have been expected. Instead, he shrewdly confided to one of his advisors, "I've learned in groups like this, don't speak all the time. But when you do, make it important. That way people will look to you." Sitting next to Bill in the first plenary session, Mickey Kantor watched him wearing his half glasses, concentrating hard on his briefing book. "Then I saw he had a crossword puzzle down in one corner of the book and was working on it," Kantor recalled. "For him, it was a way to keep his mind on what he was doing. It was not a distraction but a way of keeping his concentration."

On her first foreign trip, Hillary behaved like a conventional First Lady and said little. With her mother as a companion, she visited Kabuki theaters, tea ceremonies, and shrines. But she did break ranks once to get a briefing on municipal development because, she confessed, "I'm such a government junkie."

ON THEIR WAY HOME, Bill and Hillary were joined by Chelsea for a short vacation in Hawaii, where Hillary also met with local officials to discuss the state's progressive health-care program. Bill was back at his desk on Wednesday, July 14, but Hillary, Chelsea, and Dorothy Rodham stayed away for another week, stopping first in Santa Barbara to visit the Thomasons—who had fled Washington under withering criticism for Harry's role in the travel-office affair—and then briefly in Little Rock.

At the White House, Staff Secretary John Podesta had finished an internal investigation of the travel office and issued a report that reprimanded William Kennedy. Vince Foster felt deeply responsible for the imbroglio, especially its impact on Kennedy. While Hillary later said she couldn't re-call talking to Foster after the middle of June, his notes showed he had spo-ken with her twice about the travel office, and Nussbaum remembered seeing Foster in an agitated state after a conversation with Hillary in early July.

"Vince was obsessing about the attacks being made on us, expressing concern," recalled Nussbaum. "He thought Congress would investigate and that we should get lawyers." Hubbell later wrote that Foster "couldn't bear the thought" of being "grilled by caustic congressmen." "My God, what have we done?" Foster said to David Watkins, expressing concern that Hillary's role in the firings would come to light. He urged Watkins to pro-tect "the client" at all costs. Foster faced the possibility that in shielding Hillary's involvement, he might have to mislead congressional investiga-tors under oath—a grim prospect for a man who took pride in being a straight arrow. In a notebook later released to investigators, Foster crypti-cally wrote, "defend/HRC role—whatever it was in fact, or might have been."

Foster was also under scrutiny for his part in keeping the health-care task force secret. When *The Wall Street Journal* took aim at Foster in two editorials, Nussbaum saw his colleague's pained reaction and tried to josh him out of it, but to no avail. By mid-July, Foster had lost fifteen pounds and seemed unusually subdued. "He wasn't functioning well," recalled Nussbaum. "I got worried. I told him to take a rest or vacation."

Foster's wife, Lisa, and their two children had recently moved to Wash-ington, but their arrival didn't appreciably cheer him up. He twice con-fided to Lisa that he felt under pressure and was thinking of returning to Arkansas. To Webb Hubbell he bemoaned his dealings with Hillary, say-ing, "It's not the same, Hub," adding that on one matter after another she kept saying, "Fix it, Vince!" or "Handle it, Vince!" Hillary later testified that "he like everybody would say things about, you know, how tough this was, and how different it was, and how stressful it was. And I would, you know, express the same feelings. . . . He never confided in me. He never told me . . . that he took the *Wall Street Journal* editorial seriously. If I had known that, I would have, you know, said something funny or dismissive."

On Wednesday, July 14, Foster met with Susan Thomases at her hotel in Washington. He confided that he felt overworked and that he feared he had "let the President and Hillary down" in the travel-office situation. Two days later, Vince and Lisa drove to an inn on the eastern shore of Maryland for a getaway weekend. At dinner that night, Foster cried when his wife asked him "if he felt trapped." The Hubbells were staying with friends nearby and invited the Fosters to join them for Saturday dinner and to unwind at poolside the next day. Foster seemed relaxed, and he deflected Hubbell's inquiries about his apparent troubles by saying "not here, this feels too good."

The Wall Street Journal ran a third editorial on Monday the nineteenth, nicking Foster lightly in passing. McLarty was worried about him, but Foster reassured him that he was looking forward to taking it easy again on the weekend. The same day, Foster called his doctor in Little Rock, who gave him a prescription for the antidepressant Desyrel. That evening, Foster did something Hubbell later described as "highly unusual": He turned down an invitation to join Bill, Hubbell, and Bruce Lindsey at the White House for a screening of the new Clint Eastwood film, In the Line of Fire.

Bill later gave conflicting accounts about the invitation. At first, the White House said Bill had called because he knew Foster was "having a rough time at work." He then insisted he had been unaware of Foster's distress and phoned him only because he had been feeling "lonesome" with Hillary away. Bill reported that Foster had told him he had had "a great time" on the eastern shore. When Foster said he needed to discuss some issues, Bill agreed to meet him in the Oval Office on Wednesday the twenty-first. Yet years later in his memoir, Bill shifted his account once more, saying he knew Foster had been upset by the travel office and assaults on his integrity. In calling Foster, Bill said he "was hoping to give him some encouragement" and had tried to convince him to "shrug off the Wall Street Journal editorials," although he "could tell" he "hadn't convinced him."

TUESDAY, JULY 20 —the six-month anniversary of the Clinton presidency— was a buoyant moment at the White House. Hillary was due back the next morning after an eighteen-day absence, her longest stretch away from Washington. Bill had an upbeat meeting with House Democrats about the final push to pass his economic package. In the Rose Garden, he announced his selection of federal judge Louis Freeh as his new director of the FBI.

Afterward, Nussbaum reported to Foster that Bill's nominee for the Supreme Court, Ruth Bader Ginsburg, was breezing through her confirmation hearings in the Senate Judiciary Committee. She had been suggested by Pat Moynihan back on May 12 and advocated for strongly by Nussbaum. Bill and Hillary were eager to appoint the second woman to the court, following Ronald Reagan's choice of Sandra Day O'Connor in 1981. Nussbaum and Foster oversaw the search, keeping Hillary informed. She met the candidates, consulted with Bill on his thinking, and concurred with his final choice. Although Gore felt that Ginsburg was "charismatically challenged," Bill had successfully cast her as a compelling moderate (although she had been the principal litigator for the liberal American Civil Liberties Union's women's-rights project) in an effort to smooth her approval by the Senate.

"We hit two home runs," Nussbaum jubilantly told Foster, referring to Freeh and Ginsburg. Foster flickered a smile and said, "I'll see you later." Alone in his office, Foster had lunch on a tray from the White House Mess. When he had finished, he gave his package of M&M's to his secretary and said he had to go out but would be back. At 1:00 p.m., he pulled out of the White House driveway in his gray Nissan.

That night, the President was being interviewed by CNN's Larry King in the Residence when an aide told Mack McLarty that Foster had been found dead in Fort Marcy Park, Virginia, on the other side of the Potomac River. He had died from a gunshot in his mouth, and his father's .38-caliber Colt revolver, dating from 1913, was found at his side. It was the same method of suicide used by a Marine officer distraught about testifying against his commanding officer in *A Few Good Men*, a film Foster had recently watched. In the pocket of his trousers was a note with the names of two Washington psychiatrists. Foster was forty-eight.

McLarty instantly called Hillary in Little Rock, who burst into tears. She urged the Chief of Staff to end the CNN interview so Bill wouldn't hear the news on the air. When McLarty told him, Bill also began to weep. After he called Hillary, Bill said, "I want to see Lisa."

With McLarty at his side, Bill hurried to the Fosters' Georgetown home to comfort the widow of a man with whom he had played mumblety-peg as a child. Bill silently hugged all the assembled friends and family members and steadied the mood. He later said that everyone was "remembering and crying and laughing and talking" about Foster until nearly 2:00 a.m.

The behavior of White House officials, Clinton friends, and Hillary herself in the hours and days following Foster's death was to haunt the administration for years, raising questions about what, if anything, the Clintons had to hide that was in their personal attorney's files. Nussbaum was chastised for working with Hillary's Chief of Staff, Maggie Williams, and another aide to comb Foster's office for a suicide note on Tuesday night, for failing to seal the office the following morning, for conducting his own search in the presence of U.S. Park Police and FBI agents two days after the suicide, and for unilaterally removing sensitive files.

He gave a sheaf of these documents to Williams, who locked them away in the Residence for five days before handing them over to Clinton attorney Robert Barnett. Investigators later questioned why the documents went through an intermediary rather than directly to Barnett, and they tried to learn if the Clintons had inspected the files first—something they emphatically denied doing.

Amid an atmosphere of suspicion, the notion later took hold that key Whitewater papers went missing in the process. It did indeed appear that Hillary's records of her legal work for Madison Guaranty, annotated with red ink in Foster's handwriting, had been part of another batch of personal files in his office. Two days after Foster's death, according to Bob Woodward, Hillary had asked Carolyn Huber, the First Couple's administrative assistant, "to transfer the documents to a locked closet in the personal quarters of the White House." Although later the subject of a subpoena, the billing records were not retrieved for more than two years.

Among the suspicious activities later revealed by investigators was a series of phone calls from Susan Thomases the night of Foster's death and in subsequent days—including five calls to Hillary's office and three to McLarty's office. Thomases also phoned Nussbaum, who later testified that she asked "what was going on with respect to an examination of Mr. Foster's office" and whether "it was proper to give people access to the office at all." Thomases had known Foster for more than two decades, and he had unburdened himself to her the previous week, but her role in managing the Whitewater matter during the campaign suggested an effort to shield potentially damaging documents that had been in his custody. Nussbaum later said that "nobody was thinking about Whitewater. This just concerned the Clintons' private financial files. I made decisions and acted the way a lawyer acts. But I understand the perception issue now." Hillary said she had been on the phone from Little Rock because she "craved information like oxygen" and was "frantic because I felt so far away." But the appearance of concealment was enough to trigger what became five separate federal inquiries.

Webster Hubbell saw the death of his old friend and colleague as "the pivotal moment. Before, there was hope. To me, the astonishing thing was how fast everything began to unravel." In Nussbaum's view, "Vince Foster's death was a history-changing event of the Clinton era, like Monica Lewinsky. The actual death created suspicion, and the Independent Counsel launched an investigation. It became one of those events that brought suspicion, mistrust, and shame to the administration and became a black mark. The irony is that Vince thought he was finding peace, but instead he brought wrath down on the Clintons."

Chapter Six

—

As the shock of Foster's death subsided, almost all of his old friends said he had been suffering from depression, and they second-guessed themselves about not recognizing the seriousness of the problem. Hillary later wrote that she "would wake up in the middle of the night worrying that the actions and reactions concerning the travel office helped drive Vince Foster to take his own life. . . . I will go to my grave wishing I had spent more time with him and had somehow seen the signs of his despair."

Hillary was familiar with the malady that afflicted her close friend. Her chronically depressed uncle—Hugh Rodham's brother—had been a frequent visitor during her girlhood and had slept on the family's sofa when he was being treated at a nearby psychiatric hospital. Webster Hubbell recalled that Hillary "seemed to know" that Foster had anguished about not being able to talk to her anymore. "She realized afterward the effect she had on him," said Mary Mel French. "She felt responsible for it. She didn't mean to, and she never realized he couldn't take that."

The Foster death "ripped a hole through Hillary," Ann McCoy said. Following Foster's funeral in Arkansas, Hillary had difficulty getting out of bed for several days, until finally she told herself, "I'm going to go over to my office." That day—Monday, July 26—one of Nussbaum's associates found a torn-up note on yellow paper at the bottom of Foster's briefcase. The lawyers pieced it together and placed it on a conference table. It wasn't a suicide note but rather a list of grievances and concerns that Foster had jotted down in the days before his death.

Nussbaum went to Hillary's office to tell her he had "found something Vince wrote that may help explain why he did what he did." Hillary "looked startled," Nussbaum recalled. She followed him to the table, glanced at the note, said, "I can't deal with this. Do whatever you think has to be done," and abruptly left the room. Nussbaum then went to Bill, who listened to the description of the note's contents and said, with less emotion than Hillary, "Do what you think is right." Not only did Foster's words show how distraught he had been, they indicated that the travel-office mess had been at the center of his concerns. "I was not meant for the job in the spotlight of public life in Washington," Foster wrote. "Here ruining people is considered sport." And, he added, "The public will never believe the innocence of the Clintons and their loyal staff." After the note's release two weeks later, that comment was interpreted to mean either that he believed the Clintons were blameless or that he worried about information that could damage Bill and Hillary's reputation.

BY THE END OF JULY, Bill and Hillary had collected themselves and turned their attention to the most important task of Bill's presidency: using every tactic in their repertoire to prod the House and Senate to pass his economic plan before the August congressional recess. "I did what I often do when faced with adversity," Hillary recalled. "I threw myself into a schedule so hectic that there was no time for brooding."

The House and Senate had narrowly approved versions of the plan in May and June. The House bill had included the BTU tax championed by Al Gore because of its potential environmental benefits. Among other goals, the ambitious tax was intended to encourage the use of natural gas rather than coal and oil. Bill had promised Democratic congressmen that he would keep the complex and controversial tax at all costs and that they wouldn't pay a political penalty for their vote.

But ten days later, in an Oval Office meeting with Senate leaders, Bill agreed to drop the BTU levy when Pat Moynihan and George Mitchell said it was probably unenforceable and the Senate wouldn't accept it. Instead, Bill said he would support a gasoline tax, even though he had campaigned against one in 1992. Asked about his change of heart, Bill said, "I wasn't opposed to a gasoline tax, only to its size."

"Bill Clinton showed he is a wonderful hack," said Lawrence O'Donnell, Democratic chief of staff for the Senate Finance Committee, "and that he will find a way to whatever compromise it takes to get him to a political place he needs. The BTU tax was the biggest thing Bill Clinton had talked about for the first six months, and he dropped it just like that." "Members of the House were not pleased," said White House advisor William Galston. "It cost him. Once people have relied on you and risked something to themselves on a venture, it's harmful if you reverse yourself." For Al Gore, it was an even greater loss, but he didn't complain publicly, and he maintained his loyalty.

All the Republican lawmakers remained implacably opposed to any new taxes, and Democrats were still fractured between advocates of greater spending cuts and those who favored higher taxes. Back on July 3, on the eve of their departure for the Asia summit, the Clintons had met in the Solarium with their top advisors. Concerned that the economic plan was in jeopardy, Hillary had aimed a withering indictment at the staff for failing to sell the plan's benefits to the public. "We need a war room," she announced, summoning her favorite tactic. Bill had picked up her frustration and barked to McLarty and Gore, "I want it solved . . . before I get home." "It was a call to arms," said one participant.

Now, at the beginning of August, House and Senate Democratic negotiators had settled on the final version of the legislation, which included a modest 4.3-cent-per-gallon gasoline tax. The war room ordered by Hillary had been honing its sales pitch in an effort to pull wavering Democrats into line. But the chances of victory were still only fifty-fifty.

The House vote was scheduled for Thursday, August 5, and Bill was furiously making promises to some forty fence-sitting Democrats, enlisting Hillary's help for health-care trade-offs. Secretary of the Treasury Lloyd Bentsen, who had watched eight presidents during his career as a senator, told Bob Woodward that he had "never seen any of them so personally involved in lobbying as Bill Clinton."

The last holdout was first-term Pennsylvania representative Marjorie Margolies-Mezvinsky, who had been elected by a margin of only 1,373 votes in a suburban Philadelphia district where Republicans outnumbered Democrats by two to one. She correctly feared that her conservative constituents would run her out for endorsing higher taxes, but she succumbed to Bill's entreaties. "What he said to me on the night of the vote," she recalled, "was that without this, the country would have come to a screeching halt." When the legislation squeaked through by 218 to 216 late that Thursday night, Republicans on the House floor chanted, "Bye-bye Marjorie!" (She would indeed be defeated in 1994.) In the Oval Office, the President and his advisors hugged and hollered as Bill plucked twenty-dollar bills out of James Carville's wallet and flung them around the room—emblems of his "tax the rich" policies about to be fulfilled.

In the Senate, five Democrats out of fifty-six opposed the bill, and one remained undecided—Bob Kerrey of Nebraska, who had been an opponent of Bill in the 1992 primaries, with the strong backing of Pat Moynihan. Kerrey was brainy and charismatic, a former Navy SEAL who had lost the lower part of his right leg in the Vietnam War. The Kerrey-Clinton rivalry had been pointedly personal. As Bill told Gennifer Flowers in a tape-recorded conversation four months before the first primary, "I might lose the nomination to Bob Kerrey. He's single, won the Medal of Honor, and looks like a movie star. Because he's single, nobody cares if he's screwing." During the campaign, Kerrey had criticized Bill for duplicity, and later Hillary had vetoed him as a vice-presidential prospect.

On August 5, one day before the Senate vote, Kerrey called Bill at 8:00 a.m. to say he was against the economic package because it didn't go far enough on entitlement reform and contained taxes that could harm economic growth. Bill erupted in anger and accused Kerrey of wanting to "bring this presidency down." When Kerrey said he resented such an accusation, Bill shouted "Fuck you!" before both men hung up on each other.

Scarcely two hours later, Bill called Moynihan to say Kerrey "had got out of bed in a bad mood and was planning to vote no." Bill added that Kerrey didn't seem to grasp what a negative vote would do "to me and to the cause." Moynihan was noncommittal about lending a hand, and when Bill called back at 1:00 p.m. for a progress report, Moynihan told him he had not tried to dissuade Kerrey, but "other efforts" would be made later in the day.

At 6:00 p.m., Moynihan's wife, Liz, a shrewd political strategist who managed his campaigns, called Kerrey from their farm in upstate New York. "I wish you were President," she told the Nebraska senator. "You are a person of character." She said she knew he was against the legislation be-cause it was a "bad bill," adding, "Pat thinks the same. But he feels we can-not have another President fail. We cannot have the United States at the end of the Cold War as dilapidated as the Soviets. It is necessary to stay alive and be a player." She added that the Clintons "don't seem to know what they are up to on anything. You be the alternative and stay alive. Don't let those people do you in."

The next morning, Bill invited Kerrey to the White House Residence. Before the meeting began, Gergen cautioned Bill, "Don't make it per-sonal. Talk about your shared principles." The President and the senator spent ninety minutes together on the Truman Balcony, and Kerrey pledged his support for the legislation. In return, Bill agreed to appoint a commis-sion on "economic priorities," to be headed by Kerrey. Like so many such groups, this one was destined to become a mere "debating society." The real turning point had been Liz Moynihan's persuasion, and Bill knew it.

On Friday evening, August 6, Kerrey joined the "yea" votes, and the Senate deadlocked at 50–50, with Al Gore breaking the tie to ensure pas-sage. Kerrey took the occasion to castigate the President, calling him "green and inexperienced" and urging him to return to the "high road" by emphasizing the notion of shared sacrifice. After the vote, Hillary said to Bill, "Every woman in the Congress voted for you. They've got more balls than the men." The next day, Bill called Liz Moynihan to say she had "saved his administration."

OVER THE FOLLOWING DAYS, yet another struggle took place within the White House as various factions jockeyed for a spot atop the President's agenda. Having helped win passage of the economic package, Hillary felt entitled to advance her health-care plan, which she now promised to de-liver to Congress in September. At the end of April, on the evening of Bill's hundredth day in office, the Clintons had waved farewell to the more than five hundred consultants to the health-care task force on the South Lawn, and since then Ira Magaziner and his staff had been laboriously writing the intricate legislation.

At the same time, Al Gore was promoting his pet project, the Reinvent-ing Government (REGO) initiative, which sought to make the federal bureaucracy more efficient. The economic team and other key advisors, including Mack McLarty, Mickey Kantor, and David Gergen, were likewise urging Bill to use his momentum to push for congressional ratification of the North American Free Trade Agreement (NAFTA). The treaty, which was designed to lower trade barriers among the United States, Canada, and Mexico, had been negotiated by the Bush Administration and was slated to expire if not ratified by January 1, 1994. Liberal Democrats, including Hillary, opposed it primarily because it could take jobs away from American workers. But as an advocate of global economic cooperation, Bill was drawn to its free-trade philosophy. With its Republican pedigree, the treaty also promised to appeal to the sort of bipartisan coalition that could restore Bill's centrist bona fides. His main challenge would be bringing reluctant Democrats around.

In a series of daily "sequencing" meetings in the Solarium starting on Saturday, August 7, each West Wing faction made its case. "The economic team loved NAFTA, hated health care, and didn't know what to make of REGO," said Bruce Reed. "The health-care team hated NAFTA and didn't know what REGO was. The REGO people hated health care and didn't know what to make of NAFTA. The President loved all three with equal passion — whichever he was focused on that day."

As usual, Hillary was backed by Bill's quartet of liberal consultants, with Paul Begala working behind the scenes on Capitol Hill to defer consideration of NAFTA and press congressmen to give health care precedence. "Look," Hillary said in one Solarium meeting, "we have postponed health care until after the budget. We can't hold it up any longer."

It fell to Mickey Kantor, the U.S. Trade Representative responsible for implementing NAFTA, to reason with Hillary. One day in August, he sat her down on a bench behind the White House and tried to strike a compromise. "I said, 'If you want to drop NAFTA, we can kill it, but we shouldn't,'" Kantor recalled. "I said, 'The way to do it is to introduce health care, spend a month on it, and then do NAFTA, then go back to health care.'" With misgivings, Hillary acquiesced to the proposed sequence (including some events to introduce REGO in early September), and Bill announced that William Daley, a son of the late Richard Daley, longtime mayor of Chicago, would run the task force for NAFTA. A formidable lawyer, Daley had considerable standing in the Democratic party, with access to the labor unions leading the opposition.

BILL CLINTON WAS exhausted by mid-August. After the Solarium meetings ended on the twelfth, he took two days off in Vail, Colorado, to play golf with Jack Nicklaus, former President Gerald Ford, and Kenneth Lay, chairman and chief executive of the Enron energy company. The other men were bemused by Bill's unconventional approach to the game. After replaying numerous shots off the tee, he said he had scored an eighty, prompting Nicklaus to mutter to Ford, "an 80 with 50 floating mulligans." Nicklaus later estimated that Bill's real score was over one hundred.

Bill found more pliable golfing partners when he joined some old friends on the fairways around Fayetteville, Arkansas, during a visit to Jim and Diane Blair's house in nearby Beaver Lake. But he hadn't yet officially begun the holiday his aides had been imploring him to take. He gave speeches in Oklahoma, Missouri, and Colorado before heading back to the White House for health-care briefings from Ira Magaziner. "Mr. President, if you don't go on vacation, the American people are going to think you're weird," Paul Begala told him.

"I *am* weird," Bill replied.

Finally, on Thursday, August 19, 1993, his forty-seventh birthday, Bill set out for ten days in Martha's Vineyard with Hillary and Chelsea. The well-heeled summer folk on the Massachusetts island embraced the Clintons with an unabashed enthusiasm denied them by the capital panjandrums. There were a number of prominent Washingtonians on the island, but their clannishness was neutralized by the remote location and the presence of influential New Yorkers (opera star Beverly Sills, TV newsmen Mike Wallace and Walter Cronkite) and Hollywood celebrities (Christopher Reeve, Michael J. Fox, and Glenn Close). "It was unconditional love," said one veteran Vineyard vacationer. "Everywhere else, the Clintons were being judged."

Their cicerone was Vernon Jordan, who arranged at the last minute for Bill and Hillary to stay, rent free, in a modest and secluded gray shingled cottage on fifteen acres belonging to Robert McNamara, John F. Kennedy's Secretary of Defense, with a grand view of Oyster Pond and the Atlantic Ocean beyond. Jordan and his wife, Ann, were the Clintons' most prominent black friends, unmatched power players in political and corporate circles. With his silky manner and striking good looks, Jordan deployed his sexual magnetism so skillfully that Washington writer Marjorie Williams likened it to a "sophisticated weapon" that he would fine-tune, "turning up the dial until it is set on 'Stun.'"

Vernon Jordan had declined an administration post, preferring to kibitz from the sidelines, away from the intrusive press. Ann Jordan extended her help on White House social matters to organizing a schedule on the Vineyard that would introduce the President and First Lady to anyone they wished to know. Vacationers on the island for two decades, the Jordans rented in the fashionable white area of Chilmark rather than Oak Bluffs, the heart of the African-American community.

On their first evening, the Clintons attended a birthday party for Bill at the Jordans'—only four tables of eight on their screened-in porch, with a dress code of shirtsleeves and sweaters. The crowd included *Washington Post* chairman Katharine Graham, authors William and Rose Styron, and Jacqueline Kennedy Onassis and her longtime companion, Maurice Tempelsman. At dinner, Jackie and Chelsea flanked the President, who talked with them both about books and travel. "It was clear that Bill passed along books to Chelsea," said a guest who sat nearby.

Vernon Jordan "rose like Lawrence Welk" to lead the singing of "Happy Birthday to You." Chelsea paid tribute to her "wonderful father," and Hillary raised a glass to say, "I love you, Mr. President." More friends came for an after-dinner sing-along around a piano in the living room. Warmed up by Cole Porter and George Gershwin tunes, Bill belted out "Georgia on My Mind" and "(Sittin' on) the Dock of the Bay" as he wrapped his arm around Hillary. The Clintons lingered until 1:00 a.m., an extraordinary hour in a place where bedtime was usually 10:00 p.m. "Bill stayed and stayed and talked, so everyone stayed," said one guest. "People were telling him about their favorite places and beaches. Everyone wanted a piece of both of them."

Bill slept most of the next day, forcing Jordan to cancel their first golf match. But Bill played nearly every subsequent day, while Hillary preferred to read and take walks with Chelsea around Oyster Pond. She also befriended a group of women close to Ann Jordan that included Rose Styron, children's advocate Lucy Hackney, and broadcasters Diane Sawyer and Charlayne Hunter-Gault, who took her to the beach and invited her to lunch. Hillary was particularly eager to know William Styron, because she had read his book about depression, *Darkness Visible: A Memoir of Madness.* They ended up taking two long walks together to talk about Vince Foster, and Styron tried to reassure her that she shouldn't feel guilty about having brought Foster to Washington. One afternoon, Jackie Onassis invited the Clinton family for a four-hour sail on Tempelsman's yacht, and Massachusetts senator John Kerry treated them to a cruise as well.

Bill and Hillary were out nearly every night, either to private homes or restaurants, circulating among the same group of thirty or forty island luminaries. "I don't care about the food, just give me a fun place to eat," Bill said. The Clintons were feted by singer Carly Simon and by Sheldon Hackney, the historian who was serving as Chairman of the National Endowment for the Humanities. Katharine Graham invited them to two dinner parties, the first at Vernon Jordan's request, since she had planned it to honor her houseguests, Republican foreign-policy advisors Henry Kissinger and Lawrence Eagleburger. "Kay said, 'I am not changing the guest list,'" said one of her friends who was there that first Friday night. But Bill inevitably became the de facto guest of honor, presiding exactly as he did at White House social events. Graham insisted that he lead "general conversation" during dinner and told Carly Simon to "hush" when she was talking to Webster Hubbell. After dinner, "Clinton was talking about health care ad nauseam," said a guest. "Henry Kissinger didn't know anything about it. There were people clustered around Clinton. It was like watching a continuous film loop. As the group changed, Clinton would start over."

Another evening, the Jordans arranged a dinner at a restaurant with Paul Allaire, the chairman of Xerox, and his wife, Kay. "Clinton really wanted to talk to Paul about NAFTA, to get the view of business," recalled Kay Allaire. "Hillary made clear that she opposed NAFTA. The President was curious, asking lots of questions, listening carefully. Hillary remained aloof and said little. You could tell that she was taking it all in, that her mind was spinning. She was analyzing the situation, and she was sizing us both up."

THE CLINTONS RETURNED to Washington in time for Bill to preside over a White House interfaith prayer breakfast on Monday, August 30. During afternoons on the Vineyard, he had read Yale law professor Stephen Carter's new book, *The Culture of Disbelief*, an exploration of the hostility toward religion in contemporary culture, particularly in the media and the liberal political establishment. Bill cited Carter's thinking in his remarks, which he expanded into a series of speeches during the month of September. His theme was the difficulty of making changes in modern society and the need to reinforce the basic family-centered values underlying American life.

But as he was speaking these lofty words, Bill knew that his own values were being called into question by fresh revelations about his behavior in Arkansas. He had been aware since mid-August that four state troopers from his Little Rock security detail—Roger Perry, Larry Patterson, Danny Ferguson, and Ronnie Anderson—were telling the press that he had used them to facilitate his womanizing. They had been provoked initially by the Flowers revelations—when Patterson had been warned to keep quiet by Buddy Young; the head of the security team—and then by the troopers' resentment toward Bill's early actions as President, especially his policy toward gays in the military and the prominent role he had given to Hillary. The troopers' path to the media had been smoothed by a Little Rock lawyer named Cliff Jackson, who had attended Oxford University on a Fulbright fellowship when Bill was there as a Rhodes Scholar. Jackson had long harbored deep suspicions about Bill's character and had become an abiding enemy.

The troopers' primary contact was *Los Angeles Times* reporter Bill Rempel, who had been on their trail since the campaign. He met with them for the first time in Hot Springs on August 14, as did David Brock, a writer for the right-wing *American Spectator*. In case the mainstream press turned fainthearted about pursuing the story, Jackson had brought in Brock at the suggestion of well-connected conservative activists. Shortly afterward, the President called Buddy Young, who had become the administration's regional head of the Federal Emergency Management Agency (FEMA). Bill told Young he had heard rumors that the troopers wanted to publish a book based on their tales.

Young called three of the troopers to fish for information. One of them, Roger Perry, later said that Young told him he would be "destroyed" if he went public—a claim Young denied. After the phone calls, Young reported to the President that Perry was "giving information out or something but I didn't know what." Subsequently, Bill himself talked to Danny Ferguson by phone three times. "Troopers being talked to by lawyer—offered big $. He says GOP in on," Bill wrote. In addition to probing Ferguson about the troopers' plans, the President discussed the possibility of a federal job "just like Buddy's" or a position as a U.S. marshal. This was Bill's way of dealing with impending personal problems through oblique but unmistakable inducements meant to quiet potential troublemakers—an approach that would prove disastrous with Monica Lewinsky.

By September, inquiries by the government and by journalists into Bill and Hillary's Arkansas finances were also advancing. The Resolution Trust Corporation investigation into Madison Guaranty, led by a dogged federal employee named L. Jean Lewis, had gained momentum during the summer. On September 24, an RTC senior vice president briefed the general counsel of the Treasury Department, Jean Hanson, on nine "criminal referrals"—an array of conspiracy and fraud charges against Madison and McDougal, including bogus check writing and phony loan originating, that were finally being referred to the Justice Department after months of delays. The briefing indicated that the Clintons were "potential witnesses." Hanson transmitted the information to the acting head of the RTC, Deputy Treasury Secretary Roger Altman, and to Bernie Nussbaum at the White House.

Reporters at *The Washington Post*, as well as Jeff Gerth of *The New York Times*, who had written the original Whitewater account in March 1992, were all chasing the RTC story and an array of other allegations regarding the McDougals, the Clintons, and various Arkansas figures. White House officials—Nussbaum, Lindsey, and Gergen among them—found themselves fielding the inquiries and casting about for facts. On October 1— eight days before the Department of Justice received the criminal referrals on Madison Guaranty—Bruce Lindsey told Bill the extent of the charges. The President merely replied with a "hmmmm," according to James Stewart, author of *Blood Sport*, a chronicle of the Clinton investigations. With virtually no information forthcoming from the White House, reporters grew increasingly suspicious that the Clintons had something to hide.

IF BILL FELT ANXIOUS about the Arkansas probes, he didn't show it. Revived by his Martha's Vineyard interlude, he immersed himself in a whirlwind of activity that Gergen called "among the most productive of his presidency." He launched Al Gore's REGO initiative on the South Lawn on September 7 and a week later stood in the same place to preside over the signing of the Oslo Accords between Israel and the Palestine Liberation Organization.

Secret negotiations leading to the agreement had been conducted in Norway for months without any involvement of the United States. Bill learned of the deal—intended to give the Palestinians a role in governing the disputed territories of the West Bank and Gaza Strip—through a phone call from Israeli prime minister Yitzhak Rabin on September 9. But he was quick to recognize its potential and invited Rabin and Yasser Arafat, the PLO chairman, to the White House for a historic handshake four days later. Bill was "only too happy to claim credit," Robert Reich observed, as he watched his old friend standing between the two leaders. "It's a gift from heaven. . . . Forget Norway. Bill is reconciling these age-old antagonists." The previous night, Bill had been awake until 3:00 a.m. reading the Book of Joshua, and in his brief speech to the gathering of three thousand, he referred not only to the Bible but to the Koran. "He is the nation's Preacher-in-Chief," Reich noted. "This is his true calling."

The next day, Tuesday the fourteenth, Bill kicked off his campaign for NAFTA in an East Room ceremony attended by Presidents Carter, Ford, and Bush. He ad-libbed much of the speech, which won raves in the press. At a subsequent event on the South Lawn highlighting American products exported to Mexico, Bill was in high spirits as he spotted a replica of the White House made of LEGO bricks. "Secretary Reich could almost live there!" exclaimed Bill, and his diminutive Labor Secretary couldn't help laughing.

But the main event in this period was Bill's introduction of Hillary's health-care plan in a speech to a joint session of Congress on Wednesday, September 22. The unveiling followed a campaign of carefully timed trial balloons and press briefings that had begun with the leak of a 246-page draft of the plan. Three days after that, on September 13, *Time* hit the newsstands with a cover announcing the "inside story of the most sweeping reform since the New Deal." But the magazine sounded an alarm by remarking on the plan's "sheer size, audacity and intrusiveness into personal and business decisions" and concluding that the scheme "would push Americans away from private doctors and into less expensive group medical practices such as health maintenance organizations."

In speeches in Washington, D.C., and Minneapolis, Hillary sought to warm up public opinion by emphasizing the "underlying principles" of the new policy. Since her string of populist attacks against doctors, health-insurance companies, and pharmaceutical firms for "price gouging," she had shifted her rhetoric to describe the benefits for consumers. But she hadn't been entirely consistent in her message. In June, she had been enthusiastically applauded by two thousand doctors at the American Medical Association convention for criticizing managed care, which required third-party approval of treatments ordered by doctors. Dana Priest of *The Washington Post* pointed out that it was unclear how Hillary's criticism "squared with the Administration's proposed health care plan which, at its core, rests on the belief that managed care is the most cost-effective way to provide medical care."

Even more problematic for Hillary was the reaction of the powerful health-insurance industry, which she had been bashing. Its newly appointed chief lobbyist, A. Willis Gradison Jr., "radiated reasonableness" and tried to bridge the gap with her in May, but she had spurned his overtures. At the end of the summer, Gradison approved a ten-million-dollar television advertising campaign. Its centerpiece was a commercial featuring a middle-class couple named Harry and Louise sitting at a kitchen table and fretting over the impact of the plan's bureaucracy on ordinary citizens. The devastatingly effective TV spot, which began running in early September, had a succinct punch line: "There's got to be a better way." In her Minnesota speech on September 17, Hillary warned against "scare tactics" that were "already filling the airwaves"—the first sign of worry in the White House.

On Sunday the nineteenth, things got worse when Pat Moynihan appeared on NBC's *Meet the Press.* The previous Friday, he had spoken with economist William Baumol, with whom he had been consulting as details of the plan emerged. Baumol told him that the administration's estimates of future Medicare and Medicaid costs were "mind-bogglingly unrealistic" and invited "year after year reduction in service and promises the administration can't deliver." Under questioning from *Meet the Press* host Tim

Russert, Moynihan dismissed the plan's "fantasy numbers" and insisted that there was "no health-care crisis."

Up in the Solarium that afternoon, Hillary read through the speechwriters' draft of her husband's remarks and ordered a new version, producing what she later described as "panic." She and Bill summoned a dozen advisors to join them for a brainstorming session over nachos and guacamole. Hillary suggested that the theme for the speech be "health care reform [as] part of the American journey," proposed an outline, and dispatched the speechwriters.

The next day, Hillary tried to repair the damage from Moynihan's comments by meeting with a bipartisan group of two hundred senators and representatives. She countered that the plan would actually cut costs by slowing the growth rate of Medicare and Medicaid and that it made "budgetary sense."

On Tuesday evening, George Stephanopoulos gave Bill the revised speech, which he took to the Residence, where Hillary was waiting. "The President was late coming home—again," Stephanopoulos recalled. Yet "for all the tension that constantly crackled between them," their advisor imagined them "truly at home working through the speech together." The Clintons agreed that the "American journey" revision was awful—not in Bill's voice, Hillary said—and needed to be completely rewritten. Bill sat down for one of his all-nighters, and when Hillary awoke at 4:00 a.m., she added what she felt the speech needed.

On Wednesday morning, Stephanopoulos found the couple in their dining room, its oak table littered with heavily edited pages, as Bill continued to work through the text and Hillary rubbed his shoulders. Once again, they sent the edited version back to the speechwriters to make sense of their scribbles.

Several hours later, their modus operandi as a couple was on full display during a luncheon with a select group of reporters in the Family Dining Room on the ground floor of the Residence. It was clear, as Gwen Ifill wrote in The New York Times, that Hillary was "the power beside rather than behind the throne," showing herself a "master of policy detail. . . . The couple that so actively resisted the notion of a co-presidency only last year had no such trouble today." Hillary was Bill's "reality compass, steering him back to the goal at hand when his digressive style leads him astray."

Afterward, political consultant Mandy Grunwald announced, "Hillary's a celebrity, and that's a tremendous advantage."

Bill tinkered with the text through three practice runs in the Family Theater, standing behind the lectern known as the "Blue Goose." With the final speech in hand, Stephanopoulos squeezed his small frame onto the jump seat of the presidential limousine for the ride to the Capitol with Bill and Hillary. Bill kept fixing sentences while Hillary sat motionless, with a "tight smile" and "fixed gaze, the hands folded firmly in her lap, holding everything inside," wearing the "look of a wife who always had to worry for two."

As Bill began to speak in the House chamber, he momentarily seemed disoriented—his February 17 economic address was scrolling through the TelePrompTer. Barely missing a beat, he began a riff that lasted seven minutes before technicians fixed the glitch, and he continued for the remaining forty-seven minutes with the correct speech. Only his advisors knew what had happened. But this was Bill at his rhetorical best, facing a high-wire challenge that tapped into his storehouse of knowledge "from a lifetime of hard study and sympathetic listening," his remarkable memory, and the extemporaneous skill that set him apart from every other politician, his wife included.

Even with a prepared text, he loved to "arc off into ideas as they occurred to him [and] return for a brief touchdown to reconnect with the structure of the written version," wrote Strobe Talbott. Stephanopoulos likened his boss to a "jazz genius . . . losing himself in a wonky melody." There was something musical in the rise and fall of Bill's gravelly baritone and the way he tapped the lectern with his slender fingers. His manner was invariably relaxed, the style so conversational that he paradoxically lacked eloquence. For all his rhetorical mastery, his words rarely endured on the page—at least in part because his body language and inflection made them compelling. But he also didn't invoke the elegant images and memorable phrases of great orators. Rather, his approach came straight out of the spontaneous exchanges of Southern Baptist church services.

Bill paid tribute to Hillary during his health-care speech, calling her a "talented navigator" with a "rigorous mind, a steady compass, a caring heart." At the end, he received a bipartisan standing ovation. "Too bad it would be the high point of the health care fight," Stephanopoulos later wrote. The President's approval ratings shot to 56 percent in the Gallup and *USA Today*–CNN polls after hovering around the mid-forties since early July, but shortly afterward they dropped back down.

Hillary's peak moment came the following week, with star turns before five House and Senate committees in three days, a performance that earned rave reviews from seasoned lawmakers and skeptical reporters alike. "This is Eleanor Roosevelt time," said one of her aides. In her first four hours with two House committees, she spoke seamlessly, with perfect diction and impressive recall, consulting neither her notes nor any of her nine aides sitting nearby. "She can sling 'unfunded mandates' and 'historical reimbursement patterns' with the best of them," wrote columnist Mary McGrory. Moynihan aide Lawrence O'Donnell found Hillary to be "utterly fearless," yet without projecting "an unreasonable confidence level." When Republican Richard Armey sarcastically referred to a "government-run health care system," she linked him to Dr. Jack Kevorkian, the pathologist notorious for his role in assisting suicides. "The reports of your charm are overstated," Armey said, flushing noticeably, "and the reports on your wit are understated." After Armey left the room, the next Republican questioner, Harris Fawell, told Hillary he would "proceed with caution" after "you impaled my colleague."

ON A WEST COAST SWING to promote the health-care plan on October 3, Bill learned that American Black Hawk helicopters had been shot down in Somalia, resulting in the deaths of eighteen troops—the first American servicemen to die in battle during his presidency. They had been part of a humanitarian mission ordered by President Bush the previous December to alleviate suffering in a civil war, and their presence had indeed saved thousands of lives. The bloody fight in the streets of Mogadishu against forces led by Somali warlords came after American soldiers had launched a manhunt for the killers of twenty-four Pakistanis in the UN peacekeeping force.

Bill returned to Washington and was preoccupied by the Somalia situation, along with unrest in Russia, for the next several weeks, leaving Hillary alone to carry the banner for health care. Then, with the vote on NAFTA approaching, the time came for Bill to turn his complete attention to it for nearly two months to ensure its passage.

The White House publicity campaign included eighteen events featuring the President. NAFTA was easier to promote than health care, especially after Mickey Kantor negotiated supplemental agreements on environmental standards and labor practices in Mexico that allayed some Democrats' concerns about pollution and worker safety. Bill gave dinners at the White House and dispensed favors to one hundred undecided lawmakers. With only days to go, Al Gore solidified the vote by handily winning a televised debate with Ross Perot who—like liberal Democrats—feared a loss of American jobs. The once-powerful presidential contender was reduced to a "whiny crank." The final tally for NAFTA on November 17 was 234 votes to 200 in the House, with 132 Republicans joining 102 Democrats to vote for the treaty. The Senate vote was 61 to 38.

The bipartisan victory pushed Bill's approval ratings consistently above 50 percent for the first time since the previous April, starting with a *USA Today*–CNN poll in the first week of December 1993 that bumped him to 52 percent. "It's a measure of how much the world and rules have changed when Republicans pitch in to help Bill Clinton realize George Bush's legacy," cracked Wayne Berman, a Republican lobbyist who had worked with Mack McLarty on strategy.

WITHIN DAYS OF THAT TRIUMPH, Senate Majority Leader George Mitchell finally introduced the Clinton health-care bill on the final day of the legislative session. In an attempt to regain momentum, Bill and Hillary had delivered the much-delayed legislation to congressional leaders in a ceremony in the Capitol's Statuary Hall on October 27, in which Bill had said plaintively, "Please help us." The 240,000-word measure ran to 1,342 pages and took weeks for lawmakers to digest.

The particulars proved even more intricate and intrusive than anticipated. Aside from the layers of government regulation, the Clinton plan featured social engineering that alarmed the medical profession. In an effort to equalize care around the country, there were incentives for doctors to leave cities and live in rural areas. Even more ominously, teaching hospitals were required to increase the number of general practitioners to 55 percent, with a corresponding decrease in the number of specialists—an ill-conceived policy aimed at a profession in which 67 percent were specialists. When the wife of a thoracic surgeon expressed her concern to Hillary at a gathering of doctors in Georgia, Hillary smiled and said, "Oh, don't worry about it." But Hillary herself was concerned about the growing resistance. In mid-November, one of her friends noted in a journal that Hillary had complained angrily about "what she called the conspiracy of the medical profession to block her attempt to emphasize family practice, general practice, and pediatrics."

"I understood the core of the plan," said Robert Rubin, "but I had no idea what all the ramifications would have been." Even Bill said "my brain aches" from studying its details. The President proved surprisingly ineffective at explaining it to Americans—mainly because the ambiguities and complexities defied easy description.

At a moment when Hillary should have been reaching out, she went on the attack again. Her first broadside came on November 1 when she openly denounced the "Harry and Louise" ads, accusing the health-insurance industry of lying by saying that the plan would limit choice. She bitterly condemned the greed of health insurers, who she said were pushing the United States "to the brink of bankruptcy." Less understandable was her salvo a week later against a moderate proposal (mercifully only three hundred pages long) introduced in the House by Tennessee Democrat Jim Cooper with forty-nine cosponsors from both parties. "She really trashed southern moderate conservatives in her own party," said longtime hospital lobbyist Michael Bromberg. "They were the swing vote . . . this big group in the middle." Their principal offense was failing to guarantee universal coverage.

Bill and Hillary later blamed the "Harry and Louise" ads and Republican opponents for undercutting the chances of reform. They said the crucial blow came from a memo written by conservative Republican strategist William Kristol on December 2, exhorting Republican leaders to block passage of the legislation rather than find a compromise. Kristol wrote that health-care reform could only benefit the Democratic party, which would be seen as "the generous protector of middle class interests." "I don't think we really had a chance" after the memo circulated among Republicans, Bill recalled seven years later—although he gave no hint of such feelings at the time.

Widespread disillusionment across party lines had in fact set in about the Clinton plan. Pat Moynihan's misgivings had grown even deeper after Robert Reischauer, director of the Congressional Budget Office since

1989, told him "the notion that this could work in the real world is absurd" and described the bill as "an act of hubris." Daniel C. Tosteson, dean of the Harvard Medical School, was equally scathing, telling Moynihan that American medicine "would be put in jeopardy" by the "foolhardy" Clinton plan. "What is now a triumph of American civilization could be destroyed."

Public support for health reform, which peaked at 67 percent immediately after Bill's speech in September, had drifted down to the upper forties by December. Americans had begun to fear that an "overbearing government program" would "destroy their own health care arrangements" and "make them worse off," wrote Yale political scientist Jacob Hacker in *The Road to Nowhere,* a comprehensive study of the plan.

Simply put, the Clinton plan "had something that alienated every sector, and it was way too complicated," said health-industry lobbyist Pamela Bailey. "Hillary never made clear what she was giving people." Both Bill and Hillary overestimated their powers of persuasion and felt "that they were smarter than anyone else," wrote political journalist Elizabeth Drew. Hillary in particular wouldn't brook compromise, dismissing as "incrementalists" those who challenged her comprehensive approach. "Compromise to her was changing a few words around the margin," said Bromberg. Hillary had also frozen out many potential allies, not only in the health-care industry but among moderate Democrats in Congress such as Jim Cooper and John Breaux of Louisiana. Yet for all the obstacles, the Clintons remained determined to push through their vision of national health care—a political quest that united their fates and tested their marriage.

HILLARY CELEBRATED HER forty-sixth birthday on October 26 with a lively White House costume party. Hollywood wardrobe consultants originally planned to dress Bill and Hillary as Rhett Butler and Scarlett O'Hara, but her office vetoed the scheme. "They thought that bringing back the Confederacy was not a good idea," said a friend of Hillary. The First Couple instead impersonated James and Dolley Madison, Hillary in a black wig and a wide hoopskirt, Bill in a peruke and colonial costume complete with tights. Bruce Lindsey wore a nun's habit, Vernon Jordan came as Michael Jordan, and Bernie Nussbaum was a gladiator, because, he later said, "I was my client's protector."

His services were much in demand just five days later when *The Washington Post* broke the RTC story on page one. The reporter, Susan Schmidt, noted that government investigators had been exploring whether Madison Guaranty funds had been diverted to Bill Clinton's gubernatorial campaign and to the misbegotten Whitewater investment. The White House had been steeling itself for this, and a group of Treasury officials and West Wing advisors including Nussbaum and Lindsey had met on October 14 to discuss strategies for dealing with reporters—the first of several such contacts. Roger Altman later acknowledged that these meetings reflected "bad judgment" because they concerned an ongoing Justice Department investigation that should have remained confidential.

The first week of November brought a flurry of reports in the *Post*, *The New York Times*, and *The Wall Street Journal*, each picking a different angle of questionable Arkansas financial dealings. In his *Washington Post* article on November 2, reporter Michael Isikoff was the first to disclose that Vince Foster had spent some of his time on Whitewater business.

The most potentially damaging allegations were that Bill had pressured David Hale, a Little Rock municipal judge and investment manager, into using funds from the federal Small Business Administration to make a fraudulent three-hundred-thousand-dollar loan to Susan McDougal in 1985, and that the McDougals had siphoned a portion of that amount into Whitewater. Hale insisted that Bill made the personal plea and knew that some of the funds would go to his joint venture with the McDougals—charges Bill was repeatedly to deny. Jeff Gerth grilled Hale for five hours and was "impressed" by his "exceedingly detailed" and "internally consistent" story, according to author James Stewart. But Hale's credibility was clouded by his indictment on September 23 in Arkansas for conspiracy and lying to the Small Business Association about his lending practices.

With the reemergence of Whitewater and its tangle of related transactions and ventures, Bob Barnett, Bill and Hillary's personal lawyer at Williams and Connolly, had to step aside because his wife, Rita Braver, was a CBS reporter assigned to the White House. In his place, the Clintons hired his colleague David Kendall, an old friend from Yale days. One of Kendall's first acts was to take possession of Vince Foster's files, which Barnett had been holding. Webster Hubbell turned over additional documents on Madison Guaranty that he had gathered when he was doing damage control on the original Whitewater story during the 1992 campaign.

There was no shortage of unanswered questions, chief among them how the Clintons could have failed to know the details of Whitewater when their share of the mortgage was being paid by McDougal with funds coming from Madison Guaranty. On November 17, *The Washington Post* submitted twenty questions in writing to the White House but received no reply. Bill and Hillary instinctively resisted releasing any information, maintaining that these were private matters. Kendall, Nussbaum, and Lindsey agreed that turning over documents to the press was a "slippery slope." But the Clintons' reluctance compounded the impression that they were stonewalling. Whitewater may well have only been, as Arkansas journalist Max Brantley described it, "an embarrassing sweetheart deal that went bad." But the more the Clintons held back, the more the press went elsewhere to uncover information about dealings that seemed unethical at best and illegal at worst.

MID-NOVEMBER BROUGHT a lull in the Whitewater coverage, although Clinton lawyers continued to scour documents from Washington to the Ozarks. Bill and Hillary spent the four-day Thanksgiving holiday at Camp David with a large crowd of family and friends. Bill's mother was gravely ill by then, sustained by blood transfusions. But she wore a black wig streaked with her distinctive white patch, paraded around in a red leather jacket and red boots, and sipped scotch with her husband as they talked to the off-duty Marines in the camp's bar.

Bill practiced endlessly at the driving range with his new Big Bertha golf club and joined in some fiercely competitive bowling with Hugh and Tony Rodham. But he and Hillary were also in the mood to talk policy with Strobe Talbott, who had come for the weekend with Brooke Shearer and their two sons. In a discussion about Russia, Hillary chimed in about the need to strongly support Yeltsin's stumbling efforts to establish democracy. "Democracy comes by fits and starts after all those years of dictatorship," she observed. "Russia's not doing that badly when you compare it to Asia. We've got to give them time."

Against that backdrop of evident tranquility and compatibility—and with the allegations of the Arkansas troopers very much in the air—Bill had an encounter on the Monday after Thanksgiving that would yet again call his judgment into question. At 3:00 p.m., he ushered into the Oval Office an attractive forty-seven-year-old blonde named Kathleen Willey, a Democratic party supporter he had first met at a fund-raiser four years earlier. She told the President that she and her husband were experiencing serious financial difficulties, and she asked to be moved from her volunteer job in the White House to a paid position. Unknown to either the President or Willey at the time, her husband had committed suicide that very day.

In sworn testimony five years later, Willey said that after giving her coffee in his private kitchen, Bill told her he would try to help her. She recounted that Bill then stopped her in the hallway near his hideaway office, embraced her in "more than just a platonic hug," attempted to kiss her, touched her breasts, and put her hands on his aroused genitals. After she resisted and pulled herself free, she recalled him saying that "he had wanted to do that for a long time."

Bill was to emphatically deny having made any sexual advance, although he later conceded, "I put my arms around her. I may have even kissed her on the forehead," but he insisted there was "nothing sexual about it," and he was only trying to "help her calm down" and "reassure her."

Willey returned to the Oval Office ten days later, her first time back in the White House after her husband's death. "I was in a very desperate situation" she recalled. "I still needed to work there." Bill repeated his intention to assist her—although she noted that he seemed distracted as she spoke. She told him she considered his behavior during their previous meeting "unfortunate and inappropriate" but that she wanted to put it "behind her." He responded, she recalled, with "a blank stare." Still, she got a part-time paying job in the White House counsel's office that tided her over for ten months.

Two witnesses later said Willey had reported Bill's unwanted groping to them shortly after the first encounter. White House secretary Linda Tripp, who was to become infamous for revealing Monica Lewinsky's liaisons with Bill Clinton, characterized Willey as "flustered, happy and joyful" rather than "appalled" by the President's actions. The other woman, a friend named Julie Hiatt Steele, first said Willey had confided that Bill had crudely made a pass at her, but then Steele claimed she had lied about it at Willey's request. In the end, it was a matter of he said–she said. When Tripp spitefully took the story public in 1997, two women who worked in the West Wing remembered experiences with Bill "uncomfortably similar to what Willey described: innocent conversations that pivoted in an instant into fervid advances," causing the women to feel "angry and embarrassed, asking themselves if they had somehow sent a wrong signal," wrote Clinton biographer John Harris. These incidents, he added, "showed how the controversies over Clinton and sex . . . were not strange aberrations."

ASIDE FROM TRIPS to places like Hanover, New Hampshire, and Boston to explain the more confusing elements of the health-care plan, Hillary was helping Bill orchestrate his first major staff change. Since the tragedy in Somalia, Bill had been edging toward replacing Defense Secretary Les Aspin, whom he held accountable for the loss of life. Aspin's departure was announced on December 15, and Hillary had worked closely with her husband to make sure he carried it out.

One of Bill's advisors observed at the time that Hillary was "heavy into all personnel issues in the White House. When it came to getting rid of someone who was not serving Bill well, he tended to be forgiving, and she was not." In choosing Aspin's successor, her emphasis was "loyalty to Bill and the need to help him rather than having another agenda." They ultimately settled on William Perry, a self-effacing mathematician who had proved his reliability as Deputy Secretary of Defense.

As Hillary was enforcing tough-minded policies in the West Wing, she incongruously appeared in the pages of *Vogue*, photographed by Annie Leibovitz. Wearing a $975 black velvet dress by Donna Karan, she struck a "dishy, dreamy" pose that *The Economist* described as her new "pussycat" look. It was the latest in a series of makeovers the public had observed since inauguration day: one moment a formal blond flip, the next a tousled haircut by New York stylist Frédéric Fekkai. At an age when most women had settled on a way to present themselves, Hillary was experimenting with a persona to match her unparalleled copresident role, but she ended up telegraphing an uncertain self-image. "We sense that we aren't seeing the 'real' Hillary, and this makes us very nervous," wrote Martha Sherrill in *Mirabella* magazine.

BY THE MIDDLE OF DECEMBER, Bill had been dealing with his former Arkansas bodyguards for four months, while Hillary had been in the dark about them. She later wrote that she learned the details of their allegations only after the White House received a fax of the article David Brock had written for *The American Spectator* and David Kendall briefed her on its "vile stories" in a phone call on Saturday, December 18. But by James Stewart's account, Hillary was part of a group including David Gergen, George Stephanopoulos, and Bernie Nussbaum that convened on Thursday the sixteenth to discuss a phone inquiry from *Los Angeles Times* reporter Bill Rempel and his colleague Douglas Frantz. The reporters had secured affidavits from all the troopers, and they had completed a draft of their story. The White House group felt "especially awkward discussing the troopers' allegations in front of Hillary," Stewart wrote, "but she didn't seem to flinch." Hillary agreed with the advisors' strategy to "ignore any specific allegations."

Clinton loyalist Betsey Wright had been alerted and was already working to contain the potential damage by pressing Brock for information about his story. But Gergen was unnerved when she dismissed the allegations as "old news" and said that "as far as she could tell, the troopers were telling the truth."

White House aides kept Rempel and Frantz at bay, hoping they would be scooped by the right-wing *American Spectator*, which would be "easily discredited." Brock's story proved to be sexually explicit and lurid in its details about Bill and Hillary's screaming matches and profanities. Brock also included the tidbit that Bill once told Larry Patterson that after researching the Bible he had concluded "oral sex isn't considered adultery." But the most worrying disclosure was Bill's flurry of ill-advised phone calls to the troopers and the strong suggestion that he had dangled the prospect of a federal job to keep Ferguson quiet. *The American Spectator* went public on Sunday, December 19, and CNN followed up with interviews of Perry and Patterson. The White House tersely responded that the charges were "ridiculous"—a nondenial denial, in Washington parlance.

Behind the scenes, the Clintons were consulting their advisors about a counterattack. Dee Dee Myers believed that Brock's account of Bill's womanizing was exaggerated. "Clinton had admitted he had been unfaithful," Myers recalled. "I didn't think he needed his troopers to get women." She was more concerned with the disclosure that he had called the troopers over the previous months. The idea that he would pursue a quid pro quo made sense to her "because Bill Clinton thought he could talk people into things." George Stephanopoulos knew "something was up" and had a "sickening sense of déjà vu" when he asked about the calls and Bill shifted into "fast talking lawyerly hyperexplanation." "I just want a nice job at FEMA after this is over," remarked White House Communications Director Mark Gearan, the beginning of a mordant running joke inside the West Wing.

Hillary was leading the strategy, much as she did during the campaign. "My memory of Hillary's approach was similar to the Gennifer Flowers episode," Myers recalled. "Go after specific things about the story—dates and times. Attack the motives and the details. It was a time-honored tradition." White House aides didn't directly confront the sexual allegations, because they believed the public had already discounted that aspect of Bill's character. But at Hillary's urging they did decide to portray the stories as partisan attacks timed to coincide with Bill's rise in the polls, despite the fact that the investigations had begun months earlier, when his approval rating was around 44 percent. "Hillary's view was that there were people in Arkansas determined to destroy the Clinton presidency," said a senior White House official. "We would have meetings, and she made Bill stay focused. It was powerful to see her do it."

The White House canceled its daily briefings on Monday and Tuesday as advisors, including Bruce Lindsey and David Gergen, met one-on-one with reporters in an effort to undermine the troopers. The aides asserted that the President's accusers were only trying to make money and that the half-dozen women described in the account had not confirmed their tales. California private investigator Jack Palladino, who had intimidated Bill's alleged paramours during the campaign, pitched in to charge that the troopers had cheated on their expense accounts.

On Tuesday the twenty-first, the *Los Angeles Times* finally ran a front-page story headlined "Troopers Say Clinton Sought Silence on Personal

Affairs." Like the Brock article, this account portrayed Bill as a reckless womanizer who had assignations in parking lots and private homes as well as the governor's mansion. Rempel and Frantz quoted Bruce Lindsey admitting that the President had called Ferguson but adding that the conversations were neither "inappropriate" nor "improper." The confirmation inescapably made Bill seem guilty of something untoward. But the most intriguing revelation was that between 1989 and 1991 Bill had made at least fifty-nine phone calls to one woman—left unnamed in the story but later identified as Arkansas energy-company executive Marilyn Jo Jenkins—and that he had been with her as recently as the previous January. On a single day—July 16, 1989—he had called her home eleven times.

The afternoon the trooper story broke, Hillary gave an interview to wire-service reporters, and the "second biggest gun" at the White House, in the words of *The New York Times*, lobbed some carefully targeted mortars. She condemned the "outrageous, terrible stories" and indicated that the Clintons were the victims of a political conspiracy. "I find it not an accident," she said, that whenever Bill was succeeding, they faced "yet a new round" of attacks "that people plant for political and financial reasons." She said Cliff Jackson belonged to a group "obsessed" with bringing down her husband.

In an effort to refute the jobs-for-silence charge, Betsey Wright secured an affidavit from Danny Ferguson's Little Rock lawyer. The statement was "curiously legalistic," *Newsweek* noted, specifying only that Bill had not offered jobs "in exchange" for keeping quiet. Bill was too cunning for such a bold transaction when an inference was sufficient. Ferguson later tried to explain that while Bill "didn't say those words," his meaning was clear. But the press read the affidavit as a denial, which opened the way to further assaults on the troopers. On Christmas Eve, *The New York Times* and the *Los Angeles Times* alleged that two of them had made a fraudulent automobile-insurance claim three years earlier.

Bill was confronted with direct questions about the allegations in several previously scheduled interviews on Wednesday, December 22. "We did not do anything wrong," he told a group of wire-service reporters, adding that it was "not appropriate" for him to deny the specific charges. "So none of this actually happened?" asked a reporter in a subsequent radio interview. "I have nothing else to say," Bill stammered, as his customary verbal facility failed him. "We . . . we did, if, the, the, I, I. The stories are just as they have been said. . . . They're outrageous, and they're not so."

The revelations that became known as Troopergate "took a toll on the Clintons," said Nussbaum. Bill later wrote that the stories "hit Hillary hard because she thought we'd left all that behind in the campaign." "Trooper-gate had enormous consequences," said a senior White House official. "It colored the way Hillary operated. She may not have believed it in toto, but there is no question she was angry because she was humiliated."

Within days, the Troopergate coverage subsided—much as the Flowers saga had two years earlier. Once again, the mainstream press had little ap-petite for sexual misconduct, and reporters were readily diverted by a new round of allegations about Whitewater—this time focusing on the removal of Whitewater files from Vince Foster's office after his death, along with questions about Bill and Hillary's claim of a sixty-nine-thousand-dollar loss from the land venture.

But now, in addition to insistent press queries, Republicans began call-ing for the appointment of an independent counsel to investigate the vari-ous charges under the "Whitewater" rubric. Bill had begun to waver on yielding to a document request from *The Washington Post,* while Hillary remained adamantly opposed. On this matter, Hillary "had a veto," George Stephanopoulos recalled, because her reputation as a lawyer and the stew-ard of Clinton family finances was at stake. "It's embarrassing," Hillary said. "It makes us look unsavory. It makes me look incompetent." David Gergen believed that Hillary was mostly concerned about potentially dam-aging information—such as the one-hundred-thousand-dollar windfall profit she had made from investing in commodities futures in 1978 and 1979—which had not yet surfaced in the press.

Bernie Nussbaum shared Hillary's belief that the press would never be satisfied and that "there would be no end." Hillary said she feared the press would "pull quotes out of context," said one top White House aide. "Her view was, 'You can't buy peace with *The Washington Post,* and they would spend the next seven years of the Bill Clinton presidency dealing with what happened in Arkansas.' " But Gergen was convinced that disclosure "would have punctured" the pressure for a special prosecutor.

That may have been wishful thinking, because Justice Department lawyers were preparing subpoenas for Whitewater documents as part of their probe of the RTC evidence on Madison Guaranty, as well as for a new investigation into the circumstances of Foster's death. On December 23, the White House preemptively announced that papers from Foster's office would be turned over "voluntarily." The strategy was to "get out ahead" of the subpoena and "not appear to be reacting," said a senior White House official.

Bill and Hillary's first Christmas in the White House was a subdued affair. Virginia Kelley, who had been staying in the Residence all week, was in unmistakable decline. In an attempt to raise Bill's spirits, Webster Hubbell and Marsha Scott joined him for an exuberant last-minute shopping spree in the mall at Washington's Union Station. The next day, the Clintons returned to Arkansas, where Bill played cards and gabbed with old friends in Hot Springs before saying good-bye to his mother, who was heading out to Las Vegas for a New Year's Eve concert featuring Barbra Streisand. Bill, Hillary, and Chelsea flew to Hilton Head, South Carolina, for Renaissance Weekend, their annual celebration of "personal and national renewal" in high-minded seminars with several hundred government officials, academics, businessmen, journalists, and professionals. It had been a turbulent first year in the White House, but the coming twelve months were to prove no less challenging, a time when the personal and political collided in even more startling ways.

Chapter Seven

———

THE CLINTONS' SECOND YEAR IN THE WHITE HOUSE WAS DOMINATED BY their dogged efforts to reform the nation's health-care system and to contain the spreading inquiries into their Arkansas past. It was a period marked by anger and frustration, by internal strife and external challenges. It ended with a defeat that changed the contours of American politics and profoundly affected the remaining years of the Clinton presidency.

As soon as the calendar turned to 1994, Bill and Hillary found themselves struggling with a growing clamor for a special prosecutor to investigate the Whitewater charges. "The pressure on us at the time was blistering," said one of Bill's top advisors. "It was, 'What are you hiding?' The White House staff didn't know, and you couldn't get information out of the Clintons."

Hillary was driven to distraction by the mere thought of a special prosecutor. Deputy Treasury Secretary Roger Altman even wrote in his diary in early January, "On Whitewater, Maggie [Williams] told me that HRC was 'paralyzed' by it." Hillary's concern was not so much her oft-stated "zone of privacy" but rather, according to Williams, that she didn't want anyone "poking into 20 years of public life in Arkansas."

It was Hillary who held power of attorney in their Whitewater dealings and who had represented Madison Guaranty before a state regulator appointed by Bill. With her good name on the line, she dug in deeply, while Bill's placatory nature nudged him in the other direction. "There was profound tension between them," said a top White House official. "At the time, she felt he was under the enormous sway of a staff she had little regard for, and she was ample in her expression of that."

Twice within a week, Hillary cried in conversations with her husband's advisors. On January 4, she arrived unannounced at a meeting in Mack McLarty's office, so disconcerting the dozen participants that they froze in place "like a Henry Moore sculpture," recalled one official. After they briefed her on the arguments for a special counsel, she wheeled on George Stephanopoulos. Her eyes brimming with tears, she accused him of giving up on the Clintons when they had been attacked during the run-up to the New Hampshire primary. "You never *believed* in us," she said. Turning to the rest of the group, her mood shifted as she waved her hand dramatically and said, "John Kennedy had *men* around him. Do you think John Kennedy would have put up with this?" "On one level it was comical," said one participant. "But her ferocity was breathtaking. No one wanted to deal with her."

Three days later, Hillary called David Gergen early in the morning before he was due to appear live on the *Today* show. Once again, she started to weep, saying, "You can tell your friends at the *Post* that we've learned our lesson. We came here to do good things, and we just didn't understand so many things about this town."

Shortly before 2:00 a.m. on January 6, Virginia Kelley lost her battle with cancer. Later that morning, Senate Minority Leader Bob Dole appeared on television to say that Whitewater "cries out" for a special prosecutor. Bill was "stunned," he later wrote. "I would have thought that even the press and my adversaries would take a time out on the day of my mother's death."

Bill buried his mother on Saturday, January 8, after three thousand people filled the Hot Springs Convention Center to remember her life. The reception at the Western Sizzlin Steakhouse offered a buffet loaded with "fried meats, slow cooked vegetables, mashed potatoes, and industrial sized coffee pots." Standing among the good ol' boys, Barbra Streisand "recoiled a bit" when asked if she ate such food in Hollywood.

That night, Bill flew to Europe for a NATO meeting in Brussels, followed by visits to the Czech Republic, Ukraine, Russia, Belarus, and Switzerland. On his first day away, Bill learned that Pat Moynihan had called for a special prosecutor on *Meet the Press*. By Monday, eight other

Democratic senators, including Bill Bradley and Bob Kerrey, were echoing the senior senator from New York, whose view was "get it all out, deal with it right away, answer all questions, and give up records." The editorial pages of *The New York Times* and *The Washington Post* favored an independent investigation, and Treasury Secretary Lloyd Bentsen advised the President to "lance the boil."

By the time Bill arrived in Prague on Tuesday the eleventh, reporters were baying for a response. In an interview with Dan Rather of CBS, Bill said that he was exploring the question of a special counsel, but insisted, "not a single soul has alleged that I've done anything wrong." In the evening, Bill put his concerns temporarily aside when he played "Summertime" and "My Funny Valentine" on the saxophone in a Prague pub while Czech president Václav Havel pounded a tambourine.

Back in Washington, Bill's political advisors leaned on Hillary to reconsider her opposition to a prosecutor. They were concerned about lingering questions from reporters: Did Madison Guaranty money help fund Bill's gubernatorial campaign? Had the bank been treated leniently by state regulators as a quid pro quo? Had the Clintons received unusual advantages in Whitewater and other investments? Had investigations into these matters been impeded by the White House? There were lots of "furry, complicated nutball details that imply wrongdoing by *somebody,*" as *Newsweek* described the situation.

But Hillary argued that under the terms of the expired Independent Counsel Law and its pending replacement, a credible charge of criminality was required for a special investigation—a threshold Hillary insisted had not been met. She said they would set a "terrible precedent" by authorizing a special investigation without specific evidence of wrongdoing. Bernie Nussbaum vigorously supported her position—as did Susan Thomases. Janet Reno said she preferred to wait for the new Independent Counsel Law to be enacted in several months; she thought that any prosecutor she appointed would be perceived as no more independent than the career officials already working on the case in the Justice Department. "Nothing legally compelled Janet Reno to do anything," said Bernie Nussbaum. "She didn't want to do it. She would have trusted me. I would have argued to her that there was no underlying basis."

On Tuesday evening, Hillary suggested that the advisors assemble in the Oval Office and call Bill in Prague, where it was after midnight. Bill was on the speakerphone with Mack McLarty and David Gergen, while George Stephanopoulos, Bernie Nussbaum, and David Kendall were among those with Hillary.

"Dan Rather asked me about Whitewater," Bill said. "I gotta do something. I gotta find a way out. What is the choice?" The political advisors urged him to ask Reno to make the appointment. Stephanopoulos told him that they couldn't ignore the pressure from the press and leaders of the Democratic party; they needed to eliminate the distractions from the fight for health-care reform, and Reno would select a fair-minded investigator. The Clintons would be better off with her appointee than with the choice of a panel of judges under a revived Independent Counsel Law.

Nussbaum argued that the independent counsel was an "evil institution" with a history of troublemaking. He predicted that a special prosecutor "would investigate until the end of the presidency." As an alternative, Nussbaum proposed that Bill and Hillary "offer to testify before the Senate Judiciary Committee as long as you have to, turn over every document about Whitewater. We have a Democratic Senate, a Democratic staff. I would rather have them question you than an Independent Counsel, who has his own career and lots of FBI agents to investigate you forever."

Bill told Nussbaum his proposal was "crazy," and Stephanopoulos backed him up. "Think of the publicity, the TV all over the world," they said.

"So what?" Nussbaum replied. "I would rather you are on TV all over the world and have publicity for 30 days than have the Independent Counsel for the next seven years trying to bring you down. You and Hillary could go and hold hands and talk about your investment in Whitewater." But the political advisors feared that in such a forum the Clintons would seem evasive, and Hillary's combative personality would be off-putting.

After nearly an hour of discussion, Hillary offered to summarize the main points. When she turned to Nussbaum's arguments, she framed them in her own words, "in a disciplined and organized fashion—very effectively, because she believed it," Nussbaum recalled. She then asked everyone except David Kendall to leave so she and Bill could speak privately with their lawyer. By the end of their conversation, they had decided to ask for the special prosecutor and directed Nussbaum to prepare a letter to the Attorney General.

The strain on Bill was evident Wednesday morning in Prague when he yanked off his microphone following a Whitewater query from an NBC correspondent. "You had your two questions," he sputtered. "I'm sorry you're not interested in the trip." Later that day, after a meeting in the Kiev airport with Ukrainian president Leonid Kravchuk, Bill held another press conference. When a reporter noted that former President Jimmy Carter had also urged the appointment, Bill snapped, "I have nothing to say about that on this trip."

Hillary was solicitous when she visited Bernie Nussbaum in his office to discuss the letter. "Bill feels he has to appoint an Independent Counsel," she said. "It's the only way to get on with our agenda." Nussbaum believed that if Hillary had held her ground, "I don't think he would have overruled her. He wanted to do it, and she was worn down. The pressure got to her." Bill also appealed to Hillary by emphasizing that her issue—health care—could proceed only if they removed Whitewater from the headlines. "But the issue was broader than health care," said Nussbaum. "He was so distraught by what he considered the continual media harping on Whitewater. He started believing he couldn't function. He would be talking about eastern Europe with Dan Rather, who would ask about Whitewater."

Bill later lamented that calling for the special prosecutor was "the worst presidential decision I ever made." He was to insist that he had erred because he had been exhausted, grieving over his mother and suffering from "poor judgment." Like Hillary, he blamed "people in the White House who couldn't stand the heat of the bad stories."

But Bill himself had reacted to that heat more intensely than anyone. He deeply resented being interrupted when he was showing leadership in foreign policy. He was working hard to support Boris Yeltsin while allaying the Russian leader's anxieties about eastern European countries eager to join NATO. Bill's solution, the interim Partnership for Peace, was a sleight of hand that he sold to all parties, including Russia, with his distinctive blend of intellectual finesse and folksy informality—calling the leaders of Poland, Hungary, the Czech Republic, and Slovakia "guys" when he convened them for lunch. At the same time, he was conducting delicate negotiations with Ukraine about dismantling nuclear weapons. During his air-port meeting, Bill "was in the moment," said U.S. Ambassador William Miller. "I was aware that other things were going on, but very heavy issues were at stake. We were dealing with the third-largest nuclear arsenal in the world."

Hillary kept a decidedly low profile once she caught up with her hus-band in Moscow on January 14, after the White House announced Bill's request for a special prosecutor. With Yeltsin's wife, Naina, Hillary obedi-ently took tours of facilities devoted to children. Bill was again at the top of his game, wearing a tie with a "Carpe Diem" motif for a televised town meeting. Speaking mostly without notes, he talked about the need for Rus-sia to apply its long tradition of greatness to a new role as partner in the world community. "He focused on a psychological and emotional dy-namic," said speechwriter Eric Liu. "He emphasized that even though there had been the loss of the Soviet Union, there was still a great Russian civilization."

ON THE FIRST ANNIVERSARY of the Clinton inaugural, Janet Reno selected sixty-three-year-old Robert Fiske, a respected New York lawyer and former federal prosecutor, to investigate the charges against Bill and Hillary. He was a moderate Republican described by Reno as "ruggedly independent." That evening in a chat with Larry King on CNN, Bill expressed relief over the appointment. "The main thing I want to do is just have that turned over to him so we can go back to work," he said. "I don't want to be dis-tracted by this anymore."

Bill and Hillary's unequivocal priority was health-care legislation, but they were at odds over its breadth. In theory, Bill shared Hillary's commit-ment to the plan they had given to Congress—even her belief that any of the interlocking pieces could not be removed without jeopardizing the en-tire scheme. In practice, Bill was inclined to strike a political compromise and accept one of the more modest alternative bills that enjoyed bipartisan support. But Hillary opposed any halfway measures, and she got her way, at least in part because of the humiliation she had endured from the Troopergate stories. "I cannot recall him publicly confronting her on any health-care issue after that," recalled David Gergen.

On Friday, January 21, Hillary rebuffed an important overture from the health-care industry to reach an accommodation. The Healthcare Leadership Council—thirty chief executives of insurance companies, medical-device manufacturers, pharmaceutical companies, and hospitals—had been trying to talk to her for months, and she agreed to meet with them for the first time in Washington's Madison Hotel on a day so frigid that government offices were shut down. Her mood at the outset was pleasant, even lighthearted as she walked around the room to shake hands with everyone. In her opening remarks, the group's president, Pamela Bailey, encouraged Hillary to adopt one of the other bills that relied on less regulation. Hillary's expression, recalled Bailey, was "stony faced."

Each industry representative was scheduled to make a brief pitch, but the discussion quickly grew contentious when several participants objected to the Clinton plan's price controls, and Hillary insisted that they didn't exist. "She was *lecturing,* sort of strident," recalled Michael Bromberg, the lobbyist for private hospitals. "How are we going to reach a compromise if we can't even agree on what the facts are?" Bromberg asked Hillary. "It seems we have a language barrier." Bromberg said Hillary "stiffened so noticeably. Her body language was *angry.* . . . She really believes that if you criticize one page of a 1,364-page bill you're the enemy."

As he had in two previous private meetings with Hillary, Bromberg told her that "the President was in a win-win position, because any bill that passed, even if it was 50 percent of their bill, he would be the first President in history" to reform health care. Hillary shot back, "Bill and I didn't come to Washington to fudge the issue, to do business as usual and compromise." She added, "You're either for universal coverage, or you're not. You're going to help us get there, or you're not."

Hillary took the same unyielding approach in deliberations over the State of the Union address, which was scheduled for Tuesday, January 25. The "Gang of Four" political consultants proposed that Bill wave a fountain pen and vow to veto any bill that did not provide universal coverage, a theatrical flourish that Hillary pushed him to use. In a Cabinet Room meeting with Democratic leaders, she advocated the veto threat while Bill "sat mum," recalled Gergen, who was desperate to prevent it. Gergen asked Tom Foley, Speaker of the House, for his reaction. Foley replied that such a "categorical threat" was "dangerous," arguing that "Presidents should not lock themselves into irrevocable positions on important and controversial legislation." When Gergen entreated Hillary to reconsider, she replied, "No, we're going ahead." At that moment, Gergen watched the seesaw relationship between Bill and Hillary flip out of balance. "Might he have passed a bipartisan reform plan if the shadow of his past had not hung over his relationship with his wife?" Gergen wondered.

Bill stayed up all night to rewrite the ninth draft of the speech, and when he slid into the limousine for the ride to the Capitol, he had the final version wrapped inside his daily crossword puzzle. The address contained something for everyone, "co-opting GOP ideas, honoring middle of the road Democrats . . . soothing liberals with big talk of new programs." To minimize the heavy hand of government regulation in his health-care plan, he renamed it "guaranteed private health insurance." The climactic moment came when he warned, "If you send me legislation that does not guarantee every American private health insurance that can never be taken away, you will force me to take this pen, veto the legislation, and we'll come right back here and start all over again."

Scarcely a week later, the U.S. Chamber of Commerce, the Business Roundtable, and the National Association of Manufacturers declared their opposition to the Clinton health plan. Hillary went on the warpath once more, blasting insurance and drug companies for "fraud, waste and abuse," even as Bill's aides were telling reporters that their boss might make a deal with Tennessee Democrat Jim Cooper, whose bill did not call for mandatory coverage. "It is unclear what the White House strategy is, to cast blame and identify villains or to forge a bipartisan consensus," Pamela Bailey told *The Washington Post*. "We have very much seen mixed signals over the last few weeks." The health-care industry was facing "Bill's White House and Hillary's White House," said Michael Bromberg. Bill was regarded as someone who "wanted to get things done . . . but the view of her was that she was much to the left, and had friends to the left, and would never compromise. . . . The question that everybody asked" was "Which White House was in charge?"

BILL AND HILLARY'S HOPE that the Fiske appointment would remove the spotlight from their Arkansas days proved to be illusory. On February 11, a twenty-seven-year-old former Arkansas government employee stood behind a lectern at the Conservative Political Action Conference in Washington and announced to a crowd of reporters that on May 8, 1991, Bill had made an unwanted sexual advance to her in Little Rock's Excelsior Hotel, where he had taken a room during a conference. Paula Corbin Jones seemed an unlikely match for a powerful public official: small and uncertain, with teased dark hair, heavy makeup, a long nose, and a tendency to misspeak, such as when she said "hisself" rather than "himself."

Her revelation had been prompted by the *American Spectator* article, which had mentioned that a woman named "Paula" had been escorted to Bill's room by a trooper and had emerged after an hour, remarking that she was "available to be the governor's regular girlfriend." Jones had complained about her encounter at the time to a colleague and a friend, as well as three family members, but had otherwise kept quiet until the article had appeared. Now she said she had been offended by the implication of consensual sex and had sought redress through a lawyer. She had ended up with Cliff Jackson and other right-wing Clinton critics as her advocates.

When pressed by reporters, Jones declined to offer details. She said only that the President had asked her to engage in "a type of sex" that was "humiliating" to her. Given Bill's official position, she considered his overture to be harassment. The White House countered that the incident had "never occurred," and Bill had never met her. George Stephanopoulos called her announcement "a cheap political fund-raising trick."

Stephanopoulos wanted to believe the President's denial because there had been "no nervous chatter. He didn't over-explain." Given Jones's partisan allies, Stephanopoulos thought her charges were a "set-up job." So did the mainstream media, which mostly ignored the Jones press conference. The *Los Angeles Times* gave it some space, but *The New York Times* printed only four paragraphs deep inside the paper. ABC's evening newscast made a brief mention, while NBC, CNN, and CBS said nothing. *The Washington Post* spiked a brief story by investigative reporter Michael Isikoff because the allegations needed more verification, but gave him the green light to keep digging—not only to determine the truth of Jones's charges, but to learn whether Bill's behavior was part of a larger story. His colleague Ann Devroy reported to Stephanopoulos, "Isikoff totally believes this." She added that *Washington Post* editor Leonard Downie suspected a "pattern of compulsive sexual behavior that still defined Clinton's character."

The White House dispatched Betsey Wright to talk to trooper Danny

Ferguson, who confirmed that he had indeed taken Jones to Bill's room. Stephanopoulos was angry when he realized Bill had misled his advisors by saying he didn't recall meeting Jones and had never been alone with her. It reminded him of the "worst moments" of the 1992 campaign. In his efforts to dissuade Downie, Stephanopoulos shifted his strategy from denial to arguing that while Bill may have been a womanizer, sexual harassment "wasn't his style." If Bill had engaged in flirtation with Jones, Stephanopoulos insisted that it "does not belong on the front page of the *Post*." Downie's reaction was "polite but imponderable."

IN SUBSEQUENT WEEKS, the press reported that Nussbaum and Deputy Treasury Secretary Roger Altman had been informed six months earlier that the Clintons might be called to testify in the RTC investigation of Madison Guaranty. Altman raised suspicions of impropriety when he changed his version of events four times. The disclosure of possible attempts to influence the investigation had instant repercussions. On Friday, March 4, Robert Fiske issued subpoenas to ten officials, four of them close to Hillary, including Bernie Nussbaum.

That morning, Hillary called Nussbaum into her office. Anonymous White House officials had been quoted in press reports suggesting Nussbaum had committed "ethical breaches" by talking to Treasury officials and would probably resign. "There is a lot of pressure," Hillary said to her old friend, letting him know that she would do nothing to save him. "The press makes things look so bad." "She felt she couldn't fight it, so she stepped back," recalled Nussbaum.

Nussbaum then met with Bill, who told him, "You have become so controversial, you have to go. If you go, we will have peace, and I'll be able to pass health care." Nussbaum protested that if Bill threw him overboard, "all you will do is feed the beast and undermine yourself." Bill seemed momentarily rattled, but several hours later instructed Mack McLarty to show Nussbaum a letter from Democratic senator Carl Levin saying that the White House Counsel had to go. The next day, Nussbaum sent the President his letter of resignation, maintaining that he had acted "in an absolutely legal and ethical manner." Four months later, Fiske would clear both Nussbaum and Altman of acting illegally in connection with the RTC investigation. "I was struck," wrote FBI Director Louis Freeh, a close ally of Nussbaum, "at how easily Clinton played hardball politics even with his loyal and closest friends."

The ink was barely dry on Nussbaum's signature when Bill reached out to seventy-eight-year-old Lloyd Cutler, a bona fide Washington wise man with a secure spot in the capital Establishment. "We had all this noise out there," said a senior White House official. "Bringing in Lloyd would be seen as calming the waters." During a two-hour meeting with Bill on Sunday, March 6, 1994, in the Residence, Cutler agreed to serve for six months on the condition that the White House turn over all documents to Fiske, including some Foster files that had been previously withheld. That afternoon, the White House staff threw a pep rally in the East Room to bolster the Clintons.

BY THEN, HILLARY was coming under renewed scrutiny for being "the recurrent thread in a weave of deals, political friendships, and business associations" being scrutinized by Robert Fiske. Albert Hunt, a liberal columnist for *The Wall Street Journal,* concluded that the "bunker mentality" at the White House was "a reflection of Hillary Clinton," and *Newsweek* described a "fear wall" around the First Lady, who "can't see or won't acknowledge that her own actions contributed to the problem." *Time* portrayed her as a "queen on a chessboard," deriving power from "unrestricted movement." Michael Barone of *U.S. News & World Report* wondered if she had become a "political liability" by displaying "startlingly bad judgment" on "issue after issue," and Maureen Dowd of *The New York Times* raised anew "embarrassing ethical questions" about Hillary's behavior in Arkansas.

Every few days, Hillary met with David Kendall for briefings, passing along information to Bill when necessary. On the advice of Kendall, Hillary had stopped reading the press; in early March, she told a conference on children and television violence, "My husband and I never watch the news." "I'm going through one of my not-reading phases, so I don't know what's going on in the world," she said one afternoon in the White House. By then, she had come to rely on her staff to summarize what she needed to know.

Bill sprang to his wife's defense by insisting, "I have never known a person with a stronger sense of right and wrong," and Al Gore praised her at the Democratic National Committee spring meeting in Cleveland, where delegates wore badges that read, "Don't Pillory Hillary." Allies such as Eleanor Roosevelt biographer Blanche Wiesen Cook said that Hillary was being assaulted because Americans "have trouble stomaching the idea of women as powerful people."

Hillary launched her own counteroffensive by giving interviews to the three news magazines as well as the Sunday-morning talk shows. She said investing in Whitewater had been a mistake and "we never intended to do anything wrong." She also signaled that she and the President were prepared to pay back taxes and penalties on Whitewater if it turned out they had underpaid based on inflated losses on their tax returns.

The next day at a health-care event in Denver, Hillary acknowledged they were "trying to get an exact figure" for losses—although a year earlier Vince Foster had learned that the Clintons' accountant could document less than one tenth of the amount originally claimed. The Clintons would eventually revise the estimate from $5,878 to $46,636, while an independent auditor's calculation would come to $38,809—all because of sloppy financial record keeping by the Clintons and McDougals. Bill and Hillary's back taxes and interest amounted to nearly $15,000.

The Clinton Administration got another jolt on Monday, March 14, when Webb Hubbell suddenly resigned amid allegations of "billing irregularities" at the Rose law firm. Still in Colorado, Hillary had no comment, but Bill told reporters at a dinner in Boston that he found any impropriety "hard to believe" and called Hubbell "one of the most widely esteemed people I've ever known." During his speech, Bill conflated his frustrations about the faltering health-care plan with his fury about the Whitewater investigations. He raged about the "politics of personal destruction" by Republicans determined to "take off after" Hillary instead of pursuing health-care reform. The "opposition party" could only say "no," a word he repeated nine times, his voice rising until he was shouting and banging on the podium. It was a rare and unnerving public glimpse of his volcanic temper.

Three years later, *The New York Times* disclosed that Bill and Hillary had not been caught unawares. Both Jim Blair and David Kendall had learned that Rose "had strong proof of wrongdoing by Hubbell, and warned [the] Clintons that Hubbell needed to resign . . . as quickly as possible." Although the embezzlement allegations had no direct link to Bill and Hillary, it later emerged that Hubbell had worked with Hillary on a shady real-estate partnership between his father-in-law, Seth Ward, and Jim McDougal. He had also been custodian of the trove of Madison Guaranty and Whitewater documents, which he had turned over to David Kendall four months earlier. Within days of Hubbell's resignation, Robert Fiske took charge of investigating him, and the case merged into the collective Whitewater controversies.

Hubbell recalled receiving a "pretty reserved" letter from Bill accepting the resignation, but "I never heard from Hillary at all." He understood they were "under heavy fire," but "it still hurt." Hillary, though, distinctly remembered meeting with Hubbell in the Solarium "to ask what was happening." She said that Hubbell told her he was in a dispute over billing with their former partners and that he was seeking business opportunities "until this misunderstanding blows over."

Those "business opportunities" turned out to be surprisingly lucrative. Mack McLarty took Hillary aside at a meeting to assure her that he would "try to help" their good friend. Mickey Kantor, Vernon Jordan, and Erskine Bowles, director of the Small Business Administration, pitched in as well to drum up consulting contracts for Hubbell totaling nearly seven hundred thousand dollars over the following eighteen months. The clients included Sprint, Time Warner, Revlon, and the Los Angeles Airport Commission. Clinton political supporters Truman Arnold—who served as finance chairman of the DNC—and Bernard Rapoport also hired the disgraced lawyer for unspecified duties, and the Riady family, Clinton intimates from Arkansas days, paid him one hundred thousand dollars, again for unspecified services. Hubbell's friends and colleagues later said they acted out of "human compassion." But like so much in the Whitewater miasma, the magnitude of the compensation—and the vagueness of the services Hubbell provided while under criminal investigation—looked sufficiently irregular to trigger official probes into whether the cash payments from Bill and Hillary's associates were intended to ensure Hubbell's silence.

FOUR DAYS AFTER THE Hubbell bombshell, Hillary's ethics came into question again in a page-one story by Jeff Gerth in *The New York Times*, which revealed that in the late 1970s she had made a one-hundred-thousand-dollar profit from highly speculative trading in cattle-futures contracts. The windfall had provided the down payment for a house Bill and Hillary bought in 1980 and was largely offset by the sixty-nine thousand dollars that the Clintons claimed in Whitewater losses, which significantly reduced the amount they owed in taxes. After persistent questioning, the White House admitted that Hillary had invested only one thousand dollars, which gave her a 10,000 percent return in merely nine months.

Hillary made things worse by changing her explanation for dabbling in the tricky world of future cattle prices. At first, she said she had done the trading herself, after "reading the *Wall Street Journal*" and seeking advice from "numerous people," including longtime friend Jim Blair, a lawyer for Tyson Foods. She was then forced to concede that Blair had executed thirty of her thirty-two trades directly with Arkansas commodities broker Robert L. "Red" Bone. There were suggestions that Blair had put only profitable trades in Hillary's account, while he had absorbed her losses—which, if true, would have amounted to an indirect payoff from Tyson.

It also turned out that in addition to her $100,000 gain, Hillary had earned profits of $6,498 on trades in copper, sugar, wheat, and lumber futures, and she now owed $3,315 in taxes and interest on those transactions. In 1983, she had put $2,104 into a cellular-phone franchise operated by a policy advisor to the governor and walked away with a profit of $46,000. She had dabbled in oil-drilling and real-estate partnerships as well. "She would call me all the time to see how her stocks were doing," said her broker, Roy Drew. "Some investors I never heard from. Some call every day, even when nothing has changed. She was closer to the latter."

After her years of inveighing against Reagan-era greed, the portrait of "Yuppie Hillary" offered a "gloriously fat target," wrote *Newsweek*'s Joe Klein. Her financial activities ran counter to her "carefully cultivated reputation as a preacher of a moralistic 'politics of meaning'—Saint Hillary the commodities speculator is an odd image," noted *Time*.

A *New York Times* editorial at the end of March summed up the pervasive mistrust of the Clintons by observing that "at every turn of their financial life . . . [they] were receiving financial favors from individuals who had something to gain from having friends in high places." Bill and Hillary, the editorial concluded, "seemed to have extraordinary indifference to, or difficulty in understanding, the normal division between government and personal interests."

Although Bill's approval ratings were steadily above 50 percent, a *Los Angeles Times* poll released on Thursday, April 21, showed that Hillary's favorable ratings had dropped to 44 percent from 56 percent in January. That day, Hillary decided to make a bold move advocated by White House Counsel Lloyd Cutler. She would hold a press conference on Friday the twenty-second in which she would answer all questions from reporters about the Clinton finances. Although Eleanor Roosevelt had held more than three hundred news conferences, Hillary for weeks had been resisting any wide-ranging exchange with the press corps. She much preferred the controlled environment of one-on-one interviews or off-the-record chats with small groups. The summons to the press went out Friday morning for the afternoon gathering.

Hillary's advisors counseled her to admit her misjudgments and to be conciliatory. She decided to wear a pink St. John Knits sweater set trimmed in black. Commentators interpreted her choice as an effort to use the ultimate feminine hue to modulate her hard-nosed image. Hillary insisted that her outfit was simply what she "felt like wearing."

Sitting in a wooden armchair in the State Dining Room for what became known as the "Pink Press Conference," Hillary parried questions for sixty-eight minutes without consulting any notes. She remained calm and expressed regret that she had failed to be "more accessible to you." The changing stories about the commodities trading were due to "White House disorganization." She patiently described her trading through Blair and said that in July 1979 she had stopped when she was pregnant with Chelsea because "I just could not bear the risk anymore." She had "absolutely no reason to believe that I got any favorable treatment" vis-à-vis Tyson Foods. She pointed out that Don Tyson had even supported Bill's opponent for governor in 1980. No one inquired about the important legislation sought by Tyson to raise the weight limit on trucks for the chicken business that passed in 1983 with Bill's help.

Asked about allegations of Reagan-era greed, she said that she was only fulfilling an "obligation" to take care of her family financially. She drew laughter when she referred to her "zone of privacy" by declaring, "I've been rezoned."

Her responses on Whitewater-related matters were more elusive. She said she had "absolutely" no knowledge of any transfer of funds from Madison Guaranty to Whitewater or to Bill's gubernatorial campaign. But she deflected other questions, saying she couldn't remember details from sixteen years earlier. Her most memorable line came after she was asked, "If you know that your mortgages are being paid, but you aren't putting money into the venture, and you also know the venture isn't cash flowing, wouldn't you question the source of the funds being used to your benefit? Would you just assume your partner was making those multi-thousand dollar payments out of the goodness of his heart?"

"Well, shoulda, coulda, woulda, we didn't," she replied with surprising flippancy. And when asked why Maggie Williams was involved in the removal of documents from Vince Foster's office, Hillary said, "I don't know that she did remove any documents." Three months later, the press revealed that Hillary had in fact instructed Williams to move the papers to the White House Residence before turning them over to attorney Bob Barnett, prompting Time's Michael Kramer to write, "Slick Willie, meet Slippery Hillary."

In the days after her "cozy fireside chat," Hillary won high marks for being "confident" and "unflappable." But she did little to put to rest some of the central questions about Whitewater. A New York Times editorial noted that it remained unclear "whether wealthy benefactors who did business with the state government were padding the Clinton family income," and Hillary could still not explain "why Mr. McDougal wound up losing a lot more money than the Clintons did in what was supposedly a 50-50 deal." Hillary's explanation—that for a decade she was unaware of the facts—struck the Times as a "strange confession of ignorance from a woman who had spent the previous hour insisting that she maintained hawk-like vigilance over her commodities trades and was deeply concerned with building a family nest egg."

Hillary joined David Kendall following the press conference for a drink in the West Sitting Hall of the Residence. "You know, they're not going to let up," she told her lawyer. "They're just going to keep on coming at us, no matter what we do."

———

WHILE HILLARY HAD effectively submerged her combative instincts with the press that afternoon, it was increasingly evident that the Clintons had become notably conspiracy-minded in their outlook. Their capacious demonology included Republicans in Arkansas and Washington, the national press corps, the Washington Establishment, and, most recently, the medical profession and its allies. They considered their critics in the press to be a faultfinding mob that had been gulled by right-wing operatives into writing about Whitewater and sexual misdeeds.

Hillary was famous for holding grudges; she thought nothing of turning her back when encountering those she felt had wronged her. There was also plenty of evidence that Bill had "a long memory for slights along the way," said Mike McCurry. "That is not unreasonable. It is very human." But Bill was more inclined, after battling with an adversary, to "start bringing you back into the fold," as writer James Morgan once observed. Bill would shake hands and feign affability—then afterward comment to friends or aides, "Thank God that's over."

However angry the Clintons were with each other, they invariably took far greater umbrage at their enemies. As early as 1978, after Bill had defeated four rivals in his first gubernatorial primary, he singled out the "social ultra-conservatives" who said, " 'this guy is being foisted on us'—like I'm a creation of the media who's been cloned somehow with an Ivy League education and long hair." These adversaries, he added, made their "biggest mistake" by their "sneering" attacks on his wife as a feminist and social activist. In September 1991, when he was encouraging Gennifer Flowers to conceal their affair, Bill's first instinct was to urge her to sign an affidavit blaming "a Republican" for suggesting that she falsely claim to be Bill's lover. By the 1992 campaign, Bill was telling *Time* about the Republican party's "politics of personal destruction," with an apparatus "that rivals the KGB."

Virginia Kelley had harbored similarly aggrieved feelings about the Hot Springs medical establishment. For more than three decades, Bill had absorbed her complaints about the "backstabbing" by the "vicious circle" trying to end her career as a nurse anesthetist, stories that he took to heart and that contributed to his own feelings of persecution. The antecedents in

Hillary's background were harder to detect, although the closely knit Rodhams did have an "us against the world" mentality of fierce independence.

Bill and Hillary had first seized on a national Republican conspiracy against them in the summer of 1991, when Bill told her his apocryphal Roger Porter story. Three years later, Hillary said that "with all this stuff that's been dumped on us, that's basically how we still see it. And that's where it kind of keeps us going." Porter's alleged assertion that "we will do everything we can to destroy you personally" allowed Hillary to dismiss allegations about Bill's misbehavior by viewing each of them as a politically motivated smear. After Porter's supposed "shot across the bow," Hillary discounted "the inevitable attacks" that followed. Her counteroffensive, as she articulated it to Bill's advisors in the 1992 campaign, became "pound the Republican attack machine and run against the press." Whatever the nature of the opposition—political candidates or health-insurance companies—Hillary's first line of defense was a vigorous offense focusing on designated enemies.

By early 1994, the Clintons had consolidated all their adversaries—political zealots, investigators for government agencies, women who felt Bill had wronged them, former allies and employees—into a menacing monolith with considerable financial resources. Bill's public posture, as he told Ted Koppel in January on *Nightline*, was that Whitewater "never crosses my mind." But he later admitted that he and Hillary "talked about it all the time. For three months there I thought I was lost in the funhouse. . . . I had to fight hard to keep my mind and my spirit in the right frame." One cabinet officer felt that something had snapped in both Clintons, saying, "They've become paranoid. They think people are out to get them—this right-wing conspiracy stuff. They feel sorry for themselves."

In interviews with selected reporters in the spring of 1994, Hillary further expanded her conspiracy theories. Sidney Blumenthal of *The New Yorker*, Hillary's steadfast friend in the press, listened sympathetically to her account, convinced that "she only wanted me to understand." In early March, she told Meryl Gordon of *Elle* magazine that there was a "well organized and well financed attempt to undermine my husband, and by extension, myself, by people who have a different political agenda or have another personal and financial reason for attacking us." A week later, she insisted to *Time* that she was the victim of a Republican plot explicitly intended to discredit her. "I do not even want to spend time thinking about the people who I know spend their entire day thinking about how to destroy my husband and me," she told Patricia O'Brien of *Working Woman*. Hillary's mood, O'Brien noted, was "choreographed tranquility" that barely disguised "simmering frustration." Speaking with freelance writer James Stewart, Hillary "railed against the tactics of the right-wing media and think tanks, wondering how they were being financed."

On April 13, the same day she spoke to Stewart, Hillary first passed along the Roger Porter anecdote to Bob Woodward, describing him only as a somebody in the Bush White House. Woodward learned his identity, checked out the story, and recounted it with skepticism in *The Agenda*, his book about the Clinton White House. He declined to mention Porter by name, but he noted the story's importance to the Clintons as evidence that they were being hounded by "vast and entrenched interests" hostile to their ideas rather than to them as individuals. Several weeks later, talking to Arkansas journalist John Brummett, Bill named *The Washington Times*, the editorial page of *The Wall Street Journal*, and talk-radio hosts as "part of a national thing." He contended that the "unlimited money" from right-wing sources had underwritten a "spooky . . . national strategy" that was "reckless and intense. . . . They were just mad that I won."

While political opponents certainly targeted Bill and Hillary's ideology, many of their antagonists reacted to them in a more visceral way. Even Bill conceded, "I tended to make enemies effortlessly, just by being me." He won over friends with his gregariousness and eagerness to please, but these same traits struck critics as evidence of a narcissistic personality. He also alienated people by playing fast and loose with the truth. Hillary's air of rectitude and steely self-possession made her an even easier target. Neither of them conceded that their own conduct—their questionable activities in Arkansas and their vagueness when queried about them—was a major cause of their troubles in the White House.

Chapter Eight

—

WHEN THE CLINTONS LEARNED IN EARLY MAY 1994 THAT PAULA JONES was preparing a sexual-harassment suit against Bill, they immediately turned to Washington trial lawyer Robert Bennett. He had been added to their legal team at the suggestion of Lloyd Cutler, who thought Bennett's expansive personality would be more effective with reporters than Kendall's intense and somewhat stiff manner. Jones initially asked neither for a financial settlement nor an outright apology. Her lawyers said she would be satisfied with a statement from Bill that cleared her name. Bill insisted that he had not harassed Jones, saying such conduct was not his style—as Stephanopoulos had argued to Leonard Downie—although he acknowledged that he might have met her. Nonetheless, both Cutler and Bennett urged Bill to settle. Even if he prevailed in a trial, they said, he would be tarnished by investigations of his sexual history.

On Wednesday, May 4, *The Washington Post* ran a page-one story by Michael Isikoff that gave credence to Jones's claims, adding to the pressure on the White House. For several frantic days, Bennett tried to negotiate a settlement. The two sides came close to agreeing on a statement in which Bill would say he did not recall meeting her "in a room" but that he wouldn't "challenge the claim that we met there." He would add that Jones "did not engage in any improper or sexual conduct" and would express his "regret" over the "untrue assertions which have been made about her conduct."

Jones's lawyers thus told Bennett they would delay their lawsuit. White

House operatives then leaked to reporters that Jones would not take legal action because "she knew she had no case." Jones felt the White House was acting in bad faith, so her lawyers insisted that the agreement should suspend the statute of limitations and give her the right to file suit if anyone in the President's camp further denigrated her in the press. The President's team said no, on the grounds that such a condition would undercut the settlement. "Bennett felt that real progress was being made until the White House spin stopped the talks," wrote *Newsweek*.

On Friday, May 6, Jones filed suit alleging that Bill Clinton had engaged in "odious, perverse and outrageous conduct," that his actions had created a "hostile work environment" for the $10,270-per-year clerk, and that he and Danny Ferguson, among others, had defamed her. She asked for $700,000 in damages and described the particulars she had withheld three months earlier.

She claimed Bill had first engaged in small talk and told her, "I love your curves." She said that moments later he dropped his trousers and underwear and asked her to perform oral sex, beckoning her to "kiss it." She was able to describe the furniture in the hotel room—a sofa and chairs but no bed—and how it was arranged. Five witnesses also confirmed that she recounted the incident shortly after it happened. *Newsweek*'s Joe Klein pointed out that Jones's tale had "heft only because there have been so many others, and because it reinforces a widely held suspicion about the precise nature of the President's problem."

To buttress her allegation, Jones shockingly claimed that she could identify "distinguishing characteristics in Clinton's genital area." A year earlier, Bill had relished the tale of John and Lorena Bobbitt, and now his own private parts had become comic fodder for the likes of Jay Leno and David Letterman. "It can't help Bill Clinton to have the national imagination supplied with one more image of him as the Libido in Chief," wrote *Time*.

The Clinton camp opened a tough campaign to discredit Jones. Bennett called the charges "tabloid trash," and James Carville famously said, "Drag $100 through a trailer park and there's no telling what you'll find." The notion of portraying Jones as "trailer-park trash" caused concern within the White House because, said one senior official, "it did antagonize her."

Now that the seamy allegations were in the open, the Clintons strongly opposed settlement. "There is no question Clinton was really offended by the Paula Jones suit," said one of his advisors. "He was outraged. That was a very big factor in not settling." Another crucial factor was Hillary, whose first and abiding instinct was to fight. Bill told his advisors that a settlement would tacitly admit his guilt, and "he couldn't do that to Hillary. . . . He could not put his wife through that kind of humiliation."

Although both Bill and Jones denied they had had consensual sex, some of his advisors believed otherwise. For one thing, Bill seemed overly defensive after Jones had left his room, saying—according to Danny Ferguson—"She came up here, and nothing happened." Ferguson offered other intriguing details. When Jones and a coworker had initially seen Bill at the conference, "they were kind of giggling about the governor's pants being too short," and Jones had asked the trooper to tell Bill "she thought he was good looking, had sexy hair." "There is no dispute that she went into the room," said a top Clinton advisor, noting that she tried to see Bill several times afterward while delivering mail to the Governor's office. "Maybe she felt rejected and used," said the advisor. "A lot of things make sense if you assume there was a consensual relationship: his history, her history—all that explains why she kept looking for him."

The White House decided its best strategy was to delay the lawsuit. "Your mission is to get beyond the 1996 election," Lloyd Cutler told Bennett. On August 10, the Clinton team filed a motion in federal court to dismiss Jones's claim on the grounds of presidential immunity. They argued that a President shouldn't be subject to civil suits while in office because they could impair his ability to govern. By tying up the case in the courts and the appeals process, the Clintons and their lawyers ensured that nothing would happen for three more years—but in doing so, they kept alive a legal action that would harm Bill in ways that far transcended the embarrassment of Jones's allegations.

DURING THIS FRAUGHT PERIOD, when Bill was by his own account "lost in the funhouse" of financial and sexual allegations, he neglected a foreign-policy tragedy in Rwanda. Beginning in early April, more than eight hundred thousand Tutsis—the ethnic minority that had traditionally dominated Rwanda's economic and political life—were slaughtered by the majority Hutus. The sectarian genocide continued for nearly three months while the United States and other western nations did nothing. The American passivity had its roots in the Clinton Administration's handling of what became known as "Black Hawk Down," the killing of eighteen American servicemen in Somalia the previous October by supporters of warlord Mohammed Farrah Aidid.

Bill had been shaken by TV images of triumphant Somalis dragging mangled bodies of American soldiers through the streets of Mogadishu, and he had decided to remove all U.S. troops from the country—a judgment backed by Hillary. Years later, in a heated defense of his foreign policy on Fox News, he blamed "all the right-wingers who . . . were all trying to get me to withdraw from Somalia in 1993 the next day." In fact, congressional leaders from both parties—notably West Virginia Democrat Robert Byrd—called for a quick pullout. Two of the strongest advocates of remaining in Somalia to defeat Aidid's forces were Republicans: Senator Richard Lugar said it would be "a disgrace to cut and run," and House Minority Whip Newt Gingrich encouraged Bill to "use overwhelming power and get the job done." But the Democrat-controlled Congress was threatening a "vote to 'bring the boys home,' " recalled Stephanopoulos.

The Clinton Administration settled on a compromise plan to temporarily reinforce U.S. troops and then to withdraw on March 31, 1994. "The early-departure policy," noted *Time*, "had one immediate success: It calmed the revolt in Congress." But privately, Bill fretted, "I hope I didn't panic and announce the pullout too soon." He told Stephanopoulos that he believed "Americans are basically isolationist. . . . Right now the average American doesn't see our interest threatened to the point where we should sacrifice one American life."

Bill's announced intention to abandon Somalia served to embolden other enemies abroad. Osama bin Laden, leader of the then little-known but increasingly powerful al-Qaeda terrorist group, remarked afterward that the "jihad in Somalia" had demonstrated "the weakness, frailty, and cowardice of U.S. troops. . . . They fled in the heart of darkness." By one account, bin Laden even considered the withdrawal from Somalia "his first victory against America." An investigation by the 9/11 Commission revealed that his operatives had in fact been directly involved in the attack on American forces.

Closer to home in Haiti, a mob supporting the ruling military junta had gathered in Port-au-Prince and shouted, "Another Somalia!" The Clinton Administration had been trying for months to force the generals out and restore democratically elected Jean-Bertrand Aristide to power. On October 11, 1993, only eight days after the battle in Mogadishu, a gang of thugs prevented the USS *Harlan County* from docking in Port-au-Prince. The American ship was carrying two hundred troops to help with Haitian reconstruction, and its forcible rejection was "a terrible humiliation on top of Somalia," recalled National Security Advisor Tony Lake.

After these setbacks, Bill had become reluctant to commit U.S. troops anywhere in the world. Nevertheless, by the spring of 1994, Lake was pressing Bill to consider doing so in Haiti, arguing that only "force" or a "credible threat" could bring Aristide back. Instead, Bill took a more cautious approach and tightened economic sanctions.

He was also struggling to define a policy toward Bosnia, where in early April NATO had conducted air strikes for the first time against Serb artillery emplacements that were pounding Muslim towns and cities. A year earlier, Bill had abandoned his campaign pledge to bomb Serbian positions and help the Muslims arm themselves, and since then he had shifted between what *Time* called "high-minded declarations and failure to implement them" in Bosnia. Tony Lake later wrote, "We seemed unable or unwilling to bring American power to bear in effective ways."

Within days of the American departure from Somalia on March 31, gun battles erupted among warring clans, and the country edged toward anarchy. A thousand miles to the west, the Hutus started their massacres after the presidents of Rwanda and Burundi were killed in a plane crash. Bill recalled being "obsessed with Bosnia and all the other stuff" at the time and determined to avoid entangling the United States in military conflicts with no obvious national interest. Bill later said he didn't understand the magnitude of the Rwanda killing because it was carried out rapidly with machetes rather than guns. A senior foreign-policy advisor remembered learning "there was a lot of bloodshed, but we didn't know the scope." Still, the foreign-policy team held no meetings in which military intervention in Rwanda was even debated—"a sin not of commission but omission, but a sin nonetheless," said Lake. The Somalia experience, he said, "was part of the intellectual and political landscape of what we could not do."

———

THE TUG-OF-WAR OVER health care persisted through the spring and summer of 1994 with a series of public-relations blitzes fashioned by White
House political operatives as part of the "permanent campaign," a style of
governing never before used by an American president. Bill had devised
the nonstop campaign a decade earlier in Arkansas, and at its core was the
use of constant polling—public-opinion surveys, tracking polls, and focus
groups—to determine what aspects of policies resonated with voters and
what language appealed to them. While the Bush White House spent
$216,000 on polling in each of its first two years, the Clinton Administra-
tion's expenditure in the first year alone amounted to $1,986,410.

This was the principal franchise of the Gang of Four political consultants who churned out a stream of memos advising Bill and Hillary on policy as well as rhetoric. The consultants' guidance—with numbers supplied
by pollster Stan Greenberg—provided ammunition for the war rooms that
Hillary particularly favored and helped the President and First Lady time
their public appearances to whip up maximum support for their programs.

With the Clinton health-care plan losing altitude by the week, Bill and
Hillary needed a new strategy. Since February, they had both been attacking the "Harry and Louise" ads for ignoring "real people." They even tried
to "expose the scare tactics" with ridicule. For the annual Gridiron Club
dinner in March, they taped a video parody in which they sat together on
a sofa, pretending to be Harry and Louise. The audience laughed at such
lines as "It says here on page 3,764 that under the Clinton health security
plan we could get sick" and "On page 27,655 it says that eventually we're
all going to die." But their performance was overshadowed by Al Gore, "the
undisputed star" of the evening. Playing on his reputation for being
wooden, he was rolled to the podium leaning stiffly upright on a hand
truck, and he mocked himself relentlessly with zingers such as "Al Gore is
an inspiration to the millions of Americans who suffer from Dutch Elm
Disease," and "When people ask me what it's like being number two at the
White House, I tell them, 'She seems to enjoy it.' "

By late March, Stan Greenberg's polling had determined that the problem with the Clinton health plan was the sales pitch. The consultants test-
marketed simplified talking points and gave Bill and Hillary a new script to

use in a series of speeches and town meetings. The White House acknowledged that it was trying to "jump-start" the Clinton plan and, as *Time* described it, "avoid some of the phrases that seem to conjure images of a sprawling, socialist nightmare." Still, Robert Reich worried at the end of April that Bill was "bogged down in health care," which was "draining his energies and his political capital."

Hillary continued to insist that universal coverage was the "sine qua non of health care reform." As a consequence, the White House, "abetted by a handful of health-care zealots in the Congress," kept pursuing what *Newsweek*'s Joe Klein called "a myopic and ahistorical approach," a fifty-one-vote strategy to "ram through" the Clinton bill, even though that slender majority didn't exist.

A bipartisan parade of moderate leaders in Congress, including Pat Moynihan and Republican senators Robert Packwood of Oregon and John Chafee of Rhode Island, implored the Clintons to compromise and as a first step accept coverage of 91 percent of Americans instead of everyone, as one alternative bill would. On Sunday, June 19, Moynihan went on *Meet the Press* to declare that a bill with universal coverage had "no chance" in Congress. But Moynihan also let the White House know he had good reason to believe that Senate Minority Leader Robert Dole and other senators would help forge an incremental bill.

That evening, Bill and Hillary summoned a dozen advisors to the Map Room in the Residence. Bill was scheduled to appear on the *Today* show the next morning, and some on his staff saw an opening for him to seek middle ground. But Hillary and her allies urged Bill "not to give an inch," recalled David Gergen. Just as Treasury Secretary Bentsen was poised to present a formula for striking a deal with Congress, Bill "exploded" and his face "flushed with anger" as he shouted, "As long as I am President, I plan to keep fighting for serious reform. I did not get elected to compromise on this issue. We can't trust the Republicans, and I am not backing down! We won't compromise!"

On *Today*, Bill held firm, saying "the so-called 91 per cent solution . . . essentially would guarantee what we have now." In a subsequent meeting behind closed doors in the OEOB with health-care allies, Hillary pounded a lectern and emphasized her husband's veto pledge. The next day at a luncheon on Capitol Hill, she said, "It is time to be a conviction politician as opposed to those who crawfish around." And when Democratic leaders asked Hillary on July 1 for ideas for a fresh start, she moved even farther left, suggesting an outright government-guaranteed program based on Canada's national health plan.

Yet during a phone conversation with Moynihan on June 29, Bill's resolve seemed to weaken. "In a big democracy," Moynihan said, "you never get 100 percent of anything. Sometimes you're lucky if you get 90 percent." Bill replied that he had been thinking of that, and he was open to discussing whether full coverage was "a reasonable definition." Some three weeks later, Bill decided to think out loud, and he paid a heavy price at home.

He had traveled to Maine on July 18 for a fund-raising event with Senator George Mitchell, who had been trying to craft a bill providing 95 percent coverage. The next day, Bill addressed the National Governors Association in Boston. During the question-and-answer period, he was asked to comment on the status of health-care reform. He said he would welcome a "phased-in, deliberate effort" to increase the number of insured "somewhere in the ballpark of 95 per cent upwards" and declared that he was "open to any solution" on financing greater coverage.

"I was shocked," said Donna Shalala, who was sitting in the audience. "Ira [Magaziner] was mortified. The President caught everyone by surprise." Back in the West Wing, an aide reported Bill's remarks to Hillary. She picked up the phone and said to the White House operator, "Get me the President." Moments later, Bill came on the line. "What the fuck are you doing up there?" she screamed. "I want to see you as soon as you get back." Her tone was as "hard-edged" as her advisors had ever heard. Several hours later, Bill arrived by helicopter and walked into the Diplomatic Reception Room, where an aide was waiting to escort him upstairs.

The next day, Bill retracted his comments and even apologized, saying that universal coverage remained the administration's goal. But the Clinton plan had crashed. In the following weeks, every imaginable bloc in the Senate and the House scrambled to improvise a "less bureaucratic, more voluntary" plan.

On July 22, Hillary set out from Portland, Oregon, on a "Health Security Express" bus caravan. She had flogged her ideas to some three hundred local and national groups in thirty states over the previous ten months, and this was her final push. At every stop, she was plagued by protesters. Bill met her eight days later in Independence, Missouri, conjuring up the fighting spirit of Harry Truman. "This is not socialized medicine," Bill insisted. "This is not a government takeover."

Far from being resigned, Hillary seemed intent on making a last stand when she met with Bill's advisors on July 28. She wanted "massive retaliation," a "fiery" speech by the President before a joint session of Congress that would attack the Republicans for wrecking health-care reform. When Stephanopoulos told her Congress wouldn't agree, she asked for an address from the Oval Office. Again, Stephanopoulos turned her down, saying the networks wouldn't consider a plea for health care urgent enough to give away ten minutes of airtime. Bill's aides finally settled on a presidential press conference in the East Room on August 3.

On the morning of the second, Hillary was sobbing when she called Stephanopoulos. She had just learned that Maggie Williams and Roger Altman would be testifying before Congress the next day. She was convinced that instead of having a chance to make the case for health-care reform, Bill would be inundated with Whitewater inquiries. Struck by the "absurdity" of the situation, Stephanopoulos had to spend twenty minutes calming down the distraught First Lady. Bill ended up handling all the questions capably, but his performance at the news conference did nothing to advance the health-care cause.

As remnants of the massive Clinton plan were stuffed into different Democratic initiatives, the atmosphere was "frantic, almost hallucinatory . . . marked by slapdash, panic-stricken deal-making," while Bill and Hillary continued to stiff-arm moderates in both parties. On August 9, Hillary decided to take off after the Republicans herself in an interview with a small group of reporters, accusing the GOP of political opportunism and "personal vicious hatred that . . . is being aimed at the President and to a lesser extent myself." Yet only two weeks later, Bill dialed Robert Packwood for a late-night conversation. "Is there any chance for a health bill?" he asked.

The Republican senator told him there was, but "it won't be one you'll like." He outlined several variations of a modest package of reforms that he urged Bill to sign despite his veto threat. He told the President that if he rejected the legislation, "You'll be vetoing something that a lot of Americans want."

"What would you suggest I do?" Bill asked.

In a flash of candor, Packwood said, "The best thing would be to let it die in Congress and then blame it on the Republicans." But the GOP, he added, would probably hold the White House responsible for the failure.

On September 26, 1994, one year and four days after Bill's triumphant speech to Congress, Senate Majority Leader George Mitchell officially announced that comprehensive health insurance could not be enacted into law. The centerpiece of Bill Clinton's first term had never even come to a vote in the House or Senate. It expired, Hillary later wrote, "with barely a whimper." Neither Bill nor Hillary spoke about their defeat that day, although each offered explanations in the months and years to come.

Both of them continued to insist that their "Big Bang" approach was correct and that their opponents had misunderstood and distorted their plan. Hillary admitted that she had "alienated" some experts and potential allies and that she and Bill had tried to do "too much, too fast." But she never acknowledged the damage done by her antagonistic tactics: her war room, her sharp-edged speeches, and her need to single out "enemies." Even twelve years later, she persisted in blaming everyone else—the "powers of the status quo and special interests and political partisanship," along with the Democratic congressional leaders who gave her bad advice and a "Washington system" outraged that "he put his *wife* in charge." In the end, neither Bill nor Hillary ever conceded their plan's structural or substantive defects. Nor did Bill recognize that he needed a coalition of Democratic and Republican moderates to help pass such a sweeping plan.

With his eye fixed firmly on Hillary's future in politics, Bill repeatedly insisted over the years that she was not at fault for the failure of health care. On the eve of the congressional elections in November 1994, he told Larry King on CNN that Hillary was "never hired. She was a volunteer." Her role, he said, was merely to "try to get the work product up, and then be the spokesperson." Fifteen months later, he said the decisions on health care "were my mistakes. . . . I don't think these had anything to do with her being involved in it. . . . I just think it's wrong to put it on her."

As governor, Bill had developed theories about reforming the health-care system, and he and Hillary had engaged in what she termed a "rolling conversation" about how to put those ideas into practice. But for all of Bill's efforts at revisionism, Hillary bore responsibility for attempting to create what Moynihan called "perhaps the largest and most expensive entitlement in history." George Stephanopoulos, who watched her as closely as anyone, believed that "her leadership was more than the political system could bear. . . . The plan, like the woman who guided it, was ambitious, idealistic, and highly logical; but it was also inflexible, overly complex, and highly susceptible to misinterpretation."

HILLARY VIEWED HEALTH CARE as "part of the American journey," a theme she had tried unsuccessfully to include in Bill's first health-care speech. Since her husband had taken office, she had been talking about devising an overarching "narrative" for his administration. Back on July 3, 1993, when she had castigated Bill's top advisors in the Solarium for mishandling his economic plan, she had described Bill as the man "who was going to lead us on this journey." But a year later, no one had yet come up with directions for the trip.

Beginning in mid-May 1994, Hillary tried to address the problem again with a series of meetings, first at Blair House and then in the Map Room. The participants included the Gang of Four and a select group of West Wing staff members who were cautioned by Maggie Williams, "Don't tell, just come."

In the meetings, Hillary expressed her frustration that the administration ran on tactics rather than strategy and that everything was geared to the headline of the day. She asked various advisors to prepare paragraphs distilling core messages—"what we are about in domestic and foreign policy."

The gatherings were a classic expression of Hillary's emphasis on process and her continuing role in trying to shape the administration's policy. "This was all driven by Hillary," said one participant. "It was her correct thinking. They needed a narrative of what the Presidency was about and how what they did flowed from that."

Staff members submitted paragraphs that Hillary and her staff parsed and massaged. But in the end, no mission statement appeared. "The problem was coming to an agreement about the narrative," said a Clinton advisor. The centrist and liberal factions in the White House were as split as ever—a reflection of the President's own intellectual divisions.

It was also impossible to impose an orderly scheme on a White House "so disorganized that information is hard to come by," noted Robert Reich in early June. "The decision-making 'loop' depends on physical proximity to Bill—who's whispering into his ear most regularly, whose office is closest to The Oval, who's standing or sitting next to him when a key issue arises."

At the moment Reich was writing those words in his journal, the dysfunction of the Clinton White House burst into the open with the publication of *The Agenda*. Using his signature fly-on-the-wall technique, Bob Woodward offered an in-depth examination of the making of the Clinton economic policy, drawing attention to Bill's tirades and vacillation, the pervasive role of the consultants, and Hillary's ubiquitous presence in key decisions. Every important player in the administration including the President and First Lady had talked to Woodward—largely at the urging of Stephanopoulos, who persuaded them that the book would burnish their legacy. But its unflinching portrait rocked the White House and had significant repercussions.

The book landed on the fourth day of the President and First Lady's successful trip to Italy, France, and England to mark the fiftieth anniversary of the Normandy invasion. Bill had delivered a series of well-received tributes to the "Greatest Generation" from the vantage point of a Baby Boomer struggling to meet the challenges of the coming new century. "We are the children of your sacrifice," he said. On D-Day, Bill's handlers created a carefully crafted photo opportunity in which the President walked on Omaha Beach with three World War II veterans, then continued on his own, stopping to gather stones before kneeling to arrange them in the shape of a cross. The maneuver irked the watching journalists, who judged it a contrivance—"acting out an intimate communion with God in front of a platoon of cameras," wrote Michael Kelly in *The New York Times Magazine*. But the choreographed moment played well on television.

Both Clintons drew appreciative crowds throughout Europe, although Hillary's wardrobe received mixed reviews. Somewhat surprisingly, her staff issued bulletins with detailed sartorial descriptions—the "lovely U-shape opening at the neck," the "linen blend"—that were a throwback to the Jacqueline Kennedy era. French journalist Anne-Elisabeth Moutet commented that Hillary had "great style" and dressed "powerfully," while the Italians were less kind about her "uncertain creations." "Up close," wrote one journalist, Hillary was "very pink, like a little pig, but cute. It's said that she uses tons of Estee Lauder powder. It does her good." Designer Sonia Rykiel was puzzled by the way Hillary "changes her hair, changes the colors she wears, changes her clothes" and observed that she hadn't yet found out "who she really is."

By the end of the trip, Bill and Hillary had been fully briefed on *The Agenda*, and they were enraged, particularly at Stephanopoulos, who was quoted telling Panetta, "The worst thing about [Bill] is that he never makes a decision." When Stephanopoulos tried to give Bill some unfavorable polling results, the President stared at him hard with "suppressed rage" and said coldly, "I didn't need that now, George. I didn't need you to bring me down." Hillary blamed *The Agenda* for a drop in Bill's approval ratings to the low forties starting in late June 1994—a particular disappointment, since Stephanopoulos had assured them that after the D-Day trip those numbers would rise. She bluntly told Stephanopoulos that the book epitomized "the whole problem with this administration . . . people who go out there with no loyalty to the President . . . just seeking to aggrandize themselves. I hope they're *satisfied!*"

The first visible reaction to *The Agenda* came on June 27, with the appointment of Leon Panetta, the Budget Director, to replace Mack McLarty, who once likened the Chief of Staff's job to a "javelin catcher." Bill had been discussing the possibility of a change with Hillary as well as with Vernon Jordan and other advisors for several months. But according to Stephanopoulos, the Woodward book "crystallized" the sense that Bill needed someone more muscular than his old friend from Hope. Bill named McLarty as "counselor to the president" and shifted David Gergen—who had been on the outs with Hillary for months—to the State Department. McLarty described his own continuing role as Bill's "security blanket."

Bob Rubin, among others, felt regret about the shift. He thought that McLarty's voice of moderation had smoothed the work of the Clinton economic team and prevented infighting. But the gentle, courtly manner of "Mack the Nice" couldn't rein in the headstrong prima donnas in the West Wing. McLarty was also "intimidated by Hillary," said one of Bill's senior advisors. "He thought she was very smart and very combative. I had a sense that the last place Mack wanted to be was in a fight with Hillary." But above all, Bill made it difficult for McLarty to stand up to him and impose discipline. Bill had served notice from the beginning that he didn't want a strong Chief of Staff. He preferred to think of McLarty as his "reality check," but whenever that translated to mild criticism Bill would say, "You hurt my feelings." "Mack tried to do some things, and Clinton wasn't ready," said Mike McCurry.

When McLarty stepped down, he cracked that the White House needed a Chief of Staff who could "read Machiavelli in the original Italian." A son of Italian immigrants who grew up as a Republican and became a fervid deficit hawk as a Democratic congressman, Panetta had enough distance from Bill to bring some rigor to his Oval Office operations. Panetta leavened his enforcer role with affability, filling the West Wing with a booming laugh. His first move was to schedule a daily early-morning meeting of the top advisors before Bill arrived at the Oval Office.

Beyond the Panetta appointment, *The Agenda* "had a huge impact," said a senior West Wing official. "It changed the way the White House worked." Bill and Hillary convened smaller meetings, and whenever they were in a large group they refrained from the sort of outspoken comments that had typified the first eighteen months. "I have learned never to say anything—anything—in a meeting larger than three people," said Bill. Hillary stopped attending so many sessions with Bill's staff "because she thought they could betray her," a senior official said.

At that stage, Hillary was still in the forefront on health care, but she was sharpening her skills as a back-channel operator as well. In early July, Robert Reich complained to her that his memos to the President were being leaked. "Send them to *me*," she said. "I'll make sure they get to him. Use blank sheets of paper without any letterhead or other identifying characteristics. Just the date and your own initials." Reich followed her instructions explicitly, and Hillary's skillful hidden hand helped him a half-dozen times. "The memos did get to Bill," Reich recalled. "They weren't leaked."

BY MIDSUMMER, the Paula Jones case had slipped below the radar, and the Clintons were finding some respite in a brief burst of party giving. After a seventeen-month wait, they had their first State Dinner, in honor of Emperor Akihito and Empress Michiko of Japan. As a warm-up for that event, they hosted the wedding of Hillary's brother Tony to Nicole Boxer, the daughter of California senator Barbara Boxer. Two hundred and fifty guests attended the black-tie gathering, with music courtesy of Daddy-O and the Sax Maniacs. Several weeks later, Bill and Hillary gave a dinner in the Rose Garden for 150 that even included members of the news media along with such celebrities as Whoopi Goldberg. When a *Washington Post* reporter spotted Brit Hume, one of Bill's adversaries in the White House press corps, the ABC correspondent laughed and yelled, "I'm in the tank! I am now on the team!"

Whitewater still nagged at the Clintons, however. David Hale had pleaded guilty in March to two felony counts on his indictment for fraudulent lending practices, and he was cooperating with Robert Fiske's investigation. Bill would later write in his memoir that Hale, a "Republican municipal judge," had been "adopted" by right-wingers and had fed "damaging but erroneous stories" to reporters. In fact, according to longtime Arkansas political reporter John Brummett, Hale was a "veteran Democratic party operative," who claimed to have made loans not only to Clinton but to his successor, Jim Guy Tucker, and other members of the Democratic political elite.

Fiske came to the White House Residence on Sunday, June 12, to interview the Clintons under oath—Bill for ninety minutes and Hillary for an hour. Bill was in what his friend Terry McAuliffe called his "Big St. Bernard" frame of mind, eager to ingratiate as he gave his inquisitor a tour of his Treaty Room office. Hillary's mood, on the other hand, was of "studied detachment," and she "somewhat breezily told how little she knew" about either the circumstances of Foster's death or the White House—Treasury contacts.

The special prosecutor's probe of Webster Hubbell was gathering momentum, even as Bill and Hillary continued to include Webb and his wife, Suzy, in White House receptions and movie nights. Hubbell was living well on the earnings from his contracts, taking first-class flights back to Little Rock and finding time to play golf in Bali on a trip to Indonesia. By June, Fiske had documented enough evidence of Hubbell's theft from his partners and his clients to begin drawing up an indictment. Over the July Fourth weekend, Bill invited his old friend out to Camp David to play golf. As they sat on the terrace afterward, Bill brought up "all this stuff about your Rose firm billings." "Did you do anything that's going to get you in trouble?" he asked. Hubbell averted his eyes and replied, "No. I can work this thing out." Bill said he was "glad to hear it" and didn't raise the matter again.

On June 30, Fiske had issued his first two reports, one concluding that Foster had indeed committed suicide and the other saying that the contacts between the White House and the Treasury Department on the Madison Guaranty investigation had been proper. The same day, Bill signed the new Independent Counsel Law. It was now up to a panel of judges designated by William Rehnquist, Chief Justice of the Supreme Court, to either reappoint Fiske or substitute a new prosecutor.

The panel made its selection on August 5, replacing Fiske with forty-eight-year-old Kenneth Starr, a former federal appeals-court judge and Solicitor General for George Bush. Starr's conservative connections instantly put Bill and Hillary on edge; the new prosecutor had also gone on record with his belief that Paula Jones could legally challenge a sitting President. *Newsweek* columnist Jonathan Alter was in the White House to interview Hillary on the day of Starr's appointment. "She ranted for over an hour" about the "wimpy mainstream media" that had been cowed by the "right-wing attack machine." Alter was taken aback by her vehemence, "a side I had never seen. The bark was really stripped off."

The White House had been careful eight months earlier to acknowledge Robert Fiske's credentials as an experienced and responsible prosecutor. But this time Hillary prodded Bill's advisors to condemn Starr as a partisan. Lloyd Cutler and David Kendall recommended restraint, as did Cutler's successor, Abner Mikva, who considered Starr a friend and assured the Clintons that "we would get along." Cutler, who was just ending his promised six-month stint, was particularly concerned about antagonizing Starr. But in the following days, James Carville — Bill and Hillary's surrogate — went on the attack anyway, drawing the battle lines before the first shot was fired.

The Starr appointment occurred in the middle of hearings by the Senate Banking Committee, which was conducting its own investigation of the White House–Treasury contacts. The senators zeroed in on Roger Altman, Deputy Secretary of the Treasury, grilling him about whether he had lied to the committee by changing his story. They didn't charge him with perjury, but on August 17 he and Jean Hanson, Treasury's general counsel, resigned under pressure. Altman, who had known Bill since Georgetown days, had become a "fall guy," noted Robert Reich. "Now he leaves Washington under a dark cloud. . . . He's been treated despicably."

FACING THE CERTAIN collapse of health-care reform, Bill threw all his energy into anticrime legislation that was also foundering in Congress. For his own legacy and for the coming midterm elections, Bill needed to demonstrate that he was tough on crime, which should have been fairly routine in an election year. But when the House handily defeated the bill on August 11, Bill and his advisors were stunned. Republicans had denounced its thirty-three-billion-dollar price tag as excessive, so Bill authorized Leon Panetta to negotiate a compromise. At a time when Hillary was castigating the GOP as obstructionist on health care, a group of Republican moderates worked with the White House for more than a week to find common ground. Bill agreed to cut the cost by 10 percent, and when pressed further by Republicans he authorized an additional cut of $650 million, which added twenty votes to his side. But in defiance of the National Rifle Association, Bill insisted on including a ban on assault weapons that some Democrats worried could hurt them in the midterm contests. Panetta and congressional leaders negotiated all night on Friday the nineteenth and throughout the following day until they struck the final deal. The House passed the thirty-billion-dollar bill on Sunday, August 21, and the Senate followed four days later. Bill had won, but as usual the victory was more fraught than it needed to be.

The wrangling over the bill had delayed the Clinton family's second Martha's Vineyard vacation. When they finally arrived at the island on the twenty-sixth, they enjoyed more generous accommodations than the spartan McNamara house, where they stayed the previous summer. This time they were guests of Democratic contributor Richard Friedman, a Boston real-estate developer, and once again they paid no rent for their ten-day stay. Friedman's twenty-acre Oyster Pond estate featured a spacious nineteenth-century shingled house, hammocks, horses, a pet pig, and a guest cottage, where Bill could retreat to work and read.

Bill and Hillary easily resumed their favorite vacation routines. They bought stacks of books at the Bickerton & Ripley bookstore in Edgartown and took sailing excursions with singer James Taylor and Senator John Kerry. After several rounds of golf, Bill told reporters he had shot an eighty, which immediately raised eyebrows. That August, the press began to focus on Bill's liberal interpretation of golf rules, especially his frequent use of mulligans—not only off the tee but on the fairway and around the green—and his tendency to pocket distant putts rather than play them out. Commentators saw a reflection of Bill's character in his self-deluding habit of claiming low scores that didn't correspond to the quality of his play. Gerry Callahan of the *Boston Herald* recounted that "after 10 days of preferred lies and unlimited mulligans," a TV camera caught Bill on the green taking the same shot three times until he sank the putt and then claiming a par on the hole. "The leader of the free world was doing what he does best: cheat," wrote Callahan.

Not surprisingly, Bill blamed Republicans for the challenges to his honesty on the golf course. "It was part of their strategy to deny my legitimacy," he said eight years later. "They just decided from the day I was elected to just keep attacking me." Friends and frequent golfing partners such as Terry McAuliffe explained that Bill simply liked to practice while he played and that he would take the first shot for his score. But *New York Times* reporter Don Van Natta, who once played a round with the President, observed that when faced with two or three of his balls on the fairway, Bill invariably took the one in the best position, claiming he couldn't remember which was the first shot. "It is a shell game with golf balls," wrote Van Natta, who coined the term "Billigans" to describe Bill's "devious" do-over shots. The reporter also observed that Bill would take a "gimme" on putts as long as fifty feet. When Bill claimed a twelve or thirteen handicap, few golf professionals found him credible. Tiger Woods said Bill used "interesting math," and Raymond Floyd observed, "If you shoot an 8, you write an 8. That's golf to me."

In the evenings on the Vineyard, the Clintons slipped into the social swim of cocktail gatherings and dinners hosted by the Jordans and Katharine Graham. They dined quietly with Maurice Tempelsman and Caroline and John Kennedy Jr., whose mother had died of cancer three months earlier. At the Graham dinner, Bill quoted from William Styron's *The Confessions of Nat Turner*, and on another evening he recited a long passage from Faulkner's *The Sound and the Fury*.

The Styrons invited the Clintons to a dinner that also included Carlos Fuentes and Gabriel García Márquez, Bill's "literary hero." A dozen guests sat around a large table with Bill and Hillary at either end. Bill "commanded the conversation for the whole group," recalled historian Sheldon Hackney. "Hillary deferred to him, didn't chip in. He was President, on the spot. She didn't intrude. She isn't shy, but she didn't take over." Hackney observed the different ways Bill and Hillary displayed their intelligence and concluded, "She's not as showy as he is."

Most of the talk that evening concerned Cuba. García Márquez, a close friend of Fidel Castro, was lobbying the President to improve relations with Havana. "I got the very distinct feeling Bill Clinton was sympathetic to the complications of Cuba and Castro, that he wanted to lift the trade sanctions and wanted closer ties," said Rose Styron. "There was no way he would be able to do that at the moment, but as soon as he was re-elected, that was what he would like to do. He was not explicit. It was just a firm impression, and García Márquez and others at the table had it, too."

The Styrons were surprised to learn later that like so many others, they had mistaken Bill's expressions of understanding for agreement. Under the influence of Cuban-American Democrats in Florida, Bill actually became strongly anti-Castro in his efforts to win the state in the 1996 election. These Cuban Americans—known in the White House as the "core group"—had raised substantial sums for him in 1992 and promised to do more if he took a hard line on Cuba. An important member of this group was Hugh Rodham's wife, Maria Victoria Arias, a Miami lawyer. Through frequent phone calls to Hillary, Arias transmitted the core group's anti-Castro strategy to Bill. In February 1996, when the Cuban government shot down two private American planes that had been dropping propaganda leaflets over Havana, Bill warned Castro of military reprisals if Cuba took further hostile action. Shortly afterward, Bill signed the Helms-Burton bill, which strengthened the thirty-four-year-old trade embargo against Cuba and added tough new sanctions.

THE AUTUMN OF 1994 brought a reprieve from scandal news and a boost from some foreign-policy successes. The U.S. trade embargo on Haiti had failed to dislodge General Raoul Cedras and his junta and had pushed the population close to starvation. Under pressure from his foreign-policy team, Bill finally decided to authorize a military invasion of Haiti on September 19. He also directed his pollsters to test various arguments he could make to justify the use of force. In a speech from the Oval Office on Thursday, September 15, Bill outlined the case for intervention, appealing to Cedras directly to leave on his own before the United States forced him from power. Stan Greenberg's soundings had helped Bill "market" the decision by emphasizing human rights and the need to support a democratic government. But Bill remained concerned about any loss of American life, so two days later he directed former President Jimmy Carter, along with Senator Sam Nunn from Georgia and former Chairman of the Joint Chiefs Colin Powell, to travel to Haiti to negotiate directly with Cedras. Just hours before the planned invasion, the delegation persuaded Cedras to leave and arranged for the "permissive entry" of fifteen thousand American troops without a shot being fired. A month later, Jean-Bertrand Aristide returned to Haiti, and Bill won accolades for what became known as an "intervasion."

Around the same time, Saddam Hussein of Iraq began menacing neighboring Kuwait by massing troops on the border, as he had prior to his invasion in 1991. Bill ordered thirty-six thousand troops to the region, and Saddam pulled back. Noting Bill's forceful responses to the dictators in Haiti and Iraq, the New York *Daily News* proclaimed "CLINTON 2, BULLIES 0!"

Within days, Bill also announced North Korea's agreement to stop producing plutonium in its efforts to build a nuclear bomb. The North Koreans had come to the negotiating table only after the United States threatened sanctions and increased its troop deployment around the Korean peninsula. It was highly unlikely that Bill Clinton would have used military power against the North Koreans, but the saber rattling by the world's only superpower was effective. Under the terms of the accord, the North Koreans would shut down their old nuclear-power plants and replace them with facilities designed to produce nonweapons-grade plutonium. They also pledged to dispose of their spent fuel rods, which could be used in the production of nuclear weapons. In exchange, the United States guaranteed investments of four billion dollars from an international consortium to build new reactors and agreed to supply the North Koreans with free fuel oil. Senator Robert Dole worried that the United States had given away too much in exchange for insufficient guarantees of compliance. His concerns proved prescient several years later when the North Koreans se-

cretly started a program to enrich uranium for nuclear weapons—a violation of the agreement that was not confirmed until 2002. But in the autumn of 1994, the Clinton Administration counted the accord as a
diplomatic success.

THESE ACHIEVEMENTS BRIEFLY nudged Bill's approval ratings to 48 percent, but they reverted to the low forties in the weeks before the congressional elections. By mid-October, the White House was beginning to worry
about what one Clinton Administration advisor called a potential "GOP
surge at the polls" that "could be devastating." Just as George Bush didn't
benefit from the improving economy during the 1992 campaign, Bill was
unable to persuade the electorate that his economic plan was helping
them. To keep the lid on inflation, Alan Greenspan's Federal Reserve
Board had raised short-term interest rates six times since January, which in
turn had elevated the cost of mortgages and other forms of consumer
credit. The economy was growing and the deficit shrinking, but voters
weren't feeling any relief.

The Republicans also succeeded in solidifying an impression of Bill
Clinton among independent voters as a tax-and-spend liberal Democrat
preoccupied by the status of homosexuals in the military and committed to
intrusive big government, symbolized by Hillary's failed health-care plan.
Among conservative Republicans, two other measures stimulated voter
turnout: the Brady Act, which put limits on the sale of handguns and
which Bill had signed in late 1993, and the recently enacted assault-
weapons ban. At the same time, the NAFTA treaty alienated liberal Democrats, who felt less inclined to go to the polls.

The Republicans capitalized on their growing advantage by offering a
dramatic "Contract with America" on the steps of the Capitol on September 27. The brainchild of Newt Gingrich, the Contract called for ten legislative initiatives that included a balanced-budget amendment, a cut in
the capital-gains tax, deregulation, and term limits for congressmen. Not
only were Republicans offering popular programs designed to energize
voters on Election Day, they were "nationalizing" the congressional elections as an anti-Clinton referendum.

By the time Gingrich released the Contract, Bill had already been in
touch with Dick Morris, his former political guru from Arkansas days. In-

tense, fast-talking and self-absorbed, Morris was a master of the political dark arts—one of the few people who could hold Bill in thrall with his baroque evaluations of candidates, voters, polling statistics, and issues. After falling out with Bill in 1990 over polling techniques, Morris had turned to Republican clients. Bill had not enlisted Morris in 1992 because, he said, the consultant "was compromised in the eyes of virtually all Democrats." But now that Bill sensed electoral trouble, he had no such qualms. Morris's knowledge of the opposition added to his allure.

During the first two years of the Clinton presidency, Hillary had been talking to Morris once or twice each month, soliciting his advice "on her own work and on her own political style." Morris had also used Hillary to pass along ideas to Bill, and Hillary had shared her reactions to events—telling Morris at the time of the debacle in Somalia, for example, that she favored immediate withdrawal of American troops.

When Bill had first lost reelection as governor in 1980, Hillary had recruited Morris to orchestrate his comeback. Instead of flinching from Morris's attack politics, Hillary had said, "We need to learn how the bad boys do it," and she readily adopted his principal lesson: "You must create an enemy. That is the best way to define yourself. It's all for a good cause, but you have to target a whipping boy."

In 1993 and 1994, Morris had found the Clintons less receptive to his tactical advice. Hillary had resisted Morris's suggestions on her health-care plan, even at the eleventh hour, when he told her failure would "seriously injure the administration in general and her reputation in particular." "You've got to do it all or nothing," she said when he pressed her to back a limited bill.

In early October, Bill called Morris to request a poll on midterm election strategy. With the results in hand, Morris briefed Bill and Hillary together on the phone, telling them to emphasize the administration's "bite-size achievements" that would resonate with voters. He warned them that Democrats could lose fifty seats in the House and control of the Senate as well. He also urged Bill to avoid the campaign trail and concentrate on looking presidential. But Bill's advisors said surveys showed that voters disliked the Republican Contract and that he should campaign against it.

Bill did scuttle one series of speeches for candidates in Rhode Island, New York, Iowa, and Michigan in late October and hastily scheduled a four-day swing with Hillary through six countries in the Middle East. The purpose of the trip, noted *Time*, was "a prime-time TV triumph to boost his party's mid-term election chances." The centerpiece was the signing of a peace treaty between Israel and Jordan on an asphalt strip in the middle of a minefield on the border of the two countries—a compelling image showing Bill and Hillary in an act of statesmanship. Bill spoke to the parliaments in Jordan and Israel, visited U.S. troops in Kuwait, and met with leaders in Saudi Arabia, Egypt, and Syria. But the visits were more symbolic than substantive and barely registered with voters back home.

On his return to Washington, Bill jumped into an eight-day, "scare out the vote" campaign, blasting the Contract with America and claiming that Republicans intended to cut two thousand dollars from the annual benefits of Social Security recipients. Ironically, a CBS poll in that final week determined that 71 percent of voters were unaware of the Contract. By making himself so visible, Bill actually helped the Republicans highlight voter disaffection with his leadership.

Bill later blamed his advisors for pushing him onto the campaign trail, writing that he was "surprised to find my schedule packed with trips." He would rebuke Stephanopoulos for "talking me into attacking" the Contract, although it was Bill who had insisted on talk-radio appearances and campaign rallies. Advising Bill to stay at home during a political season, Stephanopoulos noted, was "like asking him not to breathe." Even Hillary acknowledged that Bill had been unable to "resist the lure of the campaign trail."

Feeling frustrated and wounded over her health-care defeat, Hillary had already begun to reassess her role in the weeks before Election Day. Her aides made it known that she was contemplating a profile more like Eleanor Roosevelt's public ambassadorship, using her travels to bring "voices from the real world . . . back to the policy table." Friends also came forward to emphasize Hillary's determination to remain a force in Bill's administration. "She's an incredibly patient, tenacious person, and she knows you don't always win on the first shot," said Susan Thomases. Diane Blair added that she had "never heard a shred of defeatism in [Hillary's] voice."

Hillary said she was "charged up" about the midterm elections and intended to campaign "to turn these numbers around." One of her first stops was Florida, where her forty-four-year-old brother Hugh was making a futile run for the U.S. Senate. Influential Florida Democrats had pleaded with the Clintons to dissuade Rodham. Fund-raiser Jeffrey Orseck told them that "it would hurt Bill in the next presidential election to have such a weak candidate for the Senate in Florida." "It's not the worst idea I ever heard, but pretty close to it," Bill told one of his friends. Yet Bill deferred to Hillary, who told Orseck that "it was her brother, and whatever he wanted to do she would back him 100 percent."

Hillary spent a weekend in early October stumping for "my little brother," a guaranteed gag line given his super-size proportions. Campaign manager Tony Rodham showed up for his brother's rallies "unshaven and bleary eyed," while Hugh gave rambling speeches, and Hillary laughed every time he repeated his jokes. In her own remarks, she said little about Hugh, spending most of her time reciting a list of her husband's accomplishments in the White House. Her performance was "so controlled," noted Lloyd Grove of *The Washington Post*, "that she didn't even crack a smile" when one speaker referred to "Hill and Billary."

Her most noteworthy contribution to the campaign was an interview with *Newsweek*'s Kenneth Woodward about religion. Since the publication of "Saint Hillary" in May 1993, she had kept her spiritual views out of the public arena. But in her daily life, Hillary's religiosity was apparent to friends and staff. In Arkansas, she had frequently given guest sermons at churches around the state on "What It Means to Be a Methodist." She kept handy not only the Bible but the Book of Resolutions of the United Methodist Church, as well as her notebook stuffed with scripture and inspirational quotes. She routinely said grace before meals, and she belonged to a women's prayer group including the spouses of Republicans James Baker and Jack Kemp. Hillary welcomed the group's intercessory prayers, as well as daily scripture readings and "faith messages" they sent by fax.

A Southern Baptist, Bill had grown up in the tradition of sin and redemption. He enjoyed quoting liberally from the Bible and belting out hymns, while Hillary's brand of religion was more intellectual and restrained. Drawing from the teachings of John Wesley and other theologians, she saw herself as an instrument for carrying out good works as a way to achieve a higher purpose. The Methodist notion that "we know what's good for you" was an essential part of her psyche. "Hillary is as pious as she is political," wrote Woodward. "Methodism for her is not just a church but an extended family of faith that defines her horizons."

After three months of requests from *Newsweek*, Hillary's agreement to speak about spiritual matters in late October had an inevitable political cast. Her message reflected her effort as a Democrat to recapture themes of morality and virtue from the Republicans. She said she had "a great deal of sympathy for Christian fundamentalists" and lamented that the media had done "a great disservice" to "what is loosely called the religious right" by subjecting them to stereotypes. She said flatly that abortion was "wrong" but that it should not be "criminalized," and she allowed that she was "not comfortable" with the distribution of condoms in schools.

Washington Post columnist Mary McGrory considered Hillary's remarks "startling" because they conflicted with Bill's views and even Hillary's own "not so long ago." But the First Lady's pronouncements had no discernible impact on the electorate. Election Day surveys showed that 38 percent of voters considered themselves "conservative," eight points more than in 1992, and 33 percent identified with the religious right, compared with 24 percent two years earlier.

In an effort to keep Bill buoyant in the closing days of the campaign, some of his advisors tried to minimize the damage to the Democrats. Two days before the polls opened, he was unrelentingly upbeat on *Larry King Live* during a campaign swing through Seattle. "I also just like to see the American people," Bill said. "I like to see them excited and energized again." Still glowing from the adoring crowds, he touted his achievements at home and abroad and expressed confidence that the Democrats would hold the Congress "if the American people know what has been done."

But Morris continued to predict a catastrophe, and he was right. On Tuesday, November 8, Bill and Hillary sat at their kitchen table in the Residence and watched the grim returns on television. Their first reaction was instinctively defiant. In midafternoon, they sent out word to aides to prepare a speech announcing the launch of "a new agenda for a new American century." But as the magnitude of the losses became apparent, the Clintons scuttled their lofty rhetoric. They scrambled to reach Susan Thomases, who had been consulting with Hillary several times per month, both in visits to the White House and in so many late-night phone conversations that she became known as "the midnight caller." But she had taken her phone off the hook, causing the Clintons to have the Secret Service track her down. When Bill and Hillary finally found her, she recommended they convene a half-dozen allies to figure out a recovery plan.

The Democrats ended up losing fifty-four seats in the House and eight in the Senate, their biggest defeat in nearly five decades and the first time they had lost control of the House since 1954. Later in the evening, Bill met with a group of West Wing advisors in the Residence to assess the results. As they walked down the ramp from the Solarium, Bill turned to the group and said, "Well, this could be liberating." "It was a classic optimistic moment," recalled one advisor. "He didn't show how upset he was." Bill retired to the Treaty Room where he stayed up until 2:00 a.m. calling Democrats who lost.

The first term of the Clinton Administration effectively ended that night, as did Bill and Hillary's presentation of themselves as virtual copresidents. They had learned through crushing defeats that they could not simply push through their ideas as they had in Arkansas, nor could they share power so overtly. While the public face of their professional relationship was to change, they remained staunch partners, joined by their enduring commitment to politics and policy.

Chapter Nine

—

THE MORNING AFTER THE ELECTORAL EARTHQUAKE, THE ATMOSPHERE in the West Wing was "eerily quiet," recalled Robert Reich. The President and First Lady were holed up in the Residence, not to be disturbed. At a 7:45 a.m. meeting in the Roosevelt Room, an aide read the list of the House Democrats who had been defeated. Each time a name was mentioned, people moaned, "He couldn't have lost." The roster included seemingly entrenched incumbents like Speaker of the House Tom Foley of Washington and Dan Glickman of Kansas. "Name after name was read, like the tolling of a bell," recalled domestic-policy advisor William Galston. "It was more than the loss of a majority. It was the collapse of a whole way of thinking."

With the exception of Bill's defeat in 1980, the Clintons had moved from success to success, but now they faced a repudiation of their activist style of leadership. Surveys on Election Day showed widespread anger at the Clinton Administration, particularly among middle-class Americans earning between $30,000 and $75,000 a year, who felt that Bill Clinton had betrayed their vote in 1992 for tax cuts and more modest government and for reforming welfare, health care, and campaign financing. Taken together, Republican congressional candidates won 54 percent of the vote.

While voters were upset about tax increases, including the 4.3 cents per gallon gasoline tax, Hillary's health-care plan was central to their dissatisfaction—even according to surveys taken by Stan Greenberg. In the second year of the Clinton presidency, Bill and Hillary spent more time speaking publicly about health care than about any other issue. Voters saw the proposal as "a return to liberal fundamentalism," wrote Bill's speechwriter Michael Waldman.

The rejection at the polls was as personal as it was political. *Newsweek* focus groups identified Bill as "weak" and as a "playboy" with "too many holdover hippie ideas." Research conducted by Dick Morris found that two thirds of voters objected to Bill's character. Those who didn't consider him immoral found him wishy-washy, largely because Hillary was too powerful. Morris discovered that voters viewed the Clinton marriage as a "zero-sum game" in which Hillary's dominance signaled Bill's weakness—quite the opposite of the "force multiplier" that Bill and Hillary's friends saw in the relationship.

The Clintons reacted to the 1994 results with a combination of bewilderment, self-pity, recrimination, anger, rationalization, and denial. Hillary once observed that she "seemed to be buffeted by every gust of wind, while Bill just sailed along." Yet the electoral results jolted both Clintons equally. "It was a kick in the solar plexus," said one of their old friends. "They couldn't take it other than personally," said Abner Mikva.

Bill decided to hold a press conference at midday in the East Room, although his staff wisely postponed its start by an hour so he could take a nap after his late night. Even so, when he was preparing in the small dining room adjacent to the Oval Office, he seemed "a little disoriented" to Robert Rubin. Facing reporters, Bill looked drained and exhausted, "pretty much in the Ancient Mariner mode, haunted and babbling," wrote Mary McGrory. While he accepted his "share of responsibility," everything else he said belied that concession. Voters "were not satisfied with the progress we have made," he said, but they "still want the same goal." When asked by ABC's Brit Hume if he believed he was "going in the right direction, but perhaps need to go farther and faster with the same agenda," Bill was momentarily stumped. He replied that voters had just not appreciated his many accomplishments. He faulted himself for failing to communicate effectively with the public, which struck analysts as disingenuous, given his rhetorical skills.

On Thursday, November 10, in a speech at Georgetown University, he repeated his theory that voters had failed to grasp reality. Even a year later, at a lunch with reporters, he bemoaned an "anxious mood, a negative mood, a frustrated mood about the government" in the electorate that had turned on Democrats, once again saying he had "inadequately filled" his responsibility for articulating his vision from the "bully pulpit." By then, he had also stripped away every factor in the electoral defeat except the Brady Act and the assault-weapons ban, which had provoked the National Rifle Association to attack him. Asked about gays in the military, he said, "I didn't take that on. That was an issue that was visited on the presidency." Such moments inspired Senator Bob Kerrey to remark, "Clinton's an unusually good liar."

A dozen years after the fact, Hillary insisted that she "didn't take it personally" when voters swept out the Democratic Congress. But on election night she had felt "deflated and disappointed," wondering "how much I was to blame for the debacle: whether we had lost the election over health care; whether I had gambled on the country's acceptance of my active role and lost." After several weeks of reflection, Hillary concluded that the Democrats lost seats because of the public's mistaken "perception" that her health-care plan was "Big Government." But a month later, in January 1995, she edged closer to candor when she spoke off the record to a group of gossip columnists and feature writers, telling them that on health care she had been "naive and dumb" and hobbled by "a lack of politically savvy advice"—comments she disavowed when they were published. By the time she wrote her memoir in 2003, she acknowledged only that people felt "disappointment" over the failure of her health-care initiative, which "kept a lot of Democrats at home and kind of inspired a lot of opposition on the other side." For her part, she "probably in some way helped to contribute to those losses," which made her feel "terrible." Whenever they could, Bill and Hillary each went out of their way to say that Bill never blamed her for the collapse of health-care reform.

Like her husband, Hillary believed their political mistakes were a matter of poor public relations rather than a referendum on Clintonism. She, too, held the public responsible for failing to understand the value of their programs. "She is really angry," said one longtime friend of the Clintons. "She's angry at the election results, angry at how she's treated in the press. That's the way it is with Hillary. It's everyone else's fault."

Bill also kept assigning blame elsewhere. Speaking with Douglas Eakeley, his friend from Oxford and Yale Law, he banged on about the Republicans' unfair campaigning. "He seemed depressed and self-indulgent," said Eakeley. At a Christmas party, Bill cornered Arkansas journalist Max Brantley and spoke incessantly about the need for a Democratic answer to conservative talk-show host Rush Limbaugh. Bill started spending less time in the Oval Office and more in the second-floor Treaty Room, talking on the phone for hours and reading speeches from the 1992 campaign to rediscover the reasons he was elected.

Bill took his dyspepsia public in late January 1995 at the Alfalfa Club dinner, a prestigious Washington gathering known for its lighthearted, bipartisan spirit. As he had done at his first White House Correspondents Association dinner in May 1993, Bill delivered a speech that flouted the tradition of humorous self-deprecation. Instead, he indulged in self-pitying sarcasm ("We deserved to lose in November. All we did was a good job") mixed with edgy insults. At one point he asked Republican senator Pete Domenici, "Do you dye your hair?" The audience of five hundred chief executives and capital movers and shakers laughed weakly but mostly responded with a "collective incredulous gape." *The Washington Post* delivered its verdict in a headline: "Instead of Cutting Loose, He Falls Flat."

HILLARY HAD INITIALLY confined her postelection thoughts to a small circle of friends and staff. At first, she confided to Dick Morris that she was "confused.... I don't know what works or what doesn't work." In one evening strategy meeting several weeks after Election Day, Hillary arrived looking "bedraggled," her mood "bitter" and "surly," recalled one of her advisors, who sensed a "noticeable shift in her relationship with her husband." She was struggling with a loss of overt power and with her concern that her advice would no longer be viewed as valuable in the West Wing.

During an emotional meeting with ten aides, all of them women, in the White House on November 29, Hillary was close to tears as she confessed her uncertainty about how to recast herself as First Lady. Her aides exhorted her to recommit herself to her job, and that evening in a forum on First Ladies at the Mayflower Hotel, she arrived in a bright blue suit with gold buttons and presented a decidedly cheerful face. She vowed to help with health-care reform in an "incremental" way. Picking up the thread from the plan she had hatched several weeks earlier to emulate Eleanor Roosevelt's public-ambassador role, Hillary pledged that she would "get out more" and be "better integrated in the community." "I, for better or for worse," she said, "have spoken out on public issues for 25 years."

That week, she embarked on a four-day media blitz, barreling back into the political fray, telling one audience, "There's nothing like a good fight for advocates to get energized," and in another speech attacking as "unbelievable and absurd" a welfare-reform proposal from Newt Gingrich that would place poor children in orphanages. But such outspokenness was already on the wane as she slowly came to grips with the need to develop a new role.

Hillary now eagerly listened to Dick Morris's reading of voter surveys. He told her she had to withdraw from policy meetings and confine herself to exercising her influence within the White House informally and invisibly. He said the public preferred to see her "not as a policy maker, but an advocate" and that she should have no special title as she had had for health care. Voters wanted at least the illusion of a traditional First Lady— "to see Hillary *in public* so they wouldn't spend their time morbidly imagining what she was doing *in private*," Morris said. His proposals tapped into Hillary's messianic urge to take up the cause of those less fortunate and cut her loose from writing legislation, working with task forces, and testifying before Congress. He recommended that she write a weekly column on noncontroversial topics, along the lines of Eleanor Roosevelt's "My Day." Hillary also decided to prepare a book about "raising children in today's world," an anodyne subject that would allow her to promote progressive policy prescriptions.

Hillary remained committed to "systemic change," but she was practical enough to embrace a more familiar First Lady focus on women and children, which took on added significance because of her years of legal work and affiliation with the Children's Defense Fund. "She was not intellectually chastened, but she was politically chastened," said one of her advisors who worked outside the White House. "She would no longer be seen as the leading character in the play. But she was not stepping back internally."

She drew inspiration for her comeback by reading *The Return of the Prodigal Son* by a Jesuit priest named Henri Nouwen. Two friends had given her the book as a gift, and she seized on the "epiphany" of its essential message—that one should practice "the discipline of gratitude." She was so pleased about her discovery that she described it at some length to writers for both *The Washington Post* and *The New Yorker*. Whatever her ups and downs, she said she was learning to dedicate time each day "to remember and be grateful for all that I have."

Hillary's methodical approach to gratitude reflected the rigor she applied to every aspect of her life. "She knows what she needs," said Betsey Wright, "and she makes sure she gets it. . . . Even her rest and recreation is purposeful. She knows that she needs to laugh, and she gets that for herself." Hillary could literally "walk into a room, clap her hands, and say, 'It's time to have some fun now,' " said one of her friends. "She sort of decides when she's ready to cut loose, and then it's back to business."

Unlike Eleanor Roosevelt, who fell periodically into prolonged dark moods, Hillary was never one to lapse into a lethargic funk. When she was a child, her mother had urged her to imagine having a carpenter's level inside her when she was under stress. "Try to keep that bubble in the center," she would say. Now Hillary's mental imagery helped maintain her equipoise—and her determination to plow ahead.

HILLARY'S REPOSITIONING AS First Lady was part of a larger strategy for both Clintons as they faced the 1996 presidential campaign. They recognized that Republicans would immediately go on the offensive, so Bill and Hillary began developing a defensive approach to governing. They had spent their first two years in the White House like boxers constantly on the attack, determined to knock out the Republicans for good, even as they absorbed one well-aimed shot after another. Now the Clintons became counterpunchers, waiting for their opponents to commit themselves. Bill and Hillary would shift right or left to dodge haymakers, then bloody their opponents with quick combinations. They would strike only at propitious moments and not try to slug it out with everybody. "We'll be defined by our fights," Bill said to Robert Reich in mid-January. "We've got to pick them carefully."

Fittingly, their coach would be Dick Morris, who understood the thinking of Republicans better than anyone. The Clintons' comeback would also be guided, to a degree unprecedented in politics, by market research. Relying on psychographic techniques devised to sell consumer products, Morris and pollsters Mark Penn and Doug Schoen would "rebrand" the

Clintons by invoking popular microissues, refining phrases for speeches, and even prescribing destinations for Bill and Hillary's vacations.

Bill had summoned Morris to work on November 9, 1994, with an early-morning postelection phone call. "We talked," Morris wrote, "for the next twenty-two months." In late November, they convened for the first time in the Treaty Room, followed soon afterward by a meeting that included Hillary. Morris found Bill to be surprisingly sullen and withdrawn from the staff that he bitterly referred to as "the children who helped me get elected." Bill agreed to meet secretly with Morris once a week—usually Wednesday evenings—in the Residence, where discussions of political strategy were allowed by law. Morris went by the code name "Charlie," and in the West Wing his identity was known only to Bill's two assistants, Nancy Hernreich and Betty Currie. The clandestine arrangement appealed to Hillary, who hated leaks, and especially to Bill, the self-confessed "secret keeper." Bill told Morris, "I like subterfuge, that's why I like you."

For nearly two years, the President and his consultant were so attuned that they could anticipate each other's thoughts. Bill would sometimes play game after game of solitaire as they talked, his hands moving "to their own rhythm as if disembodied, ceaselessly moving, moving, moving," Morris recalled. Morris frequently consulted what he called his "prayer book," a Casio personal organizer that contained his polling data. Mostly they spent their hours together dissecting research and crafting new tactics for the presidency.

On November 12, Bill confided to his longtime friend and advisor Mickey Kantor that he had enlisted Morris. During an economic summit in Indonesia, Bill spent two hours with Kantor hashing over the election results, still "distraught" and filled with recriminations. "He said he was getting the blame, and it was unfair," recalled Kantor. "He was being self-pitying. But the more he talked, the more optimistic he became." Bill explained that he had hired Morris because he needed someone "outside the milieu." "Morris is politically brilliant," Bill said. "He will help me through." Bill essentially assigned Kantor to be Morris's "control." "I want you to brief Dick," said Bill. "Tell him what is going on politically."

Otherwise, Bill kept his closest advisors in the dark as he ran what Stephanopoulos later called a "covert operation against his own White House." Stephanopoulos felt a pronounced estrangement from the President, who "didn't fully trust me or my judgment." Bill also disengaged from his Gang of Four consultants, rather than officially fire them. Mandy Grunwald went to work for Hillary; Paul Begala returned to Texas after Bill stopped calling him; and James Carville and Stan Greenberg were limited to consulting for the Democratic National Committee.

For the first month, it was only Bill, Hillary, and Morris in the weekly meetings in the upstairs Yellow Oval Room. Their initial collaboration was a twelve-minute televised speech from the Oval Office that Bill gave in mid-December, outlining a "middle-class bill of rights" conceived mainly by Morris. After conducting several polls, Morris sketched out much of the framework, and Bill dictated the text into a tape recorder. Bill consulted with Morris in Paris, where he was on vacation, and they faxed drafts back and forth. Hillary chipped in by ensuring that the proposal included tax deductions for education. In the days preceding the speech, Stephanopoulos picked up an "unfamiliar frequency" in Bill's monologues, but when he asked, "Who came up with this language on the middle-class bill of rights?" Bill pretended he didn't hear the question.

In essence, Morris recommended that Bill co-opt the most moderate Republican policies and reposition them as his own: a balanced budget, welfare reform, smaller and more efficient government, fewer regulations. That way, Bill would neutralize Republican appeal and gain the upper hand for the presidential campaign. Morris called his theory "triangulation," which meant pushing Bill back toward the center almost as a de facto third-party leader, placing him at the apex of a triangle that had conservative Republicans and liberal Democrats at the other two points. Bill was to seek to capture the 19 percent of the disaffected, moderate swing voters who had identified with Ross Perot in 1992 but had defected to the Republicans two years later.

The plan included an array of tax cuts for the middle class and subsidies for college tuition. Bill pledged to cut spending by seventy-five billion dollars to offset the tax breaks, and he vowed to preserve funding levels for the two big federal health-care plans—Medicare for the elderly and Medicaid for the poor—both of which the Republicans had targeted for budget reductions. *Time* called the speech a "dramatic course correction," and Republican party chairman Haley Barbour observed that Bill "shares with the hummingbird the amazing ability to turn 180 degrees in a wink."

Even Clinton's team at first dismissed triangulation as opportunistic and lacking substance. Stephanopoulos called it "a fancy word for betrayal," and Carville disparaged its emphasis on the "small stuff" as "stupid." But triangulation was to prove to be a cunning political tactic. "The internal doubters could see that 65 percent supported *x* policy, as opposed to what they believed," said one top official. "It would shut people up so the President could get on doing what was needed."

WHILE THE PRESIDENT worked on his master strategy with Morris, he conducted a parallel series of debates with his advisors about how to "restart" his administration. Once again, the liberal and moderate factions vied to gain advantage. Robert Reich and his like-minded allies wanted to shore up the Democratic base by going after "special interest" tax subsidies for business, which he called "corporate welfare." On the opposing side were William Galston, Bruce Reed, and others in the newly emboldened DLC wing who urged Bill to move back to the center. After two years of mostly ignoring them, "he was now in a mood to listen," said Galston.

But Bill was also governing more by indirection—a shift in his management style that Morris immediately observed. After being burned by so many talkative staff members, Bill now transmitted his instructions through hints rather than direct orders. "With his unbelievably acute powers of observation, his radar-like sensitivity to the moods and thoughts of others, he knew well how each of his key staff people would respond to any situation," Morris said. If someone made a mistake, Bill could readily distance himself, and if an initiative succeeded he could take credit. "Without clear verbal or written instructions," Morris noted, "he could not be quoted, or, if things screwed up, blamed."

Bill's intentions were consequently subject to more misinterpretation than ever. After a couple of meetings in which he seemed to "nod approvingly" at Reich's populist ideas, the Labor Secretary gave a speech attacking "corporate welfare," which angered Bob Rubin as well as Lloyd Bentsen. Several days later, Bentsen indicated in a television interview that Reich had been speaking out of school, a reversal that reinforced an impression of White House disarray.

Bill continued his obsessive quest for guidance from new sources. At the end of 1994, he and Hillary organized a motivational seminar at Camp

David with a group of "personal development" gurus—Tony Robbins, Stephen Covey, Marianne Williamson, Jean Houston, and Mary Catherine Bateson. Houston focused particularly on Hillary's role, telling her that she represented a "new story" for American women and that she should persevere in setting "a new pattern of possibility for women" and finding "the place and the role in which she could really express the fullness of what she was."

On Saturday, January 14, 1995, the Clintons and Gores attended the grandly titled Camp David Seminar on the Future of Democracy, a retreat designed for intellectual stimulation rather than spiritual sustenance. To help set the stage for the State of the Union address, Bill Galston invited a dozen scholars equally divided between liberals and New Democrats to "replicate the stresses and strains inside the Democratic party." The President was in an expansive mood, while Hillary remained cool and correct. As they settled around a conference table in Laurel Lodge at Camp David, everyone received thick briefing books to supplement the presentations. This was the realm of sociology and political science, of lectures on societal trends—an earnest counterpoint to Dick Morris's severely practical politics.

But as the proceedings grew contentious after more than three hours, Bill became "visibly uncomfortable," recalled political-science professor Benjamin Barber, a representative of the liberal wing. Bill was more intent on mollifying the rival groups than choosing a course of action from one faction or the other. "I think we can do both," said Bill in his typically conciliatory manner. Hillary was her old self as well, speaking with what Barber called "warrior forcefulness on behalf of traditional Democratic politics. . . . [She] seemed to be playing conscience to a President who sometimes was all politics." She denounced oligopolies and monopolies that sought to thwart progressive ideas. "Her hard, angry rhetoric resonated with the ancient ardor of class war," Barber observed. It was "a somewhat uninformed and vaguely sophomoric interpretation of the American economy," said a White House official who had heard her speak that way before. Her statements reflected beliefs that "she had to unlearn later," Barber wrote. Newsweek's Joe Klein had observed that Hillary "may well be the most influential of the many insiders who disdain the DLC and see Clinton's 'New Democrat' persona as a tactic rather than a strategy."

Somewhat surprisingly, Hillary also attacked working-class white south-
erners who had forsaken the Democratic party, and in an oblique way she
took on her husband as well. "Screw 'em," she said, "you don't owe them a
thing, Bill, they're doing nothing for you." Bill rose to their defense, "as if
rehearsing an old but honorable debate he had been having with his wife
for decades," Barber recalled.

"I know these boys," Bill said. "I grew up with them. Hardworking poor
white boys who feel left out." He pointed out that liberal reforms had often
"come at their expense" and that the Democrats had to "find a way to include these boys in our programs." Hillary had no rejoinder, but during
cocktails after the seminar she stood apart, "opaque and unsmiling." When
Harry Boyte, director of the University of Minnesota's Center for Democracy and Citizenship, tried to instruct her on citizenship training, she
"abruptly turned away," announcing that it was time for dinner—a low-
calorie menu designed by Oprah Winfrey that didn't keep Bill from eating
two desserts.

The "big think" seminar had no discernible impact on the State of
the Union address. In the week leading up to the speech on Tuesday, January 24, Bill was less visible than usual, as he operated on two tracks. His
speechwriters and West Wing staff worked on one draft, while he and Morris, sequestered upstairs in the Residence, hammered out the essential
message based on "the mother of all polls" that honed his Republican-
inspired themes: further paring the deficit, eliminating traditional welfare
in favor of work programs, cutting taxes, and shrinking the federal bureaucracy. They called it the "New Covenant," resurrecting a theme Bill had
used early in the 1992 campaign.

To avoid detection, Morris wrote the speech on a dusty IBM typewriter
scavenged by a White House usher. Every time Morris handed him a type-
written page, Bill adapted it in longhand on lined paper, which is what his
speechwriters were accustomed to seeing. Hillary acted as Morris's beard,
leading the staff in the West Wing to believe that she and Bill were collab-
orating on the text and needed privacy. George Stephanopoulos realized
only in retrospect that when he came upstairs to ask Bill and Hillary why
they had cut a line criticizing Republican tax cuts for the wealthy, "the edit
had come from Dick . . . hiding in the family room next door."

Bill's address ran a record one hour and twenty-one minutes, largely because he had larded the core points with an exhaustive recitation of every policy that had caught his fancy. There were also 105 interruptions for applause, 92 for him and the rest for the 13 honored guests he singled out in the gallery. Commentators dismissed the entire exercise as self-indulgent and bloated, but the public reacted favorably, and Bill's approval ratings temporarily lifted as high as 51 percent from the mid- to low forties.

At Morris's suggestion, Hillary dropped out of the weekly political-strategy meetings in January. Pollsters Doug Schoen and Mark Penn started attending soon afterward. By March, they were joined by Al Gore, Leon Panetta, and his two deputies, Erskine Bowles and Harold Ickes, whose friendship with the Clintons dated back to the antiwar movement. A son of FDR's Secretary of the Interior, Ickes was a Manhattan über-liberal, fierce in his loyalties and so profane that he could "string together grammatical sentences using nothing but obscenities." He wore ill-fitting suits, always used his tea bags twice, and rarely slept more than a few hours per night.

Ickes had been slated for the Deputy Chief of Staff position after the 1992 election but had been sidelined when allegations surfaced that his law firm represented New York unions with links to organized crime. Bill had typically delayed telling him the bad news until hours before he announced his White House staff, embarrassing his old friend even more. Ickes had decamped to New York for six months to clear his name and became Deputy Chief of Staff early in 1994, overseeing scandal management. It was widely assumed that ideologically and politically Ickes had "a direct line" to Hillary. In Morris's strategy sessions, Ickes became the consultant's chief adversary.

FOR THE FIRST SEVERAL months of 1995, Speaker of the House Newt Gingrich, not Bill Clinton, held the public imagination, as the Republican-dominated House passed one measure after another from the Contract with America. On Friday, April 7, Bill had been scheduled to address a group of newspaper editors in Dallas on the subject of education, but he changed course when he heard that Gingrich planned a televised speech that evening about Republican progress on the Contract. Bill surprised his senior staff by moving to preempt the Speaker with a point-by-point rebuttal of the Contract that he and Morris had crafted.

By then, Morris's secret role was out in the open. Bill recognized that he could no longer balance an official West Wing run by Leon Panetta with Morris's clandestine operation. "Leon put his foot down and said, 'No more parallel universe,' " recalled Mike McCurry, who had come aboard as Bill's Press Secretary in January. Hillary advised Bill that throwing Morris into the "mix of egos, attitudes and ambitions in the West Wing" would improve everyone's performance. With his staccato patter, robotic focus, and disregard for niceties, Morris alienated nearly everyone. Stephanopoulos considered him a "small sausage of a man" who looked like a "B movie mob lawyer" with a "pasty face." Reich was "struck by the economy of his fawning." Morris's compensation was also a source of envy: a $240,000 annual salary from the Clinton reelection campaign, along with luxurious accommodations in the $440 per night King Suite at the Jefferson Hotel, right down the corridor from Bob Rubin, who considered him "talented but unusual."

The weekly meetings in the Yellow Oval Room of the Residence expanded to some twenty participants; most evenings they began at 10:00 and lasted until well after midnight. "They were filibusters by Morris," said Mickey Kantor. "It was as if the rest of us were props on a stage, listening to Morris trying to convince the President to do things. It was Morris's one-ring circus." But Kantor understood Morris's value more than his colleagues did. "He is a political savant, but he is so cut off from reality in other ways, especially in how you deal with human beings," Kantor said. "Yet he was a force for stabilization. He focused the President. He could define the issues—whether you agreed or not—precisely with language that literally came out of his head." Bill could distinguish between Morris's good and bad ideas, and he was indifferent to the consultant's off-putting mannerisms. "Clinton was picking Morris's brain like he did with everyone," said Kantor. "He was drawing energy and thoughts, putting them in his own head, rolling them around, and coming up with his own approaches."

If Morris was the "dark Buddha whose belly Clinton rubbed in desperate times," the President found his consultant's sunny counterpoint during these months in Terry McAuliffe, an ebullient thirty-seven-year-old fundraiser with his own roster of winning schemes. They bonded when Harold Ickes invited McAuliffe for breakfast in Bill's Treaty Room office two days after Christmas, while Hillary and Chelsea were in New York City. A lawyer who had made a fortune in real estate, McAuliffe was looking for a new challenge as he wrapped up his term as finance chairman of the Democratic party. Ickes thought McAuliffe's relentlessly upbeat personality could offer Bill some "cheering up."

Although it was a Tuesday morning, Bill wore a golf shirt and jeans, and "he was uncomfortable," McAuliffe recalled. As they ate toast and drank coffee around a small table, McAuliffe presented an audacious money-raising plan to show "that Bill Clinton is viable and alive." McAuliffe's theory was simple: "You raise the most, you deserve to win." He offered to gather an unprecedented thirty-seven million dollars in six months for the Clinton-Gore reelection campaign. By building a large war chest a year and a half before the election, Bill could make it extremely difficult for any Democratic challengers to find their own sources of cash. "It was the first positive news he'd had," said McAuliffe.

Bill had been fund-raising his entire political life, starting in 1974 when he developed an extensive card file for donations from Oxford, Yale, and Georgetown friends. Twenty years later, he had picked up the phone in the Residence to solicit two million dollars for the congressional elections from forty well-heeled contributors. Investment banker Richard Jenrette took his call on October 18, and while Bill didn't specify an amount, he got the message across. Jenrette responded with a check for fifty thousand dollars, which his "Wall Street math" calculated as the amount Bill needed from each donor. Now McAuliffe wanted Bill to spend more quality time, including nights and weekends, with his wealthy supporters. "We need to give 'em the magic," he said. "To get 'em to feel good about the reelection."

Nine days later, McAuliffe sent Bill a memo detailing ways to reward existing five- and six-figure benefactors and "energize" new ones with promises of meals, rounds of golf, coffees, morning jogs, and overnights in the Residence. "Get other names at $100,000 or more, $50,000 or more," Bill scrawled on the back of the memo. "Ready to start overnights right away." This was not just the "hard" money for the reelection campaign with its limits of one thousand dollars per donor but unregulated "soft" money for the DNC to use in media campaigns and other avenues of attack.

Until then, no President had used the White House itself as a money machine. In four years, George and Barbara Bush had hosted only 273 guests for the night, few of them financial contributors. In the first term of the Clinton Administration, that number rocketed to 938 guests, many of whom stayed in the Lincoln Bedroom. The Clinton campaign maintained that no requests were actually made while their guests were in the White House. But fully one third of the Clinton overnighters made donations either before or after their visits, for a total of ten million dollars. Of all the people attending various Clinton "donor-maintenance" gatherings at the White House, 92 percent contributed a total of $26.4 million to the Democratic National Committee in 1995 and 1996. The DNC kept detailed accounts that included "projected" amounts for each event, along with the sums raised. Videotapes released to investigators in 1997 showed an eager donor actually proffering a check.

The most questionable activities were the "coffees" held in the Map Room on the ground floor of the Residence. The first few were intended as perks for established donors, but they soon became assembly-line meet and greets for virtually anyone with a fat bank account. On April 27, 1995, White House Legal Counsel Abner Mikva distributed a memo specifying that "campaign activities of any kind are prohibited in or from government buildings. This means fundraising events may not be held in the White House; also no fundraising phone calls or mail may emanate from the White House." But by then it was too late. Six coffees had already taken place in the Residence, with another scheduled for the following day. Over the next eighteen months, there were ninety-six more. Mikva had no idea such activities were under way. If he had known, "I sure as hell would have been upset about it," he later said. "And we would have put a stop to it. Any Philadelphia lawyer knows you don't raise money in a government building. And if they were budgeting money for them, they are raising money."

The 1996 fund-raising excesses prompted the same kinds of questions about ethics, conflicts of interest, and possible illegality that had dogged the Clintons in Arkansas. Although most of the malfeasance was swept under the rug during the campaign, it created significant problems in Bill's second term, and eventually nearly three million dollars in dubious contributions had to be returned following investigations by Congress and the FBI. Among the shadowy figures that climbed aboard the Democratic money bandwagon were foreigners whose contributions to the party violated federal law. During one videotaped fund-raiser, Bill blithely thanked "those who have come from other countries to be with us tonight."

The ubiquity of foreign money, especially from Chinese sources, strongly suggested attempts to buy influence. By the end of the second Clinton term in 2001, these abuses resulted in the convictions of twenty-one people for making illegal contributions. As early as 1994, a particularly energetic Chinese-American fund-raiser named Johnny Chung came to the White House for the first of forty-nine visits, half of them authorized by Hillary's office. On March 9, 1995, he arrived at the Old Executive Office Building and handed a fifty-thousand-dollar check to Hillary's chief of staff, Maggie Williams, who passed it on to the DNC. Two days later, Chung and six Chinese businessmen watched Bill deliver his eight-minute Saturday-morning radio address in the Oval Office. The price tag was roughly seven thousand dollars per head—what *Time* later called an "unusually explicit swap of money for access." Chung also had meetings with Hillary and dined with Chinese guests in the White House Mess. Not only were the Democrats eventually forced to return the $366,000 Chung raised unlawfully from foreign sources, Chung himself was to plead guilty to fraud after admitting that one hundred thousand dollars had come from the Chinese military.

The billionaire Riady family, long-standing friends of the Clintons from Arkansas and Indonesia, raised equally troubling issues of illegality, closing the circle between past and present with their commercial links to the Chinese government, their special pleadings on behalf of Asian leaders and business interests, and their payments to Webb Hubbell after he was charged with embezzlement. After contributing more than $500,000 to Bill's first campaign and $100,000 to his inauguration, Mochtar Riady met with Bill twice in the Oval Office, and his son James visited the White House at least twenty times in four years. Those visits included three private discussions with the President, several of them concerning American policy toward China and Indonesia. James Riady used funds from Lippo's overseas ventures for campaign contributions, which resulted in his guilty plea in 2001 to fraud and violations of U.S. election laws. He would also pay a fine of $8.6 million, a record amount.

Riady's accomplice in these felonies was John Huang, who had befriended the Clintons when he worked for the Riadys in Little Rock and then operated the Lippo Bank in Los Angeles. A White House memo noted that Huang had "deep Arkansas connections" and was "well known to the President." Bill named him a deputy in the Commerce Department late in 1993, and Huang moved to the DNC in late 1995 on Bill's recommendation, following an Oval Office meeting. In all, Huang visited the White House seventy-eight times in his capacity as a fund-raiser and influence peddler on behalf of Lippo and its interests in Indonesia, China, and Vietnam. Of the $3.4 million he gathered for the 1996 campaign, the Democratic party was compelled to return more than half, which had come from foreign contributors, including $450,000 from an Indonesian couple linked to the Riadys. Huang was also convicted of breaking campaign-finance laws.

The Riady family's significant financial support of Webb Hubbell was not disclosed until after the 1996 elections, but it was known within the White House. Like the Clintons, Hubbell had been close to the Riadys for more than a decade. He had been the lawyer for James Riady when he ran Little Rock's Worthen Bank, which Lippo had owned in partnership with the Stephens family for several years in the mid-eighties. Shortly after a Lippo subsidiary paid Hubbell his retainer in June 1994, Bruce Lindsey, Bill's friend and counselor, was informed. It also turned out that just two days before the payment, James Riady had met privately with Bill at the White House.

Hubbell was still on the Lippo payroll when he agreed on December 6, 1994, to plead guilty to mail-fraud and tax-evasion charges filed by Ken Starr. Only a week and a half earlier, on Thanksgiving Day, Bill and Hillary had spoken to Hubbell for the last time, when his indictment appeared imminent. "You've got to fight this," Hillary said. "You've got to get tough." Now their close friend faced a twenty-one-month prison sentence, and the Independent Counsel was pressing for his cooperation in the investigation of Hillary's role in Madison Guaranty. But along with the press and public, Starr was in the dark about the nearly seven-hundred-thousand-dollar cushion given to Hubbell by the Riadys and other Clinton allies.

Aside from the coverage of Hubbell's conviction and sentencing, the Whitewater investigations had mostly disappeared from the headlines as the Clintons sought to regain their footing after the 1994 election. But they were shaken at the end of January 1995 by the publication of *First in His Class*, an acclaimed biography of Bill by *Washington Post* reporter David Maraniss. Among its revelations was Betsey Wright's assertion that state troopers had indeed helped solicit women for Bill and that in 1987 she had dissuaded him from running for President by presenting him with a list of his purported lovers. In an interview on C-SPAN with Brian Lamb in mid-February, Bill claimed not to have read the book, although when Kenneth Starr later did an inventory of books in the Presidential Study as part of his Lewinsky investigation, he listed an "advance uncorrected proof" of *First in His Class* "with BC's notes."

Shortly after the book appeared, Dick Morris found Bill "in obvious rage" about it. Hillary was "furious," Bill told the consultant, who could see the "personal difficulties the story was causing him." Since Wright was a close and trusted friend, Hillary could not simply dismiss her statements as the work of their enemies. The White House pressured Wright to deny the account, and she issued a statement that she had been "misinterpreted," but Maraniss readily countered that he had cleared all her quotes in advance. Bill's denials "are becoming increasingly implausible," wrote Jonathan Alter in *Newsweek*.

Morris took note that Bill "never spoke of his chagrin that he had done things to bring pain to Hillary, he just railed against his misfortune at its coming out. Nowhere was there any contrition for the adultery—just a furious rage that the world was making trouble for him in his marriage." Hillary was angry enough to kick Bill out of their White House bedroom and stop speaking to him for a few weeks.

Hillary had reacted that way before in Arkansas. During periods of estrangement, she and Bill had slept in separate rooms in the governor's mansion. Bill always managed to win her back—not necessarily easily. "He has been so sweet to her," said Mary Mel French, "partly because he has been a bad boy." Bill's "need to be loved, and to be forgiven, has something to do with Hillary and the difficulties of being loved by her and forgiven by her," said one old friend.

BY THE TIME THE Clintons flew to Canada for an official visit at the end of February, they had made peace once again. Hillary had already embarked on a full public schedule of traditional First Lady duties to soften her image. She had dined with *Washington Post* food critic Phyllis Richman to share her views on White House menus and Bill's more nutritious diet. (Bill later told a TV interviewer that his favorite foods still included burritos and deep-dish pizza.) Speaking at the dedication of Eleanor Roosevelt College in San Diego on January 26, Hillary had urged students to "find ways to work together" rather than "fall prey to those who wish to divide." At Morris's suggestion, she had begun a series of "listening sessions" on breast-cancer awareness in January. While unveiling a $358,000 redesign of the Blue Room and East Room in the Residence on February 17, she gently deflected questions about her position by saying, "The stories come and go, and I stay the same." There were occasional flashes of the old confrontational Hillary in an interview she gave to CNN, when she denounced the Republicans for promoting tax breaks for "very rich people," but she hastened to add that she wanted to focus on "human issues," which was right out of Dick Morris's playbook.

For the Gridiron Club dinner in mid-March, Hillary spent three hours taping a five-minute spoof called "Hillary Gump." The idea came from comedian Jay Leno, who collaborated with fellow comedian Al Franken and exiled Clinton consultant Paul Begala. After the forced humor of the previous year's "Harry and Louise" routine, Hillary struck a more self-deprecating note, wearing an assortment of wigs and likening the White House to "a box of chocolates, pretty on the outside and full of nuts inside." But her husband captured the best moment in the video when he sat next to her on a park bench, and she offered him a chocolate. He selected one, gave it to her, and took the box for himself. "Cupid is as Cupid does," she said. The sketch received a standing ovation.

Hillary's most important initiative that spring was a schedule of foreign travel that helped her craft a new identity and gather international support. After a brief trip to Denmark to attend a United Nations conference on social development, she set out on Friday, March 24, 1995, for a twelve-day tour of India, Pakistan, Nepal, Bangladesh, and Sri Lanka. Hillary had originally been invited by Pakistan's Harvard- and Oxford-educated prime minister, Benazir Bhutto ("the only celebrity I had ever stood behind a rope line to see," Hillary later wrote), and Liz Moynihan had arranged much of the itinerary in India. Hillary was accompanied by Chelsea, Jan

Piercy—a classmate of Hillary from Wellesley who was the U.S. Executive Director of the World Bank—and a mostly female entourage of more than thirty aides who called the trip "The Hillaryland Tour."

At one stop after another, Hillary stressed that women and children were not "soft issues." In New Delhi, she quoted from a poem about the repression of women, saying with evident feeling, "when a woman fights for power . . . it is questioned. . . . There must be power, if we are to be heard." But she avoided any talk of such issues as nuclear proliferation and terrorism, which had caused strains in the U.S. relationship with Pakistan. Expecting more substance, the Indian press criticized her "anemic persona." Still, Hillary was invigorated as women from all walks of life listened to her message with rapt attention bordering on adoration.

When Hillary spoke to reporters while relaxing in the back of the plane in a sweatshirt and her formidably thick glasses, it was strictly off the record. In that more informal setting, she warmed up to her customary adversaries and conversed more freely than usual, touching on the need for eastern and western religions to develop a "spiritual" response to "rampant materialism and consumerism" and asking journalists to size up Newt Gingrich for her.

Hillary was fascinated by Benazir Bhutto's arranged marriage. "They bantered easily together, and seemed genuinely smitten with each other," Hillary observed after watching Benazir and her husband, Zardari, in Islamabad. Only later did it emerge that Zardari had used his position as First Spouse to enrich himself, leading to his wife's removal from power and his conviction and imprisonment for corruption.

In Nepal, Hillary met seventy-five-year-old Sir Edmund Hillary—the First Lady's alleged namesake—for the first time. Even though Dorothy Rodham had told *The Washington Post* two years earlier that she had given her daughter a "family name" because it was "unusual," Hillary insisted that she was named after the famous explorer because her mother had read an article about him. It was an odd fabrication, since Sir Edmund was still a beekeeper in New Zealand when Hillary was born in 1947 and achieved renown only after he began exploring in 1951 and climbed Mount Everest in 1953. When Hillary recounted the tale to Sir Edmund, he somewhat wistfully replied, "When people used to hear the name Hillary, they always thought of me. Now they think of a woman's name."

Back home, Hillary stayed relentlessly "on message" in her speeches and appearances. She promoted mammograms for older women, and she shared folksy chatter on *The Oprah Winfrey Show*. Wearing a new "honey-blond flip cut," Hillary told Winfrey's audience how much she missed shopping at the grocery store, which led a *Washington Post* reporter to wonder "where the other Hillary Clinton had gone—the policy maven and hard-hitting political adviser."

She was in fact thriving but operating behind the scenes. She rarely visited her West Wing office, preferring to work out of the Residence. On some matters she intervened directly—for example, when she lobbied Laura Tyson to put Ira Magaziner on the National Economic Council so he could "rehabilitate himself." He had been "in limbo" since the collapse of health care, shunned by West Wing staff for his "imperious" ways. ("They ought to make Ira Magaziner the ambassador to Kazakhstan," cracked Stanford University economist Alain Enthoven, a leading expert in health-care issues.) Tyson complied with Hillary's request, and Magaziner found his niche studying applications for the Internet, where web-pages were beginning to spread, along with the use of e-mail.

On other issues, Hillary operated through proxies. Her childhood friend Kevin O'Keefe worked in the White House Counsel's office and consulted with her when he was vetting nominees for U.S. attorney and the federal bench. Each Thursday morning, representatives from the Justice Department and the White House met to discuss the status of nominations. Hillary's deputy chief of staff, Melanne Verveer, represented Hillary's point of view and reported to her on progress. Bruce Lindsey was the President's stand-in, drawing on his encyclopedic memory for encounters that Bill had had with various nominees and any potential political pitfalls in their backgrounds. "If he didn't know the specifics, he would know something was there and would need to be checked before we did anything," recalled Eleanor Acheson, Hillary's Wellesley classmate who served as the Assistant Attorney General overseeing judicial nominations.

Verveer similarly supervised the Legal Services Corporation on Hillary's behalf, as both Clintons fought to prevent the Republican Congress from gutting the federal program that offered legal assistance to indigent clients. Hillary had served on the Legal Services board for two years in the eighties, and she knew that it was a lightning rod for right-wing criticism. Faced with the possibility of severe cuts, Hillary's office convened meetings to galvanize support for the program. "Hillary was the point person, and Melanne was very much an integral part," recalled Douglas Eakeley, who was chairman of the corporation. Although funding was reduced in 1995, the lobbying by Hillary and her staff created bipartisan backing that averted a second round of reductions the following year.

While Hillary removed herself from political meetings in January, Bill "just switched to asking her advice in private," recalled Morris, who sent her a written "agenda" before each weekly session in the Yellow Oval Room. After reading all the polling data and recommendations in the agenda, she reviewed strategy and tactics with Bill. "I know they talked at length," said Morris, "because she showed intimate familiarity with every bit of [the agenda]." At the end of May, she began meeting every other week with Morris, who kept her abreast of the strategy sessions and answered her questions. "I felt she was as much my client as her husband was," he recalled. "I needed to get instructions from her as well as from him." If Hillary wanted to make a point to Bill's West Wing staff, she would raise it one-on-one with her loyal friend Harold Ickes or his deputy, Doug Sosnik.

She kept a hand in fund-raising as well. She was present, along with Bill, Gore, Ickes, and other West Wing advisors, for Terry McAuliffe's mid-February description of his ten-page master plan for 1996, and she drilled him with questions about direct-mail literature, lists of names, and costs of postage and printing. She was instrumental in setting the timing and location of the early fund-raisers in the McAuliffe blitz. The first, which raised $1.2 million in thousand-dollar contributions, was in New Jersey—a direct warning to former senator Bill Bradley, a potential challenger to Bill.

In keeping with her more conventional role, Hillary zeroed in on the book she planned to write about child-rearing. She recruited Jean Houston and Mary Catherine Bateson—two participants in the Camp David self-help seminar—for a brainstorming session in the Residence after her return from South Asia in early April. At Houston's urging, Hillary conducted an imaginary conversation with Eleanor Roosevelt, a habit she had revealed from time to time in speeches over the previous two years. But instead of just venting about press coverage to her unseen spiritual mentor, this time Hillary tried to "dig deeper" in an hourlong session of "reflective meditation." With her eyes shut, Hillary directly addressed the former First Lady, as if in a séance. Hillary spoke of how she identified with Eleanor and how she wished to be remembered by history. Bateson talked to Hillary about the importance of symbolism for a First Lady and persuaded her that she could "advance the Clinton agenda through symbolic action."

Soon afterward, Hillary hired a collaborator, Barbara Feinman, to help her write *It Takes a Village: And Other Lessons Children Teach Us*. (The title was an adaptation of an African proverb.) Feinman was expected to write the book based on a series of interviews with Hillary, who would then edit the manuscript by a Labor Day deadline. It was a tight schedule that allowed Hillary to continue with her other duties as First Lady. The publication of the book, timed to coincide with the start of the 1996 campaign, would be Hillary's way to "re-emerge domestically."

BILL WAS STILL STRUGGLING to gain the upper hand over Newt Gingrich, who continued to take up most of the political oxygen. In a prime-time press conference on Tuesday, April 18, Bill was reduced to insisting that "the Constitution gives me relevance, the power of our ideas gives me relevance. . . . The President is relevant here." "He seemed pathetic, a goner," wrote Joe Klein.

A grim deus ex machina the next morning instantly elevated Bill's stature as a leader when a truck bomb blew up the Alfred P. Murrah Federal Building in Oklahoma City, killing 168 people, including nineteen children in a day-care center. Many people initially concluded that the bombing was the work of foreign terrorists, but authorities swiftly arrested Timothy McVeigh, an American military veteran with a deep hatred for the federal government. The White House announced that Bill would join the Reverend Billy Graham for a prayer service at the Oklahoma City Fairgrounds on Sunday the twenty-third.

That Saturday, Bill and Hillary were scheduled to submit to their first round of questioning under oath by Kenneth Starr. They prepared for the sessions by studying what Hillary later termed "trivialities and minutiae" in documents organized in large black binders. In the morning, the Clintons made a ten-minute televised appearance in the Oval Office with two dozen children of federal workers. "It's okay to be frightened by something as bad as this," Bill said. Hillary reassured them that America had "more good people than bad" and urged them to talk about their fears with their parents or other adults.

Before Bill sat down with Starr at noon, he offered him the same courtesy he had given Fiske the previous June by showing him the Treaty Room—pointing out a painting of Abraham Lincoln and the table where Lincoln's cabinet met. The deposition "couldn't have been more pleasant," recalled White House Counsel Abner Mikva. As they wrapped up after two hours, Bill asked Mikva to give Starr a tour of the Lincoln Bedroom. Overhearing her husband, Hillary whispered, "Don't you dare." Mikva obeyed her, not the President, who was heading out the door. "She was irritated," Mikva recalled. "I didn't think she was particularly angry, but irritated."

While the First Lady underwent her two hours of questioning, the President played a round of golf—a somewhat surprising activity on the eve of what he had designated a "national day of mourning." "It was his only way of relaxing," Mikva explained. "Everyone felt it was important to get him out on the golf course." The press mentioned Bill's golf only in passing.

The next day, Bill performed splendidly as "the nation's Preacher-in-Chief." He spoke of the need to "purge ourselves of the dark forces which gave rise to this evil. . . . When there is talk of hatred, let us stand up and talk against it. . . . As Saint Paul admonished us, let us not be overcome by evil but overcome evil with good." In an interview that evening on *60 Minutes*, Bill called for Congress to pass antiterrorism legislation that would "strengthen the hand of the FBI . . . in cracking terrorist networks, both domestic and foreign."

The United States had been hit for the first time by Islamist terrorists on February 26, 1993, only thirty-eight days after Bill had taken office. Six people had been killed and more than one thousand injured when a truck bomb exploded in the parking garage of the World Trade Center in New York. Only later did authorities learn that the bombers had intended to level both of the twin towers. Bill's reaction at the time had been muted, as his administration viewed the incident as a law-enforcement matter rather than as an act of war. By the spring of 1995, four Arab Islamist conspirators had been convicted, and the FBI had linked the attack to the al-Qaeda terror network led by Saudi millionaire Osama bin Laden. Still, when Mike Wallace noted in the *60 Minutes* interview that "it cost the World Trade

Center bomber . . . $3,000, $4,000 for all of what was involved" and asked what the Clinton Administration proposed to do about "terror on the cheap," Bill mentioned only that he would "try to get the legal support we need to move against terrorism."

The Oklahoma City tragedy thrust the President back to center stage, and he moved quickly to turn the situation to his political advantage. At the weekly strategy meeting on Thursday, April 27, Morris's agenda was titled "Aftermath of Oklahoma City Bombing," with "Permanent possible gain: sets up Extremist Issue vs. Republicans" listed as a priority. In the months to come, Bill extolled federal bureaucrats as "our friends and our neighbors and our relatives" even as he criticized Republicans for their "demeaning rhetoric about the nature of government and the nature of public service." Without making any explicit connection, Bill shrewdly implied that Newt Gingrich represented the sort of angry white males whose hatred led to the murders in Oklahoma City. By humanizing federal workers and undermining his Republican opposition, Bill laid the groundwork for a government shutdown in the autumn of 1995 that was to give the Democrats a significant edge in the 1996 election long before the campaign even began.

Chapter Ten

—

THE MOOD AROUND THE WEST WING IN 1995 WAS VASTLY DIFFERENT from what it had been in the first two years of the Clinton Administration, when Hillary strode resolutely through the corridors, interrupted meetings, and dressed down staff in front of her husband. With Hillary taking a lower profile, Al Gore reached the height of his effectiveness in the third year of the Clinton presidency.

Gore had proved his mettle many times over—prodding Bill on deficit reduction, saving NAFTA in his debate with Perot, educating Bill on the environment, downsizing twelve of thirteen cabinet-level departments with REGO ("Gore sideways," he would say of his "reinventing government" initiative), and opening a useful back channel to Boris Yeltsin's prime minister, Viktor Chernomyrdin, during delicate Russian-American negotiations. At the end of 1994, after Yeltsin blew up during a meeting in Budapest and threatened Bill with a "cold peace," Gore had gone to Moscow to repair the damage. Gore had also taken his lumps, most notably the defeat of the politically unpalatable BTU tax, which would have promoted conservation and alternative-energy sources by hiking fuel taxes as much as fifty cents per gallon. Now Gore had become the "closer" as well as the backbone for key decisions in domestic and foreign policy that were to reshape the Clinton presidency.

As soon as Bill brought Gore into the loop with Morris early in the year, the consultant recognized an important new ally. Gore had some apprehensions about Morris's character but appreciated the way he energized Bill. Morris also solidified his position with Gore by hiring Bob Squier, the Vice President's media consultant, to produce TV commercials for the re-election campaign.

After watching the President and Vice President navigate one crisis after another, Bill's advisors had a greater appreciation for Gore's value. "The two men need one another, and sense it," Robert Reich wrote in February 1995. "Above all, Gore is *patient*, where B wants it all now. Gore is content to wait for the right time. . . . He knows that B doesn't make firm decisions unless pressed."

Gore's self-mocking Gridiron Club skit in 1994 had neutralized the criticism of him as rigid and even awkward in public. In meetings, he could be spiky and pedantic, but he also applied what he called his "edgy" humor to good effect, notably when Bill did his "prebriefs," the mock question-and-answer reviews before meeting with reporters. In theory, these sessions were intended to find the right answers to anticipated inquiries, but the real purpose, recalled Mike McCurry, was "to drain the anger out of Clinton." Bill was often on a hair trigger, and his advisors counted on Gore to defuse the volatility with a deadpan remark—managing the President emotionally, somewhat like a controlled burn. When Bill faced a particularly provocative question, Gore would interject a vicious but funny version of what Bill obviously had on the tip of his tongue. "In a kind of disingenuous but joking way, Gore would become a foil," said one of Bill's senior advisors.

But Gore's most important job was pushing Bill toward decisions. "Once Gore has processed and made a decision, he is more of a risk taker than people think," said a senior West Wing official. "He can be bold. In meetings, Bill would ask him, and Gore would put his marker down. It worked very well, and Gore was always respectful." The President "believed Al Gore was not playing games, that he was saying what he thought," said Bill Galston. "If you were Bill Clinton, it was natural to be suspicious that the people around you had their own games—that advice was offered with one eye cocked to his interest and the other to their own. You never had that sense about Al Gore." Bill had the intellectual confidence to keep probing if necessary, but Gore could cut off debate if Bill was letting his advisors make their arguments for the second or third time.

WHEN THE REPUBLICANS announced in February 1995 that they would bring the deficit to zero in seven years, Morris's polls showed that 80 percent of the public supported the idea. He began leaning on the President to make a counterproposal, but Bill resisted. Siding with his liberal advisors, he argued that a fully balanced budget would require too many painful cuts in social programs. But by May, Bill's economic advisors said that a balanced budget with a longer time horizon could be feasible without the sort of draconian cuts proposed by the Republicans.

"We have to have a position that will be seen as reasonable," Gore argued as Bill continued to balk, in part because he was reluctant to adopt a cornerstone of the Contract with America. Bill also figured if he acquiesced, he could embolden the GOP to cut further into programs he wanted to protect. The publicly unseen factor was Hillary's opposition to balancing the budget. Rubin also remained "anti-zero deficit" until the economists "did their homework" and showed him "what a balanced budget would look like." Before Bill agreed to propose a plan of his own, "two forces had to be brought along, Rubin and Hillary," said one senior West Wing advisor.

With the White House divided in private, the President vacillated in public. During a phone interview with New Hampshire Public Radio on May 19, Bill indicated for the first time that a balanced budget could be achieved in ten years or less. "We can get there by a date certain," he said, driving George Stephanopoulos and other liberals in the West Wing "off the wall." Four days later, Bill appeared in the Rose Garden to denounce the Republican seven-year plan and emphasize the need to safeguard social programs, but he did not directly repudiate what he had said on the radio.

When the economic team and West Wing advisors met on Tuesday, May 30, Hillary was "an important new voice at the table." It was her first appearance at such a meeting since the defeat of health care. Like Rubin, she advocated taking more time to ensure that the budget experts could make an ironclad case for an administration proposal, and she emphasized the need for an effective public-relations strategy—one of her familiar themes. Morris went to work on Hillary privately. "While she worried about the risks of alienating the Democratic left," Morris recalled, she also understood the need to engage the Republicans equally in the debate. "I think we've got to do this," she eventually said. "We've got to be on the map, to take a position." In the end, Hillary was persuaded "by certain political necessities," said one of Bill's senior advisors. "She agreed to go along, but she wanted to make sure what the language was for the President's speech."

Once Rubin satisfied himself that they could present a balanced budget with "credible numbers," Bill talked with him about the political necessities. "He had a view," Rubin recalled, "that if we were going to coalesce public opinion, fiscal discipline was too abstract. The balanced budget was something people could understand, and he was right." As when he accepted deficit reduction early in 1993, the President now saw the balanced budget as a "threshold issue." He recognized that in order to advance his own progressive programs, he had to first demonstrate that he was serious about fiscal discipline. "Swing voters *care*" about the balanced budget, Bill told Robert Reich.

Bill, Hillary, Gore, and at least a half-dozen advisors worked on a five-minute speech to be televised live in prime time by the ABC, CBS, NBC, and Fox networks on Tuesday, June 13. "Make sure your speech gives something to the Democrats," Hillary admonished. She also requested that Bill refer to Gingrich as "the Speaker" rather than mention him by name. Morris tested virtually every line in his polling, but Bill continued to fiddle with wording even as Bob Squier was adjusting the lighting in the Oval Office.

In his brief address, Bill announced that he had decided to balance the budget in ten years because "the pain we'd inflict on our elderly, our students, and our economy" in the GOP seven-year plan "just isn't worth it." He promised to cut taxes on the middle class rather than the rich, and he drew sharp distinctions between his way and the Republican way, particularly on Medicare-costs savings, which both plans included. He insisted that the Republicans wanted to raise health-care premiums for the elderly, while he planned to cut Medicare costs by reducing payments to doctors and hospitals.

With Bill's embrace of a balanced budget, "the Republicans could have declared victory," said Robert Rubin. The GOP majority had dictated the outline of the administration's budget plan, and Democratic leaders in the House and Senate were furious, as were liberals in the White House and cabinet. Stephanopoulos bemoaned that "everything we Democrats cared about seemed to be imperiled." Reich bitterly noted that Bill had "thrown in the towel" and "lost the real war. . . . All that remains is a polit-ical game over who appears to have won."

Rather than take yes for an answer, the Republicans misread Bill's ac-ceptance as weakness and continued to press for their own timetable and their own terms. The Republicans could no longer claim the balanced budget as their issue, while the Democrats now had the credibility to cast themselves as moderates who wanted to save important social programs from what *Time* called the "granny-bashing extremists" in the GOP. Still, in the first months after his speech, Bill wanted to strike a deal rather than fight, and Morris was encouraging him to find a compromise with the Re-publicans.

Gore's "strong partisan streak" was pushing Bill in the other direction. As Morris observed, "Clinton is anxious to please the person at the other end of the table. Gore understands it's an adversary." Gore had been ready for a confrontation since April, when he predicted to Reich that the Re-publicans could "close down the government" if Bill didn't "cooperate on the budget." Mindful that Bill didn't like "drawing sharp lines," Gore said, "We're gonna have to fight eventually. When we do, we have to be in the strongest position possible."

THE OTHER ISSUE PREOCCUPYING the Clinton Administration during much of 1995 was the escalating conflict in Bosnia, and Gore and Hillary played visible and invisible roles in its resolution. For two years, Bill had pushed the issue to the sidelines as Serbs continued slaughtering Muslims in eastern Bosnia, while Croats battled Serbs in the western areas of the country with behind-the-scenes help from the United States. Bill had been "the constant kibitzer," denouncing atrocities and making idle threats, "try-ing to influence Balkan policy without making a real commitment" as he "strutted, retreated, and flexed atrophying muscles," Joe Klein wrote.

In May 1995, the Serbs began heavily shelling Sarajevo and inflicting numerous civilian casualties on the city's Muslim population. Bill agreed to NATO air strikes on Bosnian positions late that month—another in a series of what former Clinton foreign-policy advisor Michael Mandelbaum called "token bombings." To some extent, the United States was hamstrung, because the Europeans had consistently blocked more extensive air attacks for fear of harming their own NATO troops in the UN peacekeeping force there. This time, the Serbs retaliated by widening their shelling to cover more Muslim areas and by taking hundreds of UN peacekeepers hostage. UN rules dictated that the peacekeepers could not use weapons to defend themselves, and the NATO powers were "increasingly humiliated," said newly elected French president Jacques Chirac. The UN troops would need to be strengthened, or they might well leave in disarray.

Both Al Gore and Tony Lake had been hawks on Bosnia from the start, urging Bill to use airpower to force the Serbs to the negotiating table—although there was no support either in the administration or Congress for sending American troops to the war zone. Bill's advisors found him unwilling to advocate a more forceful approach to the Bosnian problem, and several of them tried to use Hillary to focus his attention and toughen his attitude. The most active was Richard Holbrooke, a shrewd and abrasive foreign-policy expert who had joined the State Department in July 1994 as Assistant Secretary of State for European Affairs. His relationships with Secretary of State Warren Christopher and National Security Advisor Tony Lake had frayed by the spring of 1995, when Holbrooke assumed the Bosnian portfolio and began secretly meeting with Hillary.

Two years earlier, Hillary had been dovish on Bosnia. Worried about getting into another Vietnam-style quagmire, she had helped persuade Bill to back away from the "lift and strike" plan to remove the ban on weapons to Muslim fighters while launching air strikes against Serbian military targets. Now the atmosphere had changed. Republicans as well as Democrats in the Senate were poised to pass a measure allowing the Bosnian Muslims to obtain weapons to fight the Serbs more effectively, and Bill's continued inaction threatened to harm him politically.

After several conversations with Holbrooke, Hillary became "an advocate for the use of force in Bosnia," said one of Bill's top advisors. By the end of June, Holbrooke told Hillary bluntly that Bill needed to show "engagement, not procrastinating and ducking and waiting for something better to happen." He added that Bill "was stockpiling adversity, and that it would hit him in the fall and winter before the primaries." It was also apparent, said an administration official, that Holbrooke "had been critical of Lake."

Hillary by then considered Holbrooke a valuable foreign-policy operative who was not being used effectively by her husband. She believed that Bill was sliding away from involvement in foreign policy, especially in Bosnia. She told another of her husband's advisors that Bill had to shoulder too much as spokesman for the administration. It was "unfair," she said, "to leave him out there as the only one pulling chestnuts out of the fire." Reverting to her copresident role, she asked for "a detailed plan for a foreign policy public relations campaign—communications offense and defense, not based on level of rank but communication skills." She specified that Secretary of Defense William Perry, CIA Director John Deutch, UN Ambassador Madeleine Albright, and Holbrooke all be tapped as surrogates to speak for Bill on foreign policy. Conspicuous by their omission were Christopher and Lake, neither of whom was dynamic on television.

As the pressure for action intensified on the President, his advisors made a discovery in mid-June that forced his hand. They learned that at the end of 1994, the Clinton Administration had promised its NATO allies that if the UN peacekeepers were compelled to flee Bosnia, the United States would provide troops to ensure their safe departure. This commitment to intervene had been made without anyone in the administration, from Bill Clinton on down, realizing its implications. It was a decision "few could even remember making," wrote Warren Bass of the Council on Foreign Relations. "The choice . . . was made by inertia." Despite the risk of American casualties, Bill could not backtrack on the pledge without ruining U.S. credibility with NATO.

Now with the likelihood of a Senate resolution lifting the weapons embargo, Bill faced an unpleasant scenario. Once the Muslims were free to arm themselves, the Russians would likely supply more powerful weapons to the Serbs, their longtime allies. The resulting battles would push out the British and French peacekeepers, and the United States would be compelled to send in troops to assist their withdrawal.

In mid-July, Bosnian Serb forces overran the Muslim enclave of Srebrenica, one of a half-dozen "safe areas" designated by the United Nations. As several hundred lightly armed UN peacekeepers from the Netherlands stood by, Serbian soldiers forcibly removed the Muslim men and boys and then slaughtered as many as eight thousand of them in a matter of days—the worst single act of genocide in Europe since World War II. Although Bill was horrified by the massacre, he had difficulty formulating a response. His advisors watched him "blow off steam" and complain about being boxed in by his European allies, who only wanted to "whine at us."

It was ultimately Gore who framed the issue for the President in an Oval Office meeting on Tuesday, July 18. After speaking at some length about the events in Bosnia, he concluded, "The worst solution would be to acquiesce to genocide. Why is this happening and we're not doing anything?" Gore's rare rebuke got everyone's attention. One way or another—either as participants in a humiliating retreat by UN peacekeepers or as enforcers of a negotiated settlement—thousands of American troops would be sent to Bosnia.

On July 26, the Senate passed its resolution to lift the arms embargo, 69 to 29—with plenty of votes to override any presidential veto. In the following weeks, Bill released Lake to "marry power to diplomacy" with a new and uncompromising strategy. Lake told the Europeans that the United States would authorize massive bombing of the Bosnian Serbs until they agreed to negotiate. Bill vetoed the arms-embargo resolution as expected, but Majority Leader Bob Dole decided to delay the Senate's override vote "to give diplomacy a chance." The administration could then present the measure as a threat rather than a fait accompli, increasing their leverage on the Europeans. At the same time, the Croats were making military gains against the Serbs in western Bosnia, and UN peacekeepers had moved away from the Serbian forces, which made the prospect of bombing more palatable to NATO.

Following a deadly and defiant mortar attack by the Serbs on a Sarajevo market at the end of August, Bill finally pressured NATO to deploy more than sixty warplanes in repeated strikes against Serbian artillery targets. Bill also designated Holbrooke as his chief mediator. The Serbs agreed to a cease-fire and an end to their blockade of Sarajevo in mid-September, and Holbrooke began several months of shuttling from Bosnia to Geneva before he convened an international peace conference in Dayton, Ohio, on November 1. Bill kept his distance from the talks, but Holbrooke continued his contacts with Hillary "to discuss an idea or ask me to convey information to Bill," she recalled. Bill's support for the Bosnia initiative "was driven not only by his horror at the suffering abroad and damage to our interests," Tony Lake later wrote, "but also by the sense that the ongoing conflict was starting to damage him at home."

Twenty-one days later, they had an agreement that partitioned Bosnia into two zones. The Serbs kept control of much of the territory they had captured, with the other half of the country to be governed by a federation of Muslims and Croats. Bill's principal contribution was bringing Boris Yeltsin to heel during a summit meeting in Hyde Park, New York, in late October. Russia had acquiesced to the NATO air strikes against Serbia, but Yeltsin was insisting that Russia be included in any peacekeeping force without being subjected to NATO command. Bill managed to persuade Yeltsin—who was drunk during much of the summit—to allow the Russian troops to carry out noncombat responsibilities in a "liaison relationship" with NATO. The agreement "provided for Russian military inclusion while sugarcoating their subordination," wrote Strobe Talbott. In so doing, the Clinton Administration was able to co-opt the Russians in a NATO venture, making it easier for Moscow to accept NATO's later expansion into eastern Europe.

The Dayton Accords left one dangerous loose end: the status of Kosovo, a Serbian province in Bosnia with a Muslim majority. But overall the treaty represented a diplomatic success. The United States committed eighteen thousand troops to enforce the peace, alongside forty thousand soldiers from twenty-five other countries. In his televised speech announcing the settlement, the President said American forces would be required for only a year, but in fact they were to stay for a decade. When the Serb, Muslim, and Croat leaders met in Paris in mid-December for the signing ceremony, Bill presided triumphantly along with Jacques Chirac, John Major, Helmut Kohl, and Viktor Chernomyrdin.

THERE WERE MOMENTS in the summer of 1995 when Bill's reactions to the Bosnian conflict—and the impact it was having on his presidency—spilled over in the most unlikely ways and in the most improbable settings. One evening, he was practicing on his new 1,500-square-foot putting green near the Oval Office when two members of his national-security staff, Sandy Berger and Nancy Soderberg, interrupted him to give a status report on the fall of Srebrenica. After listening to their "horrifying trail of death and depravity," he flew into a profanity-filled diatribe that lasted forty-five minutes even as he kept walking around the green and lining up putts. "I'm getting creamed!" he exclaimed, voicing his frustrations about the difficult options he faced and blasting Jacques Chirac for being impractical. "Soderberg felt almost as if she had fallen into Clinton's mind," Bob Woodward later wrote, "and they were witnessing the interior monologue of his anxiety."

Bill was similarly agitated when he learned that Air Force Captain Scott O'Grady had been lost in Bosnia after bailing out of his F-16. He immediately left a White House screening of Crimson Tide to call O'Grady's parents and reassure them that their son would be fine. Six days later, Tony Lake alerted Bill at 2:00 a.m. that O'Grady had been rescued. Afterward, Bill went up to the third floor where four women from Little Rock—journalist Gene Lyons's wife, Diane, and three of her friends—were spending the night. "Bill was so excited," Gene Lyons recalled. "He wanted to talk to someone about it, so he found them. They were all in their White House bathrobes, and someone took a picture of the four of them on a bed with Bill standing there scratching his head and talking. He needed to talk, and they were there."

On another evening, Bill let his preoccupation with Bosnia overwhelm one of his "donor maintenance" overnights at the White House. A wealthy couple who scarcely knew the Clintons had been invited to stay in the Lincoln Bedroom. They were met by Carolyn Huber, the Clintons' trusted aide from Arkansas who now worked as their personal assistant. On Huber's instructions, at 7:00 p.m. the guests went to the Solarium, where they were served pork chops for dinner. As they were eating, Bill arrived and sat down with them. He greeted them by name but made no personal inquiries or offers to show them around. Rather, he launched into an hour-long monologue about the parliamentary maneuvers that day on the arms-embargo resolution. "I was barely hanging on," recalled the husband. "My wife had read the papers, so at least she could follow what he was saying." Hillary was nowhere to be seen, and Bill gave no explanation of her whereabouts.

The next day, the couple wandered upstairs again for breakfast in the Solarium, where Bill joined them for bran muffins and coffee. Again, Bill took over the conversation, this time with a running commentary on the day's newspaper headlines, until one of his aides came to drag him away. The couple received special passes enabling them to go anywhere in the Residence and the West Wing and on the White House grounds. They swam in the White House pool and ran on the track alongside the driveway of the South Lawn. Later, they finally saw Hillary. She said she had been out of town and apologized for being "a terrible hostess." "She could have been there if she wanted," said the husband. "She clearly thought, 'It's not my thing.'" Yet despite the Clintons' nonchalance and Bill's self-absorption, the couple soon afterward contributed more than one hundred thousand dollars in soft money to the Democratic National Committee. "We did what he hoped we would do," said the husband. "We were flattered and dazzled."

If Hillary had been present for dinner and breakfast, it's unlikely the conversation would have been much different. "Even unplugged," said one of Hillary's confidantes during the White House years, "politics and policy were pretty much what they talked about." During get-togethers with old friends that summer, Bill and Hillary seemed little changed—in Bill's compulsion to dominate, Hillary's outspokenness, and their strongly congruent view of the world. In mid-July, the Clintons had a farewell dinner at Kinkead's restaurant for Robert Reich's wife, Clare, who was moving back to Boston for her work. The two couples, who had known each other for nearly three decades, began the evening chatting about books and films but quickly fell into the usual topics as Bill railed about "the latest Republican outrage." Despite his anger at Bill over capitulating on the balanced budget, Reich decided that the President's heart was "still in the right place."

Reich was even more gladdened by Hillary's passionate condemnation of corporate-executive compensation—one of the Labor Secretary's favorite populist topics. "These are *real* issues, Bill," she said, pointing out that the average CEO of a big company "is now earning 200 times the average hourly wage. Twenty years ago the ratio was about *forty* times. . . . People all over this country are really *upset* about this." When Bill demurred, saying he couldn't be "out front" on such issues, Hillary said sharply, "Well, *somebody* in the administration ought to be making these arguments," turning to Reich. "I agree," replied Bill with a nod.

Some weeks later, in a Solarium dinner with a group of friends, Bill and Hillary were both "holding forth," one of the guests later noted. Bill was particularly expansive "on the politics of reelection and the politics of persecution. On the first, we were blown away by his command of facts and his ability to improvise a steady flow of conversation with no expectation of response, all the while keeping eye contact to make sure we were paying attention." Hillary offered an analysis of Republican gains in the South because of the GOP's emphasis on values and cultural issues. "Americans think they don't know any gays," she said, "even if the choirmaster in their church goes to San Francisco for vacation. They don't think anything of it."

Hillary said she had been reading *The Haldeman Diaries*, an inside account of the Nixon Administration by H. R. Haldeman, the former Chief of Staff and central figure in the Watergate scandal, and she was struck that Nixon "played against government to stir up fear of government, even as he was President." Throughout the dinner, Bill and Hillary "made constant references to Richard Nixon as the archetypical Republican." They both considered California governor Pete Wilson to be the Republican party's "most formidable candidate" for President in 1996. Bob Dole was only "superficially formidable," Bill said. Bill also took off after the "power structure and the corruption of the press," especially *The New York Times* and *The Washington Post*, which were investigating the Clintons but "never the Whitewater prosecutor, who was wasting public money." Both Clintons "had a thing against Len Downie," editor of the *Post*, and Hillary "was taking it personally that wives were subject to criticism." As they left the dinner, one woman remarked about Bill: "I can't say that many things about any subject on earth including my own life and my own family," and her husband observed that he felt as if he had been "in the mist under the Niagara Falls of verbiage."

THE CLINTONS WERE questioned under oath by Kenneth Starr a second time for more than five hours on Saturday, July 22. Less than a month later, Starr indicted the McDougals along with Bill's successor as governor, Jim Guy Tucker, on twenty-one felony counts involving fraudulent loans from David Hale to benefit Madison Guaranty. Although Starr indicated that neither Bill nor Hillary was accused of criminal wrongdoing, among the charges was Hale's allegation that Bill twice pressured him to make a phony $300,000 loan to Susan McDougal—who then diverted as much as $50,000 into the joint Whitewater account with the Clintons.

On Capitol Hill, Republican senator Al D'Amato was presiding over Senate Whitewater Committee hearings, which forced the White House to release more than one hundred pages of Vince Foster's files on the Clintons' taxes—including his "can of worms" quote about Whitewater. Also among the newly disclosed documents was Hillary's letter to James McDougal in 1981 proclaiming the Whitewater development a "Mecca" made possible by Reaganomics.

D'Amato's witnesses included Webb Hubbell—only weeks away from entering a federal prison in Maryland—who mumbled and evaded questions; Justice Department official Philip Heymann, who complained that White House staff members had prevented him from overseeing a search of Foster's office two years earlier; and Bernie Nussbaum, who argued that he had properly dealt with Foster's documents. Both Susan Thomases and Maggie Williams had what *The New York Times* called "astounding memory lapses" about Foster's files. Challenged by D'Amato, Thomases blamed the effects of multiple sclerosis. Williams won sympathy as she fought back tears while recalling Foster's death.

The spectacle moved Joe Klein to write a column called "The Body Count." While he denounced D'Amato's "scavenger hunt through a sewer" as an "amorphous parascandal," he held the Clintons accountable for allowing Williams to spend $140,000 in legal fees so she could "walk the plank." Bill and Hillary were "the Tom and Daisy Buchanan of the Baby Boom political elite," leaving behind "too many lives and reputations . . . ruined by carelessness." Klein particularly took Hillary to task for making "the routine seem sinister" and failing to "come clean." Hillary was so shaken by the attack that she wept when she called White House lawyer Jane Sherburne. "That's not who I am," she insisted. "I take care of people."

Among the remaining subpoenas for documents by Whitewater investigators was one for Hillary's billing records from the Rose law firm. In the previous eighteen months, David Kendall and Carolyn Huber had conducted numerous searches for subpoenaed papers, since Huber was responsible for organizing and indexing Bill and Hillary's personal records.

Back in Little Rock, she had been the office manager for the Rose law firm for a dozen years. "She knew the format of Rose billing records in her sleep," Jane Sherburne later told author Gail Sheehy.

Yet in early August 1995, when a 116-page computer printout—roughly five or six inches thick—of Hillary's billing records turned up on a table in the Book Room, a storage area on the third floor of the Residence, Huber was inexplicably incurious. In later sworn testimony, she said she didn't grasp the significance of the papers, although she acknowledged that she recognized them as law-firm records. "They were folded," she said. "I didn't open 'em." If she had, she would have immediately spotted Vince Foster's precise handwriting in red ink on the documents. Nor did she admit to knowing how the printout had surfaced in the room next to an office used by Hillary. The Book Room was the location of the "locked closet," where Hillary had directed Huber to place private documents retrieved from Foster's office after his death.

In the days before the sudden appearance of the printout, a report issued by the Resolution Trust Corporation had disclosed that Hillary was one of eleven Rose lawyers who had worked on Castle Grande, a real-estate development in the mid-eighties conceived of by James McDougal and Seth Ward, Webb Hubbell's father-in-law. Castle Grande had become notorious in Arkansas for its "sham transactions" that had funneled cash into Madison Guaranty—and had led to fraud charges against McDougal. The failure of Castle Grande had also contributed to the collapse of the bank. What had not yet been revealed either to investigators or the public was that among the sixty hours of legal work Hillary did for Madison Guaranty, about half involved Ward and the Castle Grande project over a period of four months.

Hillary was not charged with criminal wrongdoing in that enterprise, but in August 1995 she faced the prospect of damage to her reputation by the disclosure of the extent of her association with such an unsavory venture. It later emerged that shortly after the RTC report came out, Seth Ward's lawyer, Alston Jennings, visited Hillary and David Kendall at the White House. Jennings said they didn't discuss Ward, but neither Hillary nor her lawyer offered an explanation of what they did discuss. Among the many unanswered questions was whether Hillary had been examining the billing records to refresh her memory before meeting with Jennings. For her part, Hillary frequently said that she didn't know how the billing records got to the Book Room table.

Huber later testified that she gathered the computer printouts and "plumped them down" in a box filled with knickknacks and memorabilia. To clear out some space for Hillary's researcher on her book project, Huber arranged to have several boxes, including the one with the billing records, moved down to her own office on the second floor of the East Wing. Huber explained that she then shoved them under a table, to be cataloged later. It took five more months for her to rediscover—again, seemingly by accident—and identify the billing records before their release to investigators and the public. Hillary considered Huber's actions an "oversight . . . an innocent and understandable mistake." To Republican investigators, and more than a few members of the press, such inattention from an experienced and efficient administrator strained credulity.

PAULA JONES HAD FADED from public view in the third year of the Clinton presidency, but her lawsuit had put the press on alert about Bill's sexual proclivities. Reporters periodically called Robert Bennett to ask about rumors, and the lawyer could always dismiss them. But he and other advisors reminded Bill that he needed to behave when he was around attractive women. "I'm retired," Bill told Bennett. But Bill also revealed his internal tensions when he said, "This is a prison. I purposefully have no drapes on the windows." Years later, as the Monica Lewinsky story was breaking, Bill told Dick Morris that since becoming President, "I've tried to shut myself down. I've tried to shut my body down, sexually, I mean. . . . But sometimes I slipped up."

The Kathleen Willey incident was not made public until August 1997, and other women on the staff were keeping their own encounters with Bill's overfamiliarity to themselves. But Bill's roving eye had raised enough suspicions to create problems for his staff. Back in April 1993, the success of Bill's first summit with Boris Yeltsin in Vancouver had been overshadowed when Bill heard that Sharon Stone, Richard Dreyfuss, Richard Gere, and Cindy Crawford were filming a movie and ill-advisedly joined them for drinks in a hotel suite. The presence of Stone caused particular concern. "It was not a good idea," recalled Dee Dee Myers. "President Bush wouldn't have a single, Hollywood actress to his room late at night, even with others present. This was not what he ought to be doing." Only weeks afterward, Stone was scheduled to attend a Clinton fund-raiser in New York. Sensing danger, one of Hillary's close friends called her to suggest an intervention. "Hillary didn't feel she should," said her friend. "She asked me to do it." "Do not have Sharon Stone sit next to the President at dinner," the friend told Bill's senior staff. They designated another woman for the seat, but Bill arranged to have Stone take her place. The image of the President chatting with the uninhibited actress "raised eyebrows," reported Maureen Dowd in *The New York Times*.

Part of the difficulty in controlling Bill's impulses came from his relationship with his staff. For all his efforts—largely at Hillary's behest—to appoint women throughout the administration, Bill's inner circle was exclusively male—the "White Boys" derided by the women of Hillaryland. Madeleine Albright, for example, "had to claw her way in," said Mary Mel French. Bill "had enormous respect for Madeleine and Donna [Shalala]," said a State Department official. "But the problem for all the women was to be taken seriously by Bill the way Hillary was. Maybe there could only be one such woman in his life."

One consequence of the heavily male presence around Bill was a boys' club atmosphere in which Bill and his aides would size up the physical attributes of women who came to the White House. After meeting with Pamela Harriman, the international femme fatale who became Bill's Ambassador to France, he observed, "Seventy-five years old, and she has really nice legs." "We were one step above locker-room talk," said a top West Wing official.

Those attitudes created a problem in April 1995 when Turkish prime minister Tansu Çiller came to the White House. "The Prime Minister was a huge flirt," recalled Laura Tyson, "the sort who would hang onto a man's every word." But as the background briefing began before the formal meeting, Bill said to his advisors, "Clearly if she asks for something, we are going to have to give it to her," as his advisors laughed and chimed in their own versions of how they would "give it to her." Tyson later complained to Robert Rubin about the inappropriate remarks. "Men are very childish left to their own devices," said the wife of one of Bill's advisors.

Whether intentionally or not, some of Bill's aides came to emulate his behavior, from his confident swagger to his tendency, as one advisor described it, "to undress women with his eyes." Dee Dee Myers likened Bill and Bruce Lindsey to "schoolboys" when they were in the presence of particularly beautiful women such as Patricia Duff, the wife of Hollywood producer Michael Medavoy. After Duff and Medavoy spent the night in the Lincoln Bedroom early in the Clinton Administration, she created a minor incident when she suggestively referred to Bill as "one full-service President." She denied any impropriety, but speculation persisted about a possible affair.

Counteracting the enablers on Bill's staff were a few "disenablers" who made it their business to keep pretty women away. Stephen Goodin, Bill's personal assistant, scanned crowds for women trying to get into photographs with his boss and gently steered him in other directions. Leon Panetta was vigilant about Barbra Streisand, who in the first year of the presidency had spent the night in the Lincoln Bedroom while Hillary was in Arkansas at her dying father's bedside. There was talk at the time of a major row between Hillary and Bill, who had an unexplained scratch on his face the morning after Hillary returned home. When Panetta later got wind of a proposed meeting between Bill and Streisand, he removed it from the schedule.

One old friend of the Clintons believed that Bill could have benefited from having one or two attractive and trustworthy female counselors to "manage" him. "There were women who had known Bill for a long time and had no interest in him romantically," said the friend, "and they could distract him, flatter him, engage him in ways that he needed but not have an improper relationship." Evelyn Lieberman, who left Hillaryland in 1994 to work on Bill's staff, did not fulfill this role but rather functioned as "the enforcer" of West Wing decorum. "She would send interns home if their skirts were too short," said Mike McCurry, for whom she worked as Deputy Press Secretary for Operations. "She sent me home to get a haircut." Lieberman, who had been a close ally of Hillary since Children's Defense Fund days, "dealt with Bill Clinton as if he were her son," said a member of the National Security Council staff. "He bickered at her, and she bickered back."

It was not until January 1996 that Lieberman secured regular access to the Oval Office as the first female Deputy Chief of Staff. The appointment was intended to mollify the women who complained that Bill was "flanked only by men in TV shots of him striding to his helicopter." But she also served as Hillary's no-nonsense representative among the White Boys. "Evelyn's role was to watch and protect," said Donna Shalala.

TWENTY-ONE-YEAR-OLD Monica Samille Lewinsky arrived at the White House on July 10, 1995, to begin an unpaid internship. "There goes trouble—or there goes something special," the official who interviewed Lewinsky for her job said to himself. With her full red lips, thick black hair, tight clothes, and saucy manner, there was nothing subtle about Monica Lewinsky. She had recently graduated with a degree in psychology from Lewis and Clark College in the Birkenstock-and-granola environs of Portland, Oregon, but she had grown up in Beverly Hills, surrounded by money and prominent people. Her job had been arranged by Walter Kaye, a family friend who had donated $468,000 to the Democratic party since the 1992 campaign.

At first, Lewinsky couldn't understand why "girls my own age" thought Bill was "cute, that he was sexy." She considered him just "an old guy." But she was intrigued by the gossip among junior staffers who made "knowing remarks about certain women in the White House who may or may not have been among his many alleged mistresses." Lewinsky had been in the White House for slightly more than two weeks when she watched the President in a South Lawn ceremony and decided that he "had a glow about him that was magnetic . . . a sexual energy."

On Wednesday, August 9, Lewinsky and Bill had their first rope-line encounter. He gave the buxom intern the "full Bill Clinton" once-over. "We shared an intense but brief sexual exchange," she recalled. The next day, the White House staff threw a surprise forty-ninth birthday party for Bill with a Wild West theme on the South Lawn. Leon Panetta and Harold Ickes rode in on horseback, and Jimmy Buffett sang for the crowd. "Happy birthday, Mr. President," Lewinsky said as Bill shook her hand and again gazed at her intently. His arm "casually but unnecessarily" brushed against her chest. When he glanced back at her, she flashed her pink pass, indicating that she was an intern. She blew him a kiss, and "he threw back his head in laughter."

That evening, Lewinsky read Gennifer Flowers's new memoir, *Passion and Betrayal*, which inflamed her imagination. Even if much could be discounted, the book contained salient details about Bill's seduction technique: the "sexy stare" that "everyone noticed, but he didn't seem to care." Flowers described their sexual encounters ("His stamina amazed me") and his fondness for phone sex. "Bill loved to talk dirty and to have me say sexy things back to him," Flowers wrote. "It was fun . . . because he got so excited."

The book's most vivid passage described an evening when Bill and Flowers began to make love, but "he suddenly jumped out of bed and backed up against the wall, shaking and crying." He refused to say what was bothering him, so she waited until he stopped crying and said that "everything was okay." Flowers decided that "maybe he finally had experienced some feelings of guilt . . . and was overwhelmed by those feelings. Maybe he had made an effort to be faithful to Hillary, just couldn't do it and was distraught by his weakness." She wrote that she was heartbroken "to think he was so torn up inside and unable to talk about it." Yet moments later he was "ready and eager for oral sex."

Henry Cisneros, who had his own travails with an extramarital affair, considered the story to be "poignant." "It conveyed the immense pent-up frustration, his desire to want to succeed—yet the internal demons," said Cisneros. "What would make a guy in that instant do that? Because he can't have his life whole, and he had to go to someone for that kind of attention. If you are a student of human flaws, imperfections, humanity, he is a complicated person." If nothing else, Flowers's book, including her insights into Bill's vulnerabilities, offered a road map for an infatuated young White House intern.

ON TUESDAY, AUGUST 15, Bill stopped to chat with a group of young staff members, including Lewinsky, who introduced herself for the first time. After he posed with them for a picture, he headed off with Hillary and Chelsea in Marine One, the dark-blue presidential helicopter, for a seventeen-day summer vacation in Jackson Hole, Wyoming. With the 1996 election approaching, Dick Morris and his pollsters had advised against the elitist precincts of Martha's Vineyard. They picked Wyoming because "swing voters liked outdoorsy vacations," although Jackson Hole was hardly a plebeian getaway.

By the time Bill touched down in Wyoming, "I was as tired as I've ever been in my life," he recalled. "I just wanted to lay around my family, or fool around on the golf course, or go climb mountains." He managed to play ninety-one holes in his first four days with imported friends such as Erskine Bowles, Vernon Jordan, and scratch golfer Bob Armstrong as his partners, and said he shot in the "mid-80s" in two rounds.

As in the Vineyard, the Clintons enjoyed their holiday free of charge — this time at a ranch owned by Senator Jay Rockefeller of West Virginia and his wife, Sharon. The First Family was entertained by the local elite, including Harrison Ford and World Bank president James Wolfensohn, who gave Bill a birthday party. At the end of the evening, adults and teenagers joined to sing "Puff the Magic Dragon" and "Don't Stop Thinking about Tomorrow," the anthem of the 1992 campaign.

Bill went horseback riding with Chelsea as well as whitewater rafting — despite press-office apprehension about the inevitable snide comments by reporters. Hillary joined them for an overnight expedition that required twenty-five Secret Service agents in night goggles guarding their campsite. But for the most part, the First Lady remained cloistered with her ghostwriter, working on the manuscript of *It Takes a Village*. Hillary was devoting time as well to "Talking It Over," her syndicated column carried in more than one hundred newspapers, which she wrote with speechwriter Alison Muscatine. Sometimes Hillary prepared a draft to be honed by Muscatine; otherwise, the aide assembled 750 words from Hillary's recent speeches. Hillary's voice was "a combination of political calculation, message discipline and statistics," wrote Lloyd Grove in *The Washington Post*. While Eleanor Roosevelt's long-running column, "My Day," had been "artless and ambling, like a letter to a friend," Hillary's weekly effort was "polished and organized, like a speech." To Maureen Dowd of *The New York Times*, Hillary's "bright copy about being a helpmeet" was a charade. "One of the smartest, strongest, most complicated women in Washington history is retreating behind a white-glove femininity," wrote Dowd.

After her successful solo trip to South Asia, Hillary had continued to dutifully accompany Bill overseas — to the G-7 meeting in Halifax and on visits to Russia and Ukraine. While Hillary was never "kept under a bushel when she was with him," said William Miller, U.S. Ambassador to Ukraine, she now preferred traveling on her own to build on her new role as an international ambassador for the rights of women and children. "I'm so totally engaged when I'm abroad," she told author Kati Marton. "It's twenty-four hours of just total immersion. And I think that in itself is very relaxing. . . . You can just give it a hundred per cent." Donna Shalala observed that international travel offered "another dimension" for Hillary. "She had never spent much time abroad, so Madeleine coached her."

In 1994, Hillary had been invited to lead the American delegation to the United Nations Fourth World Conference on Women in Beijing in September 1995. But on June 19, Chinese authorities had arrested prominent dissident Harry Wu and charged him with spying for the United States. The White House and State Department decided that Hillary could not attend the conference in an official capacity as long as Wu was imprisoned. Finally, in late August, the Chinese government tried and convicted Wu before expelling him from the country, opening the way for Hillary to attend the conference.

Hillary immediately shifted her attention to her keynote address, scheduled for September 5. "Bill and Hillary worked on the speech together," said one of Hillary's aides. "He considered her his best judge, and she considered him her best judge. They were always doing that. He liked what she was going to say, and no one else had seen it." The collaboration was another example of their "mutual dependency," the aide said.

En route to China, Hillary stopped in Hawaii with Bill for a ceremony marking the fiftieth anniversary of the end of World War II. She worked until dawn, revising her speech and putting the finishing touches on her book before sending it to the publisher. Foreign-policy experts made further additions to her address, and after the sixth draft Hillary was satisfied.

She spoke without regard to diplomatic niceties, arguing that "it is no longer acceptable to discuss women's rights as separate from human rights. . . . It is a violation of human rights when babies are denied food, or drowned, or suffocated, or their spines broken, simply because they are born girls, or when women and girls are sold into slavery or prostitution for human greed." There was no doubt that her condemnation of such practices included behavior in her host country. Her words were "the most stinging human-rights rebuke ever by a prominent American speaking for [her] government on Chinese soil," wrote *Time*.

The applause from the vast crowd of women filling the Plenary Hall lasted more than twenty minutes, and afterward delegates clamored just to touch Hillary. "The people there were stunned," said Donna Shalala, who served as a delegate to the conference. "There was no caution in that speech. I don't think Hillary expected that reaction. It got her deeply interested in international policies, and she saw an opportunity for impact." Hillary also discovered that she "loved the feeling of the crowd" and was thrilled when a *New York Times* editorial applauded her "finest moment in public life."

On her return to Washington, neither Hillary nor her publisher was satisfied with the manuscript of *It Takes a Village*. Faced with a final deadline at the end of November for publication in January, Hillary focused on adding what one reviewer was to call "long excursions into policy-wonkdom," which doubled the book's length. She enlisted the services of her own village—Maggie Williams, Alison Muscatine, and Simon & Schuster editor Rebecca Saletan, who moved into the White House for a period of time, as well as Jean Houston and Mary Catherine Bateson, each of whom stayed over for nearly a week to help with the writing. Hillary also had to keep up with the demands of her day job, such as traveling to four Latin American countries in five days during October. But for much of the autumn of 1995, she closeted herself, often until midnight, in her office on the third floor of the Residence, surrounded by manuscript pages produced with her helpers.

AS THE BUDGET BATTLE unfolded between the President and the Republicans on Capitol Hill, it now appeared that Newt Gingrich, Bob Dole, and their GOP forces were determined to carry out their "train wreck" strategy, insisting on their version of a balanced budget and threatening to shut down the government if Bill refused to sign it into law. Gingrich considered himself Bill Clinton's political and intellectual peer—and they were equally cocky and glib. The previous June, they had relished sparring over policy in a New Hampshire town meeting, trying to outdo each other with historical citations and geopolitical theories. They had even shaken hands on Gingrich's proposal for a bipartisan commission on campaign-finance and lobbying reform. "In a heartbeat I accept," Bill had said, but the commission never materialized. Bill considered "the good Newt" to be "engaging, intelligent," and often "in agreement in the way we viewed the world. I thought he was a worthy adversary, and I thought I would defeat him."

Throughout their budget negotiations, Gingrich consistently misinterpreted signals from Bill, thinking they were in agreement. Against his better judgment, Gingrich fell prey to the President's charms, later admitting that Bill knew how to "melt" him. To some extent, Gingrich and Dole were also the victims of what Stephanopoulos called an "inadvertently ingenious disinformation campaign" through secret messages transmitted by Morris to his erstwhile Republican client, Mississippi senator Trent Lott. Even as Bill was taking a "hard public line," Morris continued to reassure the GOP leaders that Bill would eventually accept their terms for a balanced budget.

Whenever Bill gave signs of wanting to compromise, his advisors rushed to stiffen his spine. "Al Gore was very important in saying this is where we have to stop, this is what we have to do," recalled Laura Tyson. "Several times in the process leading to the shutdown Gore was saying we have to stand firm." Bill was also bolstered by the success of a "stealth" media campaign devised by Morris against the Republican position on Medicare, the crucial sticking point. The TV commercials were an effective tactic by Morris "to define Newt Gingrich before he did," recalled Mike McCurry.

The Republican position on health care for the elderly was an honest attempt to control the costs of a major entitlement program by reducing its rate of growth from around 10 percent a year to 7 percent. Although the GOP was not technically advocating cuts, Bill's media team produced thirty-second commercials depicting the Republicans as hell-bent on slashing Medicare, if not eliminating it entirely. The ads, financed with some $15 million from the more than $40 million gathered by Terry McAuliffe's aggressive fund-raising drive, ran on cable television in "secondary markets" away from New York, Washington, and Los Angeles, so they would not be noticed by the national press. All told, the commercials were shown over a period of four months to voters in half the country.

"Medicare's a winner," Morris exclaimed in late September when Bill's approval ratings moved up to the low fifties. By then, Bill had become so involved in the "air war" that he was editing scripts for the commercials and poaching lines for his speeches. The Republicans made themselves even more vulnerable to attack by advocating a significant cut in the capital-gains tax. The administration could charge that this reduction would mainly help the wealthy and would be financed by the sacrifices imposed on the elderly through the Medicare proposals.

In an ironic twist, the Democrats were using the same sort of scare tactics that had been aimed at them a year earlier with the "Harry and Louise" commercials on health care. "It is amazing we were on the air unchallenged in so many markets where we had an impact on debate and on shifting public opinion of Republicans," recalled Mike McCurry. "The press didn't pick it up, and the Republicans didn't respond." When the time came to assign blame for the government shutdown, the administration's media campaign helped make the Democrats look strong and reliable and the Republicans reckless and insensitive.

Bill nearly sabotaged his administration's own message during a fundraiser in Houston in mid-October while Hillary was in Paraguay. Departing from the text of his speech, he told a group of wealthy donors that "probably there are people in this room still mad at me because you think I raised your taxes too much. It might surprise you to know I think I raised them too much, too." He claimed that Republicans had forced him to hike taxes when they wouldn't support his deficit-reduction plan—when in fact he had described tax increases in February 1993 as "necessary to pay for increased spending" well before any discussions with Republicans about deficit reduction. And he blamed liberal Democrats for insisting on higher taxes in exchange for their votes on the budget. Democrats angrily accused Bill of betrayal, and Republican National Committee chairman Haley Barbour described Bill's account as "a preposterous fairy tale." Bill hurriedly backtracked, claiming he had been misunderstood. But several days before the Houston event, he had told members of the Business Roundtable in Williamsburg, Virginia, that he had to "raise your taxes more and cut spending less than I wanted to, which made a lot of you furious."

As the budget negotiations proceeded, Bill "checked in often" to "ask what I thought," Hillary recalled. She made certain that an advisor from Hillaryland had a seat at the negotiating table alongside Bill's staff. Hillary was "the most powerful liberal in the White House," Stephanopoulos wrote. "The combative side . . . that had hampered the health care effort . . . was exactly what we needed in the budget showdown of 1995." Putting aside their past differences, she began calling Stephanopoulos several times per week, at one point confiding to him that in public she had "learned to smile and take it. I go out there and say, 'Please please kick me again, insult me some more.' You have to be much craftier behind the scenes, but just smile." Stephanopoulos couldn't help observing that like Bill she had become "the master of the public smile that masks private rage."

Bill put aside his budget worries on Saturday, November 4, after Israeli prime minister Yitzhak Rabin was assassinated by a right-wing extremist. When he heard the news from Tony Lake, Bill wept openly. The two leaders had formed a close bond, and Rabin had been at the White House only weeks earlier. According to Hillary, Bill regarded the Israeli leader as a "father figure." The following day, the President and First Lady flew to Jerusalem for the funeral on Monday, accompanied by an entourage that included Dole and Gingrich. Fearful that the Republicans might catch Bill at a weak moment, his aides kept the Republican leaders away from him on the return flight. Gingrich later petulantly told reporters that he had felt snubbed and had decided to push Bill even harder on a budget deal as a result.

The Republicans remained convinced that if Bill's veto of the seven-year budget forced a government shutdown, the American people would hold him responsible. As the deadline approached, the negotiations took a bitter turn that once again conflated the personal and political of the Clinton partnership. Late in the evening on Monday, November 13, when Bill and his advisers were meeting in the Cabinet Room with the Republican team led by Dole, Gingrich, and Dick Armey, the House Majority Leader, Armey accused Bill of "demagoguery" in trying to frighten his grandmother. Two years earlier, Armey had clashed publicly with Hillary during the health-reform debate and had called her a "Marxist" in one of his speeches. Proving himself as capable of keeping grudges as his wife, Bill had not forgiven the Republican leader for the insult. He stood up, stabbed his finger at Armey, and said, "I don't care what you said about me. But I have never said anything disparaging about your wife or any other family member." Armey stifled the urge to retort, "My wife has never tried to take over one-seventh of the economy." No one said a word, and the meeting ended with the President determined to call the Republicans' bluff.

As expected, Bill vetoed the seven-year budget plan that the House passed 237 to 189, and the Senate ratified 52 to 47. On November 14, eight hundred thousand federal workers were temporarily laid off, and all but the most essential government services were suspended. Instead of a staff of 430 people, the White House was operating with a skeleton crew of ninety. Ordinarily, Hillary might have been expected to wander over to the West Wing to offer her husband moral support if not assistance when he was so shorthanded. But on those crucial days, she was nowhere to be seen. Down to the wire on her book deadline, Hillary had immersed herself in "madly drafting and redrafting chapters in longhand"—uncharacteristically working late at night, only to begin again at 6:00 a.m.

SHORTLY BEFORE THE SHUTDOWN, Monica Lewinsky had been offered a full-time job in the White House Office of Legislative Affairs at a salary of twenty-five thousand dollars per year. But since she was still an unpaid intern, she was called in on the fourteenth to answer phones and run errands for Leon Panetta. She and Bill made eye contact on Wednesday the fifteenth outside the Chief of Staff's office, which Bill visited four or five times that day. Later in the afternoon, the President attended a birthday party for Panetta's assistant, Jennifer Palmieri, where Lewinsky caught him "smiling and looking" her way. When Bill returned to Panetta's office shortly afterward, Lewinsky made a fateful and provocative gesture, flipping up the back of her jacket to expose the straps of her thong underwear above the waistline of her slacks. Bill responded with "an appreciative look."

At 8:00 p.m., Bill was alone in George Stephanopoulos's tiny office next to the Oval Office when Lewinsky passed by. "You know I have a really big crush on you," she told him. The forty-nine-year-old President invited the twenty-one-year-old intern to his private study, and they made their way to the windowless hallway adjacent to the Oval Office, where he asked if he could kiss her. After their brief interlude, she wrote down her name and phone number before returning to her desk. Holding her pink intern pass, Bill said, "This could be a problem."

Two hours later, Bill found Lewinsky by herself in Panetta's office and asked her to join him in the Stephanopoulos cubicle. This time, he took her to his private study, where he had turned off the lights to avoid being seen through the windows he had kept uncurtained for self-protection. As they embraced, she partially undressed so he could fondle her. While Bill took a phone call from a congressman, Lewinsky performed oral sex on him. Bill was unwilling to "complete," telling her he needed time before he trusted her. "And then he made a joke," Lewinsky recalled, "that he hadn't had that in a long time."

Only five weeks earlier, Hillary had coyly suggested otherwise in a column about plans for their twentieth wedding anniversary on October 11. "How can romance thrive when you live above the office with a 'round-the-clock staff?" she had written. "It will be a little too cold this week to celebrate . . . with a dip in the pool. But I think I've come up with an equally romantic way to mark the day. You might be able to guess what it is. But sorry, I'm not telling." Commenting on Hillary's calculated allusion to a sexual assignation with her own husband, Lloyd Grove observed in *The Washington Post* that Eleanor Roosevelt "would never have touched such a topic."

On Friday, November 17, Bill was again in the West Wing late at night when Lewinsky delivered a vegetarian pizza to the Oval Office. He beckoned her to his private study, and as before they proceeded from petting to oral sex while he talked on the phone, this time with Sonny Callahan, a Republican congressman from Alabama. Following Bill's instructions, Lewinsky left his private quarters by way of the main corridor so she could avoid his assistants. He rejoined her in the Chief of Staff's office, where a White House photographer snapped pictures of him eating pizza with Lewinsky and other staff members.

After two sexual encounters, Bill had yet to call Lewinsky by name, referring to her only as "Kiddo," which was what John F. Kennedy had often called his paramours. Lewinsky wondered if Bill's "regular White House girlfriend" had been "furloughed" and would return after the shutdown had ended. But Bill let Lewinsky know he wished to keep seeing her, telling her that she could reach him on his private phone line and that she should visit him on weekends, when "no one else is around." Despite the demeaning and furtive circumstances of their encounters, Lewinsky was smitten and eager to continue.

THE GOVERNMENT CLOSURE ended on November 21 after the two sides struck a temporary deal that held until December 15. When the sides remained deadlocked, the government curtailed its operations again the next day, although fewer employees were affected. Bill then made a significant concession by submitting a new budget proposal that accepted the GOP's seven-year timetable in exchange for the Republicans' agreement to moderate some of their cuts in education, the environment, and health care. The opposing sides had narrowed their differences on Medicare spending, and Bill indicated he would even accept the very tax cut he had been condemning for months. "He would compromise on capital-gains tax cuts although the administration didn't believe it was good policy," recalled Laura Tyson. "But we went for it."

For a second time, the Republicans had a chance to declare victory and leave the field of battle. Instead, they chose to press their advantage on Medicaid. The GOP wanted to eliminate federal responsibility for the program by shifting funds entirely to the states through block grants. Bill was just as adamant that Washington continue its strong supervisory role in Medicaid.

As the stalemate persisted through the holidays, White House pollsters found that voters blamed the Republicans, not Bill, for the train wreck, and the House Speaker was tagged in the press as "the Gingrich Who Stole Christmas." It was Bob Dole, mindful of the approaching presidential primary campaign, who broke ranks and moved to end the impasse without achieving a balanced-budget deal. By early January, Gingrich fell into line, and the two sides agreed on stopgap legislation to keep the government operating until October 1996, when the fiscal year ended. The measure incorporated Republican spending cuts but also maintained programs important to Bill. "We made a mistake," Gingrich told Bill in front of congressional leaders and White House officials. "We thought you would cave."

But Bill had actually yielded in ways Republicans might have thought unlikely only a year earlier, and he eventually adopted both their tax reductions and their timetable for a balanced budget in negotiations after the 1996 election. "In the 1995 government shutdowns, everyone said it was a win for Bill Clinton," said Lawrence O'Donnell, chief of staff for Pat Moynihan's Senate Finance Committee. "But in fact Gingrich won the governing, and Clinton won the TV show with the shutdown." What counted for the 1996 campaign was that Bill had "completely dominated the public relations struggle" by making the GOP "look mean, petty and silly," wrote *Washington Post* economics columnist Robert Samuelson. Bill had goaded Republicans into paralyzing the federal government, only to engage in "Houdini-like feats of deception." It scarcely mattered that the game of chicken had cost taxpayers some $1.5 billion in lost services and revenue during the shutdowns.

THROUGH CUNNING AND DETERMINATION, Bill had revived his presidency by the end of 1995, only a year after hitting bottom. "When he won the budget battle, the 1996 campaign was over," said Mike McCurry. "Dole never made it to the starting line." Yet in his private actions in darkened rooms near the Oval Office, Bill had simultaneously jeopardized his marriage to Hillary and his own political career, not to mention the future of the Democratic party and the nation.

"The president was under great stress," said Laura Tyson. "It was not so much that he was distracted by Monica as he was in an extremely vulnerable state without his minders around. You have a man under stress with certain proclivities. To an extent, you can see his horrifying failures of judgment and why they happened. He was distracted on very significant things and didn't have people around basically to protect him." Still, after misbehaving during the government shutdown, Bill could easily have cut off Lewinsky without a word and quietly shipped her out of the White House.

Bill and Lewinsky stayed apart only for about a fortnight, during the Thanksgiving holidays and for a week afterward, when Bill and Hillary traveled to Europe. His visit to Northern Ireland—where Bill had promoted peace talks between the Catholic and Protestant antagonists—made him nearly giddy from the adulation of huge crowds chanting, "We want Bill!" At Belfast City Hall, Van Morrison sang "Have I Told You Lately That I Love You," which Bill dedicated to Hillary. "It was the beginning of two of the best days of my presidency," Bill later wrote.

The First Lady unveiled the White House Christmas decorations on Monday, December 4, and later that day Betty Currie invited Lewinsky to the Oval Office to receive a signed picture of Bill wearing a tie that the young woman had given him. Lewinsky was by then a full-time employee of the Office of Legislative Affairs in the East Wing, with a coveted blue pass that gave her ready access to West Wing offices. But that day, she and

Bill had time only for a Diet Coke and a few stolen kisses in his hideaway office.

Lewinsky had become a familiar enough presence to make her way freely to the pantry near the Oval Office at noon on New Year's Eve. As she was chatting with White House steward Bayani Nelvis, Bill appeared and sent Nelvis on an errand. Within moments, they had their third sexual tryst, following the same routine as before—although this time he took no phone calls during oral sex. When Lewinsky "told him her name because she was under the impression he had forgotten it," Bill reassured her that he knew full well who she was. Afterward, she saw him masturbate near the sink in the small bathroom off the interior hallway—one of the more disturbing images to emerge in Kenneth Starr's report nearly three years later.

The following three months were the most intense period of their two-year affair, with five more sexually intimate assignations as well as frequent phone conversations, sometimes late at night, when they would occasionally arouse each other as Bill and Gennifer Flowers had done. Otherwise, they spent "hours on the phone talking," Lewinsky later said. "It was emotional. . . . We were . . . interacting . . . talking about what we were thinking and feeling and doing and laughing. We were very affectionate."

"It is astonishing that Mr. Clinton would be so reckless to have his encounters just off the Oval Office," wrote historian and liberal commentator Garry Wills. But there was a practiced quality to Bill's behavior as he helped Lewinsky devise cover stories. She would carry an empty folder to feign delivering papers to him, or they would prearrange "to bump into each other in the hallway; he then would invite her to accompany him to the Oval Office." Bill advised her to avoid Nancy Hernreich, as well as his personal aide, Stephen Goodin. When Bill and Lewinsky were in the dim and narrow hallway outside his private study, he kept the door to the Oval Office ajar, and at least once Betty Currie stood just outside to tell Bill he had a phone call. "I did what people do when they do wrong things," Bill later admitted. "I tried to do it where nobody else was looking at it."

Lewinsky took her own precautions, such as entering and leaving the Oval Office through the door to the Rose Garden to avoid detection and referring to Bill as "her" when she paged Currie, who became their go-between. Lewinsky alerted Bill that when he called her from the Oval Office, her caller ID registered "POTUS," but when he phoned from the

Residence, only an asterisk showed up. At the same time, she was indiscreet enough to confide details of her sexual intimacy with Bill to two members of her family, seven friends, and two therapists, sometimes in calls from her White House office shortly after one of their encounters.

After all the salacious details were finally revealed, what most disturbed those who knew Bill best was not that he "slipped"—as he described it to Dick Morris—but that he carried on a prolonged affair with a junior employee half his age, in his office suite, knowing, as he admitted later under oath, that she was likely to talk about it. He did so, he said in a 2004 interview with Dan Rather, "just because I could." Yet the whole point was that he could not, which made his actions that much more compulsive and irrational. Bill Clinton's beau ideal, John F. Kennedy, had philandered in part because he knew that the press and the White House staff would protect him. Jack Kennedy *could* get away with it, but the circumstances were vastly different for Bill Clinton in 1995, not least because he was the target of a sexual-harassment lawsuit.

"One of the great turning points of the last fifty years was a blow job," said a longtime friend of Bill, years later. "It was the blow job that changed history. Objectively, it is where the most intimate aspects of Bill and Hillary's lives were exposed. The interaction between that and public policy and history, you can't avoid that. It is like a very very bright light you can't look at. There is no doubt that if Bill Clinton had kept his zipper up north instead of down south, Al Gore would have been elected President. That is a big deal."

Chapter Eleven

—

Bill faced an easy march to reelection in 1996, unchallenged in his own party, with a lackluster Republican opponent, an economy on the rebound, and an absence of foreign crises. Yet his fourth year in office was shadowed by his irrepressible appetites—not only an adolescent sexual lust but also a fixation on raising vast amounts of cash to lavish on a campaign that he could have won on a shoestring. At the same time, Hillary Clinton suffered the consequences of her own misguided actions in Arkansas and in her first year in the White House.

Before the end of the first week of the New Year, Hillary was rocked twice by the disclosure of documents that impugned her integrity. On Wednesday, January 3, the White House released a newly discovered memo written by West Wing aide David Watkins in the spring of 1993 that identified Hillary as the driving force behind the travel-office firings. Hillary had long maintained—both in public and under oath—that she had had nothing to do with those decisions. Now, Watkins's indelible words—that "there would be hell to pay" if her wishes were not carried out—undercut her denials. Besides the damning Watkins memo, notes from another White House aide quoted Susan Thomases saying, "Hillary wants these people fired." In a radio interview, Hillary tried to defend herself by saying that her "expression of concern" had been "taken to mean something more." But the documentary evidence led an official investigation to conclude that Hillary had indeed misrepresented her role.

On Thursday the fourth, Carolyn Huber, personal assistant to the President and First Lady, said she found Hillary's Rose law firm billing records, which had been subpoenaed two years earlier. According to Huber, while rearranging her East Wing office to accommodate some new built-in bookshelves, she decided to open up the thick computer printout she had removed from the Book Room of the Residence the previous August. When Huber recognized what it was, she alerted David Kendall, as well as Deputy White House Counsel Jane Sherburne. Just three days earlier, on Monday, January 1, *Newsweek* had published a report describing the notes taken by Thomases in the spring of 1992 indicating that Hillary had "numerous conferences" with Jim McDougal and other executives at Madison Guaranty. "Even more puzzling," *Newsweek* observed, "the Rose law firm's billing records—records that could clear up the confusion—have vanished. . . . The emerging record suggests that the Clintons' friends were worried about something." An FBI analysis found Hillary's and Vince Foster's fingerprints on the records—which were originally printed on February 12, 1992—along with those of four Rose employees, including Huber. At the very least, Hillary had handled the records during the 1992 campaign, and possibly again in the White House.

Huber's description of her serendipitous discovery and of the odyssey of the documents from the Residence to the East Wing prompted deep suspicion in the press and caught the attention of Independent Counsel Kenneth Starr. On January 19, after Huber testified before a grand jury examining possible obstruction of justice by the First Lady, Starr delivered an unprecedented subpoena to Hillary, ordering her to appear at the federal courthouse the following Friday.

Questions about Hillary's honesty overwhelmed her publicity campaign for *It Takes a Village*, which officially began the week of January 15. She claimed in her weekly column on Sunday, January 7, that she had "written a 320-page book in longhand over the last six months." Nowhere in *It Takes a Village* did she credit her many collaborators, notably Barbara Feinman, who had written the first version. Hillary had indeed spent many nights working on revisions in the two months before her December 1 deadline, but by no stretch had she devoted half of the year to writing the book. The press seized on the exaggeration, compelling Hillary's aides to show sheaves of handwritten foolscap pages as proof of her labors and forcing the First Lady to declare during an appearance in Chicago, "I actually wrote the book."

On one talk show after another, Hillary had little opportunity to discuss the book's substance, as she dodged pointed questions about Madison Guaranty and the travel office. "It is, at bottom, a partisan issue," she told the anchors on CBS This Morning. "It started with the Presidential campaign in 1992, and it will continue through the Presidential campaign of 1996." Asked on the same show if she would ever run for President, Hillary laughed and said, "Not in this lifetime!"

In an interview on National Public Radio, Hillary erroneously said that in early 1992 the Clinton campaign had handed over all its Whitewater and Madison Guaranty documents to The New York Times. Five days later, the White House retracted her statement, since Hillary and her advisors had in fact deliberately withheld most of the pertinent material, including her billing records, which Susan Thomases had knowingly claimed were missing. With the public disclosure of those records, Hillary and her lawyers continued to insist that they showed only "minimal" work for Madison Guaranty over a fifteen-month period in the mid-eighties. But the records also revealed her concentrated efforts on behalf of the bank's Castle Grande project—the land-development scheme she had denied knowing about when queried twice by federal investigators.

Now Hillary said she had worked on a real-estate venture called IDC, which was "not related to Castle Grande"—an assertion disputed by others, including Susan McDougal, who said that "IDC and Castle Grande were one and the same." What's more, a report issued in the fall of 1996 by the Federal Deposit Insurance Corporation was to say that Hillary had drafted documents used by Madison Guaranty to "deceive federal bank examiners" by facilitating phony payments in the Castle Grande deal. As the details of Hillary's involvement emerged, it became clear that if she had released all the records to The New York Times in the middle of the 1992 campaign, the revelations might well have scuttled her husband's candidacy.

During the first week in January 1996, Hillary's favorability ratings dropped from 59 percent to 47 percent in a CBS News poll, mainly because of her controversial activities. In The New York Times, conservative columnist William Safire called the First Lady a "congenital liar." Liberal columnist Joe Klein of *Newsweek* said she was more like a "congenital fudger." Both she and her husband tended to "lawyer the truth," Klein wrote. "Are they hiding something?" he wondered. "Undoubtedly." Writing in *The Washington Post*, Garry Wills tried to find clues to Hillary's character by analyzing *It Takes a Village*. While Bill's dysfunctional background helped explain his mendacity, Wills concluded that Hillary's "touchiness about the whole truth" originated with her complicity in "the philanderer's secret," a "devil's bargain" that she "made with her own and her husband's ambition" as she learned to survive in an atmosphere in which dishonesty was a given.

Bill told reporters he felt like punching William Safire, adding that "if everybody in this country had the character that my wife has, we'd be [in] a better place to live." Only two days earlier, on Sunday, January 7, Bill had called Monica Lewinsky for the first time in the New Year. He had initially reached her at home, and when he said he'd like her to "keep him company," she made her way to the White House through the city's biggest blizzard in a decade, with drifts as high as three feet. Bill phoned Lewinsky again in her East Wing office, and she walked over to the West Wing for a "chance encounter," followed by their customary sexual activity. Afterward, they talked for nearly an hour in the Oval Office as she sat in "her chair." She recalled thinking of Bill then as a "needy man who was not getting the kind of love and nurturing he desired."

Only hours after his rendezvous with Lewinsky, Bill joined Hillary in the Residence to greet fourteen scholars who had braved the blizzard to attend another "thinkers' dinner" to discuss ideas for the State of the Union address. Unlike the previous year's at Camp David, this gathering was more formal, as the participants sat around a large oval table in the ground-floor Family Dining Room and ate lobster and ticama salad, chicken with pumpkin gnocchi, and dried-pear mousse cake. "With the snow falling outside, it was a Currier and Ives evening," recalled Bill Galston, who organized the proceedings. Political scientist Benjamin Barber, a participant for the second time, noted that Bill was "perfectly attuned to everything going on in the room" as he nodded and took notes on brief lectures about creating a more "civil society."

No longer outspoken in a group setting, Hillary deferred to Bill, who gave a "masterful" summary of the presentations. When he later learned

what Bill had been doing with Lewinsky, Galston said, "Talk about compartmentalizing! He was totally engaged and as open, responsive, intuitive,
genial, and warm as could be imagined. But I am not surprised those two
things could have happened for him the same day." At 11:00 p.m., Hillary
tapped Galston on the shoulder and said, "Wrap this up." Her husband
was on a conversational roll, looking as if he could talk for hours. When
Galston shrugged at the futility of intervening, "she glowered at me, telling
me in essence to suck it up and get everyone moving." Hillary was the only
one with the power to end the evening. "She knew what she was doing,"
Galston said. "She was testing me, knowing I would fail."

Hillary remained outwardly unflappable as she prepared for her grand-
jury testimony on January 26. Privately, though, she was deeply rattled. "I
couldn't eat or sleep for a week," she recalled. "I lost ten pounds." Bill was
preoccupied with his State of the Union speech, which kept him in the
West Wing for part of the weekend following Hillary's summons. After arriving in the Oval Office at around 3:30 p.m. on Sunday the twenty-first,
he yielded to temptation after he encountered Lewinsky in a hallway. They
hadn't spoken since a midnight conversation the previous Tuesday, when
Hillary had been away on her book tour and Bill had tried phone sex with
Lewinsky for the first time.

He invited her into the hallway near his private study, where Lewinsky
asked him if their relationship was "just about sex." He told her their time
together was a "gift. . . . It's very lonely here and people don't really understand that." Lewinsky had scarcely begun to reply when he initiated their
sexual ritual, which ended abruptly after they heard someone in the Oval
Office. Lewinsky tried to leave but encountered a locked door. On returning to Nancy Hernreich's office, she saw Bill "manually stimulating" himself. Within moments, he was in the Oval Office, visiting with Jim and
Diane Blair, who were spending the weekend with the Clintons.

The leitmotif of Bill's State of the Union address two days later was a
"values agenda" carefully crafted with Dick Morris's research. Bill famously declared that "the era of big government is over," and he offered a
laundry list further refining small-scale ideas filched from the Republicans. The speech was a distillation of surveys conducted by Morris and his
pollsters, Mark Penn and Doug Schoen. After testing more than one hundred policies on a sample of 1,200 respondents, the consultants worked

with Bill's speechwriters to craft twenty paragraphs expressing "competing visions" that were subjected to additional testing.

The language of the final speech was based largely on the results. Bill's proposals included character education in the schools and a television ratings system to warn parents of depictions of sex and violence—initiatives designed to appeal to suburban "soccer moms" in the 1996 election. When Bill spoke of the need to strengthen American families, he turned his glistening eyes toward Hillary in the House gallery and praised her as "the person who taught me more than anyone else, over twenty-five years, about the importance of families and children—a wonderful wife, a magnificent mother, and a great First Lady. . . . Thank you, Hillary." As the applause engulfed her, she gave her husband a grateful smile.

That Friday, Hillary held her head high as she entered the federal courthouse for four hours of testimony before a Whitewater grand jury of ten women and eleven men. The press found symbolism in what appeared to be a "gold dragon" on her long black coat, although it turned out to be a beaded appliqué in a swirling design created by a friend in Little Rock. By the time Hillary left the courthouse after dark and faced the media swarm, she had displayed the toughness that Bill said was "one of the reasons I loved her."

IN THE FIRST WEEK of February, the press reported that feminist author Naomi Wolf had been consulting with Dick Morris about ways to increase Bill's appeal to women in the 1996 campaign. Wolf suggested that Bill be portrayed as the "good father," a metaphor to reinforce his role as "a mature cultural gatekeeper." Within days of that news, Bill and Lewinsky had their sixth sexual encounter near the Oval Office on Sunday, February 4. Afterward, Bill spent forty-five minutes "trying to get to know" Lewinsky—perhaps, she thought, because she had suggested he was only interested in her for sex.

Since their initial two assignations during the government shutdown, each of their meetings had occurred on a Sunday afternoon, by Bill's direction, when his aides weren't around. But for all of the couple's efforts at concealment, Lewinsky aroused suspicions in the early months of 1996 among a handful of staff members who branded her a "clutch"—the nickname for a female employee who lingered too long in the corridor near the

Oval Office. Secret Service agents had begun making bets on how long it would take Bill to appear in the West Wing whenever Lewinsky showed up on the weekends. Stephen Goodin later told a grand jury that "she seemed kind of enamored, she would kind of stare at him." Nancy Hernreich viewed Lewinsky with similar skepticism. But it was newly appointed Deputy Chief of Staff Evelyn Lieberman—Hillary's eyes and ears in such matters—who reacted most aggressively to the bumptious young woman.

Lewinsky and Lieberman had a confrontation in early January that spooked the junior employee. "You're always trafficking up this area," said Lieberman as they stood in a West Wing corridor. "You're not supposed to be here. Interns aren't allowed to go past the Oval Office." Startled, Lewinsky fled to the bathroom in tears but soon returned to tell Lieberman, "I work here. I'm not an intern." "They hired *you?*" Lieberman replied. "Evelyn didn't like the way Monica was behaving," said Mike McCurry. "She didn't like the way Monica hung around." Lewinsky believed Bill's aides were hostile to her because they "were wary of his weaknesses."

Despite Lewinsky's sense that her relationship with Bill had "started to blossom" during their tryst in early February, he ignored her for two weeks. On Monday, February 19, the Presidents' Day holiday, he called her at home but seemed distant, so she asked to see him in the early afternoon. When they met in the Oval Office, he told her he felt uncomfortable about their affair and wanted to end it. Refusing to kiss her, he gave her a hug and said she could keep visiting him as a "friend." Yet in the following weeks, "there continued to sort of be this flirtation," and he kept calling her, sometimes telling her that she "made him feel twenty-five again."

The President dictated the pace and tenor of their contacts. "I feel that he should have shown more restraint," Lewinsky later said. "It was too much of an emotional burden for someone my age." Lewinsky was in many ways immature but at other moments acted the grown-up despite being nearly thirty years Bill's junior. He once suggested they "get together" after a good-bye party for one of his advisors. She said that would be inadvisable because "people were going to be watching." Then on Friday, March 29, when Hillary was in Greece, Bill called Lewinsky after spotting her in the hall. Bill proposed she meet him outside the Family Theater, where more than two dozen friends were joining him for a screening of *Executive Decision*. Not "a good idea," she said.

Two days later, with Hillary due back in the evening from her eight-day trip, Bill called Lewinsky and suggested she come to the Oval Office "on the pretext of delivering papers." Their sex play in the hallway that Sunday afternoon included Bill's infamous use of a cigar as a dildo—a detail Lewinsky confided not only to a college friend, Catherine Allday Davis, but to former boyfriend Andrew Bleiler.

By early April, a Secret Service agent had complained to Evelyn Lieberman about Lewinsky's "unauthorized visits" to the West Wing. "I decided to get rid of her," said Lieberman, who expressed her concern to Bill that he and Lewinsky were "paying too much attention" to each other. "Everyone needed to be careful" in an election year, she said. Lieberman directed Lewinsky's boss, Tim Keating, to transfer her to the Pentagon. When Keating gave Lewinsky the word on Friday, April 5, he told her she was "too sexy" for the East Wing.

Bill was in Oklahoma City that day with Hillary to commemorate the first anniversary of the Alfred P. Murrah Federal Building bombing with a Good Friday sermon praising "the power of faith and community, the power of both God's grace and human courage." On Easter Sunday, Bill and Lewinsky had their final tryst in 1996, an interlude that included his request for oral sex while he talked on the phone with Dick Morris for ten minutes. Lewinsky was overwrought about leaving the White House, and Bill tried to soothe her by pledging to "bring you back" after the election. Somewhat mollified, she jokingly suggested that she be given the title "Assistant to the President for Blow Jobs," and Bill replied, "I'd like that."

For the rest of the year, they saw each other only at public events, although he continued to call her once a week for the first few months, and after that two or three times a month—often from the road, when he was campaigning. Their postmidnight conversations included phone sex seven times. Occasionally, he left recorded messages that she saved: "Don't worry. I'm going to take care of you. I don't want you to be unhappy." During their public encounters, Lewinsky recalled, "he was always very close to me. While others were there he'd usually hold my hand . . . sort of shaking hands and . . . would continue to just touch me somewhere." He even arranged for her family to attend his weekly radio address, and he posed for a picture with them. Evelyn Lieberman remained vigilant, once bracing Betty Currie after spotting Lewinsky at a White House ceremony. "What is

she doing here? What are you—nuts?" Lieberman sputtered. Bill's repeated contacts with Lewinsky went beyond mere temporizing and indicated a habit—or an attachment—he was loath to give up.

EVEN BEFORE BOB DOLE clinched the Republican nomination on March 19,
the press had marked him as a loser running a "discombobulated" campaign. The Clinton-Gore ticket had an easy double-digit lead that held
until just before Election Day, and Bill's approval ratings remained in the
mid- to upper fifties for the entire year. But neither Bill nor Hillary took the
outcome for granted. Speeches, rallies, seminars, and town meetings were
embedded in the DNA of a couple who had spent their entire adult lives
on a permanent campaign.

While Bill participated in the bulk of the fund-raising events, Hillary
did her share. She supervised a White House database of political supporters that the DNC used to solicit contributions, and she made calls for donations of $50,000 to $100,000 from lists that included Ralph Lauren, a
big fan who had helped her with White House Christmas decorations. "It
was logical if you couldn't have the President call, who better than the
First Lady?" said a consultant to Hillary. "As a surrogate on the phone, she
couldn't have been better."

Relishing his role as the reassuring "good father" figure, Bill pushed an
upbeat message—what a dispirited Robert Reich called the "happy talk"
campaign. It was devised by Morris and used "optimism as a weapon." Bill
"isn't a President who shares your pain," Morris explained to Reich. "He's
a President who shares your bright future. Now is not the time for the President to talk about any long-term problems. What good is a mandate if you
don't get re-elected?" Mark Penn even made an "optimism presentation"
at one of the Wednesday-night political meetings.

The pollsters had also discovered that the much-coveted swing voters
were "fact-based people" who tended to be "skeptics tired of grand
schemes and unfulfilled promises." To capture them, Bill needed to make
a "strong statistical case" for his record, in easily digestible messages. The
White House rolled these out several times per week in "pinprick events."
Such tactics represented the perfect merger of campaigning and governing
at a time when Republicans controlled both houses of Congress.

Bill regularly used "presidential directives" and "memoranda to agencies" to promote new policies, many of them already developed by his cabinet officers. The image of Bill "signing important papers" was specifically designed to appeal to the married couples whose votes the pollsters said he needed to be reelected. The upshot of all this careful calibration was a dull campaign that voters treated "like an argument going on in some other part of the house," observed *Time*'s Lance Morrow. Even Ross Perot, who entered the race again as a third-party candidate, failed to ignite much excitement until the final weeks of the contest.

In an effort to help Bill appear more presidential, his advisors showed him videotapes of Ronald Reagan that illustrated the fortieth President's "aura of command." They urged Bill to avoid appearing in jogging shorts and publicly wolfing down junk food and instead to spend more time up in the third-floor Exercise Room lifting weights and to wear more stylish suits. They trained him to stop throwing "giddy conspiratorial winks to friends in audiences"—although he plainly lapsed when he saw Lewinsky at a White House fund-raising event in May and mouthed, "I miss you."

Hillary proved as adept as her husband at preaching small-bore "values" issues. Just as she stayed away from the West Wing to avoid being labeled "copresident" by the Republicans, Hillary worked best campaigning under the radar, focusing on her kitchen-table topics of women and children. Whenever Whitewater-related questions surfaced, she claimed memory failure or ignorance. She was on the road four to five days per week, appearing before friendly and preselected audiences and avoiding big national issues.

She spoke about her religion to a convention of Methodists, emphasizing the need for society to care for its youth as she recited the words of the hymn "Jesus Loves the Little Children." She made two goodwill tours to Europe that included a visit with newly deployed American troops in Bosnia, where she compared herself to Eleanor Roosevelt visiting soldiers during World War II. While Hillary did take journalists with her overseas, she excluded them from her domestic flights, making them scramble to catch her on the road. By staying relentlessly on message, she deflected the scandals and maintained her approval rating at around 50 percent. "It's like traveling with a medium-level rock star in terms of the excitement she generates," said White House advisor Doug Sosnik, meaning to compliment the First Lady.

She made major news just once, when she told *Time* at the end of May that she and Bill were considering adoption. "I must say we're hoping that we have another child," she said. In the earlier years of her marriage, she "had a hard time getting pregnant," said her friend Ann Henry. "She had a bad case of endometriosis." Hillary's labor had been difficult as well, and Chelsea had been delivered by cesarean section to avoid a breech birth. Hillary said she and Bill had been "talking about" adoption "off and on, for a long time." They would "wait to get serious about it . . . after the election." Journalists were dubious about these previously undisclosed yearnings. Maureen Dowd imagined a White House baby shower for "Chelsea's new little sister, Tribeca." A month after winning reelection, Bill told reporters that he and Hillary had decided against adopting after all.

Hillary was temporarily knocked off stride at the end of June when Bob Woodward revealed her use of Jean Houston as a "spiritual adviser." Fearful of seeming "an eccentric figure," she and her staff downplayed the friendship with Houston, who described herself as a "sacred psychologist" and a "global midwife." Hillary was so concerned about negative fallout that she asked Penn to poll voter reactions to reports of her imaginary conversations with Eleanor Roosevelt. Some three quarters considered it a benign intellectual exercise, and only 13 percent actually believed she was trying to communicate with the dead.

THE REPUBLICAN CONGRESS played into Democratic hands by passing important legislation that Bill could use to his advantage. The biggest breakthrough came with welfare reform, which Bill decided to sign after a highly publicized meeting with key cabinet officers and advisors on July 31. When Bill had campaigned in 1992 to "end welfare as we know it," he had advocated shutting off perpetual cash payments to poor mothers with children and encouraging them to support themselves with jobs—in the spirit of providing opportunity to those who assume responsibility. But Hillary's health-care plan had pushed welfare reform aside for two years.

Once the Republicans gained power, they took over welfare policy and shaped it according to their values and priorities. While Bill and the GOP agreed on the need to end welfare benefits after five years, Bill had originally proposed $18 billion in additional spending over six years, primarily to support child care and job training. Now he faced a bill that reduced welfare spending by $55 billion over the same period, a $73 billion loss from Bill's scheme.

At the urging of Hillary and other liberal advocates, including Hillary's longtime mentor, Children's Defense Fund founder Marian Wright Edelman, Bill had vetoed two earlier Republican welfare bills in January and March 1996, saying that they were too punitive. The Republicans added some funds for child care, expanded Medicaid coverage for children, and eliminated a few cuts in other social programs. But the basic architecture of the bill was pure Republican: reversing a sixty-year-old policy of open-ended federal support by creating a program with time limits administered by the states and lump-sum contributions from the federal Treasury.

Edelman and Donna Shalala were among those forcefully urging Bill to veto the legislation a third time, mainly because it eliminated most benefits for legal immigrants and kept subsidies for child care and food stamps at what they considered unacceptably low levels. Senator Daniel Patrick Moynihan announced that the measure would result in what *The Washington Post* described as "devastating increases in the number of children living in poverty."

But political forces proved far more compelling. "The public favored work over welfare by a huge margin," said Ron Haskins, a Brookings Institution expert on welfare policy. Congressional Democrats had been at odds over welfare policy for years, and now the momentum was with the moderate reformers who had fallen in line with the Republicans. In late July, the House bill had passed, 328 to 101, with 98 Democrats voting for and 98 against. The Senate was poised to pass the legislation in early August. "Democrats in Congress were putting pressure on Bill to sign," recalled Shalala. "They didn't want to go to elections without welfare reform being passed. They did not want ads against them." With congressional investigators breathing down their necks, it was in Bill and Hillary's interest to ensure that as many Democrats were elected as possible.

Hillary acknowledged that she was "advising the President every step of the way," and her viewpoint carried the day during their private discussions at the end of July 1996. Vetoing the bill would have been "handing the Republicans a potential political windfall," she later wrote. "It was pure politics over substance," said Shalala. "Clearly, the Clintons had come to the conclusion together. It was their view of politics—fish or cut bait." In a talk with Hillary before the July 31 meeting, Shalala could read between the lines. "Bill was anguished, but Hillary was not torn," she recalled. "She was flat. She saw the political reality without the human dimension. If Hillary had opposed the bill, we would have gotten another veto."

The July 31 meeting had a "Kabuki theater" quality, in the view of one administration official, with all the actors playing out "stylized roles to a foregone conclusion." If the meeting had been pivotal, Hillary would have been there, rather than at the Summer Olympics in Atlanta. Others took note that unlike in comparable situations where the outcome was in doubt, Bill's staff had prepared only one speech—announcing that he would sign the measure.

Still, for two and a half hours, the President let the advocates and opponents have their say in the Cabinet Room, as he listened intently, took notes, and asked questions. Although Robert Reich knew it was a "Potemkin meeting," he nevertheless passionately argued for a veto, bearing in mind that Bill was "twenty points ahead in the polls." Bill responded by calling the measure "a decent welfare bill wrapped in a sack of shit." In his televised announcement from the White House Briefing Room after the meeting, Bill said he would work to revise the legislation to include legal immigrants and to increase funding for food stamps. Still, *Time* called his remarks "the best Republican speech of the year, so far."

Marian Edelman's husband, Peter, a top official working for Donna Shalala, resigned in protest, along with another advisor in the Department of Health and Human Services. Marian decried the new policy as a "moral blot" on the presidency, creating what Hillary called a "rift" that was "sad and difficult." In fact, Bill had already damaged their long friendship a year earlier when Peter was scheduled to be nominated to the federal bench— one of Hillary's spheres of interest. Because Peter was perceived as a "liberal lightning rod," Bill was told he could not be confirmed, a message he neglected to give to his old friend. "I am sure it was on his call list," said a West Wing advisor, "but he waited a long time, and it turned up in the newspapers before the call was made."

IN THE DAYS BEFORE the Democratic Convention at the end of August, the President signed the welfare bill, legislation to raise the minimum wage, and the Kennedy-Kassebaum Act, which allowed workers to carry their health insurance from one job to another and removed restrictions on coverage for preexisting ailments. "Kennedy-Kassebaum took the strongest points of consensus from the 1993 and 1994 health-care debate that we worked on and got passed," said health-care lobbyist Pamela Bailey. It was significant that during the signing ceremony on the South Lawn, Hillary was seated in the front row of the audience, rather than on the platform with her husband, as she would have been two years earlier.

The slogan of the Democratic Convention in Chicago was "Building a Bridge to the Twenty-first Century," a phrase that had been polled in several versions, with 42 percent favoring the final wording. Bill's speech was even more meticulously market tested—"every phrase, every paragraph, even the order of the sentences," noted Robert Reich with dismay, especially since the President made no mention of the new minimum-wage law. The buoyant proceedings were marred only by the abrupt resignation of Dick Morris after a tabloid revealed that for the previous year he had been consorting with a two-hundred-dollar-per-night call girl in his suite in the Jefferson Hotel.

Hillary was the star of the four-day event in her hometown, which treated her like a queen on a progress. No previous First Lady had been invited to make a speech to the delegates in prime time, and Hillary did so on Tuesday night, August 27. She spoke briskly for about ten minutes, touching on her favorite themes—women, children, health, welfare, and education—and throwing a few jabs at Dole and the Republicans. *The New Yorker* called it "liberalism lite" and observed that her four-minute standing ovation had "all the spontaneity of a plenary session of the North Korea Central Committee." Still, it was a thrilling moment for Hillary, who just "let the cheers wash over me." As she celebrated afterward with close friends in their suite, Hillary laughed and said, "Tell that fucking Sosnik I'm a mid-level rock star. Fuck him."

Throughout the campaign season, the low hum of scandal buzzed in the background, sometimes more audibly, at other times barely perceptibly. It received little notice back in January when a federal appeals court ruled that the Paula Jones lawsuit could proceed, in what turned out to be a portentous step toward the Supreme Court's agreement a year later to take up the case.

The noise level had increased on May 28 when the Starr prosecution team convicted Jim and Susan McDougal and Arkansas governor Jim Guy Tucker on multiple counts of fraud for phony transactions using money from Madison Guaranty. The trial had lasted three months and had featured testimony that the President videotaped in the Map Room of the White House. He vigorously denied David Hale's allegation that Bill had engineered a sham three-hundred-thousand-dollar loan to Susan McDougal. One curious aspect of the case was an agreement between the prosecutors and Susan McDougal's lawyers to bar any questions of a sexual nature relating to Bill Clinton—a friendship she had told one television interviewer was "too personal" to discuss.

The Castle Grande scheme figured in the conviction of Tucker, who had been a lawyer for the land-development deal in the eighties. In the middle of the trial, Webb Hubbell made a cryptic phone call from prison to his wife, Suzy, whose father, Seth Ward, had been retained by Jim McDougal to sell parcels of the Castle Grande property for Madison Guaranty at inflated prices. Like Hillary, Webb Hubbell had drafted documents for the crooked land deal while at the Rose law firm. During their phone conversation on March 25, 1996, Suzy told her husband that White House aide Marsha Scott, another old friend from Little Rock, had warned he would receive no "public support" if he were to "open up Hillary to all this." "I'm hearing the squeeze play," Suzy added.

Replied Webb, "So I need to roll over one more time." When Suzy asked whether overbilling was "an area where Hillary would be vulnerable," Webb cautioned her, "We're on a recorded phone." Talking to Scott the same day, Hubbell said, "There are issues that I have to stay away from to protect others, and I will."

Before Susan McDougal began serving her two-year prison sentence, she was summoned to testify before a Whitewater grand jury in Little Rock. When McDougal refused to answer any questions about the Clintons, Judge Susan Webber Wright sent her to jail for contempt on September 9. Two weeks later, Jim Lehrer asked Bill in a television interview whether he would pardon the McDougals. Bill replied that he had given pardons "no consideration" but went on to outline the steps he might take to do so—which was interpreted by Kenneth Starr, and by some in the press, as a hint for Susan McDougal to hang tough.

The Senate Whitewater Committee investigations had ended inconclusively in June 1996, with dueling reports from the majority and minority. The Republicans faulted the Clintons for withholding documents and their aides for "implausible" memory lapses. The Democrats maintained that Bill and Hillary were innocent in Whitewater and related dealings. The judgment of the minority echoed a report prepared by the San Francisco law firm Pillsbury, Madison & Sutro for the Resolution Trust Corporation in December 1995, which Bill and Hillary said had declared them to be innocent. But the "Pillsbury Report" had recommended only that the RTC not file a lawsuit against the Clintons to recover money lost by Madison Guaranty. Lacking crucial documents, the Pillsbury investigators had said they couldn't determine if funds from the bank had been siphoned into Whitewater. Charles E. Patterson, the law firm's senior partner, said the report "was neither a castigation nor vindication" of the Clintons. After reviewing the long-missing billing records, the RTC issued a revised report indicating that Hillary and her law firm "had far more contact" with the principals in the Castle Grande swindle "than was previously known."

None of these events had a discernible impact on the campaign, probably because the public had difficulty understanding the tangled web of financial transactions. But when revelations about campaign fund-raising improprieties began to break at the end of September, voters paid attention. The Clinton White House did everything possible—from ignoring media inquiries to telling reporters outright lies—to play down the stories before Election Day. The most egregious deception concerned donations from the Riadys, whom Bruce Lindsey claimed had made only "social" visits to the White House, even though he knew they had lobbied Bill on foreign-policy issues relating to their business interests.

Even without White House cooperation, reporters managed to uncover some of the Democrats' illegal contributions and excessive money-raising practices. Three weeks before Election Day, *Newsweek* called the campaign-finance system "out of control" and the Clinton White House "especially brazen." Several days later, the *Los Angeles Times* described a fund-raising scandal of "historic proportions."

Ross Perot seized on the emerging pattern of abuse to charge that if Bill Clinton were reelected, he would be "totally occupied" for two years "staying out of jail." Perot's numbers began to rise when he declared that he would "put a sign all across Washington: Not For Sale At Any Price."

Bill was obsessed with winning more than 50 percent of the vote, a goal that the campaign-finance revelations imperiled. His double-digit lead began to shrink. Until the final weeks, he had been running a strategically flawless campaign. He had further sealed his centrist credentials by signing the Defense of Marriage Act at the end of September. The legislation, which stipulated that marriage was legal only between a man and a woman, had been prompted by a new Vermont law permitting civil unions for homosexuals. Concerned that the other states would follow, the Republican Congress devised a preemptive measure that the Senate passed by 85 to 14 and the House by 342 to 67. Bill had decided in May—with Hillary's agreement—to back the legislation after Morris's polling showed "overwhelming support." The decision was "strategic" and "related to re-election," Morris later wrote. The President's move angered many supporters in the gay community, including David Mixner, who denounced his old friend for an "act of political cowardice."

Bill had also been doing his utmost to look presidential and remain above the fray. In early September, he flexed American military muscle by launching forty-four cruise missiles against targets near Baghdad after Saddam Hussein had sent forty thousand soldiers to a Kurd-controlled city in northern Iraq. The troops withdrew shortly afterward, but Bill's unilateral action alienated European allies who viewed it as disproportionate. White House aides subsequently admitted that there was a "domestic policy component" in the President's decision to "punish Saddam." Less than a month later, Bill hosted a thirty-six-hour summit with Yasser Arafat, King Hussein of Jordan, and Benjamin Netanyahu, the recently elected Prime Minister of Israel. After intense negotiations, the participants agreed on terms to end a recent round of fighting between Israeli and Palestinian forces and to reduce the Israeli presence in the West Bank town of Hebron.

FOR THE FINAL WEEK of the campaign, Bill reverted to type, manically crisscrossing the country, frantic to boost his lead. He slept only seven hours in the last three days as he visited twelve cities and towns in Arkansas, Louisiana, Florida, New Jersey, Massachusetts, Maine, New Hampshire, Ohio, Iowa, and South Dakota. Hoarse and haggard, he made his closing speech at 1:00 a.m. in Sioux Falls, hugged his wife and daughter, plunged into the rope line, leaped back to the stage, returned to the crowd, and took to the stage again before aides extracted him. On the return flight to Little Rock, everyone drank champagne, ate mango ice cream (Bill's favorite), and danced the Macarena. Still wired when he reached his suite at the Excelsior Hotel, he stayed up all night playing hearts with a group of aides.

On Tuesday, November 5, Bill and Hillary attended a brunch hosted by Arkansas senator David Pryor, where they seemed to be "floating serenely" at the prospect of victory. In the evening, they watched the returns with family and friends in their hotel suite, which featured an oil portrait of Bill in a gilt frame. Bill won 49 percent of the vote, Dole 41 percent, and Perot 8 percent—a decisive victory, but shy of the Clintons' expectations. Turnout was less than 50 percent, the lowest since 1924.

The voters had reelected their President on the strength of a surging economy and Bill's acceptance of Republican terms for a balanced budget and a smaller federal government. In contrast to Bill and Hillary's expansive, Roosevelt-style vision of 1993, he now provided a "Small Deal." "Clintonism," Newsweek noted, was "less an ideology than an assemblage of tactics forced on him by the necessities of dealing with a hostile Congress and of getting himself re-elected."

The President's coattails were disappointingly short. The Republicans held the House with a seventeen-seat margin and increased their Senate majority by two to fifty-five. Although Bill's plurality was six percentage points higher than in 1992, misgivings about his character persisted. In exit polls, 54 percent of voters said he was not "honest," and 59 percent said he was not telling the truth about Whitewater.

After midnight, Bill, Hillary, and Chelsea walked together along the red carpet to the stage in front of the floodlit Old Statehouse. Fireworks filled the sky, and a large crowd had assembled in the balmy weather for Bill's victory speech. "The vital American center is alive and well," he said. Yet for the first Democrat to win reelection since Franklin Roosevelt, his tone seemed subdued. "It was a pretty joyless victory celebration," recalled Mike McCurry. "We knew we were going to get clobbered on campaign-finance allegations."

On Wednesday, Bill and Hillary returned to the White House for a big South Lawn rally as the temperature rose to 63 on an overcast day. Among the well-wishers was Monica Lewinsky. Bill had effectively kept her at bay during the campaign, phoning her only when he felt the urge for long-distance companionship or for something racier. On Friday, July 19, at 6:30 a.m., before he and Hillary flew to Atlanta to open the Summer Olympics, Bill had woken up his young paramour for some phone sex, after which he exclaimed, "Good morning! What a way to start the day!" Lewinsky had made her own mischief a month later when she showed up at Bill's fiftieth birthday celebration, an elaborate fund-raiser at Radio City Music Hall in Manhattan. While he was talking to a group of admirers, she surreptitiously brushed her hand across his groin—a gesture she later said was playful rather than intended to arouse.

As Bill received congratulations from White House staff members in the rope line on the day after his reelection, Lewinsky waited for his approach. She wore her black beret because she knew "Handsome" liked it. She gave him an adoring look, and he hugged her with a familiarity that previously had gone undetected. But this time, television cameras caught her gaze and their embrace. Fourteen months later, that brief scene would be played repeatedly for a worldwide audience as the iconic image of Bill Clinton's most mortifying scandal.

Chapter Twelve

—

BILL CLINTON CONSIDERED 1997 TO BE "THE MOST NORMAL YEAR OF my presidency so far." Yet in crucial ways it was anything but. The widening campaign fund-raising investigations dominated the headlines for months, tarnishing his reputation and diverting his attention. The Paula Jones case reemerged with ever more graphic allegations about the President. And early in the year, he eagerly resumed his sexual intimacy with Monica Lewinsky, only to end it a month later—a decision that was to lead his besotted former employee to unleash a series of demands, causing him to spend inordinate amounts of time both placating her and figuring out how to make her go away. "What has been discounted in stacking up the time he was under stress is the period when the meter was running on Monica," said one of Bill's senior advisors. "When he quit screwing around with her, he had to manage the problem. The worst thing would have been to have her go dark on him. He was managing all of that, and only a few people knew, during that time before the Monica story came out. The anxiety before it happens is often worse than afterwards."

In some respects, Bill was, as he later said, "free to do my job." But the scope of his job had narrowed. He had become what he had derided in the early months of his administration—a President who governed like an Eisenhower Republican, right down to his growing preoccupation with golf, which he took to playing on weekday afternoons as well as on weekends. His main domestic accomplishment was securing the balanced-budget deal that he had pledged to achieve two years earlier under pressure from the GOP. In foreign policy, he fulfilled his vision of an expanded NATO. But otherwise he was hemmed in by the Republicans in Congress, unable to do more than tinker on the margins and unwilling to tackle major reforms of Social Security and Medicare. Even as he grew more obsessed with his legacy, it was clear that without a war or national crisis, greatness would elude him.

Hillary observed that while Bill was "looking his age," his hair nearly white after four years in office, she still "lit up" when she saw him and found herself "admiring his handsome face." Only a year younger, Hillary kept the same forces of nature at bay by dyeing her hair, which was now blonder and styled for the moment in a loose page boy. She believed that she and her husband "were each other's best friend." Yet one of the paradoxes of their relationship was summed up by Derek Shearer, a brother of Brooke and a friend of Bill since Oxford days, who observed, "His best friend is Hillary. If you're cheating on your best friend, who are you going to talk to? Bill had developed a whole way of functioning where he wasn't dealing with any of this."

THE PERIOD BEFORE THE second inaugural was far less frenetic than the first time around. On Thursday, November 7, 1996, Bill slept past noon. A visitor to the second floor of the Residence found him in sweatpants and a T-shirt in the Treaty Room, "on the phone, talking deals and leaks." Hillary was in her bathrobe, "looking exhausted. She was in the mode of fiercely protecting the President. They were supposed to go to a going-away for Warren Christopher at 2:30, and she was pissed off that the event had even been scheduled. They had been promised there would be nothing on the schedule."

The President met the press on Friday to announce the resignation of Leon Panetta and the appointment of his deputy, Erskine Bowles, as the new Chief of Staff. No one asked Bill why he had simultaneously cut loose Harold Ickes, the other Deputy Chief of Staff. Ickes had awakened at 5:15 the morning after Election Day to learn his fate from *The Wall Street Journal*. Bill had dumped him under pressure once before, during the transition in 1992, and Ickes was stunned that it was happening again after his loyal service. He had worked tirelessly to contain damage from the Whitewater scandals and had run a political operation during the 1996 campaign that had blunted any challenge to Bill from the left, by dissuading Jesse Jackson from entering the primaries.

Ickes had been hoping for the Chief of Staff position, but Bill had decided that Bowles, a genteel moderate Democrat from North Carolina, could work more effectively with the Republican Congress than could an outspoken liberal with the "mouth of a Teamster." In a meeting with the President and Vernon Jordan, Bowles set two conditions for accepting the job: Hillary had to stay out of West Wing business ("I love Hillary," Bowles told the President, "but I cannot have more than one boss"), and the abrasive Ickes had to go. "Someone came out of that meeting and called *The Wall Street Journal*," said Terry McAuliffe. Ickes confronted Bill about his mistreatment, but rather than apologize the President typically blamed the "sonofabitch" leaker. Bill tossed his old friend a meager bone by appointing him to coordinate the inaugural in January and the G-7 summit in Denver the following June. Ickes "took a long time," said McAuliffe, to get over what Jonathan Alter of *Newsweek* called Bill's "prodigious ingratitude." Bill's thoughtlessness also created tensions with Hillary, who was reported to be "deeply upset."

In the following weeks, Bill reshuffled half of his cabinet, and among the seven new faces was another woman, Alexis Herman as Labor Secretary, along with a Republican, Maine senator William Cohen as Secretary of Defense. At the farewell party for Laura Tyson, who stepped down as director of the National Economic Council, Bill made one last stab at flirtation. As they stood together holding glasses of champagne, Bill said, "Laura, you're the kind of girl back when I was in college I would have tried to get drunk."

"In college, I might have let you," Tyson cracked.

"That's the nicest thing you ever said to me," Bill replied.

DURING BILL'S POSTELECTION news conference, nearly half of the twenty-eight questions concerned scandals, mostly in campaign fund-raising. He revealed that he had recently read a book about second-term presidencies and learned that they could be derailed by an "external event" that would dash a President's "dreams or hopes or his agenda" or by a President thinking he had "more of a mandate than he does and tries to do too much" or by just "[running] out of steam." He noted with admiration that Ronald

Reagan had signed tax-reform legislation and the first major overhaul of the welfare program in his second term. Bill promised that the Clinton presidency would have a "big agenda . . . a driving agenda" in the years to come.

When asked if Hillary would be involved in implementing the administration's new welfare policy, Bill insisted that he and his wife "hadn't had much chance to talk about it" but said she should not have a specific role in the program. Hillary seemed to have other ideas in an interview with reporters from *Time* and *Newsweek* two weeks later. "I intend to speak about welfare reform and write about it," she said, adding that she looked forward to assuming "a formal role that would make sense." The published remarks in *Time* unnerved the President's staff, who feared comparisons to Hillary's failed health-care enterprise. Ultimately, Mike McCurry had to "extricate Hillary" and issue a statement denying that she would have any "formal role" in the second term.

She was instead to confine herself mainly to noncontroversial public initiatives—supporting historic preservation, holding conferences on children, promoting women's health programs. Only during her extensive overseas travels did she reveal her natural outspokenness by advocating—fiercely at times—women's rights. She rarely mentioned Bill in these speeches on female empowerment, which allowed her to finesse the obvious truth that she owed her influential position to her husband. Looking back on her state of mind at the time, she revealingly said she had become "like steel tempered in fire: a bit harder at the edges, but more durable, more flexible."

Yet Hillary's sub-rosa influence over the Clinton Administration remained strong. She installed one of her most loyal operatives, Ann Lewis, as Bill's Deputy Communications Director. And she worked quietly with her husband's top officials on their budgets and policy priorities in areas that interested her, such as the U.S. Agency for International Development. Brian Atwood, the director of USAID, said that Hillary "deserves more credit . . . than anyone" for securing an increase in funding for his agency in 1997.

The most dramatic illustration of her continuing clout was her insistence that Madeleine Albright be named Secretary of State. After meeting with the President and First Lady on the Saturday before Election Day to discuss candidates to replace Warren Christopher following his retirement, one of Bill's top advisors noted, "There was no doubt that Hillary was determined that it be a woman, and that it be Madeleine Albright." The most experienced candidate was Richard Holbrooke, who had been shrewdly cultivating Hillary for several years. But Albright, an equally skilled and blunt political operator, had forged a strong bond with the First Lady through their shared experiences as Wellesley graduates and through their travels together to China and eastern Europe. Holbrooke had strong champions in Strobe Talbott, Al Gore, and Pamela Harriman. But he also had outspoken opponents such as Tony Lake, and Hillary considered Holbrooke "too headstrong." Hillary's choice prevailed, and Holbrooke also lost the job of UN Ambassador to the "mediagenic" Bill Richardson, a veteran Mexican-American congressman.

With the pressures of reelection behind them, the prospect of big presidential decisions unlikely, and the power of their overt duopoly curtailed, Bill and Hillary had reached a moment of relative calm. "There was less whispering about screaming bouts on the second floor," said George Stephanopoulos. Despite Bill's illicit relationship with Lewinsky, he was "demonstrably affectionate" with Hillary, said one of his top advisors. "They were increasingly close to one another. Both were ambitious and had their own interests, and being able to pursue their interests was an important part of their lives. It made them happy. The space that was best for them was to spend some time together, and then to go off and pursue their own stuff separately, with constant phone calls back and forth to have an extended conversation. That was a very important part of their relationship. To be pinned down together and not pursuing their interests, neither would be happy."

IN MID-NOVEMBER, Bill and Hillary traveled to Hawaii, Australia, the Philippines, and Thailand for eleven days of going to the beach, playing golf, sightseeing, and meeting with Asian leaders. Back home, press reports revealed that the administration had concealed information about campaign-finance abuses before the election, and *The New York Times* even suggested that Bruce Lindsey resign for misleading reporters about the Riadys' meetings with the President. Asked at a press conference in Australia whether he was "trying to stonewall," Bill plunged into self-pity, comparing himself to Richard Jewell, the man falsely accused of planting a bomb at the Olympics in Atlanta. Hillary was also feeling sorry for herself, telling a group of four hundred Australian women that an American First Lady could "escape the politics of one's time" only by opting to "withdraw and perhaps put a bag over your head" and "make it clear you have no opinions and no ideas about anything." She bemoaned the criticism that resulted "if you try to be public about your concerns and your interests" and concluded: "The answer is to just be who you are and do what you can do and get through it—and wait for a First Man to hold the position." She pointedly said that in America, women were determined to "claim their share of personal, political, economic and civic power."

Hillary had no sooner left Washington in early December for a women's rights conference in Bolivia—her first solo trip out of town since the election—than Bill was on the phone to Monica Lewinsky. According to Lewinsky, they had phone sex, and they talked "long into the night"—until she realized that Bill had fallen asleep. Two weeks later, Lewinsky popped up at one of the White House Christmas receptions wearing a "semi-low-cut" red dress. Her date, Pentagon official Willie Blacklow, was "stunned" by the way the President enthusiastically hugged her in the receiving line, with Hillary at his side. "There was no question that she was something more than just another gofer," Blacklow later said.

It was otherwise a routine holiday season for the Clintons, who went twice to the Warner Theater to watch Chelsea dance for the last time in *The Nutcracker*—an annual event for the Clintons. Bill, Hillary, and Chelsea schmoozed for three days at Renaissance Weekend before escaping to St. Thomas in the Virgin Islands, where they spent the first five days of the new year.

The morning after their return, *Newsweek* hit the stands with a cover story reexamining the Paula Jones case ("Should She Be Heard?"), which infuriated the President. The magazine's dogged investigative reporter Michael Isikoff had taken his cue from a long article the previous November in *The American Lawyer*, written by the respected legal journalist Stuart Taylor, who had interviewed several of Jones's corroborating witnesses and had concluded that the evidence was "highly persuasive." After making its way through the legal system, the sexual-harassment lawsuit was about to be reviewed by the Supreme Court, and *Newsweek* predicted that there was a "good chance" the case would proceed, opening up the possibility that Bill's history as a womanizer would be scrutinized. The Paula Jones matter, Newsweek noted, had "the potential to make Bill Clinton's life hellish in the months and years ahead"—an "external event" with ramifications few could have predicted.

THE SECOND CLINTON INAUGURAL was a more restrained affair than the giddy extravaganza four years earlier. The celebrations lasted three days rather than four, and down on the National Mall there were eight big tents instead of sixty-five the first time around. The Clintons tried to minimize the amount of corporate underwriting and canceled a lavish White House reception for thirty top donors amid growing criticism of their campaign fund-raising. To set a more elegant tone, the inaugural-gala performers included Yo-Yo Ma and Mikhail Baryshnikov. Hillary had dropped her Arkansas dress designers and taken up with Oscar de la Renta, who created sophisticated ensembles for the swearing-in ceremony and inaugural balls. David Letterman impishly observed that she would need sleeves "long enough to hide her handcuffs."

Hillary had lobbied for either Stephen Breyer or Ruth Bader Ginsburg, Bill's two Supreme Court appointees, to administer the oath of office because she believed that the Chief Justice "despised us and our politics." But Bill hewed to tradition and was once more sworn in by William Rehnquist, who was as frosty as the President had been to him at the previous inaugural. "Good luck," said the unsmiling Chief Justice.

"They're going to screw you on the Paula Jones case," Hillary murmured to her husband.

Bill's inaugural address ran twenty-two minutes—eight minutes longer than his first. As before, he enlisted a large contingent of insiders and outsiders—a dozen or so, again including journalist Taylor Branch and novelist Tommy Caplan—to contribute ideas and help with the writing. Starting the day after his return from the Virgin Islands, he met with them nonstop, working up to the last minute. Compared to four years earlier, he was "less certain of what he wanted to say or how to say it," recalled his speechwriter Michael Waldman. "His sense of mandate was tenuous." Bill settled on several defining themes, emphasizing that "America stands alone as the world's indispensable nation" and proclaiming, with yet another Kennedyesque inversion, that "for any one of us to succeed, we must succeed as one America." The President and Congress, he said, needed to work together as "repairers of the breach," mindful that America's citizens demand "big things from us, and nothing big ever came from being small."

His was a rosy view of a world "no longer divided into two hostile camps," as it had been during the Cold War. He offered no hint of the simmering hatred of America and its allies among the terrorists being trained by Osama bin Laden and his al-Qaeda network under the protection of the radical Islamic Taliban government in Afghanistan. Several times in the previous two years, the President had warned of the "reckless aggression of rogue states" and the capability of "increasingly interconnected groups" to "traffic in terror" using "suitcase bombs" against their targets. But he and his top advisors were only minimally aware of the metastasizing terrorist operation of al-Qaeda—its roots, its ideology, its means and methods, and its leadership—although several of its members had already been implicated in the February 1993 World Trade Center bombings.

In 1996, the Clinton Administration had actually rebuffed requests from Sudanese leaders to help extradite bin Laden, who had been training his operatives in their country for five years. When the terrorist mastermind finally left Sudan that May, the United States passed up the chance to grab him as his plane stopped in Qatar for refueling. The reason, Bill explained, was a lack of evidence that bin Laden had committed a "crime against America. . . . We had no basis on which to hold him." Two months later, State Department analysts warned of bin Laden's intention to expand radical Islam and attack western targets, noting that Afghanistan was an "ideal haven" with the potential to make him "more dangerous to U.S. interests in the long run" than he had been while based in Sudan. Shortly afterward, bin Laden issued his first fatwa against the "infidel" United States, a prelude to his call in February 1998 for Muslims to kill Americans and their allies anywhere in the world. While counterterrorism officials in the FBI and CIA were tracking bin Laden and his network throughout these years, the President did not publicly mention his name, or that of al-Qaeda, until August 1998.

Commentators in the media were unimpressed by the second Clinton inaugural address, belittling him for platitudes and singling out his "nothing big" line for special ridicule. But a poll conducted by Mark Penn showed that the public was enthusiastic about the President's statements on race relations and the need for reconciliation. With his intellectual and visceral ability to articulate the black experience and connect to black audiences, Bill Clinton was unusually qualified to address the country's most divisive issue. His best speech of the first term had been a passionate and starkly candid discourse on violence among urban black teenagers that he delivered mostly off-the-cuff to a group of black ministers in Memphis in November 1993. The Reverend Martin Luther King Jr. "did not fight for the right of black people to murder other black people with reckless abandon," the President had said then. Despite the favorable response to the speech, the President inexplicably did not return to its resonant themes later.

After Bill's inaugural pledge to confront "the divide of race" that "has been America's constant curse," some of his advisors suggested that he launch a major initiative akin to the landmark Kerner Commission of the 1960s, which had analyzed race relations after devastating urban riots. Instead, he settled on a more limited approach by appointing a seven-member advisory panel to explore the issue as part of a "national conversation" to culminate in a report in the summer of 1998.

A successful race initiative was one path to shoring up his legacy—a growing preoccupation for Bill since Dick Morris had told him the previous summer that he was only a "borderline third tier" president. Bill fretted that he was a "person out of my time," who would have been more suited to the challenges of being president during World War II. Arthur Schlesinger compounded Bill's distress after the 1996 election when he reported that a jury of historians judged the forty-second president to be "average," on a par with William Howard Taft and George H. W. Bush. Leaders who attained greatness, in Schlesinger's view, "took risks in pursuit of their ideals." He urged Bill Clinton to "liberate himself from polls and focus groups" and to "put his first-rate intelligence to work on the hard problems."

Out of Schlesinger's nine "greats and near-greats," only two, Theodore Roosevelt and Andrew Jackson, "made their mark without a first-order crisis." Roosevelt in particular "could get the attention of his fellow citizens and make them think," wrote historian Elting Morison. "He knew how to put the hard questions a little before they became obvious to others . . .

how to move people into their thinking beyond short-run self-interest toward some longer view of the general welfare."

Bill Clinton's advisors seized on the Roosevelt comparison, noting that both men served in a time of "transition" and were skilled at using the "bully pulpit," which Bill intended to exploit more frequently during the second term in his self-proclaimed role as "the repairer of the breach." Bill's aides also touted the opportunity to reform Social Security and Medicare. "We want people to read in their history books in 2052 that Clinton preserved the Social Security system," boasted Mike McCurry.

Yet the President was reluctant to make any bold moves after he received the recommendations of his Advisory Council on Social Security in January 1997. Following two and a half years of study, the members offered three proposals for investing a portion of Social Security retirement funds in the stock market rather than the safer but lower yielding Treasury bills, although they differed on whether individuals or the government should make the investment decisions. Hillary reacted emphatically to the report, telling her husband, "We mustn't let Social Security be privatized." Concerned that he would be attacked by Republicans if he took a position, Bill put aside Social Security and assigned officials in the Treasury Department to study the matter further.

By Bill's own admission, his February 4, 1997, State of the Union address was mainly devoted to such "unfinished business" as balancing the budget and fixing the previous year's welfare bill. Beyond that, he singled out education as his top priority, calling for "a national crusade for education standards," improved programs for preschool children, and character education in the classroom. Hillary had a strong hand in this "call to action for American education." She even wrote her husband's tagline, that "politics must stop at the schoolhouse door," which she said was meant to "turn George Wallace on his head"—an allusion to the infamous vow by Alabama's segregationist governor to "stand in the schoolhouse door" to prevent black students from registering at the University of Alabama in 1963.

FOR MUCH OF THE SPRING, the President's lofty rhetoric was eclipsed by campaign fund-raising scandals that triggered probes by a twenty-five-member Justice Department task force and bipartisan appeals for Janet Reno to appoint an Independent Counsel. By February, the drip of stories that began before Election Day had turned into a torrent. The first wave brought John Huang and the Riadys, followed in quick succession by the 103 White House coffees with the President, rides on Air Force One, and accommodations in the Lincoln Bedroom for big donors, Bill's gleeful "ready to start overnights right away" memo, and Maggie Williams's acceptance of a fifty-thousand-dollar check from Johnny Chung. The two biggest splashes came from Bob Woodward, first in mid-February revealing Chinese efforts to influence the 1996 elections through contributions, and three weeks later detailing Al Gore's fund-raising activities as "solicitor in chief." Gore had earlier been criticized for attending a luncheon in April 1996 at a Buddhist temple where $140,000 was raised, some of it improbably credited to nuns and monks. Now it turned out he had called numerous donors from his office, a decidedly undignified chore for a Vice President. Much was made of Bill's supposed refusal to make the requests himself and of Gore's willingness to "eat the spinach" and call on behalf of his boss. But it later emerged that Bill had done his share of phone solicitations of wealthy benefactors from the White House as well.

Dialing for dollars from 1600 Pennsylvania Avenue wasn't just unseemly, it also was a possible violation of a law against fund-raising on federal property. Administration lawyers maintained that the statute excluded the President and Vice President because they lived and worked in government buildings, and that in any event it didn't apply to the unregulated soft money they were seeking. In a press conference, Gore insisted he had done nothing improper, but he damaged himself by robotically repeating seven times in twenty-four minutes that there was "no controlling legal authority" prohibiting his calls.

Bill made the situation worse by repeatedly denying any connection between White House events and fund-raising when evidence kept emerging to prove otherwise. As usual, he blamed the press for "one more false story we had to endure. . . . The Lincoln Bedroom was never sold." He said he invited overnight guests because "the only time I had to visit with people in an informal way was late at night," and there was "never a single case when I raised money because of this practice," even though donors acknowledged the quid pro quo. He also insisted that of those who slept in the Lincoln Bedroom, only about "one in nine" was a big contributor, when in fact the ratio was more than one in three. The coffees at the White

House, he said, were intended to help him counteract a "very isolating job. . . . I look for ways to have genuine conversation with people." Yet when videotapes of the coffees were released in the fall of 1997, the colloquies with the President were numbingly banal—what *Time* called "hour after hour of repetitious foreplay with potential donors." Bill claimed that "there was no specific price tag put on those coffees," even as DNC documents revealed that most of the guests were asked for twenty-five thousand dollars apiece, and White House Deputy Chief of Staff Evelyn Lieberman specifically called the gatherings "fundraisers" in one of her memos.

Related to the campaign-finance disclosures were continuing revelations about some of the corporate payments to Webster Hubbell when he was under investigation by the Independent Counsel for embezzlement and fraud. Press reports revealed the magnitude of the fees; the paucity of work done; the involvement of Mack McLarty, Mickey Kantor, and Erskine Bowles; Hubbell's continuing contacts with the White House after his resignation from the Justice Department; and Bill and Hillary's knowledge of the payments, including one hundred thousand dollars from the Riadys, at the time they were made. Hubbell's financial haul, wrote liberal *Washington Post* columnist Richard Cohen, was "the stuff of double-takes." Conservative columnist William Safire of *The New York Times* called it "hush money."

When asked in late January 1997 about Hubbell's lucrative retainers, Bill insisted that he first learned of them in a press report late in 1996. But two months later, he was forced to admit he had known in 1994—although he couldn't remember who told him—that some of his most generous political supporters were among those subsidizing Hubbell. Suspecting a coordinated White House effort to buy Hubbell's silence on Whitewater and related matters—what *Newsweek* described as "persistent memory lapses"—Kenneth Starr's investigators issued subpoenas to the top administration officials involved. Bill said his advisors were only trying to help an old friend; Hillary was more caustic, comparing charges of hush money to "some people's obsession with UFOs."

AFTER HER ELECTION-YEAR banishment, Monica Lewinsky was impatient to resume her affair with the President, especially since he had encouraged her with phone sex and the promise of meetings. "Every day can't be sunshine," he said when she complained that he was putting her off. She also began to press him for a transfer back to a White House job and expressed frustration when he failed to follow through on offers to help. "He was destroying her," recalled her friend Catherine Allday Davis. In addition to Davis, Lewinsky had extended her circle of confidantes to Pentagon coworker Linda Tripp, who had left the White House in August 1994. By February 1997, Lewinsky was even sharing Bill's voice-mail messages with several friends, including Ashley Raines on the White House staff.

Finally, on Friday, February 28, Bill invited Lewinsky to an evening taping of his weekly radio address. Afterward, he instructed Betty Currie to escort Lewinsky to his private study, so it would not appear that he was seeing the young woman alone. Currie obediently waited in the nearby dining room for the twenty minutes that her boss and Lewinsky were together. They exchanged belated Christmas gifts that included a special edition of Walt Whitman's *Leaves of Grass* and an antique hat pin for Lewinsky. For the first time in eleven months, they were sexually intimate, first in the hallway and then in the bathroom. When he pushed her away during oral sex, Bill said, "I don't want to get addicted to you, and I don't want you to get addicted to me." At Lewinsky's insistence, she brought him to completion for the first time, which left traces of his semen on her navy-blue dress from the Gap. "I was sick after it was over," Bill later said, "disgusted with myself" for resuming the affair after staying away for so many months.

Betty Currie was repeatedly the willing accomplice for her boss and his lover. At fifty-eight, Currie's public persona was that of a gentle den mother and devout Methodist. But she was more worldly than she appeared, a savvy veteran of campaign war rooms who had moonlighted as an assistant to biographer Kitty Kelley, a specialist in intrigue and scandal. Currie professed ignorance about the nature of Bill's relationship with Lewinsky, although she later admitted her "concern" about the amount of time they spent together in meetings that were "more personal in nature as opposed to business." She went to great lengths to conceal their encounters, asking the Secret Service to exclude Lewinsky from their entrance logs, making Bill's phone calls to Lewinsky herself to avoid the White House switchboard, and meeting Lewinsky at the White House gate and escorting her by circuitous routes to see the President.

On Thursday, March 13, Currie canceled a planned White House visit by Lewinsky when Bill left on a trip to the Carolinas and Florida primarily to play golf. Around midnight, Bill arrived at Tranquility, the seaside estate of the golfer Greg Norman in upper-crust Hobe Sound. Bill's traveling companion was Bruce Lindsey, who headed to bed while Bill stayed up to gab with Norman and his wife. At 1:20 a.m., Norman took the President outside to show him to the guest cottage, and as they descended the wooden staircase, Bill stumbled and fell, shredding the quadriceps tendon above his right knee. He was whisked to a hospital in West Palm Beach, and the press was not alerted for nearly two hours. The delay gave rise to suspicions about the circumstances of his injury, which was unusually severe for such a fall. The White House doctors said Bill had not been drinking, but rumors inevitably circulated that he had been cavorting with a woman who had been spirited away after the accident.

On Friday the fourteenth, Bill underwent two hours of surgery on his right knee at Bethesda Naval Hospital. He remained awake, listening to the music of Jimmy Buffett and Lyle Lovett and cracking jokes with his doctors. The following day, he was well enough to film a video for that night's Gridiron Club dinner, and at midday on Sunday he returned to the White House in a wheelchair dutifully pushed by Hillary.

Once he was settled, she was out the door with Chelsea for a two-week goodwill tour of six African countries, the First Lady's ninth trip abroad without her husband. This time, the Hillaryland contingent included celebrity photographer Annie Leibovitz, who had been assigned to take pictures for a *Vogue* article Hillary planned to write.

Bill was equally determined to keep to his own scheduled trip to Helsinki for his eleventh meeting with Boris Yeltsin. After consulting with his doctors, he delayed his departure by one day and took off on Wednesday the nineteenth. His principal agenda, he said on the flight, was to "push ol' Boris" to do "the right but hard thing" and agree to NATO expansion, which would help smooth Russia's admission to the G-7. Seated in a wheelchair with his leg in a cast, the President was transported from Air Force One on the platform of a Finnair catering truck. Although he was in considerable discomfort, Bill was fully prepared for the Russian leader. "He didn't need either a script or a rehearsal," wrote Strobe Talbott.

After two days of meetings—and one drunken performance at dinner by Yeltsin—the leaders appeared at a joint press conference, where they described how they had dealt with Yeltsin's objections to the "eastern expansion." "He thinks it's a mistake," Bill conceded, but they had found a way "of shifting the accent from our disagreement" to focus on shared goals. Yeltsin would accede to enlarging NATO to include former Warsaw Pact countries. To "minimize the negative consequences" and build on existing cooperation with the allies in Bosnia, he would also sign a NATO-Russia charter calling for regular consultation and economic development.

Six thousand miles away, Hillary was generating headlines of her own in Africa. Tanzanian activist Gertrude Mongella described her as "the co-pilot" of the United States, and at the University of Cape Town Hillary predicted that a woman would be elected President of the United States within two decades. She theorized that women had led other countries such as Britain because they had been leaders of the majority party in a parliamentary system and did not have to withstand the rigors of direct elections. "They do not have to go out and sell themselves to the entire country and face all the required questions that we in public life have to deal with," Hillary said, momentarily appearing to be speaking personally. "It's very difficult for women to answer many of the perceptions and stereotypes the public holds about them," she said, adding that in order to succeed, women should not be "tricked or seduced into undermining" one another.

On Saturday, March 29, Hillary and Chelsea were wrapping up their journey in Eritrea as Bill was welcoming Monica Lewinsky to the Oval Office for their final sexual encounter. He hobbled on crutches when Lewinsky arrived shortly after 2:00 p.m., bearing a copy of *Vox*, Nicholson Baker's explicit novel about phone sex that the President placed on the bookshelf of his private study between *Churchill on Courage: Timeless Wisdom for Persevering* and *UFO Crash at Roswell*. Lewinsky was "babbling on about something," when "kind of to shut me up, I think," Bill kissed and partly disrobed her. They had brief genital contact for the first time, but he resisted intercourse. Lewinsky performed their customary oral sex, and once again Bill ejaculated.

During their conversation afterward, Bill gave no hint of ending the affair, but he reiterated the need for absolute secrecy about their relationship, and he urged her if asked to say they were just friends. As Lewinsky was leaving at the end of their hour together, she gave him her updated résumé; the President kissed her on the forehead and serenaded her with Otis Redding's 1966 love song "Try a Little Tenderness." The next day, Easter Sunday, Hillary and Chelsea returned to Washington and "regaled Bill with our adventures" while he filled them in on his summit with Yeltsin.

Bill and Lewinsky did not see each other for nearly two months, although they had fraught phone conversations about her quest for a White House job. She interviewed in the press office in early May but was turned down for the position. Their dealings took an ominous turn when Marsha Scott told Bill that Walter Kaye, the Democratic donor who had originally recommended Lewinsky for an internship, might have heard from Lewinsky's mother, Marcia Lewis, that her daughter was having an affair with the President. As early as February, Kaye had picked up rumors about the affair from two New York Democrats, and over lunch that month Lewinsky's aunt, Debra Finerman, had told him the President called her niece late at night—a disclosure that "shocked" Kaye. In a phone conversation on May 17, Bill asked Lewinsky point-blank if she had confided in her mother. "Of course not," she replied, when in fact she had done so many months earlier.

A week later, on Saturday, May 24, Bill invited Lewinsky to his office at midday while Hillary and Chelsea swam outside in the White House pool. He told Lewinsky he had to end their affair, after eighteen months, because it was causing him too much "pain and torment." By way of explanation, he described the secret life "filled with lies and subterfuge" that he was to write about in his 2003 memoir. By Lewinsky's account, his private description of his instinctively deceptive nature went far beyond what he revealed in his book. He told Lewinsky that he had engaged in "hundreds of affairs" during his marriage. In 1986, at the age of forty, he had been so unhappy that he had thought of divorcing Hillary and leaving politics altogether. Instead, he told Lewinsky that he decided to stay married largely for the sake of Chelsea. Since then, he had kept a calendar on which he indicated "the days when he had been good."

Lewinsky, who later referred to their meeting as "Dump Day," recalled that they both cried and that Bill pledged to "be a very good friend . . . and help you in a lot of ways you don't even realize." As they parted, they kissed and hugged, although Lewinsky remained inconsolable.

Three days later, on May 27, 1997, the Supreme Court ruled unanimously that a sitting President could be subject to a civil lawsuit and that the Paula Jones case could proceed. Bill heard the news while he was conferring with his advisors in the American Ambassador's residence in Paris before a follow-up meeting with Boris Yeltsin. "He was blindsided," said one of his senior advisors. With even his two appointees going against him, Bill couldn't blame a conservative cabal. "From the moment he got the news, he seemed to be sleepwalking through the summit," recalled Strobe Talbott. The purpose of the Paris meeting was the ceremonial signing of the Russia-NATO charter that had been hammered out in Helsinki, so the two presidents weren't expected to do any delicate negotiating. But Bill was upset that the symbolic moment, which effectively overturned the 1945 Yalta agreement, was overwhelmed by headlines about the Jones matter. "All of a sudden we were drawn back to scandals and sleaze and scuzzy stuff," said Mike McCurry.

Bill and Hillary proceeded to the Netherlands to celebrate the fiftieth anniversary of the beginning of the Marshall Plan before traveling to London for twelve hours to visit newly elected British prime minister Tony Blair and his wife, Cherie. Despite the coverage back home, reporters declined to ask the President about the Jones case. He was conspicuously at ease in his first news conference with Blair, assuming an avuncular role and joking about resenting that the British leader was "seven years younger and has no gray hair." Blair spoke expansively about their "new generation of leadership" and their mutual interest in the "radical center of politics." He was appropriately deferential toward Bill's political achievements but confident enough to interject his point of view.

The Clintons returned to Washington that evening after dinner with the Blairs at Le Pont de la Tour on the bank of the Thames. The two couples found much in common, particularly Hillary and Cherie, an outspoken feminist with a busy career as a barrister. "The conversation never stalled," Hillary recalled, as they shared ideas about education, welfare, and "our concerns about the pervasive influence of the media."

Back in Washington, at Chelsea's commencement the following week,

Bill exhorted the 122 seniors at Sidwell Friends School to "dream big and chase your dreams" and to be "optimistic and grateful." Somewhat unusually, he also dwelled on the "dark forces" unleashed by "hatred and self-pity" and cautioned against becoming cynical or vengeful. He urged both forgiveness and humility, saying, "You're human, subject to error and frailty, incapable, no matter how intelligent you are, of ever knowing the whole truth." He seemed to be obliquely sharing his own code of survival, telling the graduates not to give "permission" to those who tried to make them feel inferior. "Too many brilliant minds and prodigious energies are spent simply putting people down," he said. "Do not be put down."

Bill was keeping away from Lewinsky during these weeks, and she was growing more agitated as White House officials gave her the runaround about a job. Bill later said he had decided to "limit the contact" with Lewinsky, even if it meant she might be "more likely to speak" about their relationship. On June 16, she met with White House Deputy Director of Personnel Marsha Scott—not knowing what Scott had heard from Walter Kaye—and was disquieted when Scott questioned her closely about her reasons for returning to the White House, "with such nasty women there and people gossiping" about her. Lewinsky was wary of Scott, a former interior designer from Arkansas who described herself as "Bill's girlfriend from our hippie days." Scott had been in the middle of some sensitive Clinton controversies—as an intermediary during Webster Hubbell's incarceration, an organizer of White House perks for big Democratic donors, the developer of the White House donor database, and now Bill's point person, along with Betty Currie, on Monica Lewinsky's employment.

After being ignored by Bill for more than a month, Lewinsky sent him a note on June 29 saying she felt "disposable, used and insignificant." When he failed to reply, she followed up with a note on July 3 containing her first implicit threat of exposure. If she didn't return to the White House, she would "need to explain to my parents exactly why that wasn't happening," she wrote. Alarmed by her tone, Bill asked her to meet him at the White House the next morning. She arrived at 8:51 a.m. on Friday, July 4, when much of Washington was shut down for the holiday. He rebuked her sharply about her note, telling her it was "illegal to threaten the President of the United States." But when she burst into tears, he comforted her with hugs, kisses on her neck, and caresses, telling her, "I wish I had more time for you. . . . I might be alone in three years." Emboldened, Lewinsky observed that Hillary had "cold eyes," adding that Bill seemed "to need so much nurturing." Instead of being chastened, Lewinsky concluded that the President was in love with her.

The same day, the Drudge Report, then a fledgling website posting gossip and titillating news articles, reported that Michael Isikoff of *Newsweek* was "hot on the trail" of a story about a "federal employee sexually propositioned by the President on federal property." The unnamed employee was Kathleen Willey, whose encounter with Bill at the end of 1993 had been leaked to Isikoff the previous March by lawyers for Paula Jones. Matt Drudge, the brash creator of the website, had recently been discovered by the mainstream press, but reporters and editors remained leery of passing along his tidbits. Lewinsky had heard about the *Newsweek* investigation from Linda Tripp (who had been interviewed by Isikoff) and shared what she knew with the President. He reassured her that the story was false, saying he would "never approach a small-breasted woman like Kathleen Willey."

Bill, Hillary, and Chelsea left that evening for a brief holiday in Majorca with King Carlos and Queen Sofia of Spain, followed by a meeting in Madrid to formally admit Poland, Hungary, and the Czech Republic into NATO. But the plan hit a snag when French president Jacques Chirac "threw a hissy fit," in the words of a senior administration official, and strenuously objected, partly because the United States was dictating the terms. On Monday evening, July 7, Tony Blair joined the Clintons in their hotel suite at a moment when Bill was beginning to waver under Chirac's bullying. Blair "was trying to stiffen Clinton's spine," recalled the top advisor. "Hillary was very much in the conversation. Clinton was getting heavy pressure from Chirac to admit the Baltic states and Romania. Blair and Hillary helped prevent that."

Following the Madrid meetings, the Clintons took separate paths, Hillary to Vienna for a forum on women entrepreneurs, and Bill to Poland, Romania, and Denmark. Two days after he arrived home, on Monday evening, July 14, Bill summoned Lewinsky to the White House. He was now concerned about the *Newsweek* investigation of the Willey accusations mentioned in what he mistakenly called "the Sludge Report," and he quizzed Lewinsky about the role of Linda Tripp. When he asked if she had spoken to Tripp about their relationship, Lewinsky lied and said no.

AT THE END of July, the President was playing golf with basketball star Michael Jordan in Las Vegas when the White House and congressional Republicans agreed on the details of a budget deal. Unlike in previous years, Bill had delegated the discussions to Bowles and his team, who worked collegially with negotiators representing Gingrich. For the first time in nearly three decades, Congress was poised to pass a balanced budget, which was made possible by a surging U.S. economy and an unanticipated flood of tax revenues. The economy had taken off in the second Clinton term due to a convergence of factors that included a drop in interest rates, low inflation, oil prices around twenty dollars per barrel, and deregulation in telecommunications that helped propel the Internet boom. The unusual windfall had given both sides new latitude at the bargaining table. Democrats accepted Republican terms for significant reductions in capital-gains and estate taxes—the largest tax cut in sixteen years. The Democrats got more money for education, as well as twenty-four billion dollars for a new health-insurance plan for five million children of the working poor. In a nod toward fiscal prudence, the program was to be funded by raising cigarette taxes fifteen cents per pack. Conservatives won some restraints on Medicare spending and permitted the administration to restore welfare benefits to legal immigrants. Overall, the deal provided less money for discretionary spending on liberal social programs in the future, prompting Republicans to wear "GOP 1997 Tax Cuts: The Reagan Legacy" T-shirts to a victory gathering on the east steps of the Capitol. The President was "euphoric" about signing an agreement marking the conclusion of a struggle that had begun with the disastrous midterm elections of 1994.

Bill had scarcely a week to savor his accomplishment before *Newsweek* broke the Kathleen Willey story after Michael Isikoff learned she had been subpoenaed by the Jones lawyers to show a "pattern of behavior" by the President. White House spokesmen called the accusation of sexual groping "preposterous," and other major news organizations backed off in the absence of definitive proof. Willey had remained silent, but *Newsweek* cited Linda Tripp as a witness to Willey's dishevelment after her Oval Office visit. Clinton lawyer Bob Bennett attacked Tripp as "not to be believed," which provoked her in unanticipated ways. She soon confided to New York literary agent Lucianne Goldberg that Monica Lewinsky was Bill Clinton's "girlfriend." Tripp also decided to begin taping her phone conversations with Lewinsky, in an effort to prove "misbehavior" by the President.

The day after the *Newsweek* story, Bennett initiated secret negotiations with Gil Davis and Joseph Cammarata, the lawyers for Paula Jones. All three attorneys were eager to settle, and they tentatively agreed on a payment of seven hundred thousand dollars and a statement from the President that Jones had engaged in no improper conduct. The President was in greater jeopardy than his attorney knew, given Tripp's machinations and the increasing likelihood that the Jones lawyers would hear about the affair with Lewinsky. Hillary remained opposed to a settlement, and she and Bill continued to believe that any deal would provoke others to file similar lawsuits. In the end, however, Paula Jones scuttled the talks by insisting for the first time that the President apologize. Her lawyers urged her to reconsider, and when, at the end of August, she refused, they quit.

Bill yielded to Lewinsky's continued entreaties and agreed to see her on Saturday morning, August 16. She brought an array of gifts for his fifty-first birthday, but she found him in a distracted and irritable mood. They quarreled over Marsha Scott, who Lewinsky felt was stringing her along about a White House job. But by the end of nearly an hour and a half together, Bill had agreed to "bend the rules" and enjoy a birthday kiss. Lewinsky tried to initiate oral sex, which he spurned, saying, "I'm trying to be good."

The next afternoon, the Clinton family left for Martha's Vineyard, returning to the Friedman compound after the two-year absence dictated by their campaign consultants. Their three-week holiday was their longest ever, and one day Hillary even joined her husband on the golf course, which she didn't enjoy because she played so poorly. Bill and Hillary made their social rounds in the evenings—a fifty-first birthday party for Bill given by Ted Danson and Mary Steenburgen, dinner with Caroline and John Kennedy Jr. at the home of their late mother—but they spent more time than usual on their own, playing Scrabble and taking walks with Chelsea, making the most of their final weeks before her departure for Stanford University. They had been remarkably successful at keeping their daughter sheltered from press scrutiny, presenting her in carefully controlled circumstances to show her at her best. The previous spring, Hillary had orchestrated her daughter's emergence as a solo player in a forum with African teenagers. Reporters commented on Chelsea's polished public speaking and her poise and maturity. Even when an African newspaper called her "ugly," she "took it in stride," according to Hillary's aides.

At seventeen, she had shed her braces, but her heavy features were unlikely to invite a second glance. Compared with her mother, who had seemed indifferent to her looks when she was her daughter's age, Chelsea had become extremely conscious of her appearance, taking after her paternal grandmother. Born without eyebrows, Virginia Kelley had prided herself on spending nearly an hour each morning meticulously applying the heavy makeup she called "paint." Chelsea, too, "put on tons of makeup every day," said one of her friends. "Her hair was always heavily gelled, the ringlets were firm. She spent forty-five minutes doing her makeup. She was pretty high maintenance getting ready."

She had also developed a preoccupation with her weight. "To some degree that must have come from the press," said a friend. "People always said, 'You are much smaller than in photos.' She liked that, and she wanted to be smaller. She didn't have the body type to be superthin, but she was as thin as her body let her be." When she was with her contemporaries, "she would either not eat or she would eat a bowl of peas or half a loaf of bread," said her friend. "She would eat a lot at one sitting—like a tub of yogurt. She never ate a typical meal. It was probably a function of ballet, because she doesn't have the right body type for ballet. She used her clothes as calibration."

Outwardly, she continued to be a biddable daughter, showing no sparks of rebellion and being always alert to her public image. She had a boyfriend, a classmate who was the son of a real-estate developer, and a tight circle of friends. Neither of her parents hovered over her social life, although once Hillary sought out the spouse of one of Bill's top advisors "to talk about her apprehensiveness about Chelsea's emerging sexuality. She said Chelsea had put on her dress to go to a formal, and Hillary could see every curve, which made her nervous."

When Chelsea's friends engaged in underage drinking, she participated, but carefully. One evening in the spring of her senior year, she attended a gathering of forty teenagers at a home in northwest Washington where the parents were absent, and several participants bought a total of four cases of beer with fake IDs. The members of Chelsea's Secret Service detail remained in their SUV outside, discouraging crashers and keeping the party under control. "Chelsea didn't push the envelope at all," said one of her friends. "She didn't really drink. She understood the cost of that, and she decided it wasn't worth it to her. She was very grown-up. She wasn't reflective about it, but her parents trained her well."

The Clinton family's trip to Stanford aboard Air Force One on Thursday, September 18, was meant to convey an air of normalcy, despite the presence of 250 journalists clamoring for tidbits. Marsha Berry, Hillary's press secretary, emphasized that Chelsea's roommate had been selected "according to the University's usual procedures," but in fact she was a friend from Washington, D.C., who had been chosen by the Clintons. Bill and Hillary dispensed with the Presidential limousine and arrived at the Palo Alto campus on Friday morning in armored Chevrolet Suburbans. Bill came dressed in khakis and a sports shirt, while Hillary looked subdued in a black floppy hat with matching pants and blouse. The First Couple clipped on name tags and toted boxes and suitcases to Chelsea's room in Wilbur Hall, which had bulletproof windows. While Hillary "got on Chelsea's nerves with all the fixing up," Bill noted, he made himself useful by taking the bunk beds apart to create separate twin beds. Once finished, he stood at the window and "stared out morosely, looking like a dazed boxer who had just been pummeled in the ring," Hillary recalled.

Chelsea's flight from the nest posed special challenges for both parents. Bill and Hillary adored their daughter, but she also served as glue for their marriage. Whenever Chelsea was in the picture, she became the inevitable symbol of a happy family. Her absence removed a crucial connection, and her parents sought to cope by planning extensive travel, much of it apart. From October through mid-November, Hillary anticipated being in the White House only two or three nights. "You can't know it's empty," Hillary said, "if you're not there."

MONICA LEWINSKY INTENSIFIED her pressure on the President that fall, finding little consolation in his gifts of a dress, a hat, and two T-shirts from Martha's Vineyard, which Betty Currie passed along to her in early September. Lewinsky and Marsha Scott were increasingly at odds, until finally in a phone conversation on September 3, Scott indicated there was no hope for a White House job. In an e-mail to a friend, Lewinsky complained that the President would "just lead me on because he doesn't have the balls to tell me the truth." She drafted a note of complaint about Scott to Bill, asserting that there were other women rumored to be his lovers who had "golden positions" at the White House "because they have your approval. . . . You and Marsha win. . . . You let me down, but I shouldn't have trusted you in the first place."

Betty Currie endured weeks of whining phone calls, tantrums, and one crying jag at the White House gate from Lewinsky. At Bill's suggestion, Currie contacted both Erskine Bowles and his deputy, John Podesta, to help in the job search. On September 30, when Hillary was in Miami addressing a women's group, Bill called Lewinsky to reassure her that Bowles could arrange a position in the White House. Around that time, the President had indeed asked his Chief of Staff to find the young woman something "in the Old Executive Office Building." But as with previous efforts, nothing came of the request.

By early October 1997, Linda Tripp had her operation to expose the President in high gear. Lewinsky had shown her the semen-stained dress from her February tryst, a devastating piece of evidence. Not only had Tripp begun taping her phone conversations with Lewinsky, she had anonymously given a tip about the former White House intern to the Jones lawyers, and she had alerted *Newsweek*'s Michael Isikoff about the affair. Tripp and her new confidante, Lucianne Goldberg, met with Isikoff on October 6 for a briefing that included the tantalizing prospect of the Jones lawyers using the Lewinsky job search to show how the President rewarded employees for sexual favors. By then, Lewinsky had shifted her sights to a post at the United Nations, telling Tripp that Bill owed it to her, along with an admission "that he helped fuck up my life." She sent a letter to the President demanding his assistance as a "solution for both of us."

At 2:30 a.m. on Friday, October 10, Bill called Lewinsky in a fury about her ultimatums. "If I had known what kind of person you really were, I wouldn't have gotten involved with you," Bill shouted. He told her that he had become "obsessed" with finding her a job. "I wake up in the morning, and it makes me sick thinking about it," he said. "My life is empty except for you and this search." By 4:00 a.m., they had both settled down, and Bill promised to help her relocate to New York.

That night, Hillary was wrapping up a visit to Panama, where she had addressed a conference on microcredit. On the flight home, she agreed to talk to reporters eager for reflections on her upcoming fiftieth birthday. Exercising her customary tight control, she allowed them to use only innocuous quotes, most of which concerned plans for resettling in Arkansas after the presidency. She warmed to comparisons of her husband to Teddy Roosevelt but "made a face" when reminded that the twenty-sixth President had run for a third term as an independent, pointing out "with seeming satisfaction" that her own husband couldn't do so because of the Twenty-second Amendment. She called Bill a "very nostalgic and philosophical man" intent on savoring every remaining moment in the White House. "He is really relishing it," she said.

The next day, the Clintons' twenty-second wedding anniversary, Betty Currie summoned the President's former lover at 8:30 a.m. for a meeting in the Oval Office. He hugged Lewinsky before they sat down in his private study to talk for almost an hour about her employment ambitions. In addition to the United Nations, she was now aiming for more lucrative jobs in the private sector. At Lewinsky's suggestion, Bill agreed to contact Vernon Jordan, who had arranged some of Webster Hubbell's sinecures in 1994—such as $63,000 from MacAndrews & Forbes, the holding company owned by Revlon chief executive Ronald Perelman. As Lewinsky left through Currie's office, Bill gave her a chaste peck on the forehead. When reporters later asked why Hillary had allowed him to spend time in the Oval Office on their anniversary, he quipped, "Her Calvinism will let me work, but no golf."

Hillary returned to Latin America on Sunday morning for a weeklong tour with her husband to Venezuela, Brazil, and Argentina. It was her third trip to the region and his first, although he told reporters about his passion for Brazilian music and brought along his favorite Antonio Carlos Jobim ("The Girl from Ipanema") recordings, which he said had "haunted my imagination for over 30 years." From country to country, the President carried his message of free trade and better education, but Hillary stole the show in a spirited speech on feminism at the fabled Colon Theater in Buenos Aires. She condemned domestic violence, railed against "consumer culture" that sought to "objectify women," and drew loud applause when she promoted abortion rights in a country that was more than 90 percent Roman Catholic. "It became clear that Hillary is a radical feminist," said Liliana Tojo, an Argentinian lawyer. "We welcome that here."

Hillary's birthday celebration at the end of the month lasted five days, starting on October 23 with a White House Conference on Child Care, which was meant to show her continuing impact on administration policies. Two days later, Bill staged an elegant dinner dance at the Ritz-Carlton ballroom. Rather poignantly, given the crisis over Monica Lewinsky brewing in the background, George Stephanopoulos noted that Hillary "seemed as happy as I'd ever seen her" as she danced with her husband. On Sunday the twenty-sixth, her actual birthday, her staff orchestrated an elaborate picnic with pumpkins and haystacks under a tent on the South Lawn. On Monday, she had a daylong party in Chicago featuring visits with friends and family to the "stations of the cross" from her childhood and teenage years, capped by a tribute from her husband at the Chicago Cultural Center.

Only days later, she was off once more on her own, this time to Dublin, Belfast, and London, where she met with Tony and Cherie Blair to map out a series of "Third Way" conferences to "move beyond . . . personality-based politics." After stopping briefly in Washington and Texas, she headed overseas again on Sunday, November 9, for ten days in formerly Soviet-dominated Kazakhstan, Kyrgyzstan, and Uzbekistan to promote women's education and economic development. Her journey had more strategic importance than met the eye, signaling administration efforts to pull the remote countries of central Asia into the American and European orbit.

With Hillary away, Bill kept his eye on Lewinsky's progress with periodic phone calls. The night before her interview with UN Ambassador Bill Richardson on October 31, the President gave her a "pep talk" and offered pointers on how to conduct herself. Curiously, neither Richardson nor his two aides queried her about her work experience. Three days later, when Richardson offered her the job, she replied only that she would consider it. She was so confident of her favored status that she kept the ambassador's office on the string for two full months before finally declining the position.

Lewinsky had become fixated on using Vernon Jordan to land something better in the public-relations field. On November 5, she met the well-connected power broker, who told her that she had been "highly recommended" by the President. But Jordan did nothing to follow up, and her agitation flared again. In yet another attempt to mollify her, Bill invited her to the White House on Thursday, November 13, when Nancy Hernreich was out testifying on campaign-finance matters. Because of mixed signals, Lewinsky ended up waiting in the President's private study with the lights off while he worked in the Oval Office. She saw Bill only long enough for a quick kiss before he hurried away for a dinner with Mexican president Ernesto Zedillo. "I am consumed with this disappointment, frustration, and anger," she wrote afterward in an unsent letter.

ON HIS ARRIVAL IN Washington that autumn to assume his post as British Ambassador, Sir Christopher Meyer was struck by the atmosphere of "Southern lethargy" in the Clinton Administration. He anticipated a boring tenure during which the President "would spend his time playing a lot of golf." Clinton speechwriter Michael Waldman also found his boss "subdued, his normal ebullience tamped down."

There was nothing physically wrong with Bill except a hearing loss "unusually severe for someone his age" that required a prescription for a pair of in-canal hearing aids in early October. Otherwise, his health was better than ever after a full recovery from his knee injury. By lifting weights, swimming, and eating more carefully, he had lost twenty pounds and now weighed 196.

Yet the sense of his puzzling lassitude was pervasive, and the notion of a minimalist Clinton presidency had taken hold, despite the fact that he had three more years in office. The White House seemed "strangely paralyzed," and many commentators had all but written off the second term, citing the profusion of "itsy-bitsy proposals for itsy-bitsy babies" and the erosion of Bill's bully-pulpit potential by the campaign fund-raising controversies. George Stephanopoulos (who had left the White House after the 1996 election for a career in journalism) pronounced Bill a "lame duck." Dick Morris wrote that Bill had "gone to sleep" and seemed preoccupied mostly with his presidential library and talking endlessly about golf. Acknowledging the President's increasing time on the fairways, Mike McCurry tried to rationalize it as "think time." But Bill himself often emphasized the game's importance as an escape, describing it as a way to "slow down," where "you literally can't think about anything else. If you do, you can't hit a shot." Reporters now routinely challenged his scores, to the point that Tim Russert confronted him in a *Meet the Press* interview on November 9. "How many mulligans do you take in the average eighteen holes?" Russert asked.

"One now," Bill tersely replied.

"One mulligan?" Russert said, barely hiding his incredulity.

"Yes," the President said.

Perhaps the biggest disappointment of the year was the flagging initiative on race, which became crippled by squabbling on its seven-member board. When the President was personally engaged with the issue, moderating a town-hall meeting at the University of Akron in early December, for instance, he was in his element, as he provoked audience members and experts with rapid-fire questions. "If we had four hours, I could sit here and listen to you all and I'd never get tired of it," he said. "We should be doing this in America on a systematic disciplined basis, community by community." But the man at the top lacked that very discipline and proved incapable of moving beyond talk to action.

In late 1997, Janet Reno rejected for the last time the appointment of an Independent Counsel for the fund-raising scandals, citing a lack of evidence that the President or Vice President had done anything illegal. A parallel investigation by Tennessee senator Fred Thompson also hit a dead end after five months of hearings into the role of foreign money in the 1996 campaign. Most of the major figures in the various illegal schemes had either taken refuge behind the Fifth Amendment or had left the country, making it nearly impossible for Thompson's investigators to show clear links to the Chinese government. Nor was much gleaned from White House insiders, particularly former Deputy Chief of Staff Harold Ickes, who remained loyal to the Clintons and "seemed to delight in snarling at senators." Still, the trail of stories about unethical practices damaged the administration and further undercut the President's credibility with the press.

The Whitewater investigations had stalled at midyear when Kenneth Starr entered "prosecutor's purgatory," *Newsweek* noted, "close enough to see a case, not yet close enough to make it." Without the testimony of Susan McDougal, the Independent Counsel couldn't prove that Bill Clinton had a role in her fraudulent loan, and Webster Hubbell's stoic silence had shielded Hillary's questionable activities on behalf of Madison Guaranty and Castle Grande.

The Paula Jones lawsuit carried on, however, with the mortifying disclosure in early October of her affidavit from May 1994 describing the "distinguishing characteristics" of the President's private parts. Maureen Dowd of *The New York Times* had already jokingly speculated about a "bald eagle tattoo," but the particulars were less exotic. When erect at nearly five and a half inches, his penis showed a curvature from his right to his left, according to Jones. Bob Bennett, appearing on CBS's *Face the Nation*, found himself rebutting the description, insisting that the President was "normal" in "size, shape, direction." He based his assessment on a rather awkward interview with Bill and a consultation with urologist Kevin O'Connell, who had examined the President, although not when he had an erection.

The lawyers for Jones had already moved to their next line of attack by targeting women with whom Bill had "proposed having" or "sought to have" sexual relationships. The names of nearly twenty of these women showed up late in the afternoon of Friday, December 5, on a witness list faxed to Bennett. Among them was Monica Lewinsky, whose name didn't ring a bell with the President's lawyer. Bennett forwarded the list to Bruce Lindsey, but Bill did not recall having seen it before he encountered Lewinsky in the receiving line at a White House Christmas party that evening. Although startled by her presence, he greeted her warmly with a hug and asked her escort, "Are you taking good care of Monica at the Pentagon?"

The next morning, Lewinsky arrived at the northwest White House gate with several presents and a forlorn letter to Bill that acknowledged, "You want me out of your life." When Secret Service officers told her the President was entertaining former Vice President Walter Mondale's pretty thirty-seven-year-old daughter, Eleanor, Lewinsky stormed off in a jealous fury to call Betty Currie. Lewinsky later reached Bill, and they had a heated conversation for almost an hour, each topping the other in adolescent petulance and self-pity. "In my life no one has treated me as poorly as I have been treated by you," Bill said. "Outside of my family and my friends and my staff I have spent more time with you than anyone else in the world. How dare you make such a scene? It's none of your business who I see." He denied Lewinsky's accusation that he was having an affair with

Eleanor Mondale. "She is a friend of mine," he insisted. "In fact I set her up with her current boyfriend."

Bill ultimately tried to pacify Lewinsky by inviting her to his office after noon. They spent nearly a half hour together in his private study, where she gave him an antique sterling-silver cigar holder, a tie, a biography of Theodore Roosevelt, and assorted knickknacks she had bought for Christmas. He sat in a rocking chair, and she perched by his feet as he stroked her hair and reminisced about his childhood. In contrast to his earlier hostility on the phone, his demeanor was "affectionate and open," she later said. After she complained that Vernon Jordan had been unresponsive, the President assured her, "Oh I'll talk to him. I'll get on it." He also vowed "not to jerk you around like I did before" and then proceeded to do just that, leading her on by inviting her back to the White House for her Christmas gift and a kiss.

Three and a half hours after Lewinsky left the White House at 1:36 p.m., Bill met in the same office with Bob Bennett and Bruce Lindsey to review the witness list. Bennett soon brought up Lewinsky, who he now knew had worked in the White House. "Not a problem," said Bill. Bennett pressed further, and Bill sputtered, "Bob, do you think I'm fucking crazy? Hey look, let's move on. I know the press is watching me every minute. The Right has been dying for this kind of thing from day one. No it didn't happen. I'm retired. I'm retired."

When Bennett eventually learned of Lewinsky's visit with Bill earlier that Saturday afternoon, he was floored—not only by the President's risky behavior with an unpredictable young woman but by his blatant lying. Bill had an opportunity to level with Bennett, who would have seen the danger and devoted his attention to settling with Jones and eliminating the prospect of an interrogation of Lewinsky. Bill's refusal to do so indicated a fundamental misunderstanding of a lawyer's role. In part, he was showing his desire to be liked by everyone. It later became apparent that because Bill was so intent on avoiding Bennett's disapproval, he could not bring himself to tell the truth, even under the protection of confidentiality.

Chapter Thirteen

——

For reasons Bill Clinton never explained, he kept Monica Lewinsky in the dark for eleven days about her appearance on the Jones witness list. During that interval, Vernon Jordan suddenly became Lewinsky's advisor and patron, treating her to lunch in his office, calling contacts at MacAndrews & Forbes, Young & Rubicam, and American Express in New York City and urging her to vent her frustrations to him rather than to the President.

Bill broke his silence at 2:30 on the morning of December 17, when he awakened Lewinsky to tell her that Betty Currie's brother had been killed in an automobile accident. Moments later, he said, "I saw the witness list *today* for the Paula Jones case, and your name is on it," adding that "it broke my heart." To avoid a subpoena, he suggested that she sign an affidavit. (Curiously, in his 2004 autobiography Bill wrote, "I told her some women had avoided questioning by filing affidavits saying that I had not sexually harassed them," although sexual harassment had never been at issue in Lewinsky's case, while rewards for sexual favors most certainly were.) Together, they reviewed the various cover stories they had discussed during their affair: that she had come to the Oval Office to visit Betty Currie or to deliver papers. Although Lewinsky later said that the President never specifically "asked me to lie" in her sworn statement, subterfuge about their affair was by then second nature to both of them. From the beginning, Bill had urged her to "deny a relationship, if ever asked about it" and had said that "if the two people who are involved say it didn't happen, it didn't happen"—an echo of his taped comment to Gennifer Flowers in September 1991: "If they ever hit you with it, just say no and go on. . . . If everybody is on record denying it . . . no problem." Lewinsky admitted under oath: "There were secrets, and inherent in a secret is a lie." So it was both implicit and obvious that her affidavit would deny a sexual relationship, because if she told the truth she would be compelled to testify in the Jones case.

Two days later, Jones's lawyers issued a subpoena to Lewinsky, adding greater urgency to the proposed affidavit. In a distraught state, she visited Jordan, who referred her to his friend attorney Francis Carter. Jordan also asked if she and the President had been involved in "any sexual relationship." She said no, but she believed that Jordan "with a wink and a nod" understood the affair was sexual. "I did not get graphic," Jordan later explained. "I did not get specific. I didn't ask her if they kissed. I didn't ask if they caressed, all of which, as I understand it, is a part of the act of sex." That evening, Jordan met Bill in the Residence to brief him on the subpoena and on Lewinsky's agitated mood. Jordan recalled that when he asked his old friend, "Have you had sexual relations with Monica Lewinsky?" Bill said, "No, never." For his part, Bill later could not recall either the question or the denial.

Linda Tripp also received a subpoena that day, and in a recorded conversation Lewinsky told her confidante that she intended to lie under oath so Bill would not "get screwed in this case." She despaired that the President wouldn't settle with Jones because "he's in denial." When asked directly if Bill expected Lewinsky to tell the truth, she replied, "No, oh Jesus. . . . Nobody saw anything happen between us."

On Sunday, December 28, Lewinsky answered a summons from Betty Currie and arrived at the Oval Office at 8:16 a.m. She and the President retreated to his private office, where he gave her an array of gifts from Martha's Vineyard and a trip to Vancouver. After telling him she was alarmed by the subpoena's request for his earlier gifts to her, including a specific reference to a "hat pin," she suggested removing the items from her apartment and giving them to "someone, maybe Betty." By Lewinsky's account, instead of sternly warning her about the illegality of hiding evidence, he responded by saying either "I don't know" or "Let me think about that." Bill later testified to the contrary, saying that he had told

Lewinsky, "If they ask you for gifts, you have to give them what you have. . . . That's what the law is." In the hour they spent together, they played with Buddy, Bill's three-month-old chocolate Labrador puppy, and they shared a "passionate" and "physically intimate" kiss. "OK Kiddo—good luck in New York, and be good," Bill said as Lewinsky left. It was their final meeting.

Later that afternoon, according to Lewinsky's detailed recollection, Currie called to report that "the President said you have something to give me," meaning the gifts. Currie drove over to pick them up, and Lewinsky bundled them into a box for the secretary to hide under her bed. When questioned under oath, Currie couldn't recall whether the President had asked her to retrieve the gifts, although she said that Lewinsky "may remember better than I." Bill denied having made such a request.

Over breakfast with Vernon Jordan three days later, Lewinsky mentioned that she had notes in her apartment "from me to the President." According to Lewinsky, Jordan told her to "go home and make sure they're not there." Thinking she was complying with his advice, she destroyed some fifty drafts of notes to Bill. Jordan initially denied he had seen Lewinsky that morning but subsequently revised his recollection and admitted they had met for breakfast and had discussed notes. He insisted, however, that he had not urged her to destroy evidence.

On New Year's Eve, Bill and Hillary presided in their customary fashion at the Renaissance Weekend celebration, seated on a dais for a question-and-answer session. As usual, Bill took up all the oxygen, and Hillary appeared noticeably detached. "You could feel the chill fifty feet away—saying nothing and avoiding eye contact," wrote liberal syndicated columnist Richard Reeves. When someone asked them to mention the most spontaneous thing they had done that year, Hillary reached for the microphone for the first time and said, "We don't do spontaneity." Then, according to Reeves, "she put the cordless microphone back in her lap and looked straight ahead, leaving her husband to babble on."

The Clintons escaped for the first four days of 1998 to St. Thomas. Most of the time they remained out of sight, playing cards and word games with Chelsea, reading books, swimming, hiking, and cycling. The day after they returned home, the *Los Angeles Times*, *The Washington Post*, and other newspapers ran a picture taken with a telephoto lens of Bill and

Hillary in bathing suits, apparently slow dancing on the beach. They appeared in profile next to an outcropping of rocks, Bill beaming down at his wife's intent gaze—not quite Burt Lancaster and Deborah Kerr in *From Here to Eternity*, but evocative enough. Skeptics in the media instantly suspected that the First Couple had knowingly posed for the photo in an effort to convey marital harmony before Bill's deposition for the Paula Jones lawsuit in mid-January. The White House expressed outrage over the "invasion of privacy," and Hillary proclaimed her displeasure, saying, "Name me any 50-year-old woman who would knowingly pose in her bathing suit, especially with her back pointed to the camera." But the picture showed Hillary's figure from a flattering angle, and Bill's slimmed-down physique was also on display. Agence France-Presse, which snapped the image, charged the White House with "loving the picture while castigating the press."

"NOW LET'S SPEND SOME money," Bill said to his staff in a meeting on Monday, January 5, to discuss a projected federal surplus. No more the "complacent coaster," as Jonathan Alter of *Newsweek* had described him, Bill told his advisors he was determined to redouble his efforts to reform Medicare and Social Security, to seek ratification for the treaty on global warming signed by Al Gore in Kyoto in December, and to enact a range of federal social programs.

At the annual White House "thinkers' dinner" two days later, the President and First Lady were "glowing" and in "total possession of their lives," said Benjamin Barber. Bill Galston gave a compelling talk on the damage being done to American society by the "collapse of traditional families and traditional marriage," a topic that Barber realized in retrospect "must have been ironic and painful" for the President. When the meeting broke up at 10:30, Hillary retired to the second floor. But after listening to the scholars for more than two hours, Bill was determined to hold forth about politics, the Republicans in particular. "God, they hate me," he said. "I mean, they really hate me." Barber had never heard the President more "harsh and partisan," making comments about the GOP that were "personal and vindictive." Hillary returned with Buddy an hour later and finally coaxed her husband upstairs just before midnight.

Earlier that day, Monica Lewinsky had signed her false affidavit declaring that she had "never had a sexual relationship with the President" and that after leaving her White House job in April 1996 she had seen him only in the presence of others. In a phone conversation with Bill the previous Monday evening, she had asked if he wanted to see her affidavit, and he said no, because he had "already seen about fifteen others," a reference to the sworn statements taken during the 1992 campaign from women—some under duress—denying sexual involvement with him. It had been a testy exchange, and to Lewinsky's dismay she was not to speak to the President again.

On Thursday, January 8, Lewinsky bungled her interview with MacAndrews & Forbes, prompting Vernon Jordan to call company chairman Ronald Perelman and apply the "Jordan magic." He endorsed Lewinsky as "a bright young girl who I think is terrific," which impressed Perelman, since in his twelve years on the board Jordan had never before called on behalf of a prospective employee. The following day, Perelman's Revlon subsidiary offered Lewinsky a public-relations position at forty thousand dollars per year, and she promptly notified Jordan. "Mission accomplished," the proud Washington fixer exclaimed to Betty Currie shortly afterward. "Thank you very much," Bill said to Jordan when he heard the news.

The Jones case moved forward even as the judge in the case, Susan Webber Wright, expressed skepticism about the validity of the sexual-harassment charge. At a conference in Little Rock on Monday, January 12, Wright told the lawyers for both sides, "I'm aware of Bill Clinton's reputation for womanizing." But she added that while he was known for "chasing skirts, you know, just having a good time," he was not known as a "harasser." During the meeting, one of the Jones lawyers told Bob Bennett that Monica Lewinsky had had an affair with the President. Back at the White House, Bennett again quizzed the President, who insisted Lewinsky had only delivered mail and pizza and had once joined Betty Currie's church group to see the White House Christmas decorations.

That same day, Linda Tripp alerted the Starr office that she had twenty-two hours of tape recordings in which Lewinsky discussed her affair with the President. Tripp also alleged that Bill and Jordan had encouraged Lewinsky to sign a false affidavit and helped her find a job to secure her silence. The involvement of Jordan provided a direct link to Webster

Hubbell, who Starr and his staff believed had double-crossed them by promising testimony on criminal conduct by the Clintons that he never delivered. The sexual behavior of the President aside, the prosecutors saw a pattern of obstruction and deception comparable to that around Hubbell's suspicious consulting contracts.

Events moved swiftly in the following days. After debriefing Tripp and listening to her tapes, FBI agents fitted her with a wire to record Lewinsky in a lunch conversation. By Thursday, the Independent Counsel had secured authorization from Janet Reno to expand his investigation to include the allegations about the President and Lewinsky. On Friday the sixteenth, as FBI agents interrogated Lewinsky in a hotel suite, Bill was immersed in six hours of preparation with lawyers for his deposition the next day. "The only thing you have to worry about is if you lie in there," Bennett warned the President. "They will try to impeach you if you lie."

After an additional ninety-minute practice session early on Saturday morning, January 17, the President was ready for the Jones lawyers awaiting him in a conference room at Bennett's law firm, three blocks from the White House. Judge Wright joined them at Bennett's request to ensure that the questioning was appropriate to the case. At the outset, Bill acknowledged his understanding of a definition of "sexual relations" stipulating that a person knowingly engaged in or caused "contact with the genitalia, anus, groin, breast, inner thigh, or buttocks of any person with an intent to arouse or gratify the sexual desire of any person. . . . 'Contact' means intentional touching, either directly or through clothing." For the first hour, Bill easily deflected questions about Kathleen Willey and other women. Usually it came down to he said–she said, although he admitted sexual intercourse with Gennifer Flowers just once in 1977.

In the second hour of questioning, the Jones lawyers turned to Lewinsky. Bill had prepared himself to lie if necessary, although he later rationalized his intention to be "truthful but not particularly helpful." He knew the Jones team had information about certain gifts, but he was surprised by the specificity of their knowledge. Caught in a trap, he relied on his semantic agility and lawyerly legerdemain, while telling numerous lies in the process. By willfully misleading rather than misremembering or being confused, he also set himself up for a perjury charge. He even played the victim, asserting that his right-wing adversaries had given him such a "high level of paranoia" that he had stripped the curtains from the windows of the Oval Office, private office, and dining room "so I could avoid the kind of questions you are asking me here today."

The President said he never had "sexual relations" or a "sexual affair" with Lewinsky, which he later insisted meant sexual intercourse to him ("If it ain't in, it ain't sin," in Arkansas parlance), although his actions—heavy petting and more—certainly conformed to the agreed-upon definition of sexual relations. He lied when he said he had not talked to Lewinsky about her possible testimony—a conversation that had occurred in the middle of the night only a month earlier. He could not recall being alone with Lewinsky, nor the particulars about any of the forty-eight gifts they had exchanged. Dozens of times he ducked, saying, "I don't recall," or "I don't know," which was remarkable for a man who could vividly remember the details of golf matches played years earlier. At one point, Bennett tried to head off the Lewinsky questions by citing her affidavit and saying, "There is absolutely no sex of any kind, of any manner, shape or form with President Clinton." Bill silently assented to this characterization, which he was to turn to his advantage seven months later by infamously relying on Bennett's use of the present tense. At the end of the six-hour deposition, Bennett concluded that Bill had comported himself well. But the veteran attorney had been disquieted by the details about Lewinsky, including her meetings with Vernon Jordan, which Bennett had not known about.

HILLARY HAD SPENT her Saturday "hunkered down" with "household tasks." She had been battling a cold all week, and Bill had left that morning also feeling unwell. On his return to the Residence, he was both "agitated" and "exhausted." He later said he felt "an anxiety" after the deposition because of the Lewinsky questions. The Clintons had intended to join Erskine Bowles and his wife, Crandall, for dinner at a restaurant that evening, but at the last minute they canceled their plans. Instead, they dined together at home, watched a movie, and by Hillary's account "had a good time." But Bill was bothered enough to meet with Bruce Lindsey in the Oval Office to review the deposition. In the early evening, he also called Betty Currie at home and asked her to meet him at the Oval Office on Sunday—a rare request.

Meanwhile, the tom-toms in the press had begun beating as early as

Friday when Michael Weisskopf of *Time* called White House sources to check out a rumor about a pending *Newsweek* story by Michael Isikoff on the President and a young woman. On Saturday morning, other news organizations picked up fragments of the tale, prompting West Wing advisors John Podesta and Doug Sosnik to compare notes with Bruce Lindsey and Cheryl Mills, another White House lawyer. By early afternoon, Lindsey had heard about the Lewinsky interrogation from Bill during a break in the deposition, while his colleagues remained in the dark. *Newsweek*'s nervous editors decided ultimately that Isikoff's story needed more verification, so at 6:00 p.m. they killed it. "We figured we had dodged it," said one West Wing official.

But details about the spiked story leaked to Matt Drudge, who posted it on the Internet at 2:32 a.m. on Sunday. Some of Drudge's facts were wrong, but others—an affair between the President and a former White House intern, sexual encounters near the Oval Office, the transfer of the young woman to the Pentagon—were dead right. A senior West Wing official—probably Lindsey, by Bill's recollection—called the Residence shortly afterward to describe the Drudge item to the President.

On ABC's Sunday-morning talk show, *This Week*, Republican commentator Bill Kristol briefly mentioned the Internet news flash before George Stephanopoulos swatted him down, declaring Drudge to be "discredited." "It was hard to believe," said a close associate of the President, "not that Bill would cheat on his wife, but that he would run a risk with that kind of woman in the Oval Office where there were guards and windows all over. It was not a place to have a tryst."

But in Little Rock, veteran journalist Max Brantley read the Drudge Report and said to himself, "It finally happened. There is something here. From 1980 on everyone said, 'It's going to be the women.' I knew reading Drudge that it wasn't fabricated." He immediately called his wife, Ellen. "This is going somewhere," he said. "It gave everyone a sick feeling here," Brantley recalled. "People who had fought Ken Starr so long, who had rallied so strongly in Bill Clinton's defense. This news made all that irrelevant and gave Bill Clinton the tools of his own end."

The Clintons attended church together that morning, which Hillary said "built us up again" (without explaining what precisely had torn them down). In the afternoon, as Hillary somewhat oddly described it, "we just stayed home and cleaned closets." She later explained that they had combed through old boxes of papers and photo albums as a reminder of their past—"that we have one . . . so much more than the extremely painful moments."

At 5:00, Bill went to the Oval Office, where he met Betty Currie. Standing by her desk, he drilled her with rapid-fire questions and assertions about Lewinsky: "You were always there when she was there, right? We were never really alone. Monica came on to me, and I never touched her, right? You can see and hear everything, right?" Although Currie was clearly incapable of answering most of his inquiries, she sensed that he wanted her to indicate agreement. When this encounter later became a matter of dispute, Bill said he merely wanted to "refresh" his "recollection," while the prosecutors insisted he was trying to influence Currie's version of events. Since she hadn't yet been called to testify, Bill was not technically guilty of witness tampering.

On Monday, January 19, the Martin Luther King Jr. holiday, Drudge published more particulars, including Monica Lewinsky's name, which fueled further inquiries from the press. "I shamed them into not using anything from Drudge," recalled McCurry. "I told them it lacked credibility. They were cowed. They wouldn't have dared to rip and read from Drudge."

Bill occupied himself with his State of the Union message, which he had been rewriting for two days. In a meeting with his speechwriters in the afternoon, he was in an "expansive, animated mood." Yet he also made nearly thirty phone calls that day to various lawyers and to Currie, who in turn frantically tried to contact Lewinsky, calling her eight times during one two-hour stretch. Lewinsky had not only gone underground, she had hired a new attorney, a medical-malpractice specialist from Los Angeles named William Ginsburg.

Hillary, who rarely gave interviews, took time during the holiday to answer questions from radio reporters for CBS and NBC. She spoke in unusual detail about her weekend activities and dismissed her husband's ordeal by deposition. "We do box it off," she said, echoing comments Bill had made the previous week about putting his worries "in a little box" so he could "do my work." She blamed the Paula Jones case on "political maneuvering" by enemies who had their own "agendas."

The Middle East peace process commanded the President's attention for most of Tuesday, with the arrival of Israeli prime minister Benjamin Netanyahu. The two men had a ninety-minute Oval Office meeting in the morning, with another session scheduled for the evening in the Residence. By 8:30 p.m., the White House was fielding inquiries from *Washington Post* reporters who had picked up Isikoff's leads. The *Post* had the essentials of the Lewinsky story, including the role of Vernon Jordan, the existence of the Tripp tapes, and the expansion of the Starr inquiry to investigate new charges of perjury and obstruction of justice against the President. "Until that moment, it had sounded like salacious gossip that doesn't go anywhere," recalled McCurry. "When it was connected to the Starr inquiry, it became something else." Bill began his discussions with Netanyahu at 9:45 p.m., before the *Post* had come off the presses. But the Israeli leader saw that, compared to their morning meeting, the President was "considerably less focused, not on top of the agenda." He thought that perhaps Bill had a health problem because he was so distracted. It was the first of numerous intrusions by the Lewinsky scandal into important presidential deliberations in the year to come.

McCurry read the bulldog edition of the *Post* at his desk as the hour approached midnight. The page-one story with the big four-column headline prominently quoted Bob Bennett. "The President adamantly denies he ever had a relationship with Ms. Lewinsky, and she has confirmed the truth of that," said Bennett. "This story seems ridiculous, and I frankly smell a rat." After assessing the damage, McCurry and his colleagues dispatched National Security Advisor Sandy Berger to brief Bill once his meeting with Netanyahu ended. Shortly after midnight, the story broke on the *Post* website as well as on ABC radio, and Bill made a series of calls to Bennett, Lindsey, and Currie until 2:30 a.m. The President left a wake-up call for 7:00 a.m., but he did not sleep.

THE FOLLOWING SEVEN DAYS, from January 21 to 27, shook the Clinton Administration to its core. Bill's first call on Wednesday the twenty-first was to Vernon Jordan at 6:30 a.m., followed by conversations with Lindsey, David Kendall, and Bennett, to whom he reiterated his earlier denials. By Hillary's account, her husband awakened her early to tell her about the *Post* story and to explain that Lewinsky was a friend he had helped with a job search. He said the young woman had "misinterpreted his attention" and that he had done "nothing improper." Against the backdrop of "more than six years of baseless claims" and countless attacks by their enemies, she professed to believe her husband. "It was one more false rumor," she said. Her description was weirdly anodyne, like "a bewildered Ozzie Nelson rousing Harriet from slumber," noted the *Post's* David Maraniss, rather than a discussion of "new sex allegations that seemed to threaten everything."

By the time Bill and Hillary called Chelsea, she was aware of the story on the *Washington Post* website. They reassured her that it was yet another attack by their conservative enemies—a message she absorbed readily after years of conditioning. Her mother said, "You need to push through this. These people are telling lies. You have heard this all your life." Jesse Jackson followed up early the next morning with the same message, "talking about a right-wing conspiracy, and her father being victimized," said one of Chelsea's classmates.

When Hillary's minister in Little Rock, Ed Matthews, asked how they were dealing with their daughter, Hillary said simply, "We know the truth." "There is something almost superficial or synthetic that seems to be what ultimately binds this family together," Matthews told author Gail Sheehy.

Watching Chelsea's reaction, one of her friends could see "such an importance placed on image in that family. It was easier to explain as, 'The conservatives are at fault, not your father.' In a typical family facing that situation, the truth would have come out organically and faster if dad and mom had moments of open discussion. But the complexity of their situation was due to these political imperatives. There was no challenge of a conversation about a parent being unfaithful, but rather, 'Your father is President, and we have goals that can't be compromised.'" For Chelsea, "there was always pressure to be the obedient child, always grown up and emotionally mature," her friend continued. "She had her image to preserve, and she couldn't say, 'This is awful, and I hate you.' Everybody preserved their image and inhibited their conversation."

THE OFFICIAL WHITE HOUSE line proclaimed that the President was "outraged by these allegations" and "has never had an improper relationship with this woman." But Hillary watched the men of the West Wing "walking around in a daze" and decided to "forge ahead" as Bill's chief defender. After a speech at Goucher College in Maryland, her mood was "chipper," and she declared that she "absolutely" considered the charges against her husband to be false. Once again, she deflected attention to the "concerted effort to undermine his legitimacy as President."

Throughout that day and in the weeks to come, Bill personally denied the allegations to one advisor and friend after another—not only that he "did not have sexual relations" with Lewinsky but that he "did not ask anybody to lie." To some, he went even further, telling Deputy Chief of Staff John Podesta, "I did not screw that girl," and "she did not blow me." Bill came close to being forthright only with fellow miscreant Dick Morris, who called at midday on Wednesday to commiserate.

Bill admitted that he did "do something. . . . With this girl I just slipped up." He added that "there may be gifts" and "messages on her phone answering machine." While Morris spoke of the national capacity for forgiveness, Bill fixated on his legal vulnerability for perjury. He readily agreed when Morris suggested taking a snap poll on voter attitudes.

At the same time, both Hillary and Bill singled out White House aide Sidney Blumenthal as their confidant. Not only was he intensely partisan and loyal, but he had such a conspiratorial cast of mind that within the West Wing he was known as "GK," short for "Grassy Knoll." Hillary summoned him in the afternoon to emphasize that Lewinsky was one of many "people in trouble" her husband had helped out of "empathy" and "religious conviction" (a reprise of what Hillary had told ABC's Sam Donaldson about Gennifer Flowers six years earlier). Blumenthal in turn recounted to Hillary some as yet unpublished Lewinsky "revelations" about Bill's voice mails, his preference for oral sex, and the supposed existence of a dress with semen stains—all of which he had heard from journalist David Brock, an apostate conservative who still maintained contact with his former allies.

Rather than dwell on the shocking substance, Hillary and Blumenthal coolly focused on the "lines of influence underlying the scandal"—further reinforcement for her entrenched belief in a cabal of right-wing enemies, as well as a convenient way to redirect her feelings. They agreed on a strategy in which Blumenthal would play an integral part: a war on Starr and his "daring political venture" to unseat her husband. She told Blumenthal that when she and Bill had earlier discussed the crisis in these terms, he had remarked, "Well, we'll just have to win."

That afternoon, Bill was noticeably less resolute in three back-to-back interviews originally scheduled to preview his State of the Union message. In the first, a 3:30 p.m. taping in the Roosevelt Room with public television's Jim Lehrer, he seized on the formulation Bennett had used in the deposition, saying a half-dozen times in slightly shaded versions, "There is no improper relationship." He also said with a straight face, "Look, you know as much about this as I do right now." Six minutes after the nearly hourlong interview had ended, Bill was in the Oval Office, speaking by phone to Morton Kondracke and Ed Henry from *Roll Call*, the Capitol Hill newspaper. Again, he relied on the present tense, shifting to the past only when prompted by Kondracke's final query: "Was it in any way sexual?"

"The relationship was not sexual," Bill said. "And I know what you mean, and the answer is no."

Mike McCurry thought Bill's performance was "weird because he wasn't being declarative. His demeanor seemed embarrassed." Before the last interview, a live broadcast at 5:08 p.m. on National Public Radio with Mara Liasson and Robert Siegel, McCurry called Bill's attention to his perplexing semantics. "OK, I'll use the past tense," said the President. He restated his denials, spoke again of the "little box" in his brain reserved for the scandal, and admitted that he was "furious" about dealing with any "distraction" from his job as President. Once more he said, "You know at least as much about it as I do," blaming his lack of knowledge about "the facts" on having "worked until 12:30 last night" with Netanyahu on Middle East peace.

Shortly after Bill wrapped up at 6:00 p.m., Blumenthal joined him in the Oval Office and found him "off-balance" and "beside himself." At first, Bill parroted Hillary's self-serving tale, explaining that he had only tried to help Lewinsky because "that's how I am." He then pivoted to a new line of thought, saying Dick Morris had told him that if Richard Nixon had gone on national television at the beginning of Watergate "explaining everything he had done wrong, making it all public, he would have survived."

An astonished Blumenthal asked the President what he had done wrong.

"Nothing," Bill hastily said.

"That's one of the stupidest ideas I've heard," replied Blumenthal. "Why would you do that if you have done nothing wrong?"

According to a senior White House official, Bill had been "seriously considering leveling with the American people" after at least one of his close advisors had counseled him to do so—a "frame of mind" partly reflected in his Lehrer interview. Now that Blumenthal helped him slam the door on that idea, Bill planted a slanderous story about Lewinsky. She had made a "sexual demand," he said, and when he rebuffed her, she had threatened to "tell others they had had an affair." She resented being known among her contemporaries as a "stalker"—a characterization she could disprove if the President had had sex with her. Portraying himself as the injured party, Bill said he had resisted Lewinsky's sexual overtures because "I've gone down that road before," and "I've caused pain for a lot of people, and I'm not going to do that again." The President even added a literary fillip when he compared himself to the persecuted hero of Arthur Koestler's *Darkness at Noon*.

By evening, Hillary had already assembled her defense team. Besides Blumenthal, she called in stalwarts Harold Ickes, Mickey Kantor, and Harry Thomason, along with James Carville as the designated attack dog for the talk shows. Thomason arrived on Thursday and settled into his room on the third floor of the Residence, where he remained for the next thirty-four days. He and Bill took Buddy for a walk that evening on the South Lawn. On the advice of Bob Bennett, Thomason refrained from questioning his old friend directly, but he got the message that "it just did not happen" with Lewinsky. Thomason also declined to ask because, he later said, "I wanted it to be true, and I felt it not to be true."

The prospect of all-out war seemed to energize Hillary, giving her an almost superhuman aura of strength and control. *The Washington Post* and *The New York Times* both reported that she was in "battle mode." In the West Wing, she strode around, "smiling and composed," recalled Michael Waldman. Only hours after Blumenthal passed on his disturbing information from Brock, Hillary was joking about her anticipated encounter with Richard Mellon Scaife, a billionaire benefactor of some of her conservative enemies, at a formal dinner that evening for the White House Endowment Fund.

Although close friends such as Diane Blair reached out to Hillary, she refrained from sharing her feelings, even with her mother. "I don't talk to Hillary about anything deeply personal concerning her marriage," Dorothy Rodham said. "We don't sit down and have those mother-daughter discussions about how she relates to her husband."

To keep her marriage going, Hillary had years earlier devised a "don't ask, don't tell" approach. "Tolerating his weakness," said Susan Thomases, "has always been part of her relationship with him." The Lewinsky story rattled Hillary because it was so irrational. But even in the face of compelling evidence, she took refuge in denial, repressing her understandable anger. "Hillary believed Bill because she had to," said another close friend. "If she just heard he had a dalliance somewhere, she would have believed that. But this—an intern, the Oval Office—it was insanity. She knew intellectually there was a problem, an addiction, but she still believed he could never be that insane." This friend was more skeptical: "It sounded very specific, not the kind of story you would make up." Hillary, however, "had more at stake."

"As angry as she was at her husband, as upset, she was not going to let their enemies destroy his presidency," said one of her top advisors. But aside from protecting her husband, Hillary's instinct for self-preservation kicked in as well. "Some say she saw her own legacy threatened," said another of her longtime advisors. "There may be some truth to that, to those who say she saw her own presidential ambitions going down the drain."

Dick Morris called Bill at 1:15 a.m. on January 22 with the results of his survey of some five hundred people—a poll commissioned by the President of the United States to determine whether he should tell the truth. Morris said that if Bill confessed to adultery, voters would forgive him, but if they knew he had lied about an affair or obstructed justice, they would not. The actual poll numbers were less definitive: 47 percent thought he should leave office for lying, and 56 percent for obstruction of justice. Still, Morris strongly advised him not to make a public confession. "Well, we just have to win, then," said Bill—his exact words to Hillary earlier in the day.

THE OBSTACLES TO VICTORY were significant in the early days. Many of those around the President believed the Lewinsky story to be true and felt uncomfortable defending him. After his ringing denial on the first day,

Bob Bennett made no further comment. The official reason was that Hillary had replaced him with David Kendall as lead lawyer. But Bennett had received a phone call from a senior White House official, a straight shooter who wanted to warn him as a friend. The official told Bennett that he was fairly certain the *Washington Post* story was correct and that he should think twice about speaking out again without knowing the facts.

Most members of the print and broadcast media believed the charges as well—not only on the merits, but because of Bill Clinton's history of dissembling. After years of what they called "truth squadding," reporters found it difficult to accept Bill's statements at face value, particularly after the recent campaign-finance evasions and deceptions. In an Oval Office meeting on Thursday, White House lawyer Lanny Davis pressed Bill to release as much information as soon as possible, pointing out that "the press assumed he had the affair—that he was presumed guilty." As Davis advised him to "take your case to the American people" and "let them judge," the President nodded in apparent agreement but expressed concern about "political fallout." Davis had the "strong impression" that Bill was "very uncomfortable about something" and was in "deep deep internal conflict."

Those outside the White House who knew Bill best saw through his deception. "I realized he was lying in a legalistic way," recalled Bernie Nussbaum. George Stephanopoulos was "livid," because "my gut told me the core of the story was true." On Thursday, he spoke on ABC News about the possibility of impeachment. Asked his advice for the President, Stephanopoulos said: "Get it out as quickly as you can. Answer all questions to the best of your ability." Several days later, Leon Panetta said that if the allegations were true, it would be better if Bill resigned and "if Gore became President and you had a new message and a new individual up there. . . . The worst scenario is if there's substance to it and it drags out."

Gore kept quiet publicly and stayed scrupulously loyal within the White House. To avoid entanglement in the investigation, he could not talk to the President about the matter. He also made it known that no one should raise the prospect of Bill's resignation with him. It was paramount that Gore "concentrate on the best interests of the country, enhance the stability of the government, avoid intrigue, and be steady and supportive," said a senior administration official.

Members of the inner circle knew how much support Bill needed—

despite all his talk about compartmentalizing his troubles. "To some extent he was capable of more than one thing simultaneously," said one of his advisors, "but as for boxing up something with a heavy emotional charge, he was no better at doing that than anyone." In the first week of the scandal, Bill's mood was mostly sorrowful, a departure from his general disposition, which was either happy or angry. "I have known Bill Clinton for decades, and I have never seen him like that," said political consultant Robert Shrum after a listless speech-writing session with the President. "He really was in another world for the weeks after Monica hit," said another top official. "For all appearances he was running the government, and occasionally he would meet with his lawyers. But he operated on almost no sleep. He didn't get his legs for about a month."

Of immediate concern was the impact of Bill's shifting and passive answers in his interviews on the first day and an equally tepid response to a question on Thursday during a photo opportunity with PLO chairman Yasser Arafat. Where, his aides wondered, was the Clintonian outrage that would have been the expected reaction to calumnies? After several reporters told McCurry the denials seemed "murky," he and a group of political advisors urged the President to make a stronger statement. The lawyers advised silence, and Hillary concurred. "We need to slow this down," she said. "Tell the boys that."

As a compromise, the legal team permitted a new group of surrogates to defend the President starting on Friday, January 23. Cabinet officers Madeleine Albright, William Daley, Richard Riley, and Donna Shalala stood on the driveway outside the White House and proclaimed that the allegations were "completely untrue." "At the cabinet meeting, he looked at us right in the eye and said he didn't do it," said Shalala. "I defended him before my instincts told me it probably was true. I would never have gone out if I had any sense that it was true."

Throughout the week, more tantalizing details emerged, many from excerpts of the Tripp-Lewinsky tapes published by Newsweek on Saturday: the President had told Lewinsky of having sex with "hundreds of women"; he had awakened Lewinsky at 2:00 or 3:00 a.m. to "talk dirty"; she had asked to be called "Assistant to the President for Blow Jobs." CNN found a video of Lewinsky flashing a seductive smile and hugging the President on a rope line in November 1996 and played it nonstop. Matt Drudge mentioned the semen-stained dress with a "potential DNA trail" on the *Today* show on Thursday, and the airwaves, newspapers, and magazines were filled with speculation about the "love dress" in the following days. But when the dress failed to turn up, critics ridiculed the media, and the stories, while never retracted, were assumed to be false. "There is no dress," Bill told his friends. ABC and *The Dallas Morning News* reported an "intimate incident" between Bill and Lewinsky supposedly witnessed by a Secret Service agent that did turn out to be wrong—a cause for White House gloating. Even so, it was remarkable that all the irrefutable elements of the Lewinsky story emerged in the first days.

The Clintons stayed in over the weekend, avoiding television-news reports and watching new films with friends—the somewhat ill-chosen *Titanic* on Friday night and on Saturday night *The Apostle*, starring Robert Duvall as a philandering Pentecostal preacher who seeks redemption through his ministry. Duvall and his costar Farrah Fawcett attended the screening and an informal dinner, which provided everyone with a much-needed diversion.

Beginning on Saturday morning, Bill's preparations for the State of the Union galvanized him with noticeable intensity. He now regarded the speech as his most important each year, his best opportunity to lay out his plans and summarize his achievements. He arrived at the Family Theater for the rehearsal in a jacket and tie rather than his customary casual attire—as if he were symbolically trying to reassert his dignity. He carried a draft covered with his thick handwriting and practiced at the "Blue Goose" lectern as he dictated changes to the speechwriters. "It was sort of surreal that he could pull himself together to pull it off," said one of his top advisors. "On some remarkable level, he was able to get into that moment, because that moment was so important to him. By the run-through we could see his concern about Monica Lewinsky shedding."

On Sunday morning, as Bill and Hillary sat in church listening to Corinthians ("Love does not delight in evil but rejoices with the truth"), the pundits on the talk shows were predicting that Bill had a fifty-fifty chance of remaining in office. "If he's not telling the truth, I think his presidency is numbered in days," said Sam Donaldson on ABC's *This Week*. Even the eccentric NBA player Dennis Rodman had an opinion. When he appeared on TV to apologize for being caught in a strip joint while skipping practice, he said, "It's not like I did something like Clinton. That dude, he's had a bad damn week."

In the afternoon, the tug-of-war continued between a half-dozen political advisors who wanted their boss to make a more emphatic statement about Lewinsky and lawyers who remained opposed to the idea. The advisors argued that Bill could not afford to "hide out until after his State of the Union." After initially resisting, Hillary agreed that Bill needed to say more—"the decisive vote," said Sidney Blumenthal. Also influential were poll results. *Newsweek* reported that voters thought that the President was lying and that Hillary didn't believe her husband either, yet 70 percent approved of his job performance. Private soundings taken by Mark Penn and Doug Schoen indicated, however, that the controversy could begin to erode the President's standing. Bill was inclined to take the guidance of his advisors but had not yet made up his mind.

Bill and Hillary hosted a Super Bowl party in the Family Theater on Sunday night. The mood was subdued, and after the game the guests watched the odd spectacle of Jesse Jackson praying in a corner with the President, telling him to "remain focused and faithful. God will prevail." Donna Shalala was even more disconcerted by the dynamic between the Clintons. "Hillary was sitting separate from Bill, and their Hollywood friend [Thomason] was there," Shalala recalled. "I thought, 'Oh my God, he did it.' He asked for my advice, and I said, 'Tell the truth.' My straight instinct was that I knew it would be a mess."

Close to midnight, Bill met in the Solarium with Thomason and Harold Ickes, both of whom advocated a muscular denial. They said he needed to set the record straight and to combat the right-wing attack on his presidency. The President responded with equal vigor, his manner distinctly different from his furtive ambivalence a few days earlier. "Fuck them, they are trying to take me down," he said. While he didn't indicate what he would say, he was determined to speak persuasively. Bill dispatched staff members to find a place in his schedule the next day, and they settled on a morning ceremony featuring Hillary and Gore speaking about an after-school child-care initiative.

THE PROCEEDINGS IN THE crowded Roosevelt Room on Monday, January 26, seemed routine, except for the added candlepower of a larger-than-usual contingent of Clinton Administration luminaries: Bill and Hillary, both Gores, Secretary of Education Richard Riley, and Senators Dianne Feinstein, Christopher Dodd, and Barbara Boxer, along with a group of private citizens involved in community learning centers. Exuding cheeriness in a canary-yellow pantsuit, Hillary led off, followed by a parade of speakers for the next hour. The Vice President departed from the original schedule to give his boss the last word, introducing him as "America's true education president." Only Hillary and her husband's top aides knew what was coming next.

Bill took the podium at 10:37 a.m. and spoke for ten minutes about the education programs he was going to unveil in his address in the Capitol the following night. After a brief pause, he continued: "Now, I have to go back to work on my State of the Union speech. And I worked on it until pretty late last night. But I want to say one thing to the American people. I want you to listen to me. I'm going to say this again. I did not have sexual relations with that woman, Miss Lewinsky. I never told anybody to lie, not a single time—never. These allegations are false. And I need to go back to work for the American people. Thank you."

It took less than a minute, but his words were to endure as the most memorable of Bill Clinton's presidency. They were indelible not so much for what he said as how he said it—his expression fierce, his jaw clenched, his tone defiant, his gestures hinting suppressed rage as he wagged his right index finger and banged the lectern several times. Just behind him, Hillary nodded her approval.

George Stephanopoulos watched "in fascinated disgust. This was Clinton at his cold-blooded worst. . . . Now, full of self-righteous fury, he was lying with true conviction. All that mattered was his survival." Some in the room with Bill were equally unpersuaded. "It was a shockingly powerful response at an unexpected moment," said a West Wing aide. "We didn't talk about it much. I thought he was lying, and I sensed a number of other people agreed." Even loyalist Sidney Blumenthal had to admit that Bill's words "caused him more lasting damage than any other of his presidency." In the end, the President's subordinates chose to suspend disbelief so they could continue working for him and because they assumed that no one could disprove his denials.

That morning, Bill Clinton had irretrievably cast his lot with Dick

Morris's advice and hardened his lie. He later said that he was only trying to spare his family hurt and embarrassment, but of equal importance was his need to save himself. He made the political calculation that "coming clean in the beginning would have been too shocking to the system," as one White House operative explained it to Bernie Nussbaum. The President concluded that the public outrage that might have forced him from office in January would abate over time. "The lie saved me," he insisted to a friend.

His timing capitalized perfectly on the rhythm of scandal, as he waited for signs of press fatigue after the six-day rush, then struck hard to create misgivings. But he also needed to divert attention from Lewinsky to his enemies. James Carville had offered a foretaste on *Meet the Press* the previous day when he announced, "There's going to be a war" between "the friends of the President and the Independent Counsel." It was Hillary's role to launch the first strike in a conflict even more intense than their initial assault following Starr's appointment in August 1994. After a strategy session in Hillaryland, the First Lady prepared to make her move on Tuesday morning, in a previously scheduled appearance on the *Today* show to highlight her work on child-care programs.

Hillary already had an eager collaborator in Blumenthal, who had created an elaborate diagram with circles and arrows to indicate links in a right-wing conspiracy. They had a series of discussions in which he shared his notes with her and encouraged her to say, "There are professional forces at work whose only purpose is to sow division by creating scandal."

On Monday afternoon, Hillary headed to New York, where CNN provided unusual live coverage of her visit to a reading program in Harlem. She smiled appreciatively as many in the African-American crowd "encouraged her to stand by her man," and she ducked questions from reporters. In the evening, she received a standing ovation at a fund-raising dinner for UNICEF. Back in her suite at the Waldorf-Astoria, the exhausted First Lady withdrew to her room, where she spoke again with Blumenthal, who coached her for the *Today* interview.

The next morning, Hillary took one more call from Blumenthal ten minutes before sitting down with *Today*'s Matt Lauer. She wore a navy-blue suit, and "she was very composed," said one of her advisors. "She is not a handwringer. She was trying to keep us from thinking the roof was falling in. All eyes were on her." In the back of her mind, she heard David Kendall's advice: "Screw 'em."

Hillary emphasized that she and the President had "talked at great length," and that he had "denied these allegations on all counts, unequivocally." She maintained that she and her husband had been "accused of everything" by "some of the very same people who are behind these allegations." She said she could stay calm because "I've just been through it so many times. . . . It's not being numb so much as being very experienced."

She was taken aback only once, when Lauer asked, "If an American President had an adulterous liaison in the White House and lied to cover it up, should the American people ask for his resignation?"

"Well," she replied, "they should certainly be concerned about it."

"Should they ask for his resignation?" he pressed.

"If all that were proven true," she hedged, "I think that would be a very serious offense," adding, "that is *not* going to be proven true."

Had the Lewinsky matter "caused pain in your marriage?" Lauer wondered.

"Absolutely not," Hillary replied. "You know we've been married for twenty-two years. . . . I have learned a long time ago that the only people who count in a marriage are the two that are in it. We know everything there is to know about each other, and we understand and accept and love each other."

The Lewinsky charges were "part of a continuing political campaign against my husband" by a "politically motivated prosecutor" who was "allied with the right-wing opponents of my husband," she said. "It's an entire operation." All the "specific allegations" were the result of an "intense political agenda." Then she took direct aim at her target. "I do believe that this is a battle," she said. "The great story here, for anybody willing to find it and write about it and explain it, is this vast right-wing conspiracy that has been conspiring against my husband since the day he announced for President."

Hillary had made similar statements periodically during her husband's presidency, but this time her attack was more effective because she framed it as a challenge to a credulous press corps that had been blind to a "great story." She had barely finished her spiel when White House operatives started "blast faxing" an eleven-page single-spaced fact sheet to journalists describing a conservative web that "strained to make the coincidental seem conspiratorial, the mundane seem sinister," in the words of *Newsweek*, which nevertheless devoted ten pages of its next issue to the conservative theories. When Hillary returned to the Residence that afternoon and saw Harry Thomason in the Solarium, she said, "I guess that will teach them to fuck with us."

Chapter Fourteen

—

T HE ACTIONS OF BILL AND HILLARY CLINTON IN THOSE FIRST WEEKS OF 1998—Bill's decision to lie, Hillary's acquiescence in that lie, and their assertion that Bill had been framed by enemies who needed to be defeated— set the course for the rest of his presidency. There was a better-than-even chance that he could have won over the public if he had made a full confession and apology at the outset. Even if he had been forced from office, Al Gore could have effectively pursued their agenda and gained a significant advantage in the 2000 election.

Instead, for the next year, Bill Clinton tied the presidency in knots—for seven months while he battled the Starr investigation until he was cornered into a quasi-admission of wrongdoing, then for five more months while he tried to stave off impeachment and conviction. Bolstered by high approval ratings fueled by the booming economy, he put on a brave face and went about his business, announcing lofty plans and making crucial decisions. But the scandal drained his energy and diverted his attention. It also exacted an opportunity cost that prevented him from carrying out many of his programs, impinged on some major actions in foreign policy, and severely limited one of the most powerful tools of the presidency—his moral authority. The recklessness of the Lewinsky affair, followed by his repeated lies under oath and in public, mocked his campaign for "personal responsibility," as well as his oath to uphold the law of the land. "His seven months of not fessing up cost him his place in history," said Dee Dee Myers. "The whole relationship did."

Bill called 1998 "the strangest year of my presidency," a characterization few would dispute. He also described himself as "trying to dodge bolts of lightning," as if he were an innocent golfer caught in a crackling electrical storm. Yet he was not the victim of events but rather, through a series of bad choices, the architect of them. "I was compelled as never before to live parallel lives," he later wrote, "except that this time the darkest part of my inner life was in full view." This was as close as he ever came to a genuine acknowledgment that everything revealed about his private behavior throughout the year was in fact true.

The Lewinsky scandal kept Hillary pinned down in the first months of what Al From, chairman of the Democratic Leadership Council, called her husband's "lost year." She had big plans to expand her domestic agenda by heading a major initiative on child care and education and to keep raising her profile overseas. Once she assumed control of Bill's defense, her immediate ambitions were limited to protecting their legacy. Projecting an image of marital togetherness, however difficult at times, became paramount, so she reverted to a subsidiary public role. Hillary paid a profound personal price, as her "armor . . . thickened," and she found herself isolated and lonely. She helped her husband "embitter an entire year, perhaps an entire era of our politics in the service of his perjuries," wrote liberal Washington journalist Marjorie Williams. "As soon as she decided to take the offensive on his behalf, she became socially if not legally as culpable as he for embroiling the country in his year-long deception."

FOR "THAT WOMAN, MISS LEWINSKY," life would never be the same. At twenty-four, she faced the prospect of conviction and imprisonment for perjury if she did not strike a deal with Kenneth Starr. And in the weeks after Bill's histrionic denial, the White House proceeded to shred her character with slanders that the Clintons condoned. Cueing off the scenario the President described to Sidney Blumenthal, West Wing "spinners went to work portraying Lewinsky as a stalker and a temptress," wrote Newsweek in its issue published on February 2. Several days earlier, The Washington Post had reported the President's dismissal of Lewinsky's claims on the Tripp tapes as "fantasy or untruthful boasting."

By the end of January, Lewinsky's lawyer, William Ginsburg, had worked out a ten-page proffer—essentially an informal account of what a witness can provide—detailing her admission of an "intimate and emotional relationship" with the President as a condition for immunity from prosecution. Ginsburg by then had made a series of missteps, starting in the original *Washington Post* story, when he acted as if the facts were unknowable by oddly saying that if Bill Clinton were guilty he was a "misogynist," and if not then the Independent Counsel had "ravaged the life of a youngster." On February 1, Ginsburg appeared on five Sunday talk shows and made misleading comments about Lewinsky's probable testimony, which alienated the Independent Counsel's office.

In an atmosphere of bad faith, the immunity talks collapsed two days later, and Lewinsky went into limbo for six months while Starr collected evidence and subpoenaed scores of witnesses to testify before his grand jury. Betty Currie was one of the first. Under questioning by FBI agents, she had initially "seemed to indicate that the President had coached her to lie," *Newsweek* later wrote. "But Currie's clear recollections seemed to fade after the White House found her a lawyer." Following conferences between her attorney and the President's legal counsel, her appearance before the grand jury became "vague and muddled."

Despite his early pledges to cooperate, Bill viewed the entire investigation as illegitimate and did everything he could to prolong it with numerous executive-privilege claims, which the courts struck down, and by refusing a half-dozen times to testify before the grand jury. At the same time, the White House redoubled its campaign to discredit Starr and his lieutenants—arguably a misuse of power by the executive branch. Calling himself the "sorcerer's apprentice," Sidney Blumenthal coordinated these operations, disguising the West Wing origins of damaging information he sent to reporters.

Other staff members tried to wall off Lewinsky-related news in an effort to maintain a sense of life as usual. "There was a pall around the subject," said a top administration official. "We wouldn't talk about it. We used a code and called it 'the other thing' and 'that thing.'" But suspending disbelief proved difficult for some. In mid-February, Mike McCurry shared his misgivings with the *Chicago Tribune* when he said, "Maybe there'll be a simple innocent explanation. I don't think so, because I think we would have offered that up already. . . . I think it's going to end up being a very complicated story. . . . I don't think it's going to be entirely easy to explain maybe."

As journalists, friends, and colleagues watched for signs of discord, the Clintons maintained their public solidarity. Most couples in similarly humiliating circumstances would have wilted under the stress. But Bill and Hillary Clinton were made of unusually strong stuff. They seemed to cleave even more tightly against forces they strongly believed were determined to bring them down. *Newsweek*'s Matthew Cooper, the husband of Hillary advisor Mandy Grunwald, wrote a story published on February 2 declaring that the First Lady was "goofy, flat-out in love with [Bill] and he with her." That weekend, Hillary had flown to the World Economic Forum in Davos, Switzerland, where she delivered a speech on civil society. Days later, Tony and Cherie Blair arrived in Washington, and the Clintons pulled out the stops for their State Dinner on February 5. The guest list included Hollywood bigwigs Barbra Streisand, Harrison Ford, Steven Spielberg, and Barry Diller. The tables were adorned with gold candles, vermeil flatware, and the "Reagan" china on terra-cotta damask tablecloths. Stevie Wonder and Elton John provided the after-dinner entertainment in a tent on the West Terrace, followed by dancing in the marble entrance hall of the State Floor.

"If you'd arrived from planet Mars, you wouldn't have known there was a scandal," recalled British Ambassador Christopher Meyer. Writing in *The New Yorker*, Tina Brown described the First Lady as "radiant" and the President as "absurdly debonair . . . a man in a dinner jacket with more heat than any star in the room," projecting "a kind of avid inclusiveness" and operating "vividly in the present tense." Dancing and laughing until nearly midnight, Bill and Hillary occupied a "parallel universe" of "brilliance" compared to the "howling darkness" shadowed by the "neo-Puritanism" of "op-ed tumbrel drivers."

"I took a lot of shit for that piece," Brown said later. "But they were totally into each other as far as I could tell. I felt they were tied together by the drama raging outside."

The image the Clintons conveyed that evening was consistent with their other official appearances. A week later, they were in the East Room with an audience of 180, presiding over the first of Hillary's Millennium Evenings, a series of lectures by scholars, scientists, and artists that she organized to celebrate the millennium. "Monica Lewinsky wasn't hanging over us at all," recalled Ellen Lovell, director of the White House Millennium Council. But it was noteworthy that Bill mentioned in his remarks that the American founders "understood that there was light and dark in human nature. They understood that we are all imperfect, but society is nonetheless improvable."

The First Couple sat in Chippendale armchairs on a platform, Hillary again wearing a bright-yellow pantsuit, with a choker of twisted pearls, her ears glittering with diamonds. When Harvard historian Bernard Bailyn described America in the eighteenth century, Hillary did her slow, metronomic nod, while Bill looked spellbound, with his chin cupped in his hand. The Clintons exchanged smiles and quick comments, then effortlessly shared tasks during the question-and-answer period, taking inquiries from the Internet in the first cybercast from the White House. After the program, they lingered at a reception, "very engaged in separate circles," recalled Lovell. "My memory was of rapt circles around Bill and Hillary, talking about issues related to the lecture."

In the company of friends, they presented a united front as well. They escaped to Camp David whenever they could throughout the winter and spring—nine times between the end of January and the end of June. On Presidents' Day weekend they invited six couples because "Bill wanted to hang out with friends and uncomplicate his life," said Georgetown classmate Tom Siebert. At one point Siebert found Bill fuming to Harry Thomason about Kenneth Starr. "It was the first I really heard him talk that way," said Siebert, "the relentless scrutiny, the loss of millions of dollars to pursue every lead about nothing, and the creation of a perjury trap." What also struck Siebert was that Bill "was assailing the process, but he wasn't assaulting the facts."

At Stanford, Chelsea was having difficulty following her mother's exhortation to "power through," despite the word out of the White House that she was coping well and, as *People* magazine reported, was keeping "her head high." The weekend that Hillary traveled to Switzerland, Bill had brought his daughter back east for a few days at Camp David because she was "distraught at school." She was losing weight, staying up until 2:00 and 3:00 a.m., and taking naps during the day. "She would get in-bed headaches when things were tense," said a classmate. "In February, she was in bed a lot." A natural procrastinator, Chelsea also began falling behind in her studies, and toward the end of the month, she told her friends that she had to get away "to take care of this."

On Monday, February 23, Hillary arrived in Palo Alto and whisked Chelsea off to Utah, where they settled into the gated Deer Valley estate of movie mogul Jeffrey Katzenberg, a major Democratic donor, near the summit of Bald Eagle Mountain. The trip was arranged so hastily that the White House could barely cobble together the necessary communications and security arrangements. Mother and daughter spent the next three days together and skied in fresh powder with four Secret Service agents and 1952 Olympic Alpine skiing medalist Stein Eriksen, the skiing director of Deer Valley.

Bill arrived on Thursday for what the White House advertised as celebration of Chelsea's eighteenth birthday on Friday. They were also joined by Terry McAuliffe, summoned by a White House aide who said, "You better get out there." "I moved quickly," McAuliffe recalled. "They brought me out to be cheerful and optimistic." McAuliffe skied with Hillary and Chelsea and then returned early to the house to play cards and talk politics with Bill, who avoided the slopes.

"It was a tough time," said McAuliffe. "We had meals together. The White House steward would say, 'Do you want wine?' They would say 'no,' and I would say, 'absolutely.' One reason the President had me around was to keep the conversation going." Later, Bill told McAuliffe that he had been "tortured" by the effect of the scandal on Chelsea. "He told me it was a living hell," recalled McAuliffe. That weekend in Utah, however, "was never living hell when I was around. I was keeping everyone up."

When Chelsea returned to Stanford after a week's absence, she got back on top of her schoolwork, but she continued to have headaches, and she developed a low-grade infection. She leaned increasingly on her boyfriend, Matthew Pierce, a religion major and member of the swim team she had been dating since early January, after another swimmer, Anthony Robinson, broke off with her. Following the Utah interlude, she spent most of her time in Pierce's room. She didn't seek counseling, and she tried to cope with her stress in her own way. "Chelsea didn't deal with issues," said a classmate. "She talked about her problems in a very reserved, calibrated way—not really what was going on inside her."

NO ONE WORKED harder at keeping a façade of strength than Bill Clinton. At his press conference with Tony Blair in early February, Bill said he would "never" consider resigning from office. "I'm just going to keep showing up for work," he said, noting that the "pain threshold" of being in public life "has been raised." "With Lewinsky we couldn't allow the perception to develop that it was affecting his job," explained one of his senior advisors. "The public could not get to the zone where it thought he did a bad thing that should have him removed from office. From our polling we understood what was holding it together, and that was that he was doing his job leading the country. If we lost that, we lost the franchise." To demonstrate presidential engagement, the White House concentrated on scheduling public appearances. "The message of the day was hewed to religiously, sometimes two or even three a day," according to Michael Waldman. "As the scandal went on, the pace of appearances accelerated." Although journalists disparaged the stage-managed events, they felt obligated to write about them. "These daily sessions showed the world a confident, unshaken Clinton focusing on the work of the people," noted Waldman.

Yet the laws of emotional and mental physics dictated that some things were lost. "In the Monica Lewinsky year, Bill Clinton missed a tremendous amount," said Mary Mel French, his Chief of Protocol. "He was working to keep himself afloat, but he had no extra time to devote to other important issues." In the view of one senior advisor, the President "never checked out, but there would be meetings when he checked out, after he would get off the phone with his lawyer. There is no way you can go through what he was going through and not be affected, whether for a few minutes or a few hours. Sometimes he would be really distracted for several days. But even half-engaged he was more effective than someone else who is fully engaged. He wouldn't give you seven ideas, he'd give you three." Donna Shalala felt the "enormous tension. . . . Everyone was rallying around [Hillary] and pissed off at [Bill]. But guess what? This was the best time to be in the cabinet, because there was no White House to interfere. It was fun. We could make decisions because the White House was distracted. The agencies were very busy and quite independent."

Against the backdrop of the ongoing investigation and press coverage, Bill "showed unbelievable personal discipline and didn't explode in public," said a senior advisor. "It was very hard, a difficult challenge to pull off. We needed to deal with the human condition. He had to vent behind closed doors." Waldman observed that before giving a speech, the President might make a "withering comment about Starr or the press, or a rueful aside about the mess he was in." Bill took refuge in golf by spending many of his Mondays on the fairways with Terry McAuliffe. "It was his down day," said McAuliffe. "At 2:00 or 3:00 p.m. he would rip out to the Army and Navy Club. He would shut off the second we got into the limo until the second we got off the course. We would talk politics, but we were generally talking golf." McAuliffe had no remedy, however, for the "Ken Starr Shank" that Bill developed whenever he was "feeling bad and distracted."

The President found his most reliable diversion in movies such as *The Full Monty*, but he skipped *Primary Colors*, which starred John Travolta as a womanizing presidential candidate and Emma Thompson as his wife — a thinly veiled portrait of the Clintons that came out in March. One dubious choice that Bill screened for a group of friends in Hillary's absence was *Dangerous Beauty*, about a sixteenth-century Venetian courtesan known for her sexual tricks and political bravery. Speechwriter Mark Katz watched as Bill sat "completely transfixed" by scenes of topless women, instructions in fellatio, and "abundant humping." The aide was amazed that afterward the President "eagerly discussed" the film's "attributes and nuances." "He was a guy who really loved this movie and didn't care who knew it," recalled Katz.

IN HIS STATE OF THE UNION address on January 27, the President spent seventy-two minutes detailing his most ambitious agenda in four years. He made no mention of the Lewinsky scandal, although he and his speechwriters were so sensitive to the possibility of double entendres that they changed "abroad" to "around the world." He proposed more spending on health, education, and child care; an opportunity for those aged sixty-two to sixty-five to "buy in" to Medicare coverage; and, with a sweeping flourish, a plan to use the budget surplus to "save Social Security first" rather than reduce taxes, as the Republicans proposed. At a party afterward in the State Dining Room, Bill entered like a boxer, his hands clasped above his head in triumph, to the cheers of his staff. More than fifty-three million viewers had watched the speech, and his approval ratings shot from the high fifties to the high sixties overnight. The next day, at a spirited rally before an overflow crowd of nearly nine thousand at the University of Illinois, the President asked the American people to "imagine the future" and to "believe in the fundamental unity of human nature." Al Gore offered a ringing endorsement of "my friend," asking the audience to "join me in supporting him and standing by his side."

But Bill could do little to put his signature proposals into practice. He arguably missed the opportunity of a generation to fix the country's major entitlements. Were it not for the Lewinsky scandal, he would have had the political momentum to apply his persuasive powers to bring about Social Security reform. Democrat John Breaux and Republican Bill Frist were ready to collaborate on Medicare legislation in the Senate, but they couldn't get the wounded President's support because he lacked the clout to forge the necessary bipartisan coalition. "Real pain would be required to solve Social Security and Medicare, but we had the money to do it right then and there," said Bruce Reed. "We could have added a private investment option on to Social Security benefits. . . . We could have brought Medicare up to date."

In the days before the Lewinsky story broke, Hillary and Bill had held hands with photogenic children and launched her $21.7 billion child-care initiative in the East Room amid much fanfare. "I thank my wife," he said, "who has been working on this for twenty-five years." In a *Newsweek* interview, she had spoken expansively about "getting our fiscal house in order," raising the minimum wage, and further changing the welfare system, but, post-Lewinsky, Hillary's bold program became "a casualty like everything else," said Reed.

The fallout from Lewinsky on foreign policy took a toll in obvious and subtle ways, with both short- and long-term consequences. Benjamin Netanyahu and Yasser Arafat had to cope with the breaking story during their White House talks, when Arafat was reported to be embarrassed by questions the President was forced to answer. But overall, the immediate discomfort didn't seem to have much impact on administration efforts to wrestle with Arab-Israeli issues.

In less visible parts of the world, there were more far-reaching costs. "Once he got into those domestic issues with Monica Lewinsky, the amount of time the President devoted to Ukraine fell off," said William Miller, the U.S. ambassador there during the first Clinton term. "Up until then, he was a tremendous asset, on the telephone several times a month, sending letters, seeing people from Ukraine constantly." Bill deputed Al Gore, Strobe Talbott, and William Perry to handle the disarmament of the country's nuclear weapons. "But it was very clear that Clinton could not be engaged because he was engaged with something else," said Miller. Bill's ability to talk directly to President Leonid Kuchma, the successor to Leonid Kravchuk, had been "key in Ukraine, to get him to do things," said Miller. "Clinton would work through problems with him, persuade and come to agreements. He was extremely effective in that mode, which required a physical presence. Kuchma needed constant reassurance, someone saying, 'We are by you shoulder to shoulder.' But those big shoulders were no longer there. That was the disengagement when the Ukrainian oligarchy and extensive corruption began to take place."

The situation in Iraq simmered throughout 1998, and Bill's personal problems came into play at several crucial points. Iraqi dictator Saddam Hussein had been a regular irritant to the Clinton Administration since its first day in office, and he had provoked U.S. forces into several attacks. The latest crisis began in November 1997 when Saddam ejected Americans on the UN inspection team monitoring weapons of mass destruction under the terms Iraq had agreed to in 1991, after losing the Gulf War. Even liberal commentators had become saber rattlers, as George Stephanopoulos suggested that his former boss "should seriously explore the assassination option" and not be deterred by "a misreading of the law or misplaced moral squeamishness." Others pointed out that Saddam had been emboldened by the Clinton Administration's limited and ineffective air strikes in 1993 and 1996.

Bill had seemed poised to act in November and December, talking of "eliminating" Saddam's arsenal, which he called "one of the three or four most significant security threats all of our people will face." Boris Yeltsin engineered a temporary reprieve when he persuaded Saddam to allow the inspectors back by promising to urge the UN to lift its sanctions on Iraq.

At the height of the preoccupation with the Lewinsky scandal in January, Saddam again expelled the inspectors. Secretary of State Madeleine Albright compared the Iraqi leader to Hitler, and the President threatened retaliatory air strikes, linking Saddam to "an unholy axis of terrorists, drug traffickers, and organized international criminals." But critics in the press found parallels in a new satirical film, *Wag the Dog*, in which a President accused of fondling a young woman (wearing a beret, no less) diverts public attention by starting a war with Albania. A bootleg copy of the film even appeared on Iraqi television.

UN Secretary-General Kofi Annan defused the standoff by convincing Saddam to reopen access to the weapons sites. In early March, the Security Council unanimously endorsed the Annan agreement but stopped short of permitting an automatic military response if Saddam blocked the inspectors again. At the same time, Iraqi officials voiced their objections to the aggressive approach of the chief UN weapons inspector, an Australian diplomat named Richard Butler.

The matter came to a head on March 3, when the Clintons were in New York City at a celebration of *Time* magazine's seventy-fifth anniversary at Radio City Music Hall. In the middle of dinner, Butler and his wife, who were also guests at the event, were called into a meeting with the Clintons and UN Ambassador Bill Richardson. "Hillary was so tough," recalled Butler's wife, Barbara. "She turned to Richard and said, 'There is nothing to discuss. You will do what we tell you to do.' Clinton didn't say anything. He was being the nice guy talking to Bill Richardson, who winked at Richard. I thought, 'Whoa, this is a focused, tough lady.' " After returning to the dinner, Butler said, "Well, Hillary certainly told me in no uncertain terms what *she* thought."

In early 1998, Kosovo, the Serbian-controlled province in Bosnia with a majority Albanian Muslim population, was also beginning to erupt. Since the Dayton Accords in 1995, the Kosovar Albanians had been confronting Serbian forces in an effort to assume control. When the predominantly Christian Serbs began to retaliate in February 1998, the Clinton Administration resisted involvement, partly because the President had his hands full. By late spring, Serbian leader Slobodan Milosevic began pressing his troops to forcibly remove ethnic Albanians from Kosovo, and the province edged toward all-out civil war.

As the United States continued to hang back, billionaire George Soros, a prominent Democratic party supporter, paid a visit to Hillary. A strong advocate of military action against Serbian aggression, Soros denounced her husband's inaction on Kosovo. "He was talking about appeasement," said a senior Clinton Administration official. "He was trying to get to Clinton through Hillary, to make Clinton more muscular." For all Soros's clout, nothing came of his visit, and Milosevic carried out his plan for ethnic cleansing, expelling hundreds of thousands of Kosovar Albanians in the following months.

During this stressful period, Bill made one conspicuous display of diplomatic skill that demonstrated what he might have achieved had he not been hobbled by scandal. From the beginning of his administration he had taken a keen interest in promoting peace between the Catholics and Protestants of Northern Ireland. His designated mediator was former senator George Mitchell, who brought British as well as Northern Irish leaders close to agreement by April. When the negotiations began to unravel, Tony Blair asked for the President's intervention, and Bill stayed on the phone most of the night on April 9 to help close the deal. "People made fun of him because he couldn't stop talking," recalled Ted Widmer, a National Security Council aide. "He did exhaust everyone until they couldn't figure out why they were disagreeing. His Southern Baptist background enabled him to talk to the extremist Protestants, and his Catholic schooling—not just the Jesuits at Georgetown but nuns who taught him in second and third grade—helped him with the other side." The Good Friday Accords announced the following day were "welcome inside the White House," recalled Widmer. "It was tangible success in the wake of Monica Lewinsky."

THE WINTER AND SPRING months brought regular disclosures that further undermined Bill's version of the Lewinsky story—most prominently, her thirty-seven visits to the White House, Bill's apparent coaching of Betty Currie, the identities of corroborating witnesses such as White House staffer Ashley Raines, the existence of Bill's phone messages to Lewinsky, excerpts from Lewinsky's e-mails (March 5, 1997: "Fuckface should [if Betty is nice] get my tie today. I sure hope he likes it"), and Marcia Lewis's admission that her daughter had been "in love" with the President.

Five years later, Barbara Walters would ask Hillary how she reacted to the "reports and mounting evidence of a relationship—late-night phone calls and logged visits and gifts. Did you just dismiss all of it?"

"I really didn't think it added up to a lot," replied Hillary. "You know, I really looked at it from the perspective of, Oh, my gosh. You know, one more hurdle to get over, one more problem to deal with. And one of the

Bill and Hillary in the White House Residence elevator on January 20, 1997, before the inaugural balls.   *"David Letterman impishly observed that she would need sleeves 'long enough to hide her handcuffs.'"*

Bill with Russian President Boris Yeltsin at the NATO Summit in Paris on May 27, 1997, the day the U.S. Supreme Court ruled unanimously that the Paula Jones lawsuit could proceed. *"From the moment he got the news, he seemed to be sleepwalking through the summit."*

36

MSL-DC-00001227

Dear Handsome,   29 June 1997
    I really need to discuss my situation with you. We have not had any contact for over five weeks. You leave on Sat. and I leave for Madrid w/ the SecDef on Monday returning the 14th of July. I am then heading out to Los Angeles for a few days. If I do not speak to you before you leave, when I return from LA it will have been two months since we last spoke. Please do not do this to me. ~~I feel disposable, used and insignificant.~~ I understand your hands are tied, but I ~~just~~ want to talk to you and look at some options. I am begging you ~~one last time~~ ~~from the bottom~~ of my heart to please let me ~~come~~ visit ~~see you~~ Tuesday evening. I will call Betty Tues. afternoon to see if it is o.k.

                                    —M

A pleading note written by Monica Lewinsky on June 29, 1997, after Bill had ignored her for a month. *"I feel that he should have shown more restraint. It was too much of an emotional burden for someone my age."*

37

Bill Clinton and his friend Vernon Jordan on the first hole of the Farm Neck Country Club in Martha's Vineyard, August 18, 1997.

"When faced with two or three of his balls on the fairway, Bill invariably took the one in the best position, claiming he couldn't remember which was the first shot."

Bill and Hillary helping Chelsea unpack in her dorm room at Stanford University on September 19, 1997.

"While Hillary 'got on Chelsea's nerves with all the fixing up,' Bill . . . made himself useful by taking the bunk beds apart."

Hillary celebrating her fiftieth birthday with her mother in Park Ridge, Illinois, on October 27, 1997.

"I don't talk to Hillary about anything deeply personal concerning her marriage. We don't sit down and have those mother-daughter discussions about how she relates to her husband."

Cabinet officers Madeleine Albright
(center), Richard Riley (to her left),
William Daley (to her right), and
Donna Shalala (far right) tell
reporters on January 23, 1998,
that the allegations about the
President and Monica Lewinsky are
"completely untrue."

*"He looked us right in the eye
and said he didn't do it. I defended
him before my instincts told me it
probably was true. I would never
have gone out if I had any sense
that it was true."*

Standing in front of a painting of
Theodore Roosevelt on January
26, 1998, Bill denies having had
sexual relations with "that woman,
Miss Lewinsky."

*"This was Clinton at his cold-
blooded worst. . . . Now, full of
self-righteous fury, he was lying
with true conviction. All that
mattered was his survival."*

Bill with Al Gore and Chief of Staff Erskine Bowles on February 2, 1998.
"He really was in another world for the weeks after Monica hit. For all appearances he was running the government. . . . But he operated on almost no sleep. He didn't get his legs for about a month."

Hillary on the *Today* show with Matt Lauer on January 27, 1998, asserting that a "vast right-wing conspiracy" was smearing her husband.
"In the back of her mind, she heard David Kendall's advice: 'Screw 'em.'"

Chelsea skiing during a hastily arranged family vacation in Deer Valley, Utah, on March 1, 1998.

"She told her friends that she had to get away, 'to take care of this.'"

Hillary with Madeleine Albright, who she insisted be appointed Secretary of State.

"Madeleine connects with HRC . . . lots of girl talk, lots of kinship, along the lines of 'we both know what assholes men can be.'"

Hillary speaking in Auburn, New York, during her "Save America's Treasures" bus tour, July 15, 1998.

"It had a barnstorming campaign feel. . . . It could have been a foretaste of her Senate campaign."

Bill prepares to address the nation after his grand jury testimony on August 17, 1998.

"Everything Bill said was exactly as Hillary wanted it."

48

49

The Clinton family sails with Walter Cronkite in Martha's Vineyard, August 25, 1998.

"I wouldn't say there was a lot of levity between the Clintons. Hillary didn't join in too much of the conversation."

Hillary, Chelsea, Bill, and their dog, Buddy, leave the White House for Martha's Vineyard on August 18, 1998.

"She would never disobey her parents or violate her image by walking with her arms crossed, or five paces behind. She was too smart for that."

Bill Clinton with Democratic senator Bob Kerrey, who would call him with an urgent message four days after the release of the Starr Report on September 11, 1998.

"Kerrey [said] that he had three options: 'to resign, to plea bargain, or to await impeachment.' Kerrey told the President he would be 'healthier and happier' if he stepped down."

House Minority Leader Richard Gephardt speaks to Bill's supporters in the Rose Garden after the House vote to impeach the President on December 19, 1998.

"It was intended to be arrogant, to pump up and restore some confidence in our ability ultimately to prevail."

Hillary launches her "Listening Tour" at the farm of Senator Daniel Patrick Moynihan in Pindars Corners, New York, July 7, 1999.

"The photograph of the two of them conveyed his approval and gave her instant credibility with New York voters who revered their senior senator."

Bill and Hillary on January 6, 2000, after moving into their new house in Chappaqua, New York, where Hillary would live for the rest of the year.

"When Hillary's advisors realized the scene might send 'a sad message,' Bill rearranged his schedule to accompany his wife to the first home they had owned since 1983."

The Clintons and Gores
at a Democratic
National Committee
fund-raising dinner on
April 24, 2000.

*"It was remarkable
how people who had
shared the same
foxhole for a decade
suddenly mistrusted
one another."*

Bill with Yasser Arafat,
chairman of the
Palestinian Authority,
at Camp David on July
24, 2000, after the
collapse of the Israeli-
Palestinian peace
negotiations.

*"Bill . . . believed—
against the advice of
many experts—that he
could work some magic
on the prickly, suspi-
cious, and often duplic-
itous leader."*

56

55

Bill addressing the delegates on August
14, 2000, at the Democratic National
Convention in Los Angeles.

*"Bill Clinton couldn't resist occupy-
ing center stage and grabbing the limelight from Al Gore during a crucial
moment in his campaign."*

58

Al Gore speaks to the Democratic National Convention on August 17, 2000.
*"I stand here tonight as my own man. If you entrust me with the presidency . . .
I will work for you every day, and I will never let you down."*

59

Bill campaigning at the New York State Fair in Syracuse on September 3,
2000.   *"Bill kept pressing the flesh while Hillary stood nearby, 'alone,
arms folded, waiting for him to join her.'"*

Hillary campaigning for the Senate in New York City with former mayor Ed Koch (right), June 2000. *"I'm at a subway station. People are kissing me, enveloping me. They throw themselves at me. I'm going through an emotional wringer."*

After Hillary's election to the Senate on November 7, 2000, she raises her hands in victory with Chelsea and New York Senator Charles Schumer (left, off camera), while Bill looks on.

"The unconventional tableau seemed 'an effort to underscore that the Senate victory was hers alone.'"

Bill and Hillary at a White House farewell party on January 6, 2001, after a surprise appearance by Fleetwood Mac to sing the 1992 campaign theme song, "Don't Stop Thinking about Tomorrow."

"If I don't sleep for the next sixteen days, it will seem like four more years."

Bill and Hillary with Al and Tipper Gore outside the White House on January 20, 2001.
"A veneer of public graciousness between the President and Vice President concealed their intensifying private anger over each other's role in the electoral outcome."

Bill Clinton delivers his nineteenth farewell address during a noisy rally at Andrews Air Force Base on January 20, 2001, following the inauguration of George W. Bush. *"It was really different, really unusual. . . . That's his style. He wanted two or three more parties."*

"Linda Bloodworth-Thomason, who knew the Clintons and their ambitions as well as anyone, wrote a short note that she left in her room [in the Residence]: 'I'll be back.'"

ways that I kept going . . . was to, you know, do what I could to try to figure out what was happening, to cross-examine my husband to feel like I knew."

"Which you did," Walters interrupted. "You asked him."

"Which I did," Hillary replied.

"Again and again?" asked Walters.

"Absolutely," said Hillary, acknowledging an undercurrent of undeniable strain in the Clinton marriage, as well as her awareness of the evidence as it accumulated. "But then to go on because . . . there was so much that literally could have knocked us off-kilter," Hillary continued. "And certainly, I could have found myself just constantly reacting to what was said."

In early March, Bill's deposition in the Paula Jones lawsuit leaked to *The Washington Post*. News reports highlighted his confirmation for the first time of sexual intercourse with Gennifer Flowers, as well as his admission of his peculiar encounter with Marilyn Jo Jenkins at 5:15 a.m. on the day he left Little Rock for Washington in 1993. In the following days, Jones's lawyers released other depositions from women linked to Bill, including Kathleen Willey. After being compelled to testify in the Jones case, she faced the Starr grand jury and then appeared on *60 Minutes* before an audience of twenty-nine million on Sunday the fifteenth.

Under questioning by Ed Bradley, Willey uncomfortably described the President's crude advances on November 29, 1993. She had credibility not only because of her Democratic party pedigree, but her dignified bearing and evident maturity. It also emerged that Washington real-estate developer Nathan Landow, who donated $247,000 to the Democrats, had brought her to his estate in October 1997 on Maryland's Eastern Shore to discuss her pending deposition in the Jones case. She alleged that he warned her it might be "better" if she refrained from telling her story under oath. Landow insisted he discussed only her "mental anguish" about the Jones case.

The President said he was "mystified and disappointed" by her account, and on Monday, March 16, the White House launched its counterattack by releasing nine "admiring" letters from Willey to Bill. West Wing officials also emphasized that she had met with him again in the Oval Office ten days after the purported harassment, and they cited a new affidavit from Julie Hiatt Steele, who said that Willey had encouraged her to lie about the episode. The sworn statement had been prepared by Steele's lawyer, Nancy Luque (who also represented Hillary's brother Hugh), in concert with Bill's attorneys.

Reporters quickly poked holes in the White House campaign to discredit Willey. *Newsweek* quoted another friend who said that on the night of the alleged incident, Willey had "described how Clinton had kissed and groped her." The friend, who asked to remain anonymous, said that Willey had been "shocked." The magazine also located several sources who contradicted the Steele affidavit. And when Communications Director Ann Lewis said Willey would not have been friendly to a man who had tried to molest her, journalists discovered a quote from Lewis in 1991 defending Anita Hill's decision to continue working for Supreme Court nominee Clarence Thomas even after he allegedly sexually harassed her. "You don't know what it's like . . . to have this really prestigious and powerful boss and think you have to stay on the right side of him," Lewis had said then, moving *Washington Post* columnist Michael Kelly to call her now a "rank hypocrite."

The Clintons found some relief on April 1 when they learned during a trip to Africa that Judge Wright had dismissed the Jones lawsuit. Wright said that even if the incident in the Excelsior Hotel had happened as Jones described it, her claim of sexual harassment did not hold up because Jones could not prove that she had been damaged as a result. Jones's lawyers filed an appeal, which meant the case could still end up in a damaging trial. But for the moment, Bill decided to celebrate somewhat imprudently by banging on a drum while chewing a cigar as he stood near the window of his hotel room in Dakar, Senegal.

The twelve-day swing through Africa was one of four overseas goodwill trips Bill and Hillary took between March and July, at least in part to get away from the unseemly problems at home. Besides their Africa sojourn, they spent five days in Chile in April, six days in Europe in May, and ten days in China in late June and early July. On foreign soil, Bill and Hillary appeared together more than they had during their travels the previous year. They also seemed to lose themselves in the discussions of policy and politics that so profoundly animated their marriage.

That dynamic was clearly evident in a roundtable discussion with young leaders in Johannesburg. Surrounded by idealistic activists working on economic and social problems, the Clintons participated in an easy give-and-take and showed their contrasting political and intellectual styles, as well as flashes of their competition. While Hillary had no hesitation about expressing herself, Bill effortlessly dominated the proceedings. "For those of you who work with children in conflict resolution," he asked, "do you ever talk to them about similar problems of people who look alike— the Irish problem, the Bosnian problem, the Middle Eastern problem?"

"The Rwanda problem," interjected Hillary.

"The Rwanda problem," Bill continued, correcting his wife without missing a beat: "Although the Hutus and the Tutsis don't look alike to those who are sensitive."

Bill also upstaged his wife by speaking expansively and passionately, hopscotching from experiences in Latvia to those in Los Angeles, connecting with his African listeners in a conversational and direct way. "I admire you all so much," he said. "When you get discouraged, just remember . . . bad things will happen when you don't have good leaders, good structures, and a good mission; good things will happen when you do."

When Hillary took her turn, she was focused and academic, emphasizing process more than people, expressing herself in lengthy and dense sentences. "Are there any thoughts being given," she inquired at one point, "as to how you could construct such a coordinated effort to try to replace the enthusiasm and, if you will, even slogans of liberation and freedom with a new sense of commitment over the long-term toward the steps that are going to be necessary to transform a transition into a stable, functioning democracy with as full participation as you can design?"

BACK IN WASHINGTON, Bill and Hillary each threw themselves into their separate schedules. Bill's appearances and pronouncements were predictable, but Hillary was quietly beginning to map out her future. She had suffered occasional misgivings about the perils of life in the spotlight, telling an interviewer just before the Lewinsky story broke that a public figure "becomes more and more on guard, less real, more hollowed out." Yet she began moving toward seeking elected office.

Those close to Hillary had been encouraging her for years to run. In 1974, Bill had said, "She could be President someday. She could go to any state and be elected to the Senate." Eighteen years later, during the 1992 campaign, he told Gail Sheehy, "It doesn't bother me for people to see her and get excited and say she would be President too. . . . Eight years of Hillary Clinton. Why not?" As recently as the 1996 convention in Chicago, "prominent Democrats" had discussed her prospects as a senator from Illinois, according to Sidney Blumenthal.

Betsey Wright had been a booster since 1972, although early in Bill's first term, when she suggested to *The New Yorker* that Hillary was contemplating a race for the White House, administration officials pressed her to retract her comments. In those heady days, "a small group around Hillary, Susan Thomases in particular, were really feeling their oats," said a cabinet officer. "Back then, at the beginning, there was a lot of loose-lipped undisciplined talk like 'We're going all the way,' and they didn't mean him." Linda Bloodworth-Thomason was more forthright than anyone, frequently saying that when Bill and Hillary "are dead and gone, each one of them is going to be buried next to a President of the United States."

When the subject came up publicly over the years, Hillary sent conflicting signals. Sometimes, she dismissed the prospect with a laugh ("Get outta here!" or "Not in this lifetime!"). At other moments, she spoke of the likelihood of a female President and mused about what it would take to get there in the American political system. In April 1998, seventy-five women active in the Democratic party met in Boston to devise a plan to elect a woman to the presidency within the decade. Their straw poll didn't include Hillary, but she won as a write-in. When a friend told Hillary of the results, she at first said, "God no!" but added that she would "monitor the group's progress."

Hillary homed in on New York rather than Arkansas or Illinois as the best state in which to pursue a Senate seat. The Empire State offered numerous advantages to anyone with presidential ambitions. As a senator from New York, Hillary would have *The New York Times* as her hometown paper, not to mention easy access to *Time, Newsweek*, and the television networks—all of which would automatically ensure that she remained a national figure who could be "quoted to devastating effect by the major media every day," said Moynihan advisor Lawrence O'Donnell. "There is no senator with easier or more powerful media access than a senator from New York. This is not something Dale Bumpers ever had."

From the first days of the Clinton Administration, when Hillary spoke on behalf of an Eleanor Roosevelt memorial in Manhattan, she had been welcomed by influential New Yorkers, and in her trips to the city she steadily enlarged her network of contacts. Before he worked in the White House, Sidney Blumenthal gave her a lunch at the prestigious Century Association, with a guest list drawn from journalism, publishing, and academia. Richard Holbrooke, the UN Ambassador after Bill Richardson became Secretary of Energy, organized dinners with figures in the arts such as Robert De Niro and Alan Alda, as well as *New York Times* publisher Arthur Sulzberger Jr. The advantage of such gatherings, Blumenthal explained, was that "no one raised the issue of the scandals," and Hillary could offer a "full articulation of her views" in a more relaxed and appreciative setting than Washington afforded. Once, as her limousine crossed the Fifty-ninth Street Bridge, Hillary said to a colleague, "I'd love to have an apartment in New York someday."

The first acknowledged overture to Hillary about running in New York came from Judith Hope, a transplanted Arkansan who served as chair of the New York Democratic party. At a White House Christmas party in December 1997, Hope told Hillary she didn't think Pat Moynihan would stand for reelection in 2000. "If he doesn't, I wish you would run," Hope said. Hillary chuckled and gave a look of "mock humility," but she took it under advisement. When the suggestion ended up in a New York gossip column, Moynihan was not amused.

By the spring, Hillary had begun campaigning for female Democratic candidates such as Representative Barbara Kennelly, who was running for Governor of Connecticut. The First Lady had to take a week off in late April to prepare for another round of grilling by Kenneth Starr on her Madison Guaranty and Castle Grande work. The Clintons' former friend James McDougal had died in prison of cardiac arrest on March 8 at age fifty-seven, and David Hale was serving time, as was the still-mute Susan McDougal. But the term of Starr's Little Rock grand jury was due to expire on May 7, and the Independent Counsel lacked the evidence to prove that the Clintons had broken the law in their Madison dealings and that Hillary had knowingly participated in Castle Grande's illegal sham transactions.

Hillary faced her nemesis for nearly five hours in the Yellow Oval Room on Saturday, April 25, while Bill was on the golf course. As before, she was vague about her legal work on Castle Grande, failing to recall whether she drafted certain documents. She finished just two hours before she and her husband were expected at the White House Correspondents Association dinner. "Hey! I read a draft of tonight's speech," she exclaimed with startling bonhomie when she encountered Mark Katz after leaving Starr. "Really funny. Great work, you guys." At dinner she received a standing ovation from a crowd well aware of her afternoon ordeal, and she smiled and waved her way through the evening.

Following the Clintons' Europe and China trips, Hillary was back on the campaign trail, starring in more than a half-dozen fund-raisers for House and Senate candidates in as many weeks. She also took a lead role in the administration's effort to shape the intellectual framework of the Democratic party for the 2000 elections. In the second week of July, she substituted for Bill at a White House seminar with scholars. The President was "oddly absent, downright invisible, as if he'd been banished," noted Benjamin Barber. Hillary was "poised and upright . . . in his place, listening discreetly, provoking us with pointed questions." Hillary "was no mere surrogate. . . . She was in some oblique manner taking over."

Later that week, Hillary hit the road for a four-day "Save America's Treasures" tour of eleven historical sites that ended in Seneca Falls, New York, for the 150th anniversary of the first American women's-rights convention. Accompanied by NBC's Katie Couric as well as Annie Leibovitz—for four years Hillary's photographer of choice—the First Lady traveled through New York State in a cavalcade of buses. "People were on the road, waving flags at her," said Ellen Lovell, who helped organize the tour. "There were the beginnings of speculation about her running in her own right. It had a barnstorming campaign feel. . . . It could have been a foretaste of her Senate campaign."

THE EUPHORIA WAS short-lived. On July 17, 1998, the day after the tour ended, Kenneth Starr served Bill with a subpoena summoning him to testify to the Washington, D.C., grand jury. The White House kept the subpoena secret while Bill's lawyers discussed terms for his appearance. Simultaneously, Monica Lewinsky's new attorneys, Washington veterans Jake Stein and Plato Cacheris, were negotiating intensively with Starr on an immunity arrangement. The famous navy-blue dress had become part of the plea bargain—a development Lewinsky's lawyers conveyed to David Kendall. Four days after Lewinsky turned twenty-five on July 23, she cut a deal that gave her and her mother full immunity from prosecution. Lewinsky had first spent five hours in a "Queen for a Day" briefing with Starr's team, displaying impressive recall and offering such details as Nancy Hernreich's yoga schedule. She in turn was taken aback by the quality and quantity of corroborating information the prosecutors had amassed from e-mails, audiotapes, gate logs, and telephone records, as well as grand-jury testimony from, among others, Secret Service agents who confirmed the timing and frequency of her Oval Office visits. Although her tale was filled with examples of her intrigues with Bill, she continued to say he had not directly told her to lie in her affidavit or hide his gifts, although he had spoken in hypothetical terms, and they had discussed cover stories. The next day, Tuesday, July 28, Lewinsky's lawyers announced her deal, and she turned over the tapes of Bill's unmistakably familiar voice-mail messages ("Hey, it's me"; "Sorry I missed you"), along with her size-twelve frock with the telltale stain.

On Wednesday, the President agreed to testify voluntarily, and Starr withdrew the subpoena. Early that evening, Bill seemed in a chipper mood as he gathered with his staff in the East Room to toast Deputy Chief of Staff Sylvia Mathews, who was moving to the budget office. Over in the West Wing, the ABC evening newscast was already breaking the story that the dress had been given to an FBI lab for testing. The next day, Starr and his investigators learned that the "DNA material" on the dress was in fact semen, and on Friday, July 31, they sent a letter to Kendall requesting a blood sample from the President to comply with "investigative demands." Hillary later wrote that she and Kendall thought Starr was possibly "bluffing . . . trying to spook Bill right before his testimony"—a far-fetched notion given the significance of the dress and the implication in the letter that semen had been detected.

Bill appeared in the Rose Garden on Friday morning surrounded by "stone-faced cabinet officials" to say he was "looking forward" to testifying (although he admitted the more obvious truth when he wrote in his memoir, "I can't say I was looking forward to it"). Significantly, he didn't repeat his denial of a sexual relationship with Lewinsky. In the afternoon, Bill and Hillary flew to East Hampton, on Long Island, for a weekend at the estate of Steven Spielberg, as well as a round of fund-raisers.

In his after-dinner remarks that night at the East Hampton home of

New York financier Bruce Wasserstein and his wife, Claude, Bill praised Hillary's Millennium Project and spoke about "this theme that Hillary and I have worked on, of one America . . . across all the lines that divide us." Standing on the terrace afterward, Hillary said to Claude Wasserstein, "Everything in my life with Bill is complicated and fascinating." At a later reception hosted by Alec Baldwin and Kim Basinger, Hillary introduced her husband to one thousand guests as he watched with obvious admiration.

"She's really popular in New York, isn't she," Bill said to Judith Hope.

"She *owns* New York," Hope replied.

"Maybe she should run for office here," said Bill. He leaped to the podium and hugged his wife before taking the microphone and delivering his remarks.

On Saturday night, the Clintons appeared at a five-thousand-dollar-per-person "gay-focused fundraiser" at the East Hampton home of composer-conductor Jonathan Sheffer and his life partner, Christopher Barley, a New York physician. "About three quarters of the seventy-five guests were gay or lesbian," said Sheffer, who raised nearly four hundred thousand dollars for the Democratic National Committee. The press declined to report the gay angle, although they "figured it out," said Sheffer. In a conversation with the President about his legal troubles, Sheffer told him "gay people have also been vilified, stereotyped, and persecuted. I felt it was important to make that connection between us."

During a White House event on Monday evening, August 3, Bill excused himself by prearrangement and slipped into the Map Room, where he was met by one of Starr's lawyers, an FBI agent, the chief DNA scientist from the FBI crime lab, the White House physician, and David Kendall. As the technician drew the required sample, Kendall tried to lighten the mood by saying he had always wanted one of his clients to give blood. The President shot him a withering look before returning to his dinner. To ensure that the meeting went undetected, the Starr team waited in the Map Room until all the guests had left. That night, a quick test indicated a DNA match to the dress, to be confirmed within days by more extensive analysis. The Independent Counsel's office kept a tight lid on the results, but Bill already knew the strong likelihood that he would be tagged. The anticipated result shaped his testimony to the grand jury, forcing him to admit an "inappropriate" relationship with Lewinsky. "If the blue dress didn't exist, it would have been a different conversation," said one of his advisors. "It would have been, 'He could choose anyone. Why would he pick an intern?' But the blue dress changed everything."

Lewinsky testified for the first time before the grand jury on Friday, August 6, and the next day Bill began preparing for his own appearance by videotape on August 17. Aside from making visits to Louisville, Chicago, San Francisco, and Los Angeles from the tenth to the twelfth, Bill met daily in the Residence with his legal advisors, led by David Kendall and Nicole Seligman, with assistance from Mickey Kantor—some forty hours of preparation in all.

The President was juggling consequential developments in foreign policy as well. On August 4, the Clinton Administration sought to block UN weapons monitors from carrying out surprise inspections in Iraq so as "to avoid a new crisis with the Baghdad government," *The Washington Post* reported. The new "go slow" approach retreated from the policy adopted six months earlier, raising the possibility that the President's "preoccupation with the Monica Lewinsky situation is responsible." Three days later, terrorist bombings at the U.S. embassies in Nairobi and Dar es Salaam killed 257 people, including twelve Americans, and injured another five thousand. A grim Bill Clinton walked into the Rose Garden to condemn the "cowardly attacks" before convening a series of meetings with his national-security team over the next week to determine who was responsible and whether and how to retaliate.

Hillary kept her schedule packed with "things to do" and "people to see." At an event in Philadelphia, she raised $150,000 for a Democratic candidate, and her staff put out the word that she "thrives on her public appearances." She also took time out for an interview with the *Arkansas Democrat-Gazette* in which she claimed that the campaign against the President was driven by "prejudice against our state. They wouldn't do this if we were from some other state."

Harry and Linda Thomason left Los Angeles that weekend to keep their old friends company. Because Linda feared flying, they made the trip by car. Bill called them frequently, and by Oklahoma he finally told Harry that there was truth to the Lewinsky story. On their arrival at the White House, the Thomasons spent most of their evenings with the Clintons in the Solarium playing Upwords, a three-dimensional Scrabble game. Using Harry as a sounding board, Bill privately told him pieces of the Lewinsky saga over the course of several days, as he rehearsed what he would reveal to Hillary.

The Clintons put out different versions of Bill's confession to his wife. The initial account in *Newsweek*, from "knowledgeable sources," placed the dramatic moment on Thursday evening, August 13, after a memorial service at Andrews Air Force Base for the families of the Africa-bombing victims. Without disclosing many details, Bill supposedly let Hillary know that his involvement with Lewinsky had been "long-running, and it had been sexual." Friends such as the Thomasons insisted that Bill had indeed previously withheld a significant amount from his wife. "Anyone who thinks Hillary knew what happened before the two of them had their conversation wasn't there," Linda told Gail Sheehy.

The next morning, a carefully planted story appeared on page one of *The New York Times*, headlined, "President Weighs Admitting He Had Sexual Contacts." According to a member of the Clinton "inner circle," the President would probably own up to a "specific type of sexual behavior" that would manage to avoid contradicting either his public denials or his Jones deposition. With Hillary an essential member of the White House legal team, it was inconceivable that such a leak could proceed without her concurrence. Yet in her memoir published five years later, Hillary recounted a puzzling exchange with lawyer Bob Barnett on the evening of Friday the fourteenth. She recalled that Barnett warned her there might be "more to this than you know," to which she replied, "I've asked Bill over and over again."

"But you have to face the fact that something about this might be true," Barnett replied, causing her to cut him off, saying, "Look, Bob, my husband may have his faults, but he has never lied to me"—an astonishing statement given Bill's history of philandering.

Both Hillary and Bill have written that he told her an unspecified "truth" about Monica Lewinsky by waking her up (just as he had done in January) on Saturday, August 15—two days after the version offered at the time. If retrospectively changing the confession from Thursday to Saturday was supposed to emphasize Hillary's shock, she undercut that intention by describing Barnett's warning the previous evening. The shifting times only add to the unreality in their accounts of the whole episode. In any event, each Clinton memoir contained its own dramatic details: Bill told of his "miserable . . . sleepless night," his repeated assurances to Hillary of his love, his admissions of his shame, and her reaction as if he had "punched her in the gut." Hillary described his pacing the room, his admission of "inappropriate intimacy" that had been "brief and sporadic," her "crying and yelling . . . 'Why did you lie to me?' " her feeling so "furious" and "dumbfounded" that she could "hardly breathe," his repeated assurances that he was only trying to protect "you and Chelsea." Hillary recounted that when she said he had to tell Chelsea, "his eyes filled with tears."

Many were skeptical that Hillary could have been so stunned after all that had come out over the previous seven months. Four out of five respondents in a *Newsweek* poll believed she had known "for some time" about her husband's affair with Lewinsky. "This is a charade," said then-conservative columnist Arianna Huffington. The most plausible conclusion was that if Hillary had been aware of the outlines, she now knew more particulars, and she was appropriately enraged at her husband—for being so foolish, for betraying her, for shaming their family, for embarrassing her before the world. "I think it was a surprise to her that he confessed to a real relationship," said Mike McCurry. "The hurt was genuine enough that it had to have been something different from what she had been hearing for the previous seven months."

One of Hillary's signature traits since the earliest years of her marriage was her ability, particularly when the stakes were high, to put her personal feelings about her husband aside in favor of their larger goals as a couple. "Hillary would get mad at him," said Betsey Wright, "and yet she could sort through that within a matter of hours." So it was not unusual, on the weekend before Bill's grand-jury testimony, that Hillary worked with the White House lawyers to help him prepare. On Sunday morning, Bill carried a Bible in one hand and gripped Hillary's hand tightly with the other as they walked into United Foundry Methodist Church, while Chelsea stayed home. In the evening Jesse Jackson spent several hours counseling Hillary and Chelsea and then prayed with all three Clintons. Jackson recited the Fifty-first Psalm, the classic prayer of contrition written by David after he had been caught committing adultery with Bathsheba: "Wash me thoroughly from my iniquity and cleanse me from my sin. . . . The sacrifice acceptable to God is a broken spirit."

In a phone conversation that day, Sidney Blumenthal was pleased to hear Hillary focusing on the "politics" rather than the "issues." She told Blumenthal that her husband "would be 'embarrassed' but that was for him to deal with." Hillary's imperturbability was also evident to Jackson, who said, "Hillary's not naive. There was no one great explosive shock and surprise moment. Hillary knows her husband well and has for 25 years. The best evidence of that is that Sunday as the drama was building, she was organizing his testimony, so she knew what it was going to be."

HILLARY'S INVOLVEMENT IN Bill's preparation made her fully complicit in his four-hour performance before the grand jury, by video hookup from the Map Room, the next day. Starting at 1:00 p.m., he engaged in a well-choreographed exercise in legal parsing and premeditated prevarication. Because he had no choice after the conclusive DNA evidence, he had to acknowledge that Lewinsky had performed fellatio on him. But he continued to lie about the array of sexual acts he had performed on *her*—all manner of fondling in ten intimate encounters—that could not be unequivocally proved. When he made his limited admission, he understandably wished to be vague, speaking only of "inappropriate and intimate" conduct "that was wrong." He further said that because this behavior did not include sexual intercourse, it "did not constitute sexual relations as I understood the term to be defined." By denying he had touched Lewinsky in a sexual manner, he could claim that her mouth on his sexual organ did not conform to the definition of sexual relations read to him at the Jones deposition. But the image created by this denial—of him receiving Lewinsky's sexual favors without so much as a tender caress—not only defied everything known about this most tactile man but made him seem like a man interested only in his own pleasure.

He lied in other ways as well, claiming that "what began as a friendship came to include this conduct," when in fact the relationship was sexual from the outset, and after several trysts he still didn't seem to know Lewinsky's name. He said their initial sexual intimacy had occurred "on certain occasions in early 1996," not during the government shutdown of November 1995 after Lewinsky famously flashed her thong. And he cynically relied on Orwellian semantics to avoid a perjury rap for his deposition. He said that he and Lewinsky hadn't been technically "alone" because other people were nearby, even if they weren't actually in the room. When asked whether Bob Bennett was speaking truthfully in the Jones deposition by saying "there is absolutely no sex of any kind, of any manner, shape or form with President Clinton," Bill flickered a smile and said, "It depends upon what the meaning of the word 'is' means." That sentence may have deflected the prosecutors but at a steep price, since it became the second-most famous quotation—after "that woman"—of Bill's eight years in office. Most of the time, the President skillfully filled the air with explanations and observations, launching into a series of well-rehearsed riffs designed to take up time. He sipped a Diet Coke, took his reading glasses on and off, and stopped five times for breaks. He remained cool even in the face of sexually explicit queries ("If Monica Lewinsky says that while you were in the Oval Office area, you touched her breast, would she be lying?"), seizing the platform whenever he had the chance to denounce Jones's lawyers and their "dragnet of discovery . . . funded by my political opponents."

When he emerged from the Map Room at 6:25 p.m., Bill's mood was as turbulent as the lashing rain and black thunderclouds outside. He had stayed up late the previous evening scribbling his thoughts on a legal pad for a televised speech scheduled for 10:00 p.m. While the President was with the grand jury, Paul Begala, Robert Shrum, and Linda Bloodworth-Thomason had a hand in various drafts of Bill's remarks, and Mark Penn submitted proposed language that he had tested with polling. Bill's original version had included a harsh denunciation of Starr, which his political advisors removed. They advocated full contrition, while Mickey Kantor and David Kendall reinforced Bill's instinct to attack.

After showering and changing clothes, the President was still fuming when he arrived in the Solarium, where his advisors were assembled, along with the Thomasons, James Carville (called in from Brazil), Tommy Caplan, and Chelsea, who was "trying to make sense of what was happening." Hillary remained in her private quarters on the second floor, in an effort to create some distance from a process in which she was already deeply invested. Throughout the day she had been in frequent contact with Sidney Blumenthal, who was in Italy attending a wedding, though he managed to fax in passages that were harshly critical of Starr.

Hillary eventually joined the group at 8:00 p.m. but said little as the factions debated the tone and substance of Bill's brief address. "Well, Bill, this is your speech," Hillary finally interjected. "You're the one who got yourself into this mess, and only you can decide what to say about it." Some in the room interpreted her comment as evidence of her detachment. But she had invoked that phrase—"Well, Bill, it's your speech, you say what you want"—numerous times over the years as a way to close debate. In fact, as Bob Barnett's wife, Rita Braver, said the next day, "Everything Bill said was exactly as Hillary wanted it."

Hillary and Chelsea left the Solarium, followed by the others, giving Bill about a half hour to finish rewriting on his own before the remarks were transferred to cue cards. Shortly before 10:00 p.m., he returned to the Map Room, where Harry Thomason had worked with Bob Squier to create an understated setting: the President in an eighteenth-century armchair, with a grandfather clock, an antique desk, and a vase of flowers—but no family photos—in the background. Harry perched on the floor next to Bill, trying to calm him down, while Linda sat on a chair nearby.

Bill spoke for four and a half minutes, and he devoted more than half of his 543 words to attacking Starr. His anger popped out in the second sentence, when he said he had had to answer "questions no American citizen would ever want to answer." He now admitted a relationship with Lewinsky "that was not appropriate" and "wrong . . . a critical lapse in judgment . . . a personal failure on my part," for which he accepted "complete responsibility." But he insisted that his answers in the Paula Jones deposition had been "legally accurate," and that he had taken no "unlawful action." He had "misled" people, but not under oath. His motivation was avoiding "embarrassment" and "protecting my family." But he also resented Jones's "politically inspired lawsuit" and criticized an independent prosecutor intent on "personal destruction" and "prying into private lives." The President now wished to deal with "this matter" privately with his family. "It's nobody's business but ours," he insisted. Blaming Starr for "the spectacle of the past seven months," he asked Americans to "move on."

His tone was defiant rather than remorseful, and it was tinged with self-pity. He made no apologies to either Monica Lewinsky or her family. And as he left the Map Room, he was still wound up.

When Rahm Emanuel ventured some instant negative reaction, Bill snapped back, "I said what I wanted to say. I don't care what these people say." A White House spokesman said the President "felt as if a burden had been lifted from his shoulders," which *Washington Post* columnist David Broder noted was "light compared to the burden of falsehood he placed on others who put their trust in him."

Bill rejoined his friends and advisors in the Solarium, where Hillary was "talking to people in a pleasant and smiling way," Ann Lewis reported. Sidney Blumenthal called to register his praise, and both Clintons said they were satisfied with the speech. As Blumenthal chatted with Carville and Penn, he could hear Bill and Hillary "bantering in the background. . . . They were still working as a team. Without that, nothing was possible."

Chapter Fifteen

———

THE NEXT DAY, HILLARY HASTENED TO ISSUE A STATEMENT THAT HER love for Bill was "compassionate and steadfast" and that "she believes in this marriage." While it was vital to reassure the public that the Clintons were not on the brink of separation or divorce, the First Couple did enter a period of carefully orchestrated estrangement. Both Clintons knew that "the President had to be seen taking his medicine—the isolation of contrition or redemption or whatever it might be," wrote Bob Woodward. They readily showed the world a coolness between them and permitted their aides to discuss the tensions that existed behind closed doors. But as with so much in their relationship, the reality was more complicated.

Bill had been in and out of the doghouse countless times in their nearly twenty-three years of marriage. For all the humiliations that Hillary had endured in the past, the magnitude of Bill's latest transgressions, which abased her in the eyes of the world, intensified her anger and deepened her sense of accumulated grievance. Adding to her anguish was the emotional and physical toll on Chelsea from her father's affair with a woman only seven years older than she. Yet there was little doubt Hillary would remain Bill's wife, because now they were partners who could not get along without each other—"an undifferentiated emotional unit," said Eleanor Acheson, Hillary's Wellesley friend and Bill's Assistant Attorney General. As Sidney Blumenthal observed, Bill and Hillary's endurance as a single political force overrode everything else.

The first visible sign of the unfolding Clinton family drama came on

Tuesday afternoon, August 18, as Bill, Hillary, and Chelsea walked across the South Lawn to Marine One for a trip to Martha's Vineyard. More than two weeks earlier, a news account had predicted that their departure would be a "tableau tailored for the cameras," but there was surprising drama in the simultaneous impression of solidarity and aloofness created by the actual sight: Chelsea between her parents, holding their hands, Hillary in sunglasses gazing straight ahead, her posture perfectly erect, and Bill with his head bowed, leading Buddy on his leash. Watching the scene, Monica Lewinsky "felt terrible for Chelsea, because no young person wants to think of their parents in terms of intimate sexual acts. I felt very very sorry for her." A friend of Chelsea took note that she was "being the supportive child. She would never disobey her parents or violate her image by walking with her arms crossed, or five paces behind. She was too smart for that."

In the helicopter to Andrews Air Force Base, Bill "had his face in a book," said Mike McCurry. "Hillary and Chelsea were both very quiet." McCurry made small talk by asking what he should do on his first visit to the Vineyard, and Chelsea and Hillary offered suggestions. "It did break the ice," said McCurry. On Air Force One, Hillary slept while Bill continued to read. Hillary's office had put out the word that the Clintons' friends should welcome them at the Martha's Vineyard airport, so a large contingent led by Vernon Jordan waited on the tarmac. When the family emerged from the airplane, Jordan immediately embraced the President. Chelsea came next, appearing thoroughly composed. "She was their ambassador," said Rose Styron. "She talked to each of us." As Chelsea walked away with her father, they were seen laughing together.

The President was preoccupied for the next three days with the Africa bombings and plans for retaliatory attacks. He had spent his last morning in the Oval Office meeting with his national-security advisors to discuss possible bombing targets. "Clinton showed no signs of the distraction, to say nothing of the despair, that most of us in the room were barely suppressing," noted Strobe Talbott. "He was focused on the topic at hand." As one senior advisor observed, the President "was the only person after his confession who wasn't set back on his heels and incapacitated. He had known that the shit was going to hit the fan, and he had had a chance to work his way through. He had this toughness about him, a higher form of self-delusion, as if he were saying, 'By God I don't care what the odds are.

I can ride this out. I'm going to hold onto this log and go over the waterfall and not drown.' "

At the Friedman compound, Bill set up a command center in the guesthouse, where he spent his fifty-second birthday conferring about the developing military plan with General Don Kerrick, the national-security aide who ran the White House Situation Room. In a revealing gesture of unity, Hillary worked closely with her husband on his speech that was to announce the bombings. "Hillary knew she had to stifle whatever anger she had," said McCurry. "She knew he had to be very sharp and make difficult decisions that were controversial. I could tell from Hillary's interaction with Kerrick and me that she knew what was about to come down. After Kerrick and the President had been on the secure phone to [Defense Secretary] Cohen and the NSC, Kerrick came out and Hillary said, 'Obviously we will have a hard time convincing the public about this. I hope you guys are doing everything you can to make sure the public knows he considered all this carefully.' She was conscious of how awkward the situation was." Hillary was referring specifically to the administration's concern that a bombing operation would be seen as a *Wag the Dog*–type attempt to divert attention from the President's Lewinsky troubles.

That night, the Clintons dispensed with the customary party to celebrate Bill's birthday and instead had a quiet meal with Vernon and Ann Jordan, who served barbecued chicken and coconut cake. After dinner, Bill returned to the makeshift Situation Room, where he spoke with CIA Director George Tenet at 1:30 a.m. An hour and a half later, the President authorized Sandy Berger to order the launching of cruise missiles at targets in Afghanistan and Sudan.

At 1:55 p.m. on Thursday, August 20, the President announced the attacks. For the first time, he told the American people about Osama bin Laden and his al-Qaeda terrorist network, which the administration had linked to the Africa bombings with "convincing evidence." He said the missile strikes were aimed at "one of the most active terrorist bases in the world," located in Afghanistan, along with a "chemical weapons–related facility in Sudan" associated with the bin Laden network. The objective was to hit "the terrorists' base of operation and infrastructure" in order to "damage their capacity to strike at Americans and other innocent people."

He immediately flew back to Washington, and at 5:30 gave a speech about the operation from the Oval Office. He called bin Laden "the pre-eminent organizer and financier of international terrorism in the world today," the leader of groups sharing "a hatred for democracy, a fanatical glorification of violence, and a horrible distortion of their religion to justify the murder of innocents." Operation Infinite Reach was intended to "counter an immediate threat." The base in Afghanistan had been chosen because "we have reason to believe that a gathering of key terrorist leaders was to take place there today." Although he emphasized that the battle against these terrorist networks would be "a long ongoing struggle between freedom and fanaticism, between the rule of law and terrorism," he was to speak publicly about bin Laden and al-Qaeda only a half-dozen more times in his presidency—in a radio address several days later, in response to a reporter's question at a press conference in early September, during an interview with *The New York Times* and in his State of the Union address the following January, in a commencement speech at the U.S. Coast Guard Academy in May 2000, and in an interview with Joe Klein two months later—all glancing references without either explanation or con-text. In 1999 and 2000, he ordered economic sanctions against the radical Taliban government in Afghanistan that harbored al-Qaeda, but he took no further military actions.

American allies—particularly Boris Yeltsin—harshly condemned the attacks as unwarranted unilateralism. At home, polls showed 73 percent support for the retaliation, but there was widespread *Wag the Dog* skepti-cism among what Bill dismissed as "the pundit class." Even more damag-ing, the attacks proved to be ineffectual—"an oafish sort of overkill," in the words of Joe Klein. Bin Laden and his entourage had left the training camp before it was bombed, and the evidence against the El Shifa pharmaceuti-cal factory in Sudan proved to be flimsy. In subsequent months, Clinton Administration officials quietly conceded the absence of proof that the factory produced chemicals for weapons or that the plant's owner was asso-ciated with bin Laden. "Virtually everything the Administration said pub-licly about El Shifa in the days after the attack has turned out to be wrong," *U.S. News & World Report* concluded a year later, after the magazine's investigation into the bombings.

Bill returned to the Vineyard on Friday afternoon, and over the next ten days he submitted to his Lewinsky punishment. Under pressure from

Hillary and his political advisors, he withdrew his invitation to Terry McAuliffe to spend three days playing golf. "It was decided that he was going to spend his time alone," said McAuliffe. "Hillary was clear that she wanted him to be alone." Bill took long walks on the beach with Buddy. No stranger to expulsion from the bedroom, he slept on the sofa downstairs, while Hillary stayed upstairs. She later wrote of her "unresolved anger," her inability to speak to Bill except in a "tirade," his apologies, and her continuing effort to find the "path to understanding." While her mortification was real, "Hillary was not jealous," said one of her friends. "Hillary has supreme confidence. She doesn't need outside reassurance, and she has no need to have her husband's love validated. She doesn't give a damn if people don't understand." What she did care about, said her friend, was "what Bill would have to do to make it OK with Chelsea."

Hillary described her daughter as "confused and hurting." It was clear that Chelsea was "pretty down" on Bill, said one of his aides. She barely spoke to her father and spent much of her time at the home of Clinton friends Jill and Ken Iscol.

The Clintons went out together far less than usual, but while Bill stayed close to home, Hillary sought the company of friends. She had lunch with Katharine Graham, who she knew "had her own experience with the agony of infidelity." Jacqueline Kennedy's longtime companion Maurice Tempelsman entertained Hillary on his yacht and told her that Bill "really loves you, and I hope you can forgive him." Something of an expert in unconventional domestic arrangements, Tempelsman had remained married to the mother of his three children even as he lived with Jackie.

On another afternoon, Hillary enjoyed a "girls' outing" on a sailboat owned by wealthy Californian Kelly Day. The group included Ann Jordan, Jill Iscol, author and prosecutor Linda Fairstein, Lucy Hackney, and actress Susan St. James. They sat on the back of the yacht in the sunshine, talked about their travels, and ate lunch. There was no raucous laughter, and no one went near the subject of the Clinton marriage. "Some in the group thought Hillary would let her hair down and talk, but no, she was so guarded," said Lucy Hackney's husband, Sheldon. "These were friends, and if she needed to talk, she would have been able to trust them. It was no surprise that she didn't. She came to conclude she couldn't afford to be unguarded about anything."

By Saturday the twenty-second, Bill and Hillary felt compelled to put in an appearance at one major social event, a dinner party at the home of investment banker Steven Rattner and his wife, Maureen White, a Democratic party fund-raiser. The Clintons didn't notify the hosts until 6:00 p.m. that they were coming. "They knew they couldn't hide," said one Vineyard resident. "Everyone was expecting to see them there." When they arrived, Bill and Hillary entered separately, reinforcing the impression that they were not speaking. According to protocol, they sat at different tables on opposite sides of the lawn. At the hostess's table, Bill engaged in a lively if somewhat elliptical conversation started by Harvard law professor Alan Dershowitz about the Bible's view of adultery. They had a spirited dialogue about the Ten Commandments, and Bill offered "a very interesting analysis of the sinners of Sodom." "Maybe they weren't talking about Monica Lewinsky specifically, but they were talking about whether there can be forgiveness," said one observer.

At the host's table, "it was like another planet," said a friend seated nearby. "Hillary would not talk about it at all." After a discussion about education in Chicago, someone finally said, "You've had a bad couple of weeks. Are you okay?"

"Oh, I'm fine," Hillary replied. "What's everyone doing for the rest of the summer?"

"That is the difference between the two of them," said the friend. "The conversation was about public-policy issues. You would have had no idea that her husband had been on national TV confessing to adultery."

Several days later, they ventured out together once more, this time for a private cruise with Walter and Betsy Cronkite. During their three-hour sail, Bill spent most of his time talking to Walter, leaving Hillary with Betsy, while Chelsea stayed in the back of the boat with the Secret Service agents. Bill asked endless questions about sailing, pored over Cronkite's nautical charts, and discussed the Civil War with the Cronkites' teenage grandson. "I wouldn't say there was a lot of levity between the Clintons," said Walter Cronkite. "Hillary didn't join in too much of the conversation."

The impression among Bill and Hillary's island friends was of a couple struggling to remain civil to each other. Yet those who knew them best could see that a reconciliation had already taken hold. "The point is that she knows all the facts now and is deeply committed to her husband," said

Lisa Caputo, Hillary's former press secretary, who saw them during their vacation. "They have an incredible connection and chemistry to them that carries them through a situation like this." *Newsweek* editor Ken Auchincloss and his wife, Lee, accidentally witnessed a striking example of this dynamic the very afternoon the Clintons arrived on the Vineyard—when by all public appearances they were thoroughly alienated. The Auchinclosses were walking near their house adjacent to the Friedman property when they spotted Bill and Hillary down the beach, "lost in conversation," recalled Lee. A few moments later, Lee and her husband saw the Clintons "locked in the most passionate embrace." The Auchinclosses continued walking, and when they looked back once more Bill and Hillary were "sitting and talking earnestly. Whatever he said must have worked."

During her weeks on the Vineyard, Hillary spoke frequently with her mother, who was staying in the Rodham cabin in Pennsylvania with Hugh and Tony and their families, as well as Harry and Linda Thomason. "Dorothy was concerned about Hillary but also about both of them," said a family friend. Through the Thomasons, the Rodhams sent the message to Bill that they still loved him, which boosted his morale. "They have always known about his problem," said the friend. "It was nothing new, just the magnitude. It wasn't like they would never speak to him again. They had no illusions that the problem had been fixed, and they were disappointed that something like this could be true. But they also did not stop caring about him."

As their vacation drew to a close, Bill and Hillary had to grapple with a growing public antagonism toward his televised remarks after his grand-jury testimony. "The selfishness" of the President's seven months of lying was "staggering," wrote David Broder, the veteran Washington political reporter. "Any business executive or military officer would be fired immediately" for what the President had done. Broder took issue with Bill's assertion that "it's nobody's business but ours," writing that "he made it our business" through his "utter disrespect for the high office he holds" and by "refusing all this time to do what he alone could do: clear up the matter." Michael Kelly, also writing in *The Washington Post*, scorched the President for using a "young female employee as a sexual service station" and for encouraging "a long and vicious campaign by his henchmen to savage those who were telling the truth. . . . Even in confessing his lying, Clinton lied."

On ABC's *This Week*, Cokie Roberts spoke directly to the President, saying, "What you have done is an example to our children that's a disgrace." Garry Wills wrote an essay in *Time* calling on Bill to resign. George Stephanopoulos in *Newsweek* noted that some Democrats were wondering if it would be better for Gore "to take the helm." On the irreverent *Imus in the Morning* radio show, a Ross Perot mimic described Bill Clinton as "a throbbing boner on which someone had put eyes and a pair of legs."

Monica Lewinsky came away from Bill's speech thinking that he was sorry only that he had been caught. "I was very hurt and angered," she said. "I felt like a piece of trash.... He was so self-righteous and self-centered.... He should have acknowledged my family." In her second appearance before the grand jury on August 20, she expressed her dismay that the President's portrayal of no-hands sex made their relationship seem "that all I did was perform oral sex on him and that that's all this relationship was, and it was a lot more than that to me." Because of his tortuous testimony, she was compelled to return to the grand jury a third time six days later to undergo detailed questioning about each of their sexual encounters. In the end, she testified that he had "touched and kissed her bare breasts" nine times, "stimulated" her genitals four times, brought her to orgasm three times, had phone sex fifteen times, and pleasured her once with the infamous cigar.

Some of the strongest criticism of the President was coming from his own party. Pat Moynihan said the speech was "not adequate" because it lacked an apology and focused on attacking Starr. Tom Daschle, Richard Gephardt, and Dianne Feinstein expressed their disapproval, and Gephardt even called Bill's behavior "reprehensible." Feinstein couldn't shake her disappointment that Bill had looked her in the eye and lied, although New Jersey senator Robert Torricelli reacted to a similar exchange by saying, "I'm not upset. You want to know why? Because I never believed him in the first place."

Bill did get strong backing from other quarters. Al Gore took time out from a vacation in Hawaii with his family to issue a statement and hold a press conference. A source close to the Vice President said Gore "felt genuinely sorry for the guy, because he was pursued by nasty partisans." On Wednesday, August 26, Pat Moynihan heard from two Vineyard luminaries calling on behalf of the President. Former Attorney General Nicholas

Katzenbach said he understood Moynihan was about to call for impeachment and urged him not to do so. Moynihan replied he "had no such thought." Manhattan district attorney Robert Morgenthau weighed in to tell the senator that Kenneth Starr was "a menace to the presidency." The next day, Bob Kerrey phoned Moynihan to report that the President had called and gone on "at great length about this and that. Finally he got to the point, which was that Moynihan was going to call for his resignation." When Bill had asked Kerrey to intercede, the senator wondered why he didn't call himself. "I couldn't do that," Bill replied. Finally, Moynihan contacted Mike McCurry, his former aide, and "asked if he would be good enough to have them knock it off."

As Bill's staff assessed the damage, they urged him to make another statement, showing greater contrition. He made an attempt on Friday, August 28, during a ceremony at the Union Chapel in predominantly black Oak Bluffs commemorating the thirty-fifth anniversary of Martin Luther King Jr.'s "I Have a Dream" speech. "This business of asking for forgiveness," he said, "it gets a little easier the more you do it. . . . In order to get it you have to be willing to give it." Not only did he neglect to say he was sorry, his slightly flippant tone struck a false note and invited even more anger from his critics.

THE CLINTONS RETURNED to Washington on Sunday morning, and the next day they were off to Moscow for Bill's fifteenth meeting with Boris Yeltsin. Hillary later said that by then she and Bill had reached a "détente if not peace," although they had work to do on their marriage. After watching the Clintons on the flight to Russia, New York Republican congressman Peter King observed, "They acted like the two happiest people in the world. They were holding hands, telling jokes, laughing. . . . They were fighting in public, and in private acting like a totally normal happy couple."

The Russia visit was intended to give Yeltsin a boost as his country was in the throes of a financial crisis. Listening to the President talk of needing to convince the Russian leader to "come to work every day" and "make the government work," Strobe Talbott "heard an echo of the advice Clinton must have been giving himself about how to handle the mess he'd made of his own public and private life: I've got to get up every day . . . just keep working away, doing the people's business, and maybe they'll let me stay in office." What Talbott called the "strangest of all summits" produced no breakthroughs, and Bill found himself uncomfortably in the middle of Yeltsin's deliberations about his nomination for prime minister. Reporters also took note that enterprising Muscovites were doing a brisk business in nesting dolls of the President, Monica Lewinsky, Paula Jones, Gennifer Flowers, and Hillary.

Three days into their trip, Bill and Hillary were jolted by a lacerating, twenty-four-minute speech by Joe Lieberman on the Senate floor. He said that the President's extramarital relationship with "an employee half his age . . . in the workplace in the vicinity of the Oval Office" was "not just inappropriate" but "immoral." Even so, if the President had "acknowledged his mistake and spoken with candor" in January he could have "lessened the harm." Lieberman was most disturbed that the President's deception was not a "reflexive . . . human act of concealment" but rather "intentional and pre-meditated," which served to "undercut the trust that the American people have in his word." By so damaging his own credibility, the President had jeopardized "his chances of moving his policy agenda forward." Bill's August 17 speech was especially disheartening because the President not only failed "to repair the damage" but showed no understanding of what he had done wrong and how "his behavior had diminished the office he holds and the country he serves. . . . The conduct the President admitted to that night was serious, and his assumption of responsibility inadequate."

Lieberman was one of the most respected voices in the Senate, a loyal Democrat with deep religious convictions as well as evident common sense. Although he reserved judgment about the wisdom of impeachment until Starr had presented his evidence, his anguished words had an electrifying effect. Watching from his office, Bob Kerrey bolted out the door and hurried to the Senate chamber to speak his mind. "I do not want my children to believe that the only standard of truth to which they, much less a President of the United States, must aspire is legal accuracy," said Kerrey. Pat Moynihan spoke in the same vein, and Marcy Kaptur, a Democratic congresswoman from Ohio, said the President's resignation "would not be satisfaction enough."

The Clintons were by then in Northern Ireland, where Hillary was again displaying unmistakable frostiness toward her husband. The next day, Bill used a photo opportunity in Dublin to respond to Lieberman by saying, "I agree with what he said. . . . I made a bad mistake, it was indefensible." And for the first time, the President said, "I'm sorry about it." The next day in Limerick, the Clintons were back in harmony as he made notes after her whispered suggestions, and they stood before a crowd of fifty thousand with their arms around each other's waists.

When Bill issued his fourth and fifth apologies the following week, White House aides were starting to call CNN the "Contrition News Network." On Wednesday, September 9, in the morning he made amends with Democratic members of the House in the Yellow Oval Room. In the afternoon, the President traveled to Florida, where he bit his lip and told Democratic supporters, "I let you down. I let my family down. I let this country down, but I'm trying to make it right." Late that day, two vans arrived at the Capitol with the Independent Counsel's report—452 pages with 1,660 footnotes, along with two sets of supplemental material filling thirty-six boxes.

After returning to the White House well past midnight, Bill gathered Democratic senators the next morning in the Yellow Oval Room for the same message he had given the House members. In the evening, it was the cabinet's turn to convene there and hear his apologetic soliloquy. His eyes at times welling with tears, he defended his record as President, asked for forgiveness, and pledged to redeem himself in the years to come. He also attributed his misbehavior with Lewinsky to his anger at the Independent Counsel's investigations over the previous four and a half years. When he asked the cabinet officers for their reactions, Madeleine Albright began by mildly expressing her disappointment but urging everyone to keep doing their jobs. Donna Shalala told him she "didn't buy" his attempt to blame his relationship with Lewinsky on Starr. "His description of why he did it was bizarre," Shalala recalled.

"Surely your personal behavior is as important as your policies," Shalala told the President. "I can't believe that is what you are telling us, that is what you believe, that you don't have an obligation to provide moral leadership." Bill visibly reddened and shot back, "If you were judging on personal behavior and not politics, then Richard Nixon should have been elected in 1960 and not John Kennedy." Other cabinet officers followed in a more conciliatory vein, touching on the need for confession and forgiveness. "There's no question you screwed up," said Bob Rubin. "But we all make mistakes, even big ones." The atmosphere remained tense until Al Gore moved to bring the meeting to a close. He expressed his "disappointment" but emphasized that everybody in the room needed to show their support. "Mr. President," he said, "I think most of America has forgiven you, but you've got to get your act together." Secretary of Agriculture Dan Glickman recalled that "a lot of us just wanted to end the meeting and get out of there." Barry McCaffrey, Director of the Office of National Drug Control Policy, turned to Donna Shalala and said, "This is the weirdest meeting I have ever been to."

Within days, the White House leaked the gist of the cabinet discussion, with an emphasis on Shalala's stern rebuke and the President's spirited rejoinder. The message was that the cabinet had vented its anger, and no one was going to resign in protest. One cabinet officer noted that "naturally [Shalala] and Clinton hugged at the end. The whole thing was just like an encounter group, with everyone sitting on couches." "The White House thought the leak was useful," Shalala recalled. "Their interpretation was that it demonstrated a strong independent cabinet who wouldn't let the President get away with it."

The morning after Bill's session with the cabinet, he made his most complete apology, which he said reflected the "rock bottom truth. . . . I don't think there is a fancy way to say that I have sinned." He had been up all night writing his remarks, and his demeanor was subdued as he stood before more than one hundred clergy in the East Room for a White House prayer breakfast. Hillary gave him "a modified Nancy Reagan gaze" of adoration as he admitted he had not been "contrite enough" in his televised statement nearly a month earlier. He said "everybody who has been hurt"—including for the first time Monica Lewinsky and her family—needed to know that his sorrow was "genuine." He asked their forgiveness, expressed his repentance, and offered his "broken spirit" to be restored, with "God's help," by his own willingness to forgive and his renunciation of pride, anger, and self-pity. To help him stay on the right path, he would seek "pastoral support." Yet as before, he declined to specify what precisely he had done wrong, and he naturally did not tell the clergymen that his grand-jury testimony, solemnly sworn to God to be "the truth, the whole truth, and nothing but the truth," had been riddled with lies and misrepresentations.

As he spoke, Bill grew more energized, drawing on his Southern Baptist roots and reading an "incredible" passage from the Yom Kippur liturgy about the "time for turning" to avoid being "trapped forever in yesterday's ways." With those words he turned his own rhetoric in a rather surprising direction. He said he needed to continue in office to teach "the children of this country . . . that integrity is important and selfishness is wrong" and by his example show that "God can change us and make us strong at the broken places." He wanted America's children to aspire "to grow up to be President and to be just like me."

Hours later, on September 11, 1998, the Starr Report hit the Internet after the House voted 363 to 63 to make it public. The lawmakers had not even reviewed it, which "horrified" Starr, who told *The New York Times* that Congress decided "that we're simply going to turn this information over to the American people." Leading the disclosure charge was Democrat John Dingell, who was joined by his party's leaders.

The narrative was filled with details of sexual acts, along with gamy glimpses — arguably unnecessary as a legal matter — of masturbation, phone sex, and the infamous cigar. Equally shocking was the high school quality of the President's relationship with Lewinsky — the petulant fights, the furtive and perfunctory encounters, the cheesy gifts, the desultory and banal chats. It was "a portrayal of a President who seems cunning but emotionally vacant, a man wasting his talents and powers on an empty affair with a woman who was in many ways still a child," *Time* observed. To Dee Dee Myers, the relationship was "so frivolous, so reckless, so small."

West Wing advisors were glued to their computers as they read the lurid stories about their boss. Mike McCurry called it his "worst day. Only then did I learn the awesome gruesomeness that nobody knew. Reading the report was the toughest time because you confronted the adolescent nature of the relationship. It was so weird to begin with, and the report made it more weird. He clearly was wrestling with a lot of stuff, with demons." Hillary let it be known that she would not read Starr's account, but in California, Chelsea read it online, which drove her father to tears.

The White House immediately leaped on the report with lengthy rebuttals attacking its eleven grounds for impeachment (among them perjury, obstruction of justice, and abuse of power) and skewering its "pornographic specificity," "biased recounting," and "unconscionable overreaching." Starr said that he had been forced to include so many sexual particulars because the President had lied so flagrantly—when he testified, for example, that he had never touched Lewinsky's genitals or breasts. Legal expert Stuart Taylor believed Starr could have made a more compelling case "if he'd written his report smartly, if he had kept the details in a sealed appendix." Richard Posner, a federal appeals-court judge and legal scholar, wrote that Starr could have "unmasked these lies simply by listing each of the ten sexual encounters by date, time and place . . . stating that in each of them Monica Lewinsky fellated the President while the President touched parts of her body enumerated in the definition of sexual relations." Posner pointed out that Starr had doubtless been frustrated by the President's "extraordinary verbal agility" and angered by the "campaign of vilification by Clinton supporters," but "we expect better from our prosecutors."

The week following the report's release was the most perilous time for the President. Calls for resignation came not only from a number of Democrats but from some of the nation's leading newspapers. On Sunday, September 13, *The Philadelphia Inquirer*, which had endorsed his candidacy in 1992 and 1996, wrote that "Bill Clinton should resign" for a half-dozen reasons, including that "his repeated, reckless deceits have dishonored his presidency beyond repair," "the impeachment anguish that his lies have invited will paralyze his administration," and "it is the honorable thing." The next day, *USA Today* argued for resignation because Bill Clinton had "resolutely failed—and continues to fail—the most fundamental test of any president: to put his nation's interests first." Noting that the Starr Report was a "salacious and flawed" document, the editorial said it also revealed a man who "lied in the nation's face and then used his considerable power to intimidate and discredit his accusers . . . who consciously skated along a thin legal edge, determined to hold onto office at any cost to the nation he is sworn to serve." His tactic of "relying on a contorted, legalistic definition of sexual relations designed to evade the truth while also tiptoeing past a perjury charge" was "fine for a criminal defendant but not for the President of the United States."

Leading Democrats in the House and Senate weighed their options that weekend. After the release of the Starr Report, liberal Democratic congressman David Obey had told Minority Leader Richard Gephardt that he and Tom Daschle needed "to go tell [Clinton] to get out." Gephardt asked Abbe Lowell, counsel for the Democrats on the Judiciary Committee, to plumb all the supporting evidence and assess the prospects for impeachment. On Sunday, September 13, Lowell reported to Gephardt that in the deposition there was "no question that he lied"; in the grand-jury testimony, perjury was a "closer call." He allowed that Vernon Jordan "probably lied through his teeth about what he knew, but there's no way to prove otherwise." Lowell found no "smoking gun" for an obstruction-of-justice charge, and he didn't believe the President's lies rose to the "high crimes and misdemeanors" standard for impeachment. Gephardt expressed his relief but couldn't help asking, "Abbe, is the cigar thing real?"

In the Senate, the stirrings for resignation were stronger. Tom Daschle knew that at least seven of his influential Democratic colleagues—Robert Byrd, Bob Graham, Dianne Feinstein, Harry Reid, Russ Feingold, Fritz Hollings, and Joseph Biden—were lining up to ask the President to consider leaving office, much as a Republican group led by Senators Hugh Scott and Barry Goldwater had done with Richard Nixon in 1974.

On Tuesday, the President announced that Gregory Craig, a seasoned trial lawyer and crisis manager he had known at Yale Law School, would lead his defense in the impeachment inquiry. The two men had spent several hours together the previous Saturday on the Truman Balcony, and Craig readily signed on when Bill asked him to be his "quarterback." Not only was Craig an experienced legal hand, he was handsome, smooth, and well liked in journalistic and political circles, so handling the media would be part of his portfolio as well. Although Bill had not read the entire Starr Report, "he'd read summaries, he'd read excerpts," Craig recalled. "He was a man in deep trouble personally, emotionally. . . . He felt a little bit out of control and almost helpless."

Shortly after his appointment was announced, Craig called Democratic senator Kent Conrad, a friend for twenty-five years. "I said, 'How we doing up there?'" Craig recalled. Conrad replied that they were "about two or three days away" from a White House visit by a senior delegation.

That day, Erskine Bowles and John Podesta had lunch with the Senate

Democrats, many of whom were deeply worried about the impact of Bill's conduct on the midterm elections only six weeks away. Biden said the party might do better with the President gone from the White House. In the evening, Bob Kerrey made his bold phone call to tell Bill his only options were to resign, plea-bargain, or wait to be impeached and that the best course would be to step down.

After some intense lobbying by senior White House officials and friends such as Terry McAuliffe, the center held and the much-feared "stampede" for resignation did not materialize. "I never thought it was a serious proposition," said Arkansas senator Dale Bumpers, a close ally of the Clintons. "I knew Clinton was a very tenacious guy, and he wouldn't consider such a thing."

The balance tipped decidedly in the President's favor a week later with the television broadcast of his four hours of grand-jury testimony. Bill and his aides knew how well he had performed, but the advance spin had him blowing his top and snarling at his interrogators—an effective effort to shape expectations. Still, it was difficult to predict the public reaction, and tensions ran high the weekend before the telecast on Monday, September 21. Early Sunday evening, Bill and Hillary flew to New York for the opening of the UN General Assembly. An aide who accompanied them on Marine One watched as they reviewed a list of invitees for a fund-raiser. "They were absolutely furious with each other, and barely talking," said the aide. "They were so absorbed looking at the invitation list, and it was tense, a tough twenty minutes."

The next day, the television networks aired split screens of Bill addressing the General Assembly on one side as he sparred with an off-camera voice asking intrusive questions on the other. Contrary to the advance billing, he did not lose his temper during his testimony, although he pushed back with precise legal arguments and frustrated his interrogators with nimble rhetorical dances. Much of the substance of his performance damaged him—the too-clever-by-half definition of "is," his parsing of "alone," his chilling insistence on a "legally accurate" description of sex. He slammed Kathleen Willey, telling the grand jurors that her credibility had been "shattered" by the "evidence" released by the White House. "You know what people down in Richmond said about her," he said. When asked if she had made a "sexual advance" to him, he replied, "On that day, no, she did not," implying she had done so on another occasion. Yet in a classic verbal jujitsu he cast Monica Lewinsky in a sympathetic light, even as he repeatedly said she had lied about their relationship. "She's a good young woman with a good heart and a good mind," he said. "I think she is burdened by some unfortunate conditions of her upbringing."

By the afternoon, White House aides knew from their soundings that the public had reacted sympathetically to the President. His style—the charm, the deferential feints, the twinges of sadness, the steely indignation—made a greater impression than what he actually said. In the end, his misdeeds were eclipsed by an impression of unfair hectoring by the prosecutors. When Bill and Hillary appeared in the early evening at a "Third Way" forum at New York University, the President appeared noticeably relaxed and in his element, sharing big ideas about a "new progressivism" with Tony Blair. At a reception afterward, the Blairs and the Clintons tucked into a corner of the NYU Law Library for private conversation.

THE OFFICIAL WORD FROM Hillaryland was that the First Lady was still "deeply angry" and unwilling to issue any public statement supporting her husband. But the day the Starr Report was released, the Clintons appeared at a dinner for Irish Americans, where Hillary "put her hand on her husband's leg. A moment later, beaming brightly, she leaned over and whispered in the President's ear." A friend told *Time* that Hillary had finally "reconnected the President's oxygen tube" that day. George Stephanopoulos detected "an apparent turning point. . . . Whatever their private turmoil, Hillary seems signed on for one more comeback."

While the press dutifully recorded every such tic or gesture as an indication of the President's standing with the First Lady, their public and private shifts between amiability and friction continued patterns that had been evident for years. "By that time there was so much in code," said one of their longtime advisors. "Who knows what was for public consumption, and what reflected their real feelings?" Another senior administration official recalled being in meetings with the two of them and sensing "that it was as normal as ever. They were going back and forth. And if there were times apart or times when it was cold for him, that was not particularly unusual. The morality tale that she was estranged until an amount of time had passed seemed inauthentic."

Divorce was out of the question, not only because it could bring down the Clinton presidency but because Bill and Hillary each had a visceral aversion to it, dating from their childhoods. Although Virginia Kelley married five times, she had hated divorcing Roger Clinton, despite the verbal and physical abuse that fifteen-year-old Bill had vividly described in a deposition as part of the legal proceedings. After only three months, she guiltily remarried Roger, and Bill tried to make amends by taking his stepfather's surname as his own. Hillary's attitude toward divorce came from her mother, who had been a victim of a Dickensian childhood that, according to Hillary, left her vowing to "break the pattern of abandonment in her family." After Dorothy's parents divorced when she was eight, she had lived with relatives who gave her scant affection, and she had been forced to find work at age fourteen. Dorothy and her stiff-necked husband "did not have a happy marriage," said a close family friend. "But she had a commitment to her children. She did stay for her children. She wanted them to have a different life, and Hugh also held the purse strings. He held onto every penny. It would have been untenable to leave."

Bill and Hillary had even more invested in their future as a couple. "Hillary assessed it smartly," said a close friend. "Nothing had changed since Little Rock. He loved her. They had been through more. He was still screwing up in the same way but got caught in a major way. She figured she shouldn't leave him for the same thing she never left him for before, in this instance only because of the magnitude of the situation."

Still, they had to cope with the extent of Bill's "problem" that had been exposed in excruciating detail by the Lewinsky affair. "Everybody has some dysfunction in their families," Hillary told Lucinda Franks of *Talk* magazine. "They have to deal with it. You don't just walk away if you love someone. You help the person." Writing in their memoirs in 2003 and 2004, Bill and Hillary each mentioned the marital counseling they undertook with a professional therapist. Bill revealed they met with the counselor once per week for nearly a year. During the first few months, he slept on a sofa in the family room between the master bedroom and the Yellow Oval Room. Hillary wrote that their counseling sessions forced them to "ask and answer hard questions." Bill recalled that he was able to "unify my parallel lives" and get to know his wife "beyond the work and ideas we shared and the child we adored."

Sparing Chelsea the pain of a highly publicized divorce was also fundamental to her parents' determination to stay together. Hillary had written in It Takes a Village, published two years before the Lewinsky affair exploded, "My strong feelings about divorce and its effects on children have caused me to bite my tongue more than a few times during my marriage." It was also essential for Bill to show Chelsea that he had changed his ways. "I think he went into therapy mainly to preserve that relationship," said Dee Dee Myers. "Hillary he figured he could always get back. She always crawled back to him."

IN THE FALL OF 1998, Hillary supported her husband in ways that served them both. Behind the scenes, she called wavering Democratic members of Congress to make the case against impeachment. Many Democrats had closed ranks behind the President after the grand-jury testimony was aired, but more than two dozen remained open to impeachment. Among them was James Moran of Virginia, who had been outspoken about the President's deplorable conduct and had called for his resignation. When Hillary contacted Moran by phone, he told her bluntly that her husband was "a philanderer and worse." Hillary coolly countered with a cogent legal brief against the Republican plan for an impeachment inquiry. She understood correctly that she couldn't change Moran's mind, but she needed to send him the message that "the Clintons would never give up, never give in." Hillary also embarked on what she called a "campaign marathon," stumping for Democratic Senate and House candidates such as Barbara Boxer, Patty Murray, Carol Moseley Braun, and Blanche Lincoln. She made a special effort on behalf of Charles Schumer, who was trying to unseat New York Republican senator Al D'Amato, one of her tormentors on Whitewater. She visited twenty states, headlined fifty fund-raisers, and appeared at thirty-four rallies. In one three-day swing, she hit New York, Colorado, California, Oregon, and Washington, where she told a crowd in Seattle that "the other Washington" was "a parallel universe" that "sort of exists out there somewhere in outer space." She kept up such a brutal pace that she developed a blood clot behind her right knee and began taking blood thinners. "She is hiding in her work and can't bear to be alone until she is so tired she must sleep," said Hillary's friend Sara Ehrman.

Hillary's efforts on the stump showed her effectiveness as a campaigner and earned the gratitude of countless influential Democrats who could help her with her own political ambitions. While appearing at an event in Chicago that October, New York congressman Charles Rangel told her she should be the next candidate from his state. "Who would want me to run there?" she asked. "She had a twinkle in her eye," Rangel recalled. "I knew then that this was more than a joke with her."

Hillary further raised her profile by resuming her foreign travel, which had been on hold for nearly a year. After a trip to Puerto Rico, she flew to Santiago, Chile, where she told South American first ladies that there was a "great opportunity for women in leadership positions. . . . Women still do not hold enough positions of authority, responsibility and power." Ten days later, she was off to the Czech Republic and Bulgaria for a "Women in the 21st Century" conference. Her absence on October 11 marked the first time since they arrived at the White House that she and her husband had been apart on their wedding anniversary.

MORE THAN EVER, BILL worked to show that he was focused on governing. He was fortunate that Erskine Bowles successfully negotiated a budget agreement with the Republican Congress that the President announced on October 16 in the Rose Garden. Both sides had made concessions, and with only eighteen days left before the midterm elections the President could boast of increased funding for education and the environment. But Bowles had been thoroughly disillusioned by the Lewinsky scandal, and he left the administration in late October; Bill named John Podesta his new Chief of Staff.

Bill made some campaign appearances during those weeks, but he was less visible than his wife. He spent even more time than Hillary working the phones to dissuade members of Congress from starting an impeachment inquiry. When Bob Dole came to the Oval Office in late September to discuss his recent visit to Kosovo, Bill "listened carefully" and then asked his help in persuading other senators to vote against conviction, if there were an impeachment trial. Dole later said that "a lot of attention was diverted" from key foreign-policy questions by the prospect of impeachment, which he said was "all consuming" for the President. Kosovo "may have been one of the casualties," said Dole.

At that moment, few in Congress or the administration were eager to militarily engage the Serbs in Kosovo. Instead, the President sent Richard Holbrooke to negotiate with Slobodan Milosevic. They worked out a stop-gap deal calling for the withdrawal of most of the Serbian troops from Kosovo, but the agreement didn't hold, and the Serbian leader readied a new plan for ethnic cleansing.

One topic that did fully engage the President's attention that fall was Middle East peace. For nine days in October he shuttled between the White House and the Wye River Conference Center in Maryland for meetings with Yasser Arafat and Benjamin Netanyahu, staying until 3:00 or 4:00 a.m. nearly every night. When the talks stalled, he was joined on the fifth day by King Hussein of Jordan, whose wife, Queen Noor, recorded in her journal, "Clinton looks totally exhausted and fed up."

Determined to keep both sides talking, the President stayed up with them all night on Thursday, October 22, until they signed the Wye River Memorandum on Friday morning. The agreement set out plans to estab-lish limited rule over the West Bank by the Palestinians, and it probably averted a major conflict in the region. All parties convened in the East Room on Friday afternoon for a signing ceremony. King Hussein said that Bill had "the tolerance and patience of Job," Arafat called him "a great leader of the world," and Netanyahu described him as "a warrior for peace. . . . He doesn't stop. He has this ability to maintain a tireless pace and to nudge and prod and suggest." Not only was the agreement a boost for Middle East peace, it affirmed the President's clout only ten days before the midterms.

That evening, in a speech to commemorate the 160th anniversary of the African Methodist Episcopal church, Bill announced that he had been awake for thirty-six hours and thirty minutes. He praised King Hussein, who had come to Wye from the Mayo Clinic, in Minnesota, where he was being treated for cancer. "Even though he was the smallest person in the room," the President said, "he was always the largest presence. Here was a man fighting for his own life, willing to take time to remind the people at the peace talks of what it was really all about." But Bill's most revealing moment came when he said that his peacemaking had been "my personal journey of atonement."

Prominent Washingtonians remained unimpressed, rankled as much by his continuing refusal to admit his lies as they were by the nature of his conduct with Lewinsky. On the eve of the election, they unloaded with a devastating catalog of criticism in a *Washington Post* article by Sally Quinn. The piece infuriated the President, who kept a copy on his desk for several weeks as an emblem of all he despised in the Washington Establishment. More than two dozen people — including politicians, journalists, historians, and past administration officials — spoke on the record to Quinn. "He came in here, and he trashed this place," said David Broder. Joe Lieberman decried "the deceit, the failure to own up to it. Before this is over, the truth must be told." NBC's Chris Matthews lamented that "Clinton lies, knowing that you know he's lying. It's brutal, and it subjugates the person who's being lied to." Democratic representative Paul McHale said the President "pervasively lied under oath. He was blatantly, intentionally untruthful." Dick Gephardt noted that "compartmentalization is a nice idea, but not a reality," and blamed the failure to enact a patients' health-care rights bill, campaign-finance reform, and comprehensive tobacco legislation on a President who was "not engaged on these issues." Robert Reich, who knew Bill Clinton better than anyone interviewed, concluded that the President would be "seriously crippled for the next two years. He'll have a few good moments. He'll go through the motions. There will be adoring crowds, he'll use his bully pulpit, and maybe he will have something he can call a victory, but essentially it's over."

BILL WATCHED THE ELECTION returns on November 3 with his staff in John Podesta's office, while Hillary invited two African-American colleagues, Maggie Williams and Cheryl Mills, to the Family Theater for a screening of Oprah Winfrey's new film, *Beloved*, based on Toni Morrison's novel about a nineteenth-century black woman haunted by her former life as a slave. By the end of the evening it was clear that the Democrats had not only avoided disaster but added five seats in the House, leaving the Republicans with 223 seats, and the Democrats 212. The Senate held steady at 55 Republicans and 45 Democrats, and Hillary was particularly gratified that Al D'Amato lost to Charles Schumer. The White House trumpeted the results as a significant comeback and a vote of confidence in the belea-guered President. Newt Gingrich took responsibility for his party's poor showing with the shocking announcement that not only would he step down as Speaker of the House but he would resign from Congress as well.

The turning point in Hillary's political life came three days later when Pat Moynihan said he would not run for a fifth term. Charles Rangel, who had already been pushing Hillary to make the race, called that evening and said, "I sure hope you'll consider running because I think you could win." Bill later wrote that he thought it "sounded like a pretty good idea," al-though Hillary said she told the New York congressman that she was "hon-ored" but "not interested" and that she considered the idea "absurd." Yet the same day, Mandy Grunwald, a key advisor to Hillary, called the Moyni-hans to assess their reaction to a Senate bid by Hillary. They both thought it was a bad idea because she didn't know the state and hadn't shown any interest in its issues or needs.

The Moynihan seat had, of course, been on the Clintons' radar for months. Shortly after the midterms, Hillary and Harold Ickes signaled that interest by inviting a group of friends to have dinner and talk about her prospects. "It was a very pragmatic political discussion," recalled Donna Shalala. "I told her not to run, that she was an outsider, had never lived in New York. We talked about the Bobby Kennedy thing, and her response was that she was looking at the polls. She said that based on Bobby Kennedy's experience [winning a Senate seat as a newcomer to the state], New Yorkers were welcoming." By Bill's account, Hillary made up her mind only days after Moynihan announced his retirement. Once she had spent time "looking around and talking to people," she said, "Okay, I want to do it. So here we go."

Over the following weeks, Hillary was a ubiquitous presence in New York. In early December, she was seen having lunch with Whoopi Gold-berg as well as editors from *Vogue*, *Time*, and *People*. She attended the Man-hattan premiere of *Shakespeare in Love*, and she appeared on *The Rosie O'Donnell Show*. But her apotheosis came with her image on the cover of the December *Vogue*, shot by her good friend Annie Leibovitz. Dressed in a black scoopneck velvet evening gown by Oscar de la Renta, Hillary smiled serenely and struck a regal pose against the gilded and silk backdrop of the White House Red Room.

Vogue editor Anna Wintour had been a Hillary fan for years, a bond doubtless strengthened by Wintour's connection to Democratic party fund-raiser Shelby Bryan. The multimillionaire communications entrepreneur had raised more than one million dollars for Democrats in 1997 at a lavish dinner of pheasant and quail pot pie at his Manhattan town house with the President as the featured speaker. Some months afterward, Bryan and Wintour began an extramarital affair. Bryan had also personally contributed twenty-one thousand dollars to the 1996 campaign, and Bill was to appoint him to his Foreign Intelligence Advisory Board in 1999. *Vogue* billed the First Lady on the cover as "The Extraordinary Hillary Clinton," and the photo spread inside featured her dressed variously in a black turtleneck or a white Ralph Lauren shirt, hair swept back, striking glamorous poses. The purpose, said Wintour, was to show how "she's emerged so triumphant this year."

Maureen Dowd of *The New York Times* took a more jaundiced view, noting that while "the President's head is on the block," Hillary "has never looked more radiant. . . . She looks as if she's traveling with her own pink baby spotlight." Her smile, Dowd wrote, seemed "a little eerie." Just as she had become the "single most degraded wife in the history of the world," Hillary had been transformed, in Wintour's words, into "an icon to American women." To Dowd, Hillary was being rewarded not "for something she has done, but for something she has endured," and she wondered how Hillary "came in as Eleanor Roosevelt and left as Madonna."

Hillary continued to carry out her assorted tasks as First Lady, but she was now intent on finding her own place in history, on her own terms. "She had always wanted to do that, rather than be the spouse of an elected official," said one of her longtime friends. "Being humiliated made her really want to leave that role." What's more, she knew if she allowed her First Lady identity to define her, she would, as another friend put it, "forever be remembered for all the scandals."

THE NOVEMBER ELECTIONS momentarily encouraged the Clintons and their advisors to think they could avoid a vote to impeach the President.

Their battle had begun in earnest on October 8, when 258 congressmen, including 31 Democrats (James Moran among them), voted to begin an impeachment inquiry, with 176 voting against. The House Judiciary Committee started its hearings on November 19, and they continued over seven days at intervals until the second week of December.

In the middle of the impeachment debate, Bill Clinton announced on November 13 that he had settled with Paula Jones for $850,000 and no apology. It was a significant sum—$150,000 more than she originally asked, although less than the $1 million her lawyers put on the table in the last round of negotiations with Bob Bennett. The decision to settle, which Hillary agreed to, avoided a protracted appeals process and the possibility that the case could still go to trial. Funds for the payment came from Bill's personal insurance policy and a trust fund established by Hugh Rodham. Hillary later admitted that failing to settle the Jones suit early was their "second biggest tactical mistake," after agreeing to ask for an Independent Counsel in January 1994.

As if on cue, the specter of yet another confrontation with Iraq also emerged in November. On October 31, the President had signed into law the Iraq Liberation Act, passed unanimously in the Senate and by a vote of 360 to 38 in the House. The law established "regime change" in Iraq as official U.S. policy. Bill emphasized his support for the Iraqi opposition's efforts to overthrow Saddam Hussein and establish a democratic government. "I categorically reject arguments that this is unattainable due to Iraq's history or its ethnic or sectarian make-up," he said. "Iraqis deserve and desire freedom like everyone else."

But as British Ambassador Christopher Meyer observed, "L'Affaire Lewinsky" made it impossible for the President to implement this policy. "I can just see Saddam Hussein licking his chops, seeing that the U.S. is less willing to respond," said former Republican senator Howard Baker. Once again, the Iraqi leader threatened the UN weapons inspectors, and once again the national-security team met to consider a military attack. "There was back-and-forth about bombing Iraq," recalled James Steinberg, Deputy National Security Advisor. "Some of us wanted to go forward, but then Clinton was uncertain. . . . Wag the Dog did become a problem. Every time we tried to do something, rather than debate the merits, the focus was on the political." The President issued a warning to Saddam toward the end of November, and his advisors recommended that he consider air strikes before the start of the Muslim holiday of Ramadan on December 19.

By early December, the President's lawyers began to grasp that their client was likely to be impeached. In the final round of hearings beginning December 8, they were adamant that Bill Clinton's conduct did not warrant "overturning the mandate of the American electorate," and they offered eloquent arguments to buttress their position. But they had to make some damning concessions as well. In his opening statement, Gregory Craig admitted that the President's testimony in the Jones deposition was "evasive, incomplete, misleading, even maddening" but did not constitute perjury. The following day, White House Counsel Charles Ruff went even farther, saying that Bill's conduct "violated his sacred obligations to his wife and daughter" and was "morally reprehensible." When asked directly by Republican James Sensenbrenner of Wisconsin if Bill Clinton had lied in his deposition and to the grand jury, Ruff essentially conceded that the President could not distinguish between truth and falsehood. "I have no doubt that he walked up to a line that he thought he understood," Ruff said. "Reasonable people . . . could determine that he crossed over that line and that what for him was truthful but misleading or non-responsive and misleading or evasive was, in fact, false. But in his mind—and that's the heart and soul of perjury—he thought he believed that what he was doing was being evasive but truthful."

Meeting in the Residence afterward, the President's team agreed that while the lawyers had made the best possible case, they needed to push for an alternative to impeachment. The notion of censure had been floating around since September 25, when Abner Mikva and Lloyd Cutler had first proposed such a condemnation coupled with a stiff fine. Hillary had opposed anything with a monetary penalty, and she was also worried that a censure would leave Bill open to criminal indictment. But with an impeachment vote in the House Judiciary Committee imminent, the Clintons agreed to accept a censure resolution with stinging language but no fine. The statement rebuked him for having "egregiously failed" in his obligation to uphold "high moral standards" and to show "respect for the truth," for having "violated the trust of the American people" and "dishonored the office" of the presidency, for having made "false statements con-

cerning his reprehensible conduct with a subordinate," and for having delayed "discovery of the truth." The resolution also stated that he could be
subject to "criminal and civil penalties" and that through his conduct he
"has brought upon himself, and fully deserves, the censure and condemnation of the American people and the Congress." For all the harshness of the
language, Bill knew that a censure resolution could be overturned by a
subsequent Congress controlled by Democrats, while impeachment was
irrevocable—the "lead item in the story of the Clinton presidency," said
Gregory Craig, "in the history books forever."

As the Judiciary Committee debated articles of impeachment on Friday, December 11, Bill appeared in the Rose Garden at 4:10 p.m., looking
hangdog, while Hillary was three thousand miles away, dedicating a flower
conservatory in San Francisco. He spoke of being "profoundly sorry for all
I have done wrong in words and deeds. . . . Quite simply I gave into my
shame." He said he had suffered the "agony" of inflicting pain on his family and that he was ready to accept the "rebuke and censure" of the Congress. He was abject, but his inability to admit that he lied failed to satisfy
moderate Republicans in the House, who might have saved him from impeachment.

Bill turned and walked back to the Oval Office, ignoring the shouted
questions from reporters. Shortly afterward, the House Judiciary Committee voted out the first article of impeachment, charging perjury before the
grand jury, followed by a second article alleging perjury in the Jones deposition and a third article, charging obstruction of justice. On Saturday afternoon, the committee voted out a fourth article, alleging abuse of power.
In all cases, the votes were along party lines, as was the final tally at the end
of the day to defeat the censure resolution.

By then, the President and First Lady were airborne to Israel and Gaza
for a four-day trip. Bill had meetings with Arafat and Netanyahu, and the
First Couple visited the grave of Yitzhak Rabin as well as Masada and the
Church of the Nativity. "The body language was interesting," recalled
Newsweek's Jonathan Alter. "They did hand-holding. They knew people
were watching." Bill was fully engaged, yet he was receiving constant bulletins from his political advisors about the possible totals on the coming
impeachment vote in the full House. During the trip home on Air Force

One, the updates grew increasingly bleak as a string of Republican moderates announced they would vote to impeach. Complicating matters was a fresh showdown in Iraq with the weapons inspectors and the unanimous recommendation by the President's national-security advisors to bomb suspected weapons facilities there. Mindful of the circumstances, Defense Secretary William Cohen told Bill, "If you don't act here, the next argument will be that you're paralyzed."

On Wednesday, December 16, Bill gave the order for the Desert Fox air strikes. Senate Majority Leader Trent Lott immediately denounced the operation as a *Wag the Dog*–style distraction from the impeachment debate, which ended up being postponed by a day. As in August, the two events were not directly linked. But in each case the political climate pushed a weakened President into ratifying the sort of military action he normally avoided, and it compressed the time available for careful consideration and planning. The bombings over the next four days inflicted damage but like earlier air strikes had no lasting consequences for Saddam.

With impeachment proceedings scheduled to begin on Friday, the Clintons greeted hundreds of guests at a Christmas reception the night before in the Map Room, now more a reminder of nightmare interrogations, grim speeches, and forensic procedures than the festivities of the season. It was especially difficult for Hillary, who had pulled a muscle in her back and was in considerable pain. Upstairs in the Residence, Hillary and Bill found relief in the company of Hugh Rodham and Harry Thomason, who were always ready to play cards or a game of Upwords. It was a surreal and tense time, when Bill's fate was out of his hands. "Bill figures he can patch up anything," said one of his close friends. "The first thing he couldn't patch up was impeachment. He thought he would make it okay. That has always been his problem."

As the House began its floor debate, Hillary appeared near the South Portico to tell reporters how proud she was of her husband's work as President and to urge Americans to "practice reconciliation." At the request of Richard Gephardt, she met with the House Democratic caucus on Saturday morning. "You may be mad at Bill Clinton," she said. "Certainly I'm not happy about what my husband did. But impeachment is not the answer." She emphasized what Bill had accomplished and what he stood for, and she said that under no circumstances would he resign. Gregory Craig called Hillary's remarks "very powerful and passionate and emotional. . . . It was a very moving moment."

"We all knew last-ditch efforts to avoid impeachment would fail," Hillary later wrote. In the afternoon, the House of Representatives passed two of the four articles of impeachment, charging the President with lying to the grand jury and with obstruction of justice by encouraging others to lie and to hide his gifts. The votes fell mainly along party lines in the first article, with five Democrats voting for and five Republicans voting against, for a 228 to 206 tally. The obstruction-of-justice vote was closer, at 221 to 212. It was a historic if ignominious moment: the second time in American history that a President had been impeached and faced a trial by the Senate, which could remove him from office. Bill heard the news in the West Wing, where he was sitting with Rev. Tony Campolo, one of three ministers who had been giving him "pastoral counseling" periodically for the previous two months.

Bill's political team organized a show of support afterward by bringing fifty Democrats on buses from the Capitol to the South Lawn for a pep rally. Even on that fateful day, the President kept the congressmen waiting in fifty-degree weather under overcast skies. Bill and Hillary emerged from the Oval Office, their arms linked but their expressions grim. Bill's eyes were puffy and rheumy, his lips pressed tight, his chin jutting defiantly as he walked to the magnolia tree planted by Andrew Jackson, the only president to incur an official censure, later expunged by the Senate. The pain in Hillary's back was intense, but her expression stayed impassive. Standing at a podium flanked by Hillary, Al Gore, and Richard Gephardt, Bill made brief remarks at 4:15 p.m., offering his thanks to his "millions upon millions" of supporters and lamenting that the House Republicans had rejected a "proportionate response" of censure. He vowed to keep working for the American people and asked for an end to the "politics of personal destruction," a deeply embedded theme dating to the 1992 campaign, when he had compared the Republicans to the KGB. He ended by affirming that he would serve as president "until the last hour of the last day of my term."

Given the gravity of the day's events, the mood of the Democratic caucus was oddly ebullient. "It was intended to be arrogant," said Gregory

Craig, "to pump up and restore some confidence in our ability ultimately to prevail." Caught up in the brash spirit of the moment, Al Gore called Bill "one of our greatest presidents" and told the House members, "History will judge you as heroes" for voting against impeachment.

It was a mark of the Clintons' resilience that only hours later they hosted a black-tie holiday party for five hundred of their most generous contributors. The lavish seated dinner took place in a heated tent behind the White House, and Bill and Hillary posed for endless photographs while making small talk. "Bill acted as if he had not a care in the world," said investment banker Sandy Robertson. "He was relaxed. Hillary looked as if nothing had happened either."

By the following night, Hillary was flat on her back and unable to attend the next few Christmas gatherings. She rebounded by the thirtieth, when she traveled to Hilton Head with Bill and Chelsea for Renaissance Weekend. On New Year's Eve, the Clintons did their usual star turn before an audience of more than one thousand. But in a departure from their routine, the schedule didn't call for a freewheeling question-and-answer session. Bill spoke for forty minutes about his budget and other policy successes of 1998, and the First Couple addressed several questions that had been submitted in advance and carefully vetted. When asked about her legacy, Hillary said with an edge of bitterness, "Oh, I don't need a legacy. I was on the cover of *Vogue*. . . . The epitaph should read, 'She was on the cover of *Vogue*.' "

"The President's speech stunned the crowd," said Jonathan Alter, a regular Renaissance guest. "He didn't mention anything about Monica or anything else. There was a level of obliviousness in both of them. They couldn't talk about those matters on any level. They couldn't even say they had been through tough times, and it would be better now. It was the elephant in the room. They were pretending it was a normal 1998." After the clock struck twelve, instead of shooting the breeze with anyone who approached them, as they had done with gusto for fifteen years, the President and First Lady made a beeline for the exit. Alter found himself directly in Bill's path. "I hope you have a better 1999 than 1998," he said.

The President glared at him and snapped, "I hope the Constitution has a better 1999, too."

Chapter Sixteen

—

BILL AND HILLARY CLINTON'S SEVENTH YEAR IN THE WHITE HOUSE brought a dramatic shift in their relationship, with the center of gravity moving from his realm to hers. He was the lame duck, crippled by scandal, and she was the rising political star. Having saved his presidency, Hillary now had the upper hand, and his legacy was tied to her political fortunes. At the same time, Hillary's ascendancy had a significant impact on the presidential prospects of Al Gore, diverting attention and resources from his candidacy and adding to the growing tensions between the Gores and the Clintons over Bill's affair with Lewinsky.

The first order of business for the Clinton White House in 1999 was ensuring that the President was not convicted by the Senate and removed from office. The chances of conviction were slim, given the difficulty of securing the necessary sixty-seven votes. But Bill's lawyers had to prepare for the worst, and both sides knew the process would be painful and difficult.

The Senate trial began on January 7, presided over by Chief Justice William Rehnquist, who several years earlier had altered his black robe by adding four gold-braid stripes on each sleeve. His somewhat ironic inspiration was the Lord Chancellor in the Gilbert and Sullivan operetta *Iolanthe*, known for singing at one point, "The constitutional guardian I / Of pretty young Wards in Chancery, / All very agreeable girls — and none / Are over the age of twenty-one. / A pleasant occupation for / A rather susceptible Chancellor!"

Hillary later wrote that she "studiously avoided watching the trial on

TV," and Bill claimed that "the only thing I've watched" was a speech in his defense by former senator Dale Bumpers of Arkansas, a friend for twenty-five years. But according to White House attorney Gregory Craig, the President and First Lady were monitoring the proceedings closely. "After my presentation, he called me up that night, and he said that he thought I did a great job," Craig recalled. "I think the First Lady called me as well and thought that I'd done a terrific job. They were following it. . . . Every now and then they would read stuff in the newspaper . . . and would call up in the evening about [how] they spotted something . . . [and] what did I think of that. I think they were reading the papers as much if not more than watching the television. . . . I think the president was following those proceedings very closely on television."

Both Clintons participated actively in what Hillary called the "strategy and presentation" of Bill's defense. *Washington Post* columnist Michael Kelly wrote near the end of the five-week trial that the President's lawyers "never really tried to refute the case against him." Rather, Kelly continued, they "attempted to explain away each act of perjury and obstruction with its own isolated and tailored excuse. The whole thing was banged together from misstatements of fact, lapses of memory and tricks of semantics." White House Counsel Charles Ruff gave the game away by saying in his argument on January 19 that "to conclude that the President lied to the grand jury about his relationship with Ms. Lewinsky, you must determine—forgive me—that he touched certain parts of her body, but for proof you have only her oath against his oath."

In the end, the congressmen who served as prosecutors in the Senate trial had difficulty proving key charges, notably that the President directed Betty Currie to retrieve gifts from Lewinsky and that Vernon Jordan's job search for Lewinsky was designed to win her silence. Senator Robert Byrd, the punctilious Democrat from West Virginia, exclaimed on ABC's *This Week*, "He lied under oath!" But White House lawyers succeeded in persuading a sufficient number of senators that the President's offenses did not meet what Ruff called the "lofty standard" in the Constitution requiring conviction because they constituted "private wrongs" rather than a "grave danger to the nation."

The dramatic turning point in the trial came with Dale Bumpers's plea for "proportionality" and "balance" on Thursday, January 21. Bumpers's legal arguments tracked those of the lawyers when he contended that the President's "terrible moral lapse of marital infidelity" was neither a "breach of the public trust" nor a "crime against society." The senator was most effective when he turned personal, on the one hand describing his friend's behavior as "indefensible, outrageous, unforgivable, shameless," but also portraying Bill's relationships with Hillary and Chelsea as "incredibly strained if not destroyed" by actions he had taken to avoid inflicting "unspeakable embarrassment and humiliation" on them, particularly on the "child that he worshipped with every fiber of his body." Bumpers later admitted that his characterization was a "gratuitous statement" based on his impression of the Clintons rather than on any direct knowledge. Bill Clinton also sought to downplay the portrayal, telling two reporters from *The New York Times* that he and his family had "come through the worst" and that Bumpers had simply been "trying to inject a human element."

Bill's State of the Union address was scheduled for January 19, the same day as Ruff's opening statement. As the day drew closer, speechwriter Michael Waldman "could see that the President—for all his surface calm—was under increasing pressure." On the morning of his address, Bill seemed exhausted, but as he left the Map Room that evening for the drive to the Capitol, his mood seemed to lift, and Hillary was "smiling and pleased." Yet Bill later confessed that he had been livid when he entered the House Chamber where he had been impeached precisely a month earlier. "I realized I had to just purge myself of any thought of anger at them," he recalled. For seventy-seven minutes he spoke with his customary rhetorical virtuosity and theatrical flair, even turning toward Hillary to mouth "I love you." Afterward, Bill was once again joined by scores of staff and friends in the State Dining Room at the Residence. But unusually, he went upstairs first, while Hillary lingered to work the room—a sign that she was already thinking more like a candidate than a First Lady.

As in the previous year, the President's State of the Union message advocated tapping into the growing budget surplus to "save" Social Security and now Medicare, too, while increasing expenditures on a range of domestic programs, including an ambitious new prescription-drug benefit for Medicare recipients. Under Bill's plan, Congress would allocate 60 percent of the surplus to extend the life of the Social Security trust fund by twenty-three years to 2055, and 16 percent to keep the Medicare trust fund solvent for ten more years, to 2020. He also wanted to earmark 11 percent of the surplus for tax credits to promote new universal savings accounts that would augment Social Security.

Bill's proposals offered a seemingly painless way to shore up two huge entitlement programs and avoid the more onerous remedies of increasing payroll taxes, reducing benefits, and raising the age of eligibility for retirement income. They also required sleight of hand, because he was not actually proposing the diversion of cash from the surplus to fill the coffers of Social Security and Medicare but rather to put IOUs in their trust funds. He envisioned using the surplus to pay down the national debt, which would create a climate for lower interest rates and presumably stimulate economic activity. The resulting revenue from that growth, by this analysis, would later pay off the IOUs—unless, of course, the federal government found other ways to spend the money.

Bill and Hillary operated in their parallel universe as the Senate trial crawled to its conclusion. They unveiled proposals to promote his agenda, distributed awards to worthy citizens, and danced the tango at a State Dinner for Argentine president Carlos Menem as seven of Bill's jurors (six Democrats and one Republican) looked on. When the Clintons traveled to St. Louis on January 26 to greet the Pope, Bill invited a group of Catholic friends to join them, and he and Hillary wandered through Air Force One, holding hands and chatting. "He was almost dismissive about the Senate trial," recalled Tom Siebert. "They're going to go through this process," said Bill, "but those who want to take me out are not going to get there."

"Then it was on to the next subject," said Siebert.

AMID HER USUAL BUSTLE of speeches and appearances, Hillary's plans for a Senate race were taking shape. She had been consulting with friends and advisers, such as Susan Thomases, for several months when New Jersey senator Robert Torricelli, the chairman of the Democratic Senatorial Campaign Committee, jumped the gun on January 3 by announcing on *Meet the Press* that Hillary would be a candidate. Irritated by the indiscretion, she sought advice from her consigliere, Harold Ickes, who told her, "If you have no interest, issue a Sherman-esque statement. If you do, say nothing." They agreed to meet in mid-February for an in-depth discussion about New York politics and the mechanics of a race there. Hillary "wanted a forum that legitimized her," said Susan Thomases. "She wanted to be empowered to take political stands and have a constituency to back her up." Bill would now be required to take an unaccustomed secondary role and to serve her as directly as she had served him for so long—in some sense the ultimate penance for his habitual womanizing.

Yet in his practical and optimistic way, Bill saw the Senate candidacy as a prize for Hillary, a lifeline for him, and a salve for their marriage. At a Democratic National Committee dinner in Washington's Corcoran Gallery of Art in mid-January, he bragged about what "Hillary has meant to the success of our endeavors. She's been on every continent. . . . She's gone to places most people in her position don't go . . . and just a thousand other things. And she has done it under circumstances I think are probably more difficult than anyone who has ever done it before. I love her for it." As she listened, Hillary dabbed her eyes in a rare display of public emotion. Bill was more specific about the future two weeks later during a dinner at Le Cirque in Manhattan. "It looks to me like that it is highly likely that I will increasingly be known as the person who comes with Hillary to New York," he told a group of well-heeled donors, adding that he was "getting ready for my next life. I'm going to be the comic that closes the show—my stand-up life."

Bill had his own purposes behind his slightly uneasy jocularity. "For Bill Clinton, there was no way for his popularity to be tested," said one of Hillary's advisors. "She would carry the burden of his behavior. Politicians are always looking for signs that they have been forgiven—or at least that the public has gone past it. She was a surrogate for him in that." Madeleine Albright told a friend she was "impressed that Clinton was eager for Hillary to win the Senate race to recompense her for all she had to put up with and also a way for him to get back into campaigning." Tom Siebert, who was to raise money for Hillary, recognized that "the Senate race kept them in public life. . . . They grabbed the brass ring early in their lives, and running for elective office was in her DNA as much as his."

The prospect of teaming up in another race had a salutary effect on the Clintons' relationship by shifting their conversation to safe ground, away from the personal issues they had been grappling with in couples' therapy. "Bill and I were talking again about matters other than the future of our relationship," Hillary later wrote. "We both began to relax. He was anxious to be helpful, and I welcomed his expertise." Susan Thomases observed, "She always had enormous respect and affection for him in the political context. He was always the strategist for himself and for her."

ON THE MORNING OF Friday, February 12, Harold Ickes arrived at the Residence for his long-planned meeting with Hillary, while senators at the other end of Pennsylvania Avenue prepared to vote in her husband's trial. As they settled into the West Sitting Hall, Ickes on the sofa in front of the lunette window and Hillary in an upholstered armchair, there were echoes of a moment decades earlier when his father, Harold Ickes, a close advisor of Franklin D. Roosevelt, had urged Eleanor to run for the Senate from New York scarcely a month after her husband had died of a cerebral hemorrhage, in April 1945. Five days after receiving the entreaty from the elder Ickes, Eleanor graciously turned him down, saying, "I feel very strongly that running for office is not the way in which I can be most useful," and remarking that she didn't wish her children to have another parent holding public office.

Lacking any such misgivings, Hillary listened intently as her Harold Ickes led her through a tutorial in the intricacies of politics in New York: Hispanics, blacks, different Jewish sects, county chairmen, upstate versus downstate, neighborhoods, finances, the carpetbagger image, and the Robert F. Kennedy precedent. They pored over a map, and Ickes briefed her on her most likely Republican opponent, New York mayor Rudolph Giuliani. They had been immersed for several hours when Bill wandered in before noon, dressed in a sweat suit and ready to chat. Hillary invited him to join them in the Private Dining Room for lunch, where Hillary sat at the head of the table, Bill on her left and Ickes on her right.

"Do you know how many votes I got in Herkimer County?" the President said, and the three of them launched into a discussion of the region in the foothills of the Adirondacks that Clinton and Gore had won in 1996 by 1,876 votes out of 26,888 votes cast. Bill then pulled out a statement he intended to read in the Rose Garden after the Senate vote and asked if he could try out a few lines. Hillary rolled her eyes and indulged him briefly before turning the conversation back to upstate electoral tallies. The President left before dessert, and the First Lady and her advisor continued their talk in the sitting room.

Sometime before 2:00 p.m., Republican congressman Peter King of New York called Hillary to tell her about the Senate vote: 55 to 45 for acquittal on the perjury charge, and acquittal on the obstruction-of-justice article on a 50 to 50 vote—both tallies far short of the two-thirds majority required for a guilty verdict. "The Senate voted not to convict," Hillary said to Ickes. Without missing a beat, she continued, "As you were saying about the Erie County board?" Now that her husband's brush with political oblivion was over, Hillary had shifted her focus entirely to her own political career.

John Podesta called Bill in the Residence with the news, and at 2:38 the President stepped into the Rose Garden alone, on an afternoon when the thermometer hit a record high for the day of seventy-four degrees and thunderclouds filled the horizon. After Mark Penn counseled him to be muted and brief in his remarks, Bill spoke just four sentences. "I want to say again to the American people how profoundly sorry I am for what I said and did to trigger these events and the great burden they have imposed on the Congress and on the American people," he said. It was time now for "reconciliation and renewal for America."

"In your heart, sir, can you forgive and forget?" yelled a reporter.

"I believe any person who asks for forgiveness has to be prepared to give it," the President replied. But when another journalist asked, "Do you feel vindicated, sir?" Clinton declined to answer and returned to the Oval Office, where Jesse Jackson awaited, ready to talk about political redemption. At Jackson's instigation, the two men sat on a sofa and prayed as the preacher invoked a verse from the Thirtieth Psalm: "Weeping may endure for a night, but joy cometh in the morning."

Upstairs in the Residence, Ickes and Hillary were still engaged in blunt conversation about her possible Senate run. "You might not be any good as a candidate," Ickes warned her. Hillary left the four-hour meeting with "a more realistic view" of what a campaign would entail. She issued a statement saying that she would give "careful consideration" to running and would make a decision later in the year. Relying on a list compiled by Ickes of one hundred influential New Yorkers, she got to work on Saturday, talking on the phone with prospective donors. The following day, Bill and Hillary flew to Mexico for a twenty-four-hour trip, both evidently rejuvenated—"all smiles and clasped hands"—as they visited the press section on

Air Force One. Hillary proudly displayed a gold heart-shaped pin Bill had given her for Valentine's Day, and he cheerfully offered reporters chocolates from a large heart-shaped box. His wife, he said, would be a "terrific senator."

Even more significant were Pat Moynihan's words on *Meet the Press*, which was turning into a campaign bulletin board for the First Lady. The senior senator praised her "magnificent, young, bright, able, Illinois-Arkansas enthusiasm. . . . She'd be welcome, and she'd win." But his words also alluded to Hillary's blurry geographic identity. Despite Moynihan's private misgivings about Hillary, he wanted a Democrat to keep his seat, and she figured to be the best prospect in a state where the value of being a political celebrity far outweighed the disadvantages of being a carpetbagger. Rather than being tied to a specific place, Hillary had an unusual advantage because, as one New York political consultant put it, "She lives on TV."

SHORTLY BEFORE THE VOTE in the Senate, Bill's friend Susan Estrich, a lawyer and former Democratic campaign manager, had tried to reassure him that he would soon see the end of his long ordeal. "It will never be over," replied the President. He could scarcely imagine how right he was. Only two days after his acquittal, *Newsweek* published an excerpt from *Uncovering Clinton*, a new book by Michael Isikoff that offered fresh details about the Paula Jones, Kathleen Willey, and Monica Lewinsky sagas. Ten days later, NBC News ran a prime-time interview with an Arkansas woman named Juanita Broaddrick, who told a compelling tale about being sexually assaulted by Bill Clinton in a hotel room in 1978, when he was Arkansas Attorney General. She had been pulled into the Paula Jones case as "Jane Doe No. 5" and had originally filed an affidavit saying the rape accusation was untrue because she "didn't want to be forced to testify." But under questioning by FBI agents, she had recanted. Four of Broaddrick's friends told NBC that she had confided in them about the alleged rape shortly after it occurred, and her sobbing description of the encounter to NBC's Lisa Myers seemed persuasive. David Kendall said the accusation of an assault was "absolutely false." But according to author Jeffrey Toobin, Bill "suggested to one friend that he had slept with Broaddrick, but that it had been a 'consensual deal.'" "The best his backers could do was to insist that this doesn't fit Bill Clinton's adulterous M.O., which they say was merely manipulative, not violent," observed Jonathan Alter in *Newsweek*. The President's supporters argued that "date rape" was prevalent in the seventies and that "horndogs like Bill Clinton routinely had their way with women who said no," wrote Alter.

The day after the Broaddrick report, Bill set out on his most extended travel schedule since the 1996 campaign. From Thursday, February 25, to Tuesday, March 16, he was away from the White House for two weeks, starting with a trip out west to deliver speeches in Tucson, San Francisco, and Beverly Hills. On the afternoon of Saturday the twenty-seventh, he joined his wife and daughter at Jeffrey Katzenberg's retreat in Deer Valley, Utah, to celebrate Chelsea's nineteenth birthday. As he had the previous year, Bill stayed inside and read, while Chelsea displayed her skiing prowess on the intermediate and advanced trails. Wearing dark ski clothes and a baseball cap, Hillary came to the slopes on Sunday morning for several runs before trudging back to Katzenberg's home at noon. The Clintons left on Monday afternoon—a day earlier than scheduled—after Bill made a sweep through Dolly's Books in Park City for some airplane reading: John Grisham's *The Testament*, Raymond Chandler's *Playback*, *India* by Stanley Wolpert, and *In Light of India* by Octavio Paz. Hillary's staff later revealed that while skiing, she reinjured the back muscle that had kept her bedridden for several days the previous December.

Even so, Hillary headed to New York two days later for forty-eight hours of what *The Washington Post* called "faux stumping." On Wednesday, March 3, she spoke at an intermediate school in Queens, a women's leadership forum in Manhattan, and at a fund-raising luncheon. The following day, she gave two speeches at the United Nations, where she condemned the "egregious and systematic trampling" of women's rights by the Taliban in Afghanistan, and visited the New York City Lab School before returning to Washington to introduce a screening of HBO's documentary *Dare to Compete: The Struggle of Women in Sports*.

On her first evening in New York, Hillary's friend Jurate Kazickas and her husband, Roger Altman, the ousted Treasury Department official–turned–private investor, gave the First Lady a dinner party in their Upper East Side town house with guests including media executives Barry Diller and Mort Zuckerman. The taboo topic that night was the TV program they were all missing: Barbara Walters's two-hour interview with Monica

Lewinsky on ABC's *20/20*, which was seen by more than seventy million viewers. "To know the world was watching Monica Lewinsky's debut as the femme fatale who swept her husband away," said Kazickas, "had to have been the worst day of [Hillary's] life."

Lewinsky revealed that she had suffered near-suicidal depression, and she took the occasion to apologize to Hillary, who she said had been in her thoughts "a lot" during her affair with the President. "I never thought she would find out," said Lewinsky, adding that her mother, Marcia Lewis, had tried unsuccessfully to persuade her to end the affair. The young woman described the President as "a good kisser" and a "very sensual man" who "struggles with his sensuality" but expressed disappointment that he seemed sorry only about being caught. When Bill Clinton "deliberately smeared" her in 1998 by describing her as a "stalker," Lewinsky said she "knew at that moment that he was definitely not the person that I had ever thought he was."

The Clintons were walloped again the following Monday when *Newsweek* ran a ten-page cover story excerpting George Stephanopoulos's memoir, *All Too Human*, about his experiences on the 1992 campaign and in the White House. In an accompanying interview, the former senior advisor said that Bill had "lost the battle with himself, tarnished his presidency, and all of us associated with it." Had he fully understood Bill's character at the beginning, Stephanopoulos said he would not have worked for him. "Knowing what we know now, I don't think he'd be fit enough to be elected," Stephanopoulos said. His words recalled a similar interview Mike McCurry had given to the BBC on the day the previous December that Bill Clinton was impeached. McCurry had called his former boss's behavior "contrary to the way you would expect a rational human being to behave." When asked if Bill was fit to be President, McCurry said, "I have enormous doubts because of the recklessness of his behavior."

Bill did himself no favors three weeks later in an interview with Dan Rather on CBS when he said, "I do not regard this impeachment vote as some great badge of shame. . . . I do not believe it was warranted, and I don't think it was right." His comments prompted *The Washington Post* to editorialize that "Mr. Clinton, for all his talk of repentance and soul-searching, never could bring himself to acknowledge the seriousness of his offense against the American judicial system."

Just how serious was made clear on April 12 by Susan Webber Wright, the presiding judge in the Paula Jones case, who issued a blistering thirty-two-page opinion holding Bill Clinton in contempt of court for his testimony about Monica Lewinsky in his deposition. His "false, misleading, and evasive answers" were "designed to obstruct the judicial process," she wrote. "Simply put, the President's deposition testimony regarding whether he has ever engaged in sexual relations with Ms. Lewinsky was intentionally false . . . notwithstanding the tortured definitions and interpretations of the term 'sexual relations.' " His "contumacious conduct"—the stubbornly disobedient way in which he testified—was unacceptable, particularly coming from "the chief law enforcement officer of this nation," and served to undermine "the integrity of the judicial system." She noted that the court took "no pleasure" in citing the President for contempt, but she believed sanctions were necessary to "redress the President's misconduct" and to "deter others" who might consider emulating him. She ordered him to reimburse her $1,202 travel costs, for supervising the deposition at the President's request, and to pay a $90,000 fine to cover the expenses of the Jones lawyers who conducted the deposition. She also referred the matter to Arkansas authorities to consider disbarment proceedings.

It was a stunning rebuke, not least because Wright was hardly a member of any "vast right-wing conspiracy." She had presided over the Jones case impartially, ruling against the plaintiff in a variety of ways. She had even excluded the President's testimony about Lewinsky as "not essential to the core issues" of the Jones case and had ultimately thrown out the Jones suit on the grounds that she had not demonstrated sexual harassment. But Susan Wright had been in the room during Bill Clinton's deposition and carried a vivid impression of his perjury. The President and his lawyers did not contest her ruling and eventually paid the required fines and expenses. Yet Bill would not accept the message that Wright was trying to send about his flouting of the judicial system. "I strongly disagreed with Wright's opinion," he wrote in his memoir. "It really burned me up to pay the Jones lawyers' expenses."

AFTER THE SENATE TRIAL, the President had even less political clout than during the height of the Lewinsky scandal, when he had failed to budge Congress on his far-reaching social-policy agenda. Public approval of his

job performance was still around 65 percent, which in ordinary circumstances would have given him great leverage. With a strong Vice President
poised to run for the presidency, Bill could have diminished his lame-duck
status by emphasizing the possible continuation of Clintonism into a third
and even fourth term. But the cumulative damage of the scandals and the
stain of impeachment had severely impaired his ability to push through his
programs. Not only had he alienated the Republican majority in the
House and Senate, he was beholden to the Democrats who had kept him
from being removed from office, particularly the party's "hard core," in the
words of David Broder of *The Washington Post,* who were "least willing to
contemplate any changes" in the major entitlement programs. "He
couldn't raise an eyebrow to Daschle or Gephardt," said a former White
House official.

Bill Clinton issued executive orders whenever he could, and he continued to use his bully pulpit—as his friend Robert Reich had predicted—to
propose programs, exhort the Congress, announce initiatives, tout achievements, mark anniversaries of laws passed in his first term, convene conferences, and promote studies. But no major legislation reflecting any of his
top priorities ever reached his desk. He exercised his greatest influence in
foreign policy, which he could conduct without Congress approving his
every move.

The situation in Kosovo was rapidly deteriorating as 1999 began. Not
only was Slobodan Milosevic continuing his systematic expulsion of ethnic
Albanians from there, but in mid-January his soldiers carried out a massacre of civilians. Madeleine Albright convened a conference in Ram-
bouillet, France, to address the crisis. But the first round of talks collapsed
at the end of the month, when the Kosovar Albanians refused to sign an
agreement that would have allowed NATO to use force against the Serbs.
Albright reconvened the group outside Paris, and this time the Albanians
signed a peace agreement on March 18 to ensure their autonomy in
Kosovo under NATO protection. The Serbs refused to sign, precipitating a
NATO plan to launch a campaign of air strikes against Serbia, as Milosevic amassed forty thousand troops on the border for a major offensive in
Kosovo.

The United States took the lead in the push toward war over Kosovo—
without a congressional authorization—at least in part because of Bill

Clinton's effort to show his mettle after impeachment and to demonstrate what Bob Woodward called "his need for personal atonement." At the same time, the President was genuinely concerned about a Russian over-reaction to any mistreatment of its longtime ally Serbia. Back in September, Boris Yeltsin had come "nearly unhinged" and had "ranted" for twelve minutes to Bill over the prospect of NATO intervention in Kosovo, according to Strobe Talbott. Now Bill sought to mitigate Russian anger by restricting NATO's response to a bombing campaign "without benefit of an authorizing United Nations resolution," which "would have required Russian acquiescence in the UN Security Council," wrote British Ambassador Christopher Meyer. The Russians decided against blocking NATO and instead watched from the sidelines.

Before giving the order to strike, Bill dispatched Richard Holbrooke on Sunday, March 21, to deliver an ultimatum to Milosevic in Belgrade. The next day, the Serbian leader rejected Holbrooke's eleventh-hour warning; on Tuesday morning, Bill met with his foreign-policy team to hone the bombing strategy. The President was bolstered in his actions by Madeleine Albright, a fervid advocate of intervention to prevent genocide. Al Gore was likewise "prepared to be very forceful," recalled Deputy National Security Advisor James Steinberg. "He would skip to the bottom line and say here is what we need to do and why." The President's advisors knew he had Hillary's support as well.

As the Kosovo crisis began to boil, the First Lady and Chelsea left Washington on Saturday the twentieth for a twelve-day spring vacation in Egypt, Tunisia, and Morocco. Hillary kept in daily contact with Bill by phone, listening to his worries that the bombing could result in more killings of Kosovars or could impair NATO's future ability to act. "You cannot let this go on," she told him. "What do we have NATO for if not to defend our way of life?"

The nineteen NATO allies launched their bombing campaign on Wednesday, March 24, and at 8:00 p.m. the President gave a televised address from the Oval Office explaining his rationale to a citizenry perplexed about the strategic significance of a small province in the middle of eastern Europe. He emphasized the need to "protect thousands of innocent people" from brutal Serbian forces, to prevent a wider war, to "defuse a powder keg at the heart of Europe," to stand with NATO allies, to uphold

American values, to protect American interests, and to promote the cause of peace. It was, he said, a "moral imperative," though he overstated the national-interest argument by describing Kosovo as "a major fault line between Europe, Asia and the Middle East" with such "ingredients for major war" as "ancient grievances" and "struggling democracies." He said that Milosevic was capable of spreading violence into Albania, Macedonia, and other neighboring countries, so he had to be stopped in Kosovo. Bill stated flatly that the campaign would be restricted to aerial bombing. "I do not intend to put our troops in Kosovo to fight a war," he said.

In making the humanitarian case, the President admitted that "the world did not act early enough" in Bosnia, leading to the death of a quarter-million people and the displacement of two million refugees—"genocide in the heart of Europe." This time, he said, the Allies could not "look the other way . . . as people were massacred on NATO's doorstep." It was, however, a "selective morality." Former National Security Advisor Tony Lake pointed out that by 1999, "deaths in the conflict in Southern Sudan had become more than one hundred times those in the terrible crisis in Kosovo, yet Kosovo was front and center on the nightly news," while the fifteen-year-long conflict in Sudan had gone "virtually unnoticed."

For all his brave words, Bill was so anxious about the possibility of a protracted conflict that five hours after his speech he woke up Madeleine Albright to ask for reassurance that "we're doing the right thing here." Albright believed the conflict would end "in a relatively short period of time" because Milosevic was a "schoolyard bully" who would readily capitulate. But her judgment had been informed by erroneous CIA predictions. Two days later, a revised intelligence report indicated that "air attacks will not suffice to shake Milosevic's confidence." Having been told by the American President that no NATO ground forces would be dispatched, Milosevic was emboldened to press his ethnic-cleansing campaign with even greater ferocity, driving a quarter million more Albanians from their homes, slaughtering untold others, and filling camps at the Kosovo border with more than eight hundred thousand refugees.

A week after the bombing campaign began, the success of what the press derisively called "Madeleine's War" was by no means assured. In a meeting with his political strategists, Bill fumed, "It's my war, and we're going to see it through." Hillary issued a statement of support from Marrakesh on March 31, blaming the NATO bombing on Milosevic's intransigence and asserting the need "to persevere until Milosevic has embraced peace." The same day, Dan Rather asked the President point-blank in a televised interview if "Milosevic is winning and we're losing." Bill said that ending the siege of Sarajevo in Bosnia took twelve days of bombing, and he bemoaned that "we live in an age where everybody wants things to operate like a thirty-second ad." But when Rather pressed for an assurance that "we are not going to have ground troops in there—no way, no how, no time," Bill dodged the question, saying, "I don't believe that is an appropriate thing to be discussing at this time."

As the bombing continued for weeks without disrupting Milosevic's attacks on the Albanian Kosovars, Tony Blair began pressing Bill Clinton to authorize a contingency plan for a land war. In late April, the two men had an "explosive phone call" in which Bill heatedly resisted Blair's arguments. Others in the administration were equally dubious, particularly William Cohen and Al Gore, who told *Newsweek* that one hundred thousand soldiers might be needed, and casualties could be high.

Bill tried another path by designating Gore to once again team with Viktor Chernomyrdin, now the former Russian Prime Minister, to lean on Milosevic through a back channel. The Russian envoy went to work—keeping in close touch with Gore—even as Pentagon planners informed the President in mid-May that NATO could not "stop a humanitarian outrage from 15,000 feet in the air." Gore came to share Albright's view that the United States needed to put troops on the ground, but Cohen continued to urge caution.

On May 31, Bill was about to give the green light for invasion preparations when he received word that Milosevic had surrendered. Chernomyrdin had told the Serbian leader that if NATO launched a full-fledged war, Moscow would not step in to help him. Without Russia's diplomatic pressure, American troops would doubtless have seen combat in the Balkans.

On June 10, seventy-eight days after the bombing began, the President announced the end of the air campaign, the withdrawal of Serbian forces from Kosovo, and the creation of a twenty-thousand-strong international security force, including seven thousand American soldiers, to keep peace in the province. Kosovo would become a protectorate of the United Nations. Its ultimate status—whether independent, partitioned, or as a province of Serbia—was to remain unresolved for years to come. But ending the "vicious campaign of ethnic cleansing" and winning the battle "for human dignity" in Kosovo, as Bill put it to U.S. fliers in Aviano, Italy, was an important achievement that raised the stature of the United States and its beleaguered President.

AL GORE HAD ALWAYS been a determined campaigner and a skilled debater. But with his sometimes preachy delivery and stiff demeanor, he was not a natural on the stump like his boss. As the 2000 campaign drew closer, Bill seized on those apparent weaknesses in private critiques to influential Democratic supporters. When San Francisco investment banker Sandy Robertson was spending the night in the Lincoln Bedroom after the State Dinner for Chinese premier Zhu Rongji on April 8, Bill invited him to the Treaty Room for late-night conversation. Dressed in a T-shirt, jeans, a Levi jacket, and track shoes, the President propped his feet on a table and unloaded on Gore's political deficiencies. "He said he was trying to get Gore to be a better campaigner," Robertson recalled. "He was worried." Bill told Robertson, "I've been working with him to get him to loosen up."

A month later, Bill went public with his concerns in an interview that *The New York Times* put on its front page. Those misgivings, plus some early missteps by Gore, led to a *Newsweek* cover story in mid-May describing his presidential campaign as "off and stumbling." Gore was irritated by the President's intrusion, although he made light of it by telling *Newsweek* that Bill was one of many who had advised him to "loosen up." But when asked what role Bill would play in the 2000 campaign, Gore said, "He's got a full time job being President—and he's doing it extremely well." Gore pointedly explained the strength of his own marriage by saying that he and Tipper shared the same values, which included being "faithful to one another and sharing life experiences."

Gore officially announced his candidacy for president on June 16, 1999, at the Smith County Courthouse in Carthage, Tennessee, his family seat. Bill and Hillary were with Chelsea in Paris on a nine-day trip that included the G-8 summit in Cologne, Germany, a visit to a refugee camp in Skopje, Macedonia, and three major speeches by Hillary—on globalization at the Sorbonne, on civil society in Fez, and on "Education for

Democracy" in Palermo. For Gore, the announcement provided an opportunity to redefine himself and to create some distance from Bill Clinton's
personal problems. Since the Lewinsky scandal had broken, Gore had expressed his dismay about Bill's conduct to a small circle of advisors but had
kept quiet publicly.

While polls showed the President's job-approval ratings holding at
around 60 percent, questions about his character were taking a toll on
Gore. A study by the Pew Research Center for the People and the Press
conducted in April found that "personal image problems and fallout from
Clinton administration scandals are contributing to Al Gore's declining favorability ratings and his poor showing in early horse race polls." The study
reported that Gore's favorability rating was 47 percent, compared to 58 percent the previous December. Seventy-four percent of those polled were
"tired of all the problems associated with the Clinton Administration"—an
alarming phenomenon that became known as "Clinton fatigue." Only 29
percent of Americans would have welcomed four more years of Bill Clinton, and 52 percent said they liked Gore better. In a hypothetical race between Gore and George W. Bush, the Texas governor led 54 percent to 41
percent, up several ticks since January.

At his announcement, Gore was surrounded by Tipper, his four children, and his mother. He repeatedly stressed the importance of family values and referred to the President only twice, in connection with Kosovo
and the economy. Later that evening, Al and Tipper sat for a 20/20 interview on ABC with Diane Sawyer. Asked about the Lewinsky affair, Gore
said, "I thought it was awful. I thought it was inexcusable. But I made a
commitment to serve this country as Vice President." He added that "as a
father" he felt the President's behavior "was terribly wrong, obviously."
Seeking to differentiate his character from Bill's, he said, "It is our own
lives we must master if we are to have the moral authority to guide our children." When Bill heard Gore's words, he erupted, "What the fuck is this
about?" Moments later in a call to Tennessee from his Paris hotel room, he
praised Gore's announcement speech. "Nice job," said Bill.

AS A SITTING PRESIDENT, Bill was in a unique position to boost his Vice
President's candidacy by scheduling White House events to highlight his
achievements. But in 1999, those resources were diverted from Gore to

Hillary "in a big way," said one member of the Gore team. "The Clintons come first. That was their basic framework." From June through December, Bill and Hillary appeared at twenty events under the aegis of the White House, including the release of a study on children and violence in the media, a report on Medicare and older women, an anniversary celebration for the Legal Services Corporation, a prayer breakfast, the fifth anniversary of AmeriCorps, a Medal of Freedom awards ceremony, and a celebration of Hillary's fifty-second birthday, where in typical style Bill larded his tribute with statistics on welfare, poverty, crime, and economic growth as he touted his wife as a "genuine visionary" needed by the Senate—the ultimate confluence of the personal and political. During the same period, Gore was featured only at a White House Conference on Mental Health (with Bill, Hillary, and Tipper). He made speeches on behalf of the administration on adolescent gun violence, a patients' bill of rights, and a Medicare prescription-drug benefit, and he announced an executive order to require environmental reviews in future international-trade negotiations.

In 1997, Hillary's office had listed thirty-one major speeches on the White House website. Two years later, that number had jumped to eighty-six—four times as many as those listed for her husband and Gore together. She ran White House symposiums on equal pay for women, youth violence, and philanthropy, and she spoke out on a spectrum of domestic and foreign issues, such as foster care for teenagers, gun control, and the plight of refugees in Kosovo. She published fifty "Talking It Over" columns in 1999, and she signed a contract to write *An Invitation to the White House*, a book on entertaining and décor, which *New York Times* columnist Maureen Dowd considered "plain weird." Dowd speculated that the First Lady's favorite recipes might include "Bill in a Stew" or "Seared Husband," and criticized her for "creating a Potemkin hearth, where she is the comfy bring the Prez his socks-and-slippers First Lady, rather than an emotionally battered wife and celebrity victim doing a county-by-county analysis of New York politics."

Hillary's most prestigious White House events were the "Millennium Evenings" that she inaugurated in 1998 just after the Monica Lewinsky story broke, and she continued them at regular intervals the following year. Most of these gatherings in the East Room—all of which were televised on

C-SPAN—featured lectures and discussions about science, history, literature, and music. But on April 12, author Elie Wiesel, a Holocaust survivor and human-rights advocate, discussed "the perils of indifference" in the modern world. It was a topic that dovetailed with the administration's actions in the Balkans, giving the audience the unusual opportunity to see the President and First Lady discussing those policies as peers.

In their prepared remarks, Bill, Hillary, and Wiesel all linked the Holocaust to Kosovo and the need to counteract "the human capacity for evil." Wiesel made the most prescient prediction of the night when he warned, "The real threat hanging on the twenty-first century, Mr. President and Hillary, is fanaticism . . . the Taliban or the Iranians . . . with nuclear power." Both Clintons skirted the issue, and Bill even naively asserted that "religion has nothing to do with it. It's about power and control." Each of them turned instead to advocating greater religious and cultural tolerance. They were remarkably congruent in their views, and as they smoothly passed the conversational baton back and forth they muffled the competitive impulses that often emerged in such settings. They spoke with evident feeling, made complementary points, and sparked off each other with an intellectual energy rooted in years of intense discourse. The Clintons were so fired up after two hours of nonstop talk—"You can tell we're obsessed with this," Bill said—that they continued the conversation with Wiesel and his wife upstairs in the Residence for two more hours.

DURING THE WINTER and spring, Hillary picked up the pace of her still-unannounced Senate candidacy. She methodically made her way through Ickes's list of one hundred key New Yorkers and by the middle of May had contacted twice that number. Among her counselors were former New York City mayors David Dinkins and Ed Koch, Robert F. Kennedy Jr., and Senator Charles Schumer. But none was more important than Pat Moynihan and his wife, Liz. Hillary's first strategy session with Senator Moynihan, a thoroughly publicized White House lunch accompanied by maps and charts, took place a week after Bill's acquittal. The half-dozen meetings with Liz Moynihan, which occurred in the White House and at the Moynihan apartment, remained private. The senator's wife was no fan of the First Lady, but she obliged with good advice on strategy and tactics (visit all sixty-two counties; stay upstate in order to control the story; culti-

vate upstate reporters, who tend to be less critical). She was also unnerv-
ingly blunt, telling Hillary during their first encounter in the Map Room,
"You lie about what happens. You mislead people. You haven't taken advice." Although Hillary was disconcerted by such candor, she continued
their meetings to take full advantage of Liz Moynihan's unrivaled experience.

After more than six years in the White House, Hillary finally settled on
a look that worked for her, with the help of Anna Wintour, Oscar de la
Renta, and hair stylist Isabel Goetz, a friend of Cristophe Schatteman.
Hillary kept her hair short but styled loosely and swept behind the ears, and
she had her heavy eyebrows thinned and lightened. She wore dark
pantsuits with open-collar shirts, to give her a more consistent appearance,
and sensible low-heeled shoes now that her doctor had banished high
heels following her back injury. She lost weight and chose long jackets to
conceal her wide hips.

Between February and May, Hillary made eight trips to New York State
to try out campaign themes and meet supporters. It was often difficult to
see where the veteran First Lady ended and the tyro candidate began. On
April 19, she went to Manhattan and Long Island for two days, ostensibly
on White House business. But her trip had all the trappings of campaign
barnstorming, including a fifty-two-minute lecture on education at Colum-
bia University and an appearance at a health-care symposium at Hofstra
University where she announced that she now believed in "the school of
smaller steps" and "incremental changes." She went flat out for twelve
hours on the first day, and in a thirteen-hour stretch on the second day she
made six appearances. Sounding as if she were already a resident, she
pitched New York State as "truly a microcosm of America" with "our
biggest, most dynamic city" as well as rural areas producing "crops that you
might be surprised to know are actually grown here. . . . So we have everything in New York that we have in America."

One cloud over her candidacy lifted when Webster Hubbell pleaded
guilty on June 30 to a felony charge of lying to federal banking regulators
about the work he and Hillary had done for Madison Guaranty, including
the Castle Grande development. Although Hillary was not named in the
forty-page indictment, she was referred to indirectly thirty-five times. If the
trial had proceeded, Kenneth Starr would have called her as a witness. Her

campaign could have faced significant problems from testimony focusing on her legal and financial dealings, not to mention the spectacle of her being questioned under oath in a courtroom. The Hubbell plea bargain, which spared him any more prison time, wrapped up Starr's Whitewater prosecutions and coincided with the final day of the Independent Counsel Law, which neither Republicans nor Democrats in Congress sought to reauthorize.

A week later, Hillary established her exploratory committee and began what she called the "listening tour" portion of her campaign at the nine-hundred-acre Moynihan farm in Pindars Corners, New York. She thought it best to keep Bill away from the event, but somewhat surprisingly she also excluded Harold Ickes because he was "too liberal."

In a nice bit of political choreography, Senator Moynihan walked slowly with Hillary down an unpaved road ("like a father giving away a bride," cracked one observer) from the old schoolhouse that served as his office. The photograph of the two of them conveyed his approval and gave her instant credibility with New York voters who revered their senior senator. Hillary and Moynihan stood before more than two hundred reporters for a brief press conference when he suddenly exclaimed, "My God, I almost forgot," proceeded to introduce her, and said, "I'm here to say that I hope she will go all the way. . . . I think she's going to win."

WITH THE HILLARY AND Gore campaigns revving up at the same time, the three-way tensions evident in the White House since 1993 became a more serious problem. "If she runs, we'd wish her well, but we sure could use her help," a top Gore aide had said back in February when Hillary first signaled her interest in the Senate race. Now Gore's campaign advisors began to worry that Hillary's candidacy would actually have an adverse effect on their candidate. "The implications for Gore are very serious," said New York's former Democratic governor Mario Cuomo. "She has to think very hard on this issue." Not only was Hillary unavailable as a campaigner, she was poaching top Democratic fund-raisers and donors who would normally concentrate on the Vice President. She had already enlisted Syracuse native Terry McAuliffe, the Democratic party's biggest rainmaker, who in the months to come cast a nationwide fund-raising net for her.

Before she officially established her exploratory committee, Hillary began directly competing with the Vice President for money, sometimes even at his own fund-raising events. When Tipper Gore's friend Melinda Blinken and a group of women planned a Gore fund-raiser in Los Angeles, Hillary insisted on being invited—over the objections of the event's organizers. Hillary then shocked the Vice President's supporters by soliciting donations for herself in front of Tipper Gore.

At a White House reception for the winners of the Women's World Cup soccer championship in late July, Hillary singled out "my dear friend Tipper Gore" as "a great athlete in her time." But by then Hillary had frozen out Tipper, who had given her steadfast support during her Lewinsky humiliation. Hillary never made clear her reasons for the snub, but Tipper Gore was reported to be stunned, believing she had been cast aside because she was no longer useful.

Bill headlined four Gore fund-raisers in August and September, two of them on the same night at Washington's Hay-Adams Hotel. He called Gore "the single most influential, effective, powerful, and important vice president" in history but did no more events for his Vice President for the rest of the year. Bill later complained that his efforts—giving Gore "high profile assignments" over the years, "making sure he received public recognition"—had been unappreciated, especially when he read suggestions that he could "cost Al the election" by associating with him. Bill recalled telling Gore in the fall of 1999 that he would "stand on the doorstep of the *Washington Post*'s headquarters and let him lash me with a bullwhip" if it would help his campaign. The story, according to one member of the Gore team, was a "form of self-pity, his way of calling Gore an ungrateful bastard."

In his travels around the country, Bill rarely missed an opportunity to make a plug for his wife. He put his fund-raising prowess at Hillary's disposal at least a half-dozen times from August through October, and he spoke extravagantly about her talents. His standard line, repeated at every stop with minor variations, was that he had known "thousands of people in public life" and that Hillary had "more heart, more intelligence, more ability, and more commitment than any person I have ever known."

Hillary was clearly more receptive to her husband's ideas than Gore was. "My impression was [of] her turning to the President for advice," said one of her campaign advisors, "how to talk about issues, how to position herself. She was very dependent on him." Suddenly, Bill became "conversant in obscure topics like upstate New York energy costs." By Bill's own admission, he talked to Hillary "all the time every day"—an acknowledgment of how much his mental energy was devoted to his wife's political success.

FOR ALL BILL'S EXPERIENCE, he couldn't prevent Hillary from making blunders in her first months of campaigning, and he made a major gaffe himself in a clemency case. Her listening tour drew mostly derision from the national press for being contrived and controlled. Liz Moynihan had advised her to "scale it down . . . not have it look presidential." Hillary traveled in a customized van with her staff members and a mandatory Secret Service contingent, and she spoke to carefully selected audiences on a tightly scripted schedule. She listened—and nodded—a great deal as she fulfilled her promise to visit every county. She also recited facts and figures in numbing detail, to the point that *Time*'s Eric Pooley called her "The Woman Who Knew Too Much." Pooley observed that unlike Bill, who enjoyed showing off his intelligence "in an inclusive way" by articulating "things people know but can't quite express," Hillary "sometimes can't help intimidating them." She concentrated on "soccer mom" issues such as education and health care to build support among female voters and often resorted to bromides to avoid controversy.

Even so, she stumbled, at first in small ways, such as when she made tone-deaf claims about her lifelong allegiance to the Yankees and her fondness for Elmira, based on a brief visit during a family trip four decades earlier. Then in early August she provoked a storm of bad publicity over an interview she gave to *Talk* magazine. Tina Brown, the editor, had persuaded her back in February to give full access to the magazine in order to "dispel stereotypes" of her as "cold and calculating." The writer was Lucinda Franks, a sympathetic Martha's Vineyard acquaintance whose husband, Robert Morgenthau, had called Pat Moynihan a year earlier to plead Bill's case.

Franks accompanied Hillary on trips to North Africa in March and Europe in May and interviewed her at length in the White House one morning when "the imprint of her pillow [was] still on her cheek." The admiring eleven-page article offered Hillary's views of her husband and her marriage. Asked if he suffered from sexual "addiction," she preferred to call it a "weakness." She blamed his behavior on a childhood "scarred by abuse" at age four when he witnessed "terrible conflict between his mother and grandmother." A psychologist had told her that "a boy being in the middle of a conflict between two women is the worst possible situation. There is always the desire to please each one."

Hillary did not admit that she and the President had been in psychotherapy, something Bob Woodward had first suggested in a book published earlier in the summer. But she did say that Bill had been "working on himself" and had "become more aware of his past and what was causing this behavior." Hillary considered her husband "a very, very good man," with whom she shared a "deep connection that transcends whatever happens." She had forgiven him, she said, as Jesus forgave Peter after three betrayals. "Jesus knew it but loved him anyway," she said. "We have love."

The searing fights of Bill's early years—not only those Hillary described but also the "raging tirades" against his grandfather by his maternal grandmother, a morphine addict who was eventually committed to a state mental hospital—had previously been disclosed by Virginia Kelley in her memoir. Virginia had pulled no punches about her mother, saying she had a "vindictive manipulative mind." In interviews during his first presidential campaign, Bill had said his troubled childhood gave him a hatred of "overt conflicts." Yet contrary to her comments to Franks, Hillary had insisted in February 1992 that "the horrors" of Bill's childhood were "way overstated. . . . The important thing is he was always surrounded by love."

To her critics in the press, Hillary's comments to *Talk* seemed like lame excuses. *The New York Times* editorialized that "blaming two deceased women for a bad home environment" was "another unseemly attempt to absolve Mr. Clinton for his irresponsible stewardship of the presidency." The same day, Maureen Dowd wrote that everyone was "fed up with the creepy dynamics of this warped marriage," which lacked even a "shred of authenticity." She marveled that Hillary actually compared herself to Jesus and Bill to Peter. Hillary's staff backpedaled furiously, claiming that she didn't actually "attribute" Bill's philandering to his dysfunctional childhood. They insisted she was only trying to explain Bill's behavior, not to excuse it. Such hairsplitting denials only angered press commentators even more.

The Clintons escaped their tormentors by returning to the friendly environs of Martha's Vineyard on Bill's fifty-third birthday. They remained there for nine days, leaving the island twice for fund-raisers in Nantucket, where Bill praised Hillary and her good works. At the end of August, they spent the weekend at Steven Spielberg's East Hampton estate and raised almost two million dollars at four events, much of it for Hillary's treasury. Bill was fired up, remarking to one group of thousand-dollar donors that Hillary had told him "you may be a lot of things, but you're not boring." Later that evening, during a youth-oriented rally at the East Hampton airport, Hillary left while Bill stayed on the rope line. "Dance with me!" shouted a young woman standing on a chair. "I wish I could!" yelled the President.

On the third leg of their vacation, they went to Skaneateles, New York, for another round of fund-raisers packed into three days. During their stay, they announced their purchase of an eleven-room Dutch Colonial home in Chappaqua for $1.7 million. As with their Arkansas financial transactions, this one had a curious wrinkle. They put down $350,000 from their blind trust fund, but because they had just $1 million in assets and more than $5 million in legal debts, they had difficulty qualifying for a standard mortgage. After several other wealthy friends (including Erskine Bowles) turned them down, Terry McAuliffe agreed to post $1.35 million as collateral for a loan. The arrangement was legal, but the press raised questions about potential conflicts from such indebtedness to their chief fund-raiser, prompting the Clintons to find a conventional thirty-year mortgage at a higher rate of 7.5 percent.

Back in Washington, they landed in hot water again over the President's offer of clemency to sixteen imprisoned Puerto Rican militants who belonged to the FALN, a terrorist group responsible for 130 bombings in New York and Chicago during the seventies and eighties. Bill's intervention seemed like a blatant effort to win the favor of New York's 1.3 million Puerto Rican voters. Hillary "strongly supported" the move, which Bill said they had not discussed in advance. "Political considerations played no role in the process," he insisted. After Hillary had told *Talk* only weeks earlier that she and Bill engaged in "constant conversation . . . in the solarium, in the bedroom, in the kitchen," Bill's claims about her being out of the loop rang false. New York political leaders (including Rudy Giuliani, Charles

Schumer, and Pat Moynihan) and law-enforcement officials sharply criticized the clemency offer, and ninety-three Democrats joined Republicans in the House to denounce it in a congressional resolution. Hillary reversed her position and called on her husband to revoke the offer. But by then it was too late, and the prisoners were released. "I did what I thought was right," Bill said, although his misjudgment and questionable motives foreshadowed the controversy he was to create with his pardons on leaving office in 2001.

Hillary's most serious misstep occurred during an image-burnishing visit to the Middle East in early November. At a day-care center in Ramallah on the West Bank, Yasser Arafat's wife, Suha, accused the Israelis of using toxic gas on a daily basis against women and children as Hillary "sat impassively" while listening to a simultaneous translation. When the speech ended, Hillary rose to kiss Suha Arafat on both cheeks. The *New York Post* responded the next day with the front-page headline "SHAME ON HILLARY," and Israeli prime minister Ehud Barak condemned the remarks. Hillary belatedly weighed in with her own rebuke of Suha, insisting that she had had to wait twenty-four hours for a more complete translation. On a trip to Istanbul with Bill a week later, Madeleine Albright "noticed the Hillary and Bill dynamic was not great," recorded one of her staff. "Hillary's debacles in the Middle East are in the air between them."

By year's end, Hillary's poll numbers had taken a beating. In March, a *New York Times*/CBS News survey had shown Hillary leading Rudy Giuliani 48 percent to 39 percent. By the end of October, Giuliani was ahead 46 to 42, largely because voters believed he would be "good at getting things done for New York." During the same period, Hillary's favorable rating plummeted from 52 to 37, and her unfavorable number rose from 22 to 38. Giuliani's favorable rating rose 5 points to 39 percent, and, even though his unfavorable score rose from 28 to 34, he was in slightly better position than Hillary by both measurements.

Amid speculation that she might drop out of the race, Hillary turned to polishing her credentials and mending fences. On the same day in mid-December that she stood with Bill at the White House while he signed foster-care legislation she had championed, she flew to New York, where she met with Orthodox Jewish leaders to allay their concerns about her commitment to Israel. But rather than announcing her candidacy as she had promised in February, Hillary instead pledged to make it official sometime early in the new year.

BACK IN THE SUMMER, when Hillary's listening tour began, a marriage expert told *U.S. News & World Report* that the Clintons would be happier if they had had a de facto separation, spending more time apart than together and living in separate states. "It's the perfect solution," said Michele Weiner-Davis, author of *Divorce Busting*. "They can stay married . . . and they don't have to deal with the day to day problems of marriage." In effect, that was the pattern the Clintons followed once Hillary began running for office. Aside from their eighteen days of vacationing and politicking in August and early September, a six-day official visit to Turkey and Greece in mid-November, and the Thanksgiving and Christmas holidays, they typically caught only a day or two together at the White House every week or so before setting out on their separate schedules.

The real surprise was how much Bill took to the road in his penultimate year in office: nearly three weeks in May, eighteen days in both June and July, virtually the entire month of August, seventeen days in September, thirteen days in October, and three weeks in November. Most of those trips were domestic—speeches from coast to coast, many at fund-raisers, as well as his "New Markets Tour" of depressed rural and urban areas targeted for investment by a public-private partnership organized by Al Gore. The President's speeches were set pieces promoting his agenda and chronicling his achievements, but he also worked hard to recapture his moral authority.

Near the end of almost every speech he invariably turned to his theory of what was "at the root of most of the world's problems"—a highly personal outlook that drew from his own experience, particularly his deep currents of anger. What was "dividing people" at a time of greater communication through technology, along with global economic interdependence, was "the oldest problem of human society—the fear of those who are different from us." He believed that fear begat hatred, which could lead to dehumanizing behavior and killing. "We're all scared," he said. "I wake up every day, and I sort of think of my life and my attitude toward the world and of its people as being governed by an internal scale." He believed that "every human being has got a little scale inside," with "the light forces" on one side and the "dark forces in our psyche" on the other. To Bill Clinton, each day brought a "big struggle to try to keep things in proper balance," to prevent the scale from tipping "dark," and making things "turn badly for people and those with whom they come in contact." The solution, he said, was to learn to respect differences and to "affirm each other's common humanity."

IN SEPTEMBER, THE PRESIDENT VETOED a Republican bill that would have cut taxes by nearly eight hundred billion dollars over ten years, legislation he considered "self indulgent" and "short term." Not long afterward, his moods seemed to get the better of him one Sunday afternoon when he impulsively went out to the Army and Navy Club to play a dozen holes by himself. He kept going when it began to pour and continued playing even in the dark, "swinging and wildly hitting balls everywhere," noted one observer. It was a "stark image of an increasingly isolated and frustrated President, heading toward the end of his second term, his temper rising and his power waning," wrote Ben MacIntyre in *The Times* of London.

When Bill was in Turkey on November 18, the White House announced agreement with Congress on the new budget. The deal increased funding for teachers, police, and land conservation. But nearly all the ideas for reform that Bill had been advocating since his State of the Union message—more stringent gun control, a patients' bill of rights, strengthening Social Security and Medicare, the prescription-drug benefit, increasing the minimum wage—were once again passed over. For Bill Clinton, it was another year of thwarted ambitions.

As the year 2000 approached, so did concerns about possible attacks on Americans, particularly after Jordanian intelligence agents and police rolled up a cell of sixteen terrorists in early December, and two weeks later an alert U.S. Customs official at the Canadian border arrested an Algerian al-Qaeda operative after making the "chance discovery" of explosives and bomb-making equipment in his car. The terrorist cell had planned to attack a hotel and three other locations in Jordan where Americans were expected to gather for Millennium Eve, and the Algerian jihadist had targeted Los Angeles International Airport. The CIA learned that more "millennium plots" could be afoot, causing intelligence and law-enforcement agencies to go on high alert. The glittery ball dropped on schedule in New York's Times Square, and the twenty-first century began without incident.

The Clintons ended the century with a multimillion-dollar extravaganza underwritten with funds raised by Terry McAuliffe. They kicked off the festivities on the Mall on the morning of Millennium Eve, addressed diplomats from around the world at the Reagan building in the afternoon, and attended a nighttime celebration at the Lincoln Memorial, which included a concert and a film about the twentieth century produced by Steven Spielberg, followed by fireworks. At the White House, Bill and Hillary hosted a Millennium Ball for one thousand guests. Bill later wrote that while he had a wonderful evening, he had been "nervous the entire time" about terrorist attacks.

He had more reason to worry than he ever imagined, because Osama bin Laden had already set in motion the plot that was to level the World Trade Center towers on September 11, 2001—an operation that cost only five hundred thousand dollars and relied on box cutters as weapons. Bill Clinton had taken some positive steps to combat terrorism in his second term—increasing funding for the CIA and FBI after his earlier cutbacks and issuing classified directives to strengthen counterterrorism operations. But his public comments about terrorism dealt with tactics such as sabotage of the Internet and the development of chemical, biological, and nuclear weapons of mass destruction rather than the motives and nature of this new enemy. Several times he brought up "enemies of the nation state" with "vast money and vast access to weapons and technology and travel: the organized crime syndicates, the narcotraffickers, the terrorists." But he would quickly jump to other topics, like "these gadgets where you can use as a telephone or a typewriter, do E-mail," which relied on miniaturization that could also "apply to biological and chemical weapons."

In the years following the 9/11 attacks, Bill Clinton said that during his presidency he had been "obsessed" with hunting down bin Laden—an urgency that was not reflected publicly either in his rhetoric or his actions at the time. Even after Osama bin Laden officially declared war on the United States in February 1998, the President did not acknowledge the threat in public. Bill mentioned bin Laden a half-dozen times, but his comments were elliptical at best. He later explained his circumspection by saying he didn't want to enhance the terrorist leader's stature "by giving him unnecessary publicity."

Yet it was within the President's power to use his persuasive and explanatory talents to "spark a full public discussion," in the words of the 9/11 Commission, about "who Usama Bin Ladin was, what kind of organization he led, what Bin Ladin or Al Qaeda intended, what past attacks they had sponsored or encouraged, and what capabilities they were bringing together for future assaults. We believe American and international public opinion might have been different—and so might the range of options for a president—had they been informed of these details."

The 9/11 Commission concluded that Bill Clinton had not taken the threat of al-Qaeda seriously enough, and that the "modest national effort to contain Serbia . . . between 1995 and 1999 . . . was orders of magnitude larger than that devoted to al Qaeda . . . the most dangerous foreign enemy then threatening the United States." On five occasions between June 1998 and May 1999, CIA and Pentagon officials had opportunities to either capture or kill bin Laden, but each time the administration pulled back, fearing collateral damage and retaliatory attacks. Other proposals for military operations also went nowhere, and diplomatic efforts to persuade the Taliban leadership to expel bin Laden were ineffective, as were economic sanctions. After "two senior State Department officials" suggested offering the Taliban a $250 million bounty for bin Laden, White House counterterrorism coordinator Richard Clarke cautioned that Hillary and Madeleine Albright would frown on rewarding a regime that repressed women.

When asked toward the end of 1999 what his "one line in history" would be, the President replied: "Turned the economy around and prepared America for a new century." In fact, the economy was shakier than it seemed, and Bill failed to grasp that dealing with Islamist terrorism was to be the biggest challenge of the twenty-first century. He could lament hatred of "the other" and describe the mental scales balancing the lightness and darkness of the soul, but the "extreme intolerance" of al-Qaeda seemed beyond his psychological scope. Al-Qaeda is "motivated by religion," wrote the 9/11 Commission, "and does not distinguish politics from religion, thus distorting both. . . . It can only be destroyed or utterly isolated." The fact that al-Qaeda offered no common ground seemed to pose an insoluble dilemma for a President who fashioned himself the mediator-in-chief.

Chapter Seventeen

—

F ROM THE DAY HE SET FOOT IN THE OVAL OFFICE, BILL CLINTON WAS preoccupied by how historians would judge him. Beginning in August 1993, he started meeting every month with his longtime friend Taylor Branch for extended late-night interviews in the Residence on the events of his presidency—some ninety sessions in all. After each meeting, Branch placed two identical audiotapes of what they had discussed into Bill's sock drawer, and while driving home to Baltimore the veteran journalist dictated his impressions into a microcassette recorder. "It was a very self-consciously concerned project to preserve a raw narrative for history," said Branch. "Bill Clinton was a history-minded president who felt he was trapped in a cocoon of misinterpretation."

Yet when queried by reporters, Bill invariably professed indifference to his legacy. "I don't think too much about it," he said to Jim Lehrer on public television's *NewsHour* in January 2000 when asked if he was "worried" about what historians would write about him. When Lehrer pressed him to respond to a *New York Times* editorial describing him as a "politician of splendid natural talent and some significant accomplishments" who "missed the greatness that once seemed within his grasp," Bill replied, "The question is how you keep score," indicating he had given more thought to the matter than he was willing to admit. "There is no such thing as history, because this thing is still going on," he added.

"This thing" at that moment was the 2000 campaign, which Bill regarded as a rich opportunity to tout his record while promoting not one but two successors: Hillary and Al Gore. Over and over, Bill reminded people it was the first election in more than twenty-five years that he was not on the ballot, and "most days I'm okay with it," although "some days I'm not so sure." He was in fact running at full tilt—to airbrush his image for posterity, to fulfill Hillary's ambitions, to gratify his immediate need to be loved and admired, and to secure a foothold for a return to the White House, albeit as a junior partner to his wife. "The stakes are far bigger than another Senate race, even far bigger than another President's race," Bill told a select group of Hillary's financial backers assembled at the home of Vernon and Ann Jordan in September 2000. "They are just as important, if not more important, than what we did in '92, because we now have the future to run ourselves, and we've got to do a good job of it."

For all his praise of Al Gore in scores of speeches, Bill's behavior throughout the year—making passive-aggressive remarks, belittling Gore in private, grabbing the spotlight with his own political star turns, and continuing to argue his innocence in various scandals—betrayed ambivalence about a Gore victory, at least one earned on the Vice President's own terms. "Clinton felt it was really important for Gore to succeed him to burnish his legacy," said a top White House official. "That was the main reason, and by that logic it was difficult for Clinton to contemplate any campaign strategy that departed from him as the center of attention. He couldn't live with that."

Bill's personal agendas created complications for Gore that grew worse over time and led to a nasty range war between the Clinton White House and the Gore campaign. "It was remarkable how people who had shared the same foxhole for a decade suddenly mistrusted one another," recalled Clinton domestic-policy advisor Bruce Reed. The tensions centered on the Lewinsky scandal and Bill's past womanizing, which Gore and his advisers believed had alienated independent voters—especially the soccer moms, who stood for traditional values. "Gore was quite offended in terms of personal morality and also political stupidity," said one of Hillary's advisors. Reed understood that "the Vice President would be disappointed by and resentful of the President's mistakes. The way it played out in the campaign was the real damage in how much it threw Gore off his game." As a result, Gore veered too far in differentiating himself from Bill and his record and had difficulty taking advantage of the Clinton Administration's legitimate successes.

To avoid associating themselves with the President's excesses, both Gore and Hillary made strategic decisions not to publicly campaign *with* Bill, even as he campaigned *for* both of them—considerably more for Hillary than for Gore—at private fund-raising events around the country. Hillary continued to vie with Gore for attention and money and to benefit enormously from Bill's advice as well as from her First Lady perch, while Gore essentially left the White House and played down his relationship with the President. Gore's attentiveness to Bill—especially through their weekly lunches—had kept their governing partnership stable, but in the absence of personal contact their misunderstandings multiplied, and they became disaffected, if not estranged, from each other.

FOR THE CLINTONS, even a matter as seemingly simple as moving into their new house in Chappaqua was fraught with political implications. On January 5, 2000, the President was overseeing peace talks between the Israelis and Syrians in Shepherdstown, West Virginia, and Hillary was scheduled to travel with her mother to 15 Old House Lane. But when Hillary's advisors realized the scene might send "a sad message," Bill rearranged his schedule to accompany his wife to the first home they had owned since 1983. Friends brought them dinner and helped them unpack boxes, move furniture, and hang paintings. They cranked up a solar-powered South African radio that Bill had bought at a Discovery Store in Washington and listened to Al Gore's debate with Senator Bill Bradley, who was challenging him for the Democratic nomination. After staying up past 1:00 a.m., Bill was off the next morning for West Virginia, where the negotiations came to naught, and Hillary returned to the campaign circuit.

Hillary lived in Chappaqua for the rest of the year, alighting in Washington periodically for official events. Between their move-in day and Election Day, Bill visited her twenty times, roughly twice per month, usually arriving in Chappaqua in the evening and departing the next morning. His stopovers often coincided with political appearances on Hillary's behalf or with events to promote his policies. "I slept with Buddy for sixteen months all during the Senate campaign," Bill later joked. For the White House

Correspondents Association dinner in April, he starred in what he called his "Home Alone Video"—with comic scenes of him forlornly clipping hedges, playing board games in the Situation Room with Joint Chiefs Chairman Hugh Shelton, screening *101 Dalmatians* in the Family Theater with Buddy, riding bicycles in the OEOB corridors with Terry McAuliffe, and running down the White House driveway holding a brown-bag lunch as Hillary pulled away in the presidential limousine. Yet he also conveyed a sense of desperately racing against the clock. "I never want to sleep," he told John Harris of *The Washington Post* in August. "I go to bed with a pile of stuff that I want to do and I just read and read and read and read. I just want to keep going."

Each of the Clintons cut a rather solitary figure. Bill corralled friends and relatives to keep him company and maintained a punishing travel schedule, while Hillary filled her life with political speeches and forums. They continued to confer by phone every day, sometimes as frequently as a half-dozen times. "Bill would be in the Solarium with all these houseguests, when Hillary would call, and they would talk and talk and talk," said Ann McCoy. But they couldn't hide the fact that they were essentially leading separate lives. When Hillary appeared alone at a Democratic-party tribute at Radio City Music Hall, Maureen Dowd of *The New York Times* saw her afterward "off by herself . . . like some astronaut floating in space." The Clinton marriage "thrives on distance," a friend of the couple explained to the columnist. "Perhaps," Dowd noted, "but most marriages don't."

TO PREPARE FOR THE formal announcement of her candidacy, Hillary went to the White House on February 4 for two days of consultations with advisors and practice sessions in the Family Theater behind the Blue Goose. Bill worked closely with her on her announcement speech, the first of many he would edit extensively throughout the campaign. As she struggled to find her public voice, Bill advised her, "You have to be totally comfortable. You have to listen to your heart and head and get rid of the awkwardness. If you do this, you give the election back to them, so you're not arrogant, you're not entitled. . . . You have to look like you're not reading the script. Give it to them. Act like one of them has been asking you."

Concerned that Bill might outshine his wife, her consultants gave him no speaking role when she officially entered the race on February 6, 2000, at the State University of New York in Purchase, some ten miles from Chappaqua. As the President stood silently behind, Senator Moynihan introduced Hillary, declaring that Eleanor Roosevelt "would love you." Hillary's speech was heavy on issues and light on political ingratiation. She delivered it without the ease Bill had been urging.

Her approach reflected the campaign strategy devised by her cadre of consultants, led by Mark Penn. On the basis of focus-group research, they concluded that Hillary needed to emphasize competence and mastery of policy. For all the sympathy generated by her stoicism during the Lewinsky scandal, voters mistrusted her, and white suburban women were among her harshest critics. In videotaped discussions, they judged Hillary "threatening and unwomanly," "ruthless and greedy for power," "very controlling," and "self-serving." The consultants concluded that Hillary's personality "was just too big a mountain to move," wrote Michael Tomasky in a book about her race for the Senate. "They . . . decided the best course was to stick to the issues and hope that people would put her personality aside." When presented with the findings, Bill "grasped immediately the implications," Tomasky wrote. The President endorsed the strategists' intention to use the issues to shape Hillary's identity.

Since Hillary's consultants also worked for Bill, he was comfortable kibitzing with them, and they respected his experience and judgment. But he also took care not to intrude too much, and he sometimes recused himself from strategy meetings for a week or ten days. "I give her my best thoughts," he said. "If they ask me to come to a meeting and sit and listen, I do it." During a Moscow summit meeting in early June, Bill was surprised by newly elected Russian president Vladimir Putin's keen interest in Hillary's race. "Putin asked about the use of Clinton's influence for his wife and would he be criticized for that," a presidential advisor recorded at the time. "Clinton said he kept his distance from direct campaigning and that he thought it would not be a problem in the end. He would be careful. Putin said the right approach is the careful one. Putin said he admired Hillary."

Hillary's unrelenting reliance on policy came to be known as the "grind-the-negatives-to-dust strategy," the same approach Penn had used to bolster Bill's job-approval ratings when the Lewinsky scandal threatened to drag them down. As he had with the President, Penn crafted anodyne, bite-sized messages for Hillary, mainly about local matters (bus routes, beach erosion), that he honed with market testing. According to James Bennet of *The New York Times*, Penn often filled Hillary's speeches with language Bill had already used. She revered Penn's advice, telling him, "Oh, Mark, what a smart thing to say!"

Always more comfortable with the issues than with the press-the-flesh aspects of political life, Hillary embraced Penn's tactics like a diligent student. Throughout the many months of her listening tour, she had toted her "First Lady Box" from one end of New York to the other, stuffing the plastic container with scribbled notes and newspaper clippings. She would gather her staff and read aloud from her cache of papers, firing off questions about "falling milk prices, high electricity rates, crime, and school overcrowding," reported *Newsweek*'s Debra Rosenberg. "Staffers came to dread the sight of that crate, knowing they would be stuck listening to Hillary for hours."

After slogging away on the campaign trail, Hillary learned to appreciate even more her husband's political talents. "Over and over she would say, 'My God, Bill made it look so easy,'" said one of her senior advisors. Hillary recognized that Bill had physical and temperamental qualities—among them a significantly higher energy level—that she could never match. "It helps to be a big man," Hillary observed. "Bill is supernatural. Bill can work a crowd. He can stretch his arm out three or four people deep. He can do it so fast. People can feel touched." At five foot four, Hillary knew she was at a disadvantage. "I'm at a subway station," she said. "People are kissing me, enveloping me. They throw themselves at me. I'm going through an emotional wringer. The amount of emotion is overwhelming. It's all projected."

Hillary's rather joyless politicking was belied by her girlish campaign slogan, "HILLARY!" Besides creating the illusion of liveliness in an otherwise colorless campaign, the punchy catchword severed the candidate from the Clinton name and became the latest version of an evolving political brand that began with "Hillary Rodham" during Bill's first term as governor, shifted to "Hillary Clinton," and then to "Hillary Rodham Clinton."

Her new persona was aimed principally at skeptical women such as Manhattan freelance writer Carol Lalli, who told *The New York Times*, "I don't know who this woman is anymore. . . . I don't know if this would be happening if it weren't for her husband's position. . . . She's been thrust upon us."

Bill was remarkably philosophical and compliant about his diminished place in her political persona. "Trashing me is fine if it helps Hillary," Bill told aide Sidney Blumenthal, who observed, "He just wanted her to win." In Bill's remarks at fund-raisers he obediently referred to her as "Hillary," never "Hillary Clinton," while he called Gore and other candidates by their full names.

From time to time, Hillary would attempt to lighten her image, suddenly becoming "as cheery and chirpy as a camp counselor." She had swapped jokes on David Letterman's *Late Show* in mid-January, but her manner seemed programmed, and her laughter forced—an impression that the *New York Post* reinforced by revealing that she had been fed her questions in advance. The same week, she unexpectedly emerged from a press conference to chat with reporters on a "presumably spontaneous stroll." Whenever she stepped outside her protective bubble to shout to reporters, "Come on, guys, let's go get some coffee," or on one occasion to ask passersby to sing with her, longtime Hillary watchers sensed an orchestrated maneuver. "She seemed fake as a senatorial candidate," said Max Brantley. "You have to do the routine of shaking hands with farm groups. She can do it, but she is not Bill. It doesn't seem real, even to me, and I like her."

She remained imperturbable in the cut and thrust of political combat. When Buffalo radio talk-show host Tom Bauerle asked her if she had ever been "sexually unfaithful," specifically with Vince Foster, she wavered only slightly before evenly replying, "Those kinds of questions are really out of bounds, and everybody who knows me knows the answer to those questions."

"Is the answer no?" Bauerle pressed.

"Well, yes, of course it's no." She also denied using either marijuana or cocaine and rebuked her interviewer several times for making such inquiries. At the Inner Circle dinner in March, an annual roast by the New York media, Hillary endured jokes at her expense ("Chappaqua . . . That's

Indian for 'the land of separate bedrooms' "), all the while maintaining her façade of good humor.

AS IN PREVIOUS YEARS, the State of the Union address on January 27, 2000, served as the script for the President in the following months. "Never before has our nation enjoyed at once so much prosperity and social progress with so little internal crisis and so few external threats," he proclaimed. His remarks ran a record-breaking eighty-nine minutes, eight minutes longer than his marathon 1995 speech. Many of his proposals were old ideas that had earlier failed to make it through Congress—and that now carried even bigger price tags. ("Last year I proposed a $1,000 tax credit for long-term care. . . . This year let's triple it.") Bill also had to accommodate the priorities of his wife and his Vice President. While writing the speech, the President's aides conducted ongoing negotiations with staff members representing both constituencies. "That is why it became an eighty-nine-minute speech," said a senior West Wing advisor. Among the programs Bill included for Gore were a proposed expansion of the Children's Health Insurance Program to cover parents, as well as an increase in tax deductions for college tuition. Bill gave Hillary a more ambitious version of a proposal he had made two years earlier to permit people near retirement to purchase Medicare—now with a cutoff age of fifty-five instead of sixty-two.

In every speech of the campaign season—right up to Election Day, November 7—the President heralded "the longest economic expansion in history." But his economic report card skipped over a downturn that started in the first quarter of 2000. The Dow Jones Industrial Average peaked at 11,722 on January 14 and then began a decline that picked up speed toward the end of the year. Even more spectacular was the collapse of the "dot-com" bubble, the giddy growth of technology stocks that had begun in the mid-nineties. Share prices began to drop after speculators had pushed the NASDAQ index to a high of 5,048 on March 10. Layoffs and job freezes spread through the industry as companies folded or severely retrenched. With their dividends and capital gains dwindling, investors experienced a "reverse wealth effect," causing a drop in consumer spending. Other gloomy signs included a decline in business investment, a slowdown in corporate earnings, a rise in unemployment, higher interest rates, and a steady increase in oil prices from a low of twelve dollars per barrel in 1999 to a then record high of thirty-five dollars at the end of 2000. While the economy had not, strictly speaking, entered a recession, most of the indicators pointed in that direction.

When the President convened a daylong White House Conference on the New Economy on April 5, none of these troubling numbers intruded on the proceedings. He presided over a series of panel discussions that focused on how to bridge a "digital divide" between the haves and have-nots, how the new economy could "empower civil society," and whether the Internet would be "atomizing or unifying." By late afternoon, "the East Room [was] nearly empty," and "the panelists were checking their watches," wrote Joe Klein, while Bill was "blissfully oblivious to the length of the program." But the day served its purpose: to spread the President's optimism about the "innovation and enterprise" of the high-technology economy and the prospect of boundless opportunities in the years ahead. It formed a perfect counterpoint to the economic conference Bill held after he had first been elected President. In each case, the message masked an emerging economic reality—a recovery in 1992 and a contraction eight years later.

FOR BILL, THE SPRING of 2000 was an especially sunny time, as he faced no major foreign or domestic crises. His biggest challenge concerned an emotional custody battle in Florida over six-year-old Elián González, who had landed in the United States in November 1999 while attempting to flee Cuba in a small boat. When the vessel capsized, Elián's mother and ten others perished, but the boy was rescued and brought to Florida, where his anti-Castro relatives tried to obtain his political asylum. With the backing of the Cuban government, Elián's father, Juan Miguel González, claimed custody rights. The U.S. Immigration and Naturalization Service ruled that father and son should be reunited and repatriated to Cuba, setting up a confrontation with the relatives who insisted that the boy belonged with them in Miami while they pressed their legal options. Janet Reno backed the INS, as did the President, First Lady, and, for a time, Al Gore.

The standoff moved into political territory at the end of March when Gore changed his position and supported the right of the relatives to keep Elián in the United States until his case had been resolved by the courts. It was a show of independence, as well as an appeal to Cuban-American voters crucial for a Florida victory in November. Reno set a deadline of mid-April for Elián's return to his father, which the relatives resisted. After a week of negotiations, she ordered the boy removed by force, and before dawn on Saturday, April 22, eight heavily armed federal agents stormed the house, where they found Elián hidden in a closet. A wire-service photographer caught the moment of discovery, with Elián in openmouthed terror as an INS agent in helmet and goggles seemingly pointed an automatic weapon at him.

Shortly afterward, he was delivered to his father. They remained in seclusion in Washington, D.C., until the family's appeals ran out, allowing Elián and Juan Miguel to return to Cuba on June 28. The case whipsawed Gore, who didn't get credit from Cuban Americans for breaking with the President and Attorney General, while the highly charged image of commando tactics galvanized the community against Democrats. After many years in the Republican column, Florida had gone for Clinton-Gore in 1996. But in 2000 the Cubans in that state were to vote for Bush by a margin of four to one. Bill later wondered if "that terrible mess with the Elián González case cost [Gore] a lot of votes in Florida. . . . It could have. And if it did, I feel very badly about it."

Bill suffered no ill effects from the González controversy as he sailed along with job-approval ratings skimming 60 percent. His life was a happy medley of White House celebrations, policy conferences, and gatherings of the party faithful. A high point was his annual St. Patrick's Day party, when he honored his maternal ancestry. He took the occasion on March 17, 2000, to pay tribute to the Irish peace process in which he had played a dominant role and to ruminate on his yearning for love and forgiveness. After singing "Danny Boy," Bill said, "I'm one of the few Americans that knows all the words to the second verse ['And when you come, and all the flowers are dying, / And I am dead, as dead I well may be, / You'll come and find the place where I am lying, / And kneel and say an 'ave' there for me . . .']. . . . And I believe the second verse is more beautiful than the first, and, really, the mark of a life well lived, if someone you really loved would kneel at your grave and tell you that they loved you."

Three months later, following a State Dinner on June 20 honoring Mohammed VI, the new king of Morocco, Bill invited documentary filmmaker Ken Burns to stay overnight at the White House along with a half-dozen other friends including actors Ted Danson and Mary Steenburgen. Hillary was exhausted and turned in at midnight, along with the other guests, but Bill insisted that Burns stay up and keep him company. From 1:00 until 5:00 a.m., Burns walked from room to room in the Residence while the President talked and sang with abandon. He eagerly showed Burns a new Bang & Olufson stereo system in his office that a friend had given him and played a Nina Simone version of a gospel hymn that "he wanted sung at his funeral." In his music room, Bill riffed on Sonny Rollins and John Coltrane, "mindful of the incredibly subtle battles within the jazz world over interpretation." He asked Burns about his latest project, but "he did most of the talking, and I was happy to listen," Burns recalled. "He was really himself, a remarkable specimen, laughing and bellowing out lyrics of country songs."

Most strikingly, the President "also called the election," said Burns. "He knew the combination of political baggage and of Al Gore's need to distance himself from that and create his own legacy, and that that would be a drag. . . . There was a completely clear-eyed understanding of the failings that had affected his own life and the electoral chances of Al Gore. There was also a concern about his legacy. Bill Clinton was more forward looking than one would expect at this twilight moment. He was making plans, talking about the book he would write, about where the country should go."

Several hours after Burns finally fell asleep close to dawn, he awoke and watched from the Solarium as the President and First Lady left for Fayetteville, Arkansas. They were going to visit their longtime friend Diane Blair, who was near death from metastatic lung cancer. She had been diagnosed in March, and since then Hillary had called her every day. During the Lewinsky scandal, Blair had stopped speaking to Bill for many months. "That was terrible for him," said one of Hillary's close friends. They eventually reconciled, and both Clintons visited her several times during the spring of 2000. "Hillary and I would get good publicity for flying down . . . to see Diane," Bill recalled. Blair and the President would sit on a sofa together and compete to finish the *New York Times* crossword puzzle, and she gave him advice about composing a farewell address for his presidency. During their final visit on June 21, Blair asked Hillary to "win this election for me."

Hillary returned to New York to campaign, and Bill went to Washington to speak that night at a "Hillary 2000" dinner. Bill seemed happiest on such occasions. In his last year as President, he headlined more than 150 fund-raisers, collecting nearly one hundred million dollars for Democratic candidates and getting a chance to talk about others in the context of his own success. In retrospect, a luncheon on March 30 for the Democratic National Committee was particularly noteworthy. It was held at the forty-million-dollar Fifth Avenue duplex apartment owned by Denise Rich, a songwriter and party giver nonpareil, known for what *Vanity Fair* writer Maureen Orth described as "flashing cleavage and major jewelry." That month Denise had been contacted by emissaries of her former husband, Marc Rich, a billionaire commodities trader who had fled the United States in 1983 to avoid a sixty-five-count felony indictment for tax evasion and money laundering. The allegations included illegal deals with Iran in the 1970s when that country was holding American citizens hostage. The team representing Marc planned to use Denise "on a 'personal' mission" to the President, "with a well-prepared script" to secure a pardon for their boss. Since 1998, Denise had raised millions for Democratic candidates and had donated significant sums to the Clintons, including $120,000 for Hillary's campaign and $450,000 for Bill's presidential library, to be built in Little Rock. "If I come here one more time," Bill Clinton told the contributors dining in Denise's apartment, "we should allocate part of the property tax assessment to me." He would do more than that in the final days of his presidency.

The President promoted Gore's candidacy that afternoon, as he did the following month at two receptions in the Vice President's honor. The first was a dinner on April 15 sponsored by David Geffen, Steven Spielberg, and Jeffrey Katzenberg of DreamWorks at the historic Greystone Mansion in Beverly Hills. Bill called Gore "the most qualified person in my lifetime to seek this job," a man who was "always there, always early" for every important decision of their two terms in office. "I can still remember every conversation we ever had at our weekly lunch," Bill added—a somewhat ill-advised boast from a man who had recalled so little about his numerous encounters with Monica Lewinsky. Less than two weeks later, the Gores and Clintons shared the stage at the New York Sheraton Hotel for a Democratic-party gala. Speaking in unusually personal terms, Bill said, "I probably know more about him than anybody but Tipper, I know what he likes and what he can't stand . . . when he's having a bad day, and how he deals with it. And by the way, he knows the same about me." The Vice President had "performed in an absolutely stunning manner," often "getting no credit" for his contribution. Bill would offer similar encomiums at numerous other gatherings, but he made only one more campaign appearance with Gore.

HILLARY CAUGHT A LUCKY break when Rudy Giuliani's campaign imploded even before he officially announced his candidacy. The New York mayor was undone by a series of dramatic revelations starting with the shocker in mid-April that his wife, Donna Hanover, would appear in *The Vagina Monologues,* Eve Ensler's play celebrating female sexuality by focusing on the vagina as a symbol of power. A week later, Giuliani revealed that he needed treatment for prostate cancer, followed quickly by tabloid reports linking him to an attractive brunette named Judith Nathan and his subsequent admission that she was indeed a "very good friend." In mid-May, Giuliani said that he and Hanover were separating, and on May 19 the mayor withdrew from the race. "Now I know why he likes opera," Hillary deadpanned to Sidney Blumenthal.

Taking Giuliani's place was forty-two-year-old Rick Lazio, a four-term U.S. representative from Long Island who called himself a "mainstream Republican." Lazio instantly accused Hillary of having "no real rationale for serving here other than as a steppingstone to some other position. . . . Her ambition is the issue." But for all his bluster, Lazio was not in Hillary's league. She might have been seriously tested had she faced a more formidable adversary, such as forty-nine-year-old Jack Quinn, a U.S. congressman since 1993 from an overwhelmingly Democratic district in upstate New York. "If the Republicans had nominated him he could have beaten her," said a top New York Democratic strategist. "It would have reminded them of the outgoing senator—a tall, white-haired Irishman popular in his constituency. He was a grown-up. Hillary ran against a kid."

Hillary accepted her party's nomination at its convention in Albany on May 16. Her consultants initially recommended keeping Bill away. But on the fifteenth Hillary decided it would "look weird" without him, so he played the same wordless backup role as in February. Moynihan also made an encore, and at a reception afterward Bill said that as Hillary was "going over all these issues" in her remarks, "Senator Moynihan looked at me, and he said, 'Good speech.' . . . I knew that she was on a roll."

Six months earlier, Hillary had pledged to finish her "already scheduled" First Lady obligations, "so I will be free come the year 2000 to spend the vast majority of my time on the Senate campaign." But she nevertheless continued to capitalize on her White House advantage during the campaign by assuming her First Lady role at events highlighting such issues as teenage pregnancy, crime prevention, and the emotional and behavioral problems of children. She joined her husband to lead the first White House conference on teenagers, spoke at the UNIFEM Forum on Microcredit at the United Nations, cohosted the final Millennium lecture in the East Room, and helped Bill mark the tenth anniversary of the Americans with Disabilities Act. In August, she enjoyed the matchless platform of a prime-time address to the Democratic Convention.

Between April and November 2000, Bill raised more than five million dollars for Hillary at thirty-four events designated for her Senate race, half of which she actually attended. ("That way she can be out getting votes," he would say to explain her absence.) Variously calling himself "surrogate in chief," "cheerleader in chief," and "spouse in chief," he unabashedly solicited contributions, even when Hillary wasn't the headliner. At a dinner for Democratic congressional candidates in Brentwood, California, he said, "A lot of you have given to Hillary. If you haven't, I hope you will." His descriptions of his wife's accomplishments were often hyperbolic. "Every year when I was Governor," he told one audience in Washington, "she gave up huge portions of her income as a private lawyer to devote time to public service." In fact, Hillary did very nicely for herself and the family bank account, especially considering she lived in a low-cost state with housing, meals, and incidentals picked up by the government. She earned a $110,000 annual salary as a partner at the Rose law firm and received nearly $65,000 each year from corporate board memberships. A special bonus was the almost $150,000 she made in profits from commodities trading (including her 10,000 percent return on cattle futures) with the help of influential patrons.

The Clintons had made a great effort during the 1996 campaign and afterward to minimize Hillary's copresidential role, but now Bill was spinning a different story of her "breathtaking range" of activities in domestic and foreign policy that included a "significant contribution to the Irish peace process." But he declined to touch on her back-channel operations and pervasive influence over personnel, notably her deep involvement in the political vetting of candidates for the federal bench and U.S. attorney positions.

The President so immersed himself in Hillary's campaign that it became an extension of himself. In some ways, their relationship had come to resemble a codependency more than a copresidency. Not surprisingly, Bill and Hillary remained in harmony over the issues. But he also believed that his enemies had "all transferred all their anger to her now." "I think half of them think it's their last chance at me," he told a group of supporters in Miami.

EVERYWHERE BILL WENT, he recited a long list of his achievements, portraying the GOP as an implacable enemy that tried to obstruct and destroy him. But no small measure of his legacy came from acquiescing to Republican initiatives on welfare reform, trade, a balanced budget, and tax reductions, particularly on capital gains, as well as restraints on spending. Both Republicans and moderate Democrats had forced him to abandon his most expensive and ambitious plans, notably for health care. He had found his greatest success as "the editor of the Gingrich revolution," in the words of Daniel Patrick Moynihan's senior aide Lawrence O'Donnell.

Although his second-term domestic priorities—gun control, a patients' bill of rights, more spending for education and the environment, prescription drugs for Medicare recipients, applying the surplus to Social Security and Medicare—had been stalled in Congress for two years, he tenaciously plugged for their passage. But by midyear he was following the pattern of his predecessors by setting his sights on foreign policy for his historic capstone.

He saw his best opportunity in achieving Middle East peace by solving the Israeli-Palestinian conflict. For fourteen days in July at Camp David he threw himself into the task with preternatural focus and persistence. Since the beginning of the Clinton presidency, Gore had banged home the idea that "decision making involves some sort of mental and emotional muscle," Bill recalled. "It's just like working out, and the more hard decisions you make, the easier they'll get." In that regard, Bill had grown impressively, and by his final year in office he conveyed a genuine sense of command, along with his innate ability to see circumstances through the eyes of others. Yet he remained convinced that his intellect and persuasiveness could prevail over deeply embedded viewpoints, and his optimism still blinded him to implacable realities. Arafat held the record among foreign leaders for meetings with Bill, who believed—against the advice of many experts—that he could work some magic on the prickly, suspicious, and often duplicitous leader.

The President's grand idea was to take all the incremental proposals dating back to the Oslo Accords of 1993 and put them in a comprehensive package that would lead to a new Palestinian state coexisting with Israel. Israeli prime minister Ehud Barak endorsed this omnibus approach, although Arafat remained skeptical. Beginning on Tuesday, July 11, the President shuttled among the Aspen, Laurel, Birch, and Holly cabins in the Maryland woods for a series of grueling talks with the opposing leaders to get them into the "right frame of mind" for their first "working dinner" on the fifth day. Barak made a breakthrough before dawn on July 18 by conceding more territory on the West Bank than had previously been discussed, by offering the Palestinians control over specified religious sites as well as certain neighborhoods in Jerusalem, and by suggesting that some Palestinian refugees could resettle in Israel under strict international controls.

For the next two days, Bill pushed the proposal hard. He impressed both sides with his detailed knowledge of conditions on the ground—drawing maps of Jerusalem, for example, from the Israeli and Palestinian perspectives. As the deliberations reached an impasse, Bill fumed at Arafat, "This is the best deal you're going to get!" "Clinton really got mad at him," said Protocol Chief Mary Mel French, who assisted him at Camp David. Bill left the negotiating teams after midnight on July 20 and flew to Okinawa for his long-scheduled appearance at the G-8 summit. Following three days of meetings, banquets, and other ceremonies, Bill returned to Camp David from Japan on Sunday the twenty-third.

Back in his rustic office at Laurel Cabin, Bill worked all night and through the next day and night until he finally stopped the talks at around 3:00 a.m. on Tuesday without an agreement. The negotiations had foundered on Arafat's insistence on explicit "sovereignty" over East Jerusalem and on the "right of return," a fervidly held principle that all Palestinians displaced by the 1948 Arab-Israeli war after the creation of the Jewish state should be permitted to reclaim the homes in Israel that they had lost. Implicit in this demand was the idea that Israel as a nation had no right to exist. The Israelis correctly feared that a flood of repatriated Palestinians would dilute the Jewish population and end Israel's unique identity.

"Arafat wasn't going to do a deal," said Deputy National Security Advisor James Steinberg. "He felt it was not in his interests. He got people stoked and walked away." The Camp David collapse severely weakened Barak, who had taken a big risk with his bold proposal and was to face the wrath of Israeli voters intent on a harder line. Columnist Joe Klein considered Barak's concessions and Bill's pressure for an agreement a "disastrous miscalculation. . . . The failure to make peace burst a precious, if precarious status quo." The breakdown seemed to dispel the illusion of moderates that lasting peace could be negotiated. "Now the veil has been taken away," said Richard Haass of the Brookings Institution. "If there is no longer the chance of peace through compromise, then why hold back the fighting? . . . That's why failure is so incredibly costly."

Two months later, following clashes between Palestinian demonstrators and Israeli soldiers in Jerusalem, the Intifada would again erupt in a spasm of violence. Palestinian militants attacked Israeli settlers in the occupied West Bank and Gaza and sent suicide bombers into Israel to terrorize the civilian population, prompting severe reprisals by the Israeli military. The bloodshed escalated throughout the fall, dimming the prospects for peace and strengthening the challenge by right-wing Likud party leader Ariel Sharon to the leadership of Barak and his Labor party. At the same time, the end of the process that began with the Oslo Accords inflamed anti-Americanism on the "Arab street," which was already the breeding ground for Osama bin Laden's followers. By the time of the Intifada, his plans for the September 11, 2001, attacks were well under way. His recruits were already in the United States, taking flight training.

Bill Clinton was upset in the aftermath of Camp David, feelings "he wore visibly," said one of his senior advisors. "It was very tough." In Hillary's absence, Chelsea had been his companion for the entire two weeks, even traveling to Japan with him. She was to accompany her father on two more trips later in the summer, to Africa and South America. Chelsea had accumulated enough credits at Stanford to take the fall term off and still graduate with her class the following June. "She spent . . . more than a third of her life in the White House," the President explained, "and she wants to have some more days there." She intended to help Hillary campaign and "to be able to keep company with her father," he said. According to a family friend, Bill had by then "completely restored" his relationship with his daughter. "I have no idea how long it took," but their differences were "not on the radar anymore. When your dad did that, you never forget, but the connections were solid."

The demands of politicking meant no time for a summer vacation, although the Clintons did take one long weekend on Martha's Vineyard in early August that was a busman's holiday of fund-raising receptions there and in Nantucket and Hyannis. As they were about to leave for Washington on Monday, August 7, Bill and Hillary heard that Al Gore had selected Joe Lieberman to be his running mate. When they asked Press Secretary Joe Lockhart for his reaction, he said, "I think it's a way of saying 'screw you' to Bill Clinton."

"I'm glad someone agrees with me," replied Hillary.

Bill, however, insisted, "No, no, you're wrong. It's a great choice." The President was similarly magnanimous when the press quizzed him that afternoon. Lieberman had been a friend for thirty years and was a "bold thinker . . . full of new ideas . . . an extraordinary human being."

Gore had chosen Lieberman on the merits, but also for his symbolic value as one of the Democratic party's strongest critics of Bill's behavior in the Lewinsky scandal. The Republicans had already put "character" in the forefront of the presidential campaign with George W. Bush's oft-repeated intention to "restore honor and dignity to the Oval Office." "The driving theme of the Republican campaign has been to clean out the stables and remove the stench," wrote Jonathan Alter in *Newsweek*. Lieberman was to serve as "Gore's air freshener."

During his all-night conversation with Ken Burns in June, Bill "spoke movingly of the Democratic National Convention that was coming," Burns recalled, "and how because he was on the backside of scandal and impeachment he had a more delicate role to play." In the intervening months, the President cast those sensible thoughts aside. While Ronald Reagan had addressed a cheering GOP Convention in 1988, he quickly stepped into the wings in deference to his Vice President's candidacy. But Bill Clinton couldn't resist occupying center stage and grabbing the limelight from Al Gore during a crucial moment in his campaign.

Four days before the convention opened in Los Angeles on Monday, August 14, Bill made headlines by engaging in a soul-baring conversation with the Rev. Bill Hybels, one of his spiritual counselors. In front of an audience of 4,500 in Hybels's suburban Chicago church, the President revisited his experiences as a "sinner" at a moment when Al Gore least needed such a reminder. Bill once again insisted that he had sufficiently apologized for his "terrible mistake," allowed that he had "nothing left to hide," and said, "I'm now in the second year of a process of trying to totally rebuild my life."

The Clintons planned their three days in California as an unprecedented extravaganza of media appearances and fund-raising. En route to Los Angeles on Friday, Bill set the stage by giving a wide-ranging interview to Ron Brownstein of the *Los Angeles Times* on Air Force One, and Hillary blocked out time on Saturday in her nineteenth-floor suite at the St. Regis Hotel to speak with reporters from New York's major newspapers, most prominently *The New York Times*, for publication in the widely read Sunday editions. Both Clintons were lined up for interviews on Saturday afternoon with Bryant Gumbel of CBS's *Early Show*, to be broadcast Monday morning, when they were also due to appear on NBC's *Today* show and ABC's *Good Morning America*. But after the session with Hybels, the Gore camp asked Bill and Hillary to stand down. "We knew Thursday night how upset the Gore folks were with Clinton's confessional on Thursday and that would be the talk of our interview," said Lynne Pitts, executive producer of *The Early Show*. The Clintons bailed out of all the morning shows, although Hillary proceeded as planned with interviews on the three network newscasts Monday night.

A more serious conflict arose from the schedule of events in which Bill and Hillary raised millions for themselves, distracting attention from the presidential race, siphoning off Democratic money, and further angering the Vice President and his team. That Saturday night, the Clintons collected $1.1 million for Hillary's war chest from a Gala Salute to President

William Jefferson Clinton at the thirty-million-dollar Mandeville Canyon estate of radio mogul Ken Roberts. Guests paid one thousand dollars per ticket for a concert, and dinner with the Clintons afterward cost twenty-five thousand dollars per couple. The evening featured a Hollywood who's who that included Shirley MacLaine and Whoopi Goldberg. For the concert, the entire Clinton clan—Chelsea, Dorothy, Bill's stepfather and brother, and the Rodham brothers—was seated with Bill and Hillary in directors' chairs decorated with the date and name of the event. Bill was in an exuberant mood, singing along with Diana Ross, Cher, and Melissa Etheridge, who announced that she had come out of the closet as a lesbian during the Clinton inaugural. Bill was so touched that his eyes filled with tears. At the dinner, Hillary spoke first, followed by Bill, who closed by saying, "I'm not going anywhere except to a different line of work."

On Sunday, the Clintons presided over two events: a reception for Hillary at Sony Pictures Studios, and a luncheon at the home of Barbra Streisand to raise money for Bill's presidential library. With a price tag of $125 million and a design meant to evoke a "bridge to the twenty-first century," the library on twenty-seven acres along the Arkansas River posed yet another diversion for prospective Democratic donors to the Gore campaign. Since early 1998, Bill had been quietly soliciting funds from his most loyal and well-heeled allies, a list that the White House kept private. Even during his "lost year" he managed to take in three million dollars, and by his final year in office Bill had picked up the pace, raising tens of millions from such stalwarts as Steven Spielberg; Haim Saban, who made billions from TV cartoon shows; Vinod Gupta, the owner of a computer-database company who pledged one million dollars; and S. Daniel Abraham, the billionaire founder of Slim-Fast Foods.

The climax for the Clintons occurred on Monday, August 14, when each gave a prime-time address—carried by all the television networks—to the convention delegates. After Hillary finished her eighteen-minute speech, the camera cut away to the President making his way through the corridors of the Staples Center—his pace deliberate, his face suffused with pleasure—as facts and figures (twenty-two million new jobs, one hundred thousand new police on the streets) were superimposed on the TV screen to celebrate his record. On entering the convention center, the camera caught the scene from behind him as he greeted the rapturous crowd. It was another Harry Thomason production, choreographed down to the minute, that commentators instantly likened to Russell Crowe's confident walk into the arena in *Gladiator*. Bill's half-hour speech was less remarkable, touching all the familiar bases and ending with taglines from his two presidential campaigns: "keep building those bridges" and "don't stop thinking about tomorrow."

When it came time for Gore to deliver his acceptance speech three nights later, he began by giving Tipper a passionate kiss—a vivid image of their devotion. The Vice President earned high marks from columnists and commentators for the balance he struck between personal touches (praise not only for his wife and children but for the example set by his parents, who "started out with almost nothing") and a muscular pledge to "fight" for a long list of policies, all of them goals from the previous eight years. Although he lauded the gains made during the nineties, he said it was time to "write a new chapter" with a decidedly populist angle. "The difference in this election," said Gore, was that "they're for the powerful. We're for the people." Even more dramatically, he sought to distance himself from Bill's overpowering presence—and implicitly from the President's personal conduct. "I stand here tonight as my own man," said Gore. "If you entrust me with the presidency, I know I won't always be the most exciting politician. But . . . I will work for you every day, and I will never let you down."

The convention gave a much-needed boost to Gore's campaign. Nearly a year earlier, he had been ridiculed for hiring feminist author Naomi Wolf as a consultant. She had advised him to wear "earth tones" and to be less of a "beta male" so as not to be overshadowed by the "alpha male" President. At around the same time, Gore had fired his longtime consultant, Bob Squier, along with Mark Penn, who disputed the idea that the country was suffering from "Clinton fatigue." Both men continued to work for the Clintons, while Gore hired consultant Carter Eskew, an old friend, and pollsters Harrison Hickman and Stanley Greenberg, Bill's numbers guru until the 1994 election debacle. The revamped Gore team moved the campaign headquarters from Washington to Nashville, cutting another symbolic cord with the White House.

While Gore was a seasoned campaigner with plenty of hands-on experience, the press portrayed him as an egghead preoccupied by abstractions and, in his own words, "one of the most introverted people in public life." Bush was untested and often incurious, but he had a snappy style and a reputation as a bipartisan deal maker. With a wink and a smile, the Texas governor promised generous tax cuts and portrayed Gore's neopopulism as a return to big-government Democratic liberalism. During the three presidential debates in October, Gore came across as patronizing and ponderous. Political commentators and television satirists had a field day mocking his exasperated sighing over Bush's simplistic or inarticulate statements. Liberal columnist Molly Ivins quipped, "George W. Bush sounds like English is his second language, and Al Gore sounds like he thinks it's yours."

Gore had particular difficulty dealing with Bush's efforts to cast doubt on his integrity by constantly referring to the "Clinton-Gore" Administration, which implicitly linked him to the President's scandals. Even the choice of Joe Lieberman couldn't dispel what Carter Eskew later called "the elephant in the living room." Bill refused to acknowledge that his behavior was a factor in the campaign. "I never believed that the American people were going to in effect vote against their own interests and their own values by holding Al Gore responsible for a personal mistake I made," Bill told Ron Brownstein before the convention.

But the problem went beyond one "personal mistake," as reminders of misconduct by both Clintons kept cropping up. Robert Ray, who succeeded Kenneth Starr as Independent Counsel, impaneled a new grand jury to review the President's sworn testimony about Monica Lewinsky and decide whether to indict him once he left office. The prosecutor also issued a series of reports on the travel office and Whitewater. Instead of absolving the Clintons by saying there was "no credible evidence" that they had committed crimes, Ray more narrowly stated that "the evidence was insufficient to prove to a jury beyond a reasonable doubt" that they had engaged in criminal conduct. Even more pointedly, he said that Hillary's sworn statements denying her involvement in the travel-office firings had been "factually false," and that there was "overwhelming evidence that she in fact did have a role in the decision." In an echo of the campaign-finance scandals that had tainted the Clinton Administration after the 1996 campaign, *Newsweek* revealed in early September that Bill and Hillary had resumed using overnights at the White House and Camp David to reward donors to her campaign and his library fund. "They do not grasp the notion of the White House as a hallowed place where hustling is off-limits," wrote Maureen Dowd in *The New York Times.*

In any number of ways, the Gore campaign found itself in a contest with Hillary's campaign. One of the most dramatic examples occurred in September as the Federal Trade Commission prepared to release a report on violence in the media. The agency's million-dollar study showed that entertainment companies were marketing violent movies, video games, and music to children under eighteen. Under ordinary circumstances, a Vice President running for the presidency would have first call on publicizing the report. But Hillary insisted she should handle the rollout because she had already called for a universal ratings system. "It was a key point of her Senate campaign," said Bruce Reed, the White House domestic-policy advisor. "The President had singled her out for that in the 2000 State of the Union, so the finding of the FTC was directly relevant to her campaign. The Vice President's campaign had concluded that cultural issues were hurting him, and they were dying to announce the report as well."

After "several painful days of negotiations," administration officials "thought we had a resolution that served everyone," said Reed. The FTC would release the report on Monday, September 11, followed by a comment from Gore, and then a separate one from the Clintons at a campaign event in New York. This strategy did not sit well with Gore and Lieberman, who decided to break the news on their own by inviting a reporter from *The New York Times* to the Vice President's residence on Sunday for an interview to be published in the Monday edition. "Every day was like that," Reed said. "It was a typical example of how people who had known and trusted each other a long time would do things they otherwise wouldn't have done."

Bill and Hillary offered their comments on Monday morning at a Jewish community center in Scarsdale. "Everything that needs to be said has been said," Bill told the audience. "But what does it all mean? How can we distill it?" He then explained why Hillary understood the issue better than anyone—presumably including Gore. "She started working on it years ago," he said, describing the significance of a "uniform unambiguous rating system" that "Hillary . . . was the first and maybe the only person to forcefully advocate in the entire country."

Hillary also continued to compete with Gore for campaign funds. By late September, she had gathered more than $22 million (compared to Rick Lazio's $15.7 million) from a surprisingly large national base of donors. Sixty percent of her money came from donors outside of New York State, including 16 percent from California alone. Charles Schumer, who ran a much tighter race against incumbent Al D'Amato in 1998, raised only 25 percent of his funds from out-of-state donors, 4 percent of them from California.

Hillary's campaign by then was sprinting toward what looked to be an effortless victory. Her surge began after her debate with Lazio on September 13 in Buffalo. She was on her own that night, with Bill in Washington, watching in the Residence. Dorothy Rodham was there to keep him company, but he was "a nervous wreck," he later said, and his mother-in-law became so upset she went off by herself to watch in another room.

Lazio hit Hillary hard, and she punched back. When Hillary repeatedly tried to tie Lazio to the discredited Newt Gingrich, the congressman retorted that "you, of all people, shouldn't try to make guilt by association." Two moments in particular had an enormous impact. Moderator Tim Russert showed a clip from Hillary's *Today* show interview on January 27, 1998, in which she said Bill had told the truth about Monica Lewinsky. Russert then asked if she regretted "misleading the American people." Hillary stumbled through her answer, frequently saying "you know" and staring at her hands as she tried to explain that she may have given a false impression but had not meant to mislead. "Well, you know, Tim, that was a very, a very painful time for me," she said, and she essentially blamed Bill, saying, "I didn't know the truth." Then, toward the end of the debate, Lazio unexpectedly walked across the stage and brandished a pledge for her to sign disavowing the use of soft money. "That was a wonderful performance," Hillary said sarcastically.

"I'm not asking you to admire it," Lazio snapped back. "I'm asking you to sign it."

In both instances, Hillary came across as the victim of heavy-handed treatment, generating sympathy that translated into higher numbers in the polls. In a *New York Times* survey conducted in the days following the debate, 48 percent of the respondents favored Hillary over 39 percent for Lazio, a comfortable lead. The newspaper's previous poll in June had shown her only five points ahead. An even more telling number was her support from the much-coveted suburban women, who had backed Lazio 43 to 36 in June and now went for Hillary 54 to 38. "She did great in the debate . . . even though it was two on one half the time," Bill told a crowd of financial backers in Philadelphia four days later. "I thought she did best when they got meanest, and that's good. . . . She showed . . . she could take a punch, and she can take a lot of them." At a fifty-third birthday fund-raiser for Hillary at Manhattan's Roseland Ballroom, Bill proudly announced that she had the "requisite aggression" to be a good New Yorker.

Even with a secure lead in the polls, Hillary continued to campaign relentlessly. After Labor Day, she spent most of her Sundays attending services at black churches around New York State, to stimulate minority turnout. In early October, she finally apologized for kissing Suha Arafat, telling a Jewish group in a synagogue on the Upper West Side that she shouldn't have reacted that way and that her actions caused a "misimpression about my strong feelings for Israel."

Hillary had become more comfortable with rope lines, at least in part because Bill had tutored her in handshaking techniques so she could avoid injuring her fingers. "I have big hands, but Hillary has little hands," he said. "A big hand can harm her with a tight squeeze." He taught Hillary to lock her thumb inside the other person's thumb so she would be "in charge of the shake . . . fingers out of the way, up the other person's wrist, and the other guy can't harm you."

But her basic style hadn't changed much. She was still uninspiring on the podium, her voice "modulating between two tones," noted Adam Nagourney of The New York Times in late September. "It is not uncommon . . . to hear the rustle of conversation rising from the back of the hall before the First Lady reaches the last page." Although Bill continually pressed her to show more "joy" in her campaigning, she more often betrayed impatience or weariness. At the New York State Fair in Syracuse on September 2, Nagourney watched a scene play out that many had witnessed over the decades. After the First Couple had spent hours shaking hands, Bill kept pressing the flesh while Hillary stood nearby "alone, arms folded, waiting for him to join her." Barely a week later, Michael Paterniti, a writer for Esquire, caught another similarly illuminating scene after Bill and Hillary had spoken about the FTC report. As Hillary sat in her van, Bill leaned in for an intense discussion, "his long fingers pointing and gesturing, his eyes fixed on her, and hers back on him," Paterniti wrote. "In the thrall of another race, they both seem in a kind of momentary rapture." It was probably fitting that exactly a month later they celebrated their twenty-fifth wedding anniversary in Chappaqua by watching the second presidential debate on television.

BILL CONTINUED TO express frustration that he couldn't publicly partici- pate in the presidential campaign as much as he wanted. "I wish I were running this year," he told Sidney Blumenthal. "I'd run their ass down." He disapproved of Gore's populist rhetoric and felt his own leadership wasn't getting enough credit for the country's progress. He sent advice through emissaries to William Daley, Gore's campaign chairman, as well as to cam- paign manager Donna Brazile. "I believe Clinton used practically every- one he could get his hands on to send messages to Al Gore," said Brazile.

But Bill also kept making counterproductive comments about the can- didate, his message, and his tactics, some of which surfaced in the press. He might voice subtle misgivings, as in a September speech in Connecti- cut when he said, "People ask me: Do you really think Al Gore is going to win? I always said yes." Or he could veer off message, when he casually said at a fund-raiser in mid-October, "Suppose Al Gore turns out to be wrong because there's a little bit of a recession, and we don't have enough money to keep all the spending commitments?" His criticisms made headlines after the third presidential debate on October 17 when Bill was reported to have told congressional Democrats that he had "almost gagged" over Gore's failure to challenge Bush's false claim of credit for a patients' bill of rights in Texas. Gore strategist Tad Devine told Steve Richetti, Bill's Deputy Chief of Staff, that the comment had helped raise Gore's unfavor- able rating by five points in a week. "The President goes out and awakens doubts about Gore, and all the bad stuff . . . begins to come to the surface," said Devine.

At the end of the month, only days before the polls opened, a new issue of *Esquire* appeared on the newsstands with Bill on the cover, striking a de- cidedly unpresidential pose: legs spread wide, huge hands clapped on his knees, his smile radiating self-satisfaction. In the magazine's "Exit Inter- view," Bill mentioned Al Gore just twice in passing, defended himself against the controversies of his presidency, castigated his critics, and said the Republicans owed him an apology. The effect was to make the campaign seem all about Bill—exactly what Gore was trying to avoid.

The colliding agendas of the President, First Lady, and Vice President were gifts to the Republicans, whose efforts to tag Gore with his boss's weaknesses were paying off. "Gore's numbers on honesty and forthrightness lag far behind Bush's," Newsweek noted the week before the election. There were other disturbing signs in the closing days as the press began to comment that the economy was "slowing, not yet ominously but noticeably." Third-party candidate Ralph Nader was also emerging as a spoiler on the left with a "noticeable little breeze at his back." Nader, who appealed to roughly 5 percent of voters, was gaining traction by portraying Gore and Bush as indistinguishable, and the Gore campaign worried that he could have an adverse impact on the returns in a half-dozen states.

After negotiations between the White House and the Gore campaign, Bill was dispatched to do eleventh-hour politicking in only three states—speeches at the convention centers in Little Rock and Pine Bluffs and get-out-the-vote rallies in San Francisco, Los Angeles, and New York City. He worked at full throttle in New York State, a safe haven where his popularity was at 70 percent, where Democrats had two million more registered voters than Republicans, and where he could keep helping his wife with his public appearances.

Hillary stumped without Bill in her campaign's final week. On the Sunday before Election Day, she and Chelsea visited seven black churches in as many hours, soaking up the gospel music and the approval of the congregations. "Brother Bill has had his season," said the Rev. Charles E. Betts Sr. "God is raising up another woman of God."

BILL, HILLARY, AND CHELSEA went to the polls at the Douglas G. Grafflin Elementary School in Chappaqua on Tuesday morning, November 7, a mild and intermittently cloudy day. When he had first pulled the lever for his wife two months earlier in the pro forma Democratic primary, Bill had called it a "most extraordinary experience. . . . I was as happy as a kid on Christmas morning." Now he and Chelsea cast their ballots first, then embraced while Hillary voted for herself.

In the evening, Marine One ferried them to Manhattan, where they had a suite of rooms at the Grand Hyatt hotel, next to Grand Central Terminal. En route, Hillary busied herself by reading *The New York Times* while Bill edited the victory speech that she was too anxious to review. In the suite swarming with staff, Hillary wore a terry-cloth hotel bathrobe as a stylist worked on her hair. At 10:40, Lazio called to concede, and Hillary "simply smiled" before giving everyone hugs.

She had won resoundingly, with 55 percent of the vote to Lazio's 43 percent. "If it had not been for your endorsement, Hillary would never have won," Bill told Daniel Patrick Moynihan as they rode the freight elevator down to the victory celebration. Dressed in a teal jacket and trousers, Hillary faced the cheering crowd from the podium in the ballroom and said, "Sixty-two counties, sixteen months, three debates, two opponents, and six black pantsuits later, because of you, we are here." Behind her, Bill could be seen brushing away tears. But when Hillary raised her arms for the victory photo, her left hand clasped Chelsea's, and her right hand held Charles Schumer's, while Bill stood on Chelsea's other side, smiling, with his hands down. The unconventional tableau seemed "an effort to underscore that the Senate victory was hers alone," noted Elisabeth Bumiller of *The New York Times.*

Al Gore's fate that night was cruelly ambiguous. He was headed toward winning the overall total by more than a half-million votes (543,895, when all the counting was eventually completed). Earlier in the evening, he had also seemed poised for victory in the decisive Electoral College as the TV networks gave him Florida, Pennsylvania, and Michigan. But around 10:00 p.m., the Florida results turned uncertain, and the state switched back into the undecided category. By around 2:00 a.m., all the networks declared that Bush had prevailed in Florida, giving him the twenty-five electoral votes he needed to win the presidency.

Gore stoically called Bush to concede and drove through the rain to War Memorial Plaza in Nashville to make his concession speech. As he was about to walk onto the platform, his aides grabbed him and said that Bush's five-figure lead had shrunk to some five hundred votes. Under election law, Gore was entitled to a recount if the margin was less than one half of one percent. Gore called Bush back and said, "Circumstances have changed dramatically since I first called you. The State of Florida is too close to call." The Vice President's words triggered a legal challenge that was to drag on for thirty-six days.

In the Grand Hyatt, Bill was transfixed by the developing drama. He had spent the evening prowling the suite, consulting with advisors, making phone calls, and planting himself only inches away from one of the living room's four TV sets. An aide thought that "he seemed to be having fun . . . as if he was watching a close and important basketball game." At 4:18 a.m., Bill reached Gore, later reporting that the Vice President had been "in a good humor, pleased that he was ahead in the popular vote." Gore congratulated Hillary, and "they had a nice little visit." Bill stayed up the rest of the night, playing Oh Hell with members of his staff before finally going to sleep at 6:00 a.m.

"Election night was so bizarre, mostly bitter," Bruce Reed recalled. "It was clear from almost the moment she got in the race that the First Lady would win and that the Vice President's camp was star-crossed from the outset. There wasn't anybody at the White House who felt much like celebrating. We were over the moon for Hillary's victory, but the prize lost was so consequential and painful that it dwarfed everything."

Almost immediately the rumors started about a Hillary presidential candidacy in 2004 or 2008. "I believe that's worse than idle speculation," Bill told CBS's Dan Rather. "Of course she'll run," said Senator Moynihan.

Chapter Eighteen

—

Bill Clinton had wanted to be president for so long that when it finally came time to leave—after eight incredibly full years of what he called "storm and sunshine"—he didn't want to go. His last two months in office were an unprecedented spectacle of sentimental journeys and no fewer than twenty farewell addresses (including two in the hours after he left office), along with a high-risk play for peace in the Middle East, "last-hurrah interviews to every publication this side of *Field and Stream*," a frantic round of parties, hasty and often ill-advised executive actions, and a last-minute dash to pack up so his successor could move into 1600 Pennsylvania Avenue. By contrast, the previous two-term president, Ronald Reagan (whose videotapes Bill had studied for bearing and style and whose organizational efficiency he admired), left office after delivering four carefully crafted speeches sharing "the lessons" he had learned in the Oval Office and one televised farewell address.

The helter-skelter finale of the Clinton presidency prompted Bob Dole to crack that Bill needed a SWAT team to remove him from the White House. University of Wisconsin political-science professor Charles O. Jones imagined aides beckoning the President to "come out from under the desk now" on January 20. As it turned out, Bill's jam-packed final days were more consequential than comic and resulted in some of the worst decisions of his presidency.

His behavior offered a mirror image of the administration's earliest days—"a chaos of innocence at the beginning and a chaos of knowing everything at the end," said Bruce Reed. The President often had good intentions, including a somewhat ironic yearning, as he said in a farewell sermon at his church, to "follow the example of the mythic Parsifal, a good man slowly wise." His ability to move and mesmerize audiences was stronger than ever, as was his command of the issues before him. And he had some admirable and productive moments, particularly in articulating his vision for an Israeli-Palestinian settlement.

But in the end, Bill's gargantuan ambitions defeated him, as he threw off the restraints his staff had painstakingly placed on him in the previous years. "All his life he has been able to have everything," said one of his senior advisors. "He wanted everything as President, wanted to make progress on every issue. But you have to choose, and he doesn't like choosing, was never good at choosing, which requires discipline. Doing a little of everything is good politics, but it is more profoundly rooted in his own desire to have everything, do everything, be everything. This made him formidable, but it meant his presidency ultimately lacked definition. He was a great President, but it was not a great presidency."

At the same time, Hillary abandoned her customary caution. Freed from her White House duties, she immersed herself in the routines of Capitol Hill and in pulling together a legislative staff, leaving her husband to his own devices. She shucked her rigid self-discipline and yielded to a level of self-celebration unusual for a freshman senator. In their last weeks, the Clintons seemed oblivious to the crushing lessons of their eight years in the White House, rewarding friends and political allies and cutting ethical corners. Later, when faced with harsh criticism of their actions, both Bill and Hillary blamed others, as they had done so many times in the past.

For more than a month, Al Gore suffered in political purgatory as his lawyers battled the Bush forces in Florida over the convoluted recount to determine the winner of the state's electoral votes. Those tense weeks also brought postmortems and recriminations over Gore's failure to easily capture the Electoral College. His popular vote was 50,999,897, exceeded only by Ronald Reagan's 1984 landslide. Even though he had received far more votes and a higher percentage than Bill Clinton had in his two presidential races, Gore found himself battling accusations from the Clinton camp that if the President had been unleashed on the campaign trail, he would have energized the Democratic base and enabled Gore to win.

The Gore-Lieberman ticket found itself on the wrong side of the classic pendulum of American politics. In 1992, the momentum was beginning to swing toward the Democrats after twelve years of GOP control of the White House, and Ross Perot helped by taking the vast majority of his votes from George H. W. Bush. But by 2000 the pendulum was moving in the other direction, propelled by the Clinton scandals that alienated religious and swing voters. Former White House aide and Gore campaign consultant Robert Boorstin told Vanity Fair's Marjorie Williams, "Did we make mistakes? Yes. Would I say that Clinton was the only reason we lost? No. Would I say with absolute zero doubt in my mind that we would have won the election if Clinton hadn't put his penis in her mouth? Yes. I guarantee it."

Other factors undeniably came into play, particularly Gore's disappointing performance in the debates and the distractions presented by the Clintons themselves. When George H. W. Bush ran in 1988, he benefited enormously from Reagan's unequivocal support. As the general campaign began in early September that year, Reagan "handed out red, white and blue ties with the legend 'Push for Bush' to cabinet members and told them he expected them to be on the road campaigning for the next two months," wrote Reagan biographer Richard Reeves. Reagan hit the hustings as well, wherever the Bush campaign directed him to go.

In Florida, Gore's support was clearly damaged by the Elián González fiasco, but the insurgent candidacy of Ralph Nader—prompted in part by a perception of Gore's vulnerability—also split the Democratic vote on the left. If Nader's 97,488 votes in Florida had been in the Gore column, the state would have been his, chads or no chads. In New Hampshire, which Clinton-Gore won in 1992 and 1996, Gore lost by 7,211, a margin that would have been erased if Nader's 22,198 votes had gone to the Democrats. Two other once-solid Clinton-Gore states that Bush won decisively were Arkansas (by 50,172 votes) and Tennessee (by 80,229 votes). Bill's home state was one of the three places where he had campaigned two days before the election, so the loss carried a special sting, as did the defeat in Gore's native Tennessee. Bill maintained that the administration's strong stand on gun control had hurt the Democrats in both those states and else-where in the South.

THE FIRST LEG OF BILL'S farewell tour was a nostalgic sweep through Ire-land and Britain with Hillary and Chelsea. He reminisced in Belfast about bringing peace to Northern Ireland, and at the University of Warwick in Coventry, England, he gave a lengthy address on the "Global Social Con-tract." His themes of American engagement in an era of globalization echoed an even longer speech he had delivered a week earlier at the Uni-versity of Nebraska. Both forums offered ideal opportunities for him to sound the alarm about the rising threat of Islamist terrorism. But as before, he only alluded to the possibility of terrorists, narcotraffickers, and orga-nized criminals "working together in lines that are quite blurred." He told his Nebraska audience that "one of the biggest threats to the future is going to be cyberterrorism—people fooling with your computer networks, trying to shut down your phones, erase bank records, mess up airline schedules, do things to interrupt the fabric of life."

While the Clintons were in Northern Ireland on Tuesday, December 12, they learned that the U.S. Supreme Court had voted 5 to 4 to stop the recount in Florida on the grounds that it was unconstitutional and could not be finished by the state-mandated deadline of midnight. With a margin of just 537 votes, Bush won Florida, its Electoral College allotment, and the presidency, giving him victory, 271 electoral votes to 266. Gore made a gracious and eloquent concession speech, saying, "I do believe, as my fa-ther once said, that no matter how hard the loss, defeat might serve as well as victory to shape the soul and let the glory out."

Bill called Gore to tell him his remarks were "fabulous," and Gore mentioned that a friend had mordantly observed, "Gore got the best of all worlds: he won the popular vote and doesn't have to do the job." It was "a great line," Bill told reporters during a rambling interview on Air Force One while flying back to Washington on the fourteenth. In a classic *tour d'horizon*, Bill reveled in the highs of his presidency (his 1995 trip to Ire-land, with "all the people filling the square" in Derry, "up the hill behind as far as you could see") and skipped lightly over the lows. He spoke expan-sively about Seamus Heaney's *The Cure at Troy*, a retelling of the Greek warrior Philoctetes' ten-year ordeal of solitude and pain after he had been abandoned by Ulysses. Bill was impressed that not only did Philoctetes forgive Ulysses but that he commented while sailing away from his island prison, "It was a fortunate wind that blew me here." The President said that for all his travails—"There were times when I felt like a piñata in somebody else's ball game"—he believed a "fortunate wind" had blown him to the White House. He said he identified with the endurance of Philoctetes and how he "just purged his soul" and was able to move on despite his mistreatment—a lesson for "people that are still mad at each other."

In the following days, Bill tried to put the best gloss on Gore's defeat. He told Dan Rather on December 18 that George Bush won "partly because of the prosperity. I think they both debated how to use the prosperity, and the country was evenly divided." Yet the next day, before meeting in the Oval Office with Bush, the President finally conceded to reporters that an economic downturn was under way. "I think there will be things to be managed," he said. "He'll have economic challenges, and you ought to give him a chance to meet them."

A veneer of public graciousness between the President and Vice President concealed their intensifying private anger over each other's role in the electoral outcome. At Gore's request, they met in the Oval Office on Thursday, December 21, to air their differences. It was an unpleasant encounter, as Gore forthrightly blamed Bill's scandals, while Bill rebuked Gore for failing to make the most of their successful record. Afterward, Bill told Sidney Blumenthal they had parted after "patching everything up," but in fact the mutual resentments among the Clintons and Gores persisted. According to David Remnick of The New Yorker, some in the Gore camp suspected that Bill "was not entirely displeased that the defeat left more room on the political stage for Hillary."

BILL SPENT MUCH of December intent on resuscitating the moribund Israeli-Palestinian negotiations. In the weeks after the Intifada exploded, he had sought to reduce the violence by working the phones with Barak and Arafat, at one point in early October scarcely sleeping for two days, and then a week later making a one-day trip to Sharm el-Sheikh, Egypt, for an emergency summit. On November 9, he summoned Arafat to the Oval Office and sternly reminded him that he had "only ten weeks left to make an agreement." To show he meant business, Bill "held his arm" and "stared straight at him."

In the middle of Bill's ongoing remonstrations, the U.S. military was hit by terrorists on October 12 when a small boat filled with explosives rammed into the navy destroyer USS *Cole* in the harbor of Aden in Yemen, killing seventeen sailors and wounding at least forty. Within weeks, U.S. intelligence agencies had "strong evidence connecting the *Cole* attack to al-Qaeda." Yet the President and his top advisors refrained from ordering the sort of retaliatory attack they had launched in August 1998 after the bombings of American embassies in Africa by al-Qaeda. White House counterterrorism chief Richard Clarke had the "impression" the White House "didn't really want to know," mainly because Bill was focused on negotiating with the Israelis and Palestinians. Both the President and National Security Advisor Sandy Berger told the 9/11 Commission they considered the link to al-Qaeda to be only a "preliminary judgment." They said that before taking action against al-Qaeda they needed "a conclusion" from CIA Director George Tenet. But the CIA chief could not remember "any discussions" with Berger or the President about retaliation or being told they were awaiting decisive "magic words" from the CIA and FBI. (Berger's credibility on these matters later became suspect when federal authorities discovered that he had stolen and destroyed highly classified documents from the National Archives during the 9/11 investigation and then lied about his actions.) The 9/11 Commission concluded that the bombing of the *Cole* "galvanized al-Qaeda's recruitment efforts," particularly when the United States failed to respond.

Barak and Arafat agreed yet again to send teams of negotiators to the United States in mid-December. This time they met at Bolling Air Force Base in Washington, D.C., but they were still "flapping around" after five days when the President brought them to the Cabinet Room on December 23. Reading from his notes, he gave them his final "parameters" for a comprehensive agreement that went beyond the proposals at Camp David. To create a Palestinian state, Israel would relinquish the Gaza Strip and about 95 percent of the West Bank and would incorporate into Israel roughly three quarters of the Jewish settlements built in the West Bank. The crucial quid pro quo at the core of the plan was a requirement that the Israelis give up sovereignty over the Temple Mount, the holiest religious site in Jerusalem, which was also the location of sacred Muslim shrines. In exchange, the Palestinians would have to abandon their insistence on an unlimited right of return to Israel for 3.7 million Palestinian refugees. *Time* called the plan Bill's "Hail Mary" play, while *The Wall Street Journal's* Robert Bartley derided it as "compulsive grandstanding." For each side, the Clinton ultimatum meant giving up principles that had deep popular support.

Ehud Barak, whose prospects for reelection hinged on securing a peace agreement, persuaded his cabinet to accept the framework "in principle." Arafat, however, sent a letter to the White House on December 27 listing twenty-six objections and questions—an obvious stalling tactic. "If you don't take this golden opportunity, you will have no mention in history, and coming generations of Palestinians will curse you," Bill said to Arafat in a tense phone call.

On the same day that Bill received the Palestinian leader's disappointing reply, he and David Kendall had a secret meeting in the Map Room with Independent Counsel Robert Ray to consider the outlines of another kind of peace agreement. Ray had spent more than a year completing the fifty-five-million-dollar investigation begun by Robert Fiske in January 1994 and pursued with singular zeal by Kenneth Starr. Ray had been weighing an indictment of Bill Clinton for perjury since he had impaneled a new grand jury the previous summer. Ray and Kendall had been quietly talking for months but making no progress until November, when the prosecutor called Monica Lewinsky back for an additional interview, and the pressure on the President intensified. Although Bill had been boasting to the press that "they have yet to come up with one example of official misconduct in office—not one," he privately told his advisors that he was concerned about being charged with a criminal offense. Before Christmas, Ray said he could fashion a settlement if the President publicly admitted lying under oath and accepted some form of sanction. Any agreement would be contingent on a separate agreement with the Arkansas Bar Association, which was considering disbarment proceedings. During their fifteen-minute Map Room meeting, Bill said nothing as Ray described his proposed deal in more detail, setting the stage for the two sides to work out specific language.

———

IN THE WEEKS AFTER her election, Hillary flew around New York State to thank supporters, attended tutorials for freshman senators, and paid homage to Robert Byrd, President pro tempore of the Senate, whose allegiance she needed to begin building her power base on Capitol Hill. On November 28, she threw herself a party in the East Room to mark the publication of *An Invitation to the White House,* her meditation on history, décor, and entertaining. The book had originally been scheduled to come out for Christmas 1999 but was postponed until after the election for fear of making her seem "fluffy" while running for office.

Before the book party, she met with top executives of Simon & Schuster, her publisher, to discuss a memoir she planned to write. Over the following days, she had similar meetings in New York with a dozen publishing houses. She offered no written proposal, but she had steep financial requirements: an advance of more than $7.5 million, half of which she wanted upon signing her contract, an unusually large amount up front. After considering bids from eight publishers, Hillary announced on December 15 that she would stay with Simon & Schuster. Her advance was nearly $8 million, significantly higher than the $7.1 million paid to the chairman of General Electric, John F. Welch Jr., but lower than Pope John Paul II's advance of $8.5 million in 1994.

Government watchdog groups immediately criticized the payment, and a *New York Times* editorial called it "an affront to common sense," adding, "No lawmaker should accept a large, unearned sum from a publisher whose parent company, Viacom, is vitally interested in government policy on issues likely to come before Congress." With a generous check in her pocket and the promise of more to come, Hillary signed another contract, this time for a $2.85 million home in Washington, D.C. Located on a cul-de-sac near Embassy Row, the five-bedroom, 5,500-square-foot brick house had a pool and a terrace. She put down $855,000 and had no trouble securing a mortgage for the balance. Emulating the upper-class habit of creating lofty identities for country estates, she called her city home "Whitehaven," after the name of her street.

On Christmas Eve, Maureen Dowd of *The New York Times* revealed that Hillary's "wealthy friends and contributors" had decided to "treat her like a bride" and buy from her registry at Borsheim's, a jewelry and gift store in Omaha owned by multibillionaire Clinton benefactor Warren Buffett. The First Lady's supporters were calling around on her behalf to solicit "housewarming presents" before her swearing-in, to circumvent the hundred-dollar limit on gifts to senators. Among the suggested items from Hillary's listed silver and china patterns were a Fabergé serving spoon for $510 and a Spode vegetable dish for $980. One of the organizers, Rita Pynoos of Beverly Hills, even proposed that contributors send five-thousand-dollar checks if they didn't know what to select, and Hillary's decorator circulated a wish list of furniture. "I got a call," said one prominent Washington Democrat. "They asked me for a couple of plates. I hadn't seen the Clintons in four years. I said I would rather not." Numerous others stepped up with extraordinary largesse. Among them were Pynoos and her husband, Morris, who gave Hillary $4,970 worth of sterling flatware, and Steven Spielberg and his wife, Kate Capshaw, who donated $4,920 worth of china.

ONE NOTEWORTHY GIFT to Hillary was from Denise Rich, who spent $7,375 for two coffee tables and two chairs. The campaign to pardon Marc Rich, which was begun the previous spring with the enlistment of Denise as a sotto-voce lobbyist, gained momentum in the fall and winter. At another fund-raiser Denise hosted on October 5, Bill said, "I don't think Hillary and I have had a better friend anywhere in America than she's been to us for the whole time I've been president. . . . A lot of you here have helped Hillary." On November 30, Denise presented the President with a new saxophone during his appearance at her biennial Angel Ball to raise money for cancer research, and once again he praised her for "everything you have done to make it possible for Hillary and me to serve."

Within a week, Bill received a letter from his close friend pleading her former husband's case, which she supported "with all my heart." She continued her campaign with a second note, a phone call, and a conversation during a White House party on December 20. By then, Denise had been joined in her efforts by Beth Dozoretz, another wealthy courtier who gave a dining-room table and server worth some seven thousand dollars to the Clinton gift collection. Dozoretz had been finance chair of the Democratic National Committee for eight months in 1999 until she was asked to resign in a shake-up of the fund-raising team. Bill and Dozoretz had a close relationship. In her official capacity, she had accompanied Bill on a dozen trips to California, New York, Illinois, Florida, Nevada, and Connecticut, and she visited the White House ninety-six times in Bill's last two years in office.

Dozoretz had been recruited to the Marc Rich cause by Jack Quinn, Bill's former White House Counsel (not the U.S. congressman from New York), who was leading the pardon team. When Dozoretz and Denise were skiing in Aspen in early January 2001, the President called Dozoretz to say he was ready to grant Rich a pardon. Denise in turn phoned Quinn to report that Bill sounded "very positive." In a later congressional inquiry into the pardon, both Denise Rich and Beth Dozoretz pleaded the Fifth Amendment.

Dozoretz's other key connection to the Rich pardon was none other than her friend Ehud Barak, who had received financial contributions to his campaign from Rich. In the middle of the delicate Israeli-Palestinian negotiations in December and January, Barak found time to argue Rich's case three times to the President, insisting that the fugitive had played a "humanitarian role in Israel." According to Maureen Orth of *Vanity Fair*, the Israeli Prime Minister also "described Rich as being very helpful to Mossad," the Israeli intelligence agency. *Newsweek*'s Joe Klein believed that the collapse of Camp David and the eruption of the Intifada had given Bill "a lingering sense of guilt" over his role in Barak's "political fate."

The most dubious player in the Rich saga was Quinn, who was retained by Rich to prepare the pardon petition and on December 11 gave his former boss a thick dossier filled with testimonials. Quinn leaned on Bruce Lindsey as well as the White House Counsel's office, which he worked "pretty hard." Quinn's actions were "inexcusable," said Abner Mikva, one of his predecessors as White House Counsel. "If you feel strongly, there is nothing wrong with importuning your former employer, but not for money."

SEVERAL OTHER SUCCESSFUL pardon pleas proved nearly as controversial because they enriched Hillary's siblings. As in the Marc Rich case, Bill made his decision after bypassing the views of knowledgeable officials at the Justice Department, judges, and prosecutors.

The Rodham brothers had long been fixtures at the White House. Hugh had become a semipermanent resident of the third floor, by one account "accumulating so much stuff that when the Clintons vacated the Residence he had nearly as many boxes to move as Chelsea." He had been regularly shuttling between his Coral Gables home and Washington since he had begun keeping Bill company during the Lewinsky and impeachment travails, and then through the 2000 campaign. Hugh's wife, Maria Arias, was "bored" with the White House, according to one of the Clintons' close friends, and "she didn't think the food was good," so she rarely accompanied him. Hugh shared Bill's enthusiasm for Upwords, which they played together long into the night. When Hillary put the family on the Dean Ornish "heart healthy" diet emphasizing whole grains, fruits, and vegetables, Hugh defied her edict by snacking at McDonald's. Up in the Solarium he worked his contacts, trying to cadge tickets to the Oscars and the Super Bowl, "telling potential clients they could reach him at 'The House,' " wrote *Time*'s Margaret Carlson.

Fifty-year-old Hugh and his forty-six-year-old brother, Tony, also tried to use their White House connections to score lucrative business deals. "Hughie and Tony are smart guys who never found a niche," said a close friend of the Clintons. Hugh redeemed himself with geniality, but Tony was gruff and pushy. Both had suffered from "having had a father whose disapproval was unrelenting," said the friend.

In 1999, "The Boys" had latched onto a $118 million business to grow and export hazelnuts from the former Soviet republic of Georgia. Their collaborator in the venture was Aslan Abashidze, a political front man for Russian efforts to undermine Georgian president Eduard Shevardnadze. The Rodhams' open cooperation with a sworn enemy of the U.S. government's ally caused such consternation in diplomatic circles that Sandy Berger intervened to ask the brothers to desist. Hugh stepped back, but Tony remained defiantly involved, insisting that he was "restructuring" the deal—a "strong business" that would soon be profitable.

Tony, whose marriage to the daughter of California senator Barbara Boxer had broken up only five years after their Rose Garden wedding, was also working as a consultant for a Tennessee-based carnival company called United Shows of America. The company's owners, Edgar and Vonna Jo Gregory, had been convicted of bank fraud in 1982. Tony had met them at a Clinton-Gore fund-raiser in 1996, and they had subsequently hired him as a "consultant," paying him $244,769 over two and a half years. With Hillary's help, Tony had arranged carnival attractions at South Lawn events in 1998 and 2000, but the Gregorys were otherwise unable to document any work he had done for them.

When the Gregorys submitted a pardon application, Tony lobbied his brother-in-law on their behalf, saying that they were having difficulty securing contracts for their business because they were convicted felons. In March 2000, Bill granted them clemency, an act that received no publicity at the time. In addition to federal prosecutors, Justice Department officials and the sentencing judge opposed the pardons. Jeff Sessions, the U.S. attorney who prosecuted the Gregorys in Alabama, said that "pardons should follow normal procedures, and in this case it is clear President Clinton didn't follow that protocol."

In the spring of 2000, Tony received the first of sixteen checks totaling $109,000 that the Gregorys designated as loans—none of which he repaid. Tony later insisted that "on the pardon issue, I never received a dime," but an investigation by the House Government Reform Committee concluded that "the most valuable thing that Rodham did for the Gregorys was to obtain presidential pardons. . . . There is a substantial question as to whether the Gregorys paid Rodham for his efforts to obtain presidential pardons for them."

The following winter, it was Hugh's turn to make six figures on a pardon deal—an even more lucrative four-hundred-thousand-dollar "success fee." His clients were Almon Glenn Braswell, a Floridian convicted of mail fraud and perjury, and Carlos Vignali, a notorious California cocaine dealer who was midway through a fifteen-year prison sentence. In the final weeks of the Clinton presidency, Hugh lobbied Bill on behalf of both men. "I knew it was going on, and it made me ill," recalled a Clinton friend who spent time in the Residence during that period. "It was like watching a car wreck in slow motion." The Braswell application was considered exclusively by the White House Counsel's office, and Vignoli's request was handled more routinely by the Justice Department. In both cases, federal prosecutors lodged strong objections to clemency, to no avail.

AGAINST THE ADVICE of his national-security team, Bill began the new year by inviting Yasser Arafat to the Oval Office for one final attempt to turn the Palestinian leader around. They met twice on Tuesday, January 2, the first time for two and a half hours, the second for nearly an hour. Arafat held firm on the right of return, which essentially ended the prospects for peace and ensured Barak's defeat by Ariel Sharon—an outspoken opponent of the Oslo process—the following month.

Bill continued to insist he had not given up, and on January 7 he made an emotional speech to 1,100 members of the liberal Israel Policy Forum at a dinner at the Waldorf-Astoria. For the first time, he publicly endorsed the creation of a Palestinian state, and he described in some detail the elements of the plan he had proposed two weeks earlier. He vowed to use "my remaining time in office" to "narrow the differences. . . . I've got 13 days, and I'll do what I can."

He made no progress, and on Wednesday, January 17, Arafat called to say farewell. When the Palestinian leader told Bill he was a "great man," the President exploded. "The hell I am," he said. "I'm a colossal failure, and you made me one." "Clinton wanted a breakthrough in the Middle East in the worst way," recalled Tom Siebert. "He feels that Arafat killed him, that Arafat couldn't be a peacemaker and would always be a terrorist."

HILLARY WAS SWORN in with thirty-three other senators on Wednesday, January 3, as Bill, Chelsea, and Dorothy watched from the front row of the visitors' gallery in the Senate chamber. Al Gore administered the oath amid "jubilant faces," wrote columnist Mary McGrory, which could only remind him of "his excruciating loss." The freshman New York senator was dressed in the same vibrant teal pantsuit she had worn to her victory celebration on election night, and Bill had a matching tie, along with a HILLARY! button on his lapel. Once again, the President's eyes filled with tears, and he jumped up to applaud at the end of the ceremony. Afterward, Hillary hosted the largest reception. She was honored that evening at a party in the Grand Ballroom of the Mayflower Hotel given by major Democratic donor Walter Kaye, the man who had originally promoted Monica Lewinsky for a White House internship—an awkward coincidence that fazed neither Bill nor Hillary. In his remarks to the partygoers, Bill showered thanks on Kaye and his wife, Thelma, and spoke of his "enormous pride" in Hillary's achievement.

The next night, the Clintons went across town to an "I Survived the Clinton Presidency" party at Nightclub 9:30. "If I don't sleep for the next sixteen days, it will seem like four more years," Bill told the crowd of White House aides in the cavernous rock club. For all his joking, he actually took his own comment to heart in the following weeks.

Bill's long good-bye began in earnest on Saturday the sixth with an even more elaborate party for past and present Clinton White House staff members, under a large white pavilion on the South Lawn. Bill and Hillary were driven from the White House in the bus that had transported them during the 1992 campaign. The Gores were delayed by yet another difficult ordeal—the Vice President's required appearance in the Senate chamber to supervise the official count of the Electoral College vote.

The program featured skits—Gene Sperling, director of the National Economic Council, dressed as a rapper and Bruce Reed in a school uniform—speeches, and the surprise appearance of Fleetwood Mac to sing the 1992 campaign anthem, "Don't Stop Thinking about Tomorrow." Gore did a self-deprecating routine about being unemployed, and the crowd rewarded him with sustained applause. But the jollity seemed forced, the mood bittersweet. Even worse, among the tributes and long video clips celebrating the greatest hits of the previous eight years, there was little mention of the Vice President. "You had to work hard at not having Gore included in that," a former White House aide told Marjorie Williams of *Vanity Fair*. "They obviously did."

It was Hillary's turn again the following evening, with a celebration attended by nearly three thousand supporters in Madison Square Garden. The New York State Democratic party billed it as her "real swearing-in," with prayers, songs (by Jessye Norman and Billy Joel), and a reading by Toni Morrison. Al Gore gamely joined Hillary in reenacting the oath-of-office ceremony in front of the "swinging, swaying, celebrity-studded, standing-ovation-flooded" gathering, as Tipper looked on. Bill thanked Tipper for "keeping the rest of us in good humor, always seeing the glass as half full," and complimented Al's "strength of character that very few of us could emulate if we were in the same circumstances." He also pledged to be Hillary's "de facto case worker," who would spend his time traveling around New York to "help the upstate economy"—a promise still unfulfilled six years later.

Over the next ten days Bill rocketed around the country, touching down in Michigan, Illinois, New Hampshire, and Arkansas for nostalgic reminiscences interspersed with the now-familiar recitations of his achievements and his goals for the country. More often than not, he kept his audiences waiting, explaining that he was "unavoidably detained" because "I can't stop doing my job." On one day, he packed in five appearances in East Lansing, Michigan, and Chicago. He was so carried away after speaking to supporters at the Palmer House Hilton in Chicago, he "invaded" a private dinner in a nearby room to tell the surprised guests, "America may find people who do this job better than I have, but you will never find anybody who loved doing it any more."

He made a pilgrimage to Dover, New Hampshire, where he had famously declared nine years earlier that he would "be there for you till the last dog dies." He recalled how everyone "said I was dead," but a friend had painted his portrait with "fist clenched and . . . jaw clenched" that he had later hung in his study next to the Oval Office. Without a trace of embarrassment about that room's association with Lewinsky, he said, "All the tough days I'd go back and look at that picture, and I would remind myself of why I ran for President and what we were doing." Now, with only nine days to go, he announced that "the last dog is still barking." After taking a stroll down Main Street in Manchester, with just enough time to consume some potato skins and mozzarella sticks, he flew to Boston for a rally at Northeastern University, where seven thousand fans filled the arena. He told them that in "election after election and in good times and bad, the one place that I knew would always be there" was Massachusetts.

The last full weekend of his presidency brought another whirl of parties, this time at Camp David. With his cabinet in Laurel Lodge, Bill exchanged toasts and thanks. Hillary biographer Kati Marton attended with her husband, United Nations Ambassador Richard Holbrooke. Marton recalled that several in the group "referred to the possibility that there was a 'future president' in the room. No one doubted who the object of the reference was." Hillary "looked radiant," Marton noted. The cabinet party was "wistful and fun," said Donna Shalala, while the White House staff party on Saturday night was more exuberant, with an after-dinner concert by Don Henley.

Bill's last visit to his home state as President was the most emotional of all the stops on his prolonged victory tour. Speaking for almost an hour to the Arkansas legislature, he boasted that he had recruited more than 460

Arkansans to work for his administration, and he seemed to thank most of them, even Buddy Young, the state trooper who had pressured his former subordinates to keep quiet about Bill's amorous adventures. Bill had Chelsea with him but not Hillary, who he said "learned all of her politics wrestling with you." If she hadn't followed him to Arkansas three decades earlier, "I doubt the rest of this trip would have happened," he said.

On his way out of town, he addressed a rally at the airport, as he had done in January 1993. He told the crowd of seven hundred that he would leave the White House "more idealistic and more hopeful" than when he first took the oath of office. During a ten-minute interview with Max Brantley, a small cloud passed over the President's sunny face when he was asked about "all the people from Arkansas who had paid a high price for serving in his administration. "He said it wasn't his fault," recalled Brantley. "He was mad at Kenneth Starr plenty." The moment passed, and Bill quickly rattled off his record once more. "He was expansive, feeling good," said Brantley. "He was reflecting that he was through running for office. But he had a legacy to run for, so he is still running. For him it is always a popularity contest."

THE WANING CLINTON PRESIDENCY brought a flood of appraisals, most of them tinged with high-minded regret. *The Economist* wrote of "a huge sense of talent wasted. With more discipline and less self-indulgence, how good eight years of Bill Clinton could have been." Former White House Chief of Staff Leon Panetta described "a tale of two presidencies, one was brilliant, capable of dealing with every type of policy. . . . The other presidency is one of personal weakness . . . that created a dark legacy that will forever be with him." Mike McCurry mournfully observed that "twenty years from now when people think back to the late 1990s, the only thing they will associate with that time is the rise of the Internet." Nine months later, he might well have added the rise of Islamist terrorism.

Washington Post columnist David Broder offered one of the most searching—and tough-minded—verdicts. He praised Clinton for economic growth, welfare reform, and a foreign policy that brought peace to the Balkans and Northern Ireland, yet he lamented that "there were too many jagged edges . . . too many highs and lows, too much grandeur and too much farce." The fundamental flaw, Broder said, was Bill Clinton's lifelong belief that he was "fortune's favored child," which created a sense of "immunity" and "indestructibility" that led to reckless behavior. Unknown to Broder, those patterns were continuing even in Bill's last few days on the job.

The assessment that may have hurt Bill the most was from Douglas Eakeley, his close friend since Oxford and Yale and a committed liberal. Writing in the January 4 edition of his local New Jersey paper, *The Bernardsville News*, Eakeley began, "My wife and I stayed in the Lincoln bedroom before it went on sale." He described how Bill had restored his presidency after 1994, "in a sense at his best, defining himself by the opposition." But he concluded that "the affair with Monica Lewinsky will also remain indelibly part of the story—a reflection of a tragic flaw." Recalling vividly the "expectations that greeted [Bill's] election," Eakeley expressed "a deep sense of disappointment for what might have been—Social Security and health care reform, a nation less divided, a federal government less partisan." Like others who had believed in Bill Clinton, Eakeley cited the "eight years of unprecedented peace and prosperity" on his watch, along with an important change in "the political dynamic . . . a renewed sense that the federal government matters" in making "a difference for the better in the lives of ordinary Americans." The Clinton Administration had been "some ride," Eakeley concluded. "I know he would have liked the opportunity to do it all over again, applying the lessons learned from his mistakes."

After two weeks had passed, Bill sat down to write a three-page letter to Eakeley, his thick, tight scrawl conveying a repressed fury and obvious chill. He crossed out several words, underlined others for emphasis, and signed off with an austere "Sincerely, Bill." The column had "a lot of good in it," Bill wrote on January 18. "I have no quarrel with what you said about personal misconduct." But he vehemently denied selling the Lincoln Bedroom, insisting "there was never a quid pro quo, and the evidence shows it." "If you really feel 'deep disappointment,' " Bill continued, "*then* either you don't know or you weigh things on very different scales than I do." He blamed the failure to fix Social Security on "the leadership of *both* parties," and he singled out Republican "intransigence" for the "excessive partisanship." After listing eight accomplishments in the previous year including trade bills, land conservation, sequencing the human genome, and passing a budget, Bill asserted, "I am *not* disappointed and partisanship has *not* paralyzed us." About Eakeley's observation about his old friend's yearning for a second chance at the presidency, Bill was conspicuously silent.

On the same day that Bill wrote Eakeley, he was working feverishly on his official farewell address, scheduled for a live broadcast at 8:00 p.m. In a scene evoking his first inaugural eve, he collected his aides around him in the Cabinet Room while he rewrote and read aloud. He didn't finish until fifteen minutes before airtime, when an aide took the computer disc and "sprinted away to get the words onto the TelePrompTer." His seven-minute speech, one of the shortest of his presidency, was a straightforward and un-remarkable recitation of statistics coupled with a warning that the United States "must not disentangle itself from the world."

The scene in the White House that night was chaotic, with friends, rel-atives, and staff members trying to help the Clintons pack. Aides had been working overtime to file Bill and Hillary's correspondence in acid-free blue boxes embossed with the presidential seal and to weed out unneeded pa-perwork. "We didn't have a shredder, so we put things in big bags," recalled Ann McCoy. An eighteen-wheeler carted the boxes away for storage in Lit-tle Rock until the completion of the presidential library.

Hillary was dividing her time between her new Senate duties and su-pervising the move from the Residence. Whenever she could, she stole a moment of quiet contemplation before the lunette window in the West Sit-ting Hall, her favorite spot in the White House. "She was mostly getting things done upstairs," recalled Terry McAuliffe. "He wouldn't pack. He was in the Oval Office working on everything." Ann McCoy had the feel-ing that Bill "was clinging. He stayed in the West Wing. He didn't sleep much." One cause for delay was Bill's tendency to tell stories about each item of memorabilia as it was being put away.

Among the guests in the Residence were Harry and Linda Thomason, along with Harry's brother, Danny (an optometrist from Arkansas), Tommy Caplan, and Dorothy and Hugh Rodham. Tony Rodham was staying in a hotel with a group of Russian colleagues from his still-developing hazelnut business, badgering his brother-in-law for a quick meet and greet. The Clintons had set up a long table in the Solarium that they piled with un-wanted items that had been sent to them over the years—basketballs, footed pajamas, glass bowls, parkas. "They turned it into a Goodwill store," said one observer of the scene. "They wanted to get packed, and Bill tried to unload this terrible stuff."

AFTER LITTLE IF ANY SLEEP, Bill went into overdrive on his last full day in office. That Friday morning, the White House made the stunning announcement that the President had struck a plea bargain with Robert Ray to avoid an indictment on perjury charges. Bill issued a four-paragraph statement admitting for the first time that in his Paula Jones deposition, "I tried to walk a fine line between acting lawfully and testifying falsely, but I now recognize that I did not fully accomplish this goal and that certain of my responses to questions about Ms. Lewinsky were false." At the same time, he agreed to pay a twenty-five-thousand-dollar fine to the Arkansas Bar Association, which suspended his law license for five years, instead of disbarring him permanently.

Since his meeting with Ray after Christmas, Bill had been intimately involved in the settlement negotiations, helping to shape "every clause, every word, and every comma." The thirty-two-page order from the Arkansas Supreme Court Committee on Professional Conduct stated unambiguously that "Mr. Clinton admits and acknowledges" that "he knowingly gave evasive and misleading answers" in his Jones deposition and "engaged in conduct that is prejudicial to the administration of justice." David Kendall tried to spin his client's words another way by insisting, "We have not admitted he lied."

The agreement brought the Independent Counsel's investigation to a conclusion and provoked considerable comment, much of it indignant. *The New York Times* mildly observed that "if only Mr. Clinton had owned up to his false testimony under oath earlier, he might have spared himself and the country a lot of pain," adding that he would doubtless continue "to try to portray himself as a victim rather than the prime creator of his legal troubles." Still, the *Times* concluded, "clearly the nation is better off for the fact that the legal detritus of the Clinton scandals was cleared out on the last day of the Clinton presidency." *USA Today* took a harder line, citing Bill's "hopelessly cracked ethical barometer" in his assertion that he had attempted to "walk a fine line" of legality. "How's that for a standard by which to judge presidents?" the paper asked. *The Wall Street Journal*, a longtime critic of the President's behavior, noted his "clear admission of guilt" and observed that he "would still be denying everything if it were not for his DNA on Monica's blue dress." But it was the Democratic mayor of Chicago, Richard Daley, who summed up the dismay of those even in his own party: "In *Esquire* magazine Bill Clinton came out right before the election and said the Republicans owed him an apology," Daley said. "Then the Friday before he leaves he said, 'I'm sorry I did it,' . . . and walks away. He left a lot of people disappointed."

Throughout the day and following night, Bill labored over piles of pardon applications. In his last visit to the Oval Office, Sidney Blumenthal found the President still packing up CDs, books, and golf clubs as moving men hauled out boxes. Bill asked his devoted aide whether there might be political repercussions if he granted pardons to Susan McDougal and Henry Cisneros. Blumenthal said he thought not.

Bill made no mention of Marc Rich, who was uppermost in his mind. That afternoon, he spoke again with Ehud Barak, and in the early evening Jack Quinn spent twenty minutes with the President, making his final plea. The Rich application had been managed by Beth Nolan, Quinn's successor as White House Counsel, who did not send it on to the Department of Justice—an extraordinary breach of customary procedure, which usually allows Justice months to review a pardon request, especially one from a high-profile fugitive accused of cheating the U.S. government out of nearly fifty million dollars. Quinn belatedly sent a letter to Deputy Attorney General Eric Holder justifying clemency for Rich. The Pardon Office at Justice said that Rich "did not qualify" for a pardon, and officials there warned that the prosecutors in New York City who worked on the Rich case would "go nuts" if the President granted one.

In advancing Rich's case, Jack Quinn "knew how to press Bill Clinton's buttons," said one senior White House official. "His story was that Rich was a business man who had done good deeds and was unfairly singled out by unscrupulous prosecutors." This version of events had "external validation" from Barak, Denise Rich, Beth Dozoretz, and others. That very day, Bill's plea bargain "reminded him of what he thought of prosecutors," added the senior official. Yet Bill also "considered himself a very good lawyer," said one of his close friends. "It is not as if someone pulled a fast one on him because he was tired," said the presidential advisor. "Clinton knew a lot about the case." He had been thinking about it for weeks and had even told Beth Dozoretz ten days earlier that he wanted to make it happen.

Beth Nolan, Bruce Lindsey, and Chief of Staff John Podesta all opposed the Rich pardon. "It is a legal doctrine that no one in law enforcement is supposed to help someone on the lam," said Abner Mikva. "Bruce told Clinton that." But Bill only recognized the side Quinn had presented, arguing he had faith in his former counsel's word. Shortly after his conversation with Quinn, Bill asked Nolan to check in with Eric Holder, who had received Quinn's letter about Rich just two days earlier. Holder had not consulted with the New York prosecutors, so didn't know the full details of the case. Lacking any strong objections from Holder, Nolan acceded to her boss's decision to pardon Rich. "Clinton made a controversial call on limited information," said the senior official. "He was making that call against a deadline, and he exercised bad judgment."

AS BILL CONTINUED to debate the names of other pardon applicants with his advisors, he took time out to tape his Saturday radio broadcast—an abbreviated version of the televised farewell address—which he had originally hoped to deliver live the next morning. He and Hillary then hosted a gathering of 250 people in the State Dining Room to celebrate the engagement of one of her aides, Kelly Craighead. The reception resembled a festive Hillaryland reunion. Afterward, a small group, including the Thomasons, Dorothy Rodham, and Tommy Caplan, had a buffet dinner in the Solarium amid the boxes and crates. "We've got to pack," said Hillary, as everybody polished off their apple cobbler. "We'll be up all night." Yet even then, Bill and Hillary "just wanted to keep strolling from room to room."

Harry Thomason organized a screening in the Family Theater of *State and Main*, a David Mamet satire about a Hollywood film crew's misadventures on location in a small New England town. Bill watched for a while but returned to the Oval Office and his unfinished pardon business. He didn't go back to the Residence to complete his packing until close to dawn. As he filled his suitcases, Danny Thomason—Bill's fellow chorister at the Immanuel Baptist Church in Little Rock—lay on a nearby bed while they reminisced. Linda Bloodworth-Thomason, who knew the Clintons and their ambitions as well as anyone, wrote a short note that she left in her room: "I'll be back."

Wearing a dark suit, white shirt, and blue tie, Bill left the Residence at 9:30 a.m. for his last walk to the Oval Office along the colonnade bordering the Rose Garden. He met with John Podesta, signed papers, made some phone calls, and wrote a letter for George Bush that he placed on the desk along with the note that the new president's father had left for Bill eight years earlier. It wasn't until 10:00 a.m. that the President completed his executive clemency list for release that day—140 pardons and thirty-six commuted prison sentences.

After taking a stroll in the cold drizzle with Chelsea to the Children's Garden next to the White House tennis court, Hillary joined Bill briefly in the Oval Office—now stripped of its tchotchkes and books—for a last look out the bay windows across the South Lawn. Hillary wore a royal blue–and–rust plaid suit reminiscent of her bold wardrobe choices in the early days.

The Clintons said a weepy farewell to the Residence staff in the State Dining Room before making their way to the Grand Foyer, where a combo of Marines in scarlet uniforms played sprightly tunes. White House butler Buddy Carter grabbed Hillary for an impromptu dance, and Bill cut in. As the First Couple had a last waltz around the marble entrance hall, reporters watched the sentimental moment through misted windows.

The Bushes and Cheneys arrived promptly at 10:25 a.m. for coffee and pastries with the Clintons and Gores. When it was nearly time to go, Bill was still sitting on the piano bench looking pensive and swaying to one of his favorite songs, "Our Love Is Here to Stay." Shortly before 11:00 a.m. the Clintons walked out of the White House for the final time as President and First Lady. "Bye," Bill said, before climbing into the presidential limousine.

On the platform outside the Capitol's West Front, Bill shook hands, waved, and chatted while Gore stood quietly in his place. After taking the oath of office at noon, George W. Bush delivered a crisp fifteen-minute inaugural address. It had begun to rain as George and Laura Bush entered the Capitol's Statuary Hall for the traditional postinaugural lunch.

"In the past, they shook hands, the [former] president went to a helicopter and that was it," remarked Chicago mayor Richard Daley. "This was different. . . . It was really different, really unusual. . . . That's [Clinton's] style. He wanted two or three more parties."

Instead of an inconspicuous helicopter ride, the Clintons opted for a motorcade with a media contingent to record their progress through the streets of Washington out to Andrews Air Force Base. At the airport, Bill observed the custom of reviewing a Marine honor guard and listened to his last "Hail to the Chief," followed by a twenty-one-gun salute. But he departed from tradition by staging a noisy farewell rally in an airplane hangar attended by his cabinet officers and thousands of friends, supporters, and former employees. Among the well-wishers were Tony Rodham and his Russian business associates, who would finally get their promised handshake with Bill.

"You see that sign there that says, 'Please don't go'?" Bill shouted. "I left the White House, but I'm still here. We're not any of us going anywhere. . . . You've got a senator over here who will be a voice for you." As he launched into another lengthy speech about himself and his presidency, all the television networks showed a split screen—the new president dining with members of Congress and the extraordinary scene being created by the ex-President. Bill then plunged into the crowd for extended hugging and handshaking, clearly exhausted, running on the fumes of adoration.

Ronald Reagan's exit, by contrast, had been simple and swift. He did his final review of the honor guard at Andrews, "stepping as always in sync with his escort," wrote Reagan biographer Edmund Morris. Only one cabinet officer, John Herrington, turned up, "but there was a large crowd of ordinary Americans and their children." His military review completed, Reagan climbed the stairs of his aircraft and waved.

It was not until 2:57 p.m.—one hundred minutes after the time of his arrival at Andrews—that Bill Clinton's Boeing 747, now designated Special Air Mission 28000 rather than Air Force One, took off for the forty-minute flight to New York. The crowd onboard included Hillary, Chelsea, Buddy (Socks remained in Washington with Betty Currie), Vernon Jordan, Harry Thomason, Terry McAuliffe, and most of Bill's senior White House staff. They all gathered in a conference room, where a steward served them cake and champagne as a photographer clicked away. "It was a surreal feeling," said Terry McAuliffe. "The President hadn't slept in days. But it was festive. It would be the last time we would be on this bird for a while."

In TWA's Hangar 12 at Kennedy Airport, another few thousand fans awaited, and Bill obliged them with more variations on his farewell speech. Since this was now her home turf, Hillary spoke, too, at greater length than her husband but mainly about him. "I have watched my husband for eight years give his all," she said.

The Clintons and a small entourage climbed into Hillary's van for the ride to Chappaqua, and the minute the door closed Bill "was out solid, snoring," McAuliffe recalled. They attended a brief welcoming ceremony at the Chappaqua firehouse and that night had a small dinner at home. McAuliffe left the next morning, while Hillary stayed to help unpack books and boxes before flying to Washington later in the day.

McAuliffe returned to Chappaqua on Monday to find Bill "all alone with Oscar the steward. It was weird. She was in the Senate." The two friends had lunch in a little café. It was clear, McAuliffe said, that "he was lonely already."

ON THE DAY HE LEFT OFFICE, Bill Clinton had a 68 percent approval rating in several public-opinion polls. In the following weeks, he lost nearly all that goodwill in the backlash over the Clintons' messy departure from the White House. Their financial-disclosure forms revealed that they walked away with $190,027 worth of furniture, china, flatware, art, and other gifts, nearly half of it acquired in their final year. It also turned out that they took some property that actually belonged to the permanent White House collection. To Maureen Dowd, they "seemed more like grifters than public servants." Michael Kramer of the New York *Daily News* branded them "world-class users." *Saturday Night Live* lampooned them in a skit, and members of Congress weighed in with criticism.

In an effort to contain the damage that was clouding Hillary's first weeks in the Senate, the Clintons rapidly backtracked. In early February, they agreed to pay $85,966 to reimburse everyone who had given them gifts in their last year in office "to remove any suggestion of impropriety." Several days later, they also sent back eleven items worth $28,000, including rugs, furniture, and lamps, that were from the White House collection.

But a far bigger furor erupted over Bill's last-minute pardons. It took a couple of days for the magnitude of the pardon binge to sink in. At first, the press simply noted the inclusion of friends and relatives—Susan McDougal and Bill's brother, Roger—as well as former administration figures such as Henry Cisneros and celebrities such as heiress Patty Hearst Shaw, who had been convicted of bank robbery after she had been kidnapped by a group of political radicals in the 1970s. News accounts also mentioned prominent exclusions, primarily Webster Hubbell. Hillary's former law partner hadn't applied for a pardon but had received signals from the White House that one would be forthcoming. "It was a personal decision not to pardon me," he said later. Watching the Clintons leave the White House on inauguration day, Hubbell's daughter Caroline had bitterly observed, "It has always been about them. . . . When push comes to shove, it is *still* about them."

Within forty-eight hours of Bill's departure from Washington, the Marc Rich pardon hit the headlines, and the personal and political machinations behind it became evident. "You don't pardon a traitor who has paid no price at all," said former senator Bob Kerrey. "Something got in the way of good judgment." The law-enforcement community was particularly incensed about Bill's deliberate strategy of circumventing the review processes of the FBI and Justice Department. "I worked a long time on that case," said Rudy Giuliani, who had led the Rich prosecution in the early eighties. "What the President did was an absolute outrage." Mary Jo White, the U.S. attorney in New York, said that the Rich case was one of a number that raised "serious law enforcement concerns."

Editorial comment was scathing. *The Washington Post* condemned Bill's "scandalous present to Mr. Rich" that "diminished the integrity and grandeur of the pardon power. . . . What a way to leave." *The New York Times* decried Bill's "shocking abuse of presidential power."

The egregious nature of the Rich pardon—his status as a fugitive, the gravity of his alleged crimes, and the mingling of the Clintons' quest for financial support with the exigencies of American foreign policy—drew attention to Bill's manipulation of the pardoning process. FBI Director Louis Freeh was "stunned by the fact that neither the FBI nor the Attorney General nor the Department of Justice was ever consulted about a single one of them. . . . Giving reprieves and pardons out almost as party favors and to some of those closest to him wasn't what the founding fathers had in mind. . . . Bill Clinton has now tainted the old and honorable tradition of presidential mercy . . . by his penchant for excess."

The revelations about the Rodham brothers' lobbying for pardons did not emerge until late February, sparking another wave of what *The New York Times* called "public revulsion over the former President's decisions" and adding to "the disturbing impression that Mr. Clinton's actions may have been influenced by friendships, politics, and financial contributions."

Both Bill and Hillary denied knowing that substantial six-figure fees were involved and demanded that the money be returned. But as *Time*'s Margaret Carlson pointed out, "It defies credulity to think that as Hughie was brokering the deal in the President's house, right under his nose, Bill Clinton thought his brother-in-law was working pro bono. . . . Who helps scum for free, anyway?"

Hillary scrambled to distance herself from the newest scandals, saying she was "heartbroken," "saddened," and "disappointed" over Hugh's acceptance of the fees. She said she had no involvement in any of her husband's pardons, although she admitted that "information was coming to me, information was passed on. . . . People would hand me envelopes. I would just pass them on. You know, I would not have any reason to look into them." When asked about Tony's role in the pardon of the carnival operators a year earlier, Hillary said—erroneously—that he had "a personal relationship with them. He was not paid."

The uproar over the Clintons' exit rivaled the reaction to the Lewinsky affair. Bill remained unrepentant about all of his eleventh-hour decisions, and he continued to insist that his judgments—especially on the Rich case—had been on the merits. He later said that the only regret he had about the Rich pardon was that "it was terrible politics. It wasn't worth the damage to my reputation." For her part, Hillary blamed the "culture of investigation" that "followed us out the door of the White House . . . generating hundreds of news stories over several months." The "full-blown flap" over their excessive gifts, she said, was due to "clerical errors."

As the storm eventually passed, both Bill and Hillary knew they could rely on the passage of time to help them repair the damage. They were more battle hardened than ever, ready for the long march back to Pennsylvania Avenue. Fortified by the acquisition of vast wealth to augment their high profiles and political connections, they had become a new and more powerful entity, Clinton Incorporated. Their mission remained the same: high political office, a Democratic agenda, the accumulation of power, and the pursuit of the Clinton legacy for the history books. To be sure, the principals had swapped positions. Bill had become chairman, giving up day-to-day control of the enterprise, and Hillary had taken over as CEO. But they continued to operate as force multipliers—through it all, they were still two for the price of one.

Acknowledgments

——

As a biographer living in Washington for the past sixteen years, I was riveted by the Clinton presidency, but always as a spectator, not a chronicler. Various book projects held the center of my attention, so I relied on friends in journalism to keep me posted on developments behind the headlines. The most consistently penetrating perspective came from my *Vanity Fair* colleague Marjorie Williams, who wrote about powerful figures in Washington with preternatural clarity and wit. She was a dear friend who died of cancer in January 2005, way too young, at age forty-seven. I have dedicated this book to her memory by way of thanks for her generous insights, even in her last weeks, when she was giving me ideas for sources and lines of inquiry into what had by then become my latest biographical subject.

In the spring of 2004, my editor at Random House, Jonathan Karp, proposed that I write a dual biography of Bill and Hillary Clinton, focusing on their years in the White House, to be published in the fall of 2007. I had just completed my book about Jack and Jackie Kennedy, and Jon thought I could apply my knowledge of presidential relationships to another White House couple. He also recognized that as the primaries approached, the Clinton marriage would be of paramount importance in evaluating Hillary's candidacy, and that it would be impossible to understand one Clinton without factoring in the other. I was exceedingly fortunate that when Jon left to become editor in chief of Twelve, Kate Medina, one of the most respected editors in the business, took over my project and instantly grasped how it should unfold.

Over the past three years, I have analyzed the extensive written record and interviewed numerous Clinton insiders. My aim was to take apart a familiar story and tell it in a fresh and revealing way: identifying patterns and juxtapositions not evident at the time, reconnecting the dots to gain a new understanding of tumultuous events, and recapturing the high emotions—excitement as well as dismay—of the period with the detachment that time and distance can bring.

Bill and Hillary Clinton regard themselves as students of history, but they seem determined to scrub their own and to downplay the importance of much of what they said and did when they lived at 1600 Pennsylvania Avenue. Both Clintons are deeply invested in their political sequel—she because she feels she deserves the presidency after many years in his shadow, he because he believes it will embellish his legacy and purify Clintonism—so the past is very much alive for them. It frames and marks them, and they cannot escape it.

Neither Bill nor Hillary Clinton was willing to be interviewed for this book because, as their lawyer and agent, Bob Barnett, explained to me in April 2005, "they don't want to choose one person to talk to. There's nothing in it for them, and they have already put out their own stories." Fortunately, many of Bill and Hillary's closest friends and associates felt otherwise and shared their memories and insights about a relationship they observed in a variety of settings; others had passing but vivid encounters that showed intriguing aspects of the couple's dynamic. Roughly a quarter of those I interviewed requested anonymity, and I thank everyone, named and unnamed, for their wisdom and knowledge:

Linda Aaker, Henry Aaron, Eleanor Acheson, Kay Allaire, Bob Armstrong, Pamela Bailey, Scott Barnes, Bob Barnett, William Baumol, Andrew and Darcie Baylis, Lisa Bedell, Betsy Blass, Bruce Bockman, Taylor Branch, Max and Ellen Brantley, Rita Braver, Dale Bumpers, Ken Burns, Barbara Butler, Gloria Cabe, George Campbell, Tommy Caplan, James Chace, Ellen Chesler, Henry Cisneros, Wayne Cranford, Ann Crittenden, Walter Cronkite, Lloyd Cutler, Leo Daly, Douglas and Priscilla Eakeley, Mary Mel French, David Friedman, Bill Galston, Lucy and Sheldon Hackney, Stephen Hess, Margo Howard, Martin Indyk, Ann Jordan, Hamilton Jordan, Michael Kahn, Mickey Kantor, Rick Kaplan, Alison Kitay, Polly Kraft, Anthony Lake, David Leopoulos, Eric Liu, Ellen Lovell, Gene Lyons, Ed Markey, Chris Marlowe, Capricia Marshall, Kati Marton, Terry McAuliffe, Ann McCoy, Mike McCurry, Mack McLarty, Sir Christopher Meyer, Abner Mikva, Bill and Suzanne Miller, Betty Monkman, Beadle Moore, Dee Dee Myers, Lee Auchincloss Niven, Bernie Nussbaum, Beth Nyhus, Lawrence O'Donnell, Jeffrey Orseck, Ann Pincus, Roger Porter, Eden and Jerry Rafshoon, Bruce Reed, Robert Reich, Tunkie Riley, Sandy Robertson, Robert Rubin, Cindy Samuels, Bernard Schwartz, Juan Sepulveda, Donna Shalala, Tom Siebert, Cliff Sloan, James Steinberg, Ann Stock, Rose Styron, Eric Tarloff, Susan Thomases, Lionel Tiger, Jeffrey Toobin, Mary Tydings, Laura Tyson, Benedicte Valentiner, Harry Ward, Claude Wasserstein, Ted Widmer, and Anthony Williams.

I also received invaluable assistance from journalists who covered the Clinton Administration, including my friend Martha Sherrill, who shared notes of her interviews with Clinton family members and friends during the postelection transition and the early months of the administration. Heartfelt thanks to all for giving me so much intelligent guidance: Joel Achenbach, Jonathan Alter, Jim Barnes, Michael Barone, Ann Blackman, Gloria Borger, Peter Boyer, Tom Brokaw, Tina

Brown, Elizabeth Drew, Howard Fineman, Brit and Kim Hume, Peter Kaplan, David Maraniss, Chris Matthews, Lance Morrow, Pat O'Brien, Maureen Orth, Charlie Peters, Victoria Pope, Todd Purdum, Sally Quinn, Bennett Roth, Tim Russert, Walter Shapiro, Stuart Taylor, Evan Thomas, Elsa Walsh, Susan Watters, Jacob Weisberg, and Adam Zagorin.

Other friends, family members, and acquaintances helped me in a variety of ways—with ideas, moral support, and gracious hospitality: Tom Austin, Peter and Amy Bernstein, Clara Bingham, Hayley Bower, Geraldine Brooks, Bernard and Joan Carl, Graydon Carter, Bob Colacello, Pat and Bill Compton, Mary Copeland, Jim Dunning, David Goodrich, Nancy Hereford, Robert Higdon, Walter Isaacson, Marguerite Kelly, Jim Ketchum, Leanna Landsman, Wayne Lawson, Sharon Lorenzo, Phyllis Magrab, Susan Magrino, Catherine Manning, Janet Maslin, Alyne Massey, Sandy Meehan, David Michaelis, Penne Korth Peacock, Ginny Rosenblatt, Jim and Cindy Rowbotham, Bruce Sanford, Francesca Stanfill, Will Swift, Dick and Ginny Thornburgh, Dan Yergin, and Bill Young.

All biographers—whether writing about events from centuries past or recent decades—must rely on the groundbreaking work of those who preceded them: the newspaper and magazine journalists who write contemporaneous accounts, the biographers who dig deeper into the story, and the close associates of the biographical subject who transform their experiences into memoirs. For the Clinton years, the most perceptive insiders-turned-authors were David Gergen, Robert Reich, Robert Rubin, George Stephanopoulos, Strobe Talbott, and Michael Waldman. Stephanopoulos, in particular, in both his memoir and his writing for *Newsweek,* displayed a raw candor that he later carefully masked after becoming a television talk-show moderator. Clinton political consultant Dick Morris's first book, *Behind the Oval Office,* was a detailed and straightforward account of a crucial period in the Clinton presidency, largely free of the animus that colored his later writing.

Bill and Hillary Clinton's memoirs provided helpful timelines and official interpretations, but offered little about the inner workings of their White House. It was far more productive to mine the vast archive of daily and weekly journalism, especially during the 1992 campaign and first months of the presidency, to find their less guarded and more valuable comments. Among those who covered the Clintons on a regular basis, Margaret Carlson, Eleanor Clift, Maureen Dowd, and Ruth Marcus could be counted on to capture the authentic moments.

Veteran journalist Bob Woodward's three books about the Clinton years illuminated aspects of the presidency that escaped the headlines, as did the work of Elizabeth Drew, Gail Sheehy, James Stewart, and Jeffrey Toobin. Reporters and columnists David Broder, John Harris, Michael Isikoff, Haynes Johnson, Joe Klein, Howard Kurtz, and David Maraniss expanded their knowledge into well-crafted volumes focusing on different facets of policy and politics. British journalist Andrew Morton, who became famous for his as-told-to book on Princess Diana, did the same for Monica Lewinsky, adding many important details to the story of her affair with the President.

The William J. Clinton Presidential Center, an impressive work of architecture and an intriguing museum, offers little to writers about the Clinton years. The papers of Bill and Hillary were made available only by application under the Freedom of Information Act in January 2006, subject to approval by Bill's longtime aide Bruce Lindsey, who by law can reject anything that "reveals internal White House deliberations." As archivist Richard Stalcup explained to me during my visit to the library in March 2005, "The President has the discretion to exclude all personal material, along with anything political," which in the Clinton White House covered just about everything. He advised me that there would be little likelihood of receiving any useful documents—correspondence, memos, daily office diaries, telephone logs, memoranda of conversations—prior to my spring 2007 deadline. Indeed, as of this past March, no substantive FOIA requests had been filled (nor, in some cases, even acknowledged), and *Newsday* described the library as "Little Rock's Fort Knox."

For official documents, the Clinton Library's website is less user-friendly than the online edition of the Weekly Compilation of Presidential Documents, a pilot project administered by the National Archives and Records Administration (NARA) and the Government Printing Office (GPO). The search engine on the NARA-GPO website is fast, accurate, and comprehensive, providing not only the texts of speeches and press conferences but also the President's weekly schedules, a vital guide to constructing chronologies.

I am most grateful to Liz Moynihan, the widow of Senator Daniel Patrick Moynihan, for giving me access to her late husband's papers at the Library of Congress, and to archivist John Hanes for alerting me when they were ready for review. The Moynihan memoranda of conversations during the Clinton administration opened an essential window into relations between the Clintons and Congress, particularly during the debate over health-care reform, and provided a fresh take on the atmosphere during the impeachment crisis.

Mike Hill, who must be the fastest and most resourceful researcher on the planet, helped not only with the Moynihan archive, but in finding and organizing some seven thousand pages of material—articles from newspapers, magazines, and academic journals—into twenty-eight three-ring binders. He also checked the facts in my manuscript, bringing his eagle eye to every page, and prepared the first draft of my source notes. Mike's friendship and scholarship have been a wonderful blessing, and I am endlessly thankful for his upbeat spirit.

Kate Medina and I had been acquaintances for years, and I had long admired her work at Random House, so it was an enormous pleasure to experience firsthand her astute judgment, keen intelligence, and constant encouragement. I was also lucky to work with editor Robin Rolewicz, a rising star at Random House, who diplomatically monitored my progress when I went underground for a year to write the manuscript, then became a wonderful advocate for the book as she efficiently orchestrated the publishing schedule. Kate's assistant, Abby Plesser, was also a delight to work with.

For the second time I have benefited from the wisdom and enthusiastic support of Random House president and publisher Gina Centrello, and the great instincts of Tom Perry, senior vice president and deputy publisher. Sally Marvin, director of publicity, was a smart strategist, and I much appreciated the work of her assistant, Kristina Miller, along with publicity manager Dana Maxson. Laura Goldin conducted yet another thorough and perceptive legal review. Thanks as well to Tim Mennel, a scrupulous copy editor; production editor Steve Messina, who handled my stream of e-mails with good cheer; art director Carole Lowenstein; sales director Jack Perry; and rights manager Rachel Bernstein; jacket designer Robbin Schiff; and book designer Barbara M. Bachman.

Photo researcher Carol Poticny made an impressively wide sweep to find evocative images, taking the time to survey not only the well-known photographers and agencies but also local newspapers around the country. She immediately understood that I envision the picture section as a photo essay, and she worked hard to find shots to fit into that scheme. I am also grateful to Shannon Swenson of Stream Studio Web Architects for imaginatively updating my website.

Max Hirshfeld, the photographer responsible for my author photograph, is not only a maestro behind the camera, he also knows how to create a relaxing atmosphere for a nervous subject with his wonderful wit and easy manner. Many thanks as well to Rob Conner for doing wonders with his makeup kit.

It is a great bonus to have a friend since college days still with me as counselor and champion. Amanda Urban has been my agent for all five of my biographies, and once again she offered an incisive assessment of my manuscript, along with shrewd advice on the marketing and timing of its publication.

My three dear children are busy pursuing their careers in distant cities—Kirk in St. Louis, Lisa in London, and David in Los Angeles—yet they all managed to give me not only their love and support but an adult appreciation of my writing. I knew I could always share with them the thrill of my discoveries and count on them to buck me up when my task seemed overwhelming. My daughter also filled the unusual role of source as I quizzed her about her knowledge of Chelsea Clinton from the first inaugural, when Lisa attended Chelsea's party at the White House, through their high school years.

Stephen, my beloved husband of a quarter century, has been by my side every minute of this project, believing in me and the value of my labors, even as they occupied me virtually nonstop for three years. For the third time he produced an inspired title, a four-word crystallization of the Clinton marriage and the theme of my book. His experience as a magazine editor during the Clinton years—when he ran *National Journal* as well as *U.S. News & World Report*—brought an unrivaled point of view. And thanks to his repeated exhortation, I constructed my most detailed outline, which (as he predicted) smoothed the task of writing and helped me beat my deadline by more than a month. He devoted two vacations and many evenings to editing my manuscript, yet again applying his exceptional talents to my words. Because I have sung his praises in five acknowledgments, a reader might be tempted to dismiss my enthusiasm as a wifely indulgence, so I'll give one of his former reporters, Julie Mason of the *Houston Chronicle*, the last word in summing up Steve's gifts: "He is one of the loveliest, most writerly editors I've ever worked for," Mason told *The Washington Post*. "He touches your copy and just makes it shine."

Sally Bedell Smith
Washington, D.C.
JULY 2007

Source Notes

This book is based on interviews with more than 160 people—including numerous close Clinton friends and political colleagues—who had firsthand knowledge of Bill and Hillary. Thirty-five of those individuals asked to remain anonymous, and despite their significant contributions they have been omitted from these source notes at their request. Any anonymous quotations not specifically cited below are from my confidential interviews. Other confidential quotes from trustworthy publications are specifically cited.

I read thousands of articles in newspapers, magazines, and academic journals, scores of interviews with the Clintons and their circle conducted by print and broadcast journalists, along with transcripts of less formal exchanges, more than five hundred of Bill and Hillary's speeches and comments at symposia, and the vast trove of legal documents from the numerous investigations of the Clintons. I also analyzed sixty-five books, including the memoirs of Bill and Hillary and of major participants in their administration, along with studies of foreign and domestic policy and examinations of political and legal issues. The perspectives of close observers were invaluable, and in a number of instances I interviewed the authors to expand on points they had made in their books.

In addition, I had access to unpublished interviews and journals offering intimate scenes from the Clinton marriage that illuminated the dynamic of their relationship. I was also exceedingly fortunate to be the first biographer given access to the papers of the late senator from New York Daniel Patrick Moynihan. His memoranda of conversations were especially helpful in explaining Hillary Clinton's management of her ill-fated health-care plan.

Listed below are abbreviations for frequently cited publications and manuscript collections.

FREQUENTLY CITED BOOKS

    ML: Bill Clinton, *My Life*

    LH: Hillary Rodham Clinton, *Living History*

  FiHC: David Maraniss, *First in His Class*

    OO: Dick Morris, *Behind the Oval Office*

    MS: Andrew Morton, *Monica's Story*

  ATH: George Stephanopoulos, *All Too Human*

    BS: James B. Stewart, *Blood Sport*

ARCHIVES

  DPM: Senator Daniel Patrick Moynihan Papers, Library of Congress, Washington, D.C.

  PPP: *Public Papers of the President: William Jefferson Clinton.* 1993–2001

PUBLICATIONS

  NYT: *The New York Times*

  WP: *The Washington Post*

INTRODUCTION

  ix "The truth is": *Newsweek*, March 9, 1992.

  xi beige upholstered seats: E-mail from Hayley Bower, Office of the Curator, White House, Feb. 7, 2007.

  xi "that woman, Miss Lewinsky": *PPP*, 1998, book 1, p. 111.

  xi "vast right-wing conspiracy": Matt Lauer interview with Hillary Clinton, *Today*, Jan. 27, 1998.

  xii "resurfaced following the Monica revelation": Mary Mel French interview.

  xii *Something to Talk About*: Author's screening of film.

  xii "Bill and Hillary were completely silent": Mary Mel French interview.

  xii "she was trying": Ibid.

  xiii "force multipliers": Martha Sherrill interview with Dorothy Rodham.

  xiii "The Clintons are complicated": Mary Mel French interview.

  xiii "Eleanor Roosevelt was strong": Kati Marton, *Hidden Power: Presidential Marriages That Shaped Our Recent History*, p. 306.

  xiv "Their lives had been so entwined": Mickey Kantor interview.

  xiv "force of nature": Hillary Clinton interview with Barbara Walters, ABC News, transcript, June 8, 2003.

  xiv "Iron John misty": *NYT*, Jan. 14, 1993.

  xiv "girly man": Gene Lyons interview.

  xiv "quarter inch of softness": *Time*, June 9, 1997.

  xiv "Once we were talking about an article": Laura Tyson interview.

  xv "For six months": Tunkie Riley interview.

xv   "hall monitor": *NYT*, May 18, 1992.

xv   "Salvation Army sister": *WP*, March 3, 1993.

xv   "Nothing too Hillary": *NYT*, May 18, 1992.

xv   "She reminds most men": *WP*, Jan. 15, 1995.

xv   "Unthinking emotion": Gail Sheehy, *Hillary's Choice*, p. 42.

xv   "We can't cash this": Ann McCoy interview.

xv   "You get a hug from Bill": Ibid.

xv   "You can see her sometimes": *NYT*, Jan. 20, 1997.

xv   "attuned to the glory": *The New Yorker*, Sept. 18, 2006.

xv   "obsessive personality": Hillary Rodham Clinton, *Living History*, p. 223.

xv   "I might as well try": *The New Yorker*, May 30, 1994.

xv   "She could be moody": Ann Stock interview.

xvi   "She just does everything she has to do": *Newsweek*, April 11, 1994.

xvi   *College Bowl*: *Time*, Jan. 4, 1993.

xvi   *Life* magazine: Ibid.

xvi   first student commencement speaker: *WP*, Jan. 12, 1993; *Time*, Jan. 4, 1993.

xvi   only twenty-seven women in a class of 235: *LH*, p. 44.

xvi   Early in her second year: *FiHC*, p. 246.

xvi   anti–Vietnam War activities: Robert Reich, *Locked in the Cabinet*, p. 15.

xvi   "It didn't take": *FiHC*, p. 246.

xvi   "staring": Ibid., p. 247.

xvi   "impressed and stunned": *ML*, p. 181.

xvi   "sense of strength": Ibid.

xvi   "With Hillary there was no arm's length": Ibid., p. 184.

xvi   "I have to have somebody": Virginia Kelley, *Leading with My Heart*, p. 191.

xvi   "big gangly guy": *Talk*, Sept. 1999.

xvi   "vitality that seemed to shoot": *LH*, p. 52.

xvi   "which is perfect": *City Journal*, June 18, 2003.

xvii   "wasn't afraid of me": Sheehy, p. 76.

xvii   "I don't do spontaneity": Ibid., p. 367; Eleanor Clift noted that "spontaneity has never been Hillary's style." *Newsweek*, July 20, 1992.

xvii   "Someday you'll eat your words": Bernie Nussbaum interview.

xvii   "The rumors about him": Max Brantley interview.

xvii   "recklessly chasing women": Hamilton Jordan, *No Such Thing as a Bad Day*, p. 191.

xvii   "I want a div-or-or-or-orce": *FiHC*, p. 394.

xvii   "serious threat": Sheehy, p. 182. Sheehy quoted Betsey Wright as saying, "There was only one serious threat to that marriage—the only serious relationship he had with another woman."

xviii   close to separating: *FiHC*, p. 450.

xviii   "I thought he had conquered it": *Talk*, Sept. 1999.

xviii   rumors that she was a lesbian: Frank Rich wrote, "Like every woman who challenges the male status quo, she was immediately rumored to be a lesbian," *NYT Magazine*, June 13, 1993; *Esquire*, Aug. 1993.

xviii   lack of interest in her appearance: *LH*, p. 110; Kelley, p. 199.

xviii   "Herc and the girls": *Washingtonian*, Jan. 1993.

xviii   "Hillaryland": *WP*, Oct. 30, 1992.

xviii   "she was really into her women friends": Martha Sherrill interview.

xviii   "Madeleine connects with HRC": Private journal.

xix   "those shiny divas": *NYT*, Feb. 9, 2000.

xix   only First Couple to be fingerprinted: Bob Woodward, *Shadow: Five Presidents and the Legacy of Watergate*, p. 318.

xix private quarters searched: Ibid., pp. 319–21.

xix "begin thinking about leaving": DPM, Memcon of Senator Daniel P. Moynihan, Sept. 16, 1998. The call took place Sept. 15.

xix "never entered my mind": Bill Clinton interview with Dan Rather, March 31, 1999, PPP, 1999, book 1, p. 481.

xxi "It is fascinating . . . how he and his wife": Bill Clinton interview with Terry Gross, on *Fresh Air*, NPR, June 24, 2004.

xxi "That's right, but Eleanor": *FiHC*, p. 343.

xxii For the purposes of clarity: Skip Rutherford, a friend of the Clintons from Arkansas, told Martha Sherrill that kids called her Hillary and that many called her "Hill" and called Bill "Bill." Nobody called Hillary "Mrs. Clinton." Martha Sherrill interview with Skip Rutherford.

xxii their shared love of politics: Tom Siebert, a friend of Bill Clinton since college, said of Bill and Hillary, "Politics is his passion, and it is who she is. It is in her DNA as it is in his."

CHAPTER ONE

3 "John Kennedy said": *Time*, Jan. 4, 1993.

3 "Our vote was a vindication": NYT, July 3, 1978.

3 "working unit": *NYT Magazine*, Jan. 20, 1993.

3 "Billary": WP, Jan. 20, 1993.

4 When Bill began thinking about running: ML, p. 364.

4 Bill picked up softness in that support: Michael Barone interview.

4 Bill had been bored with his job: John Brummett, *Highwire: From the Backroads to the Beltway—The Education of Bill Clinton*, p. 17.

4 "The voters were getting tired": Michael Barone interview.

5 "less than compelling": *Time*, Nov. 16, 1992.

5 he advocated ideological flexibility: *New York*, Nov. 4, 1991.

5 "mild-mannered policy wonk": David Maraniss, *The Clinton Enigma: A Four-and-a-Half-Minute Speech Reveals This President's Entire Life*, p. 93.

5 "cut the crap": Joe Klein, *The Natural: The Misunderstood Presidency of Bill Clinton*, p. 86; ML, p. 368.

5 "do everything we can to destroy you": Bob Woodward, *The Agenda: Inside the Clinton White House*, p. 393; ML, p. 368.

5 Hillary took this threat: Woodward, *Agenda*, p. 393.

5 "Bill Clinton started telling": Roger Porter interview.

6 "I never heard from or saw Roger Porter": ML, p. 369. Bill's story about Porter also suffers from its own internal contradiction. In *My Life*, he said he "liked President Bush" and found him "nowhere near as ruthless or right-wing as most of the Reaganites," but two paragraphs later he describes the supposed threat from Porter as a message "he had been designated to deliver," by the Bush White House, a deeply ruthless operation bent on destroying Bill Clinton. ML, p. 368.

6 "to talk process": *Time*, Dec. 21, 1992.

6 also received advice: Robert E. Rubin, *In an Uncertain World: Tough Choices from Wall Street to Washington*, p. 111.

6 who several years earlier had disclosed: *Newsweek*, Dec. 22, 1997.

6 "You have handled it the right way": Henry Cisneros interview.

6 "Hillary and I have talked about it": Beadle Moore interview.

6 "pervasiveness": *Newsweek*, Nov./Dec. 1992 (special election issue).

6   "Our relationship has not been perfect": *NYT*, Dec. 27, 1991; *FiHC*, p. 461; *ML*, p. 372.

6   "Specificity is a character issue this year": *New York*, Jan. 20, 1992.

7   "You're always perfect": *New York*, March 16, 1992.

7   "Billy Vote Clinton": *WP*, July 12, 1992.

7   "carried springtime": Benjamin R. Barber, *The Truth of Power: Intellectual Affairs in the Clinton White House*, p. 39.

7   "like a helium balloon": Terry McAuliffe interview.

7   "He is always evangelizing": Max Brantley interview.

7   "full intensity Clinton": Reich, p. 239.

7   more suited to a pianist or a surgeon: *LH*, p. 54.

7   hands in an antlike clasp: Ken Burns interview.

7   "basic, reflexive moves": Barber, p. 37, quoting Joe Klein in *Primary Colors: A Novel of Politics* (New York: Random House, 2006).

8   "How's your house": Sandy Robertson interview.

8   "He wasn't pretending": Jonathan Alter interview.

8   "powerful impression": *The New Yorker*, April 5, 1993.

8   "When you are talking to him": Anthony Williams interview.

8   "He has the narcissist's gift": Barber, p. 215; Dee Dee Myers said in an interview: "He would have a conversation in front of you with himself, not a conversation with you."

8   "After he had framed his policy": Eric Liu interview.

8   intensity of crowds was "overwhelming": Sidney Blumenthal, *The Clinton Wars*, p. 688.

9   more naturally reserved: Author's observations at the home of Leo and Grega Daly, June 5, 2006; Jordan, p. 190.

9   "holding court": Webster Hubbell, *Friends in High Places: Our Journey from Little Rock to Washington, D.C.*, p. 13.

9   Hillary sat patiently backstage: *Time*, Jan. 4, 1993.

9   "For Bill Clinton politics": Terry McAuliffe interview.

9   "Bill's catholic tastes": Max Brantley interview.

9   With her friends and staff: *Mirabella*, May 1992.

9   "I'm not a good actress": *Talk*, Sept. 1999.

9   Watching her walk into a Washington party: Author's observations at the home of Roger Altman and Jurate Kazickas, Feb. 13, 1995.

9   "her business face": Martha Sherrill interview with Hugh Rodham.

10   Dorothy Rodham said she pushed: Martha Sherrill interview with Dorothy Rodham.

10   dropped "g"s that belied: *WP*, Oct. 30, 1992.

10   "fugues into technocratic prose": *NYT*, July 12, 1992.

10   "Men can show emotion": Mickey Kantor interview.

10   "found himself handling poisonous snakes": *Time*, Feb. 3, 1992.

10   The first such tale: *Newsweek*, Feb. 8, 1999; *ATH*, p. 54.

10   "We have to destroy her story": *Newsweek*, Feb. 8, 1999; *ATH*, pp. 54–55.

11   "I wish I could find a way": *Time*, Jan. 27, 1992.

11   The report named five: *ML*, p. 360.

11   "less breezy" and "more agitated": *ATH*, p. 56.

11   The Clintons vigorously denied: *Newsweek*, Nov./Dec. 1992 (special election issue).

11   "practically giddy": Ibid.

11   But George Stephanopoulos was disquieted: *ATH*, pp. 57, 68.

11   "six figure amount": Gennifer Flowers, *Passion and Betrayal*, p. 108.

11   "My 12-Year Affair with Bill Clinton": *Star*, Feb. 4, 1992.

11   "I never felt he was struggling": Ibid.

11 "retired": *Star*, Feb. 11, 1992.
11 the exact language: Woodward, *Shadow*, p. 259.
11 "If they ever hit you": *Star*, Feb. 4, 1992.
11 "explaining, you know": *Newsweek*, Feb. 9, 1998.
12 "Republican harassment": *Star*, Feb. 4, 1992.
12 "He would seize on incorrect details": *Newsweek*, Sept. 21, 1998.
12 "a different man": Ibid.
12 "there was no scorn": *Newsweek*, Mar. 30, 1992.
12 "trashy supermarket" journalism: *New York*, July 13, 1992.
12 "a relationship . . . that I should not have had": *ML*, p. 387.
12 she was "frightened": *Time*, Feb. 3, 1992.
12 "clearly . . . knows her as more than": *The New Republic*, Feb. 17, 1992.
12 "assumed without asking": *Newsweek*, Feb. 2, 1998.
12 Even so, Bill apologized: *Newsweek*, Feb. 10, 1992.
12 "acts like" a Mafioso: *Star*, Feb. 11, 1992.
13 "Anybody who knows my husband": *The New Yorker*, May 30, 1994.
13 Bill had "ministered" to Lewinsky: Jeffrey Toobin, *A Vast Right Wing Conspiracy*, p. 242.
13 "nondenial denial": *Time* described it as a "contrite nondenial," May 29, 1995.
13 "the ultimate inoculation": *Newsweek*, Feb. 8, 1999.
13 "This is not an arrangement": *ML*, p. 386; *LH*, p. 107.
13 "You know, I'm not sitting here": *LH*, p. 107.
13 "had doubts about Clinton": *ATH*, p. 69.
13 Bill had arranged a $17,520 job: *Time*, Feb. 3, 1992.
13 *Newsweek*'s Jonathan Alter ruefully admitted: *Newsweek*, March 30, 1998.
14 "If you'll give": *ML*, p. 391.
14 "He showed he was capable": Max Brantley interview.
14 "*We're* declaring victory": *Newsweek*, Nov./Dec. 1992 (special election issue).
14 After reading Garry Wills's: *The New Republic*, July 27, 1992.
14 "never broken the drug laws": *ML*, p. 372.
14 "didn't inhale": *ML*, p. 404.
14 "I like to play the saxophone": *The New Republic*, April 27, 1992.
15 "He gave the impression": James Barnes interview.
15 When his induction notice surfaced: *ATH*, p. 70.
15 he was renowned: *Newsweek*, Nov./Dec. 1992 (special election issue).
15 Bill had not told his staff: *ATH*, p. 70.
15 "I've had blind dates": *Newsweek*, April 11, 1994.
15 While he was still at Oxford: *ML*, p. 159. The number was 311.
15 "political viability": *Newsweek*, July 20, 1992.
15 "I want to thank you": *ATH*, p. 74; *Newsweek*, July 20, 1992. Bill's letter was written on Dec. 3, 1969. His lottery number was announced Dec. 1, 1969; *ML*, p. 159.
15 "Some reporters were really angry": Dee Dee Myers interview.
15 "masseur's touch": *NYT*, Nov. 15, 1992.
16 "plausible deniability": *The Nation*, April 27, 1992.
16 "lax" in the "coverage": Brummett, p. 240.
16 "ability or willingness": Max Brantley interview.
16 "Hillary was assigned to neutralize": Gene Lyons interview.
16 "the TV cameras caught everything": Max Brantley interview.
16 Both Clintons felt "seared": Howard Kurtz, *Spin Cycle: How the White House and the Media Manipulate the News*, p. xxi.
16 "appalling . . . arrogance": *Time*, July 20, 1992.
16 "It's 10 o'clock, Hillary": *NYT*, Feb. 3, 1992.

16 "burned out . . . automaton": *Newsweek*, July 20, 1992.

17 "reductionist" tendencies: Ibid.

17 In particular, the Clintons: *BS*, p. 212.

17 "surprisingly positive": *ML*, p. 445.

17 "human being who struggled": *Newsweek*, Dec. 7, 1994.

17 "the ordinary confrontation": *Newsweek*, March 30, 1992.

17 "Bill is a talkative person": Gene Lyons interview.

17 "the interwoven power structure": *WP*, July 21, 1992.

17 To augment her $110,000: Ibid.

18 "making sure he was in good grace": Ibid.

18 In that atmosphere, Bill and Hillary developed: Ibid. Joe Klein wrote that the Clintons "felt entitled to take investment advice." *Newsweek*, Jan. 22, 1996. See also *WP*, Mar. 11, 2006: The Clintons took the Wal-Mart jet fourteen times in 1990 and 1991.

18 "If Reaganomics": *Time*, Aug. 21, 1995.

18 The cost of the property: *LH*, p. 87.

18 although they were equal partners: *WP*, July 21, 1992; *NYT* editorial, April 24, 1994.

18 the Clintons kept the partnership going: *Time*, April 20, 1992.

18 The Whitewater venture lost money: Brummett, p. 236.

18 the Clintons allowed the McDougals: *Time*, Aug. 21, 1995. McDougal covered more than three quarters of nearly two hundred thousand dollars in losses.

18 One of Hillary's more questionable moves: *The New Yorker*, May 30, 1994.

18 The bank eventually cost taxpayers $73 million: *NYT*, Sept. 21, 2000.

18 McDougal later claimed: *BS*, p. 194.

18 the Clintons had filed tax returns: *BS*, p. 197.

19 Hillary blunted with the help: *Newsweek*, Feb. 5, 1996.

19 "numerous" conferences: Ibid.

19 both Hubbell and his Rose colleague: Ibid.

19 "incomprehensible": *BS*, p. 209.

19 "I gave my standard answer": *ML*, p. 405.

19 "Buy one, get one free": *Newsweek*, July 20, 1992.

19 "loved the modern-marriage": *ATH*, p. 92.

19 "People call us": *NYT*, Oct. 30, 1992. In the article, Hillary also referred to her partnership with her husband as a "blue light special."

19 Out on the stump: *The New Republic*, July 27, 1992; *WP*, March 10, 1992.

19 She edited Bill's speeches: Ibid.

19 When she was dissatisfied: *WP*, Nov. 4, 1992.

20 "process person": *Time*, Nov. 16, 1992.

20 "closer": *Time*, Jan. 4, 1993.

20 "the two of them propped up": *ATH*, p. 34.

20 "it took the staff a long time": Susan Thomases interview.

20 "Hillary pounds the piano": *Working Woman*, Aug. 1992.

20 "So what if she did?": *NYT*, May 18, 1992.

20 "We will try to decide": *WP*, March 31, 1992.

20 "no attack": *WP*, Jan. 20, 1993.

20 "she would be the first": Mickey Kantor interview.

21 "bimbo eruptions": *Time*, June 6, 1994.

21 "legal rights": Bernie Nussbaum interview.

21 Subsequently, the campaign secretly paid: *Newsweek*, Feb. 9, 1998, and Aug. 24, 1998.

21 "doomsday book": *Vanity Fair*, June 2001.

21 "[The Clintons] were saying": Ibid.

21 Hillary stumbled during the Illinois primary: *ML*, pp. 396–97; *LH*, p. 108; *NYT*, March 26, 1992.

21 "I suppose I could have stayed home": *LH*, p. 109.

21 "I don't know how": *The New Yorker*, Sept. 11, 1995.

21 voters disliked Hillary's outspokenness: *NYT*, Nov. 5, 1992.

21 "Hillary problem": *Time*, Nov. 2, 1992.

21 "more than Nancy Reagan": *NYT*, Nov. 16, 1992.

21 "Manhattan Project": *Newsweek*, May 5, 1997, and Nov./Dec. 1992 (special election issue).

22 Only weeks later: *NYT*, Nov. 5, 1992.

22 "Bill and I were raised": *Newsweek*, Nov./Dec. 1992 (special election issue).

22 They stopped the "buy-one-get-one": *NYT*, July 13, 1992.

22 "thought it was funny": *WP*, Jan. 15, 1995.

22 "voice for children": Karen Lehrman, "Beware the Cookie Monster," *NYT*, July 18, 1992.

22 "the good wife of a candidate": *NYT*, Oct. 30, 1992.

22 "Hillary Nod": *The Economist*, Dec. 15, 1992.

22 "It's an absorption technique": *The New Yorker*, May 30, 1994.

22 "was in every key meeting": Mickey Kantor interview.

22 to give Bill some gravitas: *Newsweek*, Oct. 26, 1992.

22 "sort of sibling synergy": *Time*, Jan. 4, 1993.

22 "long-lost sister": *Time*, Sept. 7, 1992.

22 "If there is": Ibid.

22 Only in the last weeks: *NYT*, Oct. 30, 1992.

22 Speaking to a crowd: *Time*, Nov. 16, 1992.

23 "the real Hillary Clinton . . . popped back up": *NYT Magazine*, Jan. 17, 1993.

23 "like the dog": *Time*, Jan. 4, 1993.

23 "Bill Clinton and I": *New York*, May 22, 2006.

23 At the time, Bill claimed: *Newsweek*, Nov. 16, 1992; Brummett, p. 69. Brummett wrote, "Clinton was buoyed by the possibility that he actually might have won 62%."

23 Another cautionary signal: *U.S. News & World Report*, Nov. 16, 1992; Haynes Johnson and David S. Broder, *The System: The American Way of Politics at the Breaking Point*, p. 451.

CHAPTER TWO

24 "oscillate between": *U.S. News & World Report*, Jan. 18, 1993.

24 "Of the wasted prospects": Michael Waldman, *POTUS Speaks*, p. 24.

24 The irony was that Bill: *WP*, Nov. 13, 1992.

25 "follow Reagan's pattern": *U.S. News & World Report*, Nov. 30, 1992.

25 "sidetracked by side issues": *WP*, Nov. 15, 1992.

25 Indeed the Reagan transition: Ibid.

25 "I hope so": *WP*, Dec. 19, 1992.

25 "the right balance": *Time*, Jan. 4, 1993.

25 She was precluded: *NYT*, Nov. 16, 1992; *WP*, Dec. 19, 1992.

26 "has always used 'we' ": *Newsweek*, Dec. 28, 1992.

26 "In one of my early conversations": Donna Shalala interview.

26 Most of the staff members were in offices: *WP*, Nov. 15, 1992.

26 "nerve center": *LH*, p. 117.

26 his book-lined study or a low-ceilinged: Author's tour of governor's mansion with Wayne Cranford.

26 "Susan Thomases was running": Dee Dee Myers interview.

27 "more influential": *The New Yorker*, Jan. 25, 1993.

27 "I did micromanage": *NYT*, Jan. 14, 1993.

27 Hillary quizzed many: *NYT*, Dec. 14, 1992.

27 "My impression was she was very": Robert Rubin interview.

27 Bill selected a mixture: *WP*, Jan. 7, 1993.

27 "something more: a human dam": *Newsweek*, Aug. 24, 1998.

27 "look like America": *WP*, Nov. 7, 1992.

27 She pressed him to fill: Marton, p. 319.

27 And she specifically urged: *ATH*, p. 118; James Stewart noted that "none of the four oldest cabinet posts . . . had ever been headed by a woman, and Hillary had insisted that Justice would be." *BS*, p. 246.

28 Al Gore, by comparison: *NYT*, Jan. 15, 1993.

28 "She stayed the whole time": *WP*, Nov. 17, 1992.

28 "call the shots": *Modern Healthcare*, Nov. 21, 1992.

28 Her track record on health policy: Harry Ward interview; Max Brantley interview; *LH*, p. 94.

28 "concerned citizen": Transcript of Bob Woodward's March 11, 1994, interview with Hillary Clinton, obtained from a source.

28 But Hillary wanted to lead: *The New Yorker*, May 30, 1994.

28 "signature initiative": *LH*, p. 144.

29 "eight hundred billion dollars in annual spending—one seventh of the economy": *WP*, Feb. 7, 1993; *Time*, March 22, 1993.

29 Bill made the extravagant promise: *WP*, Dec. 6, 1992.

29 "Ira was talking about his vision": Laura Tyson interview.

29 "thinking of putting Hillary in charge": Donna Shalala interview.

29 "I don't want her to have a job": *NYT*, Jan. 14, 1993.

29 Magaziner officially accepted: *LH*, p. 143.

30 "senior adviser": *WP*, Jan. 15, 1993.

30 One of Bill's biggest miscalculations: *ML*, p. 467.

30 only one hundred out of three thousand executive-branch jobs: *U.S. News & World Report*, Jan. 18, 1993.

30 "They didn't realize": Bruce Reed interview.

30 aides began to resent the secrecy: *Time*, Jan. 25, 1993.

30 "strict quota policy": Ibid.

30 "vetoing strong candidates": Ibid.

30 "The Brady Kids": *U.S. News & World Report*, Jan. 18, 1993.

30 "the most important dinner party ever": *WP*, Jan. 15, 1993.

30 For his Chief of Staff: *ML*, p. 454.

31 his intensely personal operating style: *Time*, Nov. 16, 1992.

31 "is not Little Rock": *U.S. News & World Report*, Dec. 28, 1992.

31 "private Bible": *Time*, Nov. 16, 1992.

31 "spokes of the wheel": Ibid.

31 "I was always fascinated": *Time*, Jan. 4, 1993.

31 "a loose White House structure": Hamilton Jordan, "What Not to Do," *WP*, Nov. 9, 1992.

31 Jordan's plea to George Stephanopoulos: Hamilton Jordan interview.

31 the press concluded that his operation: *NYT*, Nov. 10, 1992; *WP*, Jan. 31, 1993.

31 "blue-sky no-pain promises": *NYT*, Nov. 9, 1992.

31 "two hard months": *WP*, Jan. 12, 1993, citing C-SPAN interview with Bill on June 15, 1992.

31 "ready on the desk": *WP*, Jan. 15, 1993.

32 the first hundred days: *WP*, Jan. 12, 1993.

32 his pledge early in the campaign: *NYT*, Feb. 18, 1993.

32   He continued to promote: *WP*, Jan. 14, 1993.

32   "absolutely not": *NYT*, Feb. 1, 1993.

32   "the press thought the most important issue": *NYT*, Feb. 15, 1993.

32   Reporters rebuked him: *NYT*, Jan. 15, 1993.

32   "Nail Bill Clinton" network: *NYT Magazine*, Jan. 17, 1993.

32   "Yes, I want to": *NYT*, Nov. 12, 1992.

32   It was an assurance he had made repeatedly: *Newsweek*, Feb. 1 and May 3, 1993.

32   Bill failed to anticipate: *NYT*, Nov. 12, 1992.

32   "immediate repeal": *Newsweek*, Nov. 23, 1992.

32   "Like so much else in those first few months": *ATH*, p. 125.

33   On the first thirty-six-hour foray: *Time*, Nov. 30, 1992; *LH*, p. 124.

33   he kept the entire U.S. Supreme Court: *WP*, Jan. 12, 1993.

33   On consecutive evenings, the Clintons attended: *ML*, p. 450.

33   "reassure the Establishment": *WP*, Nov. 19, 1992.

33   On Thanksgiving weekend, the Clintons traveled: *WP*, Nov. 22, 1992, and Jan. 4, 1993.

33   "as interconnected as laces": *WP*, Jan. 4, 1993.

33   In the campaign, Harry had helped: *WP*, Jan. 4, 1993.

33   "noble public servant": *The Man from Hope*, Mozark Productions.

33   the California trip became another cavalcade: *NYT*, Nov. 28 and Dec. 1, 1992.

34   "the one with the white legs": *NYT*, Nov. 30, 1992.

34   he capped the evening: *WP*, Nov. 30, 1992.

34   Bill presided over a two-day conference: *NYT*, Dec. 15 and Dec. 16, 1992; *NYT Magazine*, Jan. 17, 1993.

34   "tireless master": *The Economist*, Jan. 17, 1993.

34   "You watch Bill Clinton and you think": *NYT*, Dec. 15, 1992.

34   "seemed to have a compulsion": Elizabeth Drew, *On the Edge: The Clinton Presidency*, pp. 66–67.

34   Hillary was a visible presence: *WP*, Dec. 19, 1992.

34   None of the participants challenged: Brummett, p. 75.

34   "Like peacocks on audition": *NYT*, Dec. 15, 1992.

34   "create a political mood": Ibid.

34   "supreme irony": *Newsweek*, Dec. 7, 1992; see also *Time*, Nov. 23, 1992, and Jan. 4, 1993.

34   Bill Clinton "lucked out": *Newsweek*, Dec. 7, 1992.

34   Bill and his team were nevertheless: *Time*, Nov. 23, 1992.

35   So his advisors secretly: *WP*, Dec. 15, 1992.

35   "I was told they needed someone to deliver": *Time*, Jan. 4, 1993.

35   Revised estimates now pegged: Ibid.

35   "investments": *NYT*, Dec. 16, 1992.

35   "absolute consensus": Ibid.

35   It fell to political scientist: Ibid.; Joe Klein reported that Clinton "seemed piqued by the bluntness" of Kamarck's remarks. *Newsweek*, Dec. 28, 1992.

35   "bean counters": *WP*, Dec. 22, 1992.

35   "tough, tenacious": *NYT*, Dec. 25, 1992.

35   "the last woman standing": *WP*, Jan. 20, 1993.

35   The team responsible for vetting: *NYT*, Jan. 15, 1993.

36   "did not think it was a problem": Ibid.

36   "emblematic of our early troubles": *ATH*, p. 118.

36   Bill and Hillary celebrated their last: *NYT*, Dec. 26, 1992.

36   "He gets these colds": Reich, p. 14.

36   Bill's brother, Roger, showed up: *NYT*, Dec. 26, 1992.

36   Bill gave Hillary and Chelsea: *WP*, Dec. 26, 1992.

36   *Robin Hood:* NYT, Dec. 27, 1992.
36   Bernie Nussbaum got the summons: Bernie Nussbaum interview.
36   Bill was on his way home: *ML,* p. 464; *NYT,* Jan. 3, 1993.
36   "in retrospect poignant": Bernie Nussbaum interview.
37   The Clintons decided to sell their stake: *BS,* p. 234; *Newsweek,* Jan. 8, 1996.
37   Blair loaned it to him: *BS,* p. 234.
37   It fell to Foster: Ibid., pp. 252–54.
37   "Mr. No of Capitol Hill": *U.S. News & World Report,* Dec. 21, 1992.
37   "common sense on economic issues": Robert Rubin interview.
37   such an advocate of slashing: *Newsweek,* Dec. 21, 1992.
38   "The new president was slightly intimidated": Robert Reich interview.
38   "threshold issue": Rubin, p. 119.
38   "I don't think it was thirty minutes": Robert Rubin interview.
38   To some extent, he simply underestimated: *Newsweek,* Nov. 2, 1992.
38   "almost no thought": *ML,* p. 467.
38   "There was an air of distrust": See also *ATH,* p. 302: "Hillary became the object of some quiet resentment because no one was ever sure what the rules were in internal debates."

CHAPTER THREE

39   He wept as he sang: *WP,* Jan. 11, 1993.
39   With an entourage: *WP,* Jan. 16, 1993.
39   "particularly southern": *WP,* Jan. 20, 1993.
39   He freed Chelsea's pet frog: *WP,* Jan. 17, 1993.
39   slapped yellow Post-it notes: *WP,* Jan. 16, 1993.
39   kept an appreciative crowd waiting: *WP,* Jan. 12, 1993.
39   At 5:15 a.m.: Sheehy, p. 220.
39   Trooper Danny Ferguson testified: *Newsweek,* Mar. 16, 1998.
39   Bill had also phoned her frequently: Woodward, *Shadow,* p. 373.
39   One call, at 1:23 a.m.: Sheehy, p. 185.
39   "serious threat": Ibid., p. 182.
40   Both Jenkins and Bill later denied: *Time,* Jan. 3, 1994.
40   "personal crisis": Sheehy, p. 221.
40   "forlorn and wistful": Woodward, *Shadow,* p. 374.
40   Bill also eventually acknowledged: *WP,* Mar. 13, 1998.
40   After a delayed departure: *LH,* p. 120.
40   "understood the kind of complexity": Bill Clinton interview with Brian Lamb, C-SPAN, Feb. 19, 1995.
40   "some sense of despair": Bill Clinton, remarks at White House screening of Ken Burns, *Thomas Jefferson,* Feb. 11, 1997. *PPP,* 1997, book 1, p. 147.
40   "carefully to veil from the public eye": *ML,* p. 406.
40   Bill and Hillary joined Al and Tipper: *NYT,* Jan. 18, 1993.
40   "It struck me like a college-dorm": Tom Brokaw interview.
41   "the science of how they interacted": Mike McCurry interview.
41   "I *have* seen": *The New Yorker,* May 30, 1994.
41   "It was not grabbing": Linda Aaker interview.
41   Bill stood just over: Blumenthal, p. 5.
41   size-thirteen feet: Kelley, p. 210.
41   oversized head: *ATH,* p. 44.
41   "the sexiest mouth": Flowers, p. 1.

41 Tipping the scales at 226 pounds: *Newsweek*, Aug. 11, 1997.
41 When his girth increased: Drew, p. 136.
41 "white linen pants": *ML*, p. 11.
41 He thought nothing of wearing: Waldman, p. 175.
41 "Turkey Trot": *NYT*, Nov. 27, 1992.
42 "seemed to be too big": *ML*, p. 221.
42 Once she recognized the importance: Hubbell, pp. 4, 14.
42 after reading in Margaret Thatcher's: *WP*, July 23, 1992.
42 She took to wearing headbands: *LH*, p. 110; *Washingtonian*, Jan. 1993.
42 They orchestrated a makeover: *LH*, p. 111; *WP*, Jan. 13, 1993.
42 *Designing Women* consultant: *Newsweek*, Nov. 16, 1992; *WP*, July 23, 1992; *WP*, Jan. 13, 1993.
42 "We needed things": Martha Sherrill interview with Brooke Shearer.
42 "her hair on top": *WP*, Dec. 28, 1992.
42 "What did you think": Martha Sherrill interview with Sara Ehrman.
42 The most dramatic change: *LH*, p. 14; *WP*, Jan. 13, 1993.
42 her husband considered "beautiful": Sheehy, p. 87.
42 "an overweight, underdressed": *WP*, July 23, 1992.
43 "a cross between a State Dinner": *NYT*, Nov. 15, 1992.
43 The total cost came to: *Time*, Jan. 25, 1993.
43 "You have to run against 'inside Washington' ": *WP*, Nov. 15, 1992.
43 "accept Washington's hospitality": Ibid.
43 "watching on both sides": *NYT*, Jan. 17, 1993.
43 "Faces of Hope" luncheon: *NYT*, Jan. 19, 1993.
43 "I'll remember that this town": Ibid.
43 It was a five-minute video: Toobin, p. 248.
44 "We're bunker people": *WP*, Jan. 13, 1993.
44 "chauvinistic, mean-spirited": *WP*, Jan. 4, 1993.
44 reporters criticized the week's: *WP*, Jan. 22, 1993.
44 "Wal-Mart inaugural week": *Diane Rehm Show*, Jan. 19, 1993.
44 "let-'em-eat-cake": *NYT*, Jan. 20, 1993.
44 "Woodstock in a limousine": *NYT*, Jan. 20, 1993.
44 Hillary forbade: *NYT*, Feb. 8, 1993.
44 On the strength of his connections: *NYT*, Jan. 18, 1993; *Time*, Jan. 18, 1993.
44 "musically challenged": *The New Yorker*, Feb. 1, 1993.
44 "Without the fact of the shared last name": *NYT*, Jan. 18, 1993.
44 Roger had been arrested twice: *Time*, Jan. 18, 1993.
44 Now he had arranged to make: *NYT*, Jan. 18 and Jan. 20, 1993; *Time*, Jan. 18, 1993.
45 "The Brothers Karamazov": *WP*, Jan. 13, 1993.
45 embarrassed their sister: *WP*, Jan. 15, 1993; *Time*, Jan. 25, 1993.
45 "The Rodham brothers were a nightmare": Mary Mel French interview.
45 Bill's stepfather Roger had died: Kelley, pp. 176, 188, 208.
45 She wore sunglasses and a white fur coat: *NYT*, Jan. 20 and Jan. 21, 1993.
45 "Let me get this straight": Tommy Caplan interview.
45 but in fact her cancer had spread: Kelley, pp. 262, 268–69, 286.
45 In Little Rock, her public school: *NYT*, Jan. 6, 1993.
45 "very disappointed": *NYT*, Jan. 14, 1993.
46 But the Clintons said their choice: *NYT*, Jan. 6, 1993.
46 "They talk to Chels": Ann McCoy interview.
46 From the age of six: Sheehy, pp. 169–70; *Time*, Mar. 21, 1994.
46 "done a terrible job": *WP*, Mar. 10, 1992.
46 "told her that what we heard": *Newsweek*, Feb. 3, 1992.

46 "I think I'm glad": *Newsweek,* July 20, 1992.
46 "Mom is going on TV": Mickey Kantor interview.
46 "Oh, that's not true": *The New Yorker,* May 30, 1994.
46 "pretended that her life": Ibid.
46 "Chelsea watched and understood": Mickey Kantor interview.
46 "Chelsea is a lot like her mother": Sheehy, p. 170.
46 "gain mastery over her emotions": Hillary Clinton, *It Takes a Village: And Other Lessons Children Teach Us,* p. 151.
47 "unthinking emotion is pitiful": Sheehy, p. 42.
47 They filled Blair House: Benedicte Valentiner interview.
47 "We ran a continuous buffet": Ibid.
47 On their first full day: Waldman, p. 34.
47 Along with the Gore family: *WP,* Jan. 18, 1993.
47 at 2:00 a.m. a butler found: Benedicte Valentiner interview.
47 a marathon of speeches: *WP,* Jan. 19, 1993.
48 a visit to the Kennedy grave site: *WP,* Jan. 20, 1993.
48 Hillary strolled along the Mall: *The New Yorker,* Feb. 8, 1993.
48 the Clintons were nearly an hour late: *NYT,* Jan. 20, 1993.
48 "excessive beyond one's wildest dread": *WP,* Jan. 20, 1993.
48 "Thank you for sharing": Ibid.
48 "This man must have one of the highest": Ibid.
48 "the sex will be superb": *NYT,* Jan. 21, 1993.
48 "His words flew": Waldman, pp. 29–30.
48 "whoever managed to wander in": *ATH,* p. 114.
48 Bill summoned two friends who were professional writers: Tommy Caplan interview; Waldman, p. 34.
48 "rambling effort": *ATH,* p. 114.
48 his vice president dozed upright: Ibid.
49 Starting at the end of December: *NYT,* Dec. 28, 1992.
49 These clashes escalated: *NYT,* Jan. 18, 1993.
49 "alarming innocence": *The New Republic,* Feb. 8, 1993.
49 "I believe in deathbed conversions": *NYT,* Jan. 14, 1993.
49 Bill compounded the problem: *The New Republic,* Feb. 8, 1993.
49 Al Gore counteracted: Ibid.
49 "anti-war past": *WP,* Feb. 15, 1993.
49 Bill was up at 7:00 a.m.: *ATH,* p. 115.
49 He and his family went to: *ML,* p. 474; *NYT,* Jan. 21, 1993.
49 A U.S. Park Police officer later said: Sheehy, pp. 115–16, 222; *Time,* Oct. 21, 1996.
49 Bill and Hillary arrived: *WP,* Jan. 21, 1993.
50 the country had "drifted": Ibid.
50 the new President gave a round of hugs: Ibid.
50 Hillary wore a royal-blue coat: *The New Yorker,* Feb. 1, 1993.
50 broad-brimmed hat that Robert Reich likened: Reich, p. 44.
50 Soprano Marilyn Horne sang: *The New Yorker,* Feb. 8, 1993; *NYT,* Jan. 21, 1993.
50 Following a precedent: *NYT,* Jan. 21, 1993.
50 "walking at her own pace": Ibid.
50 The first party at the White House: Lisa Bedell interview; *NYT,* Feb. 2, 1993; *LH,* p. 128.
50 The inaugural balls offered: *NYT,* Jan. 20 and Jan. 21, 1993; *WP,* Jan. 20, 1993.
51 Hillary danced with her husband: *WP,* Jan. 21, 1993.
51 "I feel like I been rode hard": Ibid.
51 In one of the few quiet moments: *Newsweek,* Dec. 16, 1996. Mochtar Riady wrote a let-

ter to Bill in March 1993, thanking him for "the very personal time you and Hillary gave to my family."

51 The Clintons had been friendly: *Time*, Oct. 28, 1996, and July 28, 1997; Betsy Blass, Little Rock philanthropist, interview; *Newsweek*, Oct. 21 and Dec. 16, 1996.

51 During 1992, the Riadys had contributed: *Time*, Oct. 28, 1996, and July 28, 1997.

51 "unconscionable": *Newsweek*, Dec. 16, 1996.

51 A Chinese government company: *Newsweek*, Feb. 24, 1997.

51 "crashed into bed" and "too tired": *LH*, pp. 128, 126.

51 "I wanted to look around": *ML*, p. 479.

CHAPTER FOUR

52 "the campus": *Time*, Mar. 8, 1993.

52 known for chewing bubble gum: *Newsweek*, Mar. 1, 1993.

52 Pizza boxes and takeout: *NYT*, Feb. 15, 1993.

52 R.E.M. filled the once-hushed: *Time*, Mar. 8, 1993.

52 The White House Mess: *Newsweek*, Mar. 1, 1993; *Time*, May 10, 1993.

52 staff members referred to him: Mike McCurry interview; Strobe Talbott, *The Russia Hand: A Memoir of Presidential Diplomacy*, p. 44.

52 Now the First Couple were: *LH*, p. 137.

53 Bill turned over its décor: *ML*, p. 541.

53 "alarming yellow": Waldman, p. 105.

53 "The Redskin Room": *Time*, Dec. 6, 1993.

53 Hillary had a hand: *ATH*, p. 178; *Time*, May 10, 1993.

53 Chelsea could be glimpsed: *Newsweek*, Mar. 1, 1993.

53 At first, Bill spent as much: *NYT*, Feb. 15, 1993; *Newsweek*, Mar. 1, 1993; *ML*, p. 952.

53 "the highest office": *Newsweek*, May 26, 1997.

53 He delighted in giving: *NYT*, Feb. 15, 1993; Drew, p. 89.

53 he invited Annie Leibovitz: *Time*, Mar. 8, 1993.

53 "He was standing there in his shorts": Tom Brokaw interview.

53 "I'm not one for rules": Kelley, p. 91.

54 He dismissed signs of deference: *ATH*, p. 132.

54 In answer to a question: Mark Katz, *Clinton and Me*, p. 234.

54 "He eats like a Tasmanian devil": *NYT Magazine*, Jan. 17, 1993.

54 "I am right over Arkansas!": David Leopoulos interview.

54 "I can't make every decision": *U.S. News & World Report*, Jan. 25, 1993.

54 his reliance on only four hours: *FiHC*, p. 53; Betty Glad, "Evaluating Presidential Character," *Presidential Studies Quarterly*, vol. 28, no. 4, fall 1998, p. 866.

54 "If he could get by": Terry McAuliffe interview.

54 "sleep deprivation": *ML*, p. 81.

54 working harder than they were: *Time*, Nov. 16, 1992.

54 "It was his creative improvising time": Mike McCurry interview.

54 "wondering and worrying": *ML*, p. 150.

54 Fueled by adrenaline: Joe Klein wrote that Bill "would go on and on. He would pick up speed and intensity as the hours stretched." Klein, p. 164.

54 which he transformed from: *ML*, p. 480; *ATH*, p. 390; *NYT*, Aug. 15, 1993; *Time*, Dec. 6, 1993.

55 he typically had a half-dozen: *Time*, Feb. 7, 1994.

55 "gulping down literary caviar": *NYT*, Dec. 10, 1992.

55 His taste ran: *Time*, July 20, 1992, and Feb. 7, 1994.

55 he lugged around: *U.S. News & World Report*, Jan. 18, 1993; *ATH*, p. 35.

55 In most books he made: *ML*, p. 28; Reich, p. 24.

55 His briefing primers: *Time*, Mar. 8, 1993.

55 his habit: Talbott, p. 51.

55 "to find out what went on that day": Terry McAuliffe interview.

55 "I cut off a valuable feedback mechanism": Mike McCurry interview.

55 Occasionally, Bill's interlocutor: Bob Woodward, *The Choice: How Clinton Won*, pp. 54–55.

56 During one phone conversation: Terry McAuliffe interview.

56 "That never happened to me": Ibid.

56 Most mornings, Bill's staff: Woodward, *Agenda*, p. 255.

56 "shake awake": *Newsweek*, July 12, 1993.

56 friends contributed thirty thousand: *NYT*, Feb. 25, 1993. *WP* reported on May 5, 1993, that the White House "received some $50,000 in private donations, considerably more than the $30,000 goal."

56 "He can barely stay awake": Reich, p. 64.

56 Bill tried to compensate: Bill Clinton, interview with Dan Rather, March 24, 1993. *PPP*, 1993, book 1, p. 346.

56 "I watch your eyes": Woodward, *Agenda*, p. 387.

56 "cusswords for five minutes": Abner Mikva interview.

57 "purple fits": Woodward, *Agenda*, p. 297.

57 His admirers likened his eruptions: Rubin, p. 135.

57 "He could get really ugly": Mary Mel French interview.

57 he acted as if nothing happened: *FiHC*, p. 335.

57 earplugs to Betsey Wright: Ibid., p. 427.

57 "If you ever talk to me again": Robert Reich interview.

57 when an aide once neglected: Kim Hume, ABC News producer, interview.

57 "my daily companion": *ATH*, pp. 97, 176, 286–88.

57 "more like a battered wife": *Newsweek*, June 13, 1994.

57 "parallel lives": *ML*, p. 149.

57 "secret keeper": Ibid., p. 46.

57 "letting anyone into the deepest recesses": Ibid., p. 149.

58 "deeper and stronger": Ibid., p. 42.

58 Bill expended little effort: Eric Liu interview.

58 Robert Reich bluntly told: Robert Reich interview.

58 "He struck me as more quiet and moody": Eric Liu interview.

58 "You first meet him, it is awe": Dee Dee Myers interview.

58 "Bill Clinton has a remarkable intellect": Robert Rubin interview.

58 "I am a professional economist": Ibid.

58 "to watch him think": Brookwood Elementary School postcard of Bill Clinton's first-grade class, Arkansas Post Card Company, North Little Rock, Arkansas.

58 "astonishing" multitasking: Hubbell, p. 273.

58 his virtuoso displays: *Newsweek*, July 12, 1993.

59 "He absolutely could dual process": Robert Rubin interview.

59 Bill "would circle back and pick up": Eric Liu interview.

59 "we would be playing cards": David Leopoulos interview.

59 "He would pull back and chew on his glasses": Mack McLarty interview.

59 "He was always looking for a way": Bill Galston interview.

59 "eager and bright graduate student": Laura Tyson interview.

59 "He was not only open": Robert Rubin interview.

59 "He wanted to hear views": Anthony Lake interview; George Stephanopoulos wrote that Bill "hates open fights." *ATH*, p. 337.

60 "He didn't like a precooked answer": James Steinberg interview.

60 "If everyone was agreeing": Robert Rubin interview.

60 "in an open way to keep": Eric Liu interview.

60 "transmit mode": Talbott, p. 44.

60 kind of "catharsis": Laura Tyson interview.

60 Bill would then quiet down: Robert Rubin interview.

60 By blurring the lines: Klein, p. 59; Waldman, p. 83; John F. Harris, *The Survivor: President Clinton and His Times*, pp. 148, 170.

60 "shadow staff": *Newsweek*, June 7, 1993.

60 each of whom was paid: Drew, p. 123.

60 They shaped communications strategies: Ibid., p. 124.

60 Friends such as Harry: *Time*, May 31, 1993; *The New Yorker*, Apr. 15, 1996.

60 "it was never entirely clear": Rubin, p. 136.

61 "dysfunctional" environment: *ATH*, p. 337.

61 speaking on the phone: *ATH*, p. 131.

61 The favored metaphor for meetings: Mickey Kantor interview; David Gergen, *Eyewitness to Power: The Essence of Leadership, Nixon to Clinton*, p. 276.

61 "struggles about who": Rubin, p. 137.

61 Meetings scheduled for ten minutes: *Time*, June 7, 1993; Klein, p. 59.

61 "silver bullet": Mack McLarty interview.

61 "like a gardener": *Newsweek*, May 17, 1993.

61 "he didn't realize": Mack McLarty interview.

61 "A signature of his": Talbott, p. 185.

62 "If you go in": *Time*, Nov. 16, 1992.

62 "When he says": Ibid.

62 "Clinton Standard Time": *WP*, Jan. 12, 1993.

62 not even a group of elderly Holocaust survivors: *Time*, May 10, 1993; Clinton admitted at the time, "I had a lot of conversations this afternoon and we are a little late and for that I apologize." *PPP*, 1993, book 1, p. 473.

62 "It wasn't malicious": Ann Stock interview.

62 "We got him up": Martha Sherrill interview with Chris Emery.

62 They learned to stay at their desks: Eric Liu interview.

63 "Hillary could not do anything": Mary Mel French interview.

63 "serene, stealing time": *Newsweek*, Feb. 10, 1992.

63 "I never smoke those things": *WP*, Nov. 19, 1992.

63 At least once, though, he disobeyed: PBS *Frontline* interview with Anthony Lake, Sept. 2000.

63 "six major southern food groups": *WP*, Jan. 20, 1993.

63 "a lot of fiber and a lot of fruit": *NYT*, Feb. 2, 1993.

63 "nutritionally literate": *WP*, Apr. 2, 1994.

63 Bill rarely missed: *Time*, Nov. 18, 1996.

63 steady infusions of Diet Coke: Hubbell, p. 232.

63 Bill drank little alcohol: *WP*, Dec. 1, 1993.

63 three bases of operation: *LH*, p. 132.

64 She spent virtually no time in the East Wing: Ann McCoy interview.

64 She occupied a small corner: *WP*, Jan. 15, 1995; *Time*, May 10, 1993.

64 "about as far": *Time*, Jan. 25, 1993.

64 The office was thoroughly businesslike: *WP*, May 6, 1993; *Time*, May 10, 1993; Ann Stock interview; *LH*, p. 148.

64 In the Residence, Hillary had two: Ann Stock interview; *WP*, Feb. 17, 1995; *Time*, May 10, 1993.

64 she had more senior officials: *Time*, May 10, 1993.

64 Only one man: Ann Stock interview.

64　"upbeat, optimistic, positive": *WP*, Feb. 17, 1995.

64　"Hillaryland" lapel pins: *LH*, p. 133.

64　liberal stalwarts: *WP*, Jan. 15, 1993; *The New Yorker*, May 30, 1994.

65　Her twentysomething aides: *LH*, p. 104.

65　she maintained her lifelong capacity: *Newsweek*, Nov. 18, 1996.

65　"Hillary was always sending me plates of broccoli": Capricia Marshall interview.

65　she pulled her advisors close: *WP*, Feb. 17, 1995.

65　"White Boys": *Time*, Mar. 21, 1994.

65　"King Kong Kibitzer": *WP*, Mar. 2, 1993.

65　"There were no fights over territory": Ann Stock interview.

65　"When Hillary leans forward": *Time*, May 10, 1993.

66　"frequently reduced her personal traveling aide to tears": Woodward, *Choice*, p. 135.

66　Hillary withdrew in cool silence: Mary Mel French and Dee Dee Myers interviews.

66　"Mel, your problem is you just aren't mean": Mary Mel French interview.

66　Hillary was invariably on the move: *Time*, May 10, 1993; Ann Stock interview.

66　In the corridors of the West Wing: *WP*, Mar. 3, 1993; *Newsweek*, Mar. 1, 1993.

66　thick no-line bifocals: Martha Sherrill interview with Connie Fails, a friend from Little Rock.

66　"First Lady Box": Ann Stock interview.

66　She made many of her own calls: *Time*, May 10, 1993.

66　With a bedtime: *Time*, Jan. 4, 1993; Sheehy, p. 271.

66　National Public Radio "blaring": *PPP*, 2000, book 3, p. 2745.

66　logging time on a treadmill: *WP*, Feb. 17, 1995.

66　She conducted her meetings: Ellen Lovell interview.

66　claiming that salsa and Tabasco: *WP*, Feb. 17, 1995.

67　"[Bill] would call people to chat": Ann Stock interview.

67　She customarily made calls: Woodward, *Choice*, p. 134.

67　self-consciously "female": *The New Yorker*, Feb. 26, 1996.

67　"circle or matrix management": Ibid.

67　true believers: *The New Republic*, Feb. 20, 2006.

67　"do something about those bags": *Talk*, Sept. 1999.

67　"Hillary is direct and organized": Mickey Kantor interview.

67　"If you would say something to Hillary": Robert Rubin interview.

67　she was meticulous: Henry Cisneros interview.

67　"She didn't look back": Ann Stock interview.

67　"She thought before she spoke": Robert Reich interview.

67　Her literary tastes: *NYT*, Dec. 10, 1992; Ellen Lovell interview; *Time*, May 10, 1993.

68　"would attend all the classes": *The New Yorker*, May 30, 1994.

68　Not surprisingly, Hillary often read: *WP*, Jan. 15, 1995.

68　she had little interest in the traditional: *NYT*, Dec. 14, 1992.

68　"one of the most political jobs": Ann Stock interview.

68　"the Republican way": Martha Sherrill interview with Ann Stock.

68　During the same period three decades earlier: *National Journal*, Apr. 24, 1999; Sally Bedell Smith, *Grace and Power: The Private World of the Kennedy White House*, p. 223.

68　Once they made a commitment: Capricia Marshall interview.

68　"Ann was very helpful": Ann McCoy interview.

69　By then, Hillary was more involved: Ibid.

69　"needed to be quieter": *NYT*, Apr. 1, 1993.

69　spend more than three hundred thousand: *Time*, Dec. 6, 1993.

69　"so ablaze in color": *NYT*, Dec. 12, 1993.

69　quilts and rocking chairs: *Time*, May 10, 1993.

69　"RAISE AND SPEND": *NYT*, Apr. 1, 1993.

69 The Clintons added bookshelves: *NYT*, Dec. 10 and Dec. 14, 1992.

69 The night tables flanking: *Time*, May 10, 1993.

69 the Clinton "Family Room": *LH*, p. 328.

69 "The cooking gene": Hillary on *The Ellen DeGeneres Show*, Nov. 21, 2005.

69 Her best culinary efforts: *Working Woman*, June 1994.

69 They had an aversion to taking: Terry McAuliffe interview.

70 Their favorite gathering place: Ann McCoy interview; *NYT Magazine*, May 30, 1999; Woodward, *Choice*, p. 130; photograph at www.WhiteHouseMuseum.org/floor3/sun-room.htm.

70 Clintons "didn't waste a second": Ann Stock interview.

70 "kick back from work": Talbott, pp. 46–47.

70 "We knew that Bill Clinton was probably": Lani Guinier, *Lift Every Voice: Turning a Civil Rights Setback into a New Vision of Social Justice*, pp. 24–25.

71 most of the Clintons' private entertaining: Mary Mel French interview; *Newsweek*, May 5, 1997.

71 he had seen his favorite film: *NYT*, Dec. 10, 1992.

71 When Barbra Streisand came for the night: *Time*, May 31, 1993.

71 "The overnight guest list": Ibid.

71 On Friday afternoons: Ann Stock and Mary Mel French interviews.

71 "The people around them were loyal": Laura Tyson interview.

71 "as scary as she seems": Author's observation, Feb. 1993.

71 "probably drove people crazy": Ann McCoy interview.

72 Kathie Berlin, an executive with: *NYT*, Jan. 8, 1993.

72 "had lived what I thought": Bill Clinton, interview with *Rolling Stone*, Oct. 10, 2000; *PPP*, 2000–2002, book 3, p. 2628.

72 "very impressed by his discipline": *American Heritage*, Dec. 1994.

72 "he identified with me": Bill Clinton, interview with *Rolling Stone*, Oct. 10, 2000; *PPP*, 2000–2002, book 3, p. 2628.

73 "the job of the presidency": David Leopoulos interview.

73 Chelsea engaged in shoptalk: Drew, p. 104.

73 "living above the store": *Time*, Sept. 21, 1998.

73 "was under a kind of White House arrest": Ibid.

73 "He gives speeches": Maraniss, *Enigma*, p. 98.

73 But he made a point each night: *NYT*, Sept. 18, 1997; Bernie Nussbaum interview.

73 Hillary was usually home: Ann Stock interview; *LH*, p. 311.

73 The décor of Chelsea's suite: *LH*, p. 136; *NYT*, Aug. 15, 1993.

73 "Call my dad": *Newsweek*, Mar. 1, 1993.

73 "authoritative": *WP*, Jan. 28, 1996.

73 "close, low-key": Martha Sherrill interview with Diane Blair.

73 "Bill would go on and on": Priscilla Eakeley interview.

74 "I was up late": *Newsweek*, Nov. 18, 1996.

74 When he asked Laura Tyson for: Laura Tyson interview; *ATH*, p. 210.

74 Once when a group encountered him: Lisa Bedell interview.

74 they even excluded her: *NYT*, Dec. 7, 1993.

75 "the inevitable fallout": Hillary Rodham Clinton, *It Takes a Village*, p. 150.

CHAPTER FIVE

76 "brutal" and "automatic pilot": *LH*, p. 178.

76 "imperial mandate": *Time*, Nov. 18, 1996.

76 "Why are we here": Woodward, *Agenda*, p. 116.

76 "the steady but light wind": *WP*, May 6, 1993.

77 "joyful chaos": *Newsweek*, May 3, 1993.

77 "In the early days": Bruce Reed interview.

77 Bill's first full day in office: *NYT*, Jan. 22, 1993; *WP*, Jan. 22, 1993.

77 "We just screwed all these people": *Time*, Jan. 20, 1997.

77 Wearing a wireless microphone: *NYT*, Jan. 22 and Jan. 24, 1993; Ann Stock interview.

77 The military had sent fighter planes: *NYT*, Jan. 22, 1993.

77 A week earlier, *The New York Times* had: *NYT*, Jan. 14, 1993.

77 "technical violation": *The New Yorker*, Feb. 15, 1993.

77 "I don't want to rain": Ibid.

78 "frazzled": *ATH*, p. 109.

78 "hard look on her face": Ibid.

78 "No, he can't do that": Ibid.

78 "When you abandon people": Bernie Nussbaum interview.

78 her support for tort reform: *NYT*, Jan. 14, 1993.

78 positions that differed: *The New Republic*, Feb. 1, 1993.

78 "murky": *NYT*, Jan. 23, 1993.

78 "fully disclosed": *NYT*, Jan. 15, 1993.

78 this time in sweatpants: *ATH*, p. 120.

78 conceding that his review: *NYT*, Jan. 23, 1993.

78 Wood's path to office: *BS*, pp. 249–50.

78 Both Bill and Hillary interviewed Wood: Drew, p. 53.

78 After Wood's name leaked: *The New Yorker*, Feb. 15, 1993.

78 The crucial difference: *WP*, Feb. 6, 1993.

79 Wood had also paid: Drew, p. 53.

79 "the latest prejudice": *The New Republic*, Mar. 1, 1993.

79 "They didn't think the public would understand": Dee Dee Myers interview.

79 Wood moved even faster: *ATH*, pp. 133–34.

79 his signing that day: *PPP*, 1993, book 1, p. 50.

79 aides pored over lists: *ATH*, p. 134.

79 Bill suggested the state attorney: Hubbell, p. 188; *WP*, Feb. 12, 1993; *ML*, p. 491.

79 "Bigfoot": *WP*, Apr. 21, 1993.

79 "mixed" reviews in her handling: *Newsweek*, May 3, 1993.

79 "politically tone-deaf": *Newsweek*, Nov. 18, 1996.

80 "Janet was a different kettle of fish": Donna Shalala interview.

80 "I don't think Clinton believed he had a choice": Dee Dee Myers interview.

80 "Gender is the reason": *WP*, Jan. 25, 1998. Ruth Marcus noted in *WP*, Feb. 10, 1993, that Hillary interviewed Attorney General candidates.

80 "a Trojan horse": *Newsweek*, Nov. 21, 1994.

80 he marginalized some of his prominent: Bruce Reed interview.

80 his governing strategy was: *Newsweek*, Nov. 21, 1994.

80 Bill put down his most conspicuous: *Time*, May 31, 1993.

80 which Bill lauded: Presidential Documents Online, via GPO Access, vol. 29, no. 3, pp. 85–87.

80 "honorable compromise": Fred I. Greenstein, "The Presidential Leadership Style of Bill Clinton: An Early Appraisal," *Political Science Quarterly*, vol. 108, no. 4, winter 1993–1994, p. 601.

80 delay for six months: *NYT*, Jan. 21 and Jan. 30, 1993; Michael Kelly wrote that making gays in the military a major issue was "an accident," *NYT*, Feb. 2, 1993.

80 "looked pale and uncertain": Drew, p. 47.

80 he unveiled an initiative: *Time*, Nov. 14, 1994, and Sept. 2, 1996.

81 create 105 new government: Stanley Renshon, *High Hopes: The Clinton Presidency and the Politics of Ambition*, p. 297.

81 His appointment of Hillary: *NYT*, Feb. 28, 1993. Hillary Clinton noted in *LH*, "Few on the White House staff knew that Bill had asked me to chair the task force" (p. 143).
81 "time to get adjusted": *WP*, Mar. 31, 1992.
81 "It was a clear indication": Bruce Reed interview.
81 education establishment as "the enemy": Drew, p. 51.
81 "war room": *WP*, Jan. 26, 1993.
81 "unconscionable profiteering": Harris, p. 202; see also *NYT*, Feb. 12, 1993, and Woodward, *Agenda*, p. 163.
81 "The use of a 'war room' ": Pamela Bailey interview.
81 The task force was supposed: *LH*, pp. 153–54; *Time*, May 10, 1993; *WP*, Feb. 7, 1993.
81 hybrid structure: *WP*, Jan. 26, 1993; *NYT*, Feb. 28, 1993.
82 "as a way to buy time": *Time*, Sept. 20, 1993; see also Jacob S. Hacker, *The Road to Nowhere: The Genesis of President Clinton's Plan for Health Security*, p. 122.
82 "I had about eighteen": PBS *Frontline* interview with Michael Bromberg, June 14, 1996.
82 From the start, important groups: William Baumol interview; *Time*, Mar. 22, 1993.
82 "A lot of people didn't have a fair chance": Robert Rubin interview.
82 "galvanized every single sector": Pamela Bailey interview.
82 his misgivings about price controls: *NYT*, Feb. 28, 1993.
82 "He said to her that many of the changes": DPM, Memcon of Senator Daniel P. Moynihan, June 21, 1994.
82 "We have many health-care systems": Michael Barone interview.
82 the Clinton plan envisioned: Pamela Bailey interview.
82 Ira Magaziner anticipated: *Time*, Sept. 19, 1994.
83 the plan confounded: Donna Shalala interview.
83 "not a good omen": Reich, p. 105.
83 The President and First Lady said: William Baumol interview; *WP*, Jan. 31, 1993; Hacker, p. 107.
83 When some members of the transition team: *Newsweek*, Mar. 1, 1993.
83 Bill asked them to revise: *WP*, Jan. 23, 1993; Johnson and Broder, p. 109.
83 he knew he couldn't impose still more taxes: Hacker, p. 103.
83 "crazy process": Donna Shalala interview.
83 took Magaziner twenty-two pages: *WP*, Feb. 7, 1993; Johnson and Broder, p. 134.
83 "tollgates": *WP*, Feb. 7, 1993.
83 "working groups": Hacker, p. 123.
83 "dozens of propeller heads": Bruce Reed interview.
83 a history of impractical ideas: *Washington Monthly*, May 1993.
83 "skitters like an ice cube": *Time*, Apr. 19, 1993.
83 "He assumed you were a fool": Donna Shalala interview.
83 angered the press, Democratic leaders: Hacker, pp. 141, 230.
83 self-defeating political strategy: Pamela Bailey interview.
84 "Democrats only" approach: *LH*, pp. 150, 154; Hacker, p. 118.
84 For a brief period: *LH*, p. 154; Johnson and Broder, p. 127.
84 Another strategic mistake: Mickey Kantor interview. Al From also argued about focusing on welfare reform. Drew, p. 128.
84 pledge to "end welfare": *The New Republic*, Feb. 2, 1993.
84 Welfare reform had been one: *FiHC*, p. 418.
84 linchpin of his New Democrat: DPM, Memcon of Senator Daniel P. Moynihan, Jan. 25, 1993. Moynihan noted that Al From met with *The Wall Street Journal* and indicated that welfare reform "is one of the defining issues of the Clinton administration."
84 "the clatter of campaign promises": *WP*, Jan. 15, 1993.

84 "everything the President cares most about": *Time*, Feb. 1, 1993.

84 "Big deal": Ibid.

85 "that person would be fired": DPM, Memcon of Richard Eaton, Jan. 25, 1993.

85 "horrified" and "livid": DPM, Memcon of Senator Daniel P. Moynihan, Jan. 25, 1993.

85 "would remember this slight": *ATH*, pp. 121–22.

85 "The 'big deal' quote was from Rahm": DPM, Memcon of Senator Daniel P. Moynihan, May 21, 1996.

85 those making $200,000 per year: *Newsweek*, Mar. 16, 1992.

85 this tax would edge closer: *NYT*, Feb. 18, 1993.

85 He included a tax on energy: *ML*, p. 494; *Newsweek*, Mar. 29, 1993.

85 he removed the cap of $135,000: *NYT*, Feb. 18, 1993.

85 Bill's pollsters had concluded: Woodward, *Agenda*, p. 100.

85 *USA Today*–CNN poll: *WP*, Jan. 31, 1993.

85 Yielding to both Perot's: Woodward, *Agenda*, pp. 67–68, 84.

86 "a bunch of fucking bond traders": Ibid., p. 84.

86 "Eisenhower Republican": Ibid., p. 185.

86 He targeted the military: *NYT*, Feb. 15, 1993.

86 The remainder would come: *NYT*, Feb. 21, 1993.

86 Bill's initial ten-minute message: *WP*, Feb. 16, 1993.

86 "a place where common sense": Drew, p. 77.

86 market plummeted eighty-three points: Ibid.

86 Bob Rubin, meanwhile, picked: Woodward, *Agenda*, p. 156; *ATH*, p. 137.

86 By then, Rubin had established: *WP*, Jan. 24, 1993.

86 "working relationship": Robert Rubin interview.

86 "The Court of Appeals": Dee Dee Myers interview.

86 "understated and intense": *ML*, p. 452.

86 "Clinton was more disciplined": Jacob Weisberg interview.

87 Hillary considered Rubin "wonderful": Transcript of Bob Woodward's March 11, 1994, interview with Hillary Clinton, obtained from a source.

87 "I really paid attention": Ibid.

87 "Show me what you mean": Robert Rubin interview; Rubin, p. 128.

87 "Hillary had a certain authority": Robert Rubin interview.

87 "he seemed very engaged": Tom Brokaw interview.

87 an aide heard him singing: *Newsweek*, May 3, 1993.

87 He continued to consult: *Time*, Mar. 1, 1993.

87 invited "the kids": Ibid.

87 Hillary surprisingly agreed: Ibid.; Brummett, p. 83.

88 "immediate results": Woodward, *Agenda*, p. 196.

88 Polls taken in the spring: *Time*, May 3, 1993.

88 The Republicans were united: *Newsweek*, Mar. 8, 1993.

88 Both factions sent a harsh: *Newsweek*, May 13, 1993.

88 "The president had asked": Rubin, p. 131.

88 hitting bottom: Roper Center poll ratings, Yankelovich/*Time*/CNN, May 26–27, 1993.

88 "Incredible Shrinking President": *Time*, June 7, 1993.

88 'Hillary thinks this': Bernie Nussbaum interview.

88 "We would always say": Dee Dee Myers interview.

88 "let me think about it": *ATH*, p. 171.

88 "He depended on her": Abner Mikva interview.

88 "like a baby": Marton, p. 317.

88 "During the day": *Time*, May 10, 1993.

89 "chilling effect": *Time*, Sept. 6, 1993.

89 "would try to avoid fighting": Bernie Nussbaum interview.

89   "if they were furious with each other": Ann Stock interview.

89   "almost whistling as he whipped through papers": Gergen, p. 274.

89   "His mood would darken": Ibid. See also Marton, p. 330.

89   "nightcap": *ATH*, p. 287.

89   "It was her way of saying": Marton, pp. 323–24.

90   "She would launch a deadly missile": Gergen, pp. 298–99.

90   "demoralizing": Ibid., p. 299.

90   "got into a row": Ibid., p. 298.

90   "What the fuck": Marton, p. 324.

90   Gergen believed the First Couple: Gergen, p. 309.

91   The anecdote came from: *BS*, p. 248.

91   "thrown a lamp": *WP*, Feb. 9, 1996.

91   "pretty good arm": Hillary Clinton, interview with Barbara Walters, ABC News, Jan. 12, 1996.

91   But she never directly addressed: *The New Yorker*, Apr. 15, 1996.

91   "We have a lot of enemies": Bernie Nussbaum interview. John F. Harris and Ann Devroy wrote in *WP* that after the lamp-throwing incident appeared in the press, Hillary "freaked. She could not abide the idea of having spies in her own house." *WP*, Feb. 9, 1996.

91   Harry Thomason, who had been staying: *WP*, Jan. 12, 1996; *BS*, pp. 247, 259; Drew, p. 178.

91   had urged Hillary to replace: *BS*, p. 247.

91   "overreacting": *The New Yorker*, Apr. 15, 1996.

91   the agents switched their posts: Ibid.; *BS*, pp. 248–49; Drew, pp. 90–91.

91   "just have to get used to": Gergen, p. 292.

92   "three forces to be reckoned with": Bruce Reed interview.

92   "three-headed system": Gergen, p. 293.

92   "inevitably diminish": *Newsweek*, Jan. 25, 1993.

92   "Dudley Do-Right": *NYT Magazine*, Jan. 17, 1993.

92   "Al Gore hasn't yet realized": Ibid.

92   "would have to adjust": Ibid. *NYT* reporter Gwen Ifill also wrote that Gore's "role has often been overshadowed in news reports by accounts of the influence of Mr. Clinton's wife, Hillary." *NYT*, Feb. 19, 1993.

92   "There are a great many people": *The New Yorker*, May 30, 1994; in a September 2006 interview with the author, Washington writer Ann Crittenden said, "The summer after Bill Clinton was inaugurated, we [Crittenden and her husband, John Henry] saw Taylor Branch and his wife in Aspen. Taylor said he had recently spent time with Bill and Hillary, and they were talking about her running after him—about sixteen years of the Clintons. I was amazed by the arrogance of that." Branch later denied making such a statement.

93   "Gore gets credit": Private journal.

93   Before taking office: *Newsweek*, Sept. 2, 1996.

93   Bill also committed to a private lunch: Ibid.

93   "wonk talk": *Time*, July 17, 1996.

93   "They managed quite well": Laura Tyson interview.

93   "both loved detail": James Steinberg interview.

93   Gore avoided public disagreement: *Newsweek*, Oct. 31, 1994.

93   "The Vice President rarely spoke first": Bill Galston interview.

93   "analytical framework that is all-Harvard": Henry Cisneros interview.

94   "Gore in small settings": Donna Shalala interview.

94   "piece of artillery": *Newsweek*, Sept. 13, 1993.

94   "You just pray nobody sneezes": *Time*, Dec. 15, 1997.

94 "It takes me twice as long": *Newsweek*, Oct. 31, 1994.

94 "reinforces Hillary as a caring person": *WP*, May 18, 1993.

95 Bill and Hillary pursued: *Time*, Mar. 22, 1993; *WP*, Apr. 30, 1993.

95 She nodded and listened: *WP*, Feb. 5 and Feb. 12, 1993.

95 she talked with Ira Magaziner: *Esquire*, Aug. 1993.

95 deep-seated dislike for the national press: *ATH*, p. 147.

95 Hillary initially benefited: Drew, p. 196.

95 "icon of American womanhood": Kurtz, p. 83.

95 But Hillary had needlessly antagonized: *ATH*, p. 112; *NYT*, Jan. 22, 1993; Woodward, *Agenda*, p. 230.

95 "free to walk around": *ATH*, p. 112.

95 Weeks later, she irritated: *NYT*, Feb. 2, 1993.

95 "the biggest chip on her shoulder": Sheehy, p. 227.

96 "power-walking down the corridors": *WP*, Mar. 3, 1993.

96 "a hard pol": Ibid.

96 "creeping Rodhamism": *The New Republic*, Feb. 15, 1993.

96 "a stick that you beat": Katz, p. 181.

96 "swallowed nervous laughter": Ibid., p. 190.

96 "unfair, unjust, inaccurate": Johnson and Broder, p. 140.

96 She reminded herself: *WP*, Apr. 4, 1995.

96 Eleanor had refrained from whining: Ibid.

96 Eleanor had never taken a seat: *WP*, Mar. 14, 1994.

96 "unsmiling" and "joyless": *WP*, Mar. 3, 1993.

96 "all the conversations I've had in my head": Woodward, *Choice*, p. 130.

96 Hillary's life turned upside down: *LH*, p. 156.

96 The health-care task force proceeded: *WP*, Apr. 3, 1993.

97 She returned to Washington: *Time*, May 10, 1993.

97 uncharacteristically impassioned: Ibid.

97 "sleeping sickness": *WP*, May 6, 1993.

97 "crisis of meaning": *Time*, Oct. 19, 1992.

97 The following day, Hillary was in: *NYT*, Apr. 29, 1993.

97 She was preternaturally composed: Woodward, *Agenda*, p. 185.

97 Later that night, Hugh Rodham: *NYT*, Apr. 8, 1993; *WP*, May 3, 1993.

97 "suddenly she leaned her head": Hubbell, p. 231.

97 her father had been impossible: *The Boston Globe*, Jan. 12, 1993; Hillary Clinton, *It Takes a Village*, p. 22.

97 If Hillary forgot to replace: *LH*, p. 11; Priscilla Eakeley interview.

97 "even in the snow": Ibid.

97 "closet Democrat": Martha Sherrill interview with Dorothy Rodham.

97 "was active in Goldwater's": Ibid.

98 "was ever really conservative": *The Boston Globe*, Jan. 12, 1993.

98 "I don't care how they do things": Woodward, *Agenda*, p. 190.

98 In Little Rock, they had been coequals: Brummett, p. 159.

98 "best friends": *LH*, p. 79.

98 Atticus Finch: Ibid.

98 reserved, upright: *NYT*, July 23, 1993.

98 "People gravitated to him": Hubbell, pp. 40–41.

98 Foster said there was no truth: Bernie Nussbaum interview.

98 "I just don't think": *The New Yorker*, Sept. 11, 1995.

98 "take command": *BS*, p. 310.

98 "idolized" Hillary: Susan Thomases interview.

98 discussed his own private matters: Hubbell, p. 98.

98   But now Hillary was his boss: Sheehy, p. 233.

98   Foster was acting as personal attorney: *The New Yorker*, Mar. 23, 1998.

99   "too naïve": BS, p. 248.

99   "the client": Ibid.

99   "became a very demanding": Hubbell, p. 194.

99   "snapped at him": Ibid., p. 212.

99   "excessive costs": NYT, Aug. 15, 1993.

99   Foster was still trying to straighten: *Time*, July 24, 1995.

99   capital gain of one thousand: BS, pp. 252–54; Woodward, *Shadow*, p. 285.

99   "a can of worms": Woodward, *Shadow*, p. 285.

99   officials at the Resolution Trust: *Newsweek*, Jan. 17, 1994; BS, p. 341.

99   "on the radar screen": Bernie Nussbaum interview.

100 Foster had worked on Madison: WP, June 2, 1996; *Newsweek*, Jan. 17, 1994.

100 Hubbell, who had stolen: Hubbell, pp. 142, 149; *The New Yorker*, Jan. 8, 1996; *Time*, Apr. 14, 1997; BS, pp. 257–58; LH, pp. 266–67; *Vanity Fair*, June 2001.

100 "drove Vince batty": Bernie Nussbaum interview.

100 "financial mismanagement": LH, p. 172.

100 should be replaced: Drew, p. 178.

100 "on top of": *The New Yorker*, Apr. 15, 1996.

100 "general impatience": Ibid.

100 "We need to have our people": NYT, Oct. 19, 2000.

100 "There would be hell": NYT, Jan. 7, 1996.

100 Mack McLarty gave the order: Brummett, pp. 124–28.

101 allegations of cronyism: *Time*, May 31, 1993.

101 "direct contact": LH, p. 173.

101 "a six-figure salary": WP, May 27, 1993.

101 "sort of the equivalent of taking over": *Newsweek*, June 7, 1993.

101 "offhand comment": LH, p. 172.

101 "origin of the decision": BS, p. 277, quoting White House lawyer Neil Eggleston's statement on April 4, 1994.

101 "did not direct that any action": Ibid.

101 "factually false" and "overwhelming evidence": NYT, Oct. 19, 2000.

101 Bill was caught by White House reporters: Drew, p. 174; Dee Dee Myers interview; ATH, p. 144.

101 "When I asked how much": Dee Dee Myers interview.

102 "The underlying truth": ATH, p. 144.

102 He had proposed her: Brummett, p. 142; Blumenthal, p. 55.

102 He had actually read more: Drew, p. 206.

102 Hillary's full support: Ibid., p. 205.

102 "not to cut her loose": Bernie Nussbaum interview.

102 Guinier was furious: Guinier, pp. 125–26.

102 "Hey Kiddo!": Ibid., p. 50; *The New Yorker*, Feb. 26, 1996.

102 "messy departure": *Newsweek*, June 14, 1993.

102 Taking the advice of Al Gore: Warren Bass, "The Triage of Dayton," *Foreign Affairs*, vol. 77, no. 5, Sept./Oct. 1998, pp. 100–101.

102 "perception of drift": *Newsweek*, May 24, 1993.

102 "deep misgivings" and viewed . . . "a Vietnam": Ibid.

103 "ethnic cleansing" in Bosnia: ML, p. 512.

103 "Saint Hillary": NYT *Magazine*, May 23, 1993. Ironically, there had indeed been a St. Hilary of Poitiers in the fourth century, who wrote on the meaning of faith.

103 Hillary and her aides had meticulously: Martha Sherrill interview; *Time*, Mar. 21, 1994.

103 "the use of power to achieve": *NYT Magazine*, May 23, 1993.

103 "her staff loved": *Time*, Mar. 21, 1994.

103 Hillary was upset: *Working Woman*, June 1994.

103 "elite media": Ibid.

103 "scared of it": Ibid.

103 Bill brought veteran Republican: Woodward, *Agenda*, pp. 241–42; *ATH*, p. 149.

103 At Gergen's urging: Drew, pp. 215, 238; *WP*, June 24, 1993.

104 "pan-seared lamb cushions": Ibid.

104 "This isn't dinner": Ibid.

104 "many . . . who went to the White House": *WP*, July 18, 1993.

104 "She suddenly looked down": Eric Tarloff, e-mail to author, Jan. 5, 2005, and author's conversation with Tarloff.

104 Bill asked for regular bulletins: *ATH*, p. 205.

104 Bill and Hillary left for Tokyo: *ML*, p. 526; Talbott, p. 47.

105 he had spent months nurturing: Talbott, p. 48.

105 In April, he had met with: *ATH*, pp. 139–40.

105 "the biggest foreign policy": Talbott, p. 61.

105 He also knew he needed: Ibid., p. 83.

105 "I suspected that there was": Ibid., pp. 185–86.

105 "compelling evidence": Louis Fisher, "Military Action Against Iraq," *Presidential Studies Quarterly*, vol. 28, no. 4, fall 1998, p. 794.

105 Bill made his decision in secrecy: *ATH*, pp. 161–62.

105 "very awkward": Queen Noor, *Leap of Faith: Memoirs of an Unexpected Life*, p. 360.

106 a chance to show he could be a muscular leader: *ATH*, pp. 157–58.

106 Bill's approval ratings rose: Roper Center poll ratings, June 27–29, 1993.

106 "In hard times": *Time*, July 19, 1993.

106 "I've learned in groups": Drew, p. 245.

106 "Then I saw he had a crossword puzzle": Mickey Kantor interview.

106 On her first foreign trip: Drew, p. 244; *LH*, p. 175; *Time*, July 19, 1993.

106 With her mother as a companion: *WP*, July 12, 1993.

106 "I'm such a government junkie": Ibid.

106 Hillary also met with local: *LH*, p. 175.

106 Hillary, Chelsea, and Dorothy: Ibid.; *Time*, Aug. 30, 1993.

106 John Podesta had finished: *The New Yorker*, Sept. 11, 1995.

106 Foster felt deeply responsible: *LH*, p. 173; Hubbell, p. 235.

107 While Hillary later said: *BS*, p. 278.

107 "Vince was obsessing": Bernie Nussbaum interview.

107 "couldn't bear the thought": Hubbell, p. 235.

107 "My God, what have we done?": *BS*, p. 267.

107 Foster faced the possibility: *BS*, p. 423.

107 "defend/HRC role": *Newsweek*, Feb. 5, 1996.

107 Foster was also under scrutiny: *The New Yorker*, Sept. 11, 1995.

107 "He wasn't functioning well": Bernie Nussbaum interview.

107 Foster's wife, Lisa: *The New Yorker*, Sept. 11, 1995.

107 "It's not the same": Hubbell, p. 234.

107 "he like everybody would say things": *BS*, p. 278.

108 "let the President and Hillary down": *BS*, p. 285.

108 "if he felt trapped": *The New Yorker*, Sept. 11, 1995.

108 "not here, this feels too good": Hubbell, p. 243.

108 McLarty was worried: Ibid., p. 244.

108 The same day, Foster called: *The New Yorker*, Sept. 11, 1995.

108 "highly unusual": Hubbell, p. 244.

108 "having a rough time": *Time*, Aug. 9, 1993.
108 "lonesome": Dee Dee Myers press conference, July 19, 1993.
108 When Foster said he needed: Ibid.; Drew, p. 256.
108 "was hoping to give him some encouragement": *ML*, p. 531.
108 "hadn't convinced him": Ibid.
108 Bill had an upbeat meeting: Woodward, *Agenda*, pp. 310–11.
108 he announced his selection: Louis Freeh, *My FBI: Bringing Down the Mafia, Investigating Bill Clinton, and Fighting the War on Terror*, pp. 57, 60.
109 She had been suggested by: Bernie Nussbaum interview; DPM, Memcon of Senator Daniel P. Moynihan, May 24, 1993.
109 Nussbaum and Foster oversaw: Bernie Nussbaum interview.
109 "charismatically challenged": Drew, p. 217.
109 "We hit two home runs": Freeh, p. 61.
109 "I'll see you later": Ibid.
109 Foster had lunch on a tray: Brummett, p. 159.
109 At 1:00 p.m., he pulled: *Time*, Aug. 2, 1993.
109 Foster had been found: *NYT*, July 23, 1993; *The New Yorker*, Aug. 9, 1993; *LH*, p. 177.
109 It was the same method: *BS*, p. 287; *The New Yorker*, Sept. 11, 1995.
109 In the pocket: *Newsweek*, Aug. 9, 1993.
109 Hillary in Little Rock, who burst into tears: *LH*, pp. 175–76.
109 When McLarty told him: Mack McLarty interview.
109 "I want to see Lisa": Ibid.
109 played mumblety-peg: Hubbell, p. 253.
109 Bill silently hugged: Ibid., pp. 250–51.
110 "remembering and crying": *Newsweek*, Aug. 2, 1993.
110 Nussbaum was chastised: Drew, pp. 257, 384.
110 He gave a sheaf: *WP*, Aug. 2, 1994; *LH*, p. 178; *Newsweek*, Aug. 7, 1995.
110 Investigators later questioned: *Newsweek*, Aug. 7, 1995.
110 Amid an atmosphere: *Newsweek*, Jan. 8, 1996; Drew, pp. 384–85; Woodward, *Shadow*, p. 298.
110 annotated with red ink: Sheehy, pp. 279, 281.
110 "to transfer the documents to a locked": Woodward, *Shadow*, p. 298; *WP*, June 2, 1999.
110 Among the suspicious activities: *WP*, June 16, 1996; *Newsweek*, Aug. 7, 1995.
110 "what was going on": *Time*, Aug. 7, 1995.
110 Thomases had known Foster: Susan Thomases interview.
110 effort to shield potentially damaging documents: *WP*, June 16, 1996.
111 "nobody was thinking about Whitewater": Bernie Nussbaum interview.
111 "craved information": *LH*, p. 176.
111 trigger what became five separate federal inquiries: Harris, p. 76.
111 "the pivotal moment": Hubbell, p. 260.
111 "Vince Foster's death was a history-changing event": Bernie Nussbaum interview.

CHAPTER SIX

112 "would wake up in the middle": *LH*, pp. 173–74.
112 Hillary was familiar with the malady: Ibid., p. 5.
112 "seemed to know": Hubbell, p. 254.
112 "She realized afterward": Mary Mel French interview.
112 "ripped a hole": Ann McCoy interview.
112 "I'm going to go over to my office": Woodward, *Shadow*, p. 285.
113 "found something Vince wrote": Bernie Nussbaum interview.

113 "I was not meant for the job": *ML*, p. 532.

113 "The public will never believe": Ibid.

113 that comment was interpreted to mean: Brummett, p. 173.

113 "I did what I often": *LH*, p. 178.

113 Among other goals: Woodward, *Agenda*, pp. 235, 327.

113 Bill agreed to drop the BTU: Lawrence O'Donnell interview.

113 "I wasn't opposed": Ibid.

113 "Bill Clinton showed he is a wonderful hack": Ibid.

114 "Members of the House": Bill Galston interview.

114 For Al Gore, it was an even greater: Woodward, *Agenda*, p. 327.

114 "We need a war room": Ibid., p. 296.

114 "I want it solved": Ibid., p. 297.

114 The war room ordered by Hillary: Ibid., p. 303.

114 enlisting Hillary's help: Ibid., p. 344.

114 "never seen any of them": Ibid., p. 348.

114 The last holdout: Ibid., pp. 351–52.

115 "What he said to me": *Time*, Oct. 30, 1995.

115 "Bye-bye Marjorie!": Woodward, *Agenda*, p. 354.

115 Bill plucked twenty-dollar bills: Ibid., pp. 354–55.

115 "I might lose the nomination": *Star*, Feb. 4, 1992. Bill Clinton telephone conversation, taped by Gennifer Flowers, Sept. 23, 1991.

115 Hillary had vetoed him: Woodward, *Agenda*, p. 333.

115 Kerrey called Bill: Ibid., p. 335.

115 "bring this presidency down": *ATH*, p. 176.

115 "Fuck you!": Woodward, *Agenda*, p. 336.

115 Kerrey "had got out of bed": DPM, Memcon of Senator Daniel P. Moynihan, Aug. 5, 1993.

115 Moynihan was noncommittal: Ibid.

115 At 6:00 p.m., Moynihan's wife, Liz: *ATH*, p. 181; DPM, Memcon of Senator Daniel P. Moynihan, May 8, 1993.

116 "Don't make it personal": *ATH*, pp. 180–82.

116 Kerrey joined the "yea" votes: Ibid.

116 "green and inexperienced": *ATH*, p. 182.

116 "high road": Woodward, *Agenda*, p. 363.

116 "Every woman in the Congress": *ATH*, p. 182.

116 "saved his administration": DPM, letter to "Godfrey," April 1998.

116 At the end of April: *Time*, May 10, 1993.

117 The economic team and other key advisors: Laura Tyson interview.

117 The treaty, which was designed: *Time*, Aug. 9, 1993.

117 But as an advocate of global: Brummett, p. 33.

117 "The economic team loved NAFTA": Bruce Reed interview.

117 Hillary was backed by Bill's quartet: *Time*, Aug. 9, 1993.

117 "we have postponed": *The New Yorker*, May 30, 1994.

117 " 'If you want to drop NAFTA' ": Mickey Kantor interview; Drew, p. 289.

117 Bill announced that William Daley: *ML*, p. 540; Waldman, p. 58.

118 After the Solarium meetings: Woodward, *Agenda*, p. 368.

118 "80 with 50 floating mulligans": Don Van Natta Jr., *First off the Tee: Presidential Hackers, Duffers, and Cheaters from Taft to Bush*, p. 193.

118 Bill found more pliable: Brummett, p. 197; *Time*, Aug. 30, 1993.

118 He gave speeches: *ML*, p. 539.

118 health-care briefings: Johnson and Broder, pp. 156–57.

118   "I *am* weird": Brummett, p. 196.
118   arranged at the last minute: Drew, p. 291; *NYT*, July 29, 1994; *Time*, Aug. 30, 1993; *Newsweek*, Aug. 23, 1993.
119   "sophisticated weapon": Marjorie Williams, *The Woman at the Washington Zoo*, p. 82.
119   Vacationers on the island: *Time*, Aug. 30, 1993; Williams, p. 79.
119   On their first evening, the Clintons attended: *Time*, Aug. 30, 1993.
119   "rose like Lawrence Welk": Ibid.
119   "wonderful father" and "I love you, Mr. President": Ibid.
119   Bill slept most of the next: *Time*, Sept. 5, 1994.
119   Hillary preferred to read and take walks: *Time*, Aug. 30, 1993.
119   She also befriended a group of women: Rose Styron interview.
120   Hillary was particularly eager to know: Ibid.
120   One afternoon, Jackie Onassis: Drew, pp. 291–92; *Time*, Aug. 30, 1993.
120   Bill and Hillary were out: Lucy Hackney interview.
120   "I don't care about the food": *Time*, Sept. 5, 1994.
120   Katharine Graham invited them: *Time*, Aug. 30, 1993.
120   "Clinton really wanted to talk": Kay Allaire interview.
120   Bill to preside over: Drew, p. 293.
121   he had read Yale law professor: *Newsweek*, Nov. 7, 1994; *Time*, Sept. 5, 1994.
121   He had been aware since mid-August: BS, pp. 319–24.
121   he would be "destroyed": Ibid., p. 323.
121   "giving information out": Ibid.
122   "Troopers being talked to": Toobin, p. 22.
122   "just like Buddy's": BS, p. 324.
122   By September, inquiries by the government: Ibid., pp. 225, 227, 329, 333–34.
122   "potential witnesses": *Newsweek*, Aug. 8, 1994.
122   Hanson transmitted the information: BS, p. 334.
122   Reporters at *The Washington Post*: Ibid., p. 337.
122   White House officials: Ibid., p. 328; *Time*, Aug. 8, 1994.
122   The President merely replied with a "hmmmm": BS, p. 336.
122   reporters grew increasingly suspicious: Ibid., p. 329.
123   "among the most productive": Gergen, p. 262.
123   Secret negotiations leading to: *ML*, p. 541.
123   "only too happy to claim credit": Reich, p. 129.
123   The previous night, Bill had been: *ML*, p. 542; *ATH*, p. 189.
123   "He is the nation's Preacher-in-Chief": Reich, p. 129.
123   Bill kicked off: PPP, 1993, book 2, pp. 1777–81.
123   He ad-libbed: Waldman, pp. 60–61.
123   "Secretary Reich could almost": Ibid., pp. 63–64.
123   leak of a 246-page draft: Drew, p. 303; *Time*, Sept. 20, 1993.
123   "inside story" and "sheer size": *Time*, Sept. 20, 1993.
124   Hillary sought to warm up: *WP*, June 14 and Aug. 10, 1993.
124   "price gouging": *NYT*, May 27, 1993.
124   "squared with the Administration's": *WP*, June 14, 1993.
124   "radiated reasonableness": Johnson and Broder, p. 200.
124   At the end of the summer, Gradison approved: Ibid., p. 205.
124   "scare tactics": Ibid., pp. 204–5.
124   "mind-bogglingly unrealistic": DPM, Memcon of Senator Daniel P. Moynihan, Sept. 17, 1993.
125   "fantasy numbers": Johnson and Broder, pp. 173, 351; *LH*, p. 185.
125   nachos and guacamole: *LH*, p. 186.
125   "health care reform [as] part": Ibid.; see also *Time*, Oct. 4, 1993.

125   "budgetary sense": *NYT*, Sept. 21, 1993.

125   "The President was late coming home": *ATH*, p. 199.

125   "American journey" revision was awful: Ibid.

125   Bill sat down for one of his all-nighters: *Time*, Oct. 4, 1993.

125   Stephanopoulos found the couple: *ATH*, p. 199.

125   "the power beside": *NYT*, Sept. 22, 1993.

126   Bill tinkered with the text: *Time*, Oct. 4, 1993; Klein, p. 6.

126   "tight smile": *ATH*, p. 200.

126   he momentarily seemed disoriented: *LH*, pp. 187–88.

126   "from a lifetime of hard study": *ATH*, p. 202.

126   "arc off into ideas": Talbott, p. 116.

126   "jazz genius": *ATH*, p. 202.

126   his approach came straight out: Tommy Caplan interview.

126   "talented navigator": *ATH*, p. 203.

126   "Too bad it would be the high point": Ibid.

127   The President's approval: Roper Center poll ratings, Sept. 24–26, 1993.

127   star turns before five: *NYT*, Oct. 1, 1993.

127   earned rave reviews: *WP*, Oct. 6, 1993.

127   "This is Eleanor Roosevelt": *NYT*, Sept. 29, 1993.

127   "She can sling": *WP*, Oct. 3, 1993.

127   "utterly fearless": Lawrence O'Donnell interview.

127   "government-run health care": *WP*, Sept. 30, 1993.

127   "proceed with caution": Ibid.

127   Bill learned that: Drew, p. 316; *LH*, p. 191.

127   had indeed saved: *ATH*, p. 214.

127   The bloody fight: Ibid., pp. 210, 214; Anthony Lake, *Six Nightmares: Real Threats in a Dangerous World and How America Can Meet Them*, p. 129; *ML*, p. 550.

127   the time came for Bill to turn: Johnson and Broder, p. 189.

127   The White House publicity: Waldman, p. 63.

128   Bill gave dinners: Drew, p. 340; *Time*, Oct. 25, 1993.

128   Al Gore solidified the vote: Gergen, pp. 283–84.

128   "whiny crank": *Newsweek*, Nov. 22, 1993.

128   The bipartisan victory pushed: Roper Center poll ratings, Dec. 15–19, 1993.

128   "It's a measure": *Time*, Nov. 29, 1993.

128   Senate Majority Leader George: *WP*, Nov. 23, 1993; *LH*, p. 191.

128   In an attempt to regain: Drew, p. 310; *Time*, Nov. 8, 1993.

128   "Please help us": *Time*, Nov. 8, 1993.

128   240,000-word measure: *NYT*, July 5, 1994.

128   In an effort to equalize care: Michael Barone interview.

128   teaching hospitals were required: *WP*, Nov. 23, 1993.

128   "Oh, don't worry about it": Ibid.

129   "I understood the core of the plan": Robert Rubin interview.

129   "my brain aches": *Time*, Nov. 8, 1993.

129   The President proved surprisingly ineffective: Hacker, p. 148.

129   Her first broadside: Johnson and Broder, pp. 209–10.

129   "to the brink of bankruptcy": *NYT*, Nov. 2, 1993.

129   Less understandable was her salvo: *NYT*, Nov. 9, 1993.

129   "She really trashed": PBS *Frontline* interview with Michael Bromberg, June 14, 1996.

129   They said the crucial blow: Johnson and Broder, p. 233.

129   "the generous protector": Hacker, p. 176.

129   "I don't think we really had a chance": Bill Clinton, interview with Joe Klein, July 5, 2000. *PPP*, 2000, book 2, pp. 2079–2104.

130 "the notion that this could work": DPM, Memcon of Senator Daniel P. Moynihan, Nov. 16, 1993.
130 "would be put in jeopardy": Ibid., Jan. 25, 1994.
130 Public support for health reform: Hacker, p. 146.
130 "overbearing government program": Ibid., p. 148.
130 "had something that alienated every sector": Pamela Bailey interview.
130 "that they were smarter than anyone else": Drew, p. 305.
130 "incrementalists": Bill Galston interview.
130 "Compromise to her": PBS *Frontline* interview with Michael Bromberg, June 14, 1996.
130 The First Couple instead impersonated: *ML*, p. 555; *LH*, p. 192.
130 Bruce Lindsey wore: Hubbell, p. 291.
130 "I was my client's protector": Bernie Nussbaum interview.
131 *The Washington Post* broke: *BS*, p. 341.
131 The White House had been steeling: Drew, p. 378.
131 "bad judgment": *BS*, pp. 406, 408.
131 The first week of November: Ibid., pp. 341, 345.
131 The most potentially damaging: Ibid., p. 317; Toobin, p. 65.
131 "impressed": *BS*, p. 327.
131 With the reemergence: Hubbell, p. 267; *LH*, pp. 194–95; *BS*, p. 366.
131 Hubbell turned over additional documents: Hubbell, p. 267.
132 There was no shortage: Drew, p. 391.
132 *The Washington Post* submitted: *LH*, p. 200; *BS*, p. 342.
132 "slippery slope": *LH*, p. 200.
132 "an embarrassing sweetheart deal": Max Brantley interview.
132 Clinton lawyers continued to scour: *LH*, p. 195.
132 Bill and Hillary spent the four-day: Ibid., p. 201.
132 Bill's mother was gravely ill: *ML*, pp. 565–66; *LH*, p. 201.
132 Bill practiced endlessly: Talbott, p. 103.
132 "Democracy comes by fits": Ibid., p. 104.
133 Bill had an encounter: *Newsweek*, March 30, 1998.
133 "more than just": Excerpts of Kathleen Willey's deposition (Jan. 10, 1998), released Mar. 13, 1998.
133 "I put my arms": Bill Clinton deposition, Jan. 17, 1998.
133 "I was in a very desperate": Kathleen Willey deposition, Jan. 10, 1998.
133 he seemed distracted: Ibid.
133 "a blank stare": *Newsweek*, Mar. 30, 1998.
133 Still, she got a part-time: *Newsweek*, Aug. 11, 1997.
133 "flustered, happy and joyful": Ibid.
134 first said Willey had confided: Toobin, p. 397.
134 When Tripp spitefully took her story: *The New Yorker*, Mar. 23, 1998.
134 "uncomfortably similar": Harris, p. 229.
134 Aside from trips: *LH*, p. 204; *NYT*, Dec. 8, 1993.
134 Since the tragedy in Somalia: Drew, pp. 358, 360, 363.
134 "heavy into all personnel": Private journal.
134 They ultimately settled: *ML*, p. 576.
134 "dishy, dreamy": *NYT*, Dec. 12, 1993.
134 "pussycat": Ibid.
134 It was the latest in a series: *Newsweek*, June 7, 1993; *LH*, p. 171.
134 "We sense that we aren't": *Mirabella*, June 1994; *NYT*, June 15, 1994.
135 "vile stories": *LH*, p. 206.
135 Hillary was part of a group: *BS*, p. 356.

135 "especially awkward": Ibid.
135 "old news": Ibid.
135 "easily discredited": Ibid., p. 358.
135 Brock's story: *American Spectator*, Jan. 1994.
135 "ridiculous": *BS*, p. 359.
136 "Clinton had admitted he had been unfaithful": Dee Dee Myers interview.
136 "something was up": *ATH*, p. 228.
136 "I just want a nice job at FEMA": Dee Dee Myers interview.
136 "My memory of Hillary's approach": Ibid.
136 White House aides didn't directly confront: Drew, pp. 386–87.
136 But at Hillary's urging: Ibid.
136 The White House canceled: *BS*, pp. 361–62.
136 The aides asserted: Ibid.; Drew, p. 381.
136 California private investigator Jack Palladino: *Vanity Fair*, June 2001; *Newsweek*, Feb. 9, 1998.
136 On Tuesday the twenty-first: *Los Angeles Times*, Dec. 21, 1993.
137 "second biggest gun": *NYT*, Dec. 22, 1993.
137 "outrageous, terrible": *WP*, Dec. 22, 1993.
137 "I find it not an accident": Ibid.
137 Betsey Wright secured an affidavit: *BS*, p. 363.
137 "curiously legalistic": *Newsweek*, Jan. 3, 1994.
137 "didn't say those words": *BS*, p. 363.
137 alleged that two of them: Johnson and Broder, p. 256.
137 "I have nothing else": *Time*, Jan. 3, 1994.
138 "took a toll on the Clintons": Bernie Nussbaum interview.
138 "hit Hillary hard": *ML*, p. 565.
138 new round of allegations: *Newsweek*, Jan. 3, 1994.
138 Republicans began calling: *BS*, p. 366.
138 "had a veto": *ATH*, p. 228.
138 "It's embarrassing": *WP*, Feb. 9, 1996.
138 David Gergen believed: Gergen, p. 290.
138 investing in commodities futures: *NYT Magazine*, July 31, 1994.
138 "there would be no end": Bernie Nussbaum interview.
138 "would have punctured": Gergen, p. 290.
139 On December 23, the White House: Drew, pp. 392–93; *Newsweek*, Jan. 17, 1994.
139 In an attempt to raise Bill's spirits: Hubbell, p. 270.
139 The next day, the Clintons returned: *ML*, pp. 565–66.

CHAPTER SEVEN

140 "On Whitewater, Maggie [Williams] told me": *Newsweek*, Aug 8, 1994.
140 "poking into 20 years": Ibid.
141 Twice within a week, Hillary cried: *ATH*, p. 231.
141 On January 4, she arrived unannounced: Ibid., pp. 230–31.
141 "You never *believed* in us": Ibid., p. 232.
141 "You can tell your friends": Gergen, p. 299.
141 Shortly before 2:00 a.m. on January 6: *ML*, p. 567.
141 "I would have thought that even the press": Ibid., p. 568.
141 "fried meats, slow cooked vegetables": Brummett, p. 233.
141 "recoiled a bit": Ibid.
141 That night, Bill flew: *ML*, p. 569.

141 Bill learned that Pat Moynihan: Drew, p. 399; Woodward, *Shadow*, p. 236; WP, Jan. 12, 1994.

142 The editorial pages: *ML*, pp. 571–72.

142 "lance the boil": *BS*, p. 371.

142 "not a single soul has alleged": Drew, p. 405.

142 In the evening, Bill put: *ML*, pp. 568–70; *Newsweek*, Jan. 24, 1994.

142 "furry, complicated": *Newsweek*, Jan. 17, 1994.

142 "terrible precedent": *LH*, p. 213.

142 as did Susan Thomases: Susan Thomases interview; *Time*, Mar. 21, 1994.

142 "Nothing legally compelled Janet Reno": Bernie Nussbaum interview.

143 On Tuesday evening, Hillary suggested: *ATH*, p. 240; *BS*, p. 373; *LH*, p. 214. Bill Clinton said the conference call took place in Moscow. This is incorrect. It was Prague. *ML*, p. 572.

143 "Dan Rather asked me about Whitewater": Bernie Nussbaum interview.

143 Stephanopoulos told him that they couldn't ignore: *BS*, pp. 373–74.

143 "evil institution": Bernie Nussbaum interview.

143 "crazy": Ibid.

143 "So what?": Ibid.

143 But the political advisors feared: Drew, p. 402.

143 "in a disciplined and organized fashion": Bernie Nussbaum interview.

143 She then asked everyone except: *BS*, p. 375.

144 directed Nussbaum to prepare: Bernie Nussbaum interview.

144 "You had your two questions": *PPP*, 1994, book 1, p. 45.

144 "I have nothing to say": *BS*, p. 373.

144 "Bill feels he has to appoint": Bernie Nussbaum interview.

144 "But the issue was broader": Ibid.

144 "the worst presidential decision" and "poor judgment": *ML*, p. 574.

144 the interim Partnership for Peace: Drew, p. 409.

144 calling the leaders . . . "guys": *Newsweek*, Jan 24, 1994.

145 "was in the moment": William Miller interview.

145 Hillary kept a decidedly: *LH*, p. 217; WP, Jan. 15, 1994.

145 "Carpe Diem": Talbott, p. 114.

145 he talked about the need: Ibid., p. 116.

145 "He focused on a psychological": Eric Liu interview.

145 "ruggedly independent": *BS*, p. 398.

145 "The main thing I want to do": Bill Clinton, interview on *Larry King Live*, Jan. 20, 1994. *PPP*, 1994, book 1, p. 110.

145 Bill and Hillary's unequivocal priority: Drew, 396.

145 "I cannot recall him publicly": Gergen, p. 309.

145 Hillary rebuffed an important overture: Pamela Bailey interview; *The New Yorker*, May 30, 1994.

146 "stony faced": Pamela Bailey interview.

146 "She was *lecturing*": *The New Yorker*, May 30, 1994.

146 "It seems we have a language barrier": Ibid.

146 "the President was in": PBS *Frontline* interview with Michael Bromberg, June 14, 1996.

146 "Bill and I didn't come to Washington": *NYT*, July 5, 1994.

146 "You're either for": AP, Jan. 22, 1994.

146 "Gang of Four": *Time*, Feb. 7, 1994.

146 Bill "sat mum": Gergen, p. 309.

146 "categorical threat": Johnson and Broder, p. 269.

147 "No, we're going ahead": Gergen, p. 309.

147 "Might he have passed a bipartisan reform plan": Ibid.
147 Bill stayed up all night: *Newsweek*, Feb. 7, 1994.
147 final version wrapped inside: *Time*, Feb. 7, 1994.
147 "co-opting GOP ideas": *Newsweek*, Feb. 7, 1994.
147 "guaranteed private health insurance": Drew, p. 417.
147 "If you send me legislation": Johnson and Broder, p. 267.
147 Scarcely a week later: *WP*, Feb. 5, 1994.
147 "fraud, waste and abuse": Ibid.
147 "It is unclear what the White House strategy is": Ibid.
147 "Bill's White House": PBS *Frontline* interview with Michael Bromberg, June 14, 1996.
147 On February 11, a twenty-seven-year-old: Michael Isikoff, *Uncovering Clinton: A Reporter's Story*, pp. 6, 19, 24.
148 "hisself": Ibid., p. 19.
148 "Paula" had been escorted: *American Spectator*, Jan. 1994.
148 Jones had complained: *Time*, June 6, 1997; Isikoff, p. 49.
148 "a type of sex" . . . "humiliating": BS, p. 389.
148 "a cheap political fund-raising trick": Ibid.
148 "no nervous chatter": *ATH*, p. 267.
148 "set-up job": Ibid., p. 266.
148 but gave him the green light: Isikoff, pp. 16, 18.
148 "Isikoff totally believes this": *ATH*, p. 268.
148 "pattern of compulsive": Ibid.
148 The White House dispatched: Ibid., p. 269.
149 "worst moments": Ibid.
149 "wasn't his style": Ibid., p. 271.
149 "polite but imponderable": Ibid.
149 In subsequent weeks: *WP*, Mar. 2, 1994; *Time*, Aug. 8, 1994.
149 Fiske issued subpoenas: *Newsweek*, Mar. 14, 1994.
149 "There is a lot of pressure": Bernie Nussbaum interview.
149 "You have become so controversial": Ibid.
149 "in an absolutely legal and ethical": Ibid.
149 "I was struck": Freeh, p. 254.
150 Cutler agreed to serve: Woodward, *Shadow*, pp. 249–51.
150 White House staff threw a pep rally: *Newsweek*, Mar. 21, 1994.
150 "the recurrent thread": Ibid., Mar. 14, 1994.
150 "bunker mentality": *WP*, Mar. 7, 1994.
150 "fear wall": *Newsweek*, Mar. 14, 1994.
150 "queen on a chessboard": *Time*, Mar. 21, 1994.
150 "political liability": *WP*, Mar. 7, 1994.
150 "embarrassing ethical questions": Ibid.
150 Hillary had stopped reading: LH, p. 222.
150 "My husband and I never watch": *NYT*, Mar. 5, 1994.
150 "I'm going through one of my": Transcript of Bob Woodward's March 11, 1994, interview with Hillary Clinton, obtained from a source.
150 "I have never known": *Newsweek*, Mar. 21, 1994.
151 "Don't Pillory Hillary": *WP*, Mar. 12, 1994.
151 "have trouble stomaching": Ibid., Mar. 15, 1994.
151 "we never intended to do anything": *Time*, Mar. 21, 1994.
151 She also signaled: *NYT*, Mar. 13, 1994.
151 "trying to get an exact": BS, p. 253.
151 The Clintons would eventually revise: Ibid.
151 Bill and Hillary's back taxes and interest: LH, p. 223.

151 "billing irregularities": Hubbell, p. 278.

151 "hard to believe": Harris, p. 143.

151 "politics of personal destruction": Ibid.

151 "had strong proof": *NYT*, May 15, 1997.

152 it later emerged: *Newsweek*, Apr. 14, 1997.

152 "pretty reserved": Hubbell, p. 283.

152 "to ask what was happening": *LH*, p. 222.

152 business opportunities: *Newsweek*, Apr. 14, 1997; *Time*, Feb. 17 and Apr. 14, 1997, and Sept. 21, 1998.

152 "try to help": *Newsweek*, Apr. 14, 1997.

152 nearly seven hundred thousand: *WP*, June 29, 1999; *USA Today*, June 29, 1999.

152 paid him one hundred thousand dollars: *Newsweek*, Apr. 14, 1997.

152 "human compassion": *WP*, Apr. 2, 1997.

153 The windfall had provided the down payment: *BS*, pp. 415–16.

153 was largely offset by the sixty-nine thousand dollars: *Newsweek*, Apr. 4, 1994.

153 the White House admitted: *BS*, p. 417.

153 "reading the *Wall Street Journal*" and "numerous people": *BS*, p. 417.

153 She was then forced to concede: Ibid., p. 415. *Time* characterized the trades as being without "legally required collateral," July 24, 1995; *FiHC*, pp. 371–72.

153 It also turned out: *Time*, Apr. 25, 1994; *WP*, July 21, 1992.

153 "She would call me": *Time*, Mar. 21, 1994.

153 "Yuppie Hillary": *Newsweek*, Mar. 28, 1994.

153 "gloriously fat": Ibid., Mar. 21, 1994.

153 "carefully cultivated": *Time*, Mar. 28, 1994.

153 "at every turn": Renshon, p. 242.

154 a *Los Angeles Times* poll: Woodward, *Shadow*, p. 252; *NYT*, Apr. 3, 1994, had shown *Newsweek*'s poll with Clinton's approval at 43 percent.

154 bold move advocated by: *WP*, May 8, 2005.

154 Eleanor Roosevelt had held more than: *NYT*, Apr. 24, 1994.

154 She much preferred: *WP*, Apr. 23, 1994.

154 The summons to the press: *LH*, p. 225.

154 Hillary's advisors counseled: *WP*, Apr. 23, 1994.

154 "felt like wearing": *LH*, p. 225.

154 "Pink Press Conference": *LH*, p. 225; *WP*, Apr. 23, 1994.

154 No one inquired about: *NYT Magazine*, July 31, 1994.

154 "obligation": *WP*, Apr. 23, 1994.

155 "I've been rezoned": *LH*, p. 226.

155 "absolutely" no knowledge: Ibid., p. 225.

155 she deflected other questions: *WP*, Apr. 23, 1994.

155 "If you know that your mortgages": Roger Morris, *Partners in Power: The Clintons and Their America*, p. 387.

155 "Well, shoulda, coulda, woulda, we didn't": *WP*, Apr. 25, 1994.

155 "I don't know": *Time*, Aug. 15, 1994.

155 Three months later, the press: *WP*, Aug. 2, 1994.

155 "Slick Willie, meet Slippery Hillary": *Time*, Aug. 15, 1994.

155 "cozy fireside chat": *NYT*, Apr. 24, 1994.

155 "confident" and "unflappable": *WP*, Apr. 25, 1994.

155 "whether wealthy benefactors": *NYT*, Apr. 24, 1994.

155 "You know, they're not going to let up": *LH*, p. 226.

156 "a long memory for slights": Mike McCurry interview.

156 "start bringing you back": *WP Magazine*, July 12, 1992.

156 "social ultra-conservatives": *NYT*, July 3, 1978. Bill Clinton's admiring interlocutor in

that conversation was Howell Raines, who two decades later became the President's nemesis as the editor of the powerful editorial page of *The New York Times*.

156 Bill's first instinct: Isikoff, p. 56.
156 "that rivals the KGB": *Time*, July 20, 1992.
156 "backstabbing" by the "vicious": Kelley, p. 223.
157 Bill and Hillary had first seized: Woodward, *Agenda*, pp. 392–93.
157 "with all this stuff": Transcript of Bob Woodward's April 13, 1994, interview with Hillary Clinton, obtained from a source.
157 "we will do": Woodward, *Agenda*, p. 393.
157 "shot across the bow": Transcript of Bob Woodward's April 13, 1994, interview with Hillary Clinton, obtained from a source.
157 "the inevitable attacks": Ibid.
157 "pound the Republican attack machine": Sheehy, p. 12.
157 "never crosses my mind": Drew, p. 409.
157 "talked about it all": Johnson and Broder, p. 278.
157 "lost in the funhouse": Ibid., p. 279.
157 "They've become paranoid": Ibid., p. 280.
157 "she only wanted me": Blumenthal, p. 225.
157 "well organized and well financed": *BS*, p. 418.
157 Republican plot explicitly intended: *Time*, Mar. 31, 1994.
158 "I do not even want to spend": *Working Woman*, June 1994.
158 "railed against the tactics": *BS*, p. 38.
158 On April 13, the same day: Transcript of Bob Woodward's April 13, 1994, interview with Hillary Clinton, obtained from a source.
158 Woodward learned his identity: Roger Porter interview.
158 "vast and entrenched interests": Woodward, *Agenda*, p. 393.
158 "part of a national thing": Brummett, p. 282. Brummett's interview was on May 2, 1994.
158 "I tended to make enemies": *ML*, p. 49.

CHAPTER EIGHT

159 Her lawyers said she would: *Newsweek*, Jan. 13, 1997; Toobin, p. 44.
159 conduct was not his style: Woodward, *Shadow*, p. 255.
159 acknowledged that he might have met her: Ibid.
159 gave credence to Jones's claim: Isikoff, p. 88.
159 The two sides came close: Toobin, p. 44; *ATH*, p. 272.
160 "she knew she had no case": *Newsweek*, Jan. 13, 1997.
160 if anyone in the President's camp further denigrated: Toobin, pp. 45–46.
160 President's team said no: Ibid., p. 46.
160 "Bennett felt that real progress": *Newsweek*, Jan. 13, 1997.
160 "odious, perverse and outrageous": Isikoff, p. 93; Toobin, p. 47.
160 the $10,270-per-year clerk: *Time*, May 16, 1994.
160 "I love your curves": Ibid.
160 "kiss it": Harris, p. 290.
160 She was able to describe: *Time*, May 16, 1994; Toobin, p. 156.
160 Five witnesses: Isikoff, p. 49.
160 "heft only": *Newsweek*, Mar. 9, 1994.
160 "It can't help": *Time*, May 16, 1994.
160 "tabloid trash" . . . "Drag $100": *The New Republic*, June 16, 1997.
161 Hillary, whose first and abiding instinct: Toobin, p. 49.

161 "he couldn't do that": Ibid.
161 "She came up here": Danny Ferguson deposition, Dec. 10, 1997.
161 "they were kind of giggling": Ibid.
161 They argued that a President: Woodward, *Shadow*, p. 257.
161 "lost in the funhouse": Johnson and Broder, p. 279.
161 he neglected a foreign-policy tragedy: ML, pp. 592–93.
162 "Black Hawk Down": *Time*, Oct. 18, 1993.
162 a judgment backed by Hillary: Column by Dick Morris, *The Hill*, Sept. 26, 2006.
162 "all the right-wingers": Bill Clinton, interview on *Fox News Sunday*, Sept. 24, 2006.
162 In fact, congressional leaders: *Time*, Oct. 25, 1993.
162 Two of the strongest advocates: AP, Oct. 6, 1993.
162 "a disgrace to cut and run": *Atlanta Journal-Constitution*, Oct. 7, 1993.
162 "use overwhelming power": Ibid.
162 "vote to 'bring the boys home' ": ATH, p. 214.
162 "The early-departure policy": *Time*, Oct. 18, 1993.
162 "I hope I didn't panic": ATH, p. 215.
162 "Americans are basically isolationist": Ibid., p. 214.
162 "jihad in Somalia": Lawrence Wright, *The Looming Tower: Al-Qaeda and the Road to 9/11*, p. 189.
162 "the weakness, frailty, and cowardice": Ibid.
162 "his first victory against America": AP, June 15, 2006.
162 An investigation by the 9/11 Commission: *The 9/11 Commission Report: Final Report of the National Commission on Terrorist Attacks upon the United States*, p. 341.
163 "Another Somalia!": *Time*, Oct. 25, 1993.
163 "a terrible humiliation": Lake, p. 131.
163 Lake was pressing Bill: Ibid., p. 133.
163 Instead, Bill took a more cautious approach: ATH, p. 305.
163 He was also struggling to define: Talbott, p. 123; Lake, p. 131.
163 "high-minded declarations": *Time*, May 2, 1994.
163 "We seemed unable": Lake, p. 131.
163 Within days of the American: *Time*, May 2, 1994.
163 the Hutus started their massacres: ML, p. 592.
163 "obsessed with Bosnia": Bill Clinton, interview with Joe Klein, July 5, 2000. PPP, 2000, book 2, p. 2100.
163 didn't understand the magnitude: Bill Clinton, interview with *Rolling Stone*, Nov. 2, 2000; PPP, 2000–2001, book 3, p. 2640.
163 "a sin not of commission": Anthony Lake interview.
164 "permanent campaign": FiHC, pp. 407–9.
164 While the Bush White House spent: Gergen, p. 331, citing *The Wall Street Journal*, Mar. 23, 1994.
164 provided ammunition for the war rooms: Ibid.; *Time*, Apr. 11, 1994.
164 "real people": WP, Feb. 17, 1994.
164 "expose the scare tactics": LH, p. 229.
164 "It says here on page 3,764": Ibid.
164 "the undisputed star": WP, Mar. 21, 1994.
164 "Al Gore is an inspiration": Katz, p. 215.
164 "When people ask me": WP, Mar. 21, 1994.
164 Stan Greenberg's polling had determined: *Time*, Apr. 11, 1994.
165 "jump-start": Ibid., Apr. 18, 1994.
165 "bogged down in health care": Reich, p. 171.
165 "sine qua non": Transcript of Bob Woodward's April 13, 1994, interview with Hillary Clinton, obtained from a source.

165 "abetted by a handful": *Newsweek*, May 23, 1994.

165 "a myopic": Ibid.

165 A bipartisan parade: DPM, Memcon of Senator Daniel P. Moynihan, June 29, 1994; Bill Clinton on the *Today* show, June 20, 1994; PPP, 1994, book 1, p. 1099.

165 "no chance": WP, June 21, 1994.

165 But Moynihan also let the White House: Gergen, p. 302.

165 That evening, Bill and Hillary summoned: Ibid., pp. 299–302.

165 "not to give an inch": Ibid., p. 302.

165 Bill "exploded": Ibid., p. 303.

165 "As long as I am President": Ibid. Gergen later wrote that he looked at his watch and noted, "At 10:22 p.m. tonight health care died."

165 "the so-called 91 per cent": Bill Clinton on the *Today* show, June 20, 1994; PPP, 1994, book 1, p. 1099.

165 In a subsequent meeting: WP, May 21, 1994.

165 "It is time to be a conviction politician": DPM, Memcon of Senator Daniel P. Moynihan, June 23, 1994; WP, June 21, 1994.

166 she moved even farther left: Johnson and Broder, p. 438.

166 "In a big democracy": DPM, Memcon of Senator Daniel P. Moynihan, June 29, 1994.

166 "a reasonable definition": Ibid.

166 "phased-in, deliberate effort": *Time*, Aug. 1, 1994.

166 "open to any solution": Johnson and Broder, p. 456.

166 "I was shocked": Donna Shalala interview.

166 Bill retracted his comments: Johnson and Broder, p. 457.

166 "less bureaucratic": *Time*, Aug. 1, 1994

166 "Health Security Express": NYT, July 5, 1994; Johnson and Broder, p. 461.

167 "This is not socialized medicine": PPP, 1994, book 1, p. 1342.

167 "massive retaliation": ATH, pp. 298–99.

167 "absurdity" of the situation: Ibid., p. 300.

167 Bill ended up handling: Ibid.

167 "frantic, almost hallucinatory": *Newsweek*, Aug. 22, 1994.

167 "personal vicious hatred": NYT, Aug. 10, 1994.

167 "Is there any chance for a health bill?": *Newsweek*, Sept. 5, 1994.

168 "with barely a whimper": LH, p. 247.

168 Both of them continued to insist: LH, pp. 247, 249, 448; ML, p. 620.

168 "alienated" . . . "too much, too fast": LH, pp. 247–48.

168 "powers of the": *The Atlantic*, Nov. 2006.

168 In the end, neither Bill nor Hillary: William Baumol interview.

168 "never hired": Bill Clinton, interview on *Larry King Live*, Nov. 6, 1994; PPP, 1994, book 2, p. 2024.

168 "were my mistakes": WP, Feb. 9, 1996.

168 "rolling conversation": Transcript of Bob Woodward's April 13, 1994, interview with Hillary Clinton, obtained from a source.

168 "perhaps the largest and most expensive": DPM, Memcon of Senator Daniel P. Moynihan, May 19, 1995.

169 "her leadership was more than the political system": ATH, p. 301.

169 "part of the American journey": LH, p. 186.

169 "who was going to lead": Transcript of Bob Woodward's March 11, 1994, interview with Hillary Clinton, obtained from a source.

169 "so disorganized that information": Reich, p. 179.

170 largely at the urging of Stephanopoulos: ATH, pp. 282–84.

170 "We are the children of your sacrifice": Remarks on the fiftieth anniversary of D-Day at Pointe du Hoc in Normandy, France, June 6, 1994, and remarks on the fiftieth anniver-

sary of D-Day at the United States Cemetery in Colleville-sur-Mer, France, June 6, 1994, *PPP*, 1994, book 1, pp. 1042–43, 1044–46.

170   On D-Day, Bill's handlers: *NYT Magazine*, July 31, 1994; photo: Omaha Beach, France–June 6, David J. AKE/AFP/Getty Images. In *ML*, Bill Clinton said the walk took place on Utah Beach, but he is incorrect.

170   "acting out an intimate communion": *NYT Magazine*, July 31, 1994.

170   "lovely U-shape opening": *NYT*, July 10, 1994.

170   "great style": *WP*, June 8, 1994.

170   "very pink, like a little pig, but cute": *NYT*, July 10, 1994.

171   "changes her hair, changes the colors": *WP*, June 8, 1994.

171   "The worst thing": *Newsweek*, June 13, 1994.

171   "I didn't need that now, George": *ATH*, p. 288.

171   Hillary blamed *The Agenda*: *ATH*, p. 289; Roper Center poll ratings, June 25–28, 1994 (*USA Today* / CNN); June 25–28, 1994 (Gallup); July 1–3, 1994 (Gallup)

171   Stephanopoulos had assured them: *ATH*, p. 277.

171   "the whole problem with this administration:" Ibid., p. 289.

171   "javelin catcher": *WP*, Jan. 5, 2005.

171   Bill had been discussing: Harris, p. 149.

171   "crystallized": *ATH*, p. 284.

171   "security blanket": Brummett, p. 272.

171   Rubin, among others: Rubin, p. 144.

171   "Mack the Nice": *The New Yorker*, July 11, 1994.

172   "Mack tried to do": Michael McCurry interview.

172   "read Machiavelli": *The New Yorker*, July 11, 1994.

172   Panetta had enough distance: *ATH*, p. 285.

172   His first move was to schedule: Robert Rubin interview.

172   "I have learned": *OO*, p. 24.

172   "Send them to *me*": Reich, p. 180.

172   "The memos did get to Bill": Robert Reich interview.

172   they had their first State Dinner: *WP*, June 3 and June 14, 1994, and April 14, 2001.

172   As a warm-up: Ibid., May 30, 1994.

173   "I'm in the tank!": Ibid., June 11, 1994.

173   David Hale had pleaded guilty: *BS*, p. 414.

173   "Republican municipal judge": *ML*, p. 586.

173   "veteran Democratic party operative": Brummett, pp. 241–42.

173   Fiske came to the White House: *WP*, June 14, 1994.

173   "Big St. Bernard": Terry McAuliffe interview.

173   "studied detachment": Woodward, *Shadow*, p. 262.

173   Bill and Hillary continued to include: Hubbell, p. 287; *WP*, May 3, 1997.

173   "all this stuff": Hubbell, p. 288.

174   Fiske had issued his first: Woodward, *Shadow*, p. 262; *BS*, pp. 422–23.

174   The same day: *LH*, pp. 243–44.

174   put Bill and Hillary on edge: Drew, p. 426; *LH*, p. 244; *ML*, p. 613.

174   "She ranted for over an hour": Jonathan Alter interview.

174   The White House had been careful: Blumenthal, p. 100.

174   But this time Hillary prodded: *Newsweek*, Feb. 9, 1998.

174   Lloyd Cutler and David Kendall: Woodward, *Shadow*, pp. 265–66.

174   "we would get along": Abner Mikva interview.

174   Cutler, who was just ending: Woodward, *Shadow*, p. 267.

174   But in the following days, James Carville: Ibid., pp. 266–69.

174   The senators zeroed in: *Time*, Aug. 8, 1994.

175   "fall guy": Reich, p. 189.

175 Bill and his advisors were stunned: *ATH*, p. 293.

175 Bill authorized Leon Panetta: Ibid., p. 297.

175 Bill agreed to cut the cost: *Time*, Aug. 29, 1994.

175 Bill insisted on including: *ML*, p. 611.

175 Panetta and congressional leaders: *Time*, Aug. 29, 1994.

175 The wrangling over the bill: *WP*, Sept. 5, 1994.

175 they were guests: *Time*, Sept. 5, 1994; *Newsweek*, Aug. 25, 1997; Sheehy, p. 314; www.cnn.com/ALLPOLITICS/1997/08/17/clinton/index.html?eref=sitesearch and www .cnn.com/ALLPOLITICS/1997/08/20/clinton.vacation/index.html?eref=sitesearch.

175 They bought stacks of books: *WP*, Sept. 5, 1994.

176 "after 10 days": Van Natta, p. 195.

176 "It was part of their strategy": Ibid., p. 215.

176 explained that Bill simply liked to practice: Terry McAuliffe interview; Bob Armstrong, friend and administration official, interview.

176 "It is a shell game": Van Natta, p. 213.

176 "Billigans": Ibid., p. 214.

176 "gimme": Ibid., p. 211.

176 When Bill claimed a twelve or thirteen handicap: Bill Clinton on *Meet the Press*, Nov. 9, 1997; *PPP*, 1997, book 2, p. 1527.

176 "interesting math": *WP*, June 1, 2006.

176 "If you shoot an 8": Van Natta, p. 202.

176 In the evenings: *WP*, Sept. 5, 1994.

176 Bill quoted from William Styron's: Rose Styron interview.

176 "literary hero": *ML*, p. 614.

177 "commanded the conversation": Sheldon Hackney interview.

177 "I got the very distinct feeling": Rose Styron interview.

177 Under the influence of: *Time*, Oct. 28, 1996.

177 "core group": Ibid.

177 Bill finally decided: Lake, p. 140.

178 Stan Greenberg's soundings: *ATH*, pp. 310–11.

178 "permissive entry": *Newsweek*, Oct. 3, 1994.

178 "intervasion": Ibid., April 29, 1996.

178 Bill ordered thirty-six thousand troops: *ML*, p. 624.

178 "CLINTON, 2, BULLIES 0!": *Time*, Oct. 24, 1994.

178 Within days, Bill also announced: *ML*, pp. 624–25; Lake, p. 95.

178 Senator Robert Dole worried: *Time*, Oct. 31, 1994.

179 These achievements briefly nudged: Roper Center poll ratings, Oct. 22–25, 1994.

179 "GOP surge": *Newsweek*, Oct. 17, 1994.

179 the NAFTA treaty alienated: Peter Beinart, *New York Post*, Aug. 28, 2006.

179 "Contract with America": *ML*, p. 621; *LH*, p. 250; *OO*, p. 14; *The New Yorker*, Oct. 24, 1994.

179 "nationalizing": *Time*, Oct. 10, 1994.

179 Bill had already been in touch: *Newsweek*, Jan. 20, 1997.

180 After falling out with Bill: *Newsweek*, Nov. 18, 1996.

180 "was compromised in the eyes": *ML*, p. 370.

180 "on her own work": *OO*, pp. 23, 110.

180 telling Morris at the time: *The Hill*, Sept. 26, 2006.

180 "We need to learn": Sheehy, p. 146.

180 Hillary had resisted Morris's suggestions: *OO*, p. 111.

180 In early October, Bill called: Ibid., pp. 8, 11–12.

180 "bite-size achievements": Ibid., p. 12.

180 But Bill's advisors said surveys: *The New Yorker*, Oct. 24, 1994.

180   Bill did scuttle: *Time*, Oct. 31, 1994.
181   "prime-time TV triumph": *Time*, Nov. 7, 1994.
181   barely registered with voters: Ibid.; *Newsweek*, Nov. 7, 1994.
181   "scare out the vote": *Time*, Nov. 14, 1994.
181   Ironically, a CBS poll: Peter Beinart, *New York Post*, Aug. 26, 2006.
181   By making himself so visible: *The New Yorker*, Nov. 21, 1994.
181   "surprised to find my schedule": *ML*, p. 628.
181   "talking me into attacking": *ATH*, p. 334.
181   "like asking him not to": Ibid., p. 317.
181   "resist the lure": *LH*, p. 255.
181   Hillary had already begun to reassess: *NYT*, Sept. 28, 1994.
181   Her aides made it known: *WP*, Sept. 30, 1994.
181   "voices from the real world": Ibid.
181   "She's an incredibly patient": Ibid.
181   "charged up": Ibid.
182   "it would hurt Bill": Jeffrey Orseck interview.
182   "it was her brother": Ibid.
182   "my little brother": *WP*, Oct. 3, 1994.
182   "so controlled": Ibid.
182   she had frequently given guest sermons: *FiHC*, p. 433; *NYT Magazine*, May 23, 1993; *Newsweek*, July 20, 1992.
182   Book of Resolutions: *WP*, May 6, 1993.
182   her notebook stuffed: *LH*, p. 160.
182   She routinely said grace: Priscilla Eakeley interview.
182   she belonged to a women's prayer group: *LH*, pp. 167–68.
182   "faith messages": Ibid.
182   He enjoyed quoting: *Newsweek*, Oct. 31, 1994.
182   Drawing from the teachings: *WP*, May 6, 1993.
182   "Hillary is as pious as she is political": *Newsweek*, Oct. 31, 1994.
183   "a great deal of sympathy": Ibid.
183   "startling": *WP*, Nov. 27, 1994.
183   Election Day surveys: Peter Beinart, *New York Post*, Aug. 26, 2006.
183   "I also just like to see": Bill Clinton, on *Larry King Live*, Nov. 6, 1994; *PPP*, 1994, book 2, p. 2018.
183   Bill and Hillary sat: *LH*, p. 256.
183   "the midnight caller": *Time*, Aug. 7, 1995.
184   he stayed up until 2:00 a.m. calling Democrats: *Newsweek*, Nov. 21, 1994.
184   they could not simply push through: Donna Shalala interview.

CHAPTER NINE

185   "eerily quiet": Reich, p. 201.
185   "Name after name was read": Bill Galston interview.
185   now they faced a repudiation: *The New Yorker*, Nov. 21, 1994.
185   who felt that Bill Clinton had betrayed: *Newsweek*, Jan. 30, 1995.
185   Hillary's health-care plan was central: *Time*, Dec. 12, 1994; *NYT*, Mar. 20, 1995.
186   "a return to liberal fundamentalism": Waldman, p. 75.
186   "weak" . . . "playboy": *Newsweek*, Nov. 7, 1994.
186   Research conducted by Dick Morris: *NYT Magazine*, May 30, 1999.
186   "zero-sum game": *OO*, p. 39.
186   "seemed to be buffeted": *LH*, p. 297.

186 "They couldn't take it other than personally": Abner Mikva interview.
186 staff wisely postponed: *Newsweek*, Nov. 21, 1994.
186 "a little disoriented": Rubin, p. 154.
186 "pretty much in the Ancient Mariner": *The New Yorker*, Nov. 21, 1994.
186 "share of responsibility": Drew, p. 441.
186 "going in the right direction": *The New Yorker*, Nov. 21, 1994.
186 he repeated his theory: Ibid.
186 "anxious mood, a negative mood": Sept. 25, 1995, *PPP*, 1995, book 2, pp. 1473–86.
187 "Clinton's an unusually good liar": *Esquire*, Jan. 1996.
187 "didn't take it personally": *The Atlantic*, Nov. 2006.
187 "deflated and disappointed": *LH*, p. 257.
187 "Big Government": *Time*, Dec. 12, 1994.
187 "naive and dumb": *NYT*, Jan. 10, 1995; *WP*, Jan. 16, 1995.
187 "disappointment": Hillary Clinton, interview with Barbara Walters, ABC News, June 8, 2003.
187 a matter of poor public relations: *The New Yorker*, Nov. 21, 1994; *Newsweek*, Dec. 19, 1994.
187 "She is really angry": *Time*, Dec. 12, 1994.
188 "He seemed depressed": Douglas Eakeley interview.
188 Bill cornered Arkansas journalist: Max Brantley interview.
188 Bill started spending less time in the Oval Office: Abner Mikva interview.
188 reading speeches from the 1992 campaign: *Time*, Jan. 30, 1995.
188 Bill delivered a speech that flouted: Katz, pp. 13–15.
188 "confused . . . I don't know what works": Woodward, *Shadow*, 334.
188 "bedraggled": *WP*, Jan. 15, 1995.
188 During an emotional meeting: *LH*, p. 261.
188 she arrived in a bright blue: *WP*, Nov. 30, 1994.
189 "There's nothing like a good fight": *Time*, Dec. 12, 1994.
189 "unbelievable and absurd": *NYT*, Dec. 1, 1994.
189 Hillary now eagerly listened: *Time*, Oct. 20, 1997.
189 "not as a policy maker": *NYT Magazine*, May 30, 1999.
189 "to see Hillary *in public*": *OO*, p. 39.
189 His proposals tapped into: Dick Morris, *Rewriting History*, p. 100.
189 He recommended that she: *NYT Magazine*, May 30, 1999.
189 "raising children in today's world": *LH*, p. 263.
189 "systemic change": *WP*, Jan. 15, 1995.
189 more familiar First Lady focus: *Time*, Dec. 12, 1994.
189 She drew inspiration: *LH*, p. 267.
190 "She knows what she needs": *The New Yorker*, May 30, 1994.
190 Unlike Eleanor Roosevelt: *WP*, Jan. 15, 1995.
190 "Try to keep that bubble": Sheehy, p. 23.
190 "We'll be defined by our fights": Reich, p. 227.
190 Fittingly, their coach: Woodward, *Choice*, p. 24.
190 psychographic: *NYT Magazine*, June 18, 2000.
191 "We talked": *OO*, p. 17.
191 In late November, they convened: Ibid., p. 22.
191 "the children who helped me": *OO*, p. xxiii; also, *ATH*, p. 322.
191 Bill agreed to meet secretly: *OO*, pp. 26–28.
191 "I like subterfuge": *Newsweek*, Jan. 20, 1997.
191 For nearly two years: *OO*, p. 30; *ATH*, p. 330.
191 "to their own rhythm": *OO*, p. 31.
191 "prayer book": *Vanity Fair*, Nov. 1996.

191   Bill confided to his longtime friend: Mickey Kantor interview.
191   "He said he was getting the blame": Ibid.
191   "Morris is politically brilliant": Ibid.
191   "covert operation": ATH, p. 329.
192   "didn't fully trust me": Ibid., p. 330.
192   Bill also disengaged: OO, p. 27; Harris, p. 154.
192   Their initial collaboration: Reich, p. 218; Time, Dec. 26, 1994.
192   Morris sketched out: OO, p. 86.
192   Bill dictated: Newsweek, Nov. 18, 1996.
192   Hillary chipped in: NYT, Mar. 20, 1995.
192   "unfamiliar frequency": ATH, p. 329.
192   "Who came up with": Ibid., p. 335.
192   Morris recommended that Bill co-opt: OO, p. 37.
192   "triangulation": Time, Sept. 2, 1996.
192   capture the 19 percent: Newsweek, Nov. 21, 1994.
192   an array of tax cuts: Reich, p. 218; ML, p. 637.
192   "dramatic course correction": Time, Dec. 26, 1994.
192   "shares with the hummingbird": Ibid.
193   "a fancy word for betrayal": ATH, p. 336.
193   "small stuff": Time, Sept. 2, 1996.
193   "restart" his administration: Bill Galston interview.
193   "special interest" tax subsidies: Reich, p. 207.
193   "he was now in a mood to listen": Bill Galston interview.
193   Bill was also governing more by indirection: OO, p. 104.
193   "With his unbelievably": Ibid., p. xxiii.
193   "nod approvingly": Reich, p. 213.
194   "personal development" gurus: Newsweek, Jan 30, 1995; Katz, p. 241; ATH, p. 324; LH,
      p. 264.
194   "new story": Woodward, Choice, pp. 56–57.
194   Camp David Seminar on the Future: Center for Democracy and Citizenship, Project
      Pericles website, Macalester College, St. Paul.
194   "replicate the stresses": Bill Galston interview.
194   The President was in an expansive: Barber, p. 41.
194   after more than three hours: Newsweek, Jan. 30, 1995.
194   "visibly uncomfortable": Barber, p. 95.
194   "warrior forcefulness": Ibid., p. 96.
194   "she had to unlearn": Ibid.
194   "may well be the most influential": Newsweek, Apr. 4, 1994.
195   "Screw 'em": Barber, p. 97.
195   "I know these boys": Ibid.
195   "opaque and unsmiling": Ibid., p. 101.
195   "abruptly turned away": Ibid., pp. 101–2.
195   Bill was less visible: Newsweek, Jan. 30, 1995.
195   "the mother of all polls": OO, p. 93.
195   "New Covenant": Waldman, pp. 77–78.
195   To avoid detection: OO, p. 90; Morris, Rewriting History, p. 142.
195   "the edit had come from Dick": ATH, p. 336. See also Waldman, p. 81.
195   Bill's address ran: PPP, 1995, book 1, pp. 75–86.
196   Commentators dismissed: Newsweek, Jan. 25, 1999.
196   Bill's approval ratings temporarily: Roper Center poll ratings, Jan. 25, 1995, NBC / The
      Wall Street Journal.
196   Hillary dropped out: OO, pp. 39, 26.

196 "string together": *Newsweek,* June 19, 1995.

196 He wore ill-fitting: *NYT,* Jan. 13, 1993.

196 always used his tea bags: *ATH,* p. 325.

196 Ickes had been slated: *NYT,* Feb. 14, 1993; James Barnes interview.

196 "a direct line": *Time,* Nov. 23, 1995.

196 Ickes became the consultant's: *OO,* pp. 45, 131–32.

196 Bill had been scheduled: Waldman, p. 80; *Time,* Apr. 25, 1995.

197 "Leon put his foot down": Mike McCurry interview.

197 "mix of egos, attitudes and ambitions": *LH,* p. 289.

197 "small sausage of a man": *ATH,* p. 331.

197 "struck by the economy": Reich, p. 271.

197 a $240,000 annual salary: *The New Yorker,* Oct. 30, 1995.

197 the $440 per night King Suite: *Newsweek,* Nov. 18, 1996.

197 "talented but unusual": Robert Rubin interview.

197 The weekly meetings: Henry Cisneros interview; *OO,* p. 27.

197 "They were filibusters": Mickey Kantor interview.

197 "dark Buddha": *ATH,* p. 328.

197 an ebullient thirty-seven-year-old: *Newsweek,* March 10, 1997.

197 They bonded when Harold: Ibid.; Woodward, *Choice,* p. 51.

198 "cheering up": *Newsweek,* Mar. 10, 1997.

198 "he was uncomfortable": Terry McAuliffe interview.

198 "that Bill Clinton is viable": Ibid.

198 "You raise the most": *Newsweek,* Mar. 10, 1997.

198 He offered to gather: Terry McAuliffe interview; *Vanity Fair,* Jan. 2000.

198 "It was the first positive": *Newsweek,* Mar. 10, 1997.

198 "Wall Street math": *Newsweek,* Oct. 27, 1997.

198 "We need to give 'em the magic": Terry McAuliffe interview.

198 "Get other names at $100,000": *Newsweek,* Mar. 10, 1997.

199 In four years, George and Barbara: *Time,* Mar. 10, 1997.

199 92 percent contributed: *Vanity Fair,* Jan. 2000.

199 "projected" amounts: *Newsweek,* Mar. 10, 1997.

199 Videotapes released: *Time,* Oct. 27, 1997.

199 "coffees": Ibid., Mar. 10, 1997.

199 "campaign activities of any kind": Ibid.

199 Six coffees had already: Ibid.

199 "I sure as hell": Ibid.

199 nearly three million: *Time,* Mar. 30, 1997; Freeh, p. 256.

200 "those who have come": *Time,* Oct. 27, 1997.

200 these abuses resulted: Department of Justice press release, Jan. 11, 2001.

200 Johnny Chung came: *Time,* Mar. 3, 1997.

200 handed a fifty-thousand-dollar check: Ibid.; Mar. 17, 1997.

200 Chung and six Chinese businessmen: *Time,* Mar. 3, 1997.

200 "unusually explicit swap": Ibid.

200 Not only were the Democrats eventually: *Newsweek,* Mar. 17, 1997.

200 admitting that one hundred thousand: Kurtz, p. 323.

200 After contributing more than $500,000: *Time,* July 28, 1997; *Newsweek,* Dec. 24, 1997.

200 his son James visited: *WP,* May 27, 1997.

200 Those visits included three: *Newsweek,* Nov. 18, 1996.

200 James Riady used funds: Department of Justice press release, Jan. 11, 2001.

200 John Huang, who had befriended: Profile compiled from *WP* staff reports, July 24, 1997: www.washingtonpost.com/wp-srv/politics/special/campfin/players/huang.htm.

201 "deep Arkansas connections" and "well known": *Time,* Nov. 11, 1996.

201 Huang visited the White House seventy-eight times: "The Democratic Fund-Raising Flap: Timeline October 1996," www.cnn.com/ALLPOLITICS/1997/gen/resources/infocus/fundraising.flap/time9610.html.

201 fund-raiser and influence peddler: Department of Justice press release, Jan. 11, 2001.

201 $3.4 million he gathered: www.washingtonpost.com/wp-srv/politics/special/campfin/players/huang.htm.

201 $450,000 from an Indonesian couple: Time, Dec. 2, 1996.

201 Hubbell had been close to the Riadys: Kurtz, p. 178; Woodward, Shadow, p. 291; WP, May 27, 1997.

201 Shortly after a Lippo subsidiary: Kurtz, p. 179; Woodward, Shadow, p. 339; WP, May 27, 1997.

201 Riady had met privately with Bill: Harris, p. 269.

201 "You've got to fight": Hubbell, p. 292. Hillary's version in LH, p. 266.

201 Starr was in the dark: NYT, Apr. 23, 1997.

202 But they were shaken at the end: OO, pp. 111–14.

202 Betsey Wright's assertion: FiHC, pp. 440–41.

202 In an interview on C-SPAN: Feb. 19, 1995; PPP, 1995, book 1, pp. 225–33.

202 "advance uncorrected proof": The Starr Report: The Official Report of the Independent Counsel's Investigation of the President, OIC supplemental report, p. 2914.

202 "in obvious rage" and "furious": OO, pp. xxx–xxxi, 113.

202 The White House pressured: Maraniss, Enigma, p. 15.

202 "misinterpreted": Ibid. See also OO, pp. xxx–xxxi, 113.

202 "are becoming increasingly": Newsweek, Feb. 13, 1995.

202 "never spoke of his chagrin": OO, p. xxxi.

202 Hillary was angry enough to kick: Maraniss, Enigma, p. 21.

202 Hillary had reacted that way: Sheehy, p. 150; Esquire, Dec. 2000.

202 "He has been so sweet": Mary Mel French interview.

203 She had dined with: WP, Feb. 17, 1995.

203 Bill later told: Time, Nov. 18, 1996.

203 "find ways to work": keynote address by First Lady Hillary Rodham Clinton at the dedication of Eleanor Roosevelt College in San Diego, Jan. 26, 1995. In her remarks, Hillary also promoted historian Doris Kearns Goodwin's book about Franklin and Eleanor Roosevelt, No Ordinary Time.

203 "listening sessions": WP, May 6, 1995; OO, p. 109.

203 "The stories come and go": NYT, Feb. 18, 1995.

203 "very rich people": NYT, Mar. 20, 1995.

203 "Hillary Gump": WP, Mar. 27, 1995; NYT, Mar. 27, 1995; LH, p. 287.

203 schedule of foreign travel: LH, pp. 269, 271; WP, Apr. 3, 1995; NYT, Mar. 20, 1995.

203 "the only celebrity I had ever stood behind a rope line": LH, p. 271.

204 "The Hillaryland Tour": WP, Apr. 3, 1995.

204 not "soft issues": Ibid., Apr. 1, 1995.

204 "when a woman fights": NYT, Mar. 30, 1995.

204 But she avoided any talk: WP, Mar. 27, 1995.

204 "anemic persona": WP, Apr. 1, 1995.

204 When Hillary spoke to reporters: Klein, pp. 127–29.

204 "rampant materialism and consumerism": Ibid., p. 129.

204 "They bantered easily": LH, p. 272.

204 Hillary met seventy-five-year-old Sir Edmund Hillary: WP, Jan. 11 1993, and Apr. 3, 1995; Hillary omitted the tale from her own memoir, but Bill repeated it in his (p. 870). Dorothy Rodham said in an interview with Martha Sherrill in Jan. 1993, "I had always

heard [Hillary] in connection with my father's family.... It was a man's name of course, and I wanted an unusual name, and it was a family name and obscure. There is a Saint Hilary."

204 Sir Edmund was still a beekeeper: Morris, *Rewriting History*, pp. 11–12.

204 "When people used": *WP*, Apr. 3, 1995.

205 She promoted mammograms: Ibid., May 6, 1995.

205 "honey-blond flip cut": Ibid., May 17, 1995.

205 "where the other Hillary Clinton had gone": Ibid.

205 "rehabilitate himself": Laura Tyson interview.

205 "in limbo" and "imperious": Waldman, p. 76.

205 "They ought to make": *NYT*, Oct. 13, 1994.

205 Magaziner found his niche: Laura Tyson interview.

205 consulted with her when he was vetting: Eleanor Acheson interview.

205 "If he didn't know the specifics": Ibid.

206 "Hillary was the point person": Douglas Eakeley interview.

206 "just switched to asking her advice": *OO*, p. 39.

206 "I know they talked": Ibid.

206 meeting every other week with Morris: Ibid., p. 137.

206 "I felt she was": Ibid.

206 she would raise it one-on-one: *Time*, Oct. 20, 1997.

206 She was present: Woodward, *Choice*, pp. 103–4; Terry McAuliffe interview.

206 She recruited Jean Houston: Woodward, *Choice*, p. 130.

206 "dig deeper": Ibid.

206 "reflective meditation": *Time*, Oct. 20, 1997.

207 "advance the Clinton agenda": *LH*, p. 265.

207 to help her write *It Takes a Village*: *NYT*, Apr. 22, 1995; *WP*, Jan. 12, 1996; *Newsweek*, Jan. 15, 1996.

207 "re-emerge domestically": *WP*, Oct. 15, 1995.

207 "the Constitution": Katz, p. 240.

207 "He seemed pathetic": *Newsweek*, Dec. 18, 1995.

207 A grim deus ex machina: *ML*, pp. 650–51.

207 "trivialities and minutiae": *LH*, p. 296.

207 "It's okay to be frightened": *NYT*, Apr. 23, 1995.

207 "more good people than bad": *WP*, Apr. 23, 1995.

208 "couldn't have been more pleasant": Abner Mikva interview.

208 "Don't you dare": Ibid.

208 The President played a round: *NYT*, Apr. 23, 1995.

208 "national day of mourning": *WP*, Apr. 23, 1995.

208 "It was his only way of relaxing": Abner Mikva interview.

208 "nation's Preacher-in-Chief": Reich, p. 129.

208 "purge ourselves": *PPP*, 1995, book 1, pp. 573–74.

208 In an interview that evening: Bill Clinton, *60 Minutes* interview, Apr. 23, 1995; *PPP*, 1995, book 1, pp. 574–78.

208 Only later did: *National Review*, Sept. 11, 2006.

208 "it cost the World Trade Center bomber": Bill Clinton, *60 Minutes* interview, Apr. 23, 1995; *PPP*, 1995, book 1, pp. 574–78.

209 "try to get the legal support": Ibid.

209 "Aftermath of Oklahoma City": *OO*, p. 419.

209 "our friends": Bill Clinton, interview with *Rolling Stone*, Nov. 2, 2000; *PPP*, 2000–2001, book 2, p. 2633.

209 Bill shrewdly implied: Michael Barone interview.

CHAPTER TEN

210 Gore had proved his mettle: *Time*, Sept. 2, 1996.
210 "Gore sideways": *Newsweek*, Oct. 14, 1996.
210 opening a useful back channel: *Newsweek*, Dec. 23, 1996.
210 Gore had gone to Moscow: Talbott, pp. 141–45.
210 Gore had also taken: WP, June 16, 1999, and Oct. 18, 2006.
210 "closer": *Newsweek*, Dec. 23, 1996.
210 Gore had some apprehensions: Woodward, *Choice*, p. 127.
211 Bill's advisors had a greater: *Time*, Dec. 15, 1997.
211 "The two men need": Reich, p. 241.
211 In meetings, he could be spiky: *The New Yorker*, Dec. 8, 1997.
211 "edgy" humor: *Newsweek*, May 24, 1999.
211 "to drain the anger out of Clinton": Mike McCurry interview.
211 But Gore's most important job: *Newsweek*, Sept. 2, 1996.
211 "believed Al Gore was not playing games": Bill Galston interview.
212 When the Republicans announced: Johnson and Broder, p. 573.
212 Morris's polls showed: *Time*, Nov. 18, 1996.
212 Siding with his liberal advisors: Woodward, *Choice*, p. 206.
212 a balanced budget with a longer time horizon: Laura Tyson interview.
212 "We have to have a position": Woodward, *Choice*, p. 206.
212 he could embolden the GOP: OO, p. 160.
212 The publicly unseen factor: WP, Dec. 9, 1996.
212 "anti-zero deficit": ATH, p. 353.
212 "did their homework": Robert Rubin interview.
212 During a phone interview: ATH, p. 342; Woodward, *Choice*, p. 207.
212 "We can get there": *Time*, June 26, 1995.
212 "off the wall": ATH, p. 343.
212 Four days later, Bill appeared: Woodward, *Choice*, p. 207; ATH, p. 347.
212 "important new voice": ATH, p. 353.
212 Like Rubin, she advocated: Ibid., p. 354.
213 "While she worried about": OO, p. 163.
213 "credible numbers": Robert Rubin interview.
213 "threshold issue": Ibid.
213 "Swing voters *care*": Reich, p. 262.
213 "Make sure your speech": ATH, pp. 358–59.
213 Morris tested virtually every line: Harris, p. 184.
213 Bill continued to fiddle: *Time*, June 26, 1995.
213 "the pain we'd inflict": Woodward, *Choice*, p. 209.
213 "the Republicans could have declared": Robert Rubin interview.
214 "everything we Democrats cared about": ATH, p. 360.
214 "thrown in the towel": Reich, p. 264.
214 "lost the real war": Ibid., p. 284.
214 "granny-bashing extremists": *Time*, Sept. 2, 1996.
214 "strong partisan streak": ATH, p. 402.
214 "Clinton is anxious": *Time*, Dec. 15, 1997.
214 "close down the government": Reich, p. 256.
214 "constant kibitzer": *Newsweek*, July 10, 1995.
214 the Serbs began heavily: Talbott, p. 73; Lake, p. 142.
215 "token bombings": Michael Mandelbaum, "Foreign Policy as Social Work," *Foreign Affairs*, vol. 75, no. 1, Jan./Feb. 1996, p. 23.
215 UN rules dictated: Woodward, *Choice*, p. 255.

215 "increasingly humiliated": French president Jacques Chirac, Bill Clinton news conference with European leaders, June 14, 1995; *PPP*, 1995, book 1, p. 885.

215 Both Al Gore and Tony Lake: Woodward, *Choice*, p. 255; Lake, p. 142.

215 there was no support: *Newsweek*, June 26, 1995.

215 His relationships with: *Time*, Sept. 25, 1995.

215 Republicans as well as Democrats: Mandelbaum, "Foreign Policy as Social Work," p. 23.

215 "engagement, not procrastinating": Private journal.

216 "unfair . . . to leave him out there": Ibid.

216 "few could even remember making": Warren Bass, "The Triage of Dayton," *Foreign Affairs*, vol. 77, no. 5, Sept./Oct. 1998, pp. 100–101.

216 Bill faced an unpleasant scenario: Mandelbaum, "Foreign Policy as Social Work," p. 23.

217 Serbian soldiers forcibly removed: *The Christian Science Monitor*, July 22, 2005.

217 "blow off steam": *Time*, Aug. 28, 1995.

217 "whine at us": Woodward, *Choice*, p. 261.

217 "The worst solution would be": Ibid., p. 262.

217 "marry power to diplomacy": Lake, p. 142.

217 "to give diplomacy a chance": Mandelbaum, "Foreign Policy as Social Work," p. 23.

217 Holbrooke began several months of shuttling: Talbott, pp. 172–73; *ML*, p. 667.

217 "to discuss an idea": *LH*, p. 454.

218 "was driven not only": Lake, p. 261.

218 they had an agreement: Robert W. Merry, *Sands of Empire: Missionary Zeal, American Foreign Policy, and the Hazards of Global Ambition*, pp. 140–41.

218 Bill's principal contribution: Talbott, p. 179.

218 "provided for Russian military": Ibid., p. 186.

218 the Clinton Administration was able to co-opt: Bass, "Triage of Dayton," p. 104.

218 dangerous loose end: *NYT*, Nov. 21, 1995; Merry, p. 141.

218 But overall the treaty: *ML*, p. 685.

218 American forces would be required for only a year: Bill Clinton, televised address on the implementation of the peace agreement in Bosnia-Herzegovina, Nov. 27, 1995; *PPP*, book 2, pp. 1784–87.

218 in fact they were to stay for a decade: *WP*, Nov. 21, 2005.

218 One evening, he was practicing: *Time*, Aug. 28, 1995.

219 "horrifying trail of death": Woodward, *Choice*, p. 260.

219 he kept walking around the green: *Time*, Aug. 28, 1995.

219 "I'm getting creamed!": Woodward, *Choice*, p. 260.

219 "Bill was so excited": Gene Lyons interview.

220 "latest Republican outrage": Reich, p. 266.

220 "These are *real* issues": Ibid., p. 267.

221 "holding forth" . . . "on the politics of reelection": Private journal.

221 The Clintons were questioned: Woodward, *Shadow*, p. 286.

221 Starr indicted the McDougals: *Time*, Aug. 28, 1995; *WP*, June 2, 1996; *Newsweek*, Aug. 28, 1995.

222 On Capitol Hill: *Time*, July 24, 1995.

222 "Mecca" made possible: Ibid., Aug. 21, 1995.

222 D'Amato's witnesses: *Newsweek*, July 31, 1995; *Time*, Aug. 21, 1995; *WP*, June 19, 1996.

222 "astounding memory lapses": *NYT*, Jan. 21, 1996.

222 Thomases blamed the effects: *BS*, p. 437; *LH*, p. 297.

222 Williams won sympathy: *LH*, p. 297; Woodward, *Shadow*, p. 287.

222 "The Body Count": *Newsweek*, Aug. 7, 1995.

222 "That's not who I am": Woodward, *Shadow*, p. 288.

223 "She knew the format of the Rose billing records": Sheehy, p. 282.
223 roughly five or six inches: *WP*, June 2, 1996.
223 "They were folded": *Nightline*, transcript, Jan. 30, 1996.
223 Nor did she admit to knowing: *WP*, June 2, 1996.
223 The Book Room was the location: Woodward, *Shadow*, p. 298; Sheehy, p. 281; *WP*, June 2, 1996.
223 a report issued by: *WP*, June 2, 1996.
223 "sham transactions": Ibid.
223 It later emerged that: Ibid.
224 "plumped them down": *Nightline*, transcript Jan. 30, 1996.
224 To clear out some space: Woodward, *Shadow*, pp. 297–99.
224 "oversight": *LH*, p. 332.
224 "I'm retired": Woodward, *Shadow*, p. 259.
224 "I've tried to shut myself": *Starr Report*, p. 207.
224 Back in April 1993: *ATH*, p. 140.
224 "It was not a good idea": Dee Dee Myers interview.
225 "raised eyebrows": Drew, p. 182.
225 "had to claw her way in": Mary Mel French interview.
225 "Seventy-five years old": Dee Dee Myers interview.
225 "The Prime Minister was a huge flirt": Laura Tyson interview.
226 "schoolboys": Dee Dee Myers interview.
226 "one full-service President": *Vanity Fair*, Aug. 1999.
226 Stephen Goodin, Bill's personal assistant: Harris, p. 228.
226 There was talk: *Time*, May 31, 1993; Sheehy, p. 234.
226 When Panetta later got wind: Grand-jury testimony of Leon Panetta, Jan. 28, 1998, *Starr Report* supplemental materials, vol. 3, p. 3235.
226 "She would send interns home": Mike McCurry interview.
227 "flanked only by men": *Newsweek*, Feb. 12, 1996.
227 "Evelyn's role was to watch": Donna Shalala interview.
227 "There goes trouble": *WP*, Jan. 24, 1998.
227 She had recently graduated: Ibid.; *Starr Report*, p. 78.
227 Her job had been arranged: *WP*, Jan. 24, 1998.
227 "girls my own age": *MS*, p. 63.
227 "knowing remarks": Ibid.
227 "had a glow": Ibid., p. 64.
227 "full Bill Clinton": Ibid., p. 65.
227 "casually but unnecessarily": Ibid., p. 66.
227 "he threw back his head": Ibid.
227 Lewinsky read Gennifer Flowers's: Ibid.
228 "sexy stare": Flowers, p. 2.
228 "His stamina amazed me": Ibid., p. 32.
228 "Bill loved to talk dirty": Ibid., p. 72.
228 "he suddenly jumped out of bed": Ibid., p. 62.
228 "poignant": Henry Cisneros interview.
228 "It conveyed the immense": Ibid.
228 Bill stopped to chat: *MS*, p. 67.
228 seventeen-day summer vacation: *Newsweek*, Aug. 21 and Sept. 11, 1995; *ML*, pp. 667–68.
228 "swing voters liked": *Time*, Nov. 18, 1996.
228 "I was as tired": Bill Clinton, exchange with reporters on Air Force One, Sept. 22, 1995; *PPP*, 1995, book 2, p. 1463.

229   He managed to play ninety-one holes: ML, p. 668; Bob Armstrong interview; NYT, Aug. 21, 1995.

229   the Clintons enjoyed their holiday: ML, pp. 667–68; NYT, Aug. 21, 1995.

229   "Puff the Magic Dragon": The Washington Times, Aug. 25, 1995.

229   whitewater rafting: Kurtz, p. 48; Newsweek, Nov. 18, 1996.

229   the First Lady remained cloistered: WP, Jan. 12, 1996; NYT, Aug. 21, 1995.

229   "Talking It Over": WP, Oct. 12, 1995; NYT, July 24, 1995.

229   "a combination of political calculation": WP, Oct. 12, 1995.

229   "bright copy": NYT, Aug. 10, 1995.

229   "kept under a bushel": William Miller interview.

229   "I'm so totally engaged": Marton, p. 334.

230   "another dimension": Donna Shalala interview.

230   Hillary had been invited to lead: LH, p. 298.

230   Finally, in late August: WP, Aug. 27, 1995; NYT, Aug. 26, 1995.

230   She worked until dawn: LH, p. 302.

230   "it is no longer": NYT, Sept. 6, 1995.

230   "the most stinging": Time, Oct. 20, 1997.

230   The applause from the vast: LH, p. 303; Time, Oct. 20, 1997.

231   "The people there": Donna Shalala interview.

231   "loved the feeling of the crowd": LH, p. 308.

231   "finest moment in public life": Ibid., p. 306.

231   neither Hillary nor her publisher: Woodward, Choice, p. 272; WP, Jan. 12, 1996.

231   "long excursions into policy-wonkdom": WP Book World, Jan. 28, 1996.

231   She enlisted the services: Sheehy, p. 271; WP, Jan. 12, 1996; Woodward, Choice, p. 272.

231   Hillary also had to keep up: WP, Oct. 13, 1995.

231   "train wreck": Time, Sept. 2, 1996.

231   The previous June, they had relished: June 11, 1995; PPP, 1995, book 1, pp. 848–61.

231   "In a heartbeat I accept": Ibid.

231   "the good Newt": Bill Clinton, interview with Rolling Stone, Nov. 2, 2000; PPP, 2000–2001, book 3, p. 2640.

232   Gingrich consistently misinterpreted: Klein, p. 141.

232   knew how to "melt": Newsweek, Aug. 19, 1996.

232   "inadvertently ingenious disinformation campaign": ATH, p. 398.

232   "hard public line": Ibid.

232   Morris continued to reassure: Klein, p. 147.

232   "Al Gore was very important": Laura Tyson interview.

232   "to define Newt Gingrich": Mike McCurry interview.

232   The Republican position on health care: Newsweek, Nov. 18, 1996.

232   Bill's media team produced: Woodward, Choice, pp. 237–39; Newsweek, Nov. 18, 1996; Morris, Rewriting History, p. 132.

232   "Medicare's a winner": Newsweek, Nov. 18, 1996.

232   he was editing scripts: Woodward, Choice, p. 236.

232   The Republicans made themselves even more vulnerable: Reich, p. 281.

233   "It is amazing we were on the air": Mike McCurry interview.

233   "probably there are people": Time, Oct. 30, 1995.

233   "necessary to pay for increased spending": WP, Oct. 19, 1995.

233   Democrats angrily accused Bill: ATH, p. 395; Time, Oct. 30, 1995.

233   "a preposterous fairy tale": Time, Oct. 30, 1995.

233   "raise your taxes more": Ibid.

233   "checked in often": LH, p. 318.

233 "the most powerful liberal": *ATH*, p. 387.

234 "learned to smile": Ibid., p. 389.

234 "the master of the public smile": Ibid.

234 Rabin was assassinated: *ML*, p. 678.

234 Bill wept openly: *Newsweek*, Nov. 18, 1996.

234 "father figure": *LH*, p. 316.

234 his aides kept the Republican leaders away: *ATH*, p. 404.

234 "demagoguery": Woodward, *Choice*, p. 320.

234 called her a "Marxist": *Newsweek*, Nov. 27, 1995.

234 "I don't care": Ibid.

234 "My wife has never tried": Woodward, *Choice*, p. 321.

234 No one said a word: *Newsweek*, Nov. 27, 1995.

234 On November 14, eight hundred thousand: *LH*, p. 319.

235 "madly drafting": *LH*, p. 318.

235 Monica Lewinsky had been offered: *MS*, p. 70.

235 She and Bill made eye contact: Ibid., p. 71.

235 "smiling and looking": Ibid.

235 fateful and provocative gesture: Ibid.: *Starr Report*, p. 80.

235 "an appreciative look": *MS*, p. 72.

235 "You know I have a really big crush": Ibid.; *Starr Report*, p. 80.

235 they made their way: *MS*, pp. 73–74; *Starr Report*, pp. 80–81.

235 This time, he took her to: Grand-jury testimony of Monica Lewinsky, Aug. 20, 1998.

236 "And then he made a joke": *Starr Report*, p. 81.

236 "How can romance thrive": *WP*, Oct. 12, 1995.

236 "would never have touched": Ibid.

236 On Friday, November 17, Bill was: *MS*, p. 75; *Starr Report*, pp. 83–84.

236 a White House photographer snapped: *Starr Report*, p. 227, n. 176.

236 "Kiddo": *MS*, p. 76.

236 "regular White House girlfriend": Ibid., p. 73.

236 But Bill let Lewinsky know: Ibid., p. 75.

236 "no one else is around": *Starr Report*, p. 84.

236 When the sides remained deadlocked: *ML*, p. 690.

237 Bill then made a significant concession: *ATH*, p. 405; Rubin, p. 167; Reich, p. 287; Waldman, p. 90.

237 The opposing sides had narrowed: Woodward, *Choice*, p. 322.

237 "He would compromise on capital-gains": Laura Tyson interview.

237 the Republicans had a chance to declare victory: Rubin, p. 167; Johnson and Broder, p. 599.

237 White House pollsters found: *Time*, Nov. 18, 1996.

237 "the Gingrich Who Stole Christmas": *ATH*, p. 406.

237 "We made a mistake": *ML*, p. 694.

237 "In the 1995 government shutdowns": Lawrence O'Donnell interview.

237 "completely dominated the public relations struggle": *WP*, Dec. 27, 1995.

238 game of chicken: Robert Reich called the government shutdown an "idiotic game of bluff." Reich, p. 283.

238 cost taxpayers some $1.5 billion: Johnson and Broder reported that it cost taxpayers forty million dollars per day, p. 599.

238 "When he won the budget battle": Mike McCurry interview.

238 "The president was under great stress": Laura Tyson interview.

238 "We want Bill!": *LH*, p. 322.

238 At Belfast City Hall: *NYT* interview with Bill Clinton, Nov. 30, 2000; *PPP*, 2000, book 3, pp. 2789–2803.

238 "It was the beginning of two of the best days": *ML*, p. 686.
238 The First Lady unveiled: *NYT*, Dec. 5, 1995.
238 later that day Betty Currie invited: Grand-jury testimony of Monica Lewinsky, Aug. 20, 1998.
238 a coveted blue pass: *MS*, p. 62.
238 But that day, she and Bill: *MS*, p. 77.
239 Within moments, they had their third: *Starr Report*, pp. 85–86.
239 "told him her name": Ibid.
239 Afterward, she saw him masturbate: *Starr Report*, p. 437, n. 25.
239 "hours on the phone": Grand-jury testimony of Monica Lewinsky, Aug. 20, 1998.
239 "It is astonishing": *New York Review of Books*, Aug. 14, 2003.
239 "to bump into each other": *Starr Report*, p. 73.
239 "I did what people do": Ibid., p. 76.
239 referring to Bill as "her": Ibid., p. 222, n. 120.
239 Lewinsky alerted Bill: Grand-jury testimony of Monica Lewinsky, Aug. 20, 1998.
240 she was indiscreet enough to confide: *Starr Report*, pp. 59–60, 323–27.
240 she was likely to talk about it: Grand-jury testimony of Bill Clinton, Aug. 17, 1998.
240 "just because I could": *WP*, June 17, 2004.

CHAPTER ELEVEN

241 the White House released: *Newsweek*, Jan. 15, 1996.
241 "expression of concern": Hillary Clinton on *The Diane Rehm Show*, Jan. 15, 1996.
242 On Thursday the fourth: Woodward, *Shadow*, pp. 297, 300; Sheehy, p. 283.
242 "numerous conferences": *Newsweek*, Jan. 8, 1996. The issue was on the newsstands on Jan. 1.
242 "Even more puzzling": Ibid.
242 An FBI analysis found: *WP*, June 2, 1996.
242 At the very least, Hillary had handled: Woodward, *Shadow*, p. 324; *NYT*, June 5, 1996.
242 "written a 320-page book in longhand": *WP*, Jan. 12, 1996.
243 "I actually wrote the book": *NYT*, Jan. 18, 1996.
243 "It is, at bottom": *NYT*, Jan. 20, 1996.
243 Hillary erroneously said: *Nightline*, transcript, Jan. 30, 1996.
243 showed only "minimal" work: *Newsweek*, Jan. 15, 1996.
243 But the records also revealed: Sheehy, pp. 278–79; *Newsweek*, Jan. 22, 1996.
243 "not related to Castle Grande": *Nightline*, transcript, Jan. 30, 1996.
243 "IDC and Castle Grande were one": Ibid.
243 "deceive federal bank examiners": *Time*, Oct. 7, 1996.
243 it became clear that if she had released: *WP*, June 2, 1996.
243 Hillary's favorability ratings: *NYT*, Jan. 17, 1996.
243 "congenital liar": *NYT*, Jan. 8, 1996.
244 "congenital fudger": *Newsweek*, Jan. 22, 1996.
244 "touchiness about the whole truth": *WP*, Jan. 21, 1996.
244 "if everybody in this country": Ibid., Jan. 10, 1996.
244 Bill had called Monica Lewinsky: *MS*, p. 79; *Starr Report*, p. 87.
244 "chance encounter": *MS*, p. 81.
244 "her chair": Ibid.
244 "needy man": Ibid., p. 82.
244 "thinkers' dinner": Barber, pp. 132–57.
244 "With the snow falling outside": Bill Galston interview.
244 "perfectly attuned": Barber, p. 138.

244 he nodded and took notes: Waldman, p. 96.
244 "masterful" summary: Barber, p. 149.
245 "Talk about compartmentalizing!": Bill Galston interview.
245 "she glowered at me": Ibid.
245 "She was testing me": Ibid.
245 Hillary remained outwardly unflappable: WP, Jan. 17, 1996.
245 "I couldn't eat or sleep": LH, p. 335.
245 he yielded to temptation: Starr Report, pp. 89–90.
245 Hillary had been away on her book tour: Toobin, p. 89.
245 Bill had tried phone sex: Starr Report, pp. 89–90.
245 "just about sex": Ibid., p. 90.
245 a "gift": MS, pp. 83–84.
245 "manually stimulating": Starr Report, p. 438, n. 31.
245 Jim and Diane Blair, who were spending: Ibid., p. 231, n. 230.
245 "values agenda": Waldman, p. 114.
245 "the era of big government": Ibid., pp. 112, 114.
245 The speech was a distillation: Time, Nov. 18, 1996.
246 "competing visions": Ibid.
246 designed to appeal to suburban "soccer moms": Ibid.
246 "the person who taught me": NYT, Jan. 24, 1996.
246 Hillary held her head high: LH, p. 336; Woodward, Shadow, p. 316.
246 "one of the reasons": ML, p. 699.
246 "good father": Newsweek, Feb. 12, 1996.
246 "trying to get to know": Starr Report, pp. 91–92.
246 she had suggested: Ibid., p. 90.
246 "clutch": WP, Oct. 3, 1998.
247 Secret Service agents had begun making bets: MS, p. 94.
247 "she seemed kind of enamored": WP, Oct. 3, 1998.
247 "You're always trafficking": Grand-jury testimony of Monica Lewinsky, Aug. 20, 1998.
247 "She didn't like the way Monica": Mike McCurry interview.
247 "started to blossom": Starr Report, p. 92.
247 When they met in the Oval Office: MS, p. 87; Starr Report, p. 93.
247 "made him feel twenty-five": MS, p. 84.
247 "I feel that he should have": Ibid., p. 101.
247 "people were going to be watching": Grand-jury testimony of Monica Lewinsky, Aug. 20, 1998.
247 when Hillary was in Greece: Starr Report, p. 94.
247 Bill proposed she meet him: Ibid., p. 233, n. 263.
247 Not "a good idea": Grand-jury testimony of Monica Lewinsky, Aug. 20, 1998.
248 Hillary due back in the evening: WP, Mar. 25, 1996; LH, p. 346.
248 "on the pretext of delivering": Starr Report, pp. 95, 233, n. 269.
248 infamous use of a cigar: Starr Report, pp. 95, 233, n. 274, 324–25.
248 "I decided to get rid": Ibid., p. 98.
248 "paying too much attention": Ibid., p. 104.
248 Lieberman directed Lewinsky's boss: Ibid., p. 100; MS, p. 95.
248 "too sexy": Starr Report, p. 100.
248 "the power of faith": PPP, 1996, book 1, p. 548.
248 he talked on the phone with Dick Morris: Starr Report, p. 102.
248 "bring you back": Ibid., p. 101.
248 "Assistant to the President for Blow Jobs": Ibid. p. 238, n. 316.
248 they saw each other only: Ibid., pp. 105–6.
248 phone sex seven times: Ibid., pp. 106, 324.

248 "Don't worry": *MS*, pp. 102–3.

248 "he was always very close": Grand-jury testimony of Monica Lewinsky, Aug. 20, 1998.

248 He even arranged for her family: *MS*, p. 104.

248 "What is she": *Starr Report*, p. 234, n. 290.

249 "discombobulated" campaign: *Newsweek*, March 11, 1996.

249 She supervised a White House database: *WP*, Aug. 8, 1997.

249 Ralph Lauren, a big fan: Ibid., Dec. 6, 1994.

249 "happy talk": Reich, p. 311.

249 "isn't a President who shares your pain": Ibid., pp. 276–77.

249 "optimism presentation": *Time*, Nov. 18, 1996.

249 "fact-based people": Ibid.

249 "pinprick events": Waldman, p. 117.

249 "presidential directives": *Time*, July 22, 1996.

250 "like an argument": Ibid., Nov. 18, 1996.

250 showed him videotapes of Ronald Reagan: *Newsweek*, Sept. 2, 1996.

250 "aura of command": Ibid.

250 lifting weights: Ibid., Nov. 18, 1996.

250 "giddy conspiratorial winks": Ibid., Sept. 2, 1996.

250 "I miss you": *MS*, p. 107.

250 "values" issues: *NYT Magazine*, May 30, 1999.

250 campaigning under the radar: Woodward, *Choice*, p. 418.

250 She was on the road four to five days: *NYT*, Apr. 25, 1996.

250 she recited the words: Ibid.

250 she compared herself to Eleanor Roosevelt: *WP*, Mar. 25, 1996.

250 she excluded them from her domestic flights: *Time*, Oct. 7, 1996.

250 "It's like traveling": *NYT*, Aug. 25, 1996.

251 "I must say": *Time*, June 3, 1996.

251 "had a hard time": Martha Sherrill interview with Ann Henry.

251 Hillary's labor had been difficult: *ML*, p. 272; also *LH*, p. 83.

251 "talking about" adoption: *Time*, June 3, 1996.

251 "Chelsea's new little sister, Tribeca": *NYT*, June 16, 1996.

251 "sacred psychologist": Ibid., June 25, 1996.

251 Hillary was so concerned: *Newsweek*, Nov. 18, 1996; *OO*, pp. 286–87.

251 "end welfare as we know it": *Time*, Sept. 2, 1996.

251 Once the Republicans gained power: Ron Haskins, Aug. 24, 2006, Brookings Institution website (www.brookings.edu).

251 Bill had originally proposed $18 billion: Lawrence O'Donnell interview.

251 reduced welfare spending by $55 billion: Ibid.; Reich, pp. 319–21.

252 Bill had vetoed two: *Time*, Mar. 25, 1996.

252 The Republicans added: Ron Haskins, Aug. 24, 2006, Brookings Institution website (www.brookings.edu).

252 Edelman and Donna Shalala were among: Klein, pp. 152–53.

252 "devastating increases": *WP*, Aug. 1, 1996.

252 "The public favored": Ron Haskins, Aug. 24, 2006, Brookings Institution website (www.brookings.edu).

252 "Democrats in Congress were putting pressure": Donna Shalala interview.

252 "advising the President": *NYT Magazine*, May 30, 1999.

252 "handing the Republicans": *LH*, p. 369.

252 "It was pure politics over substance": Donna Shalala interview.

253 the July 31 meeting: *ATH*, pp. 419–21; *WP*, Aug. 1, 1996.

253 "Kabuki theater": *Time*, Aug. 12, 1996.

253 Bill's staff had prepared only one speech: Ibid.

253   he listened intently, took notes: *ATH*, pp. 419–21.
253   "Potemkin meeting": Robert Reich interview.
253   "twenty points ahead": Reich, p. 321.
253   "a decent welfare bill": *Time*, Aug. 12, 1996.
253   "the best Republican speech": Ibid.
253   "moral blot": Ibid.
253   "rift" . . . "sad and difficult": *LH*, p. 370.
253   In fact, Bill had already damaged: *The New Yorker*, Oct. 30, 1995.
254   "Kennedy-Kassebaum took the strongest points": Pamela Bailey interview.
254   a phrase that had been polled: *Time*, Nov. 18, 1996.
254   "every phrase, every paragraph": Reich, p. 326.
254   Hillary was the star: *LH*, p. 374.
254   "liberalism lite": *The New Yorker*, quoting Jeff Greenfield, Oct. 21, 1996.
254   "let the cheers": *LH*, p. 376.
254   the Starr prosecution team convicted: *Newsweek*, June 10, 1996.
255   "too personal" to discuss: *BS*, p. 443.
255   The Castle Grande scheme: *WP*, June 2, 1996.
255   Webb Hubbell had drafted: *Newsweek*, Feb. 17, 1997, and May 11, 1998.
255   no "public support": *Newsweek*, May 11, 1998.
255   When McDougal refused to answer: *NYT*, Sept. 5 and Sept. 10, 1996.
255   pardons "no consideration": Bill Clinton, interview with Jim Lehrer, PBS, Sept. 23, 1996.
255   which was interpreted: *Time*, Oct. 7, 1996. During the presidential debate on Oct. 6, 1996, Senator Robert Dole criticized Bill's remarks to Lehrer, saying, "You may be sending a signal. . . . As the President of the United States, when someone asks you about pardons, you say, 'no comment,' period." *PPP*, 1996, book 2, p. 1755.
256   "implausible" memory lapses: *WP*, June 16, 1996.
256   "Pillsbury Report" had recommended only: *NYT*, Jan. 17, 1996.
256   "was neither a castigation nor vindication": The RTC Investigation, www.cnn.com/ALLPOLITICS/1997/gen/resources/infocus/whitewater/rtc.html, citing a report in the *Los Angeles Times*.
256   "had far more contact": *WP*, June 2, 1996.
256   The Clinton White House did everything: *Newsweek*, Dec. 16, 1996.
256   only "social" visits: Woodward, *Shadow*, pp. 341–42.
256   reporters managed to uncover: *Time*, Oct. 21, 1996.
256   "out of control": *Newsweek*, Oct. 21, 1996.
256   "historic proportions": *Los Angeles Times*, Oct. 19, 1996.
256   "totally occupied": *ML*, p. 731.
256   "put a sign all across": *Time*, Nov. 11, 1996.
257   Bill was obsessed: *Time*, Nov. 18, 1996.
257   The legislation, which stipulated: "President Clinton and the Federal Defense of Marriage Act," *Lambda Line*, May 1996.
257   "overwhelming support": *New York Post*, Oct. 30, 2006.
257   "strategic" and "related to re-election": Ibid.
257   "act of political cowardice": "President Clinton and the Federal Defense of Marriage Act," *Lambda Line*, May 1996.
257   In early September, he flexed: *Time*, Sept. 16, 1996.
257   "domestic policy component": Fisher, "Military Action Against Iraq," p. 795.
257   After intense negotiations, the participants: *Time*, Oct. 14, 1996.
257   He slept only seven hours: Harris, p. 251.
257   he visited twelve cities and towns: 1996 Presidential Documents Online, via GPO Ac-

cess, pp. 2355–56, Week Ending Friday, Nov. 8, 1996: Digest of Other White House Announcements.

257 closing speech at 1:00 a.m.: *Newsweek*, Nov. 18, 1996.

258 "floating serenely": Ibid.

258 "Small Deal": Ibid.

258 "less an ideology": Ibid.

258 54 percent of voters: Ibid.

258 "The vital American center": Ibid.

258 "It was a pretty joyless victory celebration": Mike McCurry interview.

258 the temperature rose to 63: WeatherUnderground.com history, Nov. 5, 1996.

259 "Good morning!": *Starr Report*, p. 106.

259 she surreptitiously brushed: Grand-jury testimony of Monica Lewinsky, Aug. 20, 1998.

259 "Handsome" liked it: *MS*, p. 118.

CHAPTER TWELVE

260 "the most normal year": *ML*, p. 740.

260 "free to do my job": Ibid.

260 Eisenhower Republican: Woodward, *Agenda*, p. 165.

260 growing preoccupation with golf: *Time*, Oct. 20, 1997.

261 "looking his age": *LH*, p. 393.

261 now blonder: Ibid., p. 394.

261 "were each other's best friend": Ibid., p. 393.

261 "His best friend": Marton, p. 339.

261 "on the phone talking deals and leaks": Private journal.

261 cut loose Harold Ickes: James Barnes interview; *Newsweek*, Nov. 25, 1996; *PPP*, 1996, book 2, pp. 2091–2104.

261 He had worked tirelessly: *Time*, Nov. 25, 1996; *Newsweek*, Nov. 25, 1996.

262 "mouth of a Teamster": Ibid., June 19, 1995.

262 "I love Hillary": Marton, p. 320.

262 "Someone came out of that meeting": Terry McAuliffe interview.

262 "took a long time": Ibid.

262 "prodigious ingratitude": *Newsweek*, Nov. 25, 1996.

262 "deeply upset": Ibid.

262 "Laura, you're the kind of girl": Laura Tyson interview.

262 "external event": *PPP*, 1996, book 2, p. 2099.

263 "I intend to speak": *Time*, Dec. 2, 1996.

263 unnerved the President's staff: Kurtz, pp. 80–81.

263 feared comparisons: Ann Blackman, *Time* correspondent, interview.

263 "extricate Hillary": Mike McCurry interview.

263 "formal role": *NYT*, Nov. 25, 1996.

263 "like steel tempered": *LH*, p. 393.

263 "deserves more": *NYT*, Jan. 20, 1997.

264 "There was no doubt": Private journal.

264 had forged a strong bond: *LH*, p. 360.

264 "too headstrong": *Newsweek*, Dec. 16, 1996.

264 "mediagenic": Ibid., Aug. 11, 1997.

264 "There was less whispering": *ATH*, p. 437.

264 "trying to stonewall": *PPP*, 1996, book 2, p. 2132.

265 "escape the politics": *Time*, Dec. 2, 1996.

265 "claim their share": *NYT*, Jan. 20, 1997.

265 they had phone sex: *Starr Report*, p. 107.

265 "long into the night": *MS*, p. 123.

265 Lewinsky popped up at one: *Starr Report*, p. 109.

265 "semi-low-cut" and "stunned": *Newsweek*, Feb. 2, 1998.

265 "There was no question": Ibid.

265 went twice to the Warner Theater: Author's notes, Dec. 28, 1996. The Clintons also attended a performance on Dec. 24. 1996 Presidential Documents Online, via GPO Access, p. 2543, Week Ending Friday, Dec. 27, 1996: Digest of Other White House Announcements.

265 "Should She Be Heard?": *Newsweek*, Jan. 13, 1997.

265 infuriated the President: Kurtz, pp. 94–95.

265 "highly persuasive": *Time*, June 6, 1997.

266 "good chance": *Newsweek*, Jan. 13, 1997.

266 eight big tents: *Time*, Jan. 20, 1997.

266 canceled a lavish White House reception: WP, Mar. 13, 1997.

266 "long enough to hide": *NYT*, Jan. 20, 1997.

266 "despised us and our politics": *LH*, p. 396.

266 "Good luck": Ibid.

266 "They're going to screw you": Blumenthal, p. 192.

266 Bill's inaugural: *PPP*, 1997, book 1, pp. 43–46; Waldman, p. 153.

266 "less certain": Waldman, p. 150.

266 "America stands alone": *PPP*, 1997, book 1, pp. 43–46.

267 "reckless aggression" . . . "increasingly interconnected": Remarks to the United Nations General Assembly, Oct. 22, 1995; *PPP*, 1995, book 2, p. 1655.

267 "traffic in terror": Remarks on the fiftieth anniversary of the United Nations Charter, June 26, 1995; *PPP*, 1995, book 1, pp. 947–51.

267 "suitcase bombs": Remarks to the United Nations General Assembly, Oct. 22, 1995; *PPP*, 1995, book 2, p. 1655. See also Remarks on American security in a changing world, George Washington University, Aug. 5, 1996; *PPP*, 1996, book 2, pp. 1255–60.

267 minimally aware: *9/11 Commission Report*, pp. 108–9.

267 several of its members had: Freeh, p. 281.

267 In 1996, the Clinton Administration: *Vanity Fair*, June, 2004; see also *9/11 Commission Report*, pp. 109–10.

267 "ideal haven": *9/11 Commission Report*, p. 65.

267 first fatwa: Freeh, p. 290.

267 his call in February 1998: *9/11 Commission Report*, p. 69; Freeh, pp. 285, 292.

267 the President did not publicly mention: Author database search of Weekly Compilation of Presidential Documents, from Presidential Documents Online, via GPO Access, 1993–2001, keywords "Qaida" and "Usama," the official spellings used by the database.

267 belittling him for platitudes: Waldman, p. 155; Harris, p. 257.

267 But a poll conducted: *Time*, Dec. 22, 1997; Waldman, p. 155.

268 His best speech of the first term: Remarks to the convocation of the Church of God in Christ in Memphis, Nov. 13, 1993; *PPP*, 1993, book 2, p. 1984.

268 suggested that he launch a major initiative: *Time*, Dec. 22, 1997.

268 Instead, he settled on: Ibid., June 16, 1997; *Newsweek*, June 16, 1997.

268 "borderline third tier": *OO*, p. 306.

268 "person out of my time": *Time*, Feb. 17, 1997.

268 "took risks in pursuit": Arthur Schlesinger Jr., "Rating the Presidents: Washington to Clinton," *Political Science Quarterly*, vol. 112, no. 2, summer 1997. NYT *Magazine* originally published the Schlesinger survey on Dec. 15, 1996. See also *Newsweek*,

May 26, 1997, as well as Jan. 27, 1997, in which historian Alan Brinkley called Bill Clinton "legacy obsessed."

269 time of "transition": Kurtz, p. 102.
269 "bully pulpit": *Time*, Jan. 20, 1997.
269 "We want people to read": Ibid.
269 recommendations of his Advisory Council: Ibid.; *PPP*, 1997, book 1, pp. 109–17.
269 "We mustn't let Social Security": DPM, Memcon of Senator Daniel P. Moynihan, Jan. 7, 1997.
269 "unfinished business": *ML*, p. 743.
269 "a national crusade for education standards": State of the Union address, Feb. 4, 1997; *PPP*, 1997, book 1, p. 111.
269 "turn George Wallace on his head": Waldman, p. 160.
269 probes by a twenty-five-member Justice Department: *Time*, Mar. 17, 1997.
270 The first wave: Lanny Davis, *Truth to Tell: Notes from My White House Education*, pp. 73, 86.
270 "ready to start overnights": Ibid., p. 126.
270 first in mid-February: *WP*, Feb. 13, 1997.
270 "solicitor in chief": Ibid., Mar. 2, 1997.
270 "eat the spinach": Ibid.
270 But it later emerged: *WP*, June 28, 1997.
270 Administration lawyers maintained: Ibid.
270 "no controlling legal authority": *Time*, Mar. 17, 1997; *WP*, June 28, 1997.
270 "one more false story": Woodward, *Choice*, p. 441.
270 "the only time I had to visit": *ML*, p. 747.
270 "never a single case": Ibid.
270 "one in nine": *WP*, Mar. 8, 1997.
271 "very isolating": Ibid.
271 "hour after hour": *Time*, Oct. 27, 1997.
271 "there was no specific": *WP*, Mar. 8, 1997.
271 DNC documents revealed: Davis, pp. 101–2.
271 corporate payments: *WP*, June 29, 1999.
271 "the stuff of double-takes": *WP*, Mar. 28, 1997.
271 "hush money": *NYT*, May 4, 1997.
271 Bill insisted that he first learned: *Time*, Apr. 14, 1997.
271 "persistent memory lapses": *Newsweek*, Apr. 14, 1997.
271 Kenneth Starr's investigators issued: *WP*, Mar. 5, 1997.
271 Bill said his advisors were only: *Time*, Apr. 14, 1997.
271 "some people's obsession": *WP*, Apr. 11, 1997.
271 "Every day can't be sunshine": *Starr Report*, p. 109.
272 She also began to press him: Ibid., p. 121.
272 "He was destroying her": *MS*, p. 126.
272 In addition to Davis, Lewinsky had extended: Grand-jury testimony of Monica Lewinsky, Aug. 20, 1998; *MS*, p. 119; *Starr Report*, pp. 210–11.
272 By February 1997, Lewinsky was even: *Newsweek*, Feb. 23, 1998.
272 Finally, on Friday, February 28: *ML*, pp. 773–74; *Starr Report*, p. 116.
272 "I don't want to get addicted": *MS*, p. 128.
272 At Lewinsky's insistence: *MS*, p. 129; *Starr Report*, p. 118.
272 "I was sick": *Starr Report*, p. 118.
272 "disgusted with myself": *ML*, p. 773.
272 den mother: *Newsweek*, Feb. 16, 1998.
272 moonlighted as an assistant: Toobin, p. 234.

272 "more personal in nature": *Starr Report*, p. 112.
272 She went to great lengths: Ibid., p. 113.
273 Around midnight, Bill arrived: *WP*, Mar. 15, 1997; *ML*, p. 748; Van Natta, p. 201.
273 rumors inevitably circulated: Van Natta, pp. 200–201.
273 He remained awake, listening to the music: *WP*, Mar. 15, 1997; *Newsweek*, Mar. 24, 1997.
273 wheelchair dutifully pushed by Hillary: *WP*, Mar. 17, 1997.
273 she was out the door: *WP*, Mar. 15 and Mar. 27, 1997.
273 This time, the Hillaryland contingent: *LH*, p. 400.
273 Bill was equally determined: Bill Clinton, exchange with reporters, *PPP*, 1997, book 1, pp. 324–26.
273 "the right but hard thing": Talbott, p. 237.
273 transported from Air Force One: *Newsweek*, Mar. 31, 1997; Talbott, p. 237.
273 "He didn't need": Talbott, p. 238.
273 one drunken performance: Harris, p. 284.
274 "He thinks it's a mistake": *PPP*, 1997, book 1, p. 331.
274 "the co-pilot": *WP*, Mar. 27, 1997.
274 "They do not have": Ibid.
274 Hillary and Chelsea were wrapping up: Ibid., Mar. 30, 1997.
274 He hobbled on crutches: *MS*, p. 131.
274 placed on the bookshelf: *Starr Report*, OIC Supplemental Report: Catalog of Books in the West Wing Presidential Study as of 10 October 1997, p. 2919.
274 "babbling on about something": *Starr Report*, p. 119.
274 They had brief genital contact: Ibid.
274 he reiterated the need: *MS*, pp. 131–32; *Starr Report*, p. 120.
275 "Try a Little Tenderness": *MS*, p. 132.
275 "regaled Bill with our adventures": *LH*, p. 405.
275 they had fraught phone conversations: *MS*, p. 137.
275 She interviewed in the press office: Ibid.; Mike McCurry interview.
275 Marsha Scott told Bill: *MS*, pp. 138–39.
275 "shocked" Kaye: *Starr Report*, p. 122.
275 "Of course not": Ibid.
275 while Hillary and Chelsea swam: *MS*, p. 140.
275 "pain and torment": Ibid.
275 "hundreds of affairs": *Starr Report*, p. 122.
275 "the days when he had been good": *MS*, p. 140.
275 "Dump Day": Ibid.
275 "be a very good friend": Ibid., p. 141.
276 Bill heard the news: *Time*, June 9, 1997: "Clinton's entourage was thunderstruck, depressed and a little resentful."
276 "From the moment": Talbott, p. 247.
276 Bill was upset that the symbolic moment: *Time*, June 9, 1997.
276 "All of a sudden": Mike McCurry interview.
276 He was conspicuously at ease: Bill Clinton and Tony Blair, news conference, May 29, 1997; *PPP*, 1997, book 1, p. 677.
276 dinner with the Blairs: *LH*, p. 425; *ML*, p. 756.
276 "The conversation never stalled": *LH*, p. 425.
276 at Chelsea's commencement: *PPP*, 1997, book 1, pp. 706–8.
277 she was growing more agitated: *MS*, pp. 144–45.
277 "limit the contact": *Starr Report*, p. 127.
277 she met with White House Deputy: Ibid., pp. 124–26.
277 "with such nasty women there": Ibid.

277 "Bill's girlfriend from our hippie days": *Time*, Mar. 24, 1997.

277 Scott had been in the middle: Ibid.

277 "disposable": *MS*, p. 147.

277 "need to explain": *Starr Report*, p. 127.

277 "illegal to threaten": Ibid., p. 128.

278 "I wish I had": *MS*, p. 150.

278 "cold eyes": Ibid.

278 "hot on the trail:" *Starr Report*, p. 257, n. 531.

278 whose encounter with Bill at the end of 1993: Isikoff, pp. 112–14.

278 had recently been discovered: *WP*, May 19, 1997.

278 "never approach a small-breasted woman": *Starr Report*, p. 130.

278 Bill, Hillary, and Chelsea left: *ML*, p. 759; *LH*, p. 413.

278 "was trying to stiffen Clinton's spine": Private journal.

278 the Clintons took separate paths: *LH*, pp. 414–15; *WP*, July 12, 1997.

278 "the Sludge Report": *Starr Report*, p. 131.

279 When he asked if she had spoken: Ibid., p. 132.

279 the President was playing golf: *ML*, p. 760.

279 details of a budget deal: Ibid., pp. 754–55; Harris, pp. 261–63.

279 Democrats accepted Republican terms: *Time*, Aug. 11, 1997; *ML*, p. 761.

279 "GOP 1997 Tax Cuts": *Time*, Aug. 11, 1997.

279 "euphoric": *ML*, p. 761.

279 "pattern of behavior": *Newsweek*, Aug. 11, 1997.

279 "preposterous": Ibid.

280 "not to be believed": Ibid.

280 "misbehavior": *The New Yorker*, Mar. 23, 1998.

280 Hillary remained opposed: Harris, p. 292.

280 she and Bill continued to believe: Toobin, p. 119.

280 In the end, however, Paula Jones scuttled: Ibid., pp. 125–26.

280 Bill yielded to Lewinsky's continued entreaties: *MS*, p. 157; *Starr Report*, p. 135.

280 "I'm trying to be good": *Starr Report*, p. 135.

280 Their three-week holiday: *LH*, p. 415.

280 a fifty-first birthday: Ken Burns interview.

280 they spent more time than usual: *WP*, Sept. 13, 1997.

281 newspaper called her "ugly": *WP*, Mar. 26, 1997.

282 The Clinton family's trip: *Time*, Sept. 29, 1997; *WP*, Sept. 20, 1997.

282 "according to the University's usual procedures": *WP*, Sept. 20, 1997.

282 Bill and Hillary dispensed: Ibid.

282 "got on Chelsea's nerves": *ML*, p. 765.

282 "stared out morosely": *LH*, p. 420.

282 "You can't know": *WP*, Oct. 12, 1997.

282 Monica Lewinsky intensified: *Starr Report*, pp. 136–38; *MS*, pp. 159–62.

283 "just lead me on": *Starr Report*, p. 136.

283 "golden positions": Ibid.

283 At Bill's suggestion: Ibid.

283 "in the Old Executive": Ibid., p. 138.

283 Lewinsky had shown her: *MS*, p. 178. Lewinsky had not worn the dress since her encounter with the President, and she told Tripp she intended to have it cleaned. Tripp urged her not to, saying she might need the dress to protect herself.

283 Not only had Tripp begun taping: Ibid., pp. 164, 174.

283 Tripp and her new confidante: Isikoff, p. 203.

283 "that he helped": *Starr Report*, p. 140.

283 "If I had known": *MS*, p. 170; *Starr Report*, p. 141.

283 "My life is empty": *MS*, p. 170.
284 That night, Hillary was wrapping up: *Newsweek*, Oct. 20, 1997.
284 "made a face": *WP*, Oct. 12, 1997.
284 Betty Currie summoned: *Starr Report*, p. 142; *MS*, p. 171.
284 $63,000 from MacAndrews & Forbes: www.cnn.com/ALLPOLITICS/1997/05/22/
 jordan.hubbell/index.htm/?eref=sitesearch; *USA Today*, May 22, 1997.
284 Bill gave her a chaste peck: *Starr Report*, p. 142.
284 "Her Calvinism": *NYT*, Oct. 10, 1998.
284 "haunted my imagination": Remarks to the pool on Air Force One, Oct. 13, 1997; *PPP*,
 1997, book 2, p. 1350.
284 "consumer culture": *WP*, Oct. 17, 1997.
285 "It became clear": Ibid.
285 Hillary's birthday celebration: *NYT*, Oct. 26, 1997.
285 "seemed as happy": *ATH*, p. 437.
285 On Sunday the twenty-sixth: *ML*, p. 767.
285 "stations of the cross": *NYT*, Oct. 26, 1997.
285 capped by a tribute: Remarks, Oct. 27, 1997; *PPP*, 1997, book 2, p. 1439.
285 "move beyond . . . personality-based": Blumenthal, pp. 307–8.
285 she headed overseas again: *LH*, pp. 430–31; *WP*, Nov. 14, 1997.
285 "pep talk": *Starr Report*, p. 146; *MS*, p. 173.
285 Curiously, neither Richardson: *Starr Report*, p. 146.
285 Three days later: Ibid., pp. 147–48.
286 "highly recommended": *Starr Report*, p. 151.
286 Bill invited her to the White House: *MS*, pp. 181–83; *Starr Report*, pp. 152, 154.
286 "I am consumed": *MS*, p. 183.
286 "Southern lethargy": Christopher Meyer, *D.C. Confidential: The Controversial Memoirs of Britain's Ambassador to the U.S. at the Time of 9/11 and the Iraq War*, p. 85.
286 "subdued, his normal": Waldman, p. 186.
286 "unusually severe": *Newsweek*, Oct. 13, 1997.
286 Otherwise, his health: Ibid., and Aug. 11, 1997; *WP*, Aug. 6, 1997.
286 "strangely paralyzed": *Time*, Oct. 20, 1997.
286 "itsy-bitsy proposals for itsy-bitsy babies": *Time*, Aug. 25, 1997.
286 "lame duck" . . . "gone to sleep": Bill Clinton, press conference, Dec. 16, 1997; *PPP*,
 1997, book 2, p. 1774.
286 seemed preoccupied: *Newsweek*, Dec. 29, 1997.
286 "think time": *Time*, Oct. 20, 1997.
287 "slow down": Van Natta, p. 184.
287 "How many mulligans": Bill Clinton, interview on *Meet the Press*, Nov. 9, 1997, *PPP*,
 1997, book 2, p. 1527.
287 crippled by squabbling: *Time*, Dec. 15, 1997.
287 "If we had four hours": Remarks at a roundtable discussion, Dec. 3, 1997; *PPP*, 1997,
 book 2, p. 1702.
287 Janet Reno rejected: Davis, p. 197.
287 A parallel investigation: *Time*, June 16, 1997; *Newsweek*, Oct. 20, 1997.
287 "seemed to delight": *Newsweek*, Oct. 20, 1997.
287 "prosecutor's purgatory": *Newsweek*, July 7, 1997.
287 Without the testimony: Ibid.
288 "distinguishing characteristics": Toobin, pp. 137–38.
288 "bald eagle tattoo": Kurtz, p. 210.
288 When erect at: Toobin, pp. 137–38.
288 "normal" in "size": Kurtz, p. 278.
288 urologist Kevin O'Connell: Toobin, p. 138; Woodward, *Shadow*, p. 358.

288 "proposed having": *Starr Report*, p. 149.
288 The names of nearly twenty: *Starr Report*, p. 156; Woodward, *Shadow*, pp. 360–61; Toobin, p. 166.
288 "Are you taking good care": *MS*, p. 186; *Starr Report*, p. 156.
288 "You want me out": *Starr Report*, p. 156.
288 When Secret Service officers told: Ibid., p. 158; *MS*, p. 188.
288 "In my life no one has treated": *MS*, p. 188.
289 "affectionate and open": Ibid., p. 189.
289 "Oh I'll talk to him": *Starr Report*, p. 159.
289 "not to jerk you around": *MS*, p. 189.
289 Bill met in the same office: *Starr Report*, p. 161.
289 "Not a problem": Woodward, *Shadow*, p. 361.
289 "Bob, do you think": Toobin, p. 167.
289 When Bennett eventually learned: Ibid., pp. 168, 170.

CHAPTER THIRTEEN

290 Vernon Jordan suddenly became: *Starr Report*, p. 162; *MS*, pp. 190, 192; Toobin, p. 176.
290 "I saw the witness list": *MS*, p. 194.
290 To avoid a subpoena: *Starr Report*, p. 163.
290 "I told her some women": *ML*, p. 774.
290 cover stories: *Starr Report*, p. 163.
290 "asked me to lie": Grand-jury testimony of Monica Lewinsky, Aug. 20, 1998.
290 "deny a relationship": Ibid.; *Starr Report*, p. 72.
291 "There were secrets": Grand-jury testimony of Monica Lewinsky, Aug. 20, 1998.
291 Jones's lawyers issued a subpoena: *Starr Report*, p. 167; *MS*, pp. 196–97.
291 "any sexual relationship": *Starr Report*, p. 167.
291 "with a wink": Ibid., p. 168.
291 "I did not get graphic": Ibid, p. 284, n. 833.
291 "No, never": Ibid., p. 168.
291 "get screwed in this case": *Newsweek*, Feb. 2, 1998.
291 Lewinsky answered: *Starr Report*, pp. 166, 172; *MS*, pp. 202–4.
291 "someone, maybe Betty": *Starr Report*, p. 172.
292 "If they ask you for gifts": Grand-jury testimony of Bill Clinton, Aug. 17, 1998.
292 Bill's three-month-old: *LH*, p. 436.
292 "passionate": *Starr Report*, p. 172.
292 "OK Kiddo": *MS*, p. 204.
292 "the President said": *Starr Report*, p. 174.
292 "may remember better": Ibid., p. 176.
292 "from me to the President": Ibid., p. 177.
292 Jordan initially denied: Richard Posner, *An Affair of State: The Investigation, Impeachment, and Trial of President Clinton*, pp. 21–22.
292 seated on a dais: Sheehy, p. 339.
292 "You could feel": Richard Reeves, syndicated column, July 19, 2000.
292 "We don't do spontaneity": Ibid.
292 The day after they returned: *WP*, Jan. 6, 1998.
293 "invasion of privacy": *LH*, p. 438.
293 "name me any 50-year-old": *NYT*, Jan. 20, 1998.
293 "loving the picture": *WP*, Jan. 6, 1998.
293 "Now let's spend": Blumenthal, p. 313.

293   "complacent coaster": *Newsweek*, Jan. 19, 1998.

293   "glowing": Barber, p. 228.

293   "collapse of traditional families": Ibid., p. 232.

293   "God, they hate me": Ibid., p. 237.

293   Hillary returned with Buddy: Blumenthal, p. 316.

294   "never had a sexual": *MS*, p. 208.

294   "already seen about fifteen": *Starr Report*, p. 179.

294   It had been a testy exchange: *MS*, p. 205.

294   Lewinsky bungled her interview: *Time*, Sept. 21, 1998.

294   "Jordan magic": Ibid.

294   "bright young girl": *Starr Report*, p. 185.

294   "Mission accomplished": Ibid., p. 186.

294   "I'm aware of Bill Clinton's": Toobin, p. 208.

294   one of the Jones lawyers told: Woodward, *Shadow*, p. 369.

294   Linda Tripp alerted: Ibid., p. 371.

294   The involvement of Jordan: *Newsweek*, Aug. 10 and Aug. 17, 1998.

295   "The only thing": Toobin, p. 216.

295   the President was ready: Isikoff, p. 325; Toobin, p. 212.

295   "sexual relations": *Starr Report*, p. 193.

295   "truthful but not particularly": Grand-jury testimony of Bill Clinton, Aug. 17, 1998.

295   he was surprised by the specificity: Toobin, p. 223.

295   "high level of paranoia": Deposition of Bill Clinton, Jan. 17, 1998.

296   "If it ain't in": Lionel Tiger, anthropologist, interview in which he recounted hearing the expression from Arkansan Norris Church.

296   He could not recall being alone: *Starr Report*, p. 38.

296   could vividly remember the details: Van Natta, pp. 183–84.

296   "There is absolutely no sex": *Starr Report*, p. 193.

296   he was to turn to his advantage: Grand-jury testimony of Bill Clinton, Aug. 17, 1998.

296   But the veteran attorney had been disquieted: Woodward, *Shadow*, p. 382.

296   "hunkered down": *NYT*, Jan. 20, 1998.

296   "agitated" . . . "exhausted": *LH*, p. 440.

296   "an anxiety": Grand-jury testimony of Bill Clinton, Aug. 17, 1998.

296   The Clintons had intended: *LH*, p. 440.

296   "had a good time": *NYT*, Jan. 20, 1998.

296   In the early evening, he also called: *Starr Report*, p. 195.

297   Michael Weisskopf of *Time*: Davis, p. 17.

297   By early afternoon, Lindsey had heard: *Starr Report*, p. 195.

297   *Newsweek*'s nervous editors decided: Isikoff, p. 337.

297   But details about the spiked: Isikoff, p. 340; Woodward, *Shadow*, p. 386; Toobin, p. 231.

297   probably Lindsey, by Bill's recollection: Grand-jury testimony of Bill Clinton, Aug. 17, 1998.

297   "discredited": Isikoff, p. 341.

297   "It finally happened": Max Brantley interview.

297   "built us up again": *NYT*, Jan. 20, 1998.

297   "we just stayed home": Sheehy, p. 11.

298   "that we have one": *Talk*, Sept. 1999.

298   "You were always there": *Starr Report*, p. 196.

298   "refresh" his "recollection": Toobin, p. 234.

298   Drudge published more particulars: *MS*, p. 249; Waldman, p. 200.

298   "I shamed them into not using": Mike McCurry interview.

298   "expansive, animated mood": Waldman, p. 198.

298   he also made nearly thirty phone calls: Harris, p. 304.

298 "We do box it off": *U.S. News & World Report*, Feb. 2, 1998.
298 "in a little box": Ibid.
298 "political maneuvering": *NYT*, Jan 20, 1998.
299 The two men had a ninety-minute: *WP*, Feb. 8, 1998.
299 "Until that moment": Mike McCurry interview.
299 "considerably less focused": *WP*, Feb. 8, 1998.
299 "The President adamantly denies": Ibid., Jan. 21, 1998.
299 Bill made a series of calls: *Starr Report*, pp. 200–201.
299 The President left a wake-up call: Woodward, *Shadow*, p. 388.
299 he did not sleep: Harris, p. 305.
299 Bill's first call: *Starr Report*, pp. 200–201.
300 "misinterpreted his attention": *LH*, p. 441.
300 "more than six years": Ibid.
300 "It was one more false rumor": Hillary Clinton, interview with Barbara Walters, ABC News, transcript, June 8, 2003.
300 "a bewildered Ozzie": *WP*, Feb. 1, 1998.
300 "We know the truth": Sheehy, p. 17.
300 "outraged by these": *Starr Report*, p. 201.
300 "walking around in a daze" . . . "forge ahead": *LH*, p. 442.
301 "chipper": Blumenthal, p. 338.
301 "concerted effort": *LH*, p. 443.
301 "did not have sexual": *Starr Report*, p. 201.
301 "I did not screw": Grand-jury testimony of John Podesta, June 16, 1998, vol. 3, p. 3311.
301 "do something" . . . "slipped up": *Starr Report*, pp. 206–07.
301 "there may be gifts": Ibid., p. 206.
301 "Grassy Knoll": *Newsweek*, Feb. 9 and Feb. 23, 1998.
301 "people in trouble": Blumenthal, p. 339.
301 a reprise of what Hillary had told: *The New Yorker*, May 30, 1994.
301 "revelations": Blumenthal, pp. 337–38, 340.
301 "lines of influence": Ibid., p. 340.
301 "daring political venture": Ibid., p. 339.
302 "Well, we'll just have to win": Ibid., p. 340.
302 "There is no improper relationship": Bill Clinton, interview with Jim Lehrer, PBS, *PPP*, 1998, book 1, p. 89.
302 "Was it in any way sexual?": Bill Clinton, interview with Morton Kondracke and Ed Henry, *Roll Call*, *PPP*, 1998, book 1, p. 100.
302 "weird because he wasn't being declarative": Mike McCurry interview.
302 "OK, I'll use": *Newsweek*, Feb. 2, 1998.
302 "little box": Bill Clinton, interview with Mara Liasson and Robert Siegel, NPR, *PPP*, 1998, book 1, pp. 99–100.
302 "off-balance": Blumenthal, pp. 340–42.
303 "sexual demand": Ibid., p. 341.
303 By evening, Hillary had already: Toobin, p. 249; Maraniss, *Enigma*, p. 84; Sheehy, p. 16.
303 he remained for the next thirty-four days: *Starr Report*, p. 308.
303 "I wanted it to be true": Ibid.
303 "battle mode": *WP*, Jan. 24, 1998; *NYT*, Jan. 25, 1998.
303 "smiling and composed": Waldman, p. 205.
303 Hillary was joking about her anticipated: Blumenthal, p. 341.
304 "I don't talk": Sheehy, p. 14.
304 "Tolerating his weakness": Susan Thomases interview.
304 Dick Morris called Bill: Toobin, p. 244; Woodward, *Shadow*, pp. 390–91.

304 "Well, we just have to": *Starr Report*, p. 207.
305 "the press assumed": Davis, pp. 31–32.
305 "I realized he was lying": Bernie Nussbaum interview.
305 "livid": *ATH*, p. 433.
305 "Get it out as quickly": Ibid., p. 435.
305 "if Gore became President": *San Jose Mercury News*, Jan. 24, 1998; see also *Newsweek*, Feb. 2, 1998.
306 "I have known": Waldman, p. 203.
306 Where, his aides wondered: Ibid., p. 204.
306 "murky": Mike McCurry interview.
306 "We need to slow": *Newsweek*, Feb. 9, 1998.
306 "completely untrue": *Starr Report*, p. 208.
306 "At the cabinet meeting": Donna Shalala interview.
306 Tripp-Lewinsky tapes published: *Newsweek*, Feb. 2, 1998, available on Jan. 24, 1998.
307 "potential DNA trail": *Newsweek*, Dec. 28, 1998.
307 "love dress": Ibid., Aug. 10, 1998.
307 critics ridiculed: Davis, p. 258; Kurtz, p. 308; *Newsweek*, Aug. 10. 1998.
307 "There is no": *Newsweek*, Aug. 31, 1998.
307 "intimate incident": Davis, p. 258.
307 White House gloating: Katz, p. 329.
307 watching new films: *Newsweek*, Feb. 2, 1998; *NYT*, Jan. 25, 1998.
307 Bill's preparations: Klein, pp. 5–6.
307 "Love does not delight": *Newsweek*, Feb. 9, 1998.
307 "If he's not telling": Waldman, p. 210.
308 "It's not like": Stephen Smith, e-mail to author, Jan. 25, 1998.
308 "hide out until": *WP*, Feb. 1, 1998.
308 "the decisive vote": Blumenthal, p. 370.
308 *Newsweek* reported that voters: *Newsweek*, Feb. 9, 1998.
308 Private soundings: *WP*, Jan. 26, 1998.
308 had not yet made up his mind: Toobin, p. 250.
308 "remain focused": *Newsweek*, Feb. 9, 1998.
308 "Hillary was sitting separate": Donna Shalala interview.
308 Bill dispatched staff members: Toobin, p. 250.
308 The proceedings in the crowded: *PPP*, 1998, book 1, pp. 110–11.
309 "America's true education president": Toobin, p. 251.
309 "Now, I have to go back": *PPP*, 1998, book 1, p. 111.
309 "in fascinated disgust": *ATH*, p. 436.
309 "caused him more lasting damage": Blumenthal, p. 371.
310 He later said that he was only: *ML*, p. 774.
310 "coming clean in the beginning": Bernie Nussbaum interview.
310 "The lie saved me": Harris, p. 342.
310 "There's going to be": Sheehy, p. 15.
310 After a strategy session: Kurtz, p. 297.
310 Blumenthal, who had created: *The New Yorker*, Feb. 9, 1998; *Newsweek*, Feb. 23, 1998.
310 "There are professional forces": Blumenthal, p. 373.
310 "encouraged her to stand": *WP*, Jan. 27, 1998.
310 In the evening, she received: *The New Yorker*, Feb. 9, 1998.
310 Hillary took one more call: Blumenthal, p. 373.
311 "Screw 'em": *LH*, p. 445.
311 Hillary emphasized: Woodward, *Shadow*, pp. 394–95; Sheehy, pp. 6–8.
311 "blast faxing": *Newsweek*, Feb. 9, 1998.
312 "I guess that will teach them": Toobin, p. 258.

CHAPTER FOURTEEN

313 "His seven months of not fessing up": Dee Dee Myers interview.
314 "strangest year of my presidency": *ML*, p. 771.
314 "trying to dodge bolts": Interview with Joe Klein, July 5, 2000; PPP, 2000, book 2, p. 2096.
314 "I was compelled": *ML*, p. 771.
314 "lost year": *U.S. News & World Report*, Jan. 22, 2001.
314 "armor . . . thickened": *LH*, p. 443.
314 "embitter an entire": *Washington Monthly*, July 1999.
314 "spinners went to work": *Newsweek*, Feb. 9, 1998.
314 "fantasy or untruthful": *WP*, Jan. 25, 1998.
314 a ten-page proffer: *MS*, p. 265.
315 "misogynist": *WP*, Jan. 21, 1998.
315 On February 1, Ginsburg appeared: Toobin, p. 274.
315 immunity talks collapsed: Ibid., p. 278.
315 "seemed to indicate that the President": *Newsweek*, Oct. 12, 1998.
315 "vague and muddled": Ibid.
315 did everything he could to prolong: *Starr Report*, pp. 429–33; *Time*, Sept. 21, 1998.
315 "sorcerer's apprentice": Toobin, p. 280.
315 "Maybe there'll be": *Chicago Tribune*, Feb. 17, 1998.
316 "goofy, flat-out in love": *Newsweek*, Feb. 9, 1998.
316 she delivered a speech on civil society: *LH*, p. 447.
316 The guest list included: *The New Yorker*, Feb. 16, 1998; Meyer, p. 88.
316 "If you'd arrived from planet Mars": Christopher Meyer interview.
316 "radiant" . . . "absurdly debonair": *The New Yorker*, Feb. 16, 1998.
316 "I took a lot of shit": Tina Brown interview.
316 "Monica Lewinsky wasn't hanging": Ellen Lovell interview.
317 "understood that there was light": Millennium lecture, Feb. 11, 1998; *PPP*, 1998, book 1, pp. 211–12.
317 The First Couple sat: C-SPAN broadcast of Millennium lecture, Feb. 11, 1998.
317 "very engaged in separate circles": Ellen Lovell interview.
317 They escaped to Camp David: 1998 Presidential Documents Online, via GPO Access, January–June, the President's public schedule.
317 "Bill wanted to hang out": Tom Siebert interview.
317 Bill "was assailing the process": Ibid.
317 she was coping well: *WP*, Jan. 27, 1998.
317 "her head high": *Vanity Fair*, June 2002.
317 "distraught at school": *Newsweek*, Feb. 9, 1998.
318 On Monday, February 23: www.cnn.com/ALLPOLITICS/1998/02/27; *The Salt Lake Tribune*, Feb. 28, 1998.
318 Bill arrived on Thursday: www.cnn.com/ALLPOLITICS/1998/02/27; 1998 Presidential Documents Online, via GPO Access, the President's public schedule.
318 "You better get out there": Terry McAuliffe interview.
318 "It was a tough time": Ibid.
318 a religion major and member: *Vanity Fair*, June 2002.
319 "never" consider resigning: The President's news conference with Prime Minister Blair, *PPP*, 1998, book 1, pp. 184–93.
319 "The message of the day": Waldman, p. 219. Also see Mike McCurry in the *Chicago Tribune*, Feb. 17, 1998.
319 "In the Monica Lewinsky year": Mary Mel French interview.
319 "enormous tension": Donna Shalala interview.

320 "withering comment": Waldman, pp. 219–20.

320 "It was his down day": Terry McAuliffe interview.

320 "Ken Starr Shank": Van Natta, p. 186.

320 The President found his most reliable: DPM, Memcon of Senator Daniel P. Moynihan, Mar. 6, 1998.

320 *Primary Colors:* WP, Mar. 20, 1998.

320 "completely transfixed": Katz, pp. 321–23.

320 the President spent seventy-two minutes: WP, Jan. 28, 1998.

320 "abroad": Waldman, p. 214.

320 He proposed more spending: ML, p. 771.

320 At a party afterward: Waldman, p. 216.

320 his approval ratings shot: Roper Center poll ratings, Jan. 28, 1998, *USA Today* / CNN, Gallup, Yankelovich / *Time* / CNN.

321 "imagine the future": Remarks to overflow crowd at the University of Illinois, Jan. 28, 1998; *PPP*, 1998, book 1, pp. 123–26.

321 "Real pain would be required": Klein, pp. 198–99.

321 Hillary and Bill had held hands: WP, Jan. 8, 1998; *Newsweek*, Jan. 19, 1998.

321 "getting our fiscal house": *Newsweek*, Jan. 19, 1998.

321 "a casualty like everything else": Bruce Reed interview.

321 Benjamin Netanyahu and Yasser Arafat: WP, Feb. 8, 1998.

321 "Once he got into those domestic issues": William Miller interview.

322 "should seriously explore": *Newsweek*, Dec. 1, 1997.

322 "eliminating": Ibid., Mar. 2, 1998.

322 "one of the three": Ibid., Nov. 24, 1997.

322 Secretary of State Madeleine Albright: Ibid., Mar. 2, 1998.

322 "un unholy axis": Ibid.

323 A bootleg copy of the film: Renshon, pp. xviii–xix.

323 UN Secretary-General: NYT, Mar. 3, 1998; ML, p. 778.

323 "Hillary was so tough": Barbara Butler interview.

323 "Well, Hillary": Author's notes, Mar. 3, 1998.

323 In early 1998, Kosovo: *Newsweek*, Mar. 29, 1999; NYT, Apr. 18, 1999; Merry, p. 141; Meyer, p. 98.

324 When the negotiations began to unravel: Christopher Meyer interview.

324 "People made fun of him": Ted Widmer interview.

324 The winter and spring months brought: WP, Feb. 4, 1998, NYT, Feb. 6, 1998; *Newsweek*, Feb. 16, 1998; Drudge Report, www.drudgereport.com, Feb. 10, 1998.

324 "Fuckface should": *Newsweek*, Feb. 23, 1998.

324 "in love": Toobin, p. 282.

324 "I really didn't think it added up": Hillary Clinton, interview with Barbara Walters, ABC News, transcript, June 8, 2003.

325 In early March, Bill's deposition: WP, Mar. 6 and Mar. 14, 1998.

325 Under questioning by Ed Bradley: *Newsweek*, Mar. 9 and Mar. 23, 1998.

325 "mystified and disappointed": Ibid., Mar. 30, 1998.

325 the White House launched its counterattack: Ibid.

326 who also represented Hillary's brother: NYT, Feb. 22, 2001.

326 "described how Clinton had kissed": *Newsweek*, Mar. 30, 1998.

326 "You don't know what it's like": WP, Mar. 18, 1998.

326 "rank hypocrite": Ibid.

326 Judge Wright had dismissed: *Starr Report*, p. 40.

326 Bill decided to celebrate: *Newsweek*, April 13, 1998.

327 "For those of you": Bill and Hillary Clinton roundtable discussion, Mar. 28, 1998; *PPP*, 1998, book 1, pp. 459–63.

327 "becomes more and more": *NYT*, Jan. 20, 1998.

327 "She could be President": *FiHC*, p. 326.

328 "It doesn't bother me": Sheehy, p. 198.

328 "prominent Democrats" had discussed: Blumenthal, p. 676.

328 early in Bill's first term, when she suggested: *The New Yorker*, May 30, 1994.

328 "are dead and gone": Toobin, p. 399.

328 "Get outta here!": *WP*, June 11, 1994.

328 "Not in this lifetime!": *NYT*, Jan. 20, 1996.

328 At other moments, she spoke: *Time*, Jan. 2, 1996; *WP*, Mar. 27, 1997.

328 "God no!": *Newsweek*, May 11, 1998.

328 "quoted to devastating effect": Lawrence O'Donnell interview.

329 she steadily enlarged her network: Blumenthal, p. 176; Kati Marton interview.

329 "no one raised the issue of the scandals": Blumenthal, p. 176.

329 "I'd love to have an apartment": *Newsweek*, July 20, 1998.

329 The first acknowledged overture: Sheehy, p. 104; *LH*, p. 483.

329 "If he doesn't, I wish": Sheehy, p. 333.

329 Hillary had begun campaigning: *Newsweek*, May 11, 1998.

329 The Clintons' former friend: *WP*, Mar. 12, 1998.

329 the Little Rock grand jury was due: *NYT*, Apr. 26, 1998.

329 Hillary faced her nemesis: Ibid.

330 "Hey! I read": Katz, p. 325.

330 At dinner she received: *NYT*, Apr. 26, 1998.

330 Hillary was back on the campaign trail: Ibid., Aug. 12, 1998.

330 "oddly absent": Barber, pp. 268–69.

330 "Save America's Treasures": *NYT*, July 14, 1998; *Newsweek*, July 20, 1998.

330 for four years Hillary's photographer: *Newsweek*, Dec. 21, 1998.

330 "People were on the road": Ellen Lovell interview.

330 Kenneth Starr served Bill: *NYT*, Aug. 17, 1998.

330 Monica Lewinsky's new attorneys: *MS*, pp. 308–10.

331 Nancy Hernreich's yoga schedule: Woodward, *Shadow*, p. 423.

331 cover stories: *Newsweek*, Aug. 10, 1998.

331 "Hey, it's me": Ibid.

331 On Wednesday, the President agreed: *ML*, p. 796; *Starr Report*, p. 434.

331 "DNA material": Toobin, p. 307; Davis, p. 258.

331 "investigative demands": Toobin, p. 307.

331 "bluffing . . . trying to spook": *LH*, p. 465.

331 "stone-faced" . . . "looking forward": *Newsweek*, Aug. 10, 1998.

331 "I can't say": *ML*, p. 796.

332 "this theme that Hillary and I": Remarks at a DNC dinner in East Hampton, N.Y., July 31, 1998; *PPP*, 1998, book 2, pp. 1382–84.

332 "Everything in my life": Claude Wasserstein interview.

332 At a later reception: *NYT*, Aug. 10, 1998.

332 "She's really popular in New York": Sheehy, p. 333.

332 "gay-focused fundraiser": *The Advocate*, Sept. 15, 1998.

332 "About three quarters": Ibid.

332 During a White House event: Freeh, p. 265.

332 Kendall tried to lighten: Woodward, *Shadow*, p. 430.

332 That night, a quick test: Toobin, p. 307.

333 visits to Louisville, Chicago: 1998 Presidential Documents Online, via GPO Access, the President's public schedule.

333 some forty hours of preparation: Woodward, *Shadow*, pp. 431, 436.

333 "to avoid a new crisis": *WP*, Aug. 14, 1998.

333 "preoccupation with the Monica": Ibid., Aug. 15, 1998.
333 "cowardly attacks": *Newsweek,* Aug. 17, 1998.
333 convening a series of meetings: *ML,* p. 798.
333 "things to do": *NYT,* Aug. 12, 1998.
333 "thrives on her": Ibid.
333 "prejudice against our state": Ibid.
334 "knowledgeable sources": *Newsweek,* Aug. 31, 1998.
334 "long-running": Ibid.
334 "Anyone who thinks": Sheehy, p. 310.
334 "President Weighs Admitting": *NYT,* Aug. 14, 1998; *Newsweek,* Aug. 31, 1998.
334 "more to this than you know": *LH,* p. 465.
334 "truth": *ML,* p. 800.
335 "miserable, sleepless night": Ibid.
335 "punched her in the gut": Ibid.
335 "inappropriate intimacy": *LH,* p. 466.
335 "for some time": *Newsweek,* Aug. 31, 1998.
335 "This is a charade": *NYT,* Aug. 19, 1998.
335 "I think it was a surprise": Mike McCurry interview.
335 "Hillary would get mad": Sheehy, p. 188. In *The New Yorker,* Wright was quoted as saying that the Clintons were able to "separate personal emotions from the goal" (May 30, 1994).
335 Hillary worked with the White House: *NYT,* Aug. 19, 1998.
335 On Sunday morning, Bill carried: Ibid., Aug. 17 and Aug. 19, 1998; *Newsweek,* Aug. 31, 1998.
336 "Wash me thoroughly": *Newsweek,* Aug. 31, 1998.
336 "would be 'embarrassed' ": Blumenthal, p. 462.
336 "Hillary's not naive": *NYT,* Aug. 19, 1998.
336 Starting at 1:00 p.m., he engaged: Bill Clinton grand-jury testimony, Aug. 17, 1998 (Court TV transcript).
337 the lashing rain: WeatherUnderground.com, history for Aug. 17, 1998.
337 He had stayed up late: *Newsweek,* Aug. 31, 1998.
337 various drafts of Bill's remarks: Klein, p. 174; Toobin, pp. 312, 316.
337 called in from Brazil: Woodward, *Shadow,* p. 442.
337 "trying to make sense": *LH,* p. 467.
338 Throughout the day she had been: Blumenthal, p. 465; Sheehy, p. 312.
338 Hillary eventually joined the group: *LH,* p. 467.
338 "Well, Bill, this is your speech": Ibid., p. 468. Kati Marton wrote that Hillary "refused to help" with the speech (p. 343). *Newsweek* reported that Hillary's "role on Monday night was essentially passive" (Aug. 31, 1998).
338 But she had invoked that phrase: For example, Hillary said, "It's your speech, Bill, you say what you want," before the Jan. 24, 1995, State of the Union. *OO,* pp. 93–94, and *ATH,* p. 336.
338 "Everything Bill said": Author's conversation with Rita Braver, Aug. 18, 1998, Little Compton, R.I.
338 giving Bill about a half hour: *LH,* p. 468; Blumenthal, p. 464.
338 Harry Thomason had worked with: *Newsweek,* Aug. 31, 1998.
338 he devoted more than half: *PPP,* 1998, book 2, pp. 1457–58.
339 "I said what I wanted": Toobin, p. 320.
339 "felt as if a burden": *WP,* Aug. 19, 1998.
339 "talking to people in a pleasant and smiling way": Ibid.
339 "bantering in the background": Blumenthal, p. 465.

CHAPTER FIFTEEN

340 "compassionate and steadfast": Sheehy, p. 313.
340 "the President had to be seen": Woodward, *Shadow*, p. 448.
340 "an undifferentiated emotional unit": Eleanor Acheson interview.
341 "tableau tailored": *Newsweek*, Aug. 10, 1998.
341 "felt terrible": *MS*, p. 320.
341 "had his face": Mike McCurry interview.
341 "It did break the ice": Ibid.
341 Hillary's office had put out the word: *Newsweek*, Aug. 31, 1998.
341 "She was their ambassador": Rose Styron interview.
341 As Chelsea walked away: *NYT*, Aug. 19, 1998.
341 "Clinton showed no signs": Talbott, p. 277.
342 Bill set up a command center: *ML*, p. 803.
342 "Hillary knew she had to": Mike McCurry interview.
342 'Obviously we will have a hard time': Ibid.
342 quiet meal with Vernon and Ann: Woodward, *Shadow*, p. 449.
342 authorized Sandy Berger to order: *Newsweek*, Aug. 31, 1998; *ML*, p. 803; *U.S. News & World Report*, Aug. 16, 1999.
342 "convincing evidence": Remarks at Edgartown Elementary School, Aug. 20, 1998; *PPP*, 1998, book 2, p. 1460.
343 "the preeminent organizer": Ibid., pp. 1460–62.
343 he was to speak publicly: The President's radio address, Aug. 22, 1998, Presidential Documents Online, via GPO Access, vol. 34, no. 35, pp. 1649–65; *PPP*, 1998, book 2, p. 1530; *PPP*, 1999, book 1, pp. 68 and 92; *PPP*, 2000, book 2, pp. 951 and 2101. Author database search, 1998–2001, keywords "Qaida" and "Usama," the official spellings used by the government database.
343 Yeltsin—harshly condemned: Talbott, p. 277.
343 "pundit class": *ML*, p. 805.
343 "oafish sort of overkill": Klein, p. 175.
343 "Virtually everything the Administration": *U.S. News & World Report*, Aug. 16, 1999; see also *9/11 Commission Report*, p. 118.
344 "It was decided": Terry McAuliffe interview.
344 "unresolved anger": *LH*, p. 469.
344 "confused and hurting": Ibid.
344 "had her own experience": Ibid.
344 "really loves you": Ibid., p. 470.
344 "Some in the group": Sheldon Hackney interview.
345 Bill and Hillary entered: Sheehy, p. 315.
345 At the hostess's table: Ibid., pp. 315–16.
345 a private cruise: *LH*, p. 469; Walter Cronkite interview.
345 "I wouldn't say there was a lot": Walter Cronkite interview.
345 "The point is": *NYT*, Aug. 19, 1998.
346 "lost in conversation": Lee Auchincloss Niven interview.
346 "The selfishness": *WP*, Aug. 19, 1998.
346 "young female employee": Ibid.
347 "What you have done": *New York Review of Books*, Oct. 22, 1998.
347 Garry Wills wrote an essay: Ibid., Aug. 14, 2003.
347 "to take the helm": *Newsweek*, Aug. 31, 1998.
347 "a throbbing boner": Author's notes of program, Aug. 20, 1998.
347 "I was very hurt": *MS*, pp. 319–20.

347 "that all I did": *Starr Report*, p. 215, n. 44.
347 "touched and kissed her": *Newsweek*, Sept. 21, 1998. See also *MS*, p. 324.
347 "not adequate": *WP*, Aug. 20, 1998.
347 "reprehensible": Woodward, *Shadow*, p. 451.
347 "I'm not upset": *Newsweek*, Sept. 14, 1998.
348 "had no such thought": DPM, Memcon of Senator Daniel P. Moynihan, Aug. 27, 1998.
348 "a menace to the Presidency": Ibid.
348 "at great length": Ibid., Aug. 28, 1998.
348 "This business of asking": *PPP*, 1998, book 2, pp. 1472–75.
348 Bill's fifteenth meeting: *ML*, p. 807.
348 "détente if not peace": *LH*, p. 471.
348 "They acted like the two": Sheehy, p. 320.
348 "come to work every day": Talbott, p. 285.
349 "strangest of all summits": Ibid., p. 288.
349 "an employee half his age": Transcript of speech, www.cnn.com/ALLPOLITICS/1998/09/03/Lieberman.
349 Bob Kerrey bolted out: *Newsweek*, Sept. 14, 1998.
349 "I do not want": *USA Today*, Sept. 14, 1998.
349 "would not be satisfaction": Mark Shields on *The NewsHour*, Sept. 4, 1998, paraphrasing Kaptur's comments.
349 Hillary was again displaying: Sheehy, p. 320.
350 "I agree with what": *ML*, p. 808.
350 the Clintons were back in harmony: Sheehy, p. 322.
350 "Contrition News Network": *Time*, Sept. 21, 1998.
350 "I let you down": *MS*, p. 329.
350 "didn't buy": Donna Shalala interview.
350 "Surely your personal behavior": *Time*, Sept. 21, 1998.
350 "I can't believe": Harris, p. 348.
350 "If you were judging": *Time*, Sept. 21, 1998.
351 "There's no question": Rubin, p. 272.
351 "I think most of America": *WP*, June 16, 1999.
351 "a lot of us": Harris, p. 348.
351 "This is the weirdest": Donna Shalala interview.
351 "naturally [Shalala] and Clinton hugged": *Newsweek*, Sept. 21, 1998.
351 "The White House thought": Donna Shalala interview.
351 he made his most complete apology: Bill Clinton, breakfast with religious leaders, Sept. 11, 1998; *PPP*, 1998, book 2, pp. 1565–66.
351 "modified Nancy Reagan gaze": *Time*, Sept. 21, 1998.
352 "horrified" Starr: *NYT*, Aug. 10, 1999.
352 Leading the disclosure charge: Toobin, pp. 331–32.
352 "portrayal of a President": *Time*, Sept. 21, 1998.
352 "so frivolous": Klein, p. 173.
352 "worst day": Mike McCurry interview.
352 Hillary let it be known: *LH*, p. 475.
352 Chelsea read it online: Woodward, *Shadow*, p. 464; *Esquire*, Dec. 2000.
352 White House immediately leaped: Woodward, *Shadow*, p. 464.
353 "pornographic specificity": *Newsweek*, Sept. 21, 1998.
353 "if he'd written": Stuart Taylor interview.
353 "unmasked these lies": Posner, p. 80.
353 "Bill Clinton should resign": *The Philadelphia Inquirer*, Sept. 13, 1998.
353 "resolutely failed": *USA Today*, Sept. 14, 1998.
354 "to go tell [Clinton]": Toobin, p. 332.

354 "no question that he lied": Ibid., p. 335.

354 "probably lied through his teeth": Ibid.

354 "Abbe, is the cigar": Ibid, p. 336.

354 In the Senate, the stirrings: Woodward, *Shadow,* p. 469.

354 On Tuesday, the President announced: *ML,* p. 810.

354 "he'd read summaries": PBS *Frontline* interview with Gregory Craig, July 2000.

354 "I said, 'How are we doing up there?' ": Ibid.

354 "about two or three days": Ibid.

354 That day, Erskine Bowles and John Podesta: Woodward, *Shadow,* p. 469.

355 In the evening, Bob Kerrey made his bold phone call: DPM, Memcon of Senator Daniel P. Moynihan, Sept. 16, 1998.

355 After some intense lobbying: Terry McAuliffe interview.

355 "stampede": Toobin, p. 336.

355 "I knew Clinton": Dale Bumpers interview.

355 he sparred with an off-camera voice: Grand jury testimony of Bill Clinton, Aug. 17, 1998.

356 By the afternoon, White House aides: Blumenthal, pp. 483–84; PBS *Frontline* interview with Gregory Craig, July 2000.

356 "new progressivism": Blumenthal, p. 483.

356 At a reception afterward: Meyer, p. 95; Christopher Meyer interview.

356 "deeply angry": *Newsweek,* Sept. 21, 1998.

356 "put her hand": Ibid.

356 "reconnected the President's oxygen tube": *Time,* Sept. 21, 1998.

356 "apparent turning point": *Newsweek,* Sept. 21, 1998.

357 she had hated divorcing: *ML,* pp. 51–52.

357 "break the pattern": *Talk,* Sept. 1999.

357 she had lived with relatives: *LH,* p. 3.

357 "Everybody has some": *Talk,* Sept. 1999.

357 Bill revealed they met: *ML,* p. 810.

357 "ask and answer hard questions": *LH,* p. 476.

358 "unify my parallel lives": *ML,* p. 811.

358 "My strong feelings": Clinton, *It Takes a Village,* p. 43.

358 "I think he went": Dee Dee Myers interview.

358 "a philanderer and worse": *Newsweek,* Oct. 10, 1998.

358 "campaign marathon": *LH,* p. 482.

358 She visited twenty states: Sheehy, p. 329.

358 "the other Washington": *NYT,* Sept. 28, 1998.

358 she developed a blood clot: *ML,* p. 823; *LH,* p. 482.

359 "She is hiding in her work": *Daily Mail,* Sept. 23, 1998.

359 While appearing at an event: *NYT Magazine,* May 30, 1999.

359 "Who would want me to run": *NYT,* Nov. 8, 2000.

359 "great opportunity for women": www.cnn.com/ALLPOLITICS/1998/09/30.

359 "Women in the 21st Century": *NYT,* Oct. 10, 1998.

359 apart on their wedding anniversary: Ibid.

359 the President announced on October 16: *PPP,* 1998, book 2, pp. 1809–12; *ML,* p. 820.

359 he was less visible: *NYT,* Sept. 25, 1998; *Newsweek,* Oct. 19, 1998.

359 "listened carefully": *NYT,* Apr. 18, 1999.

360 few in Congress or the administration: Ibid.

360 For nine days in October: Bill Clinton remarks, Oct. 23, 1998; *PPP,* 1998, book 2, 1851–54.

360 "Clinton looks totally": Queen Noor, *Leap of Faith: Memoirs of an Unexpected Life,* p. 413.

360 Determined to keep both sides: *Newsweek*, Nov. 2, 1998.

360 "the tolerance and patience": Ibid.

360 "great leader of the world": Ibid.

360 "Even though he was the smallest": *PPP*, 1998, book 2, p. 1852.

361 The piece infuriated the President: Harris, p. 356.

361 "He came in here, and he trashed": *WP*, Nov. 2, 1998.

361 election returns on November 3: *LH*, p. 482; Sheehy, p. 324; Woodward, *Shadow*, p. 477; *ML*, p. 826.

362 "I sure hope you'll consider": *LH*, p. 483.

362 "sounded like a pretty good": *ML*, p. 826.

362 "honored" . . . "not interested" . . . "absurd": *LH*, p. 483.

362 "It was a very pragmatic": Donna Shalala interview.

362 By Bill's account, Hillary made: Remarks at a dinner for Hillary Clinton, Oct. 4, 2000; *PPP*, 2000–2001, book 2, pp. 2029–33.

362 "looking around": Ibid.

362 Hillary was a ubiquitous: *NYT*, Dec. 9, 1998; *Newsweek*, Dec. 21, 1998.

362 But her apotheosis came: *Vogue*, Dec. 1998; *LH*, p. 479.

363 a bond doubtless strengthened: *New York*, Sept. 20, 1999.

363 had raised more than one million: *NYT*, Feb. 19, 1997.

363 Bryan had also personally contributed: CQPolitics.com, Political Moneyline, www.fecinfo.com/cgi-win/x_allindir.exe, Shelby Bryan contributions.

363 "she's emerged so triumphant": www.cnn.com/STYLE/9811/24/hillary/.

363 "the President's head is on the block": *NYT*, Dec. 9, 1998.

363 "forever be remembered": Marton, p. 346.

363 The November elections momentarily: PBS *Frontline* interview with Gregory Craig, July 2000.

364 Bill Clinton announced on November 13: Toobin, p. 395.

364 "second biggest tactical": *LH*, p. 440.

364 "I categorically reject": Statement on signing the Iraq Liberation Act of 1998, Oct. 31, 1998; *PPP*, 1998, book 2, p. 1938.

364 "L'Affaire Lewinsky": Meyer, p. 229.

364 "I can just see Saddam": *WP*, Nov. 2, 1998.

364 "There was back-and-forth": James Steinberg interview.

364 The President issued a warning: *Newsweek*, Dec. 28, 1998.

365 the President's lawyers began to grasp: PBS *Frontline* interview with Gregory Craig, July 2000.

365 "overturning the mandate": Gregory Craig opening statement, Federal News Service, Dec. 8, 1998.

365 "violated his sacred obligations": Statement by White House Counsel Charles F. C. Ruff, Federal News Service, Dec. 9, 1998.

365 they needed to push for an alternative: *Newsweek*, Dec. 21, 1998.

365 The notion of censure: *NYT*, Sept. 25, 1998.

365 Hillary had opposed: *Newsweek*, Dec. 21, 1998.

365 "egregiously failed": Censure resolution, Associated Press, Dec. 12, 1998.

366 "lead item in the story": PBS *Frontline* interview with Gregory Craig, July 2000.

366 Hillary was three thousand miles away: *Newsweek*, Dec. 21, 1998.

366 "profoundly sorry for all": *PPP*, 1998, book 2, p. 2158.

366 failed to satisfy: *Newsweek*, Dec. 21 and Dec. 28, 1998.

366 "The body language": Jonathan Alter interview.

366 receiving constant bulletins: *Newsweek*, Dec. 28, 1998.

367 "If you don't act here": Woodward, *Shadow*, p. 493.

367 who had pulled a muscle in her back: *NYT*, Feb. 5, 1999.

367 "practice reconciliation": Woodward, *Shadow*, p. 495.

367 "You may be mad": *LH*, p. 489.

368 "very powerful": PBS *Frontline* interview with Gregory Craig, July 2000.

368 "We all knew last-ditch": *LH*, p. 489.

368 Bill heard the news: *Newsweek*, Dec. 28, 1998.

368 kept the congressmen waiting: Ibid.

368 fifty-degree weather: WeatherUnderground.com, history for Dec. 18, 1998.

368 The pain in Hillary's back: *LH*, p. 490.

368 "millions upon millions": *PPP*, 1998, book 2, pp. 2198–99.

368 "It was intended to be arrogant": PBS *Frontline* interview with Gregory Craig, July 2000.

369 "one of our greatest presidents": Waldman, p. 248.

369 "Bill acted as if": Sandy Robertson interview.

369 Hillary was flat on her back: *LH*, p. 490; *ML*, p. 838.

369 But in a departure from their routine: Linda Lader, co-founder of Renaissance Weekend, briefing, Hilton Head, S.C., Dec. 30, 1998.

369 "Oh, I don't need": Sheehy, p. 339.

369 "The President's speech stunned": Jonathan Alter interview.

369 "I hope you have": Ibid.

CHAPTER SIXTEEN

370 Bill's lawyers had to prepare: PBS *Frontline* interview with Gregory Craig, July 2000.

370 several years earlier had altered: Http://C-SPAN.org/questions/week136.asp.

370 "studiously avoided": *LH*, p. 492.

371 "the only thing I've watched": Bill Clinton interview with Judith Miller and William Broad, *NYT*, Jan. 21, 1999; *PPP*, 1999, book 1, p. 96.

371 "After my presentation": PBS *Frontline* interview with Gregory Craig, July 2000.

371 "strategy and presentation": *LH*, p. 492.

371 "never really tried to refute": *WP*, Feb. 10, 1999.

371 "to conclude that the President lied": White House Counsel Ruff's Opening Statement, Jan. 19, 1999, www.cnn.com/ALLPOLITICS/stories/1999/01/19/transcripts/index.html?eref=sitesearch.

371 "He lied under oath!": *Newsweek*, Feb. 1, 1999.

371 "lofty standard": www.cnn.com/ALLPOLITICS/stories/1999/01/19/transcripts/index.html?eref=sitesearch.

371 Dale Bumpers's plea: *Congressional Record*, Jan. 21, 1999.

372 "gratuitous statement": Dale Bumpers interview.

372 "come through the worst": *PPP*, 1999, book 1, pp. 90–96.

372 "could see that the President": Waldman, p. 256.

372 "smiling and pleased": Ibid., p. 258.

372 "I realized I had to": *Esquire*, Dec. 2000.

372 For seventy-seven minutes: Woodward, *Shadow*, p. 509.

372 "I love you": *ATH*, p. 442.

372 But unusually, he went upstairs: Woodward, *Shadow*, p. 509.

372 advocated tapping into: State of the Union address, Jan. 19, 1999; *PPP*, 1999, book 1, pp. 62–71; *ML*, pp. 842–43.

373 He envisioned using: www.cnn.com/ALLPOLITICS/stories/1999/02/25/clinton.arizona/.

373 "He was almost dismissive": Tom Siebert interview.

373 Hillary's plans for a Senate race: Susan Thomases interview.

373 she sought advice from her consigliere: *LH*, pp. 496–97.
374 "wanted a forum that legitimized her": Susan Thomases interview.
374 "Hillary has meant": Remarks at a DNC dinner, Jan. 15, 1999; *PPP*, 1999, book 1, p. 54.
374 "It looks to me": Remarks at a DNC dinner, Feb. 2, 1999; *PPP*, 1999, book 1, pp. 149–52.
374 "impressed that Clinton was eager": Private journal.
374 "the Senate race kept them": Tom Siebert interview.
374 "Bill and I were talking again": *LH*, p. 501.
375 On the morning of Friday, February 12: Ibid., p. 497.
375 "I feel very strongly": Eleanor Roosevelt to Harold Ickes, May 25, 1945, Eleanor Roosevelt Papers, George Washington University.
376 the thermometer hit: WeatherUnderground.com, history for Feb. 12, 1999.
376 Mark Penn counseled him: Harris, p. 361.
376 "I want to say again": *PPP*, 1999, book 1, p. 189.
376 Jesse Jackson awaited, ready to talk: *Newsweek*, Feb. 22, 1999.
376 "You might not be": Harris, p. 377.
376 "a more realistic view": *LH*, p. 498.
376 "careful consideration": *NYT*, Feb. 13, 1999.
376 she got to work on Saturday: *Newsweek*, Mar. 1, 1999.
376 "all smiles and clasped hands": *NYT*, Feb. 16, 1999.
377 "terrific senator": Ibid.
377 "magnificent, young, bright": Ibid.; *LH*, p. 498.
377 "She lives on TV": *NYT*, Feb. 17, 1999.
377 "It will never": *Newsweek*, Feb. 22, 1999.
377 fresh details: Ibid., released Feb. 14, 1999.
377 NBC News ran a prime-time interview: *WP*, Feb. 25, 1999.
377 "absolutely false": Ibid.
377 "suggested to one friend": Toobin, p. 383.
377 "The best his backers": *Newsweek*, Mar. 8, 1999.
378 his most extended travel schedule: *WP*, Feb. 26, 1999.
378 he joined his wife and daughter: *The Salt Lake Tribune*, Mar. 1, 1999.
378 Hillary came to the slopes: Ibid.
378 a day earlier: *WP*, Feb. 26, 1999; www.cnn.com/ALLPOLITICS/stories/1999/02/25/clinton.arizona/.
378 Bill made a sweep: *WP*, Mar. 2, 1999.
378 she reinjured the back: Ibid, Mar. 8, 1999.
378 "faux stumping": Ibid.
378 "egregious and systematic": *NYT*, Mar. 5, 1999.
378 a screening of HBO's documentary: clinton4.nara.gov/WH/EOP/First_Lady/html/generalspeeches/1999/19990304b.html (March 4, 1999).
378 On her first evening in New York: Sheehy, p. 342.
379 "To know the world": Ibid.
379 Lewinsky revealed that she: *MS*, pp. 357–59; "In Her Own Words," Monica Lewinsky interview with Barbara Walters, *20/20* transcript, Mar. 3, 1999.
379 "lost the battle": *Newsweek*, Mar. 15, 1999.
379 "contrary to the way": Mike McCurry, interview on BBC *Newsnight*, Dec. 19, 1998.
379 "I do not regard": Bill Clinton, interview with Dan Rather, Mar. 31, 1999; *PPP*, 1999, book 1, p. 482.
379 "Mr. Clinton, for all his talk": *WP*, Apr. 14, 1999.
380 "false, misleading": Ibid., Apr. 13, 1999.
380 She ordered him to reimburse: Ibid.

380 "not essential to the core": *Newsweek*, Feb. 9, 1998.

380 "I strongly disagreed": *ML*, p. 830.

381 "hard core": *WP*, Jan. 14, 2001.

381 The situation in Kosovo; *NYT*, Apr. 18, 1999.

381 Milosevic amassed forty thousand troops: Bill Clinton address, Mar. 24, 1999; *PPP*, 1999, book 1, pp. 451–53.

381 without a congressional authorization: Blumenthal, p. 625.

382 "his need for personal atonement": Woodward, *Shadow*, p. 517.

382 "nearly unhinged": Talbott, p. 300.

382 "without benefit": Meyer, p. 100.

382 Russians decided against blocking NATO: Talbott, p. 301.

382 Bill dispatched Richard Holbrooke: Ibid., p. 304.

382 "prepared to be very forceful": James Steinberg interview.

382 Hillary kept in daily contact: Sheehy, p. 344.

382 "You cannot let this go on": *Talk*, Sept. 1999.

382 the President gave a televised address: *PPP*, 1999, book 1, pp. 451–53.

383 "selective morality": Merry, p. 143.

383 "deaths in the conflict in Southern Sudan": Lake, p. 115.

383 "we're doing the right thing": *NYT*, Apr. 18, 1999.

383 "schoolyard bully": Merry, p. 142.

383 her judgment had been informed: *NYT*, Apr. 18, 1999.

383 "air attacks will not suffice": Ibid.

383 "Madeleine's War": Harris, p. 369.

383 "It's my war": Blumenthal, p. 639.

384 "to persevere until": *NYT*, Mar. 31, 1999.

384 "we live in an age": Bill Clinton, interview with Dan Rather, CBS, Mar. 31, 1999, *PPP*, 1999, book 1, pp. 475–85.

384 "explosive phone call": Meyer, p. 103.

384 one hundred thousand soldiers might be needed: *Newsweek*, Apr. 19, 1999.

384 Gore to once again team with Viktor: *ML*, p. 859; Talbott, p. 310.

384 "stop a humanitarian outrage": *Newsweek*, May 24, 1999.

384 Gore came to share Albright's: Blumenthal, p. 649.

384 Chernomyrdin had told the Serbian leader: Meyer, p. 103.

384 the President announced the end: *PPP*, 1999, book 1, pp. 994–97, 867–71, and 913–16.

385 "vicious campaign of ethnic cleansing": Ibid., pp. 994–97.

385 Bill seized on those apparent weaknesses: *WP*, June 16, 1999.

385 "He said he was trying": Sandy Robertson interview.

385 "off and stumbling": *Newsweek*, May 24, 1999.

386 Gore had expressed his dismay: *WP*, June 16, 1999.

386 holding at around 60 percent: Roper Center poll ratings, June 11–13, 1999: Gallup, *USA Today*/CNN.

386 "personal image problems and fallout": The Pew Research Center for the People and the Press, "Clinton Fatigue Undermines Gore Poll Standing," Apr. 17, 1999.

386 "I thought it was awful": "Speaking for Himself: Vice President Al Gore and Wife, Tipper," interview with Diane Sawyer, *20/20* transcript, June 16, 1999.

386 "What the fuck": Harris, p. 386.

387 "genuine visionary": Remarks at a birthday celebration for the First Lady, Oct. 23, 1999; *PPP*, 1999, book 2, pp. 1869–71.

387 "plain weird": *NYT*, Apr. 18, 1999.

388 "the perils of indifference": *PPP*, 1999, book 1, pp. 540–66; C-SPAN, April 12, 1999.

388 they continued the conversation: *Talk*, Sept. 1999.

388 She methodically made her way: *LH*, p. 498.
388 thoroughly publicized White House lunch: *Newsweek*, Mar. 1, 1999; Blumenthal, p. 679.
389 Hillary finally settled on a look: Sheehy, p. 331; *ML*, p. 838; *Talk*, Sept. 1999.
389 eight trips to New York: *Newsweek*, May 31, 1999.
389 two days, ostensibly on White House business: *NYT*, Apr. 20, 1999; *NYT Magazine*, May 30, 1999.
389 "truly a microcosm": *NYT*, Apr. 20, 1999.
389 Webster Hubbell pleaded guilty: *WP*, June 29 and July 1, 1999.
390 "listening tour": *NYT*, July 8, 1999; *LH*, p. 507.
390 "like a father": *NYT*, Nov. 8, 2000.
390 "My God, I almost forgot": Ibid., July 8, 1999; *LH*, p. 507.
390 "If she runs": *Newsweek*, Feb. 22, 1999.
390 "The implications": Ibid., May 31, 1999.
390 She had already enlisted: Ibid., Oct. 18, 1999.
391 "my dear friend Tipper Gore": clinton4.nara.gov/WH/EOP/First_Lady/html/generalspeeches/1999/19990719.html (July 19, 1999).
391 Bill headlined four Gore fund-raisers: Little Rock, Aug. 7; Hay-Adams Hotel, Aug. 10; and two at the Hay-Adams Hotel, Sept. 22; *PPP*, 1999, book 2, pp. 1401–2, 1426–27, 1573–74, and 1574–75 (back-to-back events).
391 "the single most influential": Remarks at Gore 2000 reception, Little Rock, ibid., pp. 1401–02.
391 "high profile assignments": *ML*, p. 872.
391 "stand on the doorstep": Ibid., p. 873.
391 "thousands of people": Remarks at a Victory 2000 dinner in East Hampton, *PPP*, 1999, book 2, pp. 1470–73.
392 "conversant in obscure topics": *Newsweek*, Oct. 18, 1999.
392 "all the time": Bill Clinton, interview with Bryant Gumbel, *The Early Show*, Oct. 31, 1999; *PPP*, 1999, book 2, p. 1937.
392 Her listening tour drew mostly derision: *NYT*, Oct. 22 and Nov. 8, 2000.
392 "scale it down": DPM, Memcon of Senator Daniel P. Moynihan, June 1999.
392 traveled in a customized van: *LH*, p. 511; Terry McAuliffe interview.
392 spoke to carefully selected audiences: *NYT*, Sept. 18 and Oct. 22, 2000; *NYT Magazine*, June 18, 2000.
392 "The Woman Who Knew Too Much": *Time*, July 19, 1999.
392 "soccer mom": *Newsweek*, July 19 and December 6, 1999.
392 she stumbled: *NYT*, July 24 and Oct. 22, 1999; *The New Republic*, Jan. 30, 2006.
392 storm of bad publicity: *Newsweek*, Aug. 16, 1999, observed that the "pundits" were "attacking Mrs. Clinton for yet again trying to excuse the inexcusable."
392 "dispel stereotypes": Ibid.
392 a sympathetic Martha's Vineyard: *Talk*, Sept. 1999.
392 "the imprint of her pillow": Ibid.
393 Bob Woodward had first suggested: *WP*, June 14, 1999.
393 "working on himself": *Talk*, Sept. 1999.
393 "raging tirades": *ML*, p. 10.
393 a morphine addict: Kelley, p. 113.
393 "vindictive manipulative": Ibid., p. 24.
393 "overt conflicts": *Newsweek*, Mar. 30, 1992.
393 "the horrors": Ibid., Feb. 3, 1992.
393 "blaming two deceased": *NYT*, Aug. 4, 1999.
393 "fed up with the creepy": Ibid.

393 "attribute": WP, Aug. 6, 1999.

394 fund-raisers in Nantucket: PPP, 1999, book 2, pp. 1461–63, 1465–66.

394 At the end of August, they spent: NYT, Aug. 30, 1999.

394 "you may be a lot of things": Remarks at a Victory 2000 dinner in East Hampton, PPP, 1999, book 2, pp. 1470–73.

394 a youth-oriented rally: PPP, 1999, book 2, pp. 1473–74.

394 "Dance with me!": NYT, Aug. 30, 1999.

394 they announced their purchase: Ibid., Sept. 3, 1999; Vanity Fair, Jan. 2000.

394 the press raised questions: Newsweek, Sept. 13, 1999; NYT, Oct. 19, 1999.

394 they landed in hot water: NYT, Sept. 7 and Sept. 10, 1999.

394 "strongly supported": Ibid., Sept. 7, 1999.

394 "Political considerations played": www.cnn.com/US/9909/22/fbi.faln.01/, Sept. 22, 1999.

394 "constant conversation": Talk, Sept. 1999.

395 "I did what I thought was right": www.cnn.com/US/9909/09/faln.clemency/, Sept. 9, 1999.

395 "sat impassively": Newsweek, Nov. 22, 1999; see also NYT, Nov. 13, 1999 ("sat silently").

395 insisting that she had had to wait: NYT, Nov. 13, 1999.

395 "noticed the Hillary and Bill dynamic": Private journal.

395 Hillary's poll numbers: NYT, Nov. 1, 1999.

395 she flew to New York: Ibid., Dec. 15, 1999.

396 "It's the perfect solution": U.S. News & World Report, July 26, 1999.

396 "at the root of most of the world's problems": Remarks at DNC Dinner, May 14, 1999; PPP, 1999, book 1, pp. 773–79.

396 "the oldest problem": Remarks at "Millennium Around the World" Celebration, Dec. 31, 1999; PPP, 1999, book 2, pp. 2354–57.

396 "We're all scared": Ibid., book 1, p. 778.

396 "every human being has got": Ibid.

397 "light forces" . . . "dark forces": Remarks at Empire State Pride Gala, Oct. 7, 1999; PPP, 1999, book 2, p. 1999.

397 "big struggle": Ibid., book 1, p. 778.

397 "affirm each other's common": Ibid.

397 the President vetoed: ML, p. 870.

397 "self indulgent": Remarks at birthday celebration for the First Lady, Oct. 23, 1999; PPP, 1999, book 2, pp. 1869–71.

397 "swinging and wildly": Van Natta, p. 187.

397 "stark image": Ibid.

397 concerns about possible attacks: 9/11 Commission Report, pp. 174–76.

397 "chance discovery": Ibid., pp. 182, 176–78.

397 The CIA learned: Ibid., pp. 179–80.

398 a multimillion-dollar extravaganza: ML, p. 881; Remarks on "America's Millennium" celebration, PPP, 1999, book 2, pp. 2353–54.

398 "nervous the entire time": ML, p. 881.

398 Bill Clinton had taken some positive: 9/11 Commission Report, pp. 100–102.

398 his public comments about terrorism: Ibid., pp. 105, 362.

398 "enemies of the nation": Bill Clinton, interview with Joe Klein, Aug. 15, 2000; PPP, 2000, book 2, pp. 2104–11.

398 "vast money": Bill Clinton, interview with Charlie Rose, Dec. 22, 1999, in ibid., 1999, book 2, pp. 2343–49.

398 "these gadgets": Ibid.

398 "obsessed": Bill Clinton on *Fox News Sunday*, Sept. 24, 2006.

398 Even after Osama Bin Laden: Freeh, p. 292; *9/11 Commission Report*, p. 102.

399 "by giving him unnecessary": *9/11 Commission Report*, p. 174.

399 "spark a full public discussion": Ibid., p. 341.

399 "modest national effort . . . the most dangerous": Ibid., pp. 340, 351.

399 On five occasions: Ibid., pp. 112–13, 114, 130, 137, 138, 140, 183.

399 "two senior State Department officials": Ibid., p. 125.

399 "Turned the economy": *PPP*, 1999, book 2, pp. 1936–40.

399 "extreme intolerance": *9/11 Commission Report*, p. 362.

CHAPTER SEVENTEEN

400 "It was a very self-consciously concerned": Taylor Branch interview.

400 "I don't think too much": Bill Clinton interview on *The NewsHour*, Jan. 26, 2000; *PPP*, 2000, book 1, pp. 121–28. Bill wrote in his memoir that "the press began to ask me about my legacy. . . . The truth is . . . I didn't have time to think about such things" (pp. 874–75).

401 "most days I'm okay": Remarks at a Democratic Senatorial Campaign Committee Dinner, March 3, 2000; *PPP*, 2000, book 1, pp. 372–76; also, remarks at a DNC dinner, March 4, 2000, pp. 384–88.

401 "The stakes are far bigger": Remarks at a dinner for Hillary Clinton, Sept. 14, 2000; ibid., book 2, pp. 1838–42.

401 "It was remarkable": Bruce Reed interview.

401 The tensions centered: *Vanity Fair*, July 2001.

401 "the Vice President would be": Bruce Reed interview.

402 On January 5, 2000: Remarks on departure for Chappaqua, N.Y., *PPP*, 2000, book 1, pp. 11–13.

402 "a sad message": *NYT*, Jan. 6, 2000.

402 Friends brought them dinner: Exchange with reporters in Chappaqua, N.Y., Jan. 6, 2000; *PPP*, 2000, book 1, pp. 11–14.

402 Bill visited her twenty times: Presidential Documents Online, via GPO Access, Digest of Other White House Announcements: Jan.–Nov. 2000. Bill visited Hillary in Chappaqua on Jan. 13; Feb. 5 and 24; Mar. 5 and 29; Apr. 5, 12, and 24; May 16 and 20; June 15 and 26; July 3 and 29; Aug. 20; Sept. 11; Oct. 8, 11, and 31; and Nov. 3.

402 "I slept with": Bill Clinton interview with Steve Holland and Debbie Charles, Reuters, Jan. 11, 2001; *PPP*, 2000–2001, book 3, pp. 2897–2904.

403 "Home Alone Video": Remarks at a "Tribute to the President" reception, Aug. 14, 2000; *PPP*, 2000, book 2, pp. 1656–57.

403 "I never want to sleep": Bill Clinton interview with John Harris, *WP*, Aug. 8, 2000; ibid., pp. 1812–23.

403 as frequently as a half-dozen: *NYT*, Oct. 10, 2000.

403 "Bill would be": Ann McCoy interview.

403 "off by herself": *NYT*, Oct. 1, 2000.

403 Hillary went to the White House: Blumenthal, p. 686.

403 Bill worked closely with her: Remarks at reception for Hillary Clinton, May 7, 2000; *PPP*, 2000, book 1, pp. 858–61; Blumenthal, p. 686.

403 "You have to be": Blumenthal, p. 687.

403 her consultants gave him no speaking role: *ML*, p. 895; Sheehy, p. 358.

404 "would love you": *NYT*, Nov. 8, 2000.

404 On the basis of focus-group research: Ibid., Feb. 25, 2001.

404 "threatening and unwomanly": Ibid.

404 "was just too big a mountain": Ibid.

404 "I give her my best thoughts": Bill Clinton, interview with John Harris, Aug. 8, 2000; *PPP*, 2000, book 2, pp. 1812–23.

404 "grind-the-negatives": *NYT*, Sept. 27, 2000.

405 "Oh, Mark": *NYT*, June 18, 2000.

405 "falling milk prices": *Newsweek*, Feb. 14, 2000.

405 "Bill is supernatural": Blumenthal, p. 688. Hillary said in an interview with *Talk*, "My energy level fades before Bill's" (Sept. 1999).

406 "I don't know who": *NYT*, Feb. 22, 2000.

406 "Trashing me is fine": Blumenthal, p. 687.

406 "as cheery and chirpy": *NYT*, Sept. 18, 2000.

406 She had swapped jokes on David Letterman's: Ibid., Jan. 13, 2000.

406 she had been fed her questions: *New York Post*, Jan. 14, 2000.

406 "presumably spontaneous": *NYT*, Jan. 14, 2000.

406 "Come on, guys": Ibid., Sept. 18, 2000.

406 "She seemed fake": Max Brantley interview.

406 "sexually unfaithful": *NYT*, Jan. 20, 2000.

406 "Chappaqua . . . That's Indian": Sheehy, pp. 361, 363.

407 "Never before has our nation": *PPP*, 2000, book 1, pp. 124–40.

407 a record-breaking eighty-nine minutes: archives.cnn.com/2000/ALLPOLITICS/stories/01/27/state.union.01/index.html.

408 "digital divide": *PPP*, 2000, book 1, pp. 625–29.

408 "atomizing or unifying": Ibid., pp. 634–37, third session.

408 "the East Room [was] nearly empty": Klein, p. 193.

408 Janet Reno backed the INS: *Newsweek*, Jan. 17, 2000.

408 Gore changed his position: *ML*, p. 905; *Newsweek*, Apr. 10, 2000.

409 she ordered the boy removed: *ML*, pp. 905–6.

409 Shortly afterward, he was delivered: Remarks on departure for Camp David, Apr. 22, 2000; *PPP*, 2000, book 1, pp. 760–61.

409 who didn't get credit: *Newsweek*, Apr. 10, 2000.

409 by a margin of four to one: Jeff Greenfield, *Oh Waiter! One Order of Crow: Inside the Strangest Presidential Election Finish in American History*, p. 181.

409 "that terrible mess with": Bill Clinton, interview with Dan Rather, Dec. 18, 2000; *PPP*, 2000–2001, book 3, pp. 2732–43.

409 the Irish peace process: *ML*, p. 688.

409 "I'm one of the few Americans": *PPP*, 2000, book 1, pp. 488–89; Meyer, pp. 111–12.

409 Bill invited documentary filmmaker: Ken Burns interview.

410 near death from metastatic lung cancer: *LH*, p. 516.

410 "Hillary and I would get good publicity": Remarks at memorial service for Diane Blair, July 25, 2000; *PPP*, 2000, book 2, pp. 1462–63.

410 "win this election": *LH*, p. 517.

411 "Hillary 2000" dinner: *PPP*, 2000, book 1, pp. 1202–6.

411 he headlined more than 150: *Esquire*, Dec. 2000.

411 a luncheon on March 30: *PPP*, 2000, book 1, pp. 568–73.

411 "flashing cleavage": Maureen Orth, *The Importance of Being Famous: Behind the Scenes of the Celebrity-Industrial Complex*, p. 133.

411 "on a 'personal' mission": Ibid., p. 146.

411 $120,000 for Hillary's campaign: *Vanity Fair*, Apr. 2004.

411 $450,000 for Bill's presidential library: Orth, p. 133.

411 "If I come here one more time": Remarks at DNC luncheon, Mar. 30, 2000; *PPP*, 2000, book 1, p. 568.

411 The President promoted Gore's candidacy. Ibid.

411 "I can still remember every": Remarks at DNC dinner, Apr. 15, 2000; *PPP*, 2000, book 2, pp. 725–28.

412 "I probably know more": Remarks at a DNC dinner, Apr. 24, 2000, ibid., pp. 770–71.

412 The New York mayor was undone: *NYT*, Nov. 8, 2000.

412 "Now I know": Blumenthal, p. 692.

412 "mainstream Republican": *NYT*, May 21, 2000.

412 "no real rationale": Ibid.

412 "look weird": Harris, p. 382.

413 "going over all these issues": *PPP*, 2000, book 1, pp. 947–48.

413 "so I will be free": *NYT*, Nov. 4, 1999.

413 But she nevertheless continued: clinton4.nara.gov/WH/EOP/First_Lady/html/generalspeeches/2000/index.html.

413 Bill raised more than five million: *NYT*, Oct. 10, 2000.

413 thirty-four events designated for her Senate race: May 7 and 16; June 21; July 29; Aug. 4, 6, 9, 10, 12, 13, and 18; Sept. 1, 2, 8, 11, 14, 15, and 17; Oct. 3, 4 (two events), 7, 19, 21, 22 (four events), 23 (two events), 24, and 31; and Nov. 4 (two events).

413 Variously calling himself: *PPP*, 2000, book 1, p. 1258, and book 2, p. 1913; *PPP*, 2000–2001, book 3, p. 2329.

413 "A lot of you": Remarks at a Democratic Congressional Campaign Committee Dinner, Sept. 23, 2000; *PPP*, 2000, book 2, p. 1920.

413 "Every year when I was Governor": Remarks at a dinner for Hillary Clinton, Aug. 9, 2000, ibid., p. 1596.

413 She earned: *WP*, July 21, 1992.

414 "breathtaking range": Remarks at a reception for Hillary Clinton, Oct. 22, 2000; *PPP*, 2000–2001, book 3, p. 2262.

414 "significant contribution": Remarks at a reception for Hillary Clinton, Oct. 31, 2000, ibid., pp. 2402–3.

414 Bill and Hillary remained in harmony: *NYT Magazine*, May 30, 1999.

414 "all transferred": Marton, p. 347.

414 "I think half of them": Remarks at luncheon for Hillary Clinton, Oct. 3, 2000; *PPP*, 2000, book 2, p. 2009.

414 "the editor of the Gingrich revolution": Lawrence O'Donnell interview.

414 "decision making involves": Remarks at DNC dinner, Apr. 15, 2000; *PPP*, 2000, book 1, p. 726.

415 Arafat held the record: Harris, p. 404.

415 The President's grand idea: *ML*, pp. 911–12.

415 "right frame of mind": Ibid., p. 912.

415 Barak made a breakthrough: Blumenthal, p. 778; Harris, p. 406.

415 He impressed both sides: *Newsweek*, July 31, 2000.

415 "This is the best deal": Harris, p. 407.

415 "Clinton really got mad": Mary Mel French interview.

415 The negotiations had foundered: *NYT*, Dec. 26, 2000; *ML*, p. 915.

416 "Arafat wasn't going to do a deal": James Steinberg interview.

416 "disastrous miscalculation": Klein, p. 202.

416 "Now the veil": *NYT*, Jan. 7, 2001.

416 the Intifada would again erupt: Joe Klein wrote that "the consequences of Clinton's . . . efforts" were "immediate and violent": Klein, p. 203.

416 By the time of the Intifada: *9/11 Commission Report*, pp. 173, 226, 227.

417 "She spent": Remarks on arrival in Providence, R.I., July 28, 2000; *PPP*, 2000, book 2, p. 1491.

417 busman's holiday: *PPP*, 2000, book 2, pp. 1558–62, 1570–72, and 1564–70.

417 "I think it's a way": Harris, p. 390.

417 "bold thinker": Exchange with reporters on Martha's Vineyard, Aug. 7, 2000, *PPP*, 2000, book 2, p. 1575.

417 "The driving theme of the Republican": *Newsweek*, Aug. 8, 2000.

417 "spoke movingly": Ken Burns interview.

418 he quickly stepped into the wings: Richard Reeves, *President Reagan: Triumph of the Imagination*, pp. 475–77.

418 couldn't resist occupying center stage: *NYT*, Aug. 15, 2000.

418 In front of an audience: *Newsweek*, Aug. 21, 2000.

418 "terrible mistake": Remarks in a discussion at the ministers' leadership conference, Aug. 10, 2000; *PPP*, 2000, book 2, pp. 1605–20.

418 unprecedented extravaganza: *NYT*, Aug. 13 and 15, 2000; Bill Clinton, interview with Ron Brownstein, *PPP*, 2000, book 2, pp. 1657–66.

418 "We knew Thursday night": *NYT*, Aug. 15, 2000.

419 the thirty-million-dollar Mandeville Canyon estate: *WP Magazine*, Oct. 9, 2005.

419 the entire Clinton clan: Remarks at a Hollywood tribute to the President, Aug. 12, 2000; *PPP*, 2000, book 2, pp. 1634–36.

419 "I'm not going": Ibid., p. 1636.

419 On Sunday, the Clintons presided: *PPP*, 2000, book 2, pp. 1638–42; Presidential Documents Online, via GPO Access, Digest of Other White House Announcements, Aug. 13, 2000.

419 With a price tag of $125 million: *Newsweek*, Oct. 18, 1999, and Jan. 31, 2000, *ML*, p. 876.

419 raising tens of millions: *Newsweek* web exclusive, article ID 005510E9DB0949CBD36C0, Sept. 6, 2000.

419 After Hillary finished: *NYT*, Aug. 15, 2000; *Newsweek*, Aug. 28, 2000.

420 commentators instantly likened: *NYT*, Sept. 24, 2000.

420 The Vice President earned: *Newsweek*, Aug. 28, 2000.

420 the balance he struck: Al Gore acceptance speech, August 17, 2000, www.cnn.com/ELECTION/2000/conventions/democratic/transcripts/gore.html.

420 She had advised him: *NYT*, Nov. 3, 1999; *Vanity Fair*, July 2001.

420 Gore had fired his longtime consultant: Blumenthal, p. 717.

421 "one of the most introverted": *NYT*, July 24, 1999.

421 "George W. Bush sounds": *The Free Press* (Columbus, Ohio), Oct. 24, 2000.

421 "the elephant in the living room": *Vanity Fair*, July 2001.

421 "I never believed": Bill Clinton, interview with Ron Brownstein, *PPP*, 2000, book 2, pp. 1657–66.

421 impaneled a new grand jury: *Newsweek*, Aug. 28, 2000; *NYT*, Sept. 21, 2000.

421 "the evidence was insufficient": *NYT*, Sept. 21, 2000.

421 "factually false": *NYT*, Oct. 19, 2000.

421 *Newsweek* revealed: *Newsweek*, Sept. 6, 2000; *NYT*, Sept. 25, 2000.

421 "They do not grasp": *NYT*, Sept. 24, 2000.

422 The agency's million-dollar study: *Newsweek*, Sept. 25, 2000.

422 "It was a key point": Bruce Reed interview.

422 "Everything that needs": Remarks to the community of Westchester County, Sept. 11, 2000; *PPP*, 2000, book 2, pp. 1778–84.

422 By late September, she had gathered: *NYT*, Sept. 27 and 30, 2000.

423 "a nervous wreck": Remarks at a reception for Mark O'Keefe and Carol Williams, Oct. 2, 2000; *PPP*, 2000, book 2, p. 2001.

423 "you, of all people": archives.cnn.com/2000/ALLPOLITICS/stories/09/14/ny.senate/index.html.

423 "misleading the American people": *NYT*, Sept. 14, 2000.

423 "That was a wonderful": archives.cnn.com/2000/ALLPOLITICS/stories/09/14/ny
   .senate/index.html.

423 In a *New York Times* survey: *NYT*, Sept. 21, 2000.

424 "She did great": Remarks at a brunch for Hillary Clinton, Sept. 17, 2000; *PPP*, 2000,
   book 2, pp. 1856–59.

424 "requisite aggression": Remarks at a birthday tribute to Hillary Clinton, Oct. 25, 2000;
   PPP, 2000–2001, book 3, pp. 2329–30.

424 she spent most of her Sundays: *NYT*, Nov. 8, 2000.

424 "misimpression about": Ibid., Oct. 6, 2000.

424 "I have big hands": Cindy Adams column, *New York Post*, Feb. 19, 2007.

424 "modulating between two tones": *NYT*, Sept. 18, 2000.

424 "joy" in her campaigning: Ibid.

424 "his long fingers": *Esquire*, Dec. 2000.

425 It was probably fitting: 2000 Presidential Documents Online, via GPO Access, Digest
   of Other White House Announcements, Oct. 11, 2000, vol. 36, no. 41, pp. 2459–60:
   "In the evening, he traveled to Chappaqua, where he watched the presidential debate."

425 "I wish I were running": Blumenthal, p. 747.

425 He disapproved of Gore's populist: *ML*, p. 927.

425 "I believe Clinton": *Vanity Fair*, July 2001.

425 "People ask me": Remarks at a luncheon, Sept. 11, 2000; *PPP*, 2000, book 2, p. 1783.

425 "Suppose Al Gore": Remarks to the Colorado Coordinated and State Democratic
   Fund, Oct. 14, 2000; *PPP*, 2000–2001, book 3, p. 2184.

425 "almost gagged": *Newsweek*, Nov. 20, 2000.

425 "The President goes out": Ibid.

425 "Exit Interview": *Esquire*, Dec. 2000.

426 "Gore's numbers": *Newsweek*, Nov. 6, 2000.

426 "slowing, not yet": Ibid.

426 "noticeable little breeze": Ibid.

426 Gore campaign worried: Ibid., Nov. 20, 2000.

426 his popularity was at 70 percent: *NYT*, Nov. 2, 2000.

426 "Brother Bill": *NYT*, Nov. 6, 2000.

426 Bill, Hillary, and Chelsea went: *ML*, p. 927; WeatherUnderground.com, history for
   Nov. 7, 2000.

426 "most extraordinary experience": Remarks at a dinner for Hillary Clinton, Sept. 14,
   2000; *PPP*, 2000, book 2, pp. 1838–42.

426 En route, Hillary busied: *Newsweek*, Nov. 20, 2000.

427 In the suite swarming: *LH*, p. 523; Blumenthal, p. 698.

427 "simply smiled": Blumenthal, p. 698.

427 "If it had not been": DPM, Memcon of Senator Daniel P. Moynihan, Nov. 15, 2000.

427 "Sixty-two counties": *LH*, p. 524.

427 Bill could be seen brushing away tears: *NYT*, Nov. 8, 2000.

427 "an effort to underscore": Ibid., Nov. 9, 2000.

427 around 10:00 p.m., the Florida: *Newsweek*, Nov. 20, 2000.

427 "Circumstances have changed": Ibid.

428 He had spent the evening prowling: Ibid.; Blumenthal, p. 698.

428 "he seemed to be having fun": *Newsweek*, Nov. 20, 2000.

428 "in a good humor": Remarks on returning from Chappaqua, N.Y., Nov. 8, 2000; *PPP*,
   2000–2001, book 3, pp. 2489–90.

428 "Election night was so bizarre": Bruce Reed interview.

428 "I believe that's worse": Bill Clinton, interview with Dan Rather, Dec. 18, 2000; *PPP*,
   2000–2001, book 3, p. 2732.

428 "Of course she'll run": *NYT*, Nov. 9, 2000.

CHAPTER EIGHTEEN

429 "storm and sunshine": Remarks at Foundry United Methodist Church, Jan. 7, 2001; *PPP*, 2000–2001, book 3, p. 2834.

429 twenty farewell addresses: University of Nebraska, Dec. 8, 2000; Odyssey Arena, Belfast, Dec. 13; University of Warwick, Dec. 14, 2000; South Lawn Celebration, Jan. 6, 2001; remarks at Foundry United Methodist Church, Jan. 7; tribute to Hillary, Jan. 7; Israeli Policy Forum, Jan. 7 (*The New York Times* called this speech Clinton's "Farewell Address"); farewell at the DNC, Jan. 8; Michigan State University, Jan. 9; James Ward Elementary School, Chicago, Jan. 9; Palmer House Hotel, Jan. 9 (also talks in the hotel lobby and a private dinner); Dover High School, N.H., Jan. 11; Northeastern University, Jan. 11; Arkansas State Legislature, Jan. 17; Little Rock, Arkansas, airport, Jan. 17; televised farewell, Jan. 17; radio farewell, Jan. 20; Andrews Air Force Base, Jan. 20; Kennedy Airport, Jan. 20.

429 "last-hurrah": *WP*, Jan. 15, 2001.

429 sharing "the lessons": Reeves, pp. 479, 485.

429 Bill needed a SWAT team: *Time*, Jan. 8, 2001.

429 "come out from under": *NYT*, Dec. 25, 2000.

430 "a chaos of innocence": Bruce Reed interview.

430 to "follow the example": Remarks at Foundry United Methodist Church, Jan. 7, 2001; *PPP*, 2000–2001, book 3, p. 2836.

431 "Did we make mistakes?": *Vanity Fair*, July 2001.

431 "handed out red, white and blue": Reeves, p. 478.

431 Bill maintained that the administration's strong stand: *ML*, p. 929.

432 The first leg of Bill's farewell tour: *PPP*, 2000–2001, book 3, pp. 2732–43, 2691–95, and 2653–61.

432 "working together in lines": Ibid., pp. 2732–43.

432 "one of the biggest threats": Ibid., pp. 2653–61.

432 they learned that the U.S. Supreme Court: *ML*, p. 933.

432 "I do believe": Vice President Al Gore concession remarks, Dec. 13, 2000, www.cnn .com/ELECTION/2000/transcripts/121300/t651213.html.

432 "Gore got the best": Exchange with reporters aboard Air Force One, Dec. 14, 2000; *PPP*, 2000–2001, book 3, pp. 2704–12.

433 "partly because of the prosperity": Bill Clinton, interview with Dan Rather, Dec. 18, 2000, ibid., p. 2732.

433 "I think there will be things": Bill Clinton, exchange with reporters, Dec. 19, 2000, ibid., p. 2729.

433 At Gore's request, they met: Harris, p. 428.

433 "patching everything up": Blumenthal, p. 774.

433 "was not entirely displeased": *The New Yorker*, Sept. 13, 2004.

433 scarcely sleeping for two days: Telephone remarks at a reception for Hillary Clinton, Oct. 7, 2000; *PPP*, 2000, book 2, pp. 2077–78.

434 "only ten weeks left": *ML*, p. 929.

434 "held his arm": Ibid.

434 the U.S. military was hit: *9/11 Commission Report*, p. 190.

434 "strong evidence": Ibid., pp. 193–94.

434 Clarke had the "impression": Ibid., p. 195.

434 "didn't really want to know": Ibid., p. 196.

434 "preliminary judgment": Ibid., p. 195.

434 "magic words": Ibid., p. 196.

434 Berger's credibility on these matters: *NYT*, Feb. 21, 2007; *WP*, Feb. 21, 2007.

434 "galvanized al-Qaeda's recruitment": *9/11 Commission Report*, p. 191.

434 "flapping around": *Time*, Jan. 8, 2001.

434 "parameters": Remarks at an Israeli Policy Forum dinner, Jan. 7, 2001; *PPP*, 2000–2001, book 3, pp. 2838–46.

435 "Hail Mary": *Time*, Jan. 8, 2001.

435 "compulsive grandstanding": *The Wall Street Journal*, Jan. 8, 2001.

435 "in principle": *Time*, Jan. 8, 2001.

435 "If you don't take": Ibid.

435 he and David Kendall had a secret meeting: *Time*, Jan. 29, 2001.

435 the pressure on the President intensified: Ibid.; *Newsweek*, Jan. 29, 2001.

435 "they have yet": *Esquire*, Dec. 2000.

435 Ray said he could fashion: *NYT*, Jan. 20 and Jan. 24, 2001; *Newsweek*, Jan. 29, 2001.

436 Hillary flew around: *NYT*, Nov. 9, 2000.

436 she threw herself a party: Remarks at "An Invitation to the White House" reception, Nov. 28, 2000; *PPP*, 2000–2001, book 3, pp. 2589–90.

436 "fluffy": *Newsweek*, Mar. 6, 2000.

436 to discuss a memoir she planned: *NYT*, Dec. 14 and Dec. 16, 2000.

436 "affront to common sense": Ibid., Dec. 22, 2000.

436 Hillary signed another contract: Ibid., Dec. 30, 2000.

436 "wealthy friends and contributors": Ibid., Dec. 24, 2000.

437 five-thousand-dollar checks: *Time*, Feb. 5, 2001.

437 wish list of furniture: Orth, p. 133. Denise Rich said "there was a list going around from the decorator."

437 extraordinary largesse: *NYT*, Jan. 25, 2001.

437 One noteworthy gift: Ibid.

437 "I don't think Hillary": *PPP*, 2000, book 2, p. 2050.

437 "everything you have done": *PPP*, 2000–2001, book 3, p. 2599.

437 "with all my heart": Orth, pp. 146–48.

437 wealthy courtier who gave: *NYT*, Feb. 3, 2001.

437 Dozoretz had been finance chair: Orth, p. 148; *NYT*, Oct. 5, 1999.

438 In her official capacity: Weekly Compilation of Presidential Documents, via GPO Access, database search 1999: http://frwebgate.access.gpo.gov/cgi-bin/multidb.cqi.

438 she visited the White House: Klein, p. 205.

438 "very positive": Orth, p. 147.

438 pleaded the Fifth Amendment: Ibid., p. 148.

438 her friend Ehud Barak: Klein, p. 205.

438 "humanitarian role": *Time*, Feb. 5, 2001.

438 "described Rich": Orth, p. 149.

438 "a lingering sense of guilt": Klein, p. 203.

438 gave his former boss a thick dossier: Orth, p. 145.

438 "pretty hard": Ibid, p. 147.

438 "inexcusable": Abner Mikva interview.

439 "accumulating so much stuff": archives.cnn.com/2001/ALLPOLITICS/02/26/pardons.rodham/index.html.

439 "telling potential clients": Ibid.

439 also tried to use their White House connections: *Time*, Nov. 1, 1999.

439 Their collaborator in the venture: Ibid.; *WP*, Feb. 26, 2001; archives.cnn.com/2001/ALLPOLITICS/02/26/pardons.rodham/index.html.

439 "restructuring": *Time*, Nov. 1, 1999.

439 "strong business": *USA Today* web chat with Tony Rodham, Feb. 18, 2001, www.usatoday.com/community/chat/2001-01-18-rodham.htm.

439 consultant for a Tennessee-based: *The Boston Globe*, Feb. 28, 2007; archives.cnn

.com/2001/ALLPOLITICS/03/03/clinton.pardons.rodh/; archives.cnn.com/2002/ALL POLITICS/03/23/clinton.pardons/index.html.

440 With Hillary's help: archives.cnn.com/2002/ALLPOLITICS/03/23/clinton.pardons/ index.html/.

440 Tony lobbied his brother-in-law: archives.cnn.com/2001/ALLPOLITICS/03/03/ clinton.pardons.rodh/.

440 "pardons should follow": archives.cnn.com/2002/ALLPOLITICS/03/23/clinton .pardons/index.html/.

440 "on the pardon issue": *The Boston Globe*, Feb. 28, 2007.

440 "the most valuable thing": archives.cnn.com/2002/ALLPOLITICS/03/23/clinton .pardons/ index.html/.

440 "success fee": *NYT*, Feb. 25, 2001.

440 Hugh lobbied Bill: Ibid., Feb. 22, 2001.

440 Against the advice: Ibid., Jan. 3, 2001; Bill Clinton, interview with Reuters, Jan. 11, 2001; *PPP*, 2000–2001, book 3, pp. 2897–2904.

441 "narrow the differences": Ibid., pp. 2838–46.

441 "great man": Blumenthal, p. 780.

441 "The hell I am": Ibid. See also *ML*, p. 944.

441 "Clinton wanted a breakthrough": Tom Siebert interview.

441 Hillary was sworn in: New York *Daily News*, Jan. 4, 2001; *WP*, Jan. 4, 2001; *USA Today*, Jan. 4, 2001; *NYT*, Jan. 4, 2001; *LH*, p. 527.

441 "jubilant faces": *WP*, Jan. 4, 2001.

441 Afterward, Hillary hosted: *USA Today*, Jan. 4, 2001.

441 "enormous pride": Remarks at a reception honoring Senator Hillary Rodham Clinton, Jan. 3, 2001; *PPP*, 2000–2001, book 3, pp. 2818–19.

441 "I Survived the Clinton Presidency": *NYT*, Jan. 6, 2001.

442 even more elaborate party: Blumenthal, p. 775; Bruce Reed interview; *Vanity Fair*, July 2001.

442 "You had to work hard": *Vanity Fair*, July 2001.

442 her "real swearing-in": *WP*, Jan. 8, 2001.

442 "swinging, swaying": Ibid.

442 "keeping the rest of us": Remarks at a tribute to Senator Hillary Clinton, Jan. 7, 2001; *PPP*, 2000–2001, book 3, pp. 2836–38.

443 "unavoidably detained": Ibid., pp. 2866–71.

443 "invaded" a private dinner: Ibid., p. 2875.

443 "be there for you": *ML*, p. 947; *PPP*, 2000–2001, book 3, p. 2885.

443 After taking a stroll: *The Boston Globe*, Jan. 12, 2001.

443 "election after election": *PPP*, 2000–2001, book 3, pp. 2892–96.

443 "referred to the possibility": Marton, p. 349.

443 "wistful and fun": Donna Shalala interview.

443 after-dinner concert: *ML*, p. 947.

443 Speaking for almost an hour: Remarks to a joint session of the Arkansas State Legislature, Jan. 17, 2001; *PPP*, 2000–2001, book 3, p. 2935.

444 "learned all of her politics wrestling": Ibid.

444 "more idealistic": Remarks to the community in Little Rock, Jan. 17, 2001; *PPP*, 2000–2001, book 3, pp. 2943–45.

444 "He said it wasn't his fault": Max Brantley interview.

444 "a huge sense": *The Economist*, Jan. 13, 2001.

444 "a tale of two": *U.S. News & World Report*, Jan. 22, 2001.

444 "twenty years from now": Ibid.

444 "there were too many jagged": *WP*, Jan. 14, 2001.

445 The assessment that may have hurt: *The Bernardsville News*, Jan. 4, 2001.
445 Bill sat down to write: Bill Clinton to Douglas Eakeley, Jan. 18, 2001, courtesy of Douglas Eakeley.
446 "sprinted away to get the words": Blumenthal, p. 786.
446 His seven-minute speech: *NYT*, Jan. 19, 2001.
446 "must not disentangle": *PPP*, 2000–2001, book 3, pp. 2952–53.
446 The scene in the White House: Terry McAuliffe interview.
446 "We didn't have a shredder": Ann McCoy interview.
446 An eighteen-wheeler: *NYT*, Jan. 6, 2001.
446 Hillary was dividing her time: *LH*, p. 527.
446 "She was mostly getting things": Terry McAuliffe interview.
446 Bill "was clinging": Ann McCoy interview.
446 One cause for delay: *Time*, Jan. 29, 2001.
446 Among the guests: Tommy Caplan interview.
446 Tony Rodham was staying in a hotel: *Time*, Jan. 29, 2001.
447 "I tried to walk": "Statement on Resolution of Legal Issues," Jan. 19, 2001; *PPP*, 2000–2001, book 3, pp. 2954–55.
447 "every clause, every word": *Time*, Jan. 29, 2001.
447 The thirty-two-page order: *The Wall Street Journal*, Jan. 22, 2001.
447 "We have not admitted": *U.S. News & World Report*, Jan. 29, 2001.
447 "if only Mr. Clinton": *NYT*, Jan. 22, 2001.
447 "hopelessly cracked ethical barometer": *USA Today*, Jan. 22, 2001.
447 "clear admission": *The Wall Street Journal*, Jan. 22, 2001.
448 "In *Esquire* magazine": *Chicago Sun-Times*, Jan. 25, 2001.
448 In his last visit to the Oval Office: Blumenthal, pp. 786–87.
448 That afternoon, he spoke again: Blumenthal, p. 783; Orth, p. 148; *NYT*, Jan. 25, 2001.
448 "did not qualify": *Time*, Feb. 5, 2001.
448 "go nuts": *NYT*, Jan. 25, 2001.
449 had even told Beth Dozoretz: Orth, p. 148.
449 "It is a legal doctrine": Abner Mikva interview.
449 Bill asked Nolan to check in: *Time*, Feb. 5, 2001.
449 he had originally hoped to deliver live: Ibid., Jan. 29, 2001.
449 "We've got to pack": Tommy Caplan interview.
449 "just wanted to keep strolling": *ML*, p. 949.
449 Harry Thomason organized a screening: *Time*, Jan. 29, 2001.
449 returned to the Oval Office: Ibid.
450 Bill left the Residence: *The Atlanta Journal-Constitution*, Jan. 21, 2001; *Newsweek*, Jan. 29, 2001; *ML*, p. 953.
450 After taking a stroll: *LH*, p. 527; WeatherUnderground.com, history for Jan. 20, 2001; *ML*, p. 952.
450 The Clintons said a weepy farewell: *LH*, pp. 527–28; *Time*, Jan. 29, 2001.
450 had a last waltz: *LH*, p. 528; New York *Daily News*, Jan. 21, 2001.
450 reporters watched the sentimental: *The Boston Globe*, Jan. 21, 2001.
450 "Our Love Is Here to Stay": *Boston Herald*, Jan. 21, 2001.
450 "Bye": New York *Daily News*, Jan. 21, 2001.
450 Bill shook hands, waved: *Vanity Fair*, July 2001.
450 "In the past": *Chicago Sun-Times*, Jan. 25, 2001.
450 the Clintons opted for a motorcade: *NYT*, Jan. 21, 2001; *The Boston Globe*, Jan. 21, 2001.
451 Among the well-wishers: *WP*, Feb. 26, 2001.
451 "You see that sign": *Boston Herald*, Jan. 21, 2001.

451 "I left the White House": New York *Daily News*, Jan. 21, 2001.

451 "stepping as always": Edmund Morris, *Dutch: A Memoir of Ronald Reagan*, pp. 652–53.

451 It was not until 2:57 p.m.: *NYT*, Jan. 21, 2001.

451 Special Air Mission 28000: New York *Daily News*, Jan. 21, 2001.

451 The crowd onboard included: Terry McAuliffe interview.

451 "It was a surreal feeling": Ibid.

451 In TWA's Hangar 12 at Kennedy: *NYT*, Jan. 21, 2001; New York *Daily News*, Jan. 21, 2001.

451 "I have watched": New York *Daily News*, Jan. 21, 2001.

452 "was out solid, snoring": Terry McAuliffe interview.

452 Hillary stayed to help unpack: *NYT*, Jan. 22, 2001.

452 "all alone with Oscar": Terry McAuliffe interview.

452 On the day he left office: Roper Center poll ratings, Jan. 18–19, *Newsweek*; Jan. 15–17, CBS.

452 Their financial-disclosure forms revealed: *NYT*, Feb. 8 and 11, 2001.

452 "seemed more like grifters": *NYT*, Jan. 25, 2001.

452 "world-class users": New York *Daily News*, Jan. 25, 2001.

452 *Saturday Night Live* lampooned: *NYT*, Feb. 3, 2001.

452 "to remove any suggestion": Ibid.

452 Several days later, they also sent: *NYT*, Feb. 8, 2001.

452 At first, the press simply noted: New York *Daily News*, Jan. 21, 2001; *NYT*, Jan. 21, 2001.

453 "It was a personal decision": *Vanity Fair*, June 2001.

453 "You don't pardon a traitor": *The New Yorker*, Feb. 5, 2001.

453 The law-enforcement community: Freeh, p. 267: The FBI "was kept in the dark about the pardons."

453 "I worked a long time": *Time*, Feb. 5, 2001.

453 "serious law enforcement concerns": *The Wall Street Journal*, Jan. 23, 2001.

453 "scandalous present": *WP*, Jan. 25, 2001.

453 "shocking abuse": *NYT*, Jan. 24, 2001.

453 "stunned by the fact": Freeh, p. 269.

454 "public revulsion": *NYT*, Feb. 22, 2001.

454 Both Bill and Hillary denied: Ibid.

454 "It defies credulity": archives.cnn.com/2001/ALLPOLITICS/02/26/pardons.rodham/index.html.

454 "heartbroken": *NYT*, Feb. 22, 2001.

454 "personal relationship": *The Boston Globe*, Feb. 28, 2007.

454 Bill remained unrepentant: *ML*, pp. 940–41.

454 "it was terrible politics": *Vanity Fair*, Apr. 2004.

454 "culture of investigation": *LH*, p. 439.

Bibliography

—

Aaker, Linda. *A Woman's Odyssey: Journals 1976–1992*. Denton: University of North Texas Press, 1994.

Barber, Benjamin R. *The Truth of Power: Intellectual Affairs in the Clinton White House*. New York: W. W. Norton, 2001.

Birnbaum, Jeffrey H. *Madhouse: The Private Turmoil of Working for the President*. New York: Random House, 1996.

Blumenthal, Sidney. *The Clinton Wars*. New York: Farrar, Straus and Giroux, 2003.

Brummett, John. *Highwire: From the Backroads to the Beltway—The Education of Bill Clinton*. New York: Hyperion, 1994.

Clinton, Bill. *Between Hope and History: Meeting America's Challenges for the 21st Century*. New York: Random House, 1996.

——. *My Life*. New York: Alfred A. Knopf, 2004.

Clinton, Hillary Rodham. *It Takes a Village: And Other Lessons Children Teach Us*. New York: Simon & Schuster, 1996.

——. *Living History*. New York: Simon & Schuster, 2003.

Clinton, Roger. *Growing Up Clinton: The Lives, Times, and Tragedies of America's Presidential Family*. Arlington, Tex.: Summit Publishing Group, 1995.

Davis, Lanny J. *Truth to Tell: Notes from My White House Education*. New York: Free Press, 1999.

Drew, Elizabeth. *On the Edge: The Clinton Presidency*. New York: Touchstone, 1994.

Flowers, Gennifer. *Passion and Betrayal*. Del Mar, Calif.: Emery Dalton, 1995.

Freeh, Louis J. *My FBI: Bringing Down the Mafia, Investigating Bill Clinton, and Fighting the War on Terror*. New York: St. Martin's, 2005.

Gergen, David. *Eyewitness to Power: The Essence of Leadership, Nixon to Clinton*. New York: Simon & Schuster, 2000.

Goldman, Peter, Thomas DeFrank, Mark Miller, Andrew Murr, and Tom Mathews. *Quest for the Presidency: 1992*. College Station: Texas A&M University Press, 1994.

Greenfield, Jeff. *Oh Waiter! One Order of Crow: Inside the Strangest Presidential Election Finish in American History*. New York: G. P. Putnam, 2001.

Guinier, Lani. *Lift Every Voice: Turning a Civil Rights Setback into a New Vision of Social Justice*. New York: Simon & Schuster, 1998.

Hacker, Jacob S. *The Road to Nowhere: The Genesis of President Clinton's Plan for Health Security*. Princeton: Princeton University Press, 1997.

Harris, John F. *The Survivor: President Clinton and His Times*. New York: Random House, 2005.

Hubbell, Webster. *Friends in High Places: Our Journey from Little Rock to Washington, D.C.* New York: William Morrow, 1997.

Isikoff, Michael. *Uncovering Clinton: A Reporter's Story*. New York: Crown, 1999.

Johnson, Haynes, and David S. Broder. *The System: The American Way of Politics at the Breaking Point*. Boston: Little, Brown, 1996.

Jordan, Hamilton. *No Such Thing as a Bad Day*. Atlanta: Longstreet Press, 2000.

Katz, Mark. *Clinton and Me*. New York: Hyperion, 2003.

Kelley, Virginia. *Leading with My Heart*. New York: Simon & Schuster, 1994.

Kelly, Michael. *Things Worth Fighting For: Collected Writings*. New York: Penguin, 2004.

Klein, Joe. *The Natural: The Misunderstood Presidency of Bill Clinton*. New York: Broadway Books, 2002.

Kurtz, Howard. *Spin Cycle: How the White House and the Media Manipulate the News*. New York: Touchstone, 1998.

Lake, Anthony. *Six Nightmares: Real Threats in a Dangerous World and How America Can Meet Them*. Boston: Little, Brown, 2000.

Maraniss, David. *The Clinton Enigma: A Four-and-a-Half-Minute Speech Reveals This President's Entire Life*. New York: Simon & Schuster, 1998.

———. *First in His Class: A Biography of Bill Clinton*. New York: Simon & Schuster, 1995.

Marton, Kati. *Hidden Power: Presidential Marriages That Shaped Our Recent History*. New York: Pantheon, 2001.

McAuliffe, Terry. *What a Party! My Life among Democrats*. New York: Thomas Dunne, 2007.

Merry, Robert W. *Sands of Empire: Missionary Zeal, American Foreign Policy, and the Hazards of Global Ambition*. New York: Simon & Schuster, 2005.

Meyer, Christopher. *D.C. Confidential: The Controversial Memoirs of Britain's Ambassador to the U.S. at the Time of 9/11 and the Iraq War*. London: Weidenfeld and Nicolson, 2005.

Morris, Dick. *Behind the Oval Office: Getting Reelected Against All Odds*. Los Angeles: Renaissance Books, 1999.

———. *Rewriting History*. New York: ReganBooks, 2004.

Morris, Edmund. *Dutch: A Memoir of Ronald Reagan*. New York: Random House, 1999.

Morris, Roger. *Partners in Power: The Clintons and Their America*. Washington, D.C.: Regnery, 1996.

Morton, Andrew. *Monica's Story*. New York: St. Martin's, 1999.

The 9/11 Commission Report: Final Report of the National Commission on Terrorist Attacks upon the United States. New York: W. W. Norton, 2004.

Noor, Queen. *Leap of Faith: Memoirs of an Unexpected Life*. New York: Miramax Books, 2003.

Orth, Maureen. *The Importance of Being Famous: Behind the Scenes of the Celebrity-Industrial Complex*. New York: Henry Holt, 2004.

Posner, Richard A. *An Affair of State: The Investigation, Impeachment, and Trial of President Clinton*. Cambridge, Mass.: Harvard University Press, 2000.

Reeves, Richard. *President Reagan: Triumph of the Imagination*. New York: Simon & Schuster, 2005.

Reich, Robert B. *Locked in the Cabinet*. New York: Knopf, 1997.

Renshon, Stanley A. *High Hopes: The Clinton Presidency and the Politics of Ambition*. New York: Routledge, 1998.

Rubin, Robert E. *In an Uncertain World: Tough Choices from Wall Street to Washington*. New York: Random House, 2003.

Sheehy, Gail. *Hillary's Choice*. New York: Ballantine, 1999.

Smith, Sally Bedell. *Grace and Power: The Private World of the Kennedy White House*. New York: Ballantine, 2006.

———. *Reflected Glory: The Life of Pamela Churchill Harriman*. New York: Simon & Schuster. 1996.

Stephanopoulos, George. *All Too Human: A Political Education*. Boston: Little, Brown, 1999.

Stewart, James B. *Blood Sport: The President and His Adversaries*. New York: Simon & Schuster, 1996.

Talbott, Strobe. *The Russia Hand: A Memoir of Presidential Diplomacy*. New York: Random House, 2002.

The Starr Report: The Official Report of the Independent Counsel's Investigation of the President. Rocklin, Calif.: Forum/Prima Publishing, 1998.

Thomas, Evan, Karen Breslau, Debra Rosenberg, Leslie Kaufman, and Andrew Murr. *Back from the Dead: How Clinton Survived the Republican Revolution*. Boston: Atlantic Monthly Press, 1997.

Toobin, Jeffrey. *A Vast Conspiracy*. New York: Touchstone, 1999.

Van Natta Jr., Don. *First Off the Tee: Presidential Hackers, Duffers, and Cheaters from Taft to Bush*. New York: Public Affairs, 2003.

Waldman, Michael. *POTUS Speaks*. New York: Simon & Schuster, 2000.

Williams, Marjorie. *The Woman at the Washington Zoo*. Ed. Timothy Noah. New York: Public Affairs, 2005.

Woodward, Bob. *The Agenda: Inside the Clinton White House*. New York: Simon & Schuster, 1994.

———. *The Choice: How Clinton Won*. New York: Touchstone, 1996.

———. *Shadow: Five Presidents and the Legacy of Watergate*. New York: Touchstone, 1999.

Wright, Lawrence. *The Looming Tower: Al-Qaeda and the Road to 9/11*. New York: Knopf, 2007.

Index

Photograph Credits

—

About the Author

SALLY BEDELL SMITH is the author of *Grace and Power: The Private World of the Kennedy White House, Diana: The Life of a Troubled Princess, Reflected Glory: The Life of Pamela Churchill Harriman,* and *In All His Glory: The Life and Times of William S. Paley and the Birth of Modern Broadcasting.* A contributing editor at *Vanity Fair* since 1996, she previously worked at *Time* and *The New York Times,* where she was a cultural news reporter. She lives in Washington, D.C., with her husband, Stephen. They have three grown children.

About the Type

This book was set in Electra, a typeface designed for Linotype by W. A. Dwiggins, the renowned type designer (1880–1956). Electra is a fluid typeface, avoiding contrasts of thick and thin strokes that are prevalent in most modern typefaces.